Alastair **Sawday's**

Special Places to Stay

French Châteaux & Hotels

"Searching for your perfect getaway is now easier than ever."

French Magazine

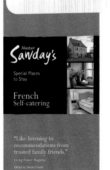

Alastair **Sawday's**

Special Places to Stay

French Self-catering

"Like listening to recommendations from trusted family friends."

Living France Magazine

Edited by Nicola Crosse

Alastair **Sawday's**

Special Places to Stay

Spain

"Indispensable."

Evening Standard

Alastair **Sawday's**

Special Places to Stay

Italy

"Delightful, hand-picked accommodation."

Italia!

Edited by Frances Oldfield

Alastair

Sawday's

Special Places to Stay

Thirteenth edition
Copyright © 2013 Alastair Sawday
Publishing Co. Ltd
Published in 2013
ISBN-13: 978-1-906136-61-1

Alastair Sawday Publishing Co. Ltd,
The Old Farmyard, Yanley Lane,
Long Ashton, Bristol BS41 9LR, UK
Tel: +44 (0)1275 395430
Email: info@sawdays.co.uk
Web: www.sawdays.co.uk

The Globe Pequot Press,
P. O. Box 480, Guilford,
Connecticut 06437, USA
Tel: +1 203 458 4500
Email: info@globepequot.com
Web: www.globepequot.com

Series Editor Alastair Sawday

Editorial Géraldine Roul, Joanne Hayers,
Patrick Henry

Senior Editor Jo Boissevain

Production Alex Skinner,
Sarah Frost-Mellor

Photo Editor Alec Studerus

Writing Jo Boissevain, Ann Cooke-Yarborough,
Monica Guy, Matthew Hilton-Dennis, Kate
Mitchell, Kerry O'Neill, Honor Peters, Annabel
Reddick, Annie Shillito

Inspections Jane Alexander, Katie Anderson,
Rose Angas, Richard & Linda Armspach, Isabelle
Browne, Jill Coyle, Penny Dinwiddie, Sarah
Dixon, Sue Edrich, Georgina Gabriel, Ann
Carisso Haine, Anne & David Hale, Diana
Harris-Sawday, Patrick Henry, Nicky Hilyer,
Rosie Jackson, Lynn Kirk, Susan Luraschi, Judith
Lott, Adeline Mandirac, Sue Nottingham,
Caroline Renouf, Géraldine Roul, Annie Shillito,
Alex Skinner, Charlie Skipwith, Victoria Thomas,
Jo Wilds, Amy Winterbotham, Ann Cooke-
Yarborough, Elizabeth Yates
*Thank you to those people who did an inspection
or two.*

Marketing & PR +44 (0)1275 395430

And thanks to Ann Cooke-Yarborough for her
invaluable support.

*We have made every effort to ensure the accuracy of the
information in this book at the time of going to press.
However, we cannot accept any responsibility for any
loss, injury or inconvenience resulting from the use of
information contained therein.*

Production: PagebyPage Co. Ltd.
Maps: Maidenhead Cartographic Services
Printing: Butler Tanner & Dennis, Frome

Distribution: Travel Alliance, Bath
DMcEntee@footprinttravelguides.com

Alastair Sawday's

Special Places
to Stay

French
Bed & Breakfast

4 Contents

This is our biggest book ever — a startling feat, for 2012 has not been a great year for the French travel world. But it does show how French B&B owners look upon Sawday's as the best port to be in a storm, let alone in good weather.

The British are sidling back into France, a touch coyly perhaps –after abandoning her during the worst of the recession. As I wrote when the financial storm blew into Europe: *Rather like a beautiful old statue, France is worth seeing however battered she is. She has lost none of her beauty, none of her special charm; all she needs is for us to show our appreciation by going there and not worshipping the false gods of long-distance holidays.*

I popped back to France for *The Independent* this year, for a nostalgic journey around some old haunts and our first B&Bs. I was welcomed as a friend by people who had been with us since 1994, as warm and genuine in their greeting as they ever had been. I was keen to know what had changed, whether our readers and web-users had changed. To my delight, we were still seen as the most open-minded and sensitive of all their visitors – keen to learn and to take things as they were found.

The drift to the cities among the young French has made it harder for B&Bs to find people to help out in the house, so they work harder. The new British passion for good food has put them on their mettle, which is fun for the brave few who have persisted in cooking for guests. The main change I would wish for is a switch from last-minute one-night stays to staying in one area. Buy our *Go Slow France* to get a feel for why this is such a lovely way of being there.

I am keen to remind you that these B&B owners are more than the sum of their parts. They feed and welcome you, but they also care for you, show you where to eat and what to see, and steer you away from error. They offer you, as one says nowadays, a complete 'experience'. They become your friends and mentors, and how precious is that in the internet age of detachment?

Alastair Sawday

Photo left: Tom Germain
Photo right: Chambres d'Hôtes Morin Salomé, entry 768

It's simple. There are no rules, no boxes to tick. We choose places that we like and are fiercely subjective in our choices. We also recognise that one person's idea of special is not necessarily someone else's so there is a huge variety of places, and prices, in the book. Those who are familiar with our Special Places series know that we look for comfort, originality, authenticity, and reject the insincere, the anonymous and the banal. The way guests are treated comes as high on our list as the setting, the architecture, the atmosphere and the food.

Inspections

We visit every place in the guide to get a feel for how both house and owner tick. We don't take a clipboard and we don't have a list of what is acceptable and what is not. Instead, we chat for an hour or so with the owner and look round - closely (it involves bouncing on beds, looking at linen, testing taps). It's all very informal but it gives us an excellent idea of who would enjoy staying there and our aim is to match places and guests. If the visit happens to be the last of the day, we may stay the night. Once in the book, properties are re-inspected every three to four years so that we can keep things fresh and accurate.

Feedback

In between inspections we rely on feedback from our army of readers, as well as from staff members who are encouraged to visit properties across the series. This feedback is invaluable to us

and we always follow up on comments. So do tell us whether your stay has been a joy or not, if the atmosphere was great or stuffy, the owners cheery or bored. Just open that place's page on our website www.sawdays.co.uk and click on the 'Tell us your thoughts' button on the lower left-hand side to send us a quick and easy email. The accuracy of the book depends on what you, and our inspectors, tell us.

A lot of the new entries in each edition are recommended by our readers, so keep telling us about new places you've discovered too. Please use the forms on our website www.sawdays.co.uk/recommend or later in this book.

However, please do not tell us if the bedside light was broken, or the shower head was scummy. Tell the owner, immediately, and get them to do something about it. Most owners are more than happy to correct problems and will bend over backwards to help. Far better than bottling it up and then writing to us a week later!

Subscriptions

Owners pay to appear on our pages. Their fee goes towards the high costs of inspecting and writing, of developing our website and producing an all-colour book. We only include places that we like and find special for one reason or another, so it is never possible for anyone to buy their way onto these pages. Nor is it possible for an owner to write their own description. We will say if the bedrooms are small, or if a main road is near. We do our best to avoid misleading people and keep up our reputation for reliability.

Disclaimer

We make no claims to pure objectivity in choosing these places. They are here simply because we like them. Our opinions and tastes are ours alone and this book is a statement of them; we hope you will share them. We have done our utmost to get our facts right but apologise unreservedly for any mistakes that may have crept in.

You should know that we don't check such things as fire regulations, swimming pool security or any other laws with which owners of properties receiving paying guests should comply. This is the responsibility of the owners.

Photo: Ferme du Ciel, entry 746

Finding the right place for you

All these places are special in one way or another. All have been visited and then written about honestly so that you can decide for yourselves which will suit you. Those of you who swear by Sawday's books trust our write-ups precisely because we don't have a blanket standard; we include places simply because we like them. But we all have different priorities, so do read the descriptions carefully and pick out the places where you will be comfortable. If something is particularly important to you then check when you book: a simple question or two can avoid misunderstandings.

Maps

Each property is flagged with its entry number on the maps at the front. These maps are a great starting point for planning your trip, but please don't use them as anything other than a general guide – use a decent road map for real navigation. Most places will send you detailed instructions once you have booked your stay.

Symbols

Below each entry you will see some symbols; they are explained at the very back of the book. They are based on the information given to us by the owners. However, things do change: bikes may be under repair or a new pool may have been put in. Please use the symbols as a guide rather than an absolute statement of fact and double-check anything that is important to you – owners occasionally bend their own rules, so it's worth asking if you may take your child or dog even if they don't have the symbol.

Children – The ♔ symbol shows places which are happy to accept children of all ages. This does not mean that they will necessarily have cots, high chairs, etc. If an owner welcomes children but only those above a certain age, we have put in these details, too. These houses do not have the child symbol, but even these folk may accept your younger child if you are the only guests. Many who say no to children do so not because they don't like them but because they may have a steep stair, an unfenced pond or they find balancing the needs of mixed age groups too challenging.

Pets – Our ♖ symbol shows places which are happy to accept pets. It means they can sleep in the bedroom with you, but not necessarily on the bed. Be realistic about your pet – if it is nervous or excitable or doesn't like the company of other dogs, people, chickens, or children, then say so.

Owners' pets – The ♘ symbol is given when the owners have their own pet on the premises. It may not be a cat! But it is there to warn you that you may be greeted by a dog, serenaded by a parrot, or indeed sat upon by a cat.

Communicating with owners

As we say below, owners are living their own lives in their own homes and, ideally, receiving guests as friends – who happen to pay them something when they leave. This is why travellers choose to stay at B&Bs rather than anonymous hotels. It is also why the owners have every right to expect to be treated like friends not machines. Yet, in the 'century of information', they are reporting more and more cases of enquirers who never reply to emails, guests who book and simply don't turn up: no email, no telephone call, no explanation, let alone an apology. It isn't for lack of the means to do it, it's because they just don't think. Let's stem the tide of thoughtlessness and keep our owners in business.

Our owners are proud of the regions in which they live and are invaluable sources of knowledge about their local areas, which they love to share. Many of our owners comment that guests who only stayed one night, en route to elsewhere, wished that they had stayed longer to explore. Guests too, having arrived and stayed for one night, have also said that they wished they had booked for longer. So do consider stopping for more than one night where you might otherwise be 'travelling through'.

Types of places

Some places have rooms in annexes or stables, barns or garden 'wings', some of which feel part of the house, some of which don't. If you have a strong preference for being in the throng or for being apart, check those details. Consider your surroundings, too: rambling châteaux may be cooler than you are used to; city places and working farms may be noisy at times; and that peacock or cockerel we mention may disturb you. Some owners give you a front door key so you may come and go as you please; others like to have the house empty between, say, 10am and 4pm. Remember that B&Bs are people's homes, not hotels.

Do expect:
• a genuine personal welcome
• a willingness to go the extra mile
• a degree of informality, even family-life chaos, i.e. a fascinating glimpse of a French way of life

Don't necessarily expect:
• a lock on your bedroom door
• gin and tonic at 2am
• your room cleaned, bed made and towels changed every day
• a private table at breakfast
• access to house and garden during the day
• an immediate response to your booking enquiry

Rooms

Bedrooms – We tell you if a room is a single, double, twin/double (i.e. with zip and link beds), suite (a room with space for seating or two rooms sharing a bathroom), family room (a double bed + single beds), or triple (three single beds). If 'antique beds' sound seductively

authentic, remember they are liable to be antique sizes too (190cm long, doubles 140cm wide); if in doubt, ask, or book a twin room (usually larger). Owners can often juggle beds or bedrooms, so talk to them about what you need before you book. It is rare to be given your own room key in a B&B and your room won't necessarily have a television.

Bathrooms – Most bedrooms in this book have an en suite bath or shower room; we only mention bathroom details when they do not. So, you may have a 'separate' bathroom (yours alone but not in your room) or a shared bathroom. Under certain entries we mention that two rooms share a bathroom and are 'let to same party only'. Please do not assume this means you must be a group of friends to apply; it simply means that if you book one of these rooms you will not be sharing a bathroom with strangers. For simplicity we may refer to 'bath'. This doesn't necessarily mean it has no shower; it could mean a shower only. If these things are important to you, please check when booking.

Sitting rooms – Most B&B owners offer guests the family sitting room to share, or they provide a sitting room specially for guests.

Meals

Unless we say otherwise, breakfast is included. This will usually be a good continental breakfast – traditionally fresh baguette or pain de campagne with apricot jam and a bowl of coffee, but brioche, crêpes, croissants, and homemade cake may all be on offer too. Some owners are fairly unbending about breakfast times, others are happy just to wait until you want it, or even bring it to you in bed.

Apart from breakfast, no meals should be expected unless you have arranged them in advance. Many places offer their guests a table d'hôtes dinner – the same food for all and absolutely must be booked ahead – but it will not be available every night. (We have indicated the distance to the nearest restaurant when dinner isn't offered; but be aware that rural restaurants stop taking orders at 9pm and often close at least one day a week.) Often, the meal is shared with other guests at a communal table. These dinners are sometimes hosted by Monsieur or Madame or both and are usually a wonderful opportunity to get to know your hosts and to make new friends among the other guests. Meal prices are quoted per person, although children will usually eat for less. Ask your hosts about reduced meal rates if you're travelling with little ones.

When wine is included this can mean a range of things, from a standard quarter-litre carafe per person to a barrel of table wine; from a decent bottle of local wine to an excellent estate wine.

Summer kitchens

Well before the ubiquitous barbecue came upon us, the French had come up with a daring idea for their places of summer residence: a minimal kitchen outside, half in the garden, and not doing 'proper' cooking. A summer kitchen is at ground level and partially open to the elements; generally under an overhang or in an adapted outbuilding, it typically contains a couple of bottled-gas burners or hotplates, a mini-refrigerator and a source of water; also crockery and cutlery. These facilities are for family and/or hosted garden meals and some owners who don't do table d'hôtes will allow guests to use the summer kitchen and picnic in their garden.

Prices and minimum stays

Most entries give a price PER ROOM with breakfast for two people. If this is not the case, we generally say so. The price range covers a one-night stay in the cheapest room in low season to the most expensive in high season. Some owners charge more at certain times (during festivals, for example) and some charge less for stays of more than one or two nights. Some owners ask for a two-night minimum stay and we mention this where possible.

Prices quoted are those given to us for 2013 onwards but are not guaranteed, so do double-check when booking.

Taxe de séjour is a small tax that local councils can levy on all paying visitors; it is rarely included in the quoted price and you may find your bill increased by €0.50–€2 per person per day to cover this.

Public Holidays

As well as the usual public holidays which we take in the UK, the French also celebrate on various other dates. It is likely that B&Bs will be booked up well in advance around these days, so do plan ahead if you are going to be travelling then.

1 January – New Year's Day
Easter Monday
1 May – May Day or Labour Day
8 May – Victory 1945 Day
Ascension Thursday and Whit Monday
14 July – Bastille Day
15 August – Assumption of the Blessed Virgin Mary
1 November – All Saints' Day
11 November – Armistice 1918 Day
25 December – Christmas

Booking and cancellation

Do be clear about the room booked and the price for B&B and for meals. It is essential to book well ahead for July and August, and wise for other months. If you practise the last-minuting habit which seems to be spreading, you deprive yourself of choice and make life harder for your hosts. Owners may send you a booking form or contrat de location (tenancy contract) which must be filled in and returned, and commits both sides. Requests for deposits vary; some are non-refundable, some owners may charge you for the whole of the booked stay in advance.

Some cancellation policies are more stringent than others. It is also worth noting that some owners will take this deposit directly from your credit/debit card without contacting you to discuss it. So ask them to explain their cancellation policy clearly before booking so you understand exactly where you stand; it may well avoid a nasty surprise.

Remember that the UK is one hour behind France and people can be upset by telephone enquiries coming through late in their evening.

Payment

Cash is usually the easiest way to pay. Virtually all ATMs in France take Visa and MasterCard. Some owners take credit cards but not all. If they do, we have given them the appropriate symbol. (Check that your particular card is acceptable.) Euro travellers' cheques will usually be accepted; other currency cheques are unpopular because of commission charges.

Tipping

Owners do not expect tips. If you have been treated with extraordinary kindness, write to them, or leave a small gift. Please tell us, too – we love to hear, and we do record, all feedback.

Arrivals and departures

Say roughly what time you will arrive (normally after 4pm), as most hosts like to welcome you personally. Be on time if you have booked dinner; if, despite best efforts, you are delayed, phone to give warning.

Closed

When given in months this means the whole of the month(s) stated. So, 'Closed: November–March' means closed from 1 November to 31 March.

Photo: Clos Saint Clement, entry 828

Alastair Sawday's

'More than a bed
for the night...'

Britain
France
Ireland
Italy
Portugal
Spain

www.sawdays.co.uk

Self-Catering | B&B | Hotel | Pub | Canopy & Stars

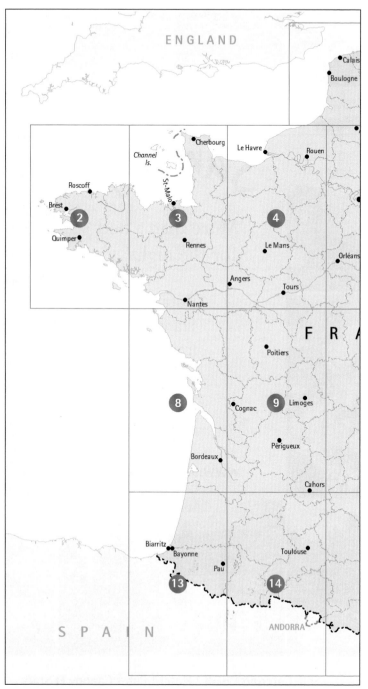

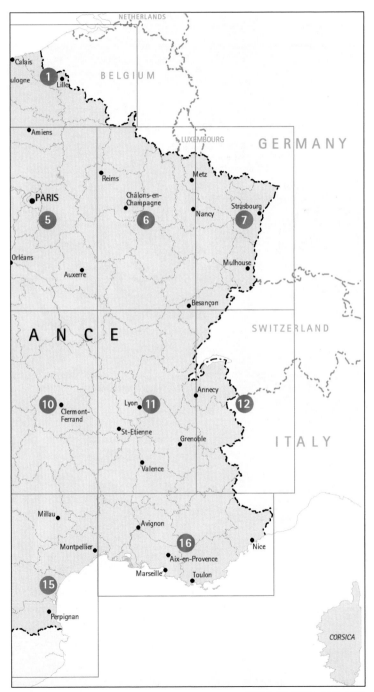

©Maidenhead Cartographic, 2013

LA CABANE DU PERCHE
Normandy - **Entry 255**

Map 1

19

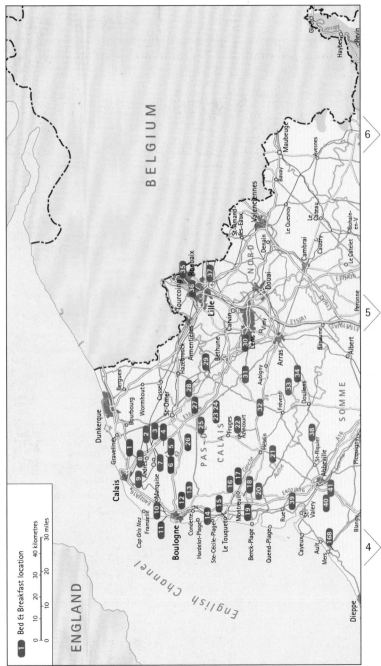

©Maidenhead Cartographic, 2013

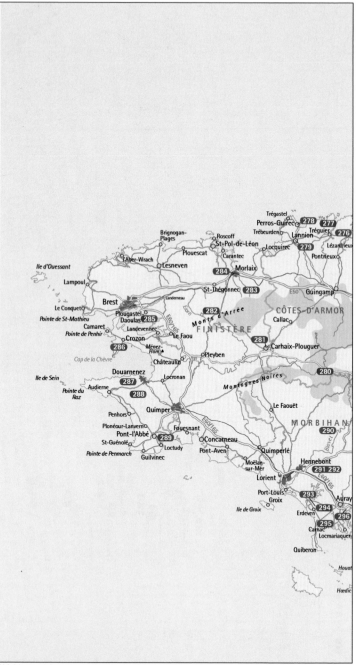

Map 3   21

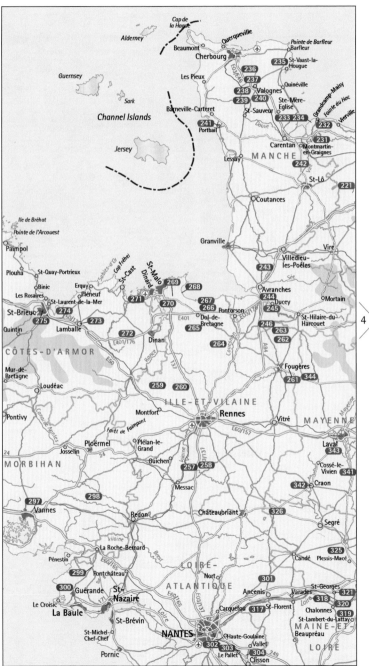

©Maidenhead Cartographic, 2013

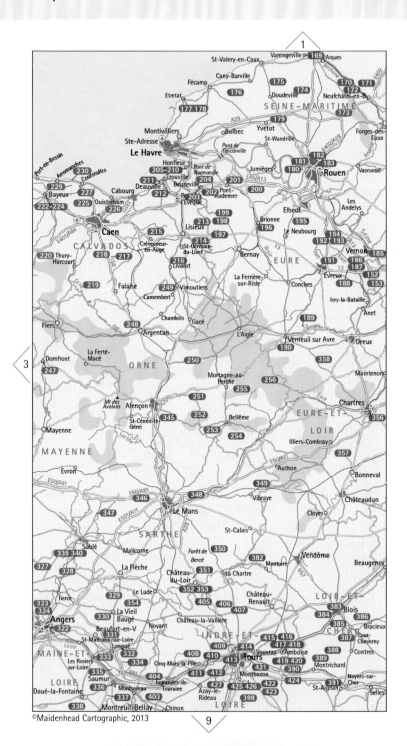

Map 5   23

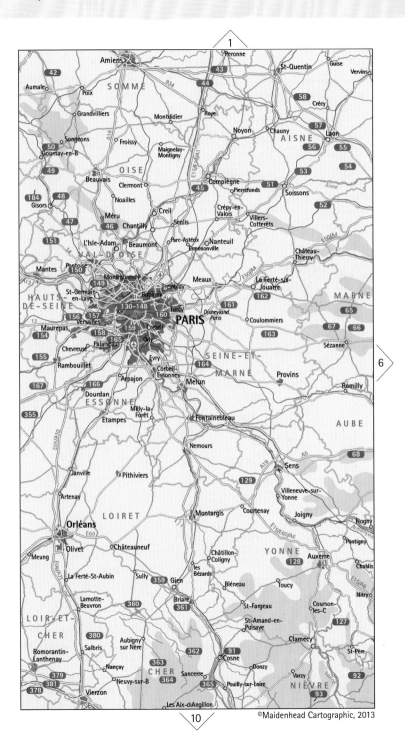

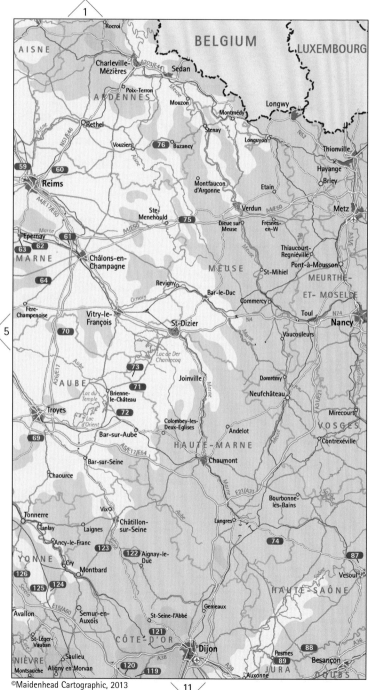

Map 7   25

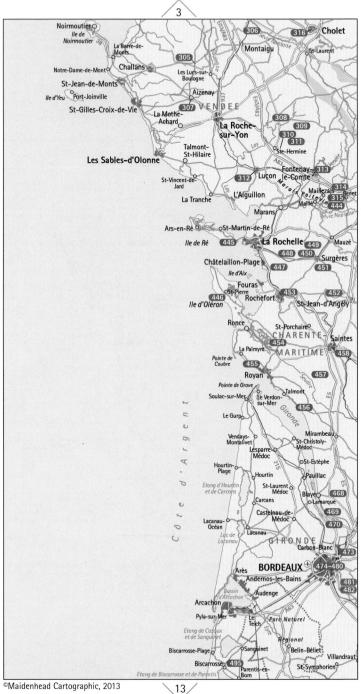

Map 9   27

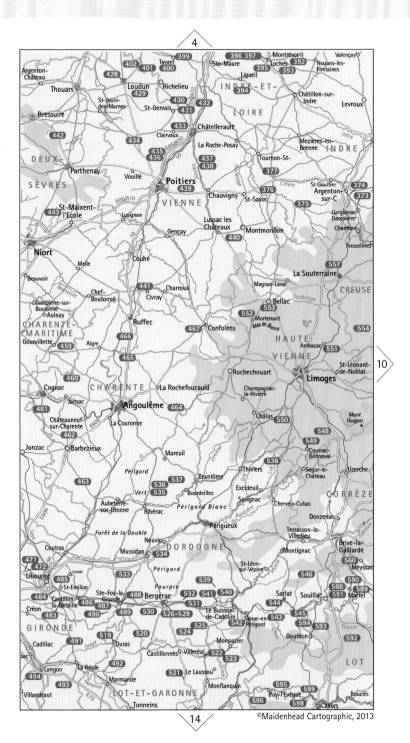

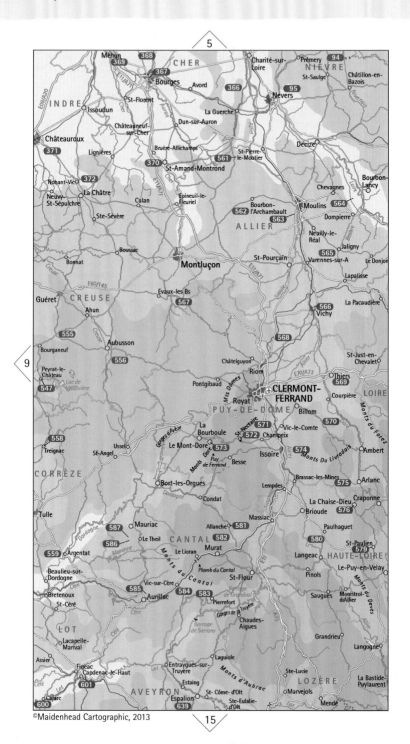

Map 11

29

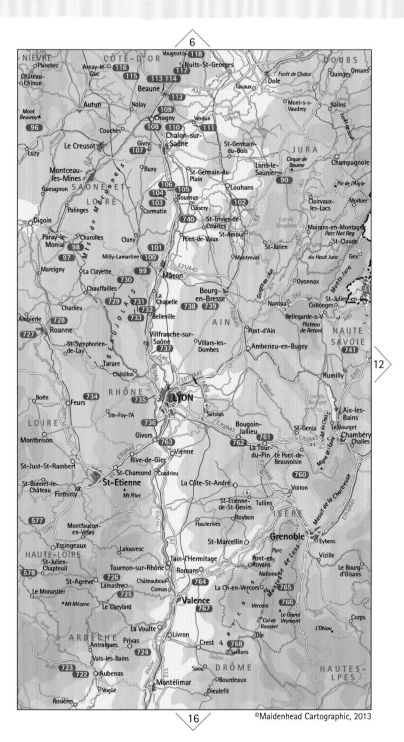

7

DOUBS

Morteau

Mouthier
Monthenoit
Doubs
Pontarlier
Cluse de
Joux
Les Hôpitaux-Neufs
Mont d'Or
Chaux-
Neuve

SWITZERLAND

Lausanne

E25/E62 Lac Léman (Lake Geneva)

Evian
Thonon 742
Sciez
743
Abondance
744
Morzine
745 746
Bonneville
Cluses
747
HAUTE
SAVOIE
748
Sallanches Servoz Argentière
Annecy 749 Le Fayet Chamonix
Thônes Combloux Chamonix-Mont-Blanc
750 752 Mont Blanc
St-
Jorioz Flumet 751
Lac
d'Annecy Megève Les
Contamines
Ugine

Albertville Roignais
Conflans Bourg-St-Maurice
754 757
Aime
756
SAVOIE 753 Mt Pourri
Aiguebelle 755 758
Moûtiers Val d'Isère
Grande
Casse
Parc National
Bonneval
de la Vanoise
Massif de la Vanoise Bessans
La Chambre St-Jean-de-Maurienne Lanslebourg
Avrieux ITALY
Modane
Valloire
759
La Grave
La Meije Le Monêtier-les-Bains
ISÈRE Chantemerle
Massif des Ecrins Mt Pelvoux Montgenèvre
Parc National Briançon
Abriès
des Ecrins Parc Nat Rég
Château-Queyras
Queyras
Vieux du Queyras
Chaillol 776 Guillestre
HAUTES-ALPES
Vars
Les Claux
Gap Embrun
Barrage de
Serre-Ponçon

11

Geneva

Mt Salève

Bonneville
Cluses

16

Map 13   31

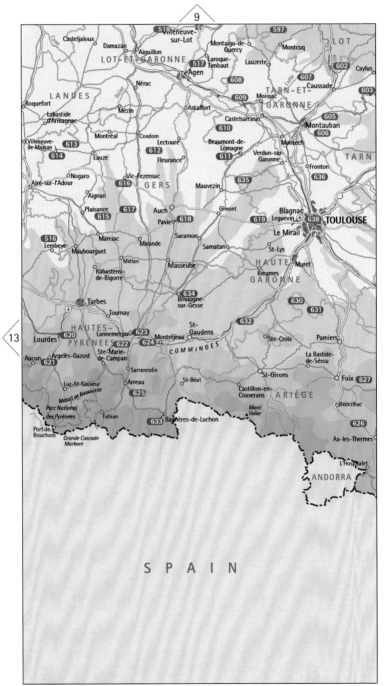

Map 15

33

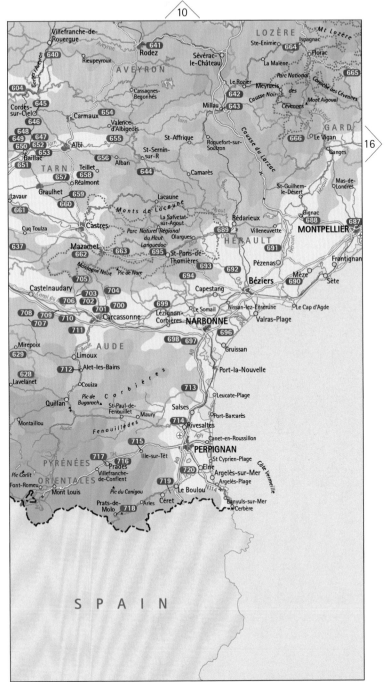

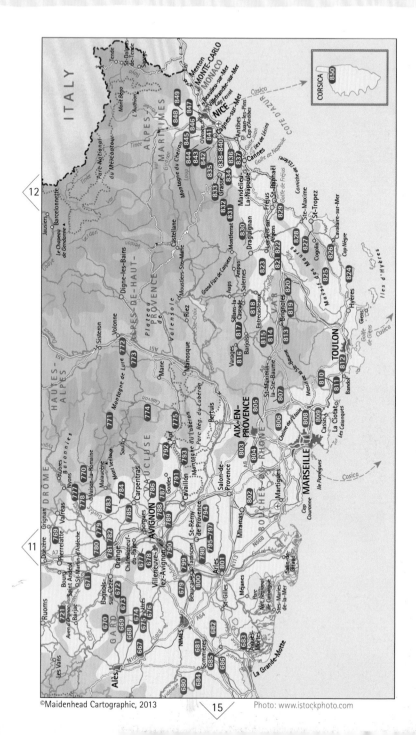

The North • Picardy

Ardres Bridge Cottage

A canal-side setting among rolling agricultural plains, usefully close to Calais. The gardens are peaceful and the owners offer friendly table d'hôtes. The ground-floor bedroom gives onto the flowery borders, the other has its own little balcony overlooking the pond, where farmyard fowl frolic, and its shower room downstairs. Both are country cosy and comfortable with floral bed linen and wooden furniture; bathrooms are among the best. You share the young and charming owners' sitting room: long and spacious with a big fire and plenty of squishy sofas; breakfast is round a farmhouse table. Utterly touching and authentic.

Cot available.

Les Fuchsias

This unusual Victorian townhouse in Bois en Ardres has a pleasingly mixed-up feel with its gingerbread cutouts, variegated roofs and lovely copsy garden of woodland thrown against lawns and fields. Francis is chatty (in English), charming and informative; Bernadette tends house, pets and guests with loving care. Guests have their own cosy, colourful sitting and breakfast rooms; for simple meals, it's a short walk to a brasserie. Inviting bedrooms have pretty duvets, fresh modern furnishings, wicker armchairs, antique samplers; the family room and the attic suite are particularly gorgeous.

Rooms	2: 1 double; 1 triple with separate shower.
Price	€50. Triple €50–€60. Extra bed €10.
Meals	Dinner with wine, €20.
Closed	Rarely.

Rooms	3: 1 suite for 4; 1 twin, 1 family room for 4 (sharing separate wc).
Price	€53–€60. Family room €53–€100. Suite €55–€100. Dog or cat €5.
Meals	Brasserie 50m, restaurants 2km.
Closed	Rarely.

Laurent Blanquart
Ardres Bridge Cottage,
678 rue du Fort Bâtard,
62610 Pont d'Ardres, Pas-de-Calais
Tel   +33 (0)3 21 96 63 92
Mobile   +33 (0)6 82 02 13 47
Email   blanquart.laurent@wanadoo.fr
Web   www.ardres-bridge-cottage.com

Bernadette Balloy
Les Fuchsias,
292 rue du Général de St Just,
62610 Bois en Ardres, Pas-de-Calais
Tel   +33 (0)3 21 82 05 25
Email   lesfuchsias@aol.com
Web   www.lesfuchsias-ardres.fr

Entry 1   Map 1

Entry 2   Map 1

La Bohême

Extrovert, excitable Sonia enjoys music, painting, cooking for and chatting with guests. Timeworn beams, dark floors, solid country furniture and knick-knackery galore: it's 'French rustique' and, like oysters or Marmite, some will love it, some won't! The overgrown garden bursts with life and secret corners, the garden-view room under the eaves is prettily done in red Jouy. In an outbuilding, the plain white and grey attic room with its big bathroom is great for a family (watch the stairs). This is lovely pony-trekking country and, if you'd like to trade car for horse, riding can be organised.

La Ferme de Wolphus

The family are truly delightful – they speak English, do wine tastings and will sell you wine and honey. Guest rooms are in a little house in the garden, breakfast is in the owners' family living room. All is straightforward, simple comfort with super new mattresses on big, adjustable beds. Basic pine furniture and slatting grace smallish, under-the-eaves rooms and shower cubicles are in the bedrooms. The closeness to ferry ports is seductive, though the nearby main road may disturb some. A lake, old trees, sheep and peacocks surround both farmhouse and outbuildings. It's basic, busy, friendly, and tremendous value.

Rooms	3: 2 doubles, 1 family room for 2-6.
Price	€55–€60. Family room €55–€135. Extra bed €20. Pets €10.
Meals	Dinner with wine, €25.
Closed	Rarely.

Rooms	3: 2 triples (sharing wc on floor below); 1 quadruple.
Price	Triple €45–€64. Quadruple €50–€77.
Meals	Restaurants 1km.
Closed	Rarely.

Sonia Benoît
La Bohême,
1947 rue de la Grasse Payelle,
62370 Zutkerque, Pas-de-Calais
Tel   +33 (0)3 21 35 70 25
Mobile +33 (0)6 16 18 71 22
Email sonia-benoit-la-boheme@wanadoo.fr
Web   perso.wanadoo.fr/sonia-la-boheme

Jean-Jacques Behaghel
La Ferme de Wolphus,
62890 Zouafques, Pas-de-Calais
Tel   +33 (0)3 21 35 61 61
Mobile +33 (0)6 43 03 93 28
Email ferme.de.wolphus@wanadoo.fr
Web   ferme-wolphus.pagesperso-orange.fr

Entry 3 Map 1

Entry 4 Map 1

Le Manoir

The trompe l'œil and frescoed friezes are lavish, from the dining panelling to the staircase 'marble'; Sylvie and Pierre are ever restoring the old house and now making a room for their disabled daughter. In spite of being known in the village as Le Château it's not really big but, with so many original details intact, it's a historian's delight. The attic rooms are romantic country-modern, those on the first floor are faded-elegant French: deep mauve and moss green fabrics and papers and some spectacular carved wardrobes and beds. Good dinner, gardens with box parterre and trees, and a living room for guests.

La Ferme de Beaupré

These lovely gentle people will take you happily into their gorgeous old house at the end of the tree-lined drive and ply you with fine home-grown organic food (ah, those breakfast jams). Lut, from Belgium, is a gracious and unpretentiously warm music teacher and mother of two boys who speaks English; Jean-Michel takes over when she is away. Perfect, peaceful bedrooms – one in taupes, off-whites, toile de Jouy and a tiny room off with a child's bed, the other modern red, white, rattan and wood. You have sole use of the living room and the garden bursts with peonies, lupins, roses and cherries. An adorable, very special place.

Minimum two nights (weekends mid-May to mid-Sept).

Rooms	5: 3 doubles, 1 triple, 1 suite for 4.
Price	€75. Triple €90. Suite €110.
Meals	Dinner with wine, €28–€40.
Closed	Rarely.

Rooms	2: 1 double, 1 family room for 4.
Price	€70. Family room €70–€110.
	Singles €60. Extra bed €20.
	€7 supplement for one night stays.
Meals	Dinner with wine, by prior arrangement, €25.
Closed	Christmas.

	Sylvie & Pierre Bréemersch		Lut & Jean-Michel Louf-Degrauwe
	Le Manoir,		La Ferme de Beaupré,
	40 route de Licques,		129 rue de Licques,
	62890 Bonningues lès Ardres,		62890 Bonningues lès Ardres,
	Pas-de-Calais		Pas-de-Calais
Tel	+33 (0)3 21 82 69 05	Tel	+33 (0)3 21 35 14 44
Email	pierre.breemersch@wanadoo.fr	Email	lut.degrauwe@nordnet.fr
Web	www.lemanoirdebonningues.com	Web	www.lafermedebeaupre.com

Entry 5   Map 1

Entry 6   Map 1

Le Manoir de Bois en Ardres

After 200 years of conversions, this house of history and unusual character stands cloister-like round its sheltered garden and old stone pond. Beyond, ponies graze beneath the mature trees of the ten-acre park: come to commune with nature. In the house and the outbuildings, lovely gently coloured rooms are a hymn to Françoise's stencil and furniture-painting skills while Thierry's collecting flair shines through the intriguing bric-a-brac. The whole atmosphere echoes this couple's joie de vivre. Just one big, attractive dayroom, for generous breakfasts of homemade jams and yogurt, fresh fruit and cheese.

Les Draps d'Or

It's been an inn since 1640 and Hilary, well integrated here, fits the tradition: vivacious, elegant and English, she enjoys receiving guests. The guest wing has its own (digicode) entrance straight off the street – you are as independent as you like. Up the narrow staircase to tidy, wood-floored rooms: blue, yellow and green; fresh, spotless and bright. The triple sports red ethnic weave curtains and a powder-blue frieze. All give onto the cobbled street but few cars pass at night. Ardres is a delightful little town and the 'Cloths of Gold' is a handy stopover on the way to Calais.

Extra twin / child's room available, sharing bathroom with triple (let to same party only).

Rooms	3: 1 suite for 4. Outbuildings: 1 twin, 1 double, sharing shower room.
Price	€78. Suite €78–€143.
Meals	Restaurant 1km.
Closed	Rarely.

Rooms	3: 2 doubles; 1 triple with separate bathroom.
Price	€62–€70. Triple €68–€100. Pets €10.
Meals	Restaurants within walking distance.
Closed	Rarely.

Françoise & Thierry Roger
Le Manoir de Bois en Ardres,
1530 rue de St Quentin,
62610 Ardres, Pas-de-Calais
Tel +33 (0)3 21 85 97 78
Mobile +33 (0)6 15 03 06 21
Email roger@aumanoir.com
Web www.aumanoir.com

Hilary Mackay
Les Draps d'Or,
152 rue Lambert d'Ardres,
62610 Ardres, Pas-de-Calais
Tel +33 (0)3 21 82 20 44
Mobile +33 (0)6 24 40 58 01
Email hilary@drapsdor.com
Web www.drapsdor.com

The North

Villa Héloïse

An endearing place with an owner to match. Chatty hard-working Marie-Christine does everything herself in her pretty red-brick home; she's even built a treehouse in the garden. Stay in the family suite in the main house, a wonderland of plants and collected items old and new, or the independent wooden-decked apartment. It comes without a sitting room but Madame has buckets of personality to make up for this, and you can dine outside on that high decked terrace. Evergreens and shrubs provide the backdrop, fields surround you, Calais and Belgium are less than 30 minutes away. Wander the dunes, cycle, fish.

Rooms	2: 1 family room for 4. Apartment: 1 double with kitchenette.
Price	Family room €55–€90. Apartment €60.
Meals	Dinner with wine, €25.
Closed	Rarely.

Marie–Christine Debriel
Villa Héloïse,
683 rue de l'Église, 62340 Andres,
Pas-de-Calais
Tel +33 (0)3 21 35 15 01
Mobile +33 (0)6 87 12 51 02
Email marie-christine.debriel@wanadoo.fr
Web villaheloise.net

Entry 9 Map 1

The North

La Villa Sainte Claire

Friendly Catherine lends you bikes – so pedal off to Wimereux, a sweet seaside town a mile down the road. Then return to a 18th-century house in the lee of a village church, its long elegant façade distinguished by tall white windows perfectly beshuttered. Fresh, spacious and uncluttered is the guest bedroom, with views to a beautiful front garden, and it's a treat to stroll the rambling grounds, dotted with statues, punctuated by topiary. Wake to fresh local croissants and organic homemade jams; set off for the markets and shops of Boulogne… and a lovely lunch in the historic old town. The coastline is wild and wonderful.

Cot available. Additional room available for 2 children.

Rooms	1 double.
Price	€90.
Meals	Restaurant 50m.
Closed	Rarely.

Catherine Debatte
La Villa Sainte Claire,
11 rue du Presbytère,
62126 Wimille, Pas-de-Calais
Tel +33 (0)3 21 91 99 58
Mobile +33 (0)6 16 70 84 26
Email contact@villa-sainte-claire.fr
Web www.villa-sainte-claire.fr

Entry 10 Map 1

Villa Fleur d'Écume

Hop over the channel and you'll soon be sunning yourself in seaside Wimereux. The Poulains' eco-friendly house looks straight out of New England with its soft blue weatherboarding and light, airy, wood-clad rooms dotted with driftwood works by their creative son. It's like staying with friends: two neat bedrooms in dusky pink and cream (one with a balcony), a lovely garden with a breakfast terrace and children's seesaw. Your helpful hosts bake bread, yogurt cake, make fruit compotes… Ask – in French please! – about beaches, restaurants, kite surfing, golf. Everything in town is an easy walk; Boulogne is a short drive.

Le Clos d'Esch

The golden stone of the oldest farmhouse in the village is now fronted by a large glass sunroom, and flowers flourish in the lower garden where two new houses stand. Discreetly friendly and obliging, new owners Olivier and Véronique (this was her pioneering parents' B&B) serve delicious breakfasts and for dinner there's a great little place five minutes away. One traditional-style bedroom is in an outbuilding overlooking courtyard and wooded hills; the triple has a wrought-iron bed with a leopard-skin cover and its own patio overlooking the garden; all are pristine, and there's a cosy sitting room too. Good value.

Rooms	2 doubles.
Price	€95. Extra bed €30.
Meals	Restaurant 500m.
Closed	Rarely.

Rooms	4: 1 double, 2 twins, 1 triple.
Price	€53–€62. Triple €68.
Meals	Auberges in village (200m).
Closed	Rarely.

Odile & François Poulain
Villa Fleur d'Écume,
2 bis av Agrippa,
62930 Wimereux,
Pas-de-Calais
Tel   +33 (0)3 21 32 75 04
Email   fleurdecumewimereux@gmail.com
Web   www.fleurdecume-wimereux.com

Véronique Boussemaere & Olivier Chartaux
Le Clos d'Esch,
62360 Echinghen, Pas-de-Calais
Tel   +33 (0)3 21 91 14 34
Mobile +33 (0)6 89 04 72 78
Email   veronique.boussemaere@wanadoo.fr
Web   www.leclosdesch.fr

Entry 11   Map 1

Entry 12   Map 1

Le Clos de Tournes

Tranquil meadows, pastoral bliss: a metaphor for your calm, smiling fishmonger hosts. Caroline grew up with B&B: her parents were pioneers, she loves it. The fine old farmhouse, with pale façade and garden dotted by shady fruit trees, is an immaculate B&B retreat, while the outbuildings house two busy gîtes. The adventurous bedrooms are a surprise after the classic French dining room (long table, high upholstered chairs). Urban-chic in deep red and mustard, one is swathed in rich oriental toile de Jouy, the other in intensely patterned wallpaper and billowing taffeta. Caroline, graceful and sociable, is an excellent cook.

Le Moulin

No more milling at the moulin, but the lake is serene and it's a treat to throw open a window and watch the ducks. All is warmly inviting at this big reassuring millhouse built in 1855 – a classically French B&B with a dark leather chesterfield and voluptuous Louis XV furniture in the sitting/dining room, and delicious breakfasts at a long elegant table. Bedrooms are pretty, one grey and white with a bergère cane bed and silver-grey scatter cushions; corridors have been revamped in warm colours. Christine is gentle, charming, welcoming – and you are a spade's throw from the local sandy beach.

Rooms	2: 1 double, 1 twin.
Price	€62. Extra bed €20.
Meals	Dinner with wine, €35. Restaurant 2km.
Closed	Rarely.

Rooms	3 doubles.
Price	€60-€75.
Meals	Restaurants 5km.
Closed	Rarely.

Caroline Boussemaere
Le Clos de Tournes,
1810 route de Tournes,
62360 Echinghen, Pas-de-Calais
Tel +33 (0)3 91 90 48 78
Mobile +33 (0)6 07 09 21 14
Email reservation@leclosdetournes.com
Web www.leclosdetournes.com

Christine Lécaille
Le Moulin,
40 rue du Centre, 62187 Dannes,
Pas-de-Calais
Tel +33 (0)3 21 33 74 74
Mobile +33 (0)6 62 27 60 33
Email christine.lecaille@free.fr
Web www.au-moulin.com

Entry 13 Map 1

Entry 14 Map 1

Villa Vertefeuille

Designed in 1913 for an actor, bought by the Simphal family in the 1930s as a summer residence, this house belongs to a lost world of easy leisure. In her boundless enthusiasm, Emmanuelle cherishes echoes of that era and, 100 years on, the family still come for summer breaks. But her renovation mostly heralds her beloved 18th century. Rooms are hugely atmospheric. Stripped, distressed château panelling clothes the big bedroom, old paintings hang near a 1720 mirror, the bathroom is fun in its shabby-chic, rough-tiled look. Pine trees shush in the big, calm and sheltering garden. Great beaches, riding and tennis are just beyond.

Rooms	1 double.
Price	€135.
Meals	Restaurants 500m.
Closed	Rarely.

Emmanuelle Simphal
Villa Vertefeuille,
Avenue des Pins,
62520 Le Touquet,
Pas-de-Calais
Tel   +33 (0)3 23 22 97 33
Email   lescernailles@hotmail.fr

Entry 15   Map 1

Le Vert Bois

Ancient peace, delightful people, fields as far as the eye can see. And it's majestic for a farm – house, outbuildings and courtyard are handsome and immaculately preserved. Étienne, Véronique and their young family grow cereals, keep cows and look after guests – charmingly – in a converted farm building. Upstairs are a fresh cosy double and a pretty twin; ceilings slope, walls are spotless, bedcovers quilted, bathrooms pristine. Breakfasts, we're told, are lovely. The fine old town of Montreuil is a walk across fields, for restaurants and "astonishing points of view". Near Calais but feels like the heart of France.

Rooms	2: 1 double, 1 twin.
Price	€65-€85.
Meals	Restaurants in town.
Closed	Rarely.

Étienne & Véronique Bernard
Le Vert Bois,
62170 Neuville sous Montreuil,
Pas-de-Calais
Tel   +33 (0)3 21 06 09 41
Mobile   +33 (0)6 08 74 79 43
Email   etienne.bernard6@wanadoo.fr
Web   gite-montreuilsurmer.com

Entry 16   Map 1

Manoir Francis

Through the gateway... to step back 400 years. Built in 1662 by the village seigneur, long, low and gleaming white in its walled garden, the old manoir stands peacefully and privately in four acres, accompanied by pigeonnier, pond, peacocks, guineafowl and geese. Bedrooms are unusual, theatrical, inviting: stunning ceiling timbers in one, warm glowing colours in another; all come with chalk-stone walls, paintings, candles, and spotless baths with shower attachments. Flexible, wildlife-loving Madame serves a lavish breakfast in the rustically splendid saddlery overlooking the paddock – and delights in her Sawday's guests!

2 child beds in one double bedroom available.

St Justin

A few bounds from Montreuil's lovely town square, this may not be the prettiest setting (edge-of-town road noise morn and eve), but it's perfect for those wanting to be near the hustle and bustle. Inside all is cosy and homely in that very French way, our favourite bedroom garnished with 19th-century coloured glass doors to a balcony overlooking garden and townscape. Weather-permitting, Madame Gobert serves a great breakfast on the crazy-paving terrace in their little garden; smiley Monsieur is a sociable soul; and river valleys, beaches and ancient ramparts are all worth a stroll. All this just a pop across the Channel, and great value too.

Rooms	3 doubles.
Price	€75.
Meals	Restaurant 5km.
Closed	15 Nov-15 Feb.

Rooms	2: 1 double, 1 twin.
Price	€58.
Meals	Restaurant 700m.
Closed	Rarely.

	Dominique Leroy
	Manoir Francis,
	1 rue de l'Église,
	62170 Marles sur Canche,
	Pas-de-Calais
Tel	+33 (0)3 21 81 38 80
Email	manoir.francis@wanadoo.fr
Web	www.manoirfrancis.com

Entry 17   Map 1

	Élisabeth Gobert
	St Justin,
	203 rue de Paris,
	Montreuil sur Mer, 62170 Écuires,
	Pas-de-Calais
Tel	+33 (0)3 21 05 49 03
Mobile	+33 (0)6 09 56 29 30
Email	elisabeth.gobert@gmail.com

Entry 18   Map 1

The North

Villa Marie

You can smell the sea air from the garden of this 1903 urban villa, built as a holiday home for a retired colonel. Vivacious Viviane gives you delicious flexibly timed breakfasts with homemade pancakes and waffles. Choose between the rooms in the main house – floral prints, antiques, crochet, sloping ceilings – or independence in the garden lodge: fresh, clean, pretty, with a charming terrace. The good-sized garden is totally walled, with fruit trees, shrubs and conifers; find a shady spot here, or head for the coast and some great seafood restaurants.

Rooms	4: 1 family suite for 4. Lodge: 1 double, 1 twin/double, 1 family suite for 3.
Price	€65-€75. Family suite €65-€125. Extra bed €20.
Meals	Kitchenette in Lodge. Restaurant 2.5km.
Closed	Rarely.

	Viviane Brocard
	Villa Marie,
	12 rue des Écoles, 62180 Verton,
	Pas-de-Calais
Tel	+33 (0)3 21 94 05 49
Mobile	+33 (0)6 20 07 82 34
Email	phbrocar@wanadoo.fr
Web	chambresdhotes-villamarie.fr

Entry 19   Map 1

The North

Ferme du Saule

Readers have called Le Saule "a little treasure". And we know that the Trunnets' smiles are genuine, their converted outbuilding handsome and perfectly finished (down to mosquito nets on windows), the ground-floor rooms solidly traditional, the beds excellent, the dayroom proud of its beautiful armoire, and you get your own little table for breakfast. Monsieur and his son are only too happy to show you the flax production process (it's fascinating); young Madame looks after her three little ones and cares beautifully for guests. Proclaimed "the best cowshed I've ever stayed in" by one happy guest.

Rooms	5: 2 doubles, 2 family rooms for 3, 1 suite for 4-5.
Price	€55. Family rooms €55-€70. Suite €55-€100. Extra bed €15. Cot €6.
Meals	Restaurants 6km.
Closed	Rarely.

	Trunnet Family
	Ferme du Saule,
	20 rue de l'Église,
	62170 Brimeux,
	Pas-de-Calais
Tel	+33 (0)3 21 06 01 28
Email	fotrunnet@wanadoo.fr
Web	perso.wanadoo.fr/fermedusaule

Entry 20   Map 1

Ferme Prévost de Courmière

In the old, old farmhouse – 1680 is inscribed in flint on the façade – find comfort and peace in great measure, fresh white and floral bed linen, real croissants, roses and peonies in the garden. With the house restoration behind them, your hospitable hosts have turned their stylish attention to the transformation of the courtyard, orchard and garden and have happily embarked on B&B. Bedrooms are pure, fresh, new and extremely charming. Breakfast is a moveable feast; dinner celebrates the most delicious Flemish dishes, served at a large table in a light, lofty room. Superb all round.

Rooms	4: 2 doubles, 1 family room for 4, 1 suite for 4, each with sitting room.
Price	€60–€70. Family room €75. Suite €75. Extra bed €20.
Meals	Dinner with wine, €30.
Closed	Rarely.

Annie Lombardet
Ferme Prévost de Courmière,
510 rue de Crécy,
62140 Capelle lès Hesdin, Pas-de-Calais

Tel	+33 (0)3 21 81 16 04
Mobile	+33 (0)6 08 28 21 66
Email	ferme-prevost-de-courmiere@wanadoo.fr
Web	prevostdecourmiere.monsite-orange.fr

Entry 21   Map 1

La Gacogne

Enter a 1750 arched orangery (the tower) filled with a very long table, an open fire and 101 curiosities. Alongside teddies are chain-mail bodices, longbows, crossbows and similar armoured reminders of Agincourt's place in history. It is a treat to be received in this most colourful and eccentric of parlours for hearty continental breakfasts (the seed cake is delicious), hosted by motherly Marie-José and knightly Patrick who've lived here for years. Small bedrooms in the outbuilding are farmhouse simple with heavy-draped medieval touches, a lush garden melts into a conifer copse and your hosts are utterly charming.

Rooms	3: 2 doubles, 1 family room.
Price	€70. Family room €80.
Meals	Restaurant 1km.
Closed	Rarely.

Patrick & Marie-José Fenet
La Gacogne,
62310 Azincourt,
Pas-de-Calais

Tel	+33 (0)3 21 04 45 61
Email	fenetgeoffroy@aol.com
Web	www.gacogne.com

Entry 22   Map 1

The North

Ferme de la Vallée

This is a real farm, so don't expect pretty-pretty – but Madame is a character and her welcome is top class. Readers return, for the authentic atmosphere and the delicious food. Amazing how much space lies behind the simple frontage of this street-side farmhouse; every little corner is crammed with 40 years' worth of collecting: porcelain, plates, jugs, crystal decanter stoppers, baskets, collectable plastics... the list is long. Come for comfy beds, generous living room areas, billiards, table football (a vintage table) and games. It's intrinsically French despite the eccentricities, and Madame is a delight.

Rooms	3: 1 double, 1 triple, 1 family suite for 4.
Price	€50. Triple €60. Family suite €75.
Meals	Dinner with wine, €20.
Closed	Never.

Brigitte de Saint Laurent
Ferme de la Vallée,
13 rue Neuve,
62190 Auchy au Bois,
Pas-de-Calais
Tel +33 (0)3 21 25 80 09
Email brigitte.de-saint-laurent@wanadoo.fr
Web fermedelavallee.free.fr

Entry 23 Map 1

The North

Les Cohettes

Elegant, vivacious Gina cares deeply that everyone be happy, adores her guests and does brilliant table d'hôtes. A full house makes quite a crowd and when B&B and gîte guests come together there can be a dozen at table. But the big garden opens its arms to all and has some comforting mature trees under which guests may link up for summer pétanque. Dark beams have been painted pale, furniture has been sanded and smudge-finished. Pretty and cosy bedrooms – in the long low farmhouse attic – are colour-coded, while the chalet suite is snug with its own little patio. The garden is peaceful and readers love it all.

Rooms	4: 2 doubles, 1 twin, 1 family room for 4.
Price	€58–€60. Family room €55–€91. Singles €50.
Meals	Dinner with wine, €25. Guest kitchen.
Closed	Rarely.

Gina Bulot
Les Cohettes,
28 rue de Pernes,
62190 Auchy au Bois, Pas-de-Calais
Tel +33 (0)3 21 02 09 47
Mobile +33 (0)6 07 06 65 42
Email ginabulot@gmail.com
Web www.chambresdhotes-chezgina.com

Entry 24 Map 1

Les Dornes

Table d'hôtes round the convivial table is the inspiration behind this B&B – which, being perfectionists, this couple do so well. Dinner, locally sourced, sounds delicious, while vegetables come from an immaculate potager. The interiors of their new but traditional village house are equally manicured: the L-shaped living room is yours to share; the bedrooms, colour-themed and French-cosy, two on the ground floor, their tiles topped by rugs, two under the eaves with honey-coloured boards; all large and super-comfortable. Historic St Omer is a must – for music and markets, bric-a-brac and breweries. Tremendous value.

La Coulonnière

Geneviève is the immaculate gardener, Dominique, a former timber importer and now deputy mayor, has limitless knowledge of the area. Both love having guests. In this new-but-traditional very French house your hexagonal bedroom in conservatory style has east-west windows that catch the sun all day. All mod cons here: electric shutters, a waterjet shower with innumerable settings, 300 channels on TV, even night lights to guide you to your loo. Best of all, your own decked terrace onto the peaceful garden. Breakfasts are superb: your generous hosts give you only the best.

Rooms	4: 3 doubles, 1 twin.
Price	€60.
Meals	Dinner with wine, €25.
Closed	Rarely.

Rooms	1 double.
Price	€110.
Meals	Restaurant 1.5km.
Closed	Rarely.

Jaqueline & Gilles Blondel
Les Dornes, 520 rue des Deux Upen,
Upen d'Aval, 62129 Delettes,
Pas-de-Calais

Tel	+33 (0)3 21 95 87 09
Mobile	+33 (0)6 88 82 55 96
Email	lesdornes@lesdornes.com
Web	www.lesdornes.com

Dominique & Geneviève Ottevaere
La Coulonnière, 26 La Place,
Hameau de Cantemerle,
62380 Wismes, Pas-de-Calais

Tel	+33 (0)3 21 39 91 51
Mobile	+33 (0)6 85 32 71 24
Email	la-coulonniere@orange.fr
Web	www.la-coulonniere.fr

Entry 25 Map 1

Entry 26 Map 1

Château de Moulin le Comte

A beautiful wooden floor in the 'green' bedroom and the black and white tiled hall are original touches still on show in this small château, renovated recently and completely by the Van der Elsts. Your Belgian hosts – father, mother, son – are serious about succeeding in their new venture and you will excuse the wonderfully kitsch china chihuahuas when you are relaxing in one of their spacious rooms; expect textured wallpapers and smart showers. Dinner in the elegant green and gold dining room might feature local watercress, colourful St Omer cauliflowers or veal with mustard, cooked by multilingual Francis.

Rooms	5: 4 twins/doubles, 1 family room.
Price	€89–€129. Family room €109–€149.
Meals	Dinner €15–€20; 5 courses, €27; 5 courses with wine, €49. Restaurant 1.5km.
Closed	Rarely.

Francis Van der Elst
Château de Moulin le Comte,
44 rue Principale, Moulin le Comte,
62120 Aire sur la Lys, Pas-de-Calais

Tel	+33 (0)3 21 88 48 38
Mobile	+33 (0)6 24 21 08 91
Email	info@chateaudemoulinlecomte.com
Web	www.chateaudemoulinlecomte.com

Entry 27   Map 1

La Peylouse Manoir

A wildly entertaining place to stay. Generous, knowledgeable and immensely hospitable hosts live in a tall, grey and red mansion furnished in a madly eclectic mix of styles amid landscaped gardens full of ancient exotic trees. Intriguing military associations too, from arms manufacture for the Sun King (the bullet workshop is still in the grounds) to barracks for the Royal Welch Fusiliers. Bedrooms range from cosy 19th-century boudoir to heavenly Art Deco to New York studio-style; all are excellent, all have views over the spectacular grounds. The canal marina is a stroll away: you could arrive by boat.

Rooms	4: 2 doubles, 2 suites.
Price	€80–€160.
Meals	Restaurant 2km.
Closed	Rarely.

Luce Rousseau
La Peylouse Manoir,
Parc et Jardins de la Peylouse,
23 rue du 8 mai 1945,
62350 St Venant, Pas-de-Calais

Tel	+33 (0)3 21 26 92 02
Email	contact@lapeylouse.fr
Web	www.lapeylouse.fr

Entry 28   Map 1

The North

Le Château de Philiomel

Overlooking a lake and leafy parkland, this commanding, Italianate mansion has the right ingredients – pillars, portico, marble fireplaces – to give you grand ideas, yet is designed with a light touch. Lofty bedrooms are hotel-perfect in muted colours with a cool mix of contemporary furniture and antiques; bathrooms are bold and modern. Elegant buffet breakfasts are taken at separate tables in an uncluttered white space of panelling, parquet and shining silver. Unwind on this private estate in immaculate solitude (the owners live next door). There are two Michelin stars within a ten-minute drive.

Ferme du Moulin

Terraced houses in front, a perfect little farmyard behind, the kindest of hosts within – it's a privilege to meet such splendid people, retired farmers of old-fashioned simple good manners, he silently earthy, she comfortably maternal, delighting in her short travels and guests' conversation. Their modest, old-fashioned French farmers' house is stuffed with collections of bric-a-brac; their genuine chambres d'hôtes are family-furnished, floral-papered, draped with all sorts and conditions of crochet; the loo is across the landing. Breakfasts are good and you are perfectly placed for those battlefields.

Indoor car park available.

Rooms	4 doubles.
Price	€85–€125.
Meals	Restaurants 2km.
Closed	Rarely.

Rooms	2: 1 double, 1 triple, each with separate bathroom, sharing wc.
Price	€45.
Meals	Restaurants 500m.
Closed	Rarely.

Frédéric Devys
Le Château de Philiomel,
Rue Philiomel, 62190 Lillers,
Pas-de-Calais
Tel   +33 (0)3 21 61 76 76
Mobile +33 (0)6 09 10 81 95
Email   contact@philiomel.com
Web   www.lechateaudephiliomel.com

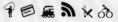

Entry 29   Map 1

Mr & Mme Dupont
Ferme du Moulin,
58 rue du Quatre Septembre,
62800 Liévin,
Pas-de-Calais
Tel   +33 (0)3 21 44 65 91

Entry 30   Map 1

La Maison de Campagne

Everyone loves it here: wine and conversation flow, and dinners are authentic and delicious. After years as a school librarian, Jacqueline threw herself into encouraging local tourism: a member of many associations and generous to a fault, she loves taking guests on walks and visits; Pierre is active in the village, too. Many drive straight past this area – take the chance to get to know it better with people who belong. You enter through the conservatory and every window looks onto flowers and meadows. Bedrooms, one on the ground floor, are simple but welcoming. Take a train to Paris for the day!

Rooms	2: 1 double with separate wc, 1 family room for 4.
Price	€50. Family room €80. Under 5's free.
Meals	Dinner €25. Wine €6-€12 per bottle.
Closed	Rarely.

Jacqueline Guillemant
La Maison de Campagne,
6 rue de l'Europe,
62127 Magnicourt en Comte,
Pas-de-Calais
Tel   +33 (0)3 21 41 51 00
Email jguillemant@gmail.com
Web   www.lamaisondecampagne.com

Entry 31   Map 1

Le Loubarré

The period of each piece shows on its face, so you expect the elegantly coffered ceilings, the deeply carved woodwork, the vast Louis XIII dresser... but nothing prepares you for the neo-gothic stone fireplace! The rooms in the stables, some up, some down, are pretty and spotless, each with good fabrics, some antiques, a neat shower room, and you can use the comfortable family sitting room. Madame loves telling tales of the house and its contents, and has some endearing dogs, goats and donkeys (and a weekend car-racing track in the valley). Both your hosts work constantly on their beloved house.

Rooms	3: 1 double, 2 twins.
Price	€56.
Meals	Guest kitchen. Restaurants within walking distance.
Closed	Rarely.

Marie-Christine & Philippe Vion
Le Loubarré,
550 rue des Montifaux,
62130 Gauchin Verloingt,
Pas-de-Calais
Tel   +33 (0)3 21 03 05 05
Email mcvion.loubarre@wanadoo.fr
Web   www.loubarre.com

Entry 32   Map 1

Château de Grand Rullecourt

A remarkable mix of place and people. This dynamic family – six fine children have grown and flown – have finished rebuilding their monumental château and brightening their escutcheon while being publishers in Paris and brilliant socialites: fascinating people, still energetic, and with a natural hospitality that makes up for any winter chill. Built in 1745, the château has many rooms and striking grandeur; come play lord and lady in chandeliered, ancestored salons, discover an aristocratic bedroom with big windows, walk the rolling green parkland as if it were your own. Breakfast is basic but it's another world.

Rooms	5: 4 doubles, 1 suite for 2-5.
Price	€100. Suite €100-€190.
Meals	Restaurants 4km.
Closed	Rarely.

Patrice & Chantal de Saulieu
Château de Grand Rullecourt,
62810 Grand Rullecourt,
Pas-de-Calais

Tel	+33 (0)3 21 58 06 37
Mobile	+33 (0)6 07 12 89 08
Email	psaulieu@routiers.com
Web	www.chateaux-chambres-hotes.com

Entry 33   Map 1

Château de Saulty

The re-lifted stately face looks finer than ever in its great park and apple orchards (15 varieties); a gorgeous setting. Inside, find a warm, embracing country house with a panelled breakfast room, an amazing, museum-worthy, multi-tiled gents cloakroom and, up the wide old stairs, quietly luxurious bedrooms, some very big, furnished with printed fabrics and period pieces. Be charmed by wooden floors and plain walls in sunny tones, perhaps an old fireplace or a mirrored armoire. Quiet and intelligent, Sylvie will make you feel welcome while serenely concocting delicious jams and managing her family. Great value.

Rooms	4: 1 double, 2 triples, 1 family room for 4.
Price	€70. Triple €80. Family room €100.
Meals	Restaurants 1km.
Closed	January.

Emmanuel & Sylvie Dalle
Château de Saulty,
82 rue de la Gare,
62158 Saulty,
Pas-de-Calais

Tel	+33 (0)3 21 48 24 76
Email	chateaudesaulty@nordnet.fr
Web	www.chateaudesaulty.com

Entry 34   Map 1

Le Jardin d'Alix

A quiet, elegant residential quarter – but hop on the tram and in 20 minutes you're in the historic centre of Lille. Alexandra's light, airy house, tucked away from the road, was built a mere half century ago by a well-known local church architect. Use your host's sitting room during the day; note the passage leading to the bedrooms has an internet post, and books galore, for the evening. Bedrooms, small and attractive, give onto the gorgeous garden – Alexandra's passion – and are hung with her paintings. Breakfast on homemade bread and jams served on fine porcelain in a spotless high-tech kitchen.

Minimum two nights.

Château de Courcelette

From the small-town back street you will enter unexpected 18th-century elegance – pilasters, panelling, marble, medallions – then a beautiful brick and cobble terrace to an acre of superb walled garden: a blissful discovery so near Lille, it is the oldest château left standing in the area. Your hosts will enchant you with their courtesy and deep love for Courcelette, their energy in preserving its classical forms, their care for your comfort; Madame bubbles and chats, Monsieur charms quietly. Pale bedrooms with original doors and handsome antiques set the tone for this quietly luxurious and civilised house. One of the best.

Rooms	2: 1 double, 1 suite.
Price	€60–€75.
Meals	Restaurants 3 minutes by tram.
Closed	Rarely.

Rooms	4: 2 doubles, 1 twin/double, 1 suite.
Price	€99. Suite €149.
Meals	Dinner with wine, €35. Guest kitchen.
Closed	Rarely.

Alexandra Hudson
Le Jardin d'Alix,
45 bis av de la Marne,
59200 Tourcoing, Nord
Tel   +33 (0)3 20 36 72 08
Email   dolcevitaanice@ymail.com
Web   www.lejardindalix.com

Catherine & Philippe Brame
Château de Courcelette,
17 rue César Parent,
59390 Lannoy, Nord
Tel   +33 (0)3 20 75 45 67
Mobile   +33 (0)6 62 45 45 67
Email   contact@chateau-de-courcelette.com
Web   www.chateau-de-courcelette.com

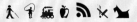

The North

Ferme de la Noyelle

The 17th-century archway leads into an enclosed farmyard where you feel sheltered and welcomed: Dominique and Nelly enjoy their guests. The moment you arrive you forget that this patch of countryside, this haven of peace, is near shopping outlets and autoroutes; they breed hens, geese, rabbits and cows. Simple guest rooms in the old stables are in new-pine cottagey style, with jolly colour matches and wide showers. No sitting room but a communal kitchen to share, and a modest restaurant in another wing, open at weekends. Good value, good dinners, and Belgium five minutes away.

Picardy

Les Mazures

An architect-designed eco house, whose beauty lies in its simplicity. And the garden is glorious, a blaze of colour and form – rock, Japanese and wild flower, carefully gauged scent and colour combos to attract bees, butterflies and other such beasties. Bright white bedrooms have their own entrance and are immaculate, paired with sparkling bathrooms. At the heart, an airy open-plan living room that guests share with owners Peter and Vincent whose nationalities (English and French) are reflected in their cooking – tasty regional and British. Birdwatching, markets and WWI cemeteries are nearby. Fresh, peaceful, convivial.

Rooms	4: 1 double, 1 twin, 1 triple, 1 family room for 4.
Price	€52. Triple €52–€72. Family room €52–€92.
Meals	Dinner with wine, €20. Guest kitchen.
Closed	Rarely.

Rooms	3: 2 doubles, 1 twin.
Price	€60.
Meals	Dinner with wine, €20. Restaurant 4km.
Closed	Rarely.

Dominique & Nelly Pollet
Ferme de la Noyelle,
832 rue Pasteur,
59262 Sainghin en Mélantois, Nord
Tel   +33 (0)3 20 41 29 82
Mobile +33 (0)6 74 85 61 79
Email   dnpollet@orange.fr
Web   perso.wanadoo.fr/dpollet

Peter Clark & Vincent Caplier
Les Mazures,
2b rue de la Prairie,
80370 Beaumetz,
Somme
Tel   +33 (0)3 22 32 80 52
Email   info@lesmazures.com
Web   www.lesmazures.com

Entry 37   Map 1

Entry 38   Map 1

Picardy

La Tour Blanche

In grand French style, stable your steeds in fine boxes beneath the immensely tall sheltering trees, swirl up the staircase to superb rooms, each a symphony in fabric and colour – red or blue, green or white – with good beds on polished floors and a gentle view of the little church: all is handsome, sober and serene. And bathrooms are brand new. Your active, intelligent young hosts happily share their generous family house and big garden with guests, two children and half a dozen horses. There are games to play, bikes to hire, Amiens to visit and the shimmering Somme estuary to walk you into bird heaven.

Rooms	3: 2 doubles, 1 suite.
Price	€90–€110. Suite €170–€215.
Meals	Dinner with wine, €40. Guest kitchen.
Closed	Rarely.

Hélène & Benoît Legru-Plancq
La Tour Blanche,
10 rue de la Ville,
80120 Forest Montiers, Somme

Tel	+33 (0)3 22 23 69 13
Mobile	+33 (0)6 88 61 31 62
Email	info@latourblanche.net
Web	www.latourblanche.net

Entry 39 Map 1

Picardy

Château de Béhen

Surrounded by wooded parkland, the handsome château started life as a holiday house. In the 1950s the Cuveliers moved in, adding paddocks, a pond for swans and a deeply traditional décor. Big bedrooms come with solid oak floors and rugs, and French flourishes. Two-tone panelling graces the first-floor rooms, those above have sloping ceilings and a beam or two; bathrooms are hotel-perfect with double basins of mottled marble. Delicious dinner is at one lively table (or a single one if preferred). Saddle up and enjoy a guided trek – for a day or even two. Fun, friendly people, donkeys to stroke and 15 horses to ride.

Rooms	6: 2 doubles, 1 twin, 1 suite, 2 family rooms.
Price	€119–€164. Suite €171–€224. Family rooms €171–€224.
Meals	Dinner, with wine, from €41 (book 2 days ahead).
Closed	Rarely.

Cuvelier Family
Château de Béhen,
8 rue du Château,
80870 Béhen,
Somme

Tel	+33 (0)3 22 31 58 30
Email	norbert-andre@cuvelier.com
Web	www.chateau-de-behen.com

Entry 40 Map 1

Picardy

Château des Alleux

Beyond the drive find kitchen garden, orangerie and glasshouse, hens in the yard, sheep in the fields and orchards for cider – the setting is stunning. The château (ring before entering), in the family for 200 years, has two stately, rather timeworn bedrooms (lovely garden view from the four-poster room). The saddlery has a low, dimly-lit modernised cottage with a kitchen: ideal for families; and a big double with a cramped shower. Dense trees protect from distant motorway hum; good home-grown meaty dinners in the warm dining room are a chance to learn about French formality, etiquette and table settings from your busy farming hosts.

Rooms	4: 2 doubles. Outbuildings: 1 double with kitchenette, 1 family suite for 4 with kitchen.
Price	€60–€70. Family suite €80–€100. Extra bed €20.
Meals	Dinner, 4 courses with wine, €20. Reservation in advance.
Closed	Rarely.

René–François & Élisabeth de Fontanges
Château des Alleux,
2 impasse du Château des Alleux,
80870 Béhen, Somme

Tel	+33 (0)3 22 31 64 88
Mobile	+33 (0)6 81 01 19 40
Email	chateaudesalleux@wanadoo.fr
Web	www.chambres-gites-somme.com

Entry 41   Map 1

Picardy

3 rue d'Inval

Imposing and old-fashioned – in the best possible sense. You soon relax into the homely atmosphere created by your calm, hospitable, country hosts – the first in the Somme to open their house for B&B. Aart keeps honey, cider and calvados in the vaulted cellars and tends the serried tulips and dahlias and the gloriously billowing shrubs; Dorette was mayor for 24 years. Her big uncluttered bedrooms (smaller on the second floor) are comfortable, modern shower rooms are big enough for a third bed, and the panelled dining room is a proper setting for a good breakfast. A great place to stay, with fishing on the lake.

Rooms	4: 1 double; 3 triples (sharing wc).
Price	€65. Triples €52–€75. Singles €30–€40.
Meals	Kitchen available. Restaurants 12km.
Closed	Rarely.

Dorette & Aart Onder de Linden
3 rue d'Inval,
80430 Le Mazis,
Somme

Tel	+33 (0)3 22 25 90 88
Mobile	+33 (0)6 33 96 52 70
Email	onderdelinden@wanadoo.fr
Web	www.lemazis.com

Entry 42   Map 5

Picardy

Maison Warlop

In serene country, a dazzling house whose hill-shaped roof becomes a timbered vault way above swathes of natural stone floor. The Picardy sky pours in and fills the vast minimally furnished living space and your hostess shows pleasure at your amazement... then serves you simple fare and good conversation. Bedrooms are pure and peaceful: white walls, patches of colour, crazy-paved floors, excellent beds and design-conscious bathrooms, 1930s antiques, no frills and touches of fun. Civilised seclusion... and a beautiful 1930s neo-gothic church next door, to which Martine has the key.

Rooms	3: 2 twins/doubles, 1 family room.
Price	€70–€125.
Meals	Dinner with wine, €26–€28.
Closed	Rarely.

Martine Warlop
Maison Warlop,
1 rue Génermont,
80320 Fresnes Mazancourt, Somme
Tel   +33 (0)3 22 85 49 49
Mobile   +33 (0)9 64 42 67 42
Email   martine.warlop@wanadoo.fr
Web   www.maison-warlop.com

Entry 43   Map 5

Picardy

Château d'Omiécourt

On a working estate, Omiécourt is a proudly grand 19th-century château and elegant family house (the Thézys have four teenage children), with tall slender windows and some really old trees. Friendly if formal, communicative and smiling, your hosts have worked hugely to restore their inheritance and create gracious French château guest rooms, each with an ornate fireplace, each named for a different period. In an outbuilding near the two pools is a neat apartment for self-caterers; there's a 'boutique', too, of pretty things. A house of goodwill where you will be very comfortable.

Minimum two nights July/Aug.

Rooms	5: 3 doubles, 1 family room, 1 suite for 3.
Price	€105–€145. Extra bed €30.
Meals	Restaurants 12km.
Closed	Rarely.

Dominique & Véronique de Thézy
Château d'Omiécourt,
80320 Omiécourt,
Somme
Tel   +33 (0)3 22 83 01 75
Email   contact@chateau-omiecourt.com
Web   www.chateau-omiecourt.com

Entry 44   Map 5

La Gaxottière

The high walls guard a secret garden, a goldfish pond, lots of intriguing mementoes and a blithe, animated hostess – a retired chemist who loves her dogs, travelling and contact with visitors. In the old house, the two mellow, beamed, fireplace'd rooms are brimful of personal collections; the bedrooms have log fires and the bathrooms are nicely old-fashioned. Françoise lives in the brilliantly converted barn where she serves breakfast; all is harmony and warmth among the antiques. Drink it all in with this great soul's talk of France and the world. Sleep in peace, wake to the dawn chorus and breakfast in the sunshine.

Le Château de Fosseuse

Your tall windows look over the great park fading away to wooded hillside (with railway); beneath your feet are 16th-century bricks. A monumental staircase ushers you up to big, canopied, glorious-viewed bedrooms that are château-worthy but not posh; behind the panelling of one is a secret staircase. Your hosts are a fascinating, cultured marriage of exquisite French manners and Irish warmth who labour on to save their family home and genuinely enjoy sharing it. Antique rugs line the hall's walls; gumboots for guests (all sizes) wait by the door; Michelin stars are a very short drive.

Rooms	3: 1 double, 1 twin, 1 single.
Price	€70. Single €40.
Meals	Dinner with wine, €20.
Closed	Rarely.

Rooms	3: 1 double, 1 triple, 1 family room for 2-4.
Price	€85. Triple €85-€110. Family room €100-€160.
Meals	Restaurant 5km.
Closed	Christmas.

Françoise Gaxotte
La Gaxottière,
363 rue du Champ du Mont,
Hameau de Varanval,
60880 Jaux, Oise
Tel   +33 (0)3 44 83 22 41
Email lagaxottiere@sfr.fr

Shirley & Jean-Louis Marro
Le Château de Fosseuse,
60540 Fosseuse, Oise
Tel   +33 (0)3 44 08 47 66
Email chateau.fosseuse@orange.fr
Web   www.chateau-de-fosseuse.com

Entry 45   Map 5

Entry 46   Map 5

Picardy

Le Clos

The sprucest of farmhouses, whitewashed and Normandy-beamed, sits in its lush secret garden, reached via a door in the wall. Indoors, you find a remarkably fresh, open-plan and modernised interior, with a comfortable sitting room to share. Your bedroom above the garage is spacious, neat, uncluttered and warm; the bedding is the best, the shower room spotless and modern with coloured towels. Dine with your informative hosts by the old farm fireplace on *tarte aux pommes du jardin*. Philippe, the chef, receives much praise. Chantal, a retired teacher, keeps you gentle company. A peaceful spot, close to Paris.

Rooms	2 family rooms for 2-3.
Price	€60-€72.
Meals	Dinner with wine, €27.
Closed	3 weeks in winter.

Philippe & Chantal Vermeire
Le Clos,
3 rue du Chêne Noir,
60240 Fay les Étangs, Oise

Tel	+33 (0)3 44 49 92 38
Email	philippe.vermeire@wanadoo.fr
Web	www.leclosdefay.com

Entry 47   Map 5

Picardy

Fosse-Valle

Everything in this smart old house is beautifully done, from the immaculately smooth white bedlinen to the delicious little sauna in the wooden garden cabin. Since moving here four years ago and starting B&B, Pascale has devoted her enthusiasm and flair to her guests. She loves chatting to her visitors over dinner, served on a pretty cloth with antique cutlery. Full of good advice, she knows the area well. Bedrooms are classic-handsome in the main house and romantic-cosy in the adorable garden cottage, every detail refined with a personal touch. Light-hearted and welcoming.

Rooms	2: 1 double. Cottage: 1 double.
Price	€145. Cottage €140. Singles €125. Extra bed €65.
Meals	Dinner €35.
Closed	Mid-December to January.

Pascale Ravé
Fosse-Valle,
5 route de Vaudancourt,
60240 Boury en Vexin, Oise

Mobile	+33 (0)6 23 05 03 72
Email	pascale.rave@fossevalle.fr
Web	www.fossevalle.fr

Entry 48   Map 5

Picardy

Les Chambres de l'Abbaye

Chloé and her artist husband have the most unusual, delightful house in a village with a fine Cistercian abbey. You are free to roam a series of beautiful rooms downstairs, read a book in the pale blue formal salon, admire Jean-François' striking, exciting pictures (though sadly illness is making it harder for him). The family suite is on the first floor, the two others higher up; all are fresh, and immaculate. You should eat well: much is homemade, including walnut wine and liqueur from their own trees. Walk it off round the partly unmanicured garden with its summerhouse and pond. It's a fascinating house and a pleasure to stay in.

Rooms	3: 2 doubles, 1 family suite for 3 (1 double, 1 single).
Price	€95. Family suite €95–€120. Singles €85.
Meals	Dinner with wine, €28.
Closed	24-26 December.

	Chloé Comte
	Les Chambres de l'Abbaye,
	2 rue Michel Greuet,
	60850 St Germer de Fly, Oise
Tel	+33 (0)3 44 81 98 38
Mobile	+33 (0)6 09 27 75 41
Email	comte.resa@free.fr
Web	www.chambres-abbaye.com

Entry 49 Map 5

Picardy

Les Jardins du Vidamé

In beautiful 17th-century Gerberoy (records go back to 923 AD), this venerable place, Ben's family home, has oodles of ancient charm in a multitude of timbers, cobbles and bricks where wisteria and untamed roses ramble. Flaubert's walls are intensely floral; photographs and mellow watercolours talk from the past; with a carved bedstead and bits of mahogany the atmosphere is of another period. Even the bathroom looks 1920s. The bigger, Maupassant room opens to the terrace. Your delightful young hosts, busy with small children and bistro, are happy to chat, and conjure up delicious organic-and-local dinners.

Rooms	2 doubles.
Price	€70–€80.
Meals	Dinner €22. Wine per glass, €3.50–€7.50. Tea room/bistro in outbuilding.
Closed	December–February.

	Céline & Ben Guilloux
	Les Jardins du Vidamé,
	4 impasse du Vidamé,
	60380 Gerberoy, Oise
Tel	+33 (0)3 44 82 45 32
Email	contact@lesjardinsduvidame.com
Web	www.les-jardins-du-vidame.com

Entry 50 Map 5

Domaine de Montaigu

Languid and pleasant gardens – pillows of lavender, dripping wisteria – hem in the large fountain'd courtyard, and neat pathways lead to stone terraces embracing the hill: welcome to this 18th-century wine domain. Gardening is one of the enthusiasms of new owner Claire (along with horses and champagne). She and Philippe love their B&B life and offer you cosy comfortable bedrooms decorated in traditional French style, three pretty with toile de Jouy. There are two sitting rooms, one large, one snug, a swimming pool for summer and a big convivial table for breakfasts of pastries and homemade jams.

Ferme de Ressons

Ressons is home to a warm, dynamic, intelligent couple who, after a hard day's work running this big farm (Jean-Paul) or being an architect (Valérie) and tending three children, will ply you in apparently leisurely fashion with champagne, excellent dinner and conversation; they also hunt. The deeply carved Henri III furniture is an admirable family heirloom; bedrooms (two en suite) are colour-coordinated, views roll for miles and sharing facilities seems easy. A house of comfort and relaxed good manners (smoking is in the study only), whose decoration and accessories reflect the owners' travels.

Rooms	4: 2 doubles, 2 family rooms.
Price	€85–€100. Family rooms €130.
Meals	Restaurant 5km.
Closed	Rarely.

Rooms	5: 1 double, 1 twin, each en suite, sharing wc; 2 doubles, 1 twin, sharing bathroom & 2 wcs.
Price	€50–€60.
Meals	Dinner €19. Wine €14; champagne €18.
Closed	Rarely.

	Philippe de Coster
	Domaine de Montaigu,
	16 rue de Montaigu,
	02290 Ambleny, Aisne
Tel	+33 (0)3 23 74 06 62
Email	info@domainedemontaigu.com
Web	www.domainedemontaigu.com

	Valérie & Jean-Paul Ferry
	Ferme de Ressons,
	02220 Mont St Martin, Aisne
Tel	+33 (0)3 23 74 71 00
Email	ferryressons@orange.fr

Entry 51   Map 5

Entry 52   Map 5

Picardy

La Quincy

The old family home, faded and weary, timeless and romantic, is well loved and lived in by this charming, natural and quietly elegant couple. Corridors cluttered with books, magazines and traces of family life lead to an octagonal tower, its great double room and child's room across the landing imaginatively set in the space. A handsome antique bed on a fine polished floor, charming chintz, erratic plumbing and two parkland views will enchant you. Shrubs hug the feet of the delicious 'troubadour' château, the garden slips into meadow, summer breakfast and dinner (good wine, book ahead) are in the orangery. Special.

Rooms	1 family room for 3.
Price	€65. Pets €8.
Meals	Occasional dinner with wine, €25.
Closed	Rarely.

Jacques & Marie-Catherine
Cornu-Langy
La Quincy,
02880 Nanteuil la Fosse, Aisne
Tel   +33 (0)3 23 54 67 76
Mobile +33 (0)7 86 99 37 95
Email   la.quincy@yahoo.fr

Entry 53   Map 5

Picardy

La Grange

Hidden down lanes, behind an undulating wall, glimpsed through wrought-iron gates, is this big converted barn; Tony and Thierry have been looking after guests, with great pleasure, for years. Rambling gardens and a bountiful vegetable plot run down to wide open pasture. Under the high glass atrium of the breakfast room lies the heart of the house with wood-burner, piano and windows opening to undulating views, while peaceful and immaculate bedrooms hop from fabric-swathed opulence to a more simple country elegance. Hosted dinners are convivial and delicious; Reims, rich in history and gastronomy, is under an hour.

Extra bed available.

Rooms	3: 2 doubles, 1 apartment (1 double, 1 twin; 1 bathroom).
Price	€67. Apartment €98–€129. Singles €59. Extra bed €20.
Meals	Dinner, 4 courses with wine, €27. Restaurant 10km.
Closed	Rarely.

Tony Bridier & Thierry Charbit
La Grange,
6 impasse des Prés,
02160 Cuiry les Chaudardes, Aisne
Tel   +33 (0)3 23 25 82 42
Email   lagrangecuiry@orange.fr
Web   lagrangecuiry.fr

Entry 54   Map 5

Picardy

Le Clos

Genuine country hospitality and warmth are yours in the big old house. Madame is kindly and direct; Monsieur is the communicator (mainly in French), knows his local history and loves the hunting horn. His 300-year-old family house is cosily unposh: floral curtains, French-papered walls, original wainscotting, funny old prints in bedrooms, comforting clutter in the vast living room, posters in the corridors. The master bedroom is superb, others are simple and fine; one has a ship's shower room, all look onto green pastures. And there's a pretty lake for picnics across the narrow road.

Rooms	4: 2 doubles, 1 twin, 1 suite for 5 (1 triple, 1 twin).
Price	€50–€60. Extra bed €20.
Meals	Occasional dinner with wine, €22.50. Restaurant in village.
Closed	Mid-October to mid-March, except by arrangement.

Michel & Monique Simonnot
Le Clos,
02860 Chérêt,
Aisne
Tel   +33 (0)3 23 24 80 64
Email   leclos.cheret@club-internet.fr
Web   www.lecloscheret.com

Entry 55   Map 5

Picardy

Domaine de l'Étang

The village on one side, the expansive estate on the other, the 18th-century wine-grower's house in between. There's a civilised mood: Monsieur so well-mannered and breakfast served with silver and fine china in the comfortably elegant guest dining room. Wake to church-spire and rooftop views in rooms with soft comfort where, under sloping ceilings, French toile de Jouy is as inviting as English chintz (your hosts spent two years in England). Bathrooms are frilled and pretty. Shrubs hug the hem of the house, a pool is sunk into the lawn behind and Laon oxen crown one of France's first gothic cathedrals.

Rooms	3: 2 doubles, 1 twin.
Price	€60–€72.
Meals	Restaurants 6km.
Closed	Rarely.

Patrick Woillez
Domaine de l'Étang,
2 rue St Martin,
02000 Mons en Laonnois, Aisne
Tel   +33 (0)3 23 24 44 52
Mobile +33 (0)6 26 62 36 41
Email   gitemons@sfr.fr
Web   www.domainedeletang.fr

Entry 56   Map 5

Picardy

Les Cernailles

As well as Emmanuelle's vibrant personality, come to be transported back to 18th-century elegance in an amazing example of how to renovate without using anything new. A few of the 27 metres of panelling that Emmanuelle – who has a passion for antiques – bought at a château auction dress the walls of the guest quarters, floors are reclaimed brick, stone or timber, each piece of furniture tells a tale, wonky Delft tiles decorate the bathrooms, Moss and period porcelain and silver decorate the breakfast table. The lovely walled garden simply begs for a crinoline, though the two fine 'grey ghost' dogs might seem out of scale.

Rooms	2 doubles.
Price	€85.
Meals	Café in village, restaurants 8km.
Closed	Rarely.

Emmanuelle Simphal
Les Cernailles,
33 av d'Île de France,
02870 Vivaise, Aisne

Tel	+33 (0)3 23 22 97 33
Email	lescernailles@hotmail.fr
Web	www.lescernailles.fr

Picardy

La Commanderie

Up here on the hill, not easy to find, is a Templar hamlet and a millennium of history: an enclosed farmyard, a ruined medieval chapel framing the sunrise, a tithe barn with leaping oak timbers – and this modern house. José-Marie, an unhurried grandmother of generous spirit, loves the history, harvests her orchards and vegetables, and welcomes genuinely. Bedrooms are in plain, dated farm style but open the window and you fall into the view that soars away on all sides of the hill, even to Laon cathedral. Homely, authentic and simple, with lived-in plumbing and great value – most readers love it.

Rooms	3: 1 double, 2 family rooms.
Price	€50-€55. Family room €60-€70.
Meals	Occasional dinner with wine, €18. Restaurants 10km.
Closed	Last week October to February, except by arrangement.

José-Marie Carette
La Commanderie,
Catillon du Temple,
02270 Nouvion & Catillon, Aisne

Tel	+33 (0)3 23 56 51 28
Mobile	+33 (0)6 82 33 22 64
Email	carette.jm@wanadoo.fr
Web	www.gite-templier-laon.com

Champagne – Ardenne

5 rue du Paradis

In this pretty Champagne village, the Harlauts produce their own delicious fruity champagne. The house, a fairly recent construction built next to old farm buildings owned by the family, has steep narrow stairs leading to a comfortable, uncluttered suite in the attic, all slanting wood-clad overheads and skylight windows. A further room lies under the eaves of the adjoining outbuilding. Both have independent access, spotless little kitchenettes and suppers can be brought on request to your own private dining table. You'll eat well: Évelyne is a great exponent of authentic country cooking.

La Closerie des Sacres

An easy drive from Reims, these former stables have changed radically. Large, cool, downstairs areas – the mangers and tethering rings remain – are pale-tiled with dark leather sofas, games and books, an open fire, a glass-topped dining table, wrought-iron chairs. And you can do your own cooking in the fully fitted kitchen. Bedrooms are solid oak-floored, draped and prettily coloured with well-dressed beds, cushions, teddy bears, electric blinds and jacuzzi baths. The Jactats have farmed here for generations and tell of the rebuilding of their village in 1925. Take time to talk, and play boules in the sheltered garden.

Rooms	2: 1 double (with extra bed), 1 family room for 4. Each with kitchenette.
Price	€62–€67. Family room €86–€110.
Meals	Supper on tray, €19 with a glass of champagne (not Sundays). Wine €8/ bottle.
Closed	December, January & Easter.

Rooms	4: 2 doubles, 1 triple, 1 suite.
Price	£94. Triple £94–£115. Suite £120–£180. Singles €78–€100.
Meals	Guest kitchen available. Restaurants 2km.
Closed	Rarely.

	Évelyne & Remi Harlaut
	5 rue du Paradis,
	51220 St Thierry,
	Marne
Tel	+33 (0)3 26 03 13 75
Email	contact@champagne-harlaut.fr
Web	www.champagne-harlaut.fr

	Sandrine & Laurent Jactat
	La Closerie des Sacres,
	7 rue Chefossez, 51110 Lavannes,
	Marne
Tel	+33 (0)3 26 02 05 05
Email	contact@closerie-des-sacres.com
Web	www.closerie-des-sacres.com

Entry 59   Map 6

Entry 60   Map 6

Champagne - Ardenne

Château de Juvigny

Oozing old-world charm, this handsome 1705 château wraps you in its warmth. The family have occupied one wing for 200 years and, thanks to Brigitte, it has a wonderfully easy-going elegance. There are chandeliers, polished floorboards, wainscotting and antiques, old-fashioned bathrooms, cracked floor tiles, rustic outbuildings. Bedrooms, in the old servants' quarters, are informally stylish with marble fireplaces, pretty bedcovers and views over the park, the formal gardens and the lake. You breakfast, colourfully, beneath a vast (and deteriorated!) portrait of an ancestor. Charming, unfussy country comfort.

Rooms	5: 3 doubles, 1 twin, 1 suite for 4.
Price	€90-€140. Suite €140-€200. Extra bed €25.
Meals	Restaurant 10km.
Closed	Mid-December to mid-March, except by arrangement.

Brigitte & Alain Caubère d'Alinval
Château de Juvigny,
8 av du Château, 51150 Juvigny,
Marne
Mobile +33 (0)6 78 99 69 40
Email information@chateaudejuvigny.com
Web www.chateaudejuvigny.com

Entry 61 Map 6

Champagne - Ardenne

Chez Éric & Sylvie

This couple have flung their rich welcome out into a lodge in the woods with a clutch of cottage-cosy bedrooms, a handsome old-fitted kitchen/diner, a piano, bar billiards and a private lake. Also on offer: a big, old-fashioned room with a small balcony and views of the vines in their own village house 2km away. Éric is a creative handyman, both are ardent trawlers of brocante stalls, the results are a personal mix of antique and retro styles against pastel paints, polished boards and well-dressed beds. Sylvie and Éric bend over backwards to bring you outstanding breakfasts, champagne receptions – and their sparkling presence.

Sawday self-catering also.

Rooms	5: 1 suite. Lodge (2km): 3 suites, 1 family suite for 3-4.
Price	€80-€115. Family suite €80-€115.
Meals	Restaurants nearby.
Closed	Rarely.

Sylvie & Éric Charbonnier
Chez Éric & Sylvie,
189 rue Ferdinand Moret,
51530 Cramant, Marne
Tel +33 (0)3 26 57 95 34
Mobile +33 (0)6 12 09 67 79
Email eric-sylvie@wanadoo.fr
Web www.ericsylvie.com

Entry 62 Map 6

Château Les Aulnois

A score of 18th-century château windows remain, gazing over topiary cones and preened gardens, sloping hills and acres of vines. Each first-floor bedroom has a matching motif for wallpapers, bedspreads and upholstered chairs; all are lofty, uncluttered, impeccable, and dressing–room bathrooms are opulent. Hospitable Madame Vollereaux adores cooking, her Aga breakfasts are fabulous, and you can gather twice-weekly at the elegant oval table for mouthwatering suppers. Don't miss the vast 1700s grape press on site, visit Épernay market and the wartime sites of Verdun and Amiens.

Sawday self-catering also.

Au Pré du Moulin

The big 1789 farmhouse deep in the country has been in the Coulmier family for two generations. Luckily, one half of the main house has been given over to guests; an interconnecting suite (poppy-print wallpaper, wooden floors) provides family-sized space to match a child-friendly garden. Elsewhere, rooms are French 'rustic chic' to a tee; white lacquered bedsteads and cornflower-blue floral details in one, stylish dark wood and Burgundian limestone with tiny black cabochons in another. Valérie and Didier are lovely, friendly and knowledgeable hosts and will share delicious organic home-grown fare with you.

Rooms	5: 2 twins/doubles, 3 suites.
Price	€150-€340. Suite €150-€340.
Meals	Dinner €45. Gourmet dinner for 4, €125. Restaurant 10-minute walk.
Closed	20 December-20 February.

Rooms	3: 1 double, 1 triple, 1 suite.
Price	€65. Triple €65-€80. Suite €95.
Meals	Dinner with wine, €25.
Closed	Christmas & New Year.

	Élisabeth Vollereaux
	Château Les Aulnois,
	61 rue du Général de Gaulle,
	51530 Pierry, Marne
Tel	+33 (0)3 26 54 27 23
Email	contact@chateau-les-aulnois.fr
Web	www.chateau-les-aulnois.fr

	Valérie & Didier Coulmier
	Au Pré du Moulin,
	4 rue du Moulin, 51130 Clamanges,
	Marne
Tel	+33 (0)3 26 64 50 16
Email	aupredumoulin@packsurfwifi.com
Web	www.aupredumoulin.fr

Champagne - Ardenne

Ferme de Bannay

The deep-country house in the pretty village is brimful of new chintz and old beams. Bedrooms dressed in ivory and white have quilted bedcovers and scatter cushions; sprays of artificial flowers brighten nooks and crannies; and there's a bathroom behind a curtain. Little English is spoken but the welcome is so endearing, the generosity so genuine, the food so delicious, that communication is easy. Just a few cows on the farm now, and the odd tractor passing, but the vegetable garden is handsome and much of the produce ends up on your (delightfully antique) plate.

Rooms	3: 1 triple, 1 quadruple, 1 suite for 2-3 with kitchen.
Price	Triple €59-€77. Quadruple €59-€94. Suite €69-€87.
Meals	Dinner with wine, €34; with champagne €50.
Closed	Rarely.

Muguette & Jean-Pierre Curfs
Ferme de Bannay,
1 rue du Petit Moulin,
51270 Bannay,
Marne
Tel +33 (0)3 26 52 80 49
Email mjpcurfs@aliceadsl.fr

Entry 65   Map 5

Champagne - Ardenne

Auprès de l'Église

New Zealanders Michael and Glenis do excellent table d'hôtes and love sharing their restored 19th-century house full of surprises: some walls are unadorned but for the mason's scribbles. The upstairs suite is separated by a fabulous wall of bookcases and an attic stair, the ground floor has a French country feel. Another big, cleverly designed room leads off the courtyard where you sit in the shade of birch trees and dine (and enjoy a champagne aperitif). Oyes church has no chiming clocks and you'll sleep deeply here. Plenty of fun and funky brocante yet the comforts are modern. Charming Sézanne is a 20-minute drive.

Sawday self-catering also.

Rooms	2 suites for 2-4.
Price	€90-€130.
Meals	Dinner with wine, €35. Child €10.
Closed	Rarely.

Glenis Foster
Auprès de l'Église,
2 rue de l'Église, 51120 Oyes,
Marne
Tel +33 (0)3 26 80 62 39
Mobile +44 (0)7808 905233
Email titusprod@me.com
Web www.champagnevilla.com

Entry 66   Map 5

La Ferme de Désiré

A quietly talkative, personable hostess and her young daughter welcome you to this majestic 17th-century family farm. Through the huge arch is a gravelled courtyard enclosed by immaculate outbuildings and farmhouse; potted palms add an exotic touch. In the converted stables, guests have a living room with original mangers, log fire and kitchen, then steep stairs up to two simply decorated, carpeted, roof-lit rooms. This is a deeply rural area with farmland reaching as far as the eye can see, close to the vineyards of Champagne.

Minimum two nights bank holiday weekends.

Domaine du Moulin d'Eguebaude

A delightful mill – and trout farm. The secluded old buildings in the lush riverside setting are home to a fish restaurant, several guest rooms and 50 tons of live fish. Delicious breakfast and dinner are shared with your enthusiastic hosts, who started the business 40 years ago; groups come for speciality lunches, anglers come to fish. Bedrooms under the eaves are compact, small-windowed, simply furnished, decorated in rustic or granny style, the larger annexe rooms are more motel-ish. Lots of space for children, and good English spoken. More guest house than B&B.

Rooms	3: 2 doubles, 1 twin.
Price	€65-€70.
Meals	Guest kitchen. Restaurant within walking distance.
Closed	Rarely.

Rooms	6: 2 doubles, 1 twin, 1 triple, 2 family rooms.
Price	€72-€77. Triple €82. Family rooms €77. Extra bed €21. Under 13s, €14.
Meals	Dinner with wine, €26. Guest kitchen.
Closed	Christmas, New Year & occasionally.

	Anne Boutour
	La Ferme de Désiré,
	51210 Le Gault Soigny, Marne
Mobile	+33 (0)6 26 68 14 10
Email	domaine_de_desire@yahoo.fr
Web	www.ferme-desire.com

	Alexandre & Sandrine Mesley
	Domaine du Moulin d'Eguebaude,
	36 rue Pierre Brossolette,
	10190 Estissac, Aube
Tel	+33 (0)3 25 40 42 18
Email	eguebaude@aol.com
Web	www.moulineguebaude.fr

Champagne - Ardenne

A L'Aube Bleue

Madame is a collector of intriguing finds (including the Peugeot 203). Her two family-friendly garden-facing bedrooms make good use of compact space: one has the double bed on the mezzanine floor and children sleep below; the other, pretty in pale colours, sleeps three. The disabled-access room, also simply furnished, is larger with a canopied bed. You breakfast at one big table next to the kitchen. Do arrange a meal in the sheltered outdoor dining area, too; it's fun and hung with agricultural bits and bobs, and the food will be good. All in a quiet village, in open country 18km south of medieval Troyes.

Rooms	3: 1 double, 1 triple, 1 family room.
Price	€59. Triple €59-€75. Family room €59-€91. Singles €49. Pets €5.
Meals	Dinner with wine, €24.
Closed	Rarely.

Christine Degois
A L'Aube Bleue,
6 rue du Viard, 10320 Assenay,
Aube

Tel	+33 (0)3 25 40 29 58
Mobile	+33 (0)6 85 10 43 50
Email	contact@chambres-hotes-aube-bleue.fr
Web	www.chambres-hotes-aube-bleue.fr

Entry 69 Map 6

Champagne - Ardenne

La Parenthèse

Lovely! A half-timbered longhouse in a drowsy village between Épernay and Troyes. Elegant Madame Debelle managed the renovation to show off timber, tile and stonework and create rustic chic bedrooms – a harmonious balance of traditional with contemporary touches. A grand fireplace takes centre stage downstairs where you breakfast at the long, benched kitchen table (homemade jams a speciality) and bedrooms have kitchenettes; the biggest has its own roof terrace. Madame can provide supper and advice on itineraries: all things Champagne, medieval Troyes. The superb Reims cathedral and the lesser-known St Rémy are an hour away.

Extra bed available.

Rooms	3: 1 twin/double, 1 double, 1 family room for 2-4.
Price	€65-€75. Family room €85-€125.
Meals	Dinner, with wine, €20. Child €10. Restaurant 10km.
Closed	Rarely.

Mathilde & Éric Debelle
La Parenthèse,
38 rue de La Lhuitrelle,
10700 Dosnon, Aube

Tel	+33 (0)3 25 37 37 26
Email	debellemathilde@hotmail.fr
Web	www.chambres-dhotes-laparenthese.com

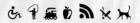

Entry 70 Map 6

Champagne - Ardenne

La Pierre Écrite

The Jeannaux, kindly people, simply love mills. This one began life in the 13th century – property then of the Earl of Champagne – and its history entwines with village folklore. Your upstairs room – modern retro style with painted panelling, brocante prints and a big monochrome shower room – overlooks the mill pond: a treat for all seasons whether dizzying with dragonflies or mist-rising on a frosty morning. Breakfast is a grand spread of sweet and savoury; there's a corner kitchen downstairs, a garden barbecue, and a decent restaurant you can easily walk to in attractive, historic and watery Soulaine-Dhuys.

Rooms	1 double.
Price	€72. Singles €60-€65. Extra bed €15.
Meals	Guest kitchenette. Restaurant within walking distance.
Closed	15 December-15 January.

Anny & Bernard Jeannaux
La Pierre Écrite,
Le Moulin, 4 rue des Tanneries,
10200 Soulaine-Dhuys, Aube
Tel   +33 (0)3 25 92 41 02
Mobile +33 (0)6 86 81 09 67
Email   lapierre.ecrite@orange.fr

Entry 71   Map 6

Champagne - Ardenne

Les Épeires

This was the family's summer house for two centuries and has been their main house for one: Madame will show you the family books, lovely old furniture and mementoes and tell you the stories (of Louis XIV's envoy to Peter the Great who was an ancestor...) in incredibly fast French. She does her own bookbinding, adores her rose garden, a jungle of perfumes and petals; she particularly loves ancient varieties and is an enthusiastic member of two specialist societies. A blithe and extrovert soul, she serves authentic French dinners before a log fire and offers you a bedroom as country-cosy as the old house, simple and clean.

Rooms	1 triple.
Price	€55-€70.
Meals	Dinner with wine, €25 (children under 12 free).
Closed	Rarely.

Nicole Georges-Fougerolle
Les Épeires,
17 rue des Écuyers,
10200 Fuligny, Aube
Tel   +33 (0)3 25 92 77 11
Email   nicolegeorges1@yahoo.fr

Entry 72   Map 6

Champagne - Ardenne

Domaine de Boulancourt

This large and splendid farmhouse is irresistible. For fishermen there's a river, for birdwatchers a fine park full of wildlife (come for the cranes in spring or autumn); for architecture buffs, the half-timbered churches are among the "100 most beautiful attractions in France". Bedrooms are comfortable and handsome; afternoon tea is served by the piano in the elegant panelled salon; dinner, possibly home-raised boar, duck or carp, is eaten at one or several tables but not with your delightful hosts who live in another wing and prefer to concentrate on their good home cooking.

Champagne - Ardenne

Le Relais du Puits

Regular guests of Michel and Évelyne in their tiny medieval village in Champagne will find this charming couple in a 'new' 200-year-old home. Just three rooms now, all reflecting Évelyne's quirky humour: snow-white Romantic, chic Belle-Époque, extravagant Medieval with a gothic, dark orange décor, daggers and tapestries. Bathrooms are gorgeous, the garden large, and dinners – Évelyne's cider chicken, Michel's chocolate mousse – fabulous value. After 18 years your hosts know just what guests want, whether it's free internet, a roaring fire in the sitting room, or bicycles for the surrounding forests and country lanes.

Rooms	5: 2 doubles, 1 twin, 1 single, 1 suite.
Price	€75-€85. Single €65-€75. Suite €85. Extra bed €20.
Meals	Dinner with wine, €30.
Closed	December to mid-March.

Rooms	3: 1 double, 1 triple; 1 twin with separate bathroom.
Price	€68. Triple €78-€100. Extra bed €20. Cot €12.
Meals	Dinner with wine, €18. Child under 10, €10. No charge for under 3's. Restaurant 8km.
Closed	Rarely.

Philippe & Christine Viel-Cazal
Domaine de Boulancourt,
Le Désert, 52220 Longeville sur la Laines,
Haute-Marne

Tel	+33 (0)3 25 04 60 18
Mobile	+33 (0)6 33 18 84 92
Email	dom.boulancourt@wanadoo.fr
Web	www.domaine-de-boulancourt.com

Évelyne & Michel Poope
Le Relais du Puits,
15 rue Augustin Massin,
52500 Pressigny, Haute-Marne

Tel	+33 (0)3 25 88 80 50
Email	e.m.poope@orange.fr
Web	www.massin-perrette.com

Entry 73 Map 6

Entry 74 Map 6

Champagne - Ardenne

La Montgonière

Knee-high wainscotting, opulent fabric, hand-painted wallpaper discovered in the attic are just some of the treats in store at this village mansion built in 1673. The first owner was seen off during the Revolution and the house was later sold to Élisabeth's family. Smiling, self-assured, she swapped law for B&B and has no regrets. Book-lined walls and elegant fauteuils encourage cogitation under the eaves, French windows open to a delightful walled garden, corridors are lined with oriental rugs. Refined living with a relaxed mood: deeply involved in musical events, Élisabeth is also an accomplished cook. A delicious address.

Rooms	3: 1 double, 1 twin, 1 suite for 3-4.
Price	€90-€140.
Meals	Dinner €25. Wine extra.
Closed	January.

Élisabeth Regnault de Montgon
La Montgonière,
1 rue St Georges, 08240 Harricourt,
Ardennes

Tel	+33 (0)3 24 71 66 50
Mobile	+33 (0)6 77 96 35 75
Email	regnault.montgon@wanadoo.fr
Web	www.lamontgoniere.net

Entry 75   Map 6

Le Mas de la Pierre du Coq, entry 785

Lorraine • Alsace • Franche Comté

Lorraine

Villa Les Roses

The restoration of these venerable buildings – one house is 400, the other 300 years old – was a labour of love: mosaic and marble flooring, a handsome oak staircase, weathered wainscotting to add charm. There are elegant terraces and superb ten-acre grounds for gîte guests and all; you breakfast – deliciously – in a big elegant sunny room at an antique table. Madame is warm, attentive and gently informal, and has redecorated her very comfortable rooms in soft pastel colours. Bathrooms are spotless and warm, there are choice antiques and religion on view, including French Catholic bibles. Delightful.

Rooms	5: 3 doubles, 1 twin, 1 family room.
Price	€60–€85.
Meals	Restaurants within walking distance.
Closed	Rarely.

Marie-Jeanne Christiaens
Villa Les Roses,
1 rue du Centre à la Vignette,
Les Islettes,
55120 Clermont en Argonne, Meuse

Tel	+33 (0)3 26 60 81 91
Mobile	+33 (0)6 87 14 06 06
Email	gites-christiaens@wanadoo.fr

Lorraine

51 rue Lorraine

Alina came from Poland with a bundle of talents; a professional gardener, she paints, embroiders, decorates. Gérard, a retired French architect, won a prize for his brilliant conversion of this dear little 200-year-old house. Their skills and taste for contemporary and ethnic styles shine through the house, their thoughtful, artistic personalities enliven the dinner table, their environmentalist passion informs their lives. Expect gorgeous vegetarian food if you ask for it; delicious meaty things too. No sitting room but comfortable, simple, spotless bedrooms, and a lovely garden and patio for summer.

Rooms	2: 1 double, 1 triple.
Price	€60–€62. Triple €72–€75.
Meals	Dinner with wine, €23–€25.
Closed	Rarely.

Alina & Gérard Cahen
51 rue Lorraine,
57220 Burtoncourt, Moselle

Tel	+33 (0)3 87 35 72 65
Email	ag.cahen@wanadoo.fr
Web	www.maisonlorraine.com

Lorraine

Château d'Alteville

A genuine eco-friendly family château (several generations run the estate) in a privileged setting: wake to a chorus of birds. Bedrooms are deliciously *vieille France*; bathrooms are functional and adequate. The real style is in the utterly French salon and the dining room – reached through halls, past library and billiards – where dinners are enjoyed by candlelight in the company of your charming hosts. David, a committed environmentalist, cooks local produce with skill, Agnieszka joyfully deals with two lovely children and fills the place with flowers. The lake on the doorstep is a marvel of peace and birdlife.

Rooms	5: 4 doubles, 1 twin.
Price	€91.
Meals	Dinner €31–€38.50 by reservation. Wine €5–€15.
Closed	Mid-October to mid-April.

David Barthélémy
Château d'Alteville,
Tarquimpol,
57260 Dieuze, Moselle
Tel   +33 (0)3 87 05 46 63
Mobile   +33 (0)6 72 07 56 05
Email   chateau.alteville@free.fr

Entry 78   Map 7

Alsace

Le Moulin

The thermal waters of Niederbronn have drawn visitors since Roman times and the town, in a half moon of hills in the Northern Vosges, retains an authentic Alsatian atmosphere. Madame and Monsieur welcome you in the same spirit to their peaceful estate where a stream-driven mill (now gîtes) sits amid ancient trees, a pool and rose walk. The elegant manor has two history-filled guest rooms, pretty in pastel and catching the morning sun, and a fire in the salon. Quietly green, your hosts run an electric car and serve home-pressed apple juice at breakfast. Roam UNESCO forests to medieval villages and ruined châteaux.

Rooms	2: 1 twin/double, 1 suite for 5 (1 double, 1 bunkroom & single).
Price	€80–€100. Suite €80–€130.
Meals	Restaurant 1km.
Closed	Rarely.

Henri & Marianne Mellon
Le Moulin,
44 route de Reichshoffen,
67110 Niederbronn les Bains,
Bas-Rhin
Tel   +33 (0)6 25 43 40 40
Email   marianne.mellon@gmail.com
Web   gite.moulin.free.fr

Entry 79   Map 7

Alsace

86 rue du Général de Gaulle

A real old Alsatian farmhouse in the wine-growing area where you can be in a bustling village street one minute and your own peaceful little world the next. It is on a main road but the bedrooms, in the separate guest wing, are at the back, protected by the courtyard. Their simplicity is reflected in the price. Your friendly hosts retired from milk and wine production in order to have more time for guests; breakfast is served in the garden or in the dining room, and Paul makes a wicked eau de vie. A useful place to know at the start of the Route des Vins, and very close to gorgeous, glamorous Strasbourg.

Rooms	3 doubles.
Price	€37-€40. Extra bed €8.
Meals	Restaurants within walking distance.
Closed	Rarely.

Paul & Marie-Claire Goetz
86 rue du Général de Gaulle,
67520 Marlenheim, Bas-Rhin
Tel +33 (0)3 88 87 52 94
Email goetz.paul@wanadoo.fr

Entry 80 Map 7

Alsace

Pierres Tombées

Escape to a rustic rural retreat where lush greenery and fresh air abound – what a charming corner of Alsace! Rumoured to have been bought by an eminent classicist for a song, this delightful cottage has won awards for its innovative architecture… light floods in from all directions, heating is directly solar, floors are of the best natural fibres and the roof is cunningly open plan. Breakfasts (and beds) are al fresco and shared with your host, Madame D'ormouse – a small lady who scurries day and night to ensure your every whim is met. The ultimate shabby-chic treat.

Rooms	1 suite.
Price	€20.
Meals	Organic, seasonal, freshly picked (by you).
Closed	Never (stays not advisable in winter).

Madame D'ormouse
Pierres Tombées,
Chemin de Terre Battue,
67480 Trou Paumé, Bas-Rhin
Tel Leave a message at bakery in town.
Email Carrier pigeon only
Web www.foin-tandis-lesoleil-brille.fr

Entry 81 Map 7

Alsace

Maison Fleurie

Bubbling, friendly and generous, Doris has been receiving guests for years: she learnt the art at her mother's knee and will greet you with the warmest welcome. Her peaceful chalet in a residential neighbourhood is a real home, surrounded by breathtaking mountain views. Both she and her husband are upholsterers so furnishings in the neat, traditional bedrooms are perfect, strong colours giving depth to modernity. Guests have their own quarters, with a log fire in the breakfast room, tables laden with goodies in the morning – try the homemade organic fruit jams and Alsace cake – and geraniums cascading. Great value.

Rooms	3: 2 doubles, 1 twin.
Price	€60–€76.
Meals	Restaurants nearby.
Closed	Rarely.

Doris Engel-Geiger
Maison Fleurie, 19 route de Neuve Église,
Dieffenbach au Val,
67220 Villé, Bas-Rhin
Tel   +33 (0)3 88 85 60 48
Mobile   +33 (0)6 25 14 15 13
Email   engel-thierry@wanadoo.fr
Web   www.lamaisonfleurie.com

Entry 82   Map 7

Alsace

La Haute Grange

On the side of a hill, looking down the valley, this 19th-century farmhouse is surrounded by forests and wildflower meadows. Rural and indulging all at once, it is a place for de-stressing… deeply comforting bedrooms, subtle and spicy colours, the whole house filled with the smell of baking in the morning. The large sitting room has an open fireplace, an honesty bar and hundreds of books; step onto the patio and enjoy the heart-lifting views. A warm, polyglot couple, Margaret and Philippe will help you plan days of discovery. Later, you can walk to the village for a choice of restaurants – a taste of Alsace with local wines.

Rooms	4: 3 doubles, 1 twin/double.
Price	€115–€150.
Meals	Restaurants 6km.
Closed	Rarely.

Margaret & Philippe Kalk
La Haute Grange,
La Chaude Côte,
68240 Fréland, Haut-Rhin
Tel   +33 (0)3 89 71 90 06
Mobile   +33 (0)6 15 72 15 15
Email   lahautegrange@aol.com
Web   www.lahautegrange.fr

Entry 83   Map 7

Alsace

Le Chat Rouge

Persevere up a steep road to find comfort and calm. Restored using a blend of wood, glass, stone and eco-friendly paints, the bright elegant guest sitting room has panoramic views and a wood-burner. Home-pressed apple juice is served at breakfast (in autumn the delicious scent of apples is everywhere). Climb your own spiral staircase (each room has one) to find floors reclaimed from oak wine casks starring in bathrooms and, on the suite's mezzanine, a daring part-glass floor! In the spreading grounds, fruit trees flower in spring and there's a sun-trap of a patio. Friendly Édith and Maurice are a mine of local information.

Minimum stay two nights in larger suite.

Rooms	2: 1 suite for 2, 1 suite for 4.
Price	Suite for 2, €130.
	Suite for 4, €150–€190.
Meals	Restaurant 3km.
Closed	Never.

Édith & Maurice Martin
Le Chat Rouge,
46 Les Champs Simon,
68370 Orbey, Haut-Rhin
Tel +33 (0)3 89 27 33 41
Email rent.redcat@gmail.com
Web www.lechatrouge-alsace.fr

Entry 84   Map 7

Alsace

Domaine Thierhurst

Your hosts are so welcoming in their sturdily luxurious modern house: he, quiet and courteous, runs the farm; she, dynamic and full of energy, opens her soul – and her house – to make you feel at home: this is real B&B and she loves it. She knows the delights of Alsace and nearby Germany intimately, concocts delicious breakfasts in the octagonal kitchen-diner and loves your amazement at the upstairs 'bathroom extraordinaire' with its vast rain shower. Pale, Turkish-rugged suites have all contemporary comforts, the large garden flowers generously, the high-quality pool is geothermally heated – dive in!

Rooms	2: 1 double, 1 suite.
Price	€120.
Meals	Restaurant 4km.
Closed	Rarely.

Bénédicte & Jean-Jacques Kinny
Domaine Thierhurst,
68740 Nambsheim, Haut-Rhin
Mobile +33 (0)6 07 97 28 22
Email domainekinny@gmail.com
Web www.kinny.fr

Entry 85   Map 7

Franche Comté

Maison d'Hôtes du Parc

Appreciate the finer things in life in Emmanuel and Mark's 1860s riverside home: gourmet cuisine, gorgeous gardens, inspired design. Polished, harmonious interiors waft with shades of mushroom, raspberry and moss, with period antiques, exquisite objets, a harp in the vast salon, a grand piano in the library. Fine china appears at four-course dinners as you chat over tender lamb cutlets with garden thyme. Rooms and suites are cosily sumptuous, views spilling over well-tended gardens of scampering roses, manicured hedges, a summer house and potager. Beyond centennial trees is a gem: Le Corbusier's sensually spiritual chapel.

Rooms	5: 2 doubles, 1 twin, 1 single, 1 suite.
Price	€100-€120. Suite €120. Single €70.
Meals	Dinner, 4 courses, €25. Restaurants nearby.
Closed	Rarely.

Emmanuel Georges
Maison d'Hôtes du Parc,
12-14 rue du Tram,
70250 Ronchamp, Haute-Saône
Tel   +33 (0)3 84 63 93 43
Email leparc-egeorges@wanadoo.fr
Web   www.hotesduparc.com

Entry 86   Map 7

Franche Comté

Château d'Épenoux

Swiss-born Susanne and Eva have given this dear little 18th-century château and its baroque chapel the facelift they deserved. Five bedrooms in the château, all generously big and different, plus apartments above the orangery, in the chapel and the manor house. The château suite, prettily papered in blue, overlooks copses and lawns; the large double is panelled in French green. Sink into wildly floral armchairs for drinks in the salon before dinner in the dining room, grand chandelier tinkling overhead. Stroll through ancient chestnut trees to the glittering pool, or visit charming Vesoul with its intriguing gothic façades.

Rooms	5: 4 doubles, 1 suite.
Price	€103-€125. Suite €125. Extra bed €27.
Meals	Dinner (weekends only) €32. Wine €12-€38.
Closed	Rarely.

Eva Holz & Susanne Hubbuch
Château d'Épenoux,
70000 Pusy & Épenoux,
Haute-Saône
Tel   +33 (0)3 84 75 19 60
Email chateau.epenoux@orange.fr
Web   www.chateau-epenoux.com

Entry 87   Map 6

Franche Comté

Les Egrignes

Refinement, loving care and high craftsmanship: you are welcomed to this exquisite house by bubbly Fabienne who, with her late husband, breathed new life into the lovely old stones and mouldings. Myriad auctions were combed for fine rugs, old mirrors, modern paintings, piano; Fabienne hung thick curtains, positioned pretty desks, carved armoires and soft sofas in vast pale-walled bedrooms and deluxe bathrooms. The garden is a marvel, the half-wheel potager is especially breathtaking. An interior designer of much flair, she is fun and excellent company. Elegant perfection.

Arrival from 5.30pm. Minimum two nights June-Sept.

Rooms	2: 1 triple, 2 suites for 2-4.
Price	Triple €95–€100. Suite €95–€100.
Meals	Summer kitchen. Restaurants 2km (Open Fri, Sat & Sun).
Closed	December/January.

	Fabienne Lego-Deiber
	Les Egrignes,
	70150 Cult, Haute-Saône
Tel	+33 (0)3 84 31 92 06
Mobile	+33 (0)6 84 20 64 91
Email	contact@les-egrines.com
Web	les-egrignes.com

Entry 88   Map 6

Franche Comté

La Maison Royale

The gaunt exterior, part of the town's 15th-century fortress, imposes – but Madame (charming, cultured, a teacher of French and Spanish) and her late husband bought the vast walls and created a house within them, her pride and joy. The courtyard has small gardens and a fountain; the huge ground-floor rooms are gorgeous; artistically marvellous bedrooms have luxury bathrooms and great views: it's like sleeping in a modern palace. It could be overwhelming but Lydie is such a delightful person that it is, in fact, unforgettably moving. And you are in one of the loveliest villages in France.

Children over 5 welcome.

Rooms	5: 4 doubles, 1 twin.
Price	€100.
Meals	Restaurants within walking distance.
Closed	October-April.

	Lydie Hoyet
	La Maison Royale,
	70140 Pesmes, Haute-Saône
Tel	+33 (0)3 84 31 23 23
Email	lydie@maisonroyalepesmes.com
Web	www.maisonroyalepesmes.com

Entry 89   Map 6

Franche Comté

Rose Art

In a lovely setting where the mountains lift up from the plain live a courteous and generous couple with all the time in the world for you, a slower, kinder, older world. Madame does artistic embroidery and her son, who speaks good English, makes organic wines and eaux de vie. It's a very average old wine merchant's house, simple, authentic and far from luxurious, but the pretty village, the rooms under the roof, the view of orchards and meadows, the brook to sing you to sleep after a good organic dinner with your adorable hosts, make it special. There's an unkempt patch of garden and a piano anyone may play – or golf down the road.

To avoid disappointment, tables d'hôtes absolutely must be booked in advance.

Ask your hosts about reduced meal rates if you're travelling with little ones.

Rooms	2: 1 twin, 1 suite for 4–5.
Price	€50.
Meals	Dinner €15. Wine €10–€12.
Closed	Rarely.

If venturing to a restaurant, be aware that rural restaurants stop taking orders at 9pm and often close at least one day a week.

Monique & Michel Ryon
Rose Art,
8 rue Lacuzon, 39570 Vernantois, Jura
Tel   +33 (0)3 84 47 17 28
Email   ryonjf@wanadoo.fr

Entry 90   Map 11

Burgundy

Burgundy

Le Prieuré St Agnan

The sunsets are special, the breakfasts are glorious with a choice of 15 teas and homemade compotes and jams. After a day scouting the best wineries, bets are on that you'll return to tea or apéritif on the garden terrace that looks over the Loire to the hills of Sancerre. This lovely 19th-century Benedictine priory is attached to the church (bells stop at 10pm). Run by sincerely friendly, unpretentious owners, it is a perfect place for those who like to wander into town and stroll home after dinner. Bedrooms are warmly immaculate, some overlooking the river; the luscious honeymoon quarters have their own terrace.

Rooms	5 doubles.
Price	€90-€130. Extra bed €20.
Meals	Restaurants within walking distance.
Closed	Rarely.

Christine Grillères
Le Prieuré St Agnan,
Impasse du Prieuré, Place St Agnan,
58200 Cosne sur Loire, Nièvre
Mobile +33 (0)6 99 03 07 75
Email prieure.saint.agnan@orange.fr
Web www.prieuresaintagnan.com

Entry 91 Map 5

Burgundy

Domaine de Drémont

Views soar from this 17th-century Burgundian farmhouse in majestically rural France. The English-French owners, quietly charming green farmers of Charolais cattle, live with their young children at one end; guest quarters – characterful, comfortable – are at the other, the atmospherically high-raftered family suite waits up outside stone stairs. Chalk-white walls, aged terracotta, the odd antique… all is spotless and unfussy. Inside: a big cosy sitting room with bold-fabric walls and stone fireplace; outside: an ancient spring-fed pool for quick plunges. Mystical Vézelay is a short drive.

Minimum three nights July / Aug.

Rooms	3: 1 double, 1 family suite; 1 double with separate shower.
Price	€50-€85. Family suite €65-€135.
Meals	Guest kitchen. Restaurant 9km.
Closed	Rarely.

Ghislaine Bentley
Domaine de Drémont,
58800 Anthien, Nièvre
Tel +33 (0)3 86 22 04 54
Email mg.bentley@wanadoo.fr
Web www.dremont.fr

Entry 92 Map 5

Burgundy

La Villa des Prés

Deep in real peace-wrapped country, this place of secluded old-style comfort and breathtaking views of the Morvan has new and rightly enthusiastic Dutch owners: it's gorgeous. Inside are open fires, antique beds, sympathetic period decorations, antique linen and super modern showers. Rooms are vast and there are two salons, one gloriously golden green, for lazing about. A baronial double stair leads down to the fine garden and the ha-ha where, rather endearingly, chickens may be roaming. A base for church, château and vineyard visits – a peaceful paradise.

Minimum three nights.

Rooms	5 twins/doubles.
Price	€80–€105.
Meals	Complimentary Sunday dinner with wine for 7-night stays. Guest kitchen. Restaurant 3km.
Closed	October–March.

	Kees & Inge Stapel
	La Villa des Prés,
	Route de Corbigny,
	58420 St Révérien, Nièvre
Tel	+33 (0)3 86 29 03 81
Mobile	+31 (0)6 51 18 89 67
Email	villa-des-pres@orange.fr
Web	www.villa-des-pres.com

Entry 93   Map 5

Burgundy

Domaine des Perrières

Make the most of seasonal farm produce and traditional French food: the visitors' book is plump with praise. Madame the farmer's wife loves cooking (delectable pastries and jams), is happy to cater for all tastes, and makes you feel at home. Wheat fields wave to the horizon, farm and cows are next door, this is 360 hectares of deepest France. Inside, in simple, straightforward rooms, all is airy and light, cheerful and double-glazed. No sitting room to share but after a day on horses or on foot (the cross-country trails are inspiring) and a long, leisurely supper, most guests retire gratefully to bed.

Extra beds available.

Rooms	2: 1 twin/double, 1 family room.
Price	€65. Family room €75.
Meals	Dinner with wine, €25.
Closed	Rarely.

	Pascale Cointe
	Domaine des Perrières,
	58330 Crux La Ville, Nièvre
Tel	+33 (0)3 86 58 34 93
Email	pbcointe58@orange.fr
Web	www.chambres-charme-bourgogne.com

Entry 94   Map 10

Burgundy

Château de Nyon

A pretty little château in a secluded valley in the heart of utterly unspoilt countryside. The remarkable Catherine inherited the house and has been doing B&B for 20 years. Her bedrooms, all on the first floor, echo the 18th-century character of the house. Toile de Jouy is charmingly splashed across pink paper and fabrics, bathrooms have big tubs or walk-in showers, glorious views to the garden reveal an avenue of lime trees and a hornbeam maze. Friendly Madame serves a beautiful breakfast of fresh pastries and home honey. It's hard to leave this blessed setting; the nearest restaurant is ten kilometres away.

Rooms	4: 2 doubles, 1 family suite for 4, 1 single.
Price	€65-€85. Family suite €150. Single €45.
Meals	Restaurant 10km.
Closed	Rarely.

Catherine Henry
Château de Nyon,
58130 Ourouër, Nièvre
Tel   +33 (0)3 86 58 61 12
Email   chateaudenyon@gmail.com
Web   www.chateaudenyon.com

Entry 95   Map 10

Burgundy

Château de Villette

Coen and Catherine – he Dutch, she Belgian – fell in love with this little château, then had their wedding here: they love their adopted country. They've opened just five rooms to guests (the suites are twin-roomed) and one very private cottage so they can spoil you properly. And get to know you over dinner. (Though, should you prefer a romantic dinner for two, they'll understand.) Bedrooms, large, light and airy, with warm colours and polished floors, are dressed in château-style finery. Views sail out of great windows to meadows and woodland and families would love it here. Beaune and the vineyards lie temptingly close.

Minimum two nights July/Aug.

Rooms	5: 1 double, 3 family suites for 5. Cottage for 2.
Price	€165-€245. Family suites €330-€390. Cottage €165-€245.
Meals	Dinner €48. Wine €18-€100.
Closed	Rarely.

Catherine & Coen Stork
Château de Villette,
58170 Poil, Nièvre
Tel   +33 (0)3 86 30 09 13
Email   catherinestork@chateaudevillette.eu
Web   www.chateaudevillette.eu

Entry 96   Map 11

Burgundy

Château de Vaulx

Vaulx was described in 1886 as "well-proportioned and elegant in its simplicity". It is as lovely now and in the most beautiful position, high on a hill with views that stretch to distant mountains. Delightful Marty will escort you to the west wing then create a delicious dinner. Expect big bedrooms full of character, a panelled drawing room with chandeliers, a huge dining room with fresh flowers, and manicured lawns and box balls tightly topiaried – stroll down the romantic avenues in dappled sunlight. In the village, a 13th-century bell tower; nearby, one of the best chocolate makers in France (monthly tastings and lessons).

Rooms	5: 2 doubles, 2 family suites for 4, 1 apartment for 5.
Price	€100–€120. Family suites €145. Apartment €190.
Meals	Dinner €30. Wine €18. Restaurant 3km.
Closed	Rarely.

Marty Freriksen
Château de Vaulx,
71800 St Julien de Civry,
Saône-et-Loire
Tel   +33 (0)3 85 70 64 03
Email   marty@chateaudevaulx.com
Web   www.chateaudevaulx.com

Burgundy

La Tour

The terraced garden is brimful of stepping stones and flowers, ginger tabbies wend through the irises, bucolic views stretch across undulating pastures: this is a deeply rural ensemble. June, widely travelled, kind, attentive, a great reader and lover of art in all its forms, lives in a long stone farmhouse in a cluster of outbuildings that go back to 1740. The airy two-bedroom suite in its own wing has a fine stone fireplace on its ground floor; floorboards are honey-coloured, the bathroom is a treat, and scrumptious breakfasts (organic jams, eggs from the hens) are served on charming country china. Lovely.

Breakfast hamper available.

Rooms	1 family suite for 2-3.
Price	€70.
Meals	Restaurants 7km.
Closed	Rarely.

June Bibby
La Tour,
71120 Marcilly La Guerce,
Saône-et-Loire
Tel   +33 (0)6 87 59 78 29
Email   bibbyjune@gmail.com
Web   www.latourbandb.com

Burgundy

La Gentilhommière de Collonges

Between Burgundy and Beaujolais, tall gates usher you straight into history. This elegant home was rebuilt from the pale stone manor burned down in the French Revolution and its fine antique furnishings testify to centuries past. In wooded gardens, the independent guest wing has good big bedrooms with working fireplaces and solid beams, stylish bathrooms and hillside views, a snug sitting room and a vast landing for delicious breakfasts. Only a hum of morning traffic reminds you of reality, and Madame's scent bottle collection is one of few signs of your very unobtrusive hosts. A perfectly private retreat.

Rooms	4: 2 doubles, 2 twins/doubles.
Price	€115–€140.
Meals	Restaurants 10-minute drive.
Closed	Rarely.

Jacques Saunier
La Gentilhommière de Collonges,
Colonge, Route Lamartine,
71960 Prissé, Saône-et-Loire
Tel   +33 (0)3 85 37 82 31
Mobile   +33 (0)6 70 17 59 18
Email   saunier.jacques@wanadoo.fr
Web   www.gentilhommieredecollonges.fr

Entry 99   Map 11

Burgundy

Le Tinailler d'Aléane

The lovely stones and cascading geraniums outside, the silk flowers, frilly lampshades and polished furniture inside have an old-world charm. The breakfast room is cosily stuffed with bric-a-brac, bedrooms are family-simple. Madame was a florist: she arranges her rooms as if they were bouquets, is always refreshing them and might put a paper heart on your pillow wishing you *bonne nuit*. (Ask for the larger room; the smaller feels cramped.) She doesn't refuse children but may well be happier if you arrive with a little dog under your arm! She delightedly arranges meals at restaurants and winery visits for non-French speakers.

Rooms	2: 1 double, 1 twin.
Price	€60–€65.
Meals	Dinner, 4 courses with wine, €25 (winter only). Restaurants 3km.
Closed	Sundays in winter.

Éliane Heinen
Le Tinailler d'Aléane,
Sommeré,
71960 La Roche Vineuse,
Saône-et-Loire
Tel   +33 (0)3 85 37 80 68

Entry 100   Map 11

Burgundy

Le Clos de Clessé

Set in a delightful, formal rose garden — clipped box hedges, gravel paths, stone-edged beds — the old manor is the enviable life's dream of your courteous Belgian hosts, excellent Cordon Bleu cooks both. Two gorgeous cottages with split-level bedrooms overlook the garden and there's a further pretty, bare-beamed room in the main house. Natural stone, old fireplaces, terracotta tiles and flagstones worn satin-smooth offset modern fittings and antique pieces perfectly. There are vineyards and châteaux galore, though the tempting, secluded pool may be as far as you'll get.

Minimum two nights June-September.

Rooms	3: 1 double. Cottage: 1 double. Cottage: 1 suite for 2-4.
Price	€100-€110. Suite €110 for 2.
Meals	Dinner with wine, €35. Restaurant 3km.
Closed	Rarely.

Tessy & André Gladinez
Le Clos de Clessé,
Ruelle Ste Marie, 71260 Clessé,
Saône-et-Loire
Tel   +33 (0)3 85 23 03 56
Email   info@closdeclesse.com
Web   www.closdeclesse.com

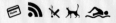

Entry 101   Map 11

Burgundy

La Ferme de Marie-Eugénie

La Ferme belonged to Marie-Eugénie's grandmother and the deft renovating flair of this ex-Parisian couple (formerly in advertising) is on show everywhere, from whitewashed beams to shabby-chic leather sofas. The pretty half-timbered barn (owners live in the cottage) overlooking a big lawned garden is now a fashionable maison d'hôtes. Be charmed by light-flooded rooms, pale tiled floors and exposed limestone walls. Bedrooms are comfortable, delightful — soft colours, modern art; there's an inviting, books-and-magazines salon and a slick dining-kitchen for delicious meals. Glossy-mag perfection meets deep rural sleepiness.

Rooms	4: 3 doubles, 1 twin.
Price	€100-€125.
Meals	Dinner €35. Wine €25-€70. Restaurants in Louhans, 9km.
Closed	Christmas.

Marie-Eugénie Dupuy
La Ferme de Marie-Eugénie,
225 allée de Chardenoux,
71500 Bruailles, Saône-et-Loire
Tel   +33 (0)3 85 74 81 84
Email   info@lafermedemarieeugenie.fr
Web   www.lafermedemarieeugenie.fr

Entry 102   Map 11

Burgundy

Château de Nobles

Oceans of history lie behind this gorgeous place (it even has a prehistoric *menhir*), its passionate owners bursting with more restoration ideas. Monsieur tends the vines and the wine: production started here in the 10th century. The bedrooms, in a renovated building near the dreamlike, 13th-15th-century château, are fresh and unfussy in a stylish way that is so very French; the bigger one is a gem, with its superb beams, vast mezzanine, little veranda, huge new bath. No guest sitting room but breakfast in the château, a delightfully lived-in listed monument, is a treat. Mellow, poetic, irresistible.

Minimum two nights at weekends.

Rooms	3: 1 double, 1 triple, 1 family room for 4.
Price	€98.
Meals	Restaurants 7km.
Closed	November–March.

Bertrand & Françoise de Cherisey
Château de Nobles,
71700 La Chapelle sous Brancion,
Saône-et-Loire

Tel	+33 (0)3 85 51 00 55
Mobile	+33 (0)6 41 94 64 79
Email	b.de.cherisey@orange.fr
Web	www.chateaudenobles.com

Burgundy

Château de Messey

A herd of fine cattle shares the buttercup meadows with this 16th-century wine estate on the Route des Vins. Wandering woodland paths, ducks on the river… it has the dreamiest setting. Three pretty country bedrooms are in the rambling rustic vine-workers' cottages, built round a grassed courtyard. The pricier ones are in the serene high-ceilinged château. Markus, who loves cooking (six minimum) and the ever-welcoming Delphine live with their three children in one of the cottages and manage it all with charming efficiency. A great, if sometimes busy, place for Tournus and other Romanesque gems.

Unfenced water.

Rooms	5: 2 twins/doubles, 2 twins, 1 triple.
Price	€107–€130.
Meals	Dinner €30. Wine €10–€15. Restaurant 2km.
Closed	Occasionally.

Delphine & Markus Schaefer
Château de Messey,
71700 Ozenay,
Saône-et-Loire

Tel	+33 (0)3 85 51 16 11
Email	info@messey.fr
Web	www.messey.fr

Burgundy

Le Crot Foulot

Gutsy Jan and Annie sold their prize-winning restaurant in Brussels and filled their cellar while putting the finishing touches to this handsome wine-grower's house. Golden stones outside, a clean minimalism inside: Belgians always pull this off with flair. An elegant glass and wood staircase leads to muted bedrooms with delicate pale timbers revealed and glorified. In the open kitchen you can watch Jan whip up his mussel mousse while a farmyard chicken sizzles with citrus fruits in the oven. Annie will have brought up the perfect nectar for the menu. All is well in Burgundy tonight!

Burgundy

Abbaye de la Ferté

A privileged spot on a handsome estate. The abbot's palace, a listed monument open to the public in summer, is all that's left of the old abbey – glimpse the vast staircase on your way to breakfast in the intimate dining room. Bedrooms are divine: one is in the dovecote by the road with its exquisite bathroom in the loft; the other is in the gatehouse, its tub armchairs dressed in deep pink. The fabulous palace gardens have grand fountains in an English-style setting. Your young hosts make it all pleasingly eccentric and fun; they are generous, too, providing log fires, tea trays, art books, a bottle of local wine.

Rooms	5: 3 twins/doubles, 1 twin, 1 family room.
Price	€105–€120. Family room €168.
Meals	Dinner €35. Wine from €15.
Closed	November-February.

Rooms	2: Dovecote: 1 suite for 2-4. Gatehouse: 1 suite for 2-4.
Price	€77–€119.
Meals	Dinner with wine, €32 (July/Aug only). Restaurants nearby.
Closed	Rarely.

Annie Coeckelberghs
& Jan Hostens
Le Crot Foulot,
71240 Jugy, Saône-et-Loire
Tel   +33 (0)3 85 94 81 07
Email   crotfoulot@orange.fr
Web   crotfoulot.com

Jacques & Virginie Thénard
Abbaye de la Ferté,
71240 St Ambreuil, Saône-et-Loire
Mobile +33 (0)6 22 91 40 11
Email   abbayedelaferte@aol.com
Web   www.abbayedelaferte.com

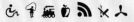

Entry 105   Map 11

Entry 106   Map 11

Burgundy

Manoir du Clos de Vauvry

A ceramic stove as big as two men dominates the breakfast room of this charming 17th-century royal hunting lodge. Summer breakfasts are on the terrace; dinners flourish home-grown produce. The whole place has an air of exaggeration: over-generous stairs, ingenious double windows, voluptuous ceilings, all totally French with floral wallpapers and embroidered bedcovers in magnificent bedrooms, 1930s tiled bathrooms (one whirlpool) and immaculate linen. This adorable couple knows everyone in wine growing and Marie helps you all she can. Burgundy has so much to offer, as well as superb wines. Wonderful.

Overflow rooms available.

Rooms	2: 1 twin, 1 suite.
Price	€75–€95. Suite €140–€160.
Meals	Dinner with wine, €32.
Closed	Rarely.

Marie & Daniel Lacroix-Mollaret
Manoir du Clos de Vauvry,
3 rue des Faussillons,
71640 Givry Sauges, Saône-et-Loire

Tel	+33 (0)3 85 44 40 83
Mobile	+33 (0)6 70 92 80 94
Email	daniel.mollaret@orange.fr
Web	www.clos-de-vauvry.com

Entry 107   Map 11

Burgundy

Clos Belloy

The two Dominques love their manor, understandably, for a timeless charm breathes from the stone of the enclosed courtyard and the house with its delicate Burgundian double staircase. Beautiful soft pale colours dress the walls in the salon, while hand-painted doors and ceilings delight in curlicues of sky blue and rose-bud pink. Meticulous bedrooms, a scattering of antiques, French windows, heavenly breakfasts, a garden full of lavender, roses and hydrangeas… it's airy, refined, light and very 18th century. Don't miss the local Rully wine, be it white chardonnay or red pinot noir.

Rooms	4: 1 double, 1 twin, 2 suites for 4.
Price	€125. Suite €170–€215. Extra bed €45.
Meals	Restaurant within walking distance.
Closed	Rarely.

Dominique & Dominique Belloy
Clos Belloy,
12 Grande Rue, 71150 Rully,
Saône-et-Loire

Tel	+33 (0)3 85 87 11 38
Mobile	+33 (0)6 14 09 63 17
Email	closbelloy@yahoo.fr
Web	www.closbelloy.fr

Entry 108   Map 11

Burgundy

La Maison Chaudenay

Bruce and Anne have settled with gusto into the ancient vibrations of 17th-century winepress, well-planned cellars, functioning bread oven and fantastic (horseless) stables that surround their gracious bourgeois house. It came complete with grand gates, veranda, parquet and a superb garden (a children's haven). Bedrooms, pale and rich, cream and floral, have taste, antiques and modern bathrooms, the fine sitting room rejoices in a beautiful carved fireplace, deep sofas, books and a stock of games. Elegant restraint and enthusiasm near one of France's best restaurants, in Chagny, near Beaune.

Minimum two nights at weekends.

Rooms	5: 4 doubles, 1 family room for 4.
Price	€70-€110. Family room €85-€130. Extra bed €20.
Meals	Summer kitchen. Restaurants 3km.
Closed	Rarely.

Anne & Bruce Leonard
La Maison Chaudenay,
26 rue de Tigny,
71150 Chaudenay,
Saône-et-Loire
Tel   +33 (0)3 85 87 35 98
Email   info@maisonchaudenay.com
Web   www.maisonchaudenay.com

Entry 109   Map 11

Burgundy

Domaine de l'Oiseau

Peeping out from under low slanting eaves and climbing plants, the lovely 18th-century buildings frame a courtyard. The village-end setting is secluded riverside woodland; feast by the pool on valley views *and* food. Bedrooms sing with serenity and good taste: the suite, graceful and feminine, in the old bakery, the rest peacefully in the Pavilion. Each has a dressing room, a small perfect bathroom and enchanting old *tomette* floor. Relax in the glorious beamed barn, now the guest library; sample the local fine wines in the cellar below under the guidance of your friendly, extrovert hosts. An exceptional place.

Rooms	4: 2 twins/doubles, 1 triple, 1 family suite for 2-4. Separate wcs.
Price	€130. Triple €140-€160. Family suite €130-€160.
Meals	Dinner with wine, from €50.
Closed	December-March.

Dominique & Philippe Monnier-Pictet
Domaine de l'Oiseau,
17 rue Chariot, 71590 Gergy,
Saône-et-Loire
Tel   +33 (0)3 85 91 61 26
Mobile   +33 (0)6 23 46 59 07
Email   info@domoiseau.com
Web   www.domoiseau.com

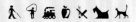

Entry 110   Map 11

Burgundy

Le Petit Clos

A sparkling outdoor pool crowns this rural idyll, a 1749 Bresse farmhouse and former château (with vines to prove it). Dainty viennoiseries and homemade yogurts appear for breakfast; Madame lights candles for evening feasts of bœuf bourguignon and crème brûlée, Monsieur offers wine tasting and local tips. Wander rose-scented gardens with a dovecote and scattered tables; the brocante-furnished bistro is perfect for intimate aperitifs. Family portraits hang on half-timbered walls, armchairs are cosy, oak staircases twist skywards and bedrooms have Jouy textiles and feminine touches. Explore historic Beaune and rural Bresse.

Minimum two nights.

Rooms	3: 2 doubles, 1 twin/double.
Price	€88. Singles €82. Extra bed €17.
Meals	Dinner €31. Wine €10–€30. Restaurant 2km.
Closed	December/January.

Élisabeth & Denis Bernard
Le Petit Clos,
10 rue de Merley, 71350 Ciel,
Saône-et-Loire
Tel   +33 (0)6 25 45 10 98
Mobile   +33 (0)6 25 45 10 98
Email   eli.ber@sfr.fr
Web   www.lepetitclosenbourgogne.fr

Entry 111   Map 11

Burgundy

Les Planchottes

If you find yourself in the Mecca of Wine, in the very heart of old Beaune, then surely you should stay with a family of wine-growers like the Bouchards. They are charming people, passionate about food, wine and matters 'green'; Cécile's breakfasts linger long in the memory. Immaculate is the conversion of this old townhouse, once three cottages: the craftsmanship of new oak and stone, the quiet good taste of the colours, the space in the comfortable bedrooms, the ultra modern bathrooms. Chill out in the walled, lush, flowered garden (complete with pet rabbit), glimpse the vineyards on the horizon. Outstanding.

Extra bed available in double room.

Rooms	2: 1 double, 1 twin.
Price	€100–€105. €5 supplement for one-night stays.
Meals	Restaurants within walking distance.
Closed	Mid-December to mid-February.

Christophe & Cécile Bouchard
Les Planchottes,
6 rue Sylvestre Chauvelot,
21200 Beaune, Côte-d'Or
Tel   +33 (0)3 80 22 83 67
Email   lesplanchottes@voila.fr
Web   lesplanchottes.fr

Entry 112   Map 11

Burgundy

Le Clos Champagne St Nicolas

Le Clos is nicely set back from the main road and Beaune is a ten-minute stroll. Built to take guests, the new wing has spanking new bedrooms, modern bits in the bathrooms and a salon overlooking the garden. Fabrics, bedding and antiques reveal Anne as a woman of taste who thinks of everything, even a guest kitchen for your morning spread of homemade jams, cake, croissants, bread, yogurt and fresh fruit. Bruno has a passion for vintage cars, especially if they're English. Knowledgeable natives and hospitable hosts, they fill you in on the sights, restaurants and vineyards over a welcoming glass of wine.

Rooms	3: 1 double, 2 twins/doubles.
Price	€110.
Meals	Guest kitchen. Restaurants within walking distance.
Closed	Rarely.

Bruno & Anne Durand de Gevigney
Le Clos Champagne St Nicolas,
114 ter route de Dijon,
21200 Beaune, Côte-d'Or
Tel   +33 (0)3 80 61 24 92
Mobile   +33 (0)6 61 82 39 63
Email   closchamp.stnicolas@free.fr
Web   closchamp.stnicolas.free.fr

Entry 113   Map 11

Burgundy

Sous le Baldaquin

Once Yves – the perfect host – swings open the huge doors of his townhouse in the heart of Beaune, the 21st-century disappears, the serene garden tugs at your soul and peace descends. Play the count, countess or courtesan as you mount the stone stair to your small perfect cocoon, past walls and ceiling painted in pale trompe-l'œil allegory. Gracious and elegant are the aubergine and willow-green taffeta drapes and beribboned baldaquin, charming the bathroom with its ancient double-basin, beautiful the view to the rambling roses. To call this romantic is an understatement – and Yves is the nicest host.

Rooms	1 double.
Price	€100–€110. Extra bed €25.
Meals	Restaurants 5-minute walk.
Closed	Rarely.

Yves Cantenot
Sous le Baldaquin,
39 rue Maufoux, 21200 Beaune,
Côte-d'Or
Tel   +33 (0)3 80 24 79 30
Mobile   +33 (0)6 80 17 72 51
Email   yves.cantenot@laposte.net
Web   www.souslebaldaquin.fr

Entry 114   Map 11

Burgundy

Burgundy

La Saura

For those wishing to escape to a sweet Côte d'Or village near Beaune – and some of the world's greatest wines – come here. The house and stables are charming and peaceful, the renovation is recent, the décor is delicious, the pool is a boon. Irresistible Madame smiles easily and loves her guests, gives you generous breakfasts before the log fire and big airy bedrooms with classic colours and lavish touches – and views; she also plans an enchanting guests' hideaway off the garden (for WiFi, books and games). Bed linen is antique and embroidered, towels carry the La Saura logo, paths lead into the hills. Bliss.

La Monastille

Stunning flagstones in the breakfast room (where baguettes and homemade jams are served) and wooden doors that creak open to cosy rooms. In a village of 50 souls (and 2,000 cows) is La Monastille, built in 1750 as a wealthy farmhouse. Generous Madame is passionate about history, antiques, food and loves her English guests. Traditional suppers at the big table feature local meat and poultry and veg from her garden. Wines flow. Bedrooms are a soothing mix of muted walls, dark old furniture and flowery bed covers, the dear little room in the tower is reached via many steps and outside is a lovely garden. A lovely restful address.

Rooms	5: 1 double. Stables: 3 doubles, 1 suite.
Price	€95–€105. Suite €115–€130. Extra bed €25.
Meals	Restaurant 2km.
Closed	20 December-31 January.

Rooms	4: 2 doubles, 2 triples.
Price	€85. Triple €105. Extra bed €20.
Meals	Dinner with wine & aperitif, €35. Restaurant 12km.
Closed	Rarely.

	Jocelyne-Marie Lehallé La Saura, Route de Beaune, 21360 Lusigny sur Ouche, Côte-d'Or
Tel	+33 (0)3 80 20 17 46
Mobile	+33 (0)6 81 29 57 42
Email	la-saura@wanadoo.fr
Web	www.la-saura.com

	Françoise Moine La Monastille, 7 rue de l'Église, 21360 Thomirey, Côte-d'Or
Tel	+33 (0)3 80 20 00 80
Email	moine.francoise@wanadoo.fr
Web	www.monastille.com

Burgundy

Les Hêtres Rouges

A pretty old Burgundian hunting lodge, 'Copper Beeches' stands in a walled garden full of ancient trees; and its village setting is a delight. There's an unexpected air of Provence inside: beautifully judged colour schemes (Madame paints), fine furniture, numerous *objets*, a tomcat or two. Your hosts extend a warm, genuine yet ungushing welcome to the weary traveller, and can organise wine tours that are perfect for you. Up a steep stair are low rooms with dark character and fine linen. Breakfast has the savour of yesteryear: yogurt, fresh bread, homemade jam, delicious coffee.

Sawday self-catering also. Cottage can be booked by the room in low season.

Rooms	2: 1 twin/double, 1 twin.
Price	€90–€104. Extra bed €32.
Meals	Restaurants 8km.
Closed	Rarely.

Jean-François & Christiane Bugnet
Les Hêtres Rouges,
10 route de Nuits, Antilly,
21700 Argilly, Côte-d'Or

Tel	+33 (0)3 80 62 53 98
Mobile	+33 (0)6 78 47 22 29
Email	leshetresrouges@free.fr
Web	www.leshetresrouges.com

Entry 117   Map 11

Burgundy

La Closerie de Gilly

A nicely grand, quintessentially French, green-shuttered façade; pretty, airy and florally friezed bedrooms with interesting prints on the walls. The ground-floor room opens straight onto the garden where chickens roam free and you can too – and breakfast alongside a beautiful Alsatian ceramic stove in the plant-filled breakfast salon. Your busy hosts – Monsieur also teaches economics – can take you on vineyard tours and conduct sessions in English on the geographical diversity of the wine areas. You are close to the impressive Château du Clos de Vougeot – and the motorway, though you wouldn't know it.

Rooms	2 doubles.
Price	€85–€90.
Meals	Restaurant 200m.
Closed	Christmas.

André & Sandrine Lanaud
La Closerie de Gilly,
16 av du Recteur Bouchard,
Gilly lès Cîteaux, 21640 Vougeot,
Côte-d'Or

Tel	+33 (0)3 80 62 87 74
Email	info@closerie-gilly.com
Web	www.closerie-gilly.com

Entry 118   Map 11

Burgundy

Domaine de Serrigny

Just yards from a pretty stretch of the Burgundy canal, a fine 18th-century house with high walls and magnificent views to perfect little Châteauneuf en Auxois. Charles and Marie-Pascale are stylish, informal and huge fun; so is their house. Fabulous antiques, interesting art and textiles, space outside for children to cavort. Bedrooms are a beautiful mix of styles with something for everyone, from grand salon to zen attic; all are delightful, bathrooms are bliss. Relax in the garden with its big lawn, colourful pots, decked pool and tennis court; have breakfast here or in the large open-plan sitting/dining room. Heaps of charm.

Rooms	3: 1 double, 1 family room for 4, 1 suite.
Price	€98–€108. Family room €122–€139. Suite €122–€139. Under 8's free.
Meals	Auberge opposite (closed Mondays).
Closed	Rarely.

Marie-Pascale Chaillot
Domaine de Serrigny, Lieu dit
"le Village", 21320 Vandenesse
en Auxois, Côte-d'Or

Tel	+33 (0)3 80 49 28 13
Mobile	+33 (0)6 86 89 90 07
Email	chaillot.mp@wanadoo.fr
Web	www.manoir-de-serrigny.com

Entry 119   Map 6

Burgundy

Wine & Water

As you sit on the sundeck of this natty hotel barge, sipping a fine burgundy, contemplating a lazy stroll or cycle into Châteauneuf, you may wonder if a more relaxing spot exists in France. Down in the open-plan saloon, large windows illuminate black leather sofas, colourful cushions and a kitchen bar where pastries and yogurts are laid out each morning by dynamic Max and Bea. Cosy up in cabins with new beds, good lights, en suite Italian showers; butterflies flutter over soft grey wallpaper. Find clever use of space, drinks in the fridge, and best quality everything. With a party of six, book a cruise down the canal.

Rooms	3: 2 twins/doubles. 1 suite.
Price	Cabin room €150. Suite €200. Dijon station pick-up, €50. Nov-April: weekend package for 6 (B&B, dinner & excursions) €1,500.
Meals	Restaurant 1km.
Closed	Never.

Beatrice & Max Renau
Wine & Water,
21320 Vandenesse en Auxois,
Côte-d'Or

Tel	+33 (0)6 14 91 02 38
Email	beatricerenau@gmail.com
Web	www.wine-water.com

Entry 120   Map 6

Burgundy

Château les Roches

A judge's passion for his mistress inspired this 1900s jewel. Built way off any beaten track, 500m high, with an unobscured view over the Serein valley and the lush forests of the Morvan, the bourgeois mansion still sits quietly behind tall gates, a haven of peace in a medieval village of 300 souls. Young Tobias, who's American, and German Marco fell just as hard as the judge and have restored it remarkably. The bones were good so they added perfect furnishings to light, spacious rooms and made the bathrooms sinful. Now they run a restaurant open to the public headed by Selby, a first-class chef. It is a perfect getaway.

Sawday self-catering also.

Rooms	6 + 1: 4 doubles, 2 family rooms for 3. Cottage for 4.
Price	€139–€179. Family room €164–€199. Cottage from €200. Cottage €950 per week.
Meals	Picnic lunch €19. Dinner €32. Wine from €16.
Closed	Rarely.

Tobias Yang & Marco Stockmeyer
Château les Roches,
Rue de Glanot,
21320 Mont St Jean, Côte-d'Or
Tel   +33 (0)3 80 84 32 71
Email   info@lesroches-burgundy.com
Web   www.lesroches-burgundy.com

Entry 121   Map 6

Burgundy

Manoir de Tarperon

Tarperon is uniquely French. An ageless charm breathes from the ancient turrets, the fine antiques, the paintings and the prints, while Soisick is young and good fun, with the unstuffy, even casual formality of a busy woman. The rooms, with family furniture, have an uncontrived, fadedly elegant décor, the bathrooms are family style, the garden is timeless, rambling, whimsical. Dinner, in the family's restaurant next door in season or table d'hôtes in the manor dining room in winter, is the very best of authentic Burgundian. All this and fly-fishing at €25 a day, and painting courses to stir your creativity.

Minimum two nights. Whole house available.

Rooms	5: 3 doubles, 1 twin, 1 triple.
Price	€75–€78. Triple €95–€105.
Meals	Dinner with wine, €30, or at family's restaurant next door.
Closed	November–March.

Soisick de Champsavin
Manoir de Tarperon,
21510 Aignay le Duc, Côte-d'Or
Tel   +33 (0)3 80 93 83 74
Email   manoir.de.tarperon@wanadoo.fr
Web   www.tarperon.fr

Entry 122   Map 6

Burgundy

Rue Hoteaux

A master stone mason built this house in the 19th century and left many marks of his consummate skill in stairs and fireplaces as well as his quarry at the back where the Escots have made a spectacular flower-filled rock garden – Madame's passion. They are a relaxed, generous couple, she bubbly and proud of her many grandchildren, he shyer but a mine of information; both love having people to stay. In the converted barn, the big ground-floor stable room has a finely clothed bed, white slatted walls and exposed beams... or climb the lovely winding stairs to the pretty attic room. Both have views on the garden.

Rooms	2: 1 triple, 1 family room for 3-4.
Price	Triple €90–€110.
	Family room €90–€130.
Meals	Restaurants 3km.
Closed	November-March.

	Gilberte & Jean Escot
	Rue Hoteaux,
	21400 Puits, Côte-d'Or
Tel	+33 (0)3 80 93 14 83
Mobile	+33 (0)6 24 83 64 18
Email	gilbertemichel2@wanadoo.fr
Web	chambrepuits.free.fr

Entry 123   Map 6

Burgundy

La Cimentelle

After an astoundingly beautiful drive you reach this handsome family house built by titans of the cement industry at the turn of the last century: the pool sits on top of the old factory. Come for extraordinary food (both hosts are gourmet cooks), thoughtfulness, friendly chat and the loveliest rooms. Three are works of art and a touch of fun: a Murano mirror, an antique desk, pink faux-baroque wallpaper and stunning white linen curtains. Swish bathrooms glow with monogrammed towels and showers in Italian mosaic. Family suites at the top of the house are huge. Don't miss it, you'll need at least two nights.

Rooms	5: 3 doubles, 2 family suites for 4.
Price	€85–€110. Family suites €140–€220.
Meals	Dinner with wine, €40.
Closed	Rarely.

	Nathalie & Stéphane Oudot
	La Cimentelle,
	4 rue de la Cimentelle,
	89200 Vassy lès Avallon, Yonne
Tel	+33 (0)3 86 31 04 85
Email	lacimentelle@orange.fr
Web	www.lacimentelle.com

Entry 124   Map 6

Burgundy

Maison Crème Anglaise

They named the gracious old house after their desserts, served with crème anglaise. From a Tintin collection to Custard the dog, this mellow old place is full of surprises. Swallows nest in a medieval archway, a staircase winds up a tower and the garden falls steeply away giving unforgettable views. Meals are accompanied by candles and flowers, bedrooms are pretty, cosy, comfy, appealing and the charming bathroom is shared. Graham and Christine, open, enthusiastic, hands-on, hold recitals, exhibitions and summer *salons de thé* in the courtyard. The hilltop village is historic, the peace is a balm. We love it all.

Minimum two nights July/Aug.

Rooms	3: 2 doubles, 1 twin, sharing bathroom.
Price	€70.
Meals	Dinner with wine, €25. Special events catered for.
Closed	Rarely.

Graham & Christine Battye
Maison Crème Anglaise,
22 Grande Rue,
89420 Montréal, Yonne
Tel   +33 (0)3 86 32 07 73
Email   grahambattye@maisoncremeanglaise.com
Web   www.maisoncremeanglaise.com

Entry 125   Map 6

Burgundy

Carpe Diem

In a tranquil Burgundy village lies this handsome old farmhouse. Peek through the gate: all is verdant with vines and the garden is picnic perfect. Eat convivially on a pretty terrace or in a grand dining room with luxurious décor and fireplace. With home-grown veg and local produce (the Charolais beef is as sweet as a nut), dinner is well worth booking. Immaculate bedrooms are romantic in toile de Jouy with pepperings of fine paintings and antiques. Ask for Chambre Diane in the main house with its big bath, or choose the beautiful stables – children will love the secret mezzanine rooms.

Children over 12 welcome.

Rooms	5: 2 doubles, 1 twin/double, 2 family rooms for 3.
Price	€93. Family room €70. Singles €62–€85.
Meals	Dinner with wine, €35. Restaurants 4km.
Closed	Rarely.

Patrick Cabon
Carpe Diem,
53 Grande Rue,
89440 Massangis, Yonne
Tel   +33 (0)3 86 33 89 32
Email   carpediem.ser@gmail.com
Web   www.acarpediem.com

Entry 126   Map 6

Burgundy

Le Charme Merry

Their table d'hôtes says it all. Delicious dinners – simple yet fine – are served in the lofty high-raftered dining room under a hooped chandelier. This winemaker's property by the village church has been immaculately restored and furnished in modernist style: cream leather sofas by open fires and beautiful bedrooms next door (two up, two down). Be delighted by à la mode fabrics and big fat pillows, exotic orchids and limestone floors, the charming owner's photographs on perfect pale walls and bathrooms worth saving up for. Outside: gravel, grass and a serene pool. Beyond: Romanesque churches and a heavenly spa.

Rooms	4 doubles.
Price	€130–€140. Extra bed €40. Cot €10.
Meals	Dinner with wine, €49. Children €15. Restaurants 13km.
Closed	January.

Nicolas & Olivia Peron
Le Charme Merry,
30 route de Compostelle,
89660 Merry sur Yonne, Yonne

Tel	+33 (0)3 86 81 08 46
Mobile	+33 (0)6 82 33 41 26
Email	olivia.peron@gmail.com
Web	www.lecharmemerry.com

Entry 127   Map 5

Burgundy

Petit Manoir des Bruyères

Fruit trees, roses galore, aviaries of canaries and rare pheasant breeds: the gardens heave with floral splendour. As for the manoir, it is unlike anything you've seen. Find a vast beamed living room, an endless polished table, rows of tapestried chairs. Bedrooms? A Louis XIV suite whose red bathroom has gold and ivory taps; another bathroom, many-mirrored, reflecting multiple magical images; a deeply, heavily pink suite with painted ceilings – wild! But such is Monique's attentiveness, the peace of the house and garden, the quality of comfort, food and wine, that we feel it's perfect for lovers of French extravaganza.

Rooms	5: 2 doubles, 1 suite. Apartment: 2 doubles.
Price	€150–€170. Suite €220. Apartment €150–€180.
Meals	Hosted dinner €46.
Closed	Never.

Monique Joullié
Petit Manoir des Bruyères,
89240 Villefargeau, Yonne

Tel	+33 (0)3 86 41 32 82
Email	jchambord@aol.com
Web	www.petit-manoir-bruyeres.com

Entry 128   Map 5

Burgundy

Château de Séréville

In this handsome, 19th-century, forested château, miles from anywhere, you are only an hour from Paris, a mile from the village. Caring, ex-Parisian hosts, a town planner and a psychoanalyst, greet you in the grand, monochrome hall which leads to rooms ranging from relatively compact to frankly huge. Décor is appropriately smart – cornices and frescoes well-cared for, objets d'art to match. Homemade jams are served with seriously good viennoiserie at breakfast – and homelaid eggs if you wish. You can withdraw to the delightfully pastel salon or the games-full library, fish in one of two lakes, play golf, bring your own horse.

Whole house available.

Rooms	4: 3 doubles, 1 suite.
Price	€95–€130. Suite €160.
Meals	Light supper €20. Wine €30. Restaurants 1.5km.
Closed	Rarely.

Jean-Marie Von Kaenel &
Christian Chavanel
Château de Séréville,
89150 La Belliole, Yonne
Tel   +33 (0)3 86 66 89 42
Email   zcch@orange.fr
Web   www.chateaudesereville.com

Entry 129   Map 5

Paris – Île de France

Paris - Île de France

Châtelet district

You will meet a most civilised couple – Mona a bubbly, award-winning artist, Jean a quietly studious former university professor – in their very personal, gently refined apartment where original timbers divide the living room and two friendly cats proclaim the cosiness. It is beautifully done and eminently French, like a warm soft nest, with antiques, lots of greenery, interesting art. Mona loves her guests and is full of good tips: the Seine and historic Paris are at the end of the road. Your attractive, compact guest quarters are nicely private with good storage space, pretty quilts and lots of light.

Minimum two nights.

Rooms	1 twin.
Price	€100.
Meals	Restaurants nearby.
Closed	Summer holidays.

Mona Pierrot
Châtelet district,
75001 Paris
Tel   +33 (0)1 42 36 50 65
Email   pierrot-jean@orange.fr

Entry 130   Map 5

Paris - Île de France

Bonne Nuit Paris

Absolute Paris, 300-year-old timbers, crazy wonky stairs and modern comforts, independent rooms and a warm welcome, little streets, friendly markets: it's real privilege. Charming, intelligent Jean-Luc serves his honey, Denise's jams and fresh bread in their generous, rambling living room upstairs. To each room, be it ground or first floor, a colourful shower, a lot of quirk (the last word in creative basins), an appealing mix of antique woodwork and modern prints, and a sense of seclusion. Simplicity, panache and personality, attention and service: these are the hallmarks. No communal space, but a lovely peaceful courtyard.

Rooms	5: 3 doubles, 2 triples.
Price	€160-€210. Triple €260-€315. Extra bed €75.
Meals	Restaurants within walking distance.
Closed	Rarely.

Denise & Jean-Luc Marchand
Bonne Nuit Paris,
63 rue Charlot, Le Marais,
75003 Paris
Tel   +33 (0)1 42 71 83 56
Mobile   +33 (0)6 72 35 90 75
Email   jean.luc@bonne-nuit-paris.com
Web   www.bonne-nuit-paris.com

Entry 131   Map 5

Paris - Île de France

Notre Dame district

At the end of the street are the Seine and the glory of Notre Dame. In a grand old building (with a new lift by the 17th-century stairs), the two unaffected rooms, one above the other, look down to a little garden. The mezzanined family room has its bathroom off the landing; a simple breakfast of shop-packed items is laid here. Upstairs is the smaller room: bed in the corner, timeworn shower room and DIY breakfast system. Madame is polyglot, active and eager to help when she is available; she leaves breakfast ready if she has to go out. She and her daughter appreciate the variety of contact guests bring. A gem in the heart of Paris.

Minimum two nights.

Rooms	2: 1 double; 1 quadruple with separate bath.
Price	€90. Quadruple €115–€140.
Meals	No breakfast in double. Continental breakfast left ready if owner has to go out.
Closed	Rarely.

Brigitte Chatignoux
Notre Dame district,
75005 Paris
Tel   +33 (0)1 43 25 27 20
Email   brichati@hotmail.com

Entry 132   Map 5

Paris - Île de France

La maison d'Anne – Paris Historic Bed & Breakfast

Dare we say unique? A four-storey 17th-century private mansion in the shadow of Notre Dame: surely the rarest B&B in Paris. Then there's the refined welcome into a lively, educated family; the basement pool, sauna and gym; the wine-and-cheese tasting in the cellar. Your suite is off the covered ground-floor courtyard: beams tell of great age, paintings of modern taste, bathroom and kitchen of Moroccan travels. Take the ancient stairs or the lift to top-floor breakfast with Anne and masses of inside lore on hidden Paris: she is charmingly erudite, her time is a gift. Extremely special and worth every centime.

Babies & children over 6 welcome. Minimum three nights.

Rooms	2: 1 triple, 1 suite.
Price	Triple €240. Suite €270. Extra bed €40.
Meals	Restaurants nearby. Kitchenette in suite.
Closed	Rarely.

Anne Cany
La maison d'Anne - Paris Historic
Bed & Breakfast,
Latin Quarter, 75005 Paris
Tel   +33 (0)1 56 81 10 85
Email   abaronnet@parsys.com
Web   www.parishistoricbnb.com

Entry 133   Map 5

Paris - Île de France

10 rue Las Cases

In a provincial-quiet city street, classy dressed stone outside, intelligence, sobriety and style inside. Madame takes you into her vast, serene apartment: no modern gadgets or curly antiques, just a few good pieces, much space, and light-flooded parquet floors. Beyond the dining room, your cosy buff bedroom gives onto a big, silent, arcaded courtyard. Your hosts have lived all over the world, and delightful Madame, as quiet and genuine as her surroundings, now enjoys her country garden near Chartres and the company of like-minded visitors – she is worth getting to know.

Minimum two nights preferred.

1 rue Lamennais

Even the air feels quietly elegant. Soisick doesn't do clutter, just good things old and new: the sense of peace is palpable (nothing to do with double glazing). Her flat turns away from the rowdy Champs-Élysées towards classy St Honoré: ask this lively active lady for advice about great little restaurants – or anything Parisian. The simple generous bedroom has size and interest – an unusual inlaid table is set off by white bedcovers – and leads to a walk-in wardrobe fit for a star and a tasteful white and grey bathroom. With three windows, parquet floor and its mix of antique and modern, the living room is another charmer.

Rooms	1 twin/double.
Price	€95.
Meals	Restaurants within walking distance.
Closed	Rarely.

Rooms	1 twin/double.
Price	€90.
Meals	Restaurants nearby.
Closed	Rarely.

	Élisabeth Marchal
	10 rue Las Cases,
	75007 Paris
Tel	+33 (0)1 47 05 70 21

	Soisick Guérineau
	1 rue Lamennais,
	75008 Paris
Tel	+33 (0)1 40 39 04 38
Email	soisick.guerineau@wanadoo.fr

Entry 134   Map 5

Entry 135   Map 5

Paris - Île de France

Côté Montmartre

Walk in and touch an 1890s heart: floral inlay on the stairs, stained-glass windows behind the lift. On the top landing, a curly bench greets you. Young and quietly smiling, Isabelle leads you to her personality-filled living room, a harmony of family antiques and 20th-century design, and a gift of a view: old Paris crookedly climbing to the Sacré Cœur. Breakfast may be on the flowering balcony, perhaps with fat cat Jules. Your big white (no-smoking) bedroom off the landing is modern and new-bedded in peaceful rooftop seclusion; the shower room a contemporary jewel. Interesting, cultured, delightful people, too.

Rooms	1 double.
Price	€135–€155. Extra bed €30.
Meals	Restaurants nearby.
Closed	Rarely.

Isabelle & Jacques Bravo
Côté Montmartre,
11 bis rue Jean Baptiste Pigalle,
75009 Paris
Tel +33 (0)1 43 54 33 09
Mobile +33 (0)6 14 56 62 62
Email isabelle.c.b@free.fr
Web www.cotemontmartre.com

Entry 136 Map 5

Paris - Île de France

52 rue de Clichy

In a smart, peaceful top-floor flat, beautifully insulated from the buzz of St Lazare (the secret is the building's inner garden), you can have one big bed or two singles in an immaculate blue bedroom, the good bathroom leading off it, the loo just over the passage. Much-travelled, interesting and attentive, Rosemary will chat about her many-facetted life, bring you breakfast on the pretty balcony or at the walnut table in her relaxing chiaroscuro living room, and point you to the Paris that suits your taste. Her flat is quietly elegant, her presence is competent and gentle, you will be well cared for.

Rooms	1 twin/double (with separate wc).
Price	€95–€125.
Meals	Restaurants 100m.
Closed	Rarely.

Rosemary Allan
52 rue de Clichy,
75009 Paris
Tel +33 (0)1 44 53 93 65
Mobile +33 (0)6 66 01 75 44
Email rosemarylouise@hotmail.fr

Entry 137 Map 5

B&B Guénot

A garden! In Paris! A restful corner and quiet, well-travelled hosts who greet you after a day of cultural excitements. The architect-renovated apartment, a delight of clever design, embraces their private garden. All rooms turn towards the greenery, including your charming compact bedroom with its timber floor, large oil painting and wonderful bathroom. Once through the door that leads off the red-leather sitting room, you are in this intimate space, enjoying a lovely wide window onto bird twitter. A generous continental breakfast – and you're ready for more museum fare.

Le P'tit Gobert

Are there just two of you, romantic in Paris? 'Bleu' is a brilliantly designed miniature dream, its plant-screened terrace a huge bonus. The light, fresh, blue and white cube has all you need – clever little shower room, good mezzanine beds, sitting space below, corner kitchen, and not a scrap more. A family, looking forward to all the city's delights? 'Rouge' is excellent value, though with less light charm. Enjoy breakfasts with your friendly, interesting hosts in their fine great modern living room upstairs. A whole group? Take the two, share the terrace (its table seats eight) and buy your own baguettes.

Minimum two nights. Sofabeds available.

Rooms	1 double.
Price	€120-€130.
Meals	Restaurants within walking distance.
Closed	Rarely.

Rooms	2: 1 twin/double with kitchenette, 1 family room for 3 with kitchen.
Price	€115. Family room €140.
Meals	Restaurants within walking distance.
Closed	Rarely.

Anne-Lise Valadon
B&B Guénot,
4 passage Guénot,
75011 Paris
Tel   +33 (0)1 42 74 23 84
Mobile   +33 (0)6 22 34 34 53
Email   anne-lise.valadon@wanadoo.fr
Web   www.bb-guenot.com

Carine Bordier
Le P'tit Gobert,
12 rue Gobert, 75011 Paris
Mobile   +33 (0)6 11 70 59 72
Email   carinebordier@gmail.com
Web   www.le-petit-gobert-paris.fr

Entry 138   Map 5

Entry 139   Map 5

Paris - Île de France

Un Ciel à Paris

For 30 years they brought up three children, taught primary kids, played the piano (Lyne), and cooked divinely (Philippe), unaware of hidden beauty overhead: the fabulous trompe-l'œil ceiling ('sky in Paris') discovered by sheer chance in 2009. Soft, warm, cocoon-like bedrooms, beautifully decorated, lightly furnished, give onto trees and a rustic house; marble-tiled shower rooms are perfect. Loving their new life as B&B hosts in this gently elegant flat where striking modern art sets off family antiques, Philippe and Lyne will give you insider advice and share their passions for art, opera and Paris.

Over 8's welcome.

Paris - Île de France

Montparnasse district

A little house in a quiet alley behind Montparnasse? It's not a dream and Janine, a live-wire cinema journalist who has lived in Canada, welcomes B&B guests to her pretty timber-ceilinged kitchen/diner; she's a night bird but her charming cat may accompany you over DIY breakfast, laid for you for the morning, and you can look forward to her cultural input in the evening. The big square bedroom across the book-lined hall, a pleasing mix of warm fabrics, honeycomb tiles, old chest and contemporary art, is ideally independent and has a good new pine bathroom. At the end of the lane you'll find glorious buzzy Paris.

Minimum two nights.

Rooms	2: 1 double, 1 triple (single bed on mezzanine).
Price	€160. Triple €210. Extra bed €50.
Meals	Restaurants nearby.
Closed	Rarely.

Rooms	1 double.
Price	€70.
Meals	Restaurants nearby.
Closed	July-September.

Lyne & Philippe Dumas
Un Ciel à Paris,
3 bd Arago, 75013 Paris
Tel   +33 (0)1 43 36 18 46
Mobile   +33 (0)6 69 73 37 26
Email   contact@uncielaparis.fr
Web   www.uncielaparis.fr

Janine Euvrard
Montparnasse district,
75014 Paris
Tel   +33 (0)1 43 27 19 43
Email   janine.euvrard@orange.fr

Entry 140   Map 5

Entry 141   Map 5

Paris - Île de France

Montparnasse district

Filled with books, paintings and objects from around the world, the Monbrisons' intimate little flat is old and fascinating. Quintessentially French Christian, knowledgeable about history, wine and cattle-breeding, and American Cynthia, an art lover, offer great hospitality, thoughtful conversation, and splendid breakfasts. They are terrifically generous. Their bedroom, quiet and snug, has a king-size bed and a good airy bathroom with views of trees. Twice a week, the open market brings the real food of France to your street; you can visit the bars frequented by Beauvoir and Sartre, or stroll to the Luxembourg Gardens.

Rooms	1 twin/double.
Price	€95.
Meals	Restaurants nearby.
Closed	Rarely.

Christian & Cynthia de Monbrison
Montparnasse district,
11 bd Edgar Quinet,
75014 Paris
Tel   +33 (0)1 43 35 20 87
Email   chris.demonbrison@free.fr

Entry 142   Map 5

Paris - Île de France

Les Toits de Paris

The attic-level flat, the guest room opposite and the most courteous young owners (with little Marius) are all of a lovely piece: modest, quiet, clothed in gentle earthy colours, natural materials and discreet manners. You will feel instantly at ease in this cultured atmosphere. Across the landing, your quiet and intimate room has a super-comfy bed, a convertible sofa and a darling little writing desk beneath the sloping beams; the beautiful bathroom has everything. Walk round 'the village', discover its quirky shops, its restaurants for all tastes and budgets – then head for the riches of central Paris.

On third floor, no lift.

Rooms	1 double & single sofabed.
Price	€130. Extra bed €20.
Meals	Restaurants nearby.
Closed	Rarely.

Matthieu & Sophie de Montenay
Les Toits de Paris,
25 rue de l'Abbé Groult,
75015 Paris
Mobile +33 (0)6 60 57 92 05
Email   resa@chambrehotesparis.fr
Web   www.chambrehotesparis.fr

Entry 143   Map 5

Paris - Île de France

Sweet Dream

You're greeted as an old friend the minute lovely Almitra opens the door to her handsome, fourth-floor (with lift) apartment in central Paris. Warm, charming and attentive, she loves her contact with international guests and has been known to offer French cookery courses and market-shopping trips. On this quiet residential street, your bedroom is a spacious double with a shallow balcony, pretty window-boxes and a neat little shower; gorgeous homemade breakfast is served in the intimate kitchen – at your leisure. There's a Parisian rent-a-bike stand right outside and you're 100 metres from the metro. Paris laps at your feet.

Paris - Île de France

Courcelles-Parc

Smart, straightforward quality, here is true city living. Sleep and relax in modern rooms on the first floor of a fine 1860s building. Sober, cool décor, superb black and white shower rooms, a personal touch in each room (grandfather's oriental screen; grandmama's decorative Hermès scarf in an elaborate frame; an antique mirror). Loving his new life, Philippe is the most attentive host and knows all the secret tips. Next morning, take the lift to the sixth floor where Nathalie will liven your breakfast in their family living room (they have two shy teenagers) with talk of art, music and *la vie parisienne.*

Rooms	1 double with separate shower.
Price	€80.
Meals	Restaurants nearby.
Closed	Rarely.

Rooms	4: 1 double (with separate wc); 1 suite for 2-3; 1 twin/double, 1 double, sharing shower.
Price	€130–€160. Suite €180–€190. Extra bed €50.
Meals	Restaurants within walking distance.
Closed	Rarely.

	Almitra De Flers
	Sweet Dream,
	54 rue Vasco de Gama,
	75015 Paris
Tel	+33 (0)1 56 56 03 60
Mobile	+33 (0)6 26 58 27 07
Email	roomsweetdream@gmail.com

	Nathalie & Philippe Lévy
	Courcelles-Parc,
	6 boulevard de Courcelles,
	75017 Paris
Tel	+33 (0)1 47 66 16 85
Email	contact@courcelles-parc.com
Web	www.courcelles-parc.com

Entry 144   Map 5

Entry 145   Map 5

Paris - Île de France

Studio Amélie

In Montmartre village, in a quiet street between bustling boulevard and pure-white Sacré Cœur, Valérie and her architect husband offer a super-chic and ideally autonomous studio off their charming, pot-planted and cobbled courtyard with your bistro table and chairs. A bed dressed in delicate red against white walls, an antique oval dining table, a pine-and-steel gem of a corner kitchen, a generous shower, a mirror framed in red. Valérie's discreet decorative flourishes speak for her calm, positive personality and her interest in other lands. A 15-minute walk from the Gard du Nord – and its stunning restaurant.

Minimum three nights. Extra bed available.

Rooms	1 twin/double with kitchenette.
Price	€110. €750 per week.
Meals	Breakfast not included. Guest kitchen. Restaurants nearby.
Closed	Rarely.

Valérie Zuber
Studio Amélie,
Montmartre, 75018 Paris
Tel   +33 (0)6 30 93 81 35
Email   studiodamelie@wanadoo.fr

Entry 146   Map 5

Paris - Île de France

Une Chambre à Montmartre

The steep climb is worth every characterful step. Up one floor, through a garden where convivial picnics happen, Claire lives at the top of a real old Montmartre house: wonky stairs, the neighbour's cat, a sense of community. The window of your independent room gives dramatically onto the whole of Paris; the Sacré Cœur peeks into a super-stylish bathroom; the bedroom is not big but hugely attractive in its mix of fascinating brocante (Claire was in antiques) and clean-limbed modernity, with space for two easy chairs. Delicious breakfast comes to you on a 1950s trolley, Claire is a mine of information.

Use funicular up hill.

Rooms	1 double.
Price	€160.
Meals	Restaurants 50m.
Closed	Rarely.

Claire Maubert
Une Chambre à Montmartre,
18 rue Gabrielle, 75018 Paris
Mobile   +33 (0)6 82 84 65 28
Email   claire.maubert@gmail.com
Web   www.chambre-montmartre.com

Entry 147   Map 5

Paris - Île de France

Belleville district

Sabine, artist and art therapist, "feeds people with colours". Jules makes the organic bread with a dazzling smile, and big, beautiful Taquin, his guide dog, loves people. Kindly and artistic, they live calmly in this bit of genuine old Paris between two tiny gardens and a tall house. The simple guest room, with good double bed and flame-covered sleigh-bed divan, a welcome tea-maker and an old-fashioned bathroom, shares a building with Sabine's studio. Healthfoody continental breakfast is in the cosy family room in the main house or outside under the birdsung tree. Such peace in Paris is rare. Lovely all round.

Minimum two nights.

Rooms	1 family room.
Price	€75.
Meals	Restaurants within walking distance.
Closed	July/August.

Sabine & Jules Aïm
Belleville district,
75019 Paris
Tel   +33 (0)1 42 08 23 71
Email   aim.jules@orange.fr

Entry 148   Map 5

Paris - Île de France

Les Colombes

On the doorstep of Paris, among leafy residential avenues in the grounds of a royal château, it's a trot from an atmospheric racecourse, almost on the banks of the Seine, with forest walks, 1600 horses in the area, good eateries and efficient trains to Paris. Your hosts offer impeccable, harmonious rooms, delicious dinners and a pretty garden to relax in. What Les Colombes lacks in old stones it makes up for in a welcome steeped in traditional hospitality – and that includes generous breakfasts, home-grown fruit and veg at dinner – and glowing antiques. Courteous, caring French hosts and great value.

Paris 15 minutes by train.

Rooms	3: 2 doubles, 1 twin.
Price	€78–€90. Extra bed €35.
Meals	Dinner with wine, €45.
Closed	Rarely.

Irène & Jacques James
Les Colombes,
21 av Béranger,
78600 Maisons Laffitte, Yvelines
Tel   +33 (0)1 39 62 82 48
Mobile   +33 (0)6 71 13 51 05
Email   jacques.james@orange.fr
Web   www.chambresdhotes-lescolombes.fr

Entry 149   Map 5

Paris - Île de France

Les Tourelles de Thun

The amazing neo-gothic brick pile rearing above its suburban street to peer across the Seine valley astonishes. Built in the 1850s by an ancestor as his summer residence and decorated with Corentin's father's varied and talented art, it has tall windows, big rooms – the modern salon is vast – and huge personality. Breakfast and dinner are in the 'medieval' dining room, the library is alive with books, scrolls and prints, there are thick carpets and deep armchairs in each big bedroom. Charming, informative and eager, Nathalie has used simple colour schemes and good fabrics to create warm comfort – and she loves cooking.

Rooms	3: 2 doubles, 1 suite (double & single with extra pullout).
Price	€88–€96. Suite €108–€158. B&B with dinner, €100 p.p. (weekdays).
Meals	Dinner with wine, €30.
Closed	Rarely.

Nathalie & Corentin Delhumeau
Les Tourelles de Thun,
25 rue des Annonciades,
78250 Meulan en Yvelines, Yvelines
Tel   +33 (0)1 30 22 06 72
Email contact@tourellesdethun.com
Web   www.chambredhotetourellesdethun.com

Entry 150   Map 5

Paris - Île de France

À l'Ombre Bleue

Let the willows weep over the village pond; you go through the high gate into a sheltered paradise. The prettiest rooms have masses of old pieces, dolls, books, pictures to intrigue you, a chirruping garden with two rescue dogs to play with and the most caring hostess to provide an exceptional brunch. Have dinner too if you can (Catherine teaches cookery and sources locally: it's delicious). The miniature garden house is a lovers' dream: tiny salon downstairs, bedroom sporting superb bath up. Fulsome towels, extras of all sorts: charming, chatty Catherine thinks of everything.

Rooms	3: 1 double & sofabed, Garden house: 1 suite (1 double, 2 singles).
Price	€85–€150. Singles €65–€85.
Meals	Dinner with wine, €25. Light supper €15.
Closed	Rarely.

Catherine Forget-Pépin
À l'Ombre Bleue,
22 rue de la Mare, Les Pâtis,
78125 Mittainville, Yvelines
Tel   +33 (0)1 34 85 04 73
Email catherine@alombrebleue.fr
Web   www.alombrebleue.fr

Entry 151   Map 5

Paris - Île de France

La Mona Guesthouse - Giverny

Blanca, a prolific artist, has Mexican panache (chat, bold colour flashes, quirky ornaments) and American friendliness. Her partner, Cathy the journalist, smiles quietly. The sheltered guest barn comes with lots of windows, white walls, Blanca-painted furniture and attention to comfort: a mixture of simplicity (hangers on hooks, shower rooms behind curtains) and luxury (fine mattresses, lovely tiling, art). The big upstairs suite thrills with Hollywood glamour. Breakfast at the kitchen table brings homemade goodies, dinners are delicious. Explore the twisty old farming village or bike out beyond.

Paris - Île de France

Au Nid de la Houssière

Bright chatty Sylvie and quiet Bruno are the perfect pair, working in harmony on their long beamy farmhouse, he the neat plumber and plasterer, she the intuitive artist mixing her own lime washes and writing pastel poetry in blue beams spanning mauve, yellow, pink walls and city-rustic lace or linen fabrics. Beautiful bathrooms, too. More good news? She loves cooking. There is space, deep comfort and a baby grand. You can breakfast – deliciously – by the log fire or at the weathered old table on the stone terrace where the westies may come to say good morning. Then off to see Giverny, Versailles, even Paris. Great value.

Third room with shower up ladder.

Rooms	3: 2 doubles, 1 suite for 2-4.
Price	€95-€100. Suite €125. Extra bed €25.
Meals	Dinner €35. BBQ available. Wine €12-€35.
Closed	Rarely.

Rooms	2 doubles.
Price	€75-€98. Extra bed €20.
Meals	Dinner with wine, €25.
Closed	Rarely.

Blanca Villalobos
La Mona Guesthouse - Giverny,
5 route de La Roche,
78270 Limetz Villez, Yvelines
Tel +33 (0)1 30 93 31 26
Mobile +33 (0)6 32 97 74 36
Email lamonaguesthouse@gmail.com
Web www.lamonaguesthouse-giverny.com

Sylvie & Bruno Delorme
Au Nid de la Houssière,
15 rue de la Houssière,
78980 St Illiers le Bois, Yvelines
Tel +33 (0)1 34 78 08 33
Mobile +33 (0)6 71 08 15 10
Email contact@nidhoussiere.fr
Web www.nidhoussiere.fr

Entry 152 Map 4

Entry 153 Map 4

Cosi à la Moutière

In an 18th-century building that once housed a legendary auberge (frequented by Orson Welles, Ava Gardner, statesmen and royals) is an elegant chambres d'hôtes in a peaceful old town. Imagine white orchids and muslin, board games and books, spaciousness and light, and stylish taupe sofas before a grand fire. Dine at one table or on the wide terrace, wake to Micaela's lemon jams, muffins and clafoutis; all is delicate and delicious. Pedal off to explore Montfort-l'Amaury's cobbled streets, return to big boutique bedrooms with monsoon showers and myriad cushions – dazzling symphonies in grey, butterscotch and white.

Rooms	3: 1 twin/double, 1 family room for 4. Annexe: 1 double.
Price	€115. Family room €125-€160. Annexe €60.
Meals	Restaurants within walking distance.
Closed	Rarely.

Micaela Tomasino
Cosi à la Moutière,
12 rue de la Moutière,
78490 Montfort l'Amaury, Yvelines

Mobile	+33 (0)6 29 37 56 23
Email	maisondecosi@yahoo.fr
Web	www.chambresdhotes-cosi.com

Entry 154   Map 5

Domaine des Basses Masures

The serene and beautiful Rambouillet forest encircles this hamlet and the house is a former stables; horses still graze in the field behind. Long, low and stone-fronted, cosily draped in Virginia creeper and wisteria, it was built in 1725. Madame, hospitable and easy-going, does B&B at one end; the gîte is at the other. The B&B bedrooms, one a triple, the other with a big double bed, are friendly and charming, with pretty paintings and mirrors on the walls. Come to walk or ride, or visit the cities and sights: Versailles is 20 minutes, Paris not much further.

Sawday self-catering also.

Rooms	2: 1 double, 1 triple.
Price	€90.
Meals	Restaurant 2km.
Closed	Rarely.

Mme Walburg de Vernisy
Domaine des Basses Masures,
13 rue des Basses Masures,
78125 Poigny la Forêt, Yvelines

Tel	+33 (0)1 34 84 73 44
Mobile	+33 (0)6 95 41 78 46
Email	domainebassesmasures@free.fr
Web	www.domaine-des-basses-masures.com

Entry 155   Map 5

Paris - Île de France

7 rue Gustave Courbet

In a residential area, behind a modest façade, is a generous interior where Madame's paintings stand in pleasing contrast to elegant antiques and feminine furnishings. Picture windows let the garden in and the woods rise beyond. The larger guest room is soberly classic with a big bathroom; the smaller one with skylight, books and bath across the landing is excellent value. Madame, charming and gracious, sings as well as she paints and enjoys cooking elegant regional dinners for attentive guests; she is very good company. Small and intimate with Paris Montparnasse station half an hour away by train and Versailles close by.

Rooms	2: 1 double; 1 double with separate bathroom.
Price	€55–€70.
Meals	Dinner with wine, €20.
Closed	Rarely.

Hélène Castelnau
7 rue Gustave Courbet,
Domaine des Gâtines,
78370 Plaisir, Yvelines
Tel   +33 (0)1 30 54 05 15
Email   hcastelnau@club-internet.fr

Entry 156   Map 5

Paris - Île de France

Villa de la Pièce d'Eau des Suisses

Ah, Versailles! The gilded grandeur of the château, the tiny backstreets of the old town, the great lake of the Swiss Guards and, in between, a discreet door opening to a rambling house warmed by cultured parents, well-mannered teenagers, friendly pets and the smell of beeswax. Bathe in books, colour and art (Laure is an accomplished artist and dress designer); a garden too. Climb two gentle floors (pictures to study at every step) to your large light room with both street and tree-lined lake views. Add unusual family furniture and a superb new biscuity shower room: this genuine family B&B is a rare privilege.

Rooms	1 twin/double.
Price	€140. Singles €130. Cot €40. Child under 12, €60.
Meals	Restaurants within walking distance.
Closed	Rarely.

Laure de St Chaffray
Villa de la Pièce d'Eau des Suisses,
6 rue de la Quintinie,
78000 Versailles, Yvelines
Tel   +33 (0)1 39 53 65 40
Mobile   +33 (0)6 22 60 05 84
Email   lauredest@live.fr
Web   www.bedinversailles.com

Entry 157   Map 5

Paris - Île de France

Maison Prairie Bonheur

Deep in the Chevreuse nature park, among great woods, rolling fields and country peace, you wouldn't know that a buzzing new town is 3km away, Paris an hour by train. Anne and Jean-François are a fine team, she doing the décor and the daily caring, he in charge of maintenance and cooking (at which he excels). In this house of many chambers (they have four children), each person counts and there's room for everyone in the big, bright veranda dayroom, the stone and glass terrace and the rambling garden. Rooms are not big but pretty and well-designed. Visit the great palaces or Paris, ride or walk and return to a cosy country home.

Rooms	5: 2 doubles, 3 family rooms for 3.
Price	€85–€105. Family room €105–€117. Extra bed €30. Exclusive use of hot tub €50.
Meals	Dinner, 3-5 courses, €25–€30. Wine from €10.
Closed	Rarely.

Anne & Jean-François Bonassies
Maison Prairie Bonheur,
Le Village, 6 chemin des Patissiaux,
78114 Magny les Hameaux,
Yvelines
Tel   +33 (0)1 30 44 26 08
Email   annebonassies@wanadoo.fr
Web   www.chambres-hotes-prairie-bonheur.com

Entry 158   Map 5

Paris - Île de France

Le Clos des Princes

Paris is 20 minutes by train, Versailles 15 by motorway. Here, behind wrought-iron gates in an elegant suburb, the French mansion sits in an exuberant town garden of pergolas, box bushes and mature trees. Your kind, attentive hosts – she an ex-English teacher, he with a passion for Sully-Prudhomme – may give you the poet/philosopher's two-room first-floor suite; he lived here in 1902. Polished floorboards, pretty prints, choice antiques, decorative perfume bottles by a claw-footed tub, all dance to the 19th-century theme. Breakfast unveils gorgeous porcelain and delicious homemade muffins and jams. Outstanding.

Sofabed available for children.

Rooms	2: 1 family room for 4; 1 suite with separate bath.
Price	Family room €95–€110. Suite €105–€120.
Meals	Restaurant 400m.
Closed	Rarely.

Christine & Éric Duprez
Le Clos des Princes,
60 av Jean Jaurès,
92290 Châtenay Malabry,
Hauts-de-Seine
Tel   +33 (0)1 46 61 94 49
Email   ce.duprez@yahoo.com
Web   www.leclosdesprinces.com

Entry 159   Map 5

Paris - Île de France

Villa Mansart

Wind your way up the handsome staircase, nudge open the attic door. The guest sitting room has sunny walls and ethnic rugs. Slim, arched bedrooms are blue or vanilla-and-orange with family furniture and windows peeping over rooftops. Breakfast on fresh fruit and mini-pastries in an elegant dining room or on the terrace. Marble steps, rescued from a local demolition, sweep down to an immaculate peaceful garden curtained by trees. Bruno and Françoise are welcoming, charming and extremely helpful when it comes to route planning. Such calm, only 20 minutes from the centre of Paris.

Extra single beds in sitting room. Free closed garage.

Rooms	2: 1 double, 1 family room.
Price	€88. Family room €118. Extra bed €30.
Meals	Restaurants nearby.
Closed	Rarely.

Françoise Marcoz
Villa Mansart, 9 allée Victor Basch,
94170 Le Perreux sur Marne,
Val-de-Marne

Tel	+33 (0)1 48 72 91 88
Mobile	+33 (0)6 62 37 97 85
Email	villamansart@yahoo.fr
Web	www.villamansart.net

Entry 160   Map 5

Paris - Île de France

Le Moulin de St Martin

Agnès is gentle, with artistic flair, Bernard is gregarious, charming, convivial: together they have created a delectable B&B. The old mill is on an island encircled by Corot's Grand Morin river; lovely old willows lap the water, the pretty villages of Voulangis and Crécy lie beyond. A warm sober elegance prevails: there are 17th-century floorboards topped by oriental rugs; Asian antiques and art in gilt frames; cherry-red toile and snowy bed linen; terraces for summer views; log fires for nights in. Disneyland Paris, a world away, maybe a short drive but, above all, fine châteaux beckon.

Minimum two nights.

Rooms	2: 1 double, 1 twin/double.
Price	€75–€95.
Meals	Dinner €28. Wine €18.
Closed	Rarely.

Bernard & Agnès Gourbaud
Le Moulin de St Martin,
7 rue de St Martin, Voulangis,
77580 Crécy la Chapelle,
Seine-et-Marne

Tel	+33 (0)1 64 63 69 90
Email	moulindesaintmartin@orange.fr

Entry 161   Map 5

Le Clos de la Rose

For seekers of garden peace, for champagne and architecture buffs (vineyards and historic Provins nearby), this gorgeous green retreat from crazed Paris — cool, quiet, stylishly homely — has been restored with fine respect for 200-year-old origins: limewash, timbers, country antiques, a gathering of books. Charming Brendan (he's Irish) and gentle, organised Véronique have a lovely family and, amazingly, time to chat over aperitifs. Bedrooms have pretty colours, antique linen and patchwork charm, the adorable cottage (with kitchen) is ideal for a longer stay. Don't miss dinner, hot or cold: you choose.

B&B & self-catering options available for cottage.

Rooms	3: 2 doubles. Cottage for 3.
Price	€72-€124. Cottage €94-€159.
Meals	Breakfast €11. Dinner €29. Wine €20-€34. Champagne €32. Restaurant 10-minute drive.
Closed	Never.

Véronique & Brendan Culligan
Le Clos de la Rose, 11 rue de la Source,
L'Hermitière, 77750 St Cyr sur Morin,
Seine-et-Marne

Tel   +33 (0)1 60 44 81 04
Mobile +33 (0)6 82 56 10 54
Email   resa@clos-de-la-rose.com
Web   www.clos-de-la-rose.com

Entry 162   Map 5

La Ferme le Merger

Monsieur bought the remote vine-covered farmhouse in this cheese-famous land after travelling the world and staying in too many soulless hotels. Visitors here are welcomed warmly by the happy Beaups, who serve French and Brazilian dishes and dine with their guests. The bedroom has matching furniture (pristine, Napoleon III-style copies), the bathroom is roomy and new, and gold taffeta curtains frame a window overlooking backyard and fields. Breakfast on the terrace on warm days — or under handsome timbers by a log fire on cool ones. Disneyland and Provins are under an hour away. Charming.

Rooms	1 double.
Price	€69.
Meals	Hosted dinner with wine, €28. Restaurants 5-minute drive.
Closed	Rarely.

Sueli Galvao da Silva-Beaup
La Ferme le Merger,
1 lieu-dit Le Merger,
77320 Choisy en Brie,
Seine-et-Marne

Tel   +33 (0)1 64 20 43 44
Email   claude.beaup@wanadoo.fr
Web   www.lemerger.skyrock.com

Entry 163   Map 5

Paris - Île de France

Ferme de Vert St Père

Cereals and beets grow in wide fields and show-jumpers add elegance to the fine landscape. A generous farm courtyard surrounded by very lovely warm stone buildings encloses peace and a genuine welcome from hosts and labradors alike, here where Monsieur's family has come hunting for 200 years. Find family furniture (the 1900s ensemble is most intriguing) and planked floors in beautiful bedrooms, immaculate mod cons and a handsome guest living room where breakfast is served at a convivial table surrounded by honey, polished floors and oriental-style rugs. Utter peace, a remote setting, and a Michelin-rated auberge in the village.

Paris - Île de France

La Candelaria

These exceptional people – an Argentine artist, an eccentric English photographer, their four excellent children – will open their unconventional arms and carry you into their wide-ranging interests: art and history, travel and ancestors. They found a near-ruin and turned it into an elegant, airy family house full of paintings, books and curiosities. Up its own steep stair, your gentle third-floor room is big, beamy, slathered in little ancestral portraits and graced by a great tin bath before the dormer window – try it. The shower room is up two high steps through a very low door. Wonderful, if not for the halt and lame.

Rooms	3: 1 family room for 3, 2 apartments for 4.
Price	Family room €70–€80. Apartment €110–€120.
Meals	Restaurant in village, 1.5km.
Closed	Christmas.

Rooms	1 double.
Price	€127.
Meals	Restaurant 2.5km.
Closed	Rarely.

	Philippe & Jeanne Mauban
	Ferme de Vert St Père,
	77390 Crisenoy,
	Seine-et-Marne
Tel	+33 (0)1 64 38 83 51
Mobile	+33 (0)6 71 63 31 36
Email	mauban.vert@wanadoo.fr
Web	vert.saint.pere.free.fr

Entry 164   Map 5

	Hugh & Celina Arnold
	La Candelaria,
	31 rue de Paris,
	91370 Verrières le Buisson, Essonne
Tel	+33 (0)6 73 87 40 35
Mobile	+33 (0)6 33 55 98 53
Email	hugh.arnold@wanadoo.fr
Web	www.lacandelaria.fr

Entry 165   Map 5

Paris - Île de France

Le Logis d'Arnière

Wonderfully preserved in authentic 1920s style: a high-windowed, fully panelled dining room with extraordinary dressers; and fabulous bathroom fittings. It is exuberantly sober and shapely with Versailles parquet and fine fireplaces as well. Tae, from Chile, uses her fine sense of style and colour to bond these antiques with richly baroque Chinese chairs and lots of South American pieces and paintings. Claude is as articulately enthusiastic as she: a fabulous couple. Quiet spot, vast natural garden, joyous hosts, resident horses, gentle labradors, swings… beautiful breakfasts set you up for Chartres, Paris, Versailles.

Rooms	2 suites for 2-5.
Price	€90-€160. Singles €70-€80.
Meals	Restaurant 200m.
Closed	Rarely.

Claude & Tae Dabasse
Le Logis d'Arnière, 1 rue du Pont-Rué,
91410 St Cyr sous Dourdan,
Essonne

Tel	+33 (0)1 64 59 14 89
Mobile	+33 (0)6 83 56 15 63
Email	taedabasse@free.fr
Web	www.dabasse.com/arniere

Entry 166 Map 5

Loire Valley

Château de Jonvilliers

Delightful hosts: Virginie beautifully French, Richard a gentle Europeanised American, and their two sons. Down a wooded drive and set in a big leafy garden, the family house has tall windows, fine proportions and the air of a properly lived-in château: elegance and deep armchairs by the marble fireplace under crystal chandeliers. The top floor has been converted into five good rooms with sound-proofing, big beds, masses of hot water, rich, bright colour schemes… and just the right amount of family memorabilia: oils, engravings, lamps, old dishes. It feels easy, intelligent and fun.

Rooms	5: 4 doubles, 1 triple.
Price	€85-€90. Triple €95-€130.
Meals	Restaurants 5km.
Closed	Rarely.

Virginie & Richard Thompson
Château de Jonvilliers,
17 rue Lucien Petit-Jonvilliers,
28320 Ecrosnes, Eure-et-Loir

Tel	+33 (0)2 37 31 41 26
Email	info@jonvilliers.com
Web	www.jonvilliers.com

Entry 167 Map 5

Normandy

Normandy

Love the land. Live the life.

Just across the Channel, Normandy is the perfect destination to get away from it all...

Steeped in our common history, Normandy invites you to go back in time to retrace the footsteps of William the Conqueror and to walk along the D-Day Beaches, the Coast of Heroes.

With its stunning coastline, picturesque ports and beaches galore, Normandy offers the visitor the choice between the elegance of the seaside resorts on the Côte Fleurie of Deauville and Cabourg, the wilder shores and fishing villages along the Cotentin peninsula to the Côte d'Albâtre with its dramatic white cliffs and secluded creeks and fishing ports. Nature lovers can head inland to get away from it all and recharge their batteries in the idyllic countryside. Cycle along the rural paths, drive though the countryside of bocage

hedgerows or just stop and wonder at the peace and quiet.

The Mont-Saint-Michel, the Wonder of the Western World which dominates the surrounding landscape, remains a must-see for all visitors. And for those who prefer the lure of the city, you are spoilt for choice between the historic delights of Caen with its imposing ducal castle, the charm of the medieval streets and cathedral of Rouen, the spectacular harbour of Cherbourg and the Unesco World Heritage site of Le Havre, famous for its impressive post-war architecture. And why not take time to stroll around the half-timbered streets of Bayeux, home to the world renowned tapestry and magnificent cathedral?

The 70th Anniversary of D-Day will be commemorated in 2014. The Battle of Normandy lasted three months after the Allies had landed and the region was indelibly marked by these historic events. A trip to its northern coastline, from Sainte-Mère-Église in la Manche to the beaches of Dieppe in Seine-Maritime, allows for a powerful first-hand experience of the forceful reminders of the

For more information please visit:
www.normandy-tourism.org

Second World War. You cannot help but be moved by a visit to one of the cemeteries, memorials and museums which offer the chance to take a quiet moment to reflect and to remember.

As the spiritual birthplace of the Impressionist movement, Normandy has inspired many great artists to create images which live on in the collective consciousness today. From Étretat and its stunning cliffs to Honfleur with its picturesque fishing port, the unique lighting, magical seascapes, dramatic monuments and dreamy countryside provided the perfect backdrop for Impressionist painters along the Channel Coast and the Seine river. Today visitors can follow in the footsteps of artists such as Monet, Boudin and Sisley whose works are on display at the region's excellent fine art museums plus take time to stroll around Giverny, once home to Claude Monet, father of the Impressionist Movement. The region will be hosting the second Normandy Impressionist Festival in spring and summer 2013, celebrating the great works of this major artistic movement.

© CDT Manche

And one of the joys of being in this part of France is the food: Normandy, home of camembert and calvados, is a true gourmet's treasure trove. How about taking the time to enjoy a typical Norman menu - a seafood platter with apple tart to follow, washed down with a glass of local cider? If you prefer home cooking, venture out to the nearest weekly market and feast your eyes on the wonderful choice of local produce.

A bientôt en Normandie!

Normandy

Manoir de Beaumont

In the old hunting lodge for guests, a vast, boar- and stag's-headed dayroom with log fire, chandelier and bedrooms above – ideal for parties. In the main house (charming, heavily wallpapered, colourful) is the handsome Jouy'd room for four. From the very lovely garden are hilltop views. Monsieur manages the Port and is a mine of local knowledge; Madame tends house, garden and guests, masterfully. Proud of their region, naturally generous, elegant, poised, they are keen to advise on explorations: nature, hiking, historical visits… Legend has it that Queen Victoria 'stopped' at this very gracious house.

Call ahead for winter bookings.

Rooms	3: 1 double, 1 quadruple, 1 suite.
Price	€51. Quadruple €58–€82. Suite €62.
Meals	Restaurant 2km. Wide choice 4.5km.
Closed	Rarely.

Catherine & Jean-Marie Demarquet
Manoir de Beaumont,
76260 Eu,
Seine-Maritime
Tel   +33 (0)2 35 50 91 91
Email   catherine@demarquet.eu
Web   www.demarquet.eu

Entry 168   Map 1

Normandy

St Mare

A fresh modern house under a steep slate roof in a lush green sanctuary; it could not be more tranquil. The garden really is lovely and worth a wander – a tailored lawn, a mass of colour, huge banks of rhododendrons for which the village is renowned (three of its gardens are open to the public). Claudine runs home and B&B with effortless efficiency and gives you homemade brioches for breakfast; smiling Remi leads you to guest quarters in a freshly wood-clad house reached via stepping stones through the laurels. Bedrooms are comfortable, sunny, spotless, shining and utterly peaceful – two are big enough to lounge in.

Extra beds available.

Rooms	3: 2 suites for 4 & kitchenette, 1 suite for 5.
Price	€75–€135.
Meals	Restaurants 20-minute walk.
Closed	Rarely.

Claudine Goubet
Rte de Petites Bruyères, 1 chemin des Sablonnières, 76119 Varengeville sur Mer, Seine-Maritime
Tel   +33 (0)2 35 85 99 28
Mobile +33 (0)6 18 92 28 20
Email   claudine.goubet@chsaintmare.com
Web   www.chsaintmare.com

Entry 169   Map 4

Normandy

Château Le Bourg

Silk bedspreads and scatter cushions, soaps, colognes and fresh roses... and Leonora's mix of English mahogany and French fabrics is as refined as her dinners. Having finished the soberly elegant bedrooms – one with boudoir touches – of her grand 19th-century mansion, she is turning her attention to the garden: it will undoubtedly delight. An intelligent hostess and fine cook, she is both entertaining and generous, handles house parties for celebrations and has a mass of books for you to browse on your return from walking the old railway line or exploring the cliffs.

Rooms	2 doubles.
Price	€100.
Meals	Dinner with wine, €30-€75.
Closed	Rarely.

Leonora Macleod
Château Le Bourg,
27 Grande Rue,
76660 Bures en Bray,
Seine-Maritime
Tel   +33 (0)2 35 94 09 35
Email   leonora.macleod@wanadoo.fr

Normandy

Les Glycines

Close to coast and ferry, in a quiet village in undulating farmland, a wisteria-hugged, red-brick house with gregarious bilingual hosts. Inside, a sitting room with sofa, wood-burner, books, DVDs; outside, a large lawn and sweet sheltered alcove for reading and dreaming. It's intimate: just two bedrooms, one sky-lit and country-pretty, one wallowing in fine fabrics and green views; awake to fresh fruit and croissants. Jenny and Christopher, who've lived in France for ten years, point you to walks, bike rides, cheese makers, cider farms... auberge meals in Londinières and gourmet offerings in Rouen.

Rooms	2 doubles.
Price	€65-€70.
Meals	Restaurants 8km.
Closed	First 2 weeks in September.

Christopher & Jenny Laws
Les Glycines,
19 rue de la Houssaye Béranger,
76270 Lucy, Seine-Maritime
Tel   +33 (0)2 35 93 12 45
Mobile   +33 (0)6 47 59 21 41
Email   kpylaws@orange.fr

Normandy

23 Grand Rue

Peter loves his wines (he was in the trade), Madeleine is energetic and vivacious, both welcome you generously at their 'maison bourgeoise' on the edge of a château village. Set back from the road behind fence and clipped hedge are four cosy classically furnished bedrooms: books and fresh flowers, immaculate duvets, smart French furniture, a calvados nightcap on the landing. Shower rooms are small and beautifully tiled. There's a conservatory for breakfast, a front room for relaxing and, at a table dressed with silver, French dinners are served. Dieppe, Rouen, Honfleur: all are wonderfully close.

Rooms	4: 2 doubles, 1 twin; 1 triple with separate bathroom.
Price	€68. Triple €80.
Meals	Dinner with wine, €27.
Closed	Rarely.

Peter & Madeleine Mitchell
23 Grand Rue,
76270 Mesnières en Bray,
Seine-Maritime
Tel   +33 (0)2 32 97 06 31
Email   info@23grandrue.com
Web   www.23grandrue.com

Entry 172   Map 4

Normandy

Le Jardin de Muriel

Standing tall and proud – backed by a beautiful flowering garden – is a red-brick townhouse owned by a gentle and pleasant couple. Muriel is a passionate gardener and amateur artist, and her pretty watercolours and drawings decorate the walls – buy any that take your fancy! Two bedrooms with views over neighbouring houses and her treasured garden have good-size bathrooms with scrummy smellies. There's also a family cottage with a kitchen and tiny intimate terrace, and a cosy salon furnished with deep-pink brocade period sofa and chairs. Head for history, culture and shopping in Rouen. Delightful.

Rooms	3: 1 double, 1 twin. Cottage for 4.
Price	€70. Cottage €77-€110.
Meals	Restaurants within walking distance.
Closed	Rarely.

Muriel & Jean-Jacques Duboc
Le Jardin de Muriel,
23 rue Paul Lesueur,
76680 St Saens, Seine-Maritime
Tel   +33 (0)2 35 59 86 18
Mobile   +33 (0)6 08 47 86 84
Email   muriel7623@gmail.com
Web   lejardindemuriel.free.fr

Entry 173   Map 4

Normandy

La Charretterie

A delicious 18th-century working farmhouse, in the family for three generations. Views sail over pastures, cows and gorgeous garden: clumps of lavender, exuberant roses, weathered teak, hazes of flowers. The Prévosts are a courteously friendly pair whose efficiency shines. Expect fresh, harmonious and beamy bedrooms, one under the eaves, the other downstairs looking on to the lawn, and two shower rooms immaculately dotted with mosaics and fresh flowers. No sitting room but a big breakfast room, warm, woody and inviting, its long table spread with homemade breads, brioche, yogurts and jams. A super stopover on the way to the coast.

Rooms	2: 1 double, 1 quadruple.
Price	€60–€70. Quadruple €70–€130.
Meals	Restaurants 3km.
Closed	Rarely.

Corinne & Arnaud Prévost
La Charretterie, 4 rue du Tilleul,
Hameau de Pierreville,
76730 Bacqueville en Caux,
Seine-Maritime
Tel   +33 (0)2 35 04 26 45
Email   arnaud.prevost@cegetel.net
Web   charretterie.perso.sfr.fr

Normandy

Le Clos du Gui Nel

Brace yourself for the last lap home or, better still, unwind in this leafy Norman oasis, neatly set between Dieppe and Le Havre. Welsh cobs graze in the lee of a little Norman church by the immaculately restored farmhouse. A deep pitched roof caps the attractive timbered façade, the stout oak doors and the high windows. No sitting room but fresh, charming, ground-floor rooms with their own entrance. If up and about early you may meet Étienne, a doctor, as he dashes off to work, or chat to Catherine about her beloved ponies as you breakfast on French pastries in the handsome dining room.

Rooms	2 doubles.
Price	€78.
Meals	Restaurant 2km.
Closed	Rarely.

Catherine & Étienne Stevens
Le Clos du Gui Nel,
4 rue de Canville, 76740 Bourville,
Seine-Maritime
Tel   +33 (0)2 35 57 02 31
Mobile   +33 (0)6 70 55 26 39
Email   contact@gui-nel.com
Web   www.gui-nel.com

Le Clos du Vivier

The lush garden shelters bees, bantams, sleek cats and a phenomenal variety of shrubs and flowering plants. Monsieur is retired and he looks after all this while Madame tends to their guests, with respect for everyone's privacy; Madame also offers guidance on hiking, and there's tennis and fishing nearby. She is an intelligent, active and graceful person, her bedrooms, some under sloping ceilings, are cosily colourful, her bathrooms big and luxurious, her breakfast richly varied. After a jaunt, you can read their books, relax among their lovely antiques or make tea in their breakfast room. The cliffs at Étretat are 20 minutes away.

Les Charmettes

Overlooking Normandy's white cliffs, loftily apart from town, is an elegant manor and garden. Courteous Raphaël, from a family of architects, took over the B&B from his mother; the rooms, rich with Art Deco, rugs and paintings, are artistic, traditional and unstuffy. Guests are welcome to relax in the salon, with its grand piano and terrace. The apartment and suite, in mahogany and marble with parquet floors and fine linen, have two bedrooms apiece. Fill up on pastries, cheese and charcuterie before a flit to beach or town; return to the walled garden's sheltering trees, to stroke Ambre the cat and relish the view. Special.

Rooms	3: 1 twin/double, 1 triple, 1 suite for 5.
Price	€90-€100. Triple €110-€120. Suite €150-€170.
Meals	Restaurants in Valmont, 1km.
Closed	Rarely.

Rooms	3: 1 twin, 1 family suite for 3. 1 apartment (2 twins, 1 bathroom).
Price	€130. Family suite €130-€170. Apartment €130-€210. Extra bed €30.
Meals	Restaurants 500m.
Closed	Rarely.

Dominique Cachera & François Gréverie
Le Clos du Vivier,
4 chemin du Vivier, 76540 Valmont,
Seine-Maritime
Tel +33 (0)2 35 29 90 95
Email le.clos.du.vivier@wanadoo.fr
Web www.le-clos-du-vivier.com

Raphaël Renard
Les Charmettes,
Allée des Pervenches,
76790 Étretat, Seine-Maritime
Tel +33 (0)2 35 27 05 54
Mobile +33 (0)6 88 15 29 76
Email raphaelrenard76@free.fr
Web www.lescharmettes-etretat.com

Normandy

Jardin Gorbeau - Étretat Guesthouse & Spa

The ingredients of a super seaside holiday in Normandy: a cosy 1820s black-and-white mansion two steps from the beach, feast-like breakfasts, leafy walled garden, big showers for sloshing off sea salt, sauna, jacuzzi… Arizona-born Jon's art collections add personality to sober French or floral décor, and a cinema room is good for quiet nights. Best bedrooms are Cosette in the main house with a secret study behind wardrobe doors, and cool Laigle in the garden house, a loft suite with coastal views. Étretat's white cliffs mirror Dover's and the GR21 cuts through this pretty town of seafood restaurants, galleries and sunsets.

Minimum two nights at weekends.

Rooms	5: 3 doubles, 1 suite, 1 quadruple.
Price	€89-€159. Suite €109-€174. Quadruple €129-€189.
Meals	Dinner €39.
Closed	Mid-November to mid-December.

Jon Cooper
Jardin Gorbeau - Étretat
Guesthouse & Spa,
27 rue Adolphe Boissaye,
76790 Étretat, Seine-Maritime
Tel   +33 (0)2 35 27 16 72
Email   info@gorbeau.com
Web   www.gorbeau.com

Entry 178   Map 4

Normandy

Manoir de la Rue Verte

The 300-year-old house stands in a classic, poplar-sheltered farmyard, its worn old stones and bricks, and less worn flints, bearing witness to its age – as does some timberwork inside. Otherwise it has been fairly deeply modernised, and filled with knick knacks and paddywhacks from everywhere. The long lace-clothed breakfast table before the winter fire is most welcoming, as are your retired farmer hosts. Madame was born here, has a winning smile and loves to talk (French only). Her pleasant rooms are in simple rural style; the only sounds are the occasional lowing of the herd and the shushing of the poplars.

Rooms	4: 1 double, 1 triple; 2 doubles sharing shower & wc.
Price	€52. Triple €75.
Meals	Auberge 1km, restaurant 4km.
Closed	Rarely.

Yves & Béatrice Quevilly Baret
Manoir de la Rue Verte,
21 rue Verte,
76970 Flamanville,
Seine-Maritime
Tel   +33 (0)2 35 96 81 27

Entry 179   Map 4

Normandy

Le Brécy

Jérôme has happy childhood holiday memories of this elegant 17th-century manor house; he and delightful Patricia moved to join grand-mère who had been living here alone for years. A long path flanked by willows leads down to the Seine: perfect (when not mud-bound!) for an evening stroll. One suite is on the ground floor, in classically French coral and cream, its windows opening to a walled garden; the second, equally refined, is in the attic. Breakfast is when you fancy: brioches, walnuts, fresh fruit in a pretty green-panelled room. Ask Patricia about the Abbey and walks to its gardens. A charming rural paradise.

Rooms	2 suites.
Price	€88–€98.
Meals	Restaurant in village.
Closed	Rarely.

Jérôme & Patricia Lanquest
Le Brécy,
72 route du Brécy,
76840 St Martin de Boscherville,
Seine-Maritime
Tel +33 (0)2 35 32 69 92
Email lebrecy@gmail.com
Web lebrecy.perso.sfr.fr

Entry 180 Map 4

Normandy

Manoir de Captot

The drive curves through paddocks and pillared gates to this serene 18th-century mansion. The forest behind may ring with the stag's call, the heads and hooves of his kin line the grand staircase. The fine classic French interior is peacefully formal: a gorgeous primrose-yellow dining room with an oval mahogany table for breakfast feasts, a collection-filled drawing room, a beautiful first-floor bedroom with the right curly antiques and pink Jouy draperies. Michelle cherishes her mansion and resembles it: gentle, attentive, courteous. Giverny is near, Rouen and its heaps of lovely restaurants are ten minutes away.

Private parking. Children over 10 welcome.

Rooms	2: 1 suite for 2-3, 1 double. Extra double occasionally available.
Price	€115.
Meals	Restaurant 900-metre walk; others in Rouen, 10-minute drive.
Closed	Rarely.

Michelle Desrez
Manoir de Captot,
42 route de Sahurs,
76380 Canteleu,
Seine-Maritime
Tel +33 (0)2 35 36 00 04
Email captot76@yahoo.fr
Web www.captot.com

Entry 181 Map 4

Normandy

Chambres avec Vue

The elegant black door hides a light, stylish interior with soul-lifting views across old Rouen to the spires of the cathedral. Dominique, a cultured hostess full of energy and enthusiasm, has a flair for decoration – as her paintings, coverings and contemporary and country furniture declare. Oriental rugs on parquet floors, French windows to balcony and garden, bedrooms brimful of interest. Nothing standard, nothing too studied, a very personal home and leisurely breakfasts promising delicious surprises. The house's hillside position in this attractive suburb is equally special. Such value!

Extra beds available. Covered garage space for one car.

Rooms	3 doubles.
Price	€63. Extra bed €25.
Meals	Restaurant 1km.
Closed	October-November.

Dominique Gogny
Chambres avec Vue, 22 rue Hénault,
76130 Mont St Aignan - Rouen,
Seine-Maritime

Tel	+33 (0)2 35 70 26 95
Mobile	+33 (0)6 62 42 26 95
Email	chambreavecvue@free.fr
Web	chambreavecvue.online.fr

Entry 182   Map 4

Normandy

Le Clos Jouvenet

From your bath you gaze upon the cathedral spire. It is a privilege to stay in these refined city surroundings, safely inside a serene walled garden above the towers of Rouen. The garden is as elegantly uncomplicated as the house and its Belgian owners, the décor classic sophisticated French to suit the gentle proportions: there are pretty pictures and prints, lots of books, handsome antique furniture and breakfast is served in the conservatory or on the terrace in warm weather. Madame is charming, Monsieur enjoys guests too, and you wake to birdsong and church bells.

Priority given to two-night stays, weekends & high season. Children over 13 welcome.

Rooms	4: 2 doubles, 2 twins/doubles.
Price	€100-€120.
Meals	Restaurants within walking distance.
Closed	Mid-December to mid-January.

Catherine de Witte
Le Clos Jouvenet,
42 rue Hyacinthe Langlois,
76000 Rouen, Seine-Maritime

Tel	+33 (0)2 35 89 80 66
Mobile	+33 (0)6 62 73 80 66
Email	leclosjouvenet@gmail.com
Web	www.leclosjouvenet.com

Entry 183   Map 4

Normandy

La Lévrière

The garden laps at the river bank where moorhens nest; trout swim, birds chirrup, deer pop by – it's the dreamiest village setting. Madame is charming and takes everything (including escapee horses) in her stride and her young family love it when guests come to stay. Breakfast is at a grey-painted table with crimson plexiglass chairs; garden loungers are a temptation to stay. Bedrooms are across the way, two in the granary, one up, one down, the third in the immaculate coach house attic with a fine garden view. Creamy walls, sweeping floors, rafters, toile de Jouy, fresh flowers... stay a long while.

Rooms	3: 1 triple, 2 suites.
Price	€85.
Meals	Restaurant 5km.
Closed	Rarely.

Sandrine & Pascal Gravier
La Lévrière,
24 rue Guérard,
27140 St Denis le Ferment, Eure

Tel	+33 (0)2 32 27 04 78
Mobile	+33 (0)6 79 43 92 77
Email	contact@normandyrooms.com
Web	www.normandyrooms.com

Entry 184   Map 5

Normandy

La Réserve

You will like Valérie, lively mother of four, the moment she opens the door to her quietly refined house. After breakfast, you will want to stay for ever: a feast for eye and palate, home-grown eggs and jams, cake of the day, cheese, cold meats and... a fruit kebab; tongues loosen, friendships bud. Outside, soft limewash walls stand among lavender-edged lawns and orchards, kindly Flaubert the Leonberger ambles, cows graze; inside are grey woodwork and gorgeous rooms, superb beds, handsome rugs on parquet floors, modern sculptures and fine antiques. Monet's ineffable gardens are just down the hill. Exceptional.

Whole house available.

Rooms	6: 2 doubles, 4 twins/doubles.
Price	€135–€165. Extra bed €40.
Meals	Restaurants 1km.
Closed	November–March, except by arrangement.

Valérie & François Jouyet
La Réserve,
27620 Giverny,
Eure

Tel	+33 (0)2 32 21 99 09
Email	mlreserve@gmail.com
Web	www.giverny-lareserve.com

Entry 185   Map 4

Normandy

Clos de Mondétour

Tiny church to one side, lazy river behind, views to weeping willows and majestic limes – the house oozes grace and tranquillity. Grégoire and Aude have created a calm, charming atmosphere inside: this is a family home. Lofty, light-drenched bedrooms with polished floorboards, antiques and monogrammed bed linen are beautifully refined; bathrooms are light and luxurious. The living area, with a striking tiled floor and bold colours, is a restful space in which to settle in front of a log fire – or enjoy a special breakfast among fresh flowers and family silver. Aude's horses graze in the meadow behind.

Rooms	3: 1 double, 1 twin/double, 1 family room for 3.
Price	€100–€120. Family room €80–€140.
Meals	Restaurants 2km.
Closed	Rarely.

Aude Jeanson
Clos de Mondétour,
17 rue de la Poste,
27120 Fontaine sous Jouy, Eure
Tel   +33 (0)2 32 36 68 79
Mobile +33 (0)6 71 13 11 57
Email aude.jeanson@closdemondetour.com
Web   www.closdemondetour.com

Entry 186   Map 4

Normandy

L'Aulnaie

Michel and Éliane have invested natural good taste in their restoration of this lovely 19th-century farmhouse in a particularly pretty village. Guests share a self-contained part of the house with its own dayroom and breakfast area – there's lots of space to settle in – with books, music and open fire. Bedrooms are gentle, beautiful, fresh, with Jouy-print fabrics, plain walls and honey-coloured floors. Enthusiastic, charming Éliane is an amateur painter and inspired gardener, pointing out the rich and the rare; lawns sweep down to a stream that meanders beneath high wooded cliffs. Such value!

Rooms	2: 1 double, 1 twin.
Price	€80.
Meals	Restaurants 2km.
Closed	Rarely.

Éliane & Michel Philippe
L'Aulnaie,
29 rue de l'Aulnaie,
27120 Fontaine sous Jouy, Eure
Tel   +33 (0)2 32 36 89 05
Mobile +33 (0)6 03 30 55 99
Email emi.philippe@worldonline.fr
Web   chambre-fontaine.chez-alice.fr

Entry 187   Map 4

Normandy

Les Granges Ménillonnes

An active farm until 1950, it sits beside a pretty garden in the prettiest countryside in the Eure valley, 20 minutes from Monet's gardens at Giverny, midway between Rouen and Paris. In converted outbuildings, big comfortable bedrooms, one with a balcony, furnished with warm colours, honeyed floorboards and country quilts beneath a riot of beams overlook cobbled paths, tumbling hydrangeas, lily pond and loungers that beckon you to doze over a book – though excellent walking abounds. Chantal and Michel, dynamic hosts, serve brilliant meals in the dining room and drinks in the salon bar – and run a proper farm shop.

Rooms	5: 2 doubles, 1 twin, 1 suite for 4, 1 suite for 7.
Price	€65–€70.
Meals	Dinner with wine, €25. Restaurant 3km.
Closed	Rarely.

Michel & Chantal Marchand
Les Granges Ménillonnes,
2 rue Grand'Cour,
27120 Ménilles, Eure

Tel	+33 (0)2 32 26 45 86
Mobile	+33 (0)6 70 46 87 57
Email	contact@lesgranges27.com
Web	www.lesgranges27.com

Entry 188   Map 4

Normandy

Manoir Les Perdrix

The young, hands-on owners of Les Perdrix are full of infectious enthusiasm for their enterprise: running a themed, welcoming, upmarket B&B. Food tastings, walking weekends – they can do it all! In the throes of serious restoration, the old house has an intimate dining room and cavernous reception room for tasty breakfasts and jolly dinners, comfortable bedrooms off a winding second-floor corridor: thick duvets and pretty linen, coordinated fabrics and polished floors, shower gels and plush bathrooms. The run-around garden – great for kids – is within earshot of the road to Verneuil.

Rooms	5: 4 twins/doubles, 1 family room.
Price	€85. Family room €95. Extra bed €20.
Meals	Dinner with wine, €16–€28.
Closed	Rarely.

Christine Vandemoortele
Manoir Les Perdrix,
Les Marnières,
27570 Tillières sur Avre, Eure

Mobile	+33 (0)6 21 21 08 52
Email	postmaster@manoirlesperdrix.fr
Web	www.normandy-guest-house.com

Entry 189   Map 4

Normandy

La Trimardière

Midway between Paris and Deauville, in the beautiful town of Verneuil sur Avre, is an 18th-century mansion in a neat French garden, immaculate inside and out. Glass decanters decorate the mantelpiece and swathes of pale pattern dress the windows, giving the lofty airy dining room a handsome allure; here Domitila serves perfect breakfasts at a big oval table. Bedrooms are on the top floors – smart, spacious, luxurious, traditional – with oriental rugs on satin-smooth floors, wonderful new mattresses, crisp snowy linen and bathrobes cosseted in hygienic packaging. Shops, restaurants, festivals wait outside the door.

Rooms	5: 2 doubles, 2 twins/doubles, 1 suite.
Price	€110–€120. Suite €120–€170. Singles €95.
Meals	Restaurant within walking distance.
Closed	Rarely.

Domitila Aranda
La Trimardière,
366 rue Gambetta,
27130 Verneuil sur Avre, Eure

Tel	+33 (0)2 32 30 28 41
Mobile	+33 (0)6 30 50 83 08
Email	latrimardiere@orange.fr
Web	www.latrimardiere.com

Entry 190   Map 4

Normandy

Clair Matin

Handsomely carved Colombian furniture, strong colours, interesting prints – not what you expect to find at an 18th-century manor with a Norman-cottage face and an unexpected turret. Your kind and very lovely Franco-Spanish hosts raised five children in South America before renovating their French home. Bedrooms, not huge, are solidly comfortable, bathrooms are immaculate and, at the huge Andean cedar breakfast table, you will find fresh breads, homemade jams and good conversation. Jean-Pierre is a passionate gardener and his plantations burst with every kind of shrub and flower: stunning!

Rooms	4: 1 double, 1 family room for 4, 2 suites for 2.
Price	€65. Family room €65–€95. Suites €80–€110.
Meals	Auberges 6km.
Closed	Rarely.

Jean-Pierre & Amaia Trevisani
Clair Matin,
19 rue de l'Église,
27930 Reuilly, Eure

Tel	+33 (0)2 32 34 71 47
Email	bienvenue@clair-matin.com
Web	www.clair-matin.com

Entry 191   Map 4

Normandy

La Londe

The big beautiful garden flows down to the river Eure – what a setting – and the old farmhouse and yesteryear buildings are as neat as new pins. Delightful Madeleine devotes herself to home and guests and bedrooms are neat, clean, pretty, sober and relaxing; the double's French windows open to the garden, the perfect small suite sits under the eaves. Expect antique lace, silver snuff boxes, a kitchen/salon for guests and very delicious breakfasts with garden views. A form of perfection in a privileged and peaceful spot: woods and water for walking, canoeing, fishing; Giverny – or Rouen – a half-hour drive.

Rooms	2: 1 double, 1 suite.
Price	€57–€62. Suite €57–€68.
Meals	Guest kitchen. Restaurants 5km.
Closed	Rarely.

Madeleine & Bernard Gossent
La Londe,
4 sente de l'Abreuvoir,
27400 Heudreville sur Eure, Eure

Tel	+33 (0)2 32 40 36 89
Mobile	+33 (0)6 89 38 36 59
Email	madeleine.gossent@online.fr
Web	www.lalonde.online.fr

Entry 192   Map 4

Normandy

Manoir de la Boissière

Madame cooks great Norman dishes with home-grown ingredients served on good china. She has been doing B&B for years, is well-organised and still enjoys meeting new people when she's not too busy. Guest quarters, independent of the house, have pretty, traditional rooms, good bedding and excellent shower rooms. Sympathetically restored 15th-century farm buildings, carefully chosen furniture – some tenderly hand-painted – and ducks and swans on the lovely pond add character. Near the motorway yet utterly peaceful – though courting peacocks in spring/summer may wake you.

Rooms	5: 2 doubles, 1 twin, 1 triple, 1 family room for 3 (with kitchenette).
Price	€65–€75.
Meals	Dinner with cider, €26. Guest kitchen.
Closed	Rarely.

Clotilde & Gérard Sénécal
Manoir de la Boissière,
Hameau la Boissaye,
27490 La Croix St Leufroy, Eure

Tel	+33 (0)2 32 67 70 85
Email	chambreslaboissiere@wanadoo.fr
Web	www.chambres-giteslaboissiere.com

Entry 193   Map 4

Normandy

La Ferme des Isles

Approach this sprawling 19th-century farm through a watercolour of mills, meadows and bridges… friendly French hosts await with a menagerie of four-legged friends. With vintage chairs, suspended lamps, billiards and book-filled mangers, it's perfect for fun social soirées and François's four-star dinners. Beams break up modern bedrooms – a triangular bath and a sunburst bed will astound you. Breakfast in the cavernous barn (on goat's cheese, grainy breads, garden fruits); end the day amongst fireplaces, convivial tables and chesterfields in stone-walled sitting and dining rooms. For nature lovers, couples and families – huge fun.

Rooms	5: 4 doubles, 1 family suite for 3.
Price	€90. Family suite €120-€150. Extra bed €20. Cot available free of charge.
Meals	Dinner, 4 courses with wine, €18-€35. Restaurants 300m.
Closed	Rarely.

François & Sophie Breban
La Ferme des Isles,
7 chemin des Isles,
27490 Autheuil Authouillet, Eure
Tel   +33 (0)2 32 36 66 14
Mobile   +33 (0)6 63 46 00 45
Email   lafermedesisles@gmail.com
Web   www.lafermedesisles.com

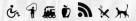

Entry 194   Map 4

Normandy

Au Vieux Logis

They are full of character and terribly French, this artist owner and her crooked house marked by the slings and arrows of 500 years: wonky floorboards, bathrooms among the beams, old-fashioned floral bedrooms and a sensuous garden full of old favourites: lilac and honeysuckle, luscious shrubs and fruit trees. Set in the middle of the village, the quiet old house has an atmosphere that inspires ease and rest. (Saint-Exupéry, author of the *Le Petit Prince* and a friend of Madame's father, stayed here.) Madame, a good, generous soul, was once an antique dealer so breakfast is served on old silver.

Rooms	4: 2 doubles, 1 quadruple, 1 triple.
Price	€50. Triple €50-€80. Quadruple €50-€100.
Meals	Dinner €17. Wine €15.
Closed	Rarely.

Annick Auzoux
Au Vieux Logis,
27370 St Didier des Bois, Eure
Tel   +33 (0)2 32 50 60 93
Email   levieuxlogis5@orange.fr
Web   www.levieuxlogis.fr

Entry 195   Map 4

Normandy

Manoir d'Hermos

The sedately old-French bedrooms with good antiques and satin touches are up the grand old staircase of this 16th-century house where brick and sandstone sit in peace by pastoral meadows, a birdy orchard and spreading lake. Madame is a most welcoming hostess, full of spontaneous smiles, who puts flowers everywhere and whose family has owned the house for 100 years. She also organises big parties (not when B&B guests are here), serves good breakfasts and brunches at one table and keeps four gentle donkeys. The orchards produce cider and trees are being planted to Napoleonic plans discovered in the archives.

Rooms	2: 1 triple, 1 quadruple.
Price	Triple €88–€117. Quadruple €136.
Meals	Restaurants 2km.
Closed	Rarely.

Béatrice & Patrice Noël-Windsor
Manoir d'Hermos,
27800 St Éloi de Fourques, Eure

Tel	+33 (0)2 32 35 51 32
Mobile	+33 (0)6 11 75 51 63
Email	contact@hermos.fr
Web	www.hermos.fr

Entry 196   Map 4

Normandy

Les Clématites

An enchanting *maison de maître*, one of several that housed the nimble-fingered ribbon weavers, with the bonus of fine table d'hôtes. Hidden amid the fields of the Normandy plains, it stands in a dream of a garden, overgrown here, brought to heel there, flanked by a majestic walnut and age-old pears, filled with shrub roses; the odd forgotten bench adds to the Flaubertian charm. Inside, Marie-Hélène, bright-eyed and eager, has used Jouy cloth and elegant colours to dress the country-French bedrooms that fill the first floor. These ex-Parisian hosts are courteous, considerate, truly endearing.

Rooms	3: 1 double, 1 twin, 1 triple.
Price	€70.
Meals	Supper, three courses with wine, €21.
Closed	Rarely.

Marie-Hélène François & Hughes de Morchoven
Les Clématites, Hameau de la Charterie,
27230 St Aubin de Scellon, Eure

Tel	+33 (0)2 32 45 46 52
Mobile	+33 (0)6 20 39 08 63
Email	la.charterie@orange.fr
Web	monsite.orange.fr/la.charterie

Entry 197   Map 4

Normandy

Le Clos Beauvallet

On the edge of a hamlet in deep Normandy is a pitch-roofed, half-timbered cottage in a big lush garden sheltered on all sides. Here live Éric and Philippe, friendly and well-travelled, who serve wonderful breakfasts (smoothies, muffins, scones, brioche, yogurt, jams: all homemade) as late as you like – and on the decked terrace on fine days. Impeccable interiors, handsome and contemporary, are splashed with modern art. Discover cider and calvados, Honfleur and Deauville, return to tranquil beds beneath sloping ceilings and rustic timbers painted white – a beautiful blend of the elegant and the ethnic. Bathrooms are delicious.

Normandy

Le Coquerel

Jean-Marc brims with ideas for your stay and love for his garden, modern art and long divine dinners with guests. He has turned the old cottage, surrounded by soft pastures, into a country gem in a flower-exuberant garden. Inside, a mix of the sober, the frivolous, the cultured and the kitsch: old and modern pieces, rustic revival and leather, paintings and brocante. Bedrooms stand out in their uncomplicated good taste, bathrooms are irreproachable, but it's your host who makes the place: duck in cider, strawberry soup and laughter, butterflies alighting on the table at breakfast.

Rooms	2: 1 double, 1 suite.
Price	€78. Suite €98.
Meals	Dinner, 5 courses, €30.
	Restaurants in Lieurey, 3km.
Closed	Rarely.

Rooms	5: 1 double, 1 twin, 1 triple,
	2 family rooms.
Price	€65-€75. Triple €75-€85.
	Family rooms €85-€105.
Meals	Dinner with wine, €28.
	Picnic available.
Closed	Rarely.

	Éric Chabbert
	Le Clos Beauvallet,
	180 impasse Beauvallet,
	27260 Morainville Jouveaux, Eure
Tel	+33 (0)2 32 20 07 68
Mobile	+33 (0)6 29 22 59 31
Email	eric.leclosbeauvallet@gmail.com
Web	leclosbeauvallet.com

Entry 198   Map 4

	Jean-Marc Drumel
	Le Coquerel,
	27560 St Siméon, Eure
Tel	+33 (0)2 32 56 56 08
Email	coquerel27@nordnet.fr
Web	www.chambredhoteducoquerel.com

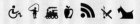

Entry 199   Map 4

Normandy

Les Aubépines

That lovely timber frame embraces a heart-warming antique clutter spread over original bricks, beams, tiles and carved family furniture. Guests share this marvellous space as family; Madame cooks with delight (maybe over the open fire), does excellent table d'hôtes and tends the intimate paradise of her garden whence views glide over forested hills; Monsieur smiles, charms – and mends everything. The delicious bedrooms are subtly lit by dormer windows, country-furnished, pastel-hued and comfortably bathroomed; the suite has steep rafters. Enchanting – they deserve a medal!

Minimum two nights.

Rooms	3: 2 twins/doubles, 1 suite for 4.
Price	€70–€75.
Meals	Dinner with wine, €25.
Closed	October–February, except by arrangement.

Françoise & Yves Closson Maze
Les Aubépines, Aux Chauffourniers,
27290 Appeville dit Annebault,
Eure

Tel	+33 (0)2 32 56 14 25
Mobile	+33 (0)6 72 26 18 59
Email	clossonmaze@orange.fr
Web	pagesperso-orange.fr/lesaubepines

Entry 200   Map 4

Normandy

Les Sources Bleues

A privileged setting on the banks of the Seine just below Rouen: once every five years the great armada comes sailing by. The garden (old trees, long grasses, the odd goat, sheep and pig) is 50m from the water's edge and there are binoculars for birdwatching. This Panda (WWF) house is for guests only: the owner lives next door, the swallows live everywhere. Old-fashioned bedrooms are in need of a lick of paint but have a certain charm, the family rooms are squeezed into the attic, and Monsieur, a great host, cooks beautifully if you fancy table d'hôtes – genuine Normandy style. There's a kitchen/diner for guests, and a sitting room too.

Rooms	4: 2 quadruples, 2 suites.
Price	Quadruples €80. Suites €58–€70.
Meals	Dinner €20. Wine €12–€15; cider €5. Kitchen available.
Closed	Rarely.

Yves Laurent
Les Sources Bleues,
Le Bourg,
27500 Aizier, Eure

Tel	+33 (0)2 32 57 26 68
Mobile	+33 (0)6 80 62 84 31
Web	www.les-sources-bleues.com

Entry 201   Map 4

Normandy

Château de Saint Maclou la Campagne

These days, the proud brick and limestone mansion is more peaceful than in the past, yet it's every bit as deliciously luxurious. Warm British hosts welcome guests into a wood-panelled drawing room where you can admire porcelains, portraits and family photographs – and snuggle before a winter fire. Breakfast at a fine mahogany table; waft up to gorgeous bedrooms in apple green, mushroom, apricot or sunny yellow, and bathrooms that are thoroughly 21st-century. A dry moat encircles the château; beyond lie vast lawns interspersed with neat hedges, an orchard and a dovecote. A fascinating slice of history in tranquil surroundings.

Whole house available.

Normandy

400 rue des Franches Terres

In a residential country lane with Norman apple-orchard views is a new peachy-painted house, a warm inviting B&B. Generous attentive Gaston (retired sea captain) and smiling Michelle (gentle seamstress) offer you a cosy bedroom with polished floorboards and rose-floral walls, and a bathroom with a big tub to sink into. Prettiness abounds in the long living room, yours to share, where a good continental breakfast is served at times to suit you. This is a great little launchpad for the port of Honfleur, rich with concerts, galleries, festivals and markets of every kind. Stay a weekend – or more!

Rooms	4 twins/doubles.
Price	€170-€220.
	Whole house €6,000-€7,000 per week.
Meals	Breakfast €12.50. Restaurant 300m.
Closed	Rarely.

Rooms	1 double.
Price	€75.
Meals	Restaurants in Honfleur, 10-minute drive.
Closed	Rarely.

Robin Gage
Château de Saint Maclou la Campagne,
352 rue Émile Desson,
27210 St Maclou, Eure

Tel +33 (0)2 32 57 26 62
Mobile +33 (0)6 75 96 87 74
Email rg@chateaudesaintmaclou.com
Web www.chateaudesaintmaclou.com

Gaston & Michelle Le Pleux
400 rue des Franches Terres,
27210 Beuzeville, Eure

Tel +33 (0)2 32 57 46 69
Mobile +33 (0)6 51 52 07 52
Email michele.lepleux@free.fr

Entry 202   Map 4

Entry 203   Map 4

Normandy

Le Moulin

You will warm to this couple who, whatever they turn their hand to – once farm and DIY store, now garden and chambres d'hôtes – turn it to perfection. The lovely half-timbered mill, operating from 1769 to 1965, is in working order still; ask Monsieur to give you a demo. Two neat, comfortable and immaculate bedrooms have carpeting or polished boards, gentle hues and dormer windows, and views of the oh-so-pretty garden; bliss to fall asleep to the sound of trickling water. Courteous and kind are the owners, bucolic is the setting. There's gourmet dining in Conteville, and a sweet, simple restaurant up the road.

Rooms	2: 1 double, 1 family suite for 3.
Price	€70. Family suite €75–€90.
Meals	Restaurant 2km–4km.
Closed	Rarely.

Madame Derouet
Le Moulin,
27210 Foulbec,
Eure

Tel +33 (0)2 32 56 55 25
Email raymond.derouet@free.fr

Entry 204   Map 4

Normandy

Le Clos Bourdet

Welcome to chic, charming B&B, off a residential street, in a big hilly garden high above town. Françoise ran a tea room for 25 years, Jean-Claude is a photographer whose black-and-white prints beautify elegant rooms. Tall windows pull in the light in a sitting room heaving with books, crowned by a chandelier. Wend your way up the corkscrew staircase (past a collection of vintage bird cages that catch the eye) to bedrooms with antique wicker chairs on seagrass floors and soft-raspberry walls showing off turquoise taffeta. There are monsoon showers and a big terrace view... such fun to be in historic Honfleur!

Parking available in the grounds.

Rooms	5: 4 doubles, 1 suite.
Price	€125–€180. Suite €190. Extra bed €45.
Meals	Restaurants within walking distance.
Closed	January.

Françoise Osmont
Le Clos Bourdet,
50 rue Bourdet,
14600 Honfleur, Calvados

Tel +33 (0)2 31 89 49 11
Mobile +33 (0)6 07 48 99 67
Email leclosbourdet@orange.fr
Web www.leclosbourdet.com

Entry 205   Map 4

Normandy

Au Grey d'Honfleur

There's a fairytale feel to this pair of tall narrow houses in a quiet cobbled backstreet. You don't quite know what to expect but you know you're somewhere rare and special. Inside, stairs and steps in all directions link little rooms; age-old beams and sloping ceilings contrast with imaginative décor and modern luxury. Josette, a globe-trotting lawyer, knows a thing or two about what's required of a guest bedroom... Looking down over the haphazard roofs of medieval Honfleur, the miniature terraced garden and fountain, delightfully formal, add to the pleasure. Breakfasts are divine.

Minimum two nights. Free public parking nearby.

Rooms	2 doubles.
Price	€125–€160.
Meals	Restaurants within walking distance.
Closed	Rarely.

Josette Roudaut
Au Grey d'Honfleur,
11 rue de la Bavole,
14600 Honfleur,
Calvados
Mobile   +33 (0)6 85 07 50 45
Email   info@augrey-honfleur.com
Web   www.augrey-honfleur.com

Entry 206   Map 4

Normandy

Le Fond de la Cour

A treat to stay in converted stables in the heart of Honfleur, with an intimate garden attached, a stroll from sumptuous seafood restaurants and medieval streets. Nab the spacious room on the first floor with pretty rooftop views, or take over the fresh green and white family apartment; both have neat bathrooms and salad-bowl basins. You're spoilt for breakfast nooks: in the shared sitting room with its corner kitchen, in Amanda and Craig's conservatory, or, a summer alternative, in their garden. End the day with a nightcap and stargazing on the terrace – and a friendly wag from the white German shepherd!

Rooms	3: 1 double, 1 twin/double, 1 family apartment for 3.
Price	€85–€115.
Meals	Guest kitchen. Restaurants 3-minute walk.
Closed	Rarely.

Amanda Ferguson
Le Fond de la Cour,
29 rue Eugène Boudin,
14600 Honfleur,
Calvados
Mobile   +33 (0)6 72 20 72 98
Email   amanda.ferguson@orange.fr
Web   www.lefonddelacour.com

Entry 207   Map 4

La Cour Ste Catherine

Through the Norman gateway into the sun-drenched courtyard; Liliane and history embrace you. The building was first a convent, then fishermen's cottages, later a *ciderie*. Now this historic quarter is a conservation area and all has been properly restored. Breakfast viennoiseries are served in the huge beamed room where the apples were once pressed; sip a summery aperitif in the courtyard with fellow guests. Bedrooms are sunny, airy, impeccable, contemporary, one in the hayloft with its own outside stair. There's a small sitting room for guests and Honfleur at your feet; your charming hosts know the town intimately.

La Lirencine

Wander the higgledy-piggledy streets of the 'city of painters', watch boats in Old Dock with its Norman harbour, amble to your pretty B&B on a peaceful backstreet. You breakfast at one table in smiley owner Annick's dining room, on croissants, fresh yogurt, home-baked breads and jams. Bedrooms in a separate building (one room is reached by steep outside stairs) vary in size, but all are attractive with lovely antiques, gorgeous linen and rooftop views. Loaf about the garden with its olive trees, tomatoes and courgettes, or visit daughter Alice's beauty parlour with its mosaic-tiled steam bath, pretty lights and calming atmosphere.

Rooms	5: 2 doubles, 1 twin/double, 1 triple, 1 family room.
Price	€90–€110. Triple €140–€170. Family room €170–€230. Extra bed €30.
Meals	Restaurants nearby.
Closed	Rarely.

Rooms	4: 1 double, 1 twin/double, 1 family room for 3, 1 suite for 4.
Price	€85. Family room €85. Suite €120. Extra bed €25.
Meals	Restaurants within walking distance.
Closed	Rarely.

	Liliane & Antoine Giaglis
	La Cour Ste Catherine,
	74 rue du Puits, 14600 Honfleur,
	Calvados
Tel	+33 (0)2 31 89 42 40
Email	coursaintecatherine@orange.fr
Web	www.coursaintecatherine.com

	Annick Proffit
	La Lirencine,
	3 Lucie Delarue Mardrus,
	14600 Honfleur, Calvados
Tel	+33 (0)6 70 70 98 65
Email	annick-proffit@club-internet.fr
Web	www.lalirencine.fr

Entry 208   Map 4

Entry 209   Map 4

Normandy

Réglisse & Pain d'Epices

Stand for a moment and appreciate the charm: two terraced fisherman's cottages in the heart of Honfleur. Behind the pretty façade of herringbone timbers are snug, spotless bedrooms full of antiques and beams – one with an ancient flint wall. Breakfast might be in your convivial hosts' cottage, decorated in warming red, or outside in the intimate courtyard where blue is the theme and flowers spill, from wheelbarrow to window sill. Six types of bread in the morning, throngs of restaurants a stroll away, and 45 minutes from the ferry ports of Caen and Le Havre – a super welcome to France!

Free parking 5 minutes from house. Cot available.

Rooms	3 doubles.
Price	€110–€120. Singles €90–€100. Extra bed €20.
Meals	Restaurants nearby.
Closed	Rarely.

Éric Blondeau & Frédéric Ledour
Réglisse & Pain d'Epices,
61 rue Haute, 14600 Honfleur,
Calvados
Tel   +33 (0)2 31 87 84 80
Mobile   +33 (0)6 78 37 47 91
Email   contact@rpe-chambres-honfleur.fr
Web   www.rpe-chambres-honfleur.fr

Entry 210   Map 4

Normandy

La Cerisée

In glamorous, horsey Deauville, a wee garden cottage all to yourselves: pink and grey kitchen/living room downstairs, airy blond bedroom up. It's a cosy, uncomplicated and imaginative mix of new-simple and antique-reclaimed – plus Isabelle's beautiful driftwood art. She is elegantly informal and stores her raw materials on the flowery patio that you share with her and Alain. Breakfast is DIY – fresh ingredients delivered to the door – but if you prefer she will happily provide in her own pretty kitchen/diner. Deauville bursts with beaches, bicycle outings, markets and luscious seafood. Great value in a fascinating area.

Rooms	1 cottage for 2-4.
Price	€110–€130. Extra person €20.
Meals	Restaurants 50m.
Closed	Rarely.

Isabelle Quinones
La Cerisée,
15 rue du Général Leclerc,
14800 Deauville, Calvados
Tel   +33 (0)2 31 81 18 29
Mobile   +33 (0)6 83 16 51 19
Email   la.cerisee@hotmail.fr
Web   chambre-hotes-deauville.com

Entry 211   Map 4

La Longère

There are two stars in this show: the whirlwind Fabienne who decorates everything from tables to crockery and delivers breakfast feasts (a party every morning!), and the seductively long, low, half-timbered 17th-century farmhouse. Fabienne and her as-generous husband throw open their home and sheltered garden, join you for dinner and perhaps drinks on the terrace; she also happily babysits. Smallish rooms are pretty with quilts and hand-painted furniture, tiles or polished floorboards; children will love the hideaway mezzanine in the family suite. An endearing hostess, and beaches five minutes away.

Minimum two nights at weekends.

Bergerie de la Moutonnière

Sheep still graze behind this charming old bergerie, the end-wing of your hospitable Dutch hosts' manor house. Great independence here: a rustic, open summer kitchen and smart little bathroom below, and a spacious suite above, tidy and homely beneath lofty rafters, with a wooden floor and wattle-and-daub walls, two armchairs, a sofa and a super-comfortable bed. Colours are dark, gentle and warm, heating is electric and staircases (inside and out) are for the sprightly. After walking, cider making, Trouville and golf, return to beautiful, peaceful grounds, with good wooden dining furniture and a barbecue on request.

Rooms	4: 2 doubles. Wing: 1 family room for 4, 1 family suite for 5.
Price	€75–€140.
Meals	Dinner with wine, €28. Restaurant 300m.
Closed	Rarely.

Rooms	Stables: 1 suite for 2 (shower room downstairs).
Price	€85.
Meals	Breakfast €7.50. Dinner with wine, €35. Summer kitchen. Restaurants 6km.
Closed	Never.

Fabienne Fillion
La Longère, Chemin de la Libération,
14800 Bonneville sur Touques,
Calvados
Tel +33 (0)2 31 64 10 29
Mobile +33 (0)6 08 04 38 52
Email fafillion@wanadoo.fr
Web www.lalongerenormandie.com

Rudolf Walthaus
Bergerie de la Moutonnière,
Le Mensil,
14590 Le Pin,
Calvados
Tel +33 (0)2 31 62 56 86
Email walthaus@mac.com
Web www.bergerienormandy.com

Entry 212   Map 4

Entry 213   Map 4

Normandy

La Baronnière

The Baron left a half-timbered glory of a manor house, expanses of grass dotted with apple trees, a stream-fed lake, sheep in a nearby pasture – enchanting. Geese gabble, chickens lay for breakfast, children rejoice (dens in trees, games on lawns). Christine, who's English, loves caring for the old house and chatting with guests; her French husband cooks beautiful meals served in the lake-view conservatory. The room in the former pantry has a Louis XIV bed on old honeycomb tiles, the other is up an outside staircase in the exquisite timbered barn. Blissful tranquillity.

Minimum two nights. Sawday self-catering also.

Rooms	2 doubles (let to same party only).
Price	€90.
Meals	Dinner with wine, €50-€60.
Closed	Rarely.

Christine Gilliatt-Fleury
La Baronnière,
14100 Cordebugle,
Calvados
Tel +33 (0)2 32 46 41 74
Email labaronniere@wanadoo.fr
Web www.labaronniere.com

Entry 214   Map 4

Normandy

Manoir de Cantepie

It may have a make-believe face, among the smooth green curves of racehorse country, but it is genuine early 1600s and astonishing from all sides. Inside, an astounding dining room, resplendently carved, panelled and painted, serves for tasty organic breakfasts. Bedrooms, all amazing value, have a sunny feel, and are delightful: one with white-painted beams and green toile de Jouy, another in yellows, a third with a glorious valley view. Madame, a beautiful Swedish lady, made the curtains and covers. She and her husband are well-travelled, polyglot and cultured: they make their B&B doubly special.

Rooms	3 doubles.
Price	€75.
Meals	Restaurant 1km.
Closed	Mid-November to February.

Christine & Arnauld Gherrak
Manoir de Cantepie,
Le Cadran,
14340 Cambremer, Calvados
Tel +33 (0)2 31 62 87 27
Email c.gherrak@dbmail.com
Web www.manoir-de-cantepie.jimdo.com

Entry 215   Map 4

Normandy

Les Costils

This Calvados farmhouse, hillside-perched with fine outbuildings, is a rural idyll. The estate, a certified organic farm, has been in charming Alain's family since the 40s; he, musician Rebeka and son Nicolas settled here in 2002. Outside, a shared orchard garden with sublime views across the (swimmable) lake and horse-scudded pastures; in the big, pretty, multi-levelled cottage natural colours with lots of wood, antique details, books and fine fabrics; breakfast comes to you here. A throng of animals, and organic garden veg too: "striving to live gently and consciously with their environment," they have created eco-nirvana.

Minimum 2 nights. Extra child bed available.

Rooms	2 cottages for 2.
Price	€70-€90. €90 for 3.
Meals	Breakfast €10. Restaurant 6km.
Closed	December-February.

Rebeka Jaqua & Alain Karmitz
Les Costils,
14140 Le Mesnil Germain,
Calvados

Tel	+33 (0)2 31 63 77 34
Email	bekajak@mac.com
Web	www.lescostils.fr

Entry 216   Map 4

Normandy

Ferme de la Ruette

The gates glide open to a gravelled sweep and a tree'd lawn framed by mellow cider-farm buildings. Elegant, compassionate Isabelle looks after house, garden, guests – and rescue cats and horses – with warmth and charm; Philippe, a friendly GP, fills the game larder. The barn houses two bedrooms, a delightful family suite under the rafters (up a steep private stair) and a cosy guest sitting room with a bar. Rooms have pretty striped wallpapers, seagrass floors and elegant Louis XV-style chairs, quirky *objets* on shelves and in crannies, beds dressed with white heirloom spreads. Vivacious, bustling Caen is an easy drive.

Rooms	3: 2 doubles, 1 family suite for 4 with kitchenette.
Price	€60-€80. Extra bed €10.
Meals	Restaurant 5km.
Closed	Rarely.

Isabelle & Philippe Cayé
Ferme de la Ruette,
5 chemin Haussé,
14190 Cauvicourt, Calvados

Tel	+33 (0)2 31 78 11 82
Mobile	+33 (0)6 28 26 22 61
Email	laruette@gmail.com
Web	www.fermedelaruette.fr

Entry 217   Map 4

Normandy

Château des Riffets

The square-set château stands handsome still as the park recovers from the 1999 storm: they lost 2,300 trees. Admire yourself in myriad mirrors, luxuriate in a jacuzzi, bare your chest to a rain shower, play the piano, and lie at last in an antique bed in one of the great, cherished bedrooms. Monsieur is a former psychologist, gracious Madame was an English teacher, and a fine breakfast is served at one big table. Take a stroll in the 30-acre wooded park, hire a nearby horse or a canoe, hone your carriage-driving skills. Period ceilings, tapestries and furniture make Riffets a stunning château experience.

Rooms	4: 2 doubles, 2 suites.
Price	€120-€170
Meals	Restaurant 1km.
Closed	Rarely.

Anne-Marie & Alain Cantel
Château des Riffets,
14680 Bretteville sur Laize,
Calvados

Tel	+33 (0)2 31 23 53 21
Mobile	+33 (0)6 14 09 74 93
Email	chateau.riffets@wanadoo.fr
Web	www.chateau-des-riffets.com

Entry 218   Map 4

Normandy

Château de la Pommeraye

For lovers of deep country and calm luxury, a fine big mansion (1646 with later additions). Your ex-Parisian host has done an immaculate restoration: handsome carpets on polished boards, big beds heaped with pillows, oils, icons and engravings. The first-floor rooms are huge with innumerable windows for vistas; the rooms above more intimate. Downstairs: pale painted wainscoting and moss-green velvet chairs, a marble fireplace for log fires, and age-old polished stone flooring; let the beauty wash over you. Visit Caen for culture and shopping, take a mini row on the moat, then enjoy a gourmet château dinner (by arrangement).

Rooms	5: 2 twins/doubles, 3 suites for 2-4. Some rooms interconnect.
Price	€160-€200. Suites €220-€280. Extra bed €40.
Meals	Breakfast €12. Dinner €35. Restaurant 4km.
Closed	Rarely.

Alexandre Boudnikoff
Château de la Pommeraye,
14690 La Pommeraye, Calvados

Tel	+33 (0)2 31 69 87 86
Email	alexandre.boudnikoff@orange.fr
Web	www.chateaudelapommeraye.com

Entry 219   Map 4

Normandy

Le Gaudin

Shooting through the centre of this 18th-century farmhouse is a chimney of 4,500 bricks. Clive knows: he built it! Every feature conveys space, age and the care and creativity of your British hosts. Exposed stone walls; an old manger, now a wine rack; Denise's upholstered coffee table; a doll's house in the sunny breakfast room, and the long table at which guests gather for Clive's superb dinners. Sophisticated bedrooms, delighting in hand-sewn fabrics, are a fanfare of colours. Pilgrims to Mont St Michel once filled their bottles at the stream in the wooded grounds; many attractions are close. No wonder people return.

Rooms	4 doubles.
Price	€70-€90.
Meals	Dinner with wine, €38.
Closed	January-March.

Clive & Denise Canvin
Le Gaudin,
Route d'Aunay,
14260 Campandré Valcongrain,
Calvados
Tel +33 (0)2 31 73 88 70
Email legaudin14@yahoo.co.uk
Web www.legaudin.co.uk

Entry 220 Map 4

Normandy

La Suhardière

Up the drive, across the spotless (non-working!) farmyard to be met by a charming, smiling hostess who delights in gardening and cooking – dinner is a wonderful affair. Beyond the dinky little hall, the salon, with its high-backed chairs, dark farmhouse beams and profusion of white lace, is a good little spot for a quiet read. The big sunny bedrooms are cosily frilly with their country furniture, framed Millet reproductions and more lace; gentle morning views over the garden drop down to the pond where you may fish: the setting is delightful. Walkers will be happy in this pretty rolling countryside.

Small dogs welcome.

Rooms	2: 1 double, 1 family room for 3.
Price	€63.
Meals	Dinner with wine, €22.
Closed	Rarely.

Alain & Françoise Petiton
La Suhardière,
14240 Livry,
Calvados
Tel +33 (0)2 31 77 51 02
Email petiton.alain@wanadoo.fr

Entry 221 Map 3

Normandy

Manoir des Doyens

The lovely old house of golden stone is the warmly natural home of interesting people: an extrovert military historian and his gentle lady. Rosemary goes the extra mile for guests and serves her own jams for breakfast. Stone stairs lead to comfortably casual, old-fashioned guest rooms and good, clean bathrooms; the courtyard houses visiting grandchildren's swings, slide, rabbits, goats and games room; the family sitting room is shared and there are always interesting people to chat to over breakfast, or a calvados. A 20-minute stroll from town but all you hear is the honk of the goose!

Guided battlefield tours can be arranged.

Rooms	3 triples.
Price	€55.
Meals	Restaurants 1km.
Closed	Rarely.

Lt Col & Mrs Chilcott
Manoir des Doyens,
Chemin des Mares, St Loup Hors,
14400 Bayeux, Calvados
Tel   +33 (0)2 31 22 39 09
Email   michaeljohn.chilcott@sfr.fr

Entry 222   Map 4

Normandy

Les Glycines

This lovely couple are kindness itself, she softly spoken and twinkling, he jovial, talkative, utterly French. Having retired from farming, they moved into the heart of Bayeux. You can glimpse the cathedral spires from their house, once part of the old bishop's palace. Beyond the gates and the wisteria, the door opens to a lofty beamed living room rejoicing in good antiques and a monumental fireplace; through another is the kitchen. Up the ancient stone stairs are pretty bedrooms – immaculate bedding, pastel-tiled showers – that look quietly over a pocket-handkerchief garden. Delicious breakfasts, history all around, and no need for a car.

Rooms	3: 2 doubles, 1 family room.
Price	€67. Family room €90.
Meals	Restaurant 50m.
Closed	Rarely.

Louis & Annick Fauvel
Les Glycines,
13 rue aux Coqs, 14400 Bayeux,
Calvados
Tel   +33 (0)2 31 22 52 32
Mobile   +33 (0)6 89 39 84 79

Entry 223   Map 4

Normandy

Normandy

Clos de Bellefontaine

Come to be pampered and effortlessly spoiled at this elegant townhouse, a ten-minute stroll from the famous Tapestry. Bedrooms are chic and gracious with choice antiques, colours are mocha and white, floors polished parquet or seagrass. Choose the top floor for snugness and charm, the first floor for grandeur and space. With a walled garden and two handsome ground-floor salons – antiques, family photographs, help-yourself refreshments – to lounge around in, you'll not miss home. Carole's breakfasts, with homemade tarts, fruit compotes and cheeses, are the highlight of the stay.

Le Manoir de Basly

In the comfortingly walled luxury of an old stone manor and well-kept antiques, this is a place of classic French refinement where you are received by gracious, friendly hosts who enjoy sharing their lifelong knowledge of their region. In the main house: two faultlessly elegant bedrooms – original stones and timbers, draped beds, delicate muslin, stitched cotton, rich brocade in soft colours – and the guests' living room. On the ground floor of the tiny cottage, the cherry on the cake: a sweet pale bedroom, more lovely furniture, a welcoming sitting area and… a wee terrace of its own. A naturally sophisticated welcome.

Secure private car park.

Rooms	2: 1 double, 1 twin.
Price	€120–€160. Extra bed €30.
Meals	Restaurants nearby.
Closed	Rarely.

Rooms	3: 1 suite. Cottage: 1 double, 1 suite.
Price	€90–€150.
Meals	Restaurants nearby.
Closed	Rarely.

Carole & Jérôme Mallet
Clos de Bellefontaine,
6 rue de Bellefontaine,
14400 Bayeux, Calvados
Mobile   +33 (0)6 81 42 24 81
Email   clos.bellefontaine@wanadoo.fr
Web   www.clos-bellefontaine.fr

Monique Casset
Le Manoir de Basly,
2 route de Courseulles,
14610 Basly, Calvados
Tel   +33 (0)2 31 80 12 08
Mobile   +33 (0)6 61 13 12 08
Email   lemanoirdebasly@wanadoo.fr
Web   www.lemanoirdebasly.com

Entry 224   Map 4

Entry 225   Map 4

Château de Bénéauville

Down the plane-flanked drive to an immaculate Renaissance château in harmonious grounds. Find painted 17th-century beams in perfect condition, heads of antelope and oryx surprising the walls, a panelled library, a powder-blue dining room, and fireplaces imposing and theatrical. Here live the Augais family, with horse, hens and handsome gundogs. In big peaceful bedrooms with tall windows are chestnut floors and grey-washed beams, oriental carpets, quilted bedspreads, boudoir armchairs, deep baths (with shower attachments) and exquisite curtain tassels. Take a dip in the discreet pool; set off for culture in Caen. Marvellous.

Ferme Le Petit Val

Close to landing beaches, village markets, the Bayeux Tapestry and jolly Caen is this perfectly maintained and very French farmstead, Outside, shrubs, conifers and a profusion of flowers; inside, country comfort and handsome furniture. It's been in the family for six generations, all is immaculate and the Lesages look after you with an easy charm. Off a Frenchly wallpapered landing, with views of garden and pretty gravelled courtyard, are the two biggest and most characterful bedrooms. Expect good china and jams at breakfast's long tables, tourist brochures on the sideboard, mountain bikes to borrow.

Rooms	2: 1 twin, 1 family suite for 3.
Price	€180-€230.
Meals	Restaurants 5km.
Closed	October-April.

Rooms	5: 1 double, 1 family room for 3. Barn: 1 double, 1 twin, 1 family room for 3.
Price	€60-€66. Family room €60-€90. Singles €54. Extra bed €25.
Meals	Restaurants 3km.
Closed	December-March.

Philippe Augais
Château de Bénéauville,
Bénéauville, 14860 Bavent,
Calvados
Tel +33 (0)2 31 72 56 49
Email reservation@chateaudebeneauville.fr
Web www.chateaudebeneauville.fr

Gérard & Anne Lesage
Ferme Le Petit Val,
24 rue du Camp Romain,
14480 Banville, Calvados
Tel +33 (0)2 31 37 92 18
Mobile +33 (0)6 87 03 85 52
Email fermelepetitval@wanadoo.fr
Web www.ferme-le-petitval.com

Entry 226 Map 4

Entry 227 Map 4

Normandy

Nuage Neuf

The views from Nuage Neuf are simply spectacular and make the somewhat steep climb – especially to the Cirrus attic room – worthwhile. The décor is simple, with pale colours throughout set off by the occasional silver lining and the beds (and, indeed, the floors and walls) incredibly soft. All rooms have showers, starting off hot in the morning, cooling rapidly towards mid-afternoon. Breakfast is served in the communal dining room and features light and airy creations made with locally sourced H and O. Your host, Rob McKenna, is well known in the area*, although the parties he throws are a little thin on atmosphere…

*and in the novels of Douglas Adams

Rooms	3 swanky suites.
Price	£1,000 per week. Not bookable through Sawday's Canopy & Stars online, nor by phone.
Meals	Restaurants: distance variable.
Closed	Never.

	Sawday's Canopy & Stars Nuage Neuf, 34 rue de Stratus, Cumulus, Manche
Tel	+44 (0)1275 395447
Email	IncrementalPrecipInducer@gmail.fr
Web	www.canopyandstars.co.uk

Entry 228   Map 5

Normandy

Le Mas Normand

A fun place, warm and colourful, and Christian a chef: the food is exceptional! Mylène is a live wire, both are sociable, informal and attentive. They've done a great job on their lovely 18th-century house: old stonework and beams, modern showers, a neo-rustic style, Provençal fabrics and soaps from Mylène's native Drôme. Bedrooms are sheer delight: the sunny much-furnished double on the ground floor, the charming suites across the yard, filled with good pieces including an *armoire de mariage*. The new family room? A big comfy eco-caravan. Ducks, geese and hens roam, the beach is a short drive. Generous and special.

Rooms	4: 1 double, 2 suites for 2-4, 1 gypsy caravan.
Price	€75. Suite €95-€140. Gypsy caravan €95-€140. Extra charge for pets.
Meals	Dinner with wine, €35-€45.
Closed	Rarely.

	Christian Mériel & Mylène Gilles Le Mas Normand, 8 impasse de la Rivière, 14114 Ver sur Mer, Calvados
Tel	+33 (0)2 31 21 97 75
Email	lemasnormand@wanadoo.fr
Web	www.lemasnormand.com

Entry 229   Map 4

Normandy

La Malposte

It's just plain lovely, this little group of stone buildings with a wooden footbridge over the rushing river, ancient steps, moss, trees, a fine garden with flowers and hens. The age-old converted mill is for the family, the hunting lodge (and an enchanting annexe) is for guests. Patricia's talented decoration weaves nostalgia with designer tones; spiral stair winds to an enchanting dayroom with guest kitchen and homemade preserves (superb fig jam); sun pours into the bedroom at the top. Woods for nut-gathering, beaches nearby, table tennis and that playful stream. Your hosts are sweet and love having families.

Unfenced water.

Rooms	4: 1 double, 1 family suite (1 double, 1 twin). Cottage: 1 double, 1 family room for 3.
Price	€88. Family room €108. Family suite €134.
Meals	Guest kitchen. Restaurants 2km.
Closed	Rarely.

Patricia & Jean-Michel Blanlot
La Malposte,
15 rue des Moulins, 14470 Reviers,
Calvados

Tel	+33 (0)2 31 37 51 29
Email	jean-michel.blanlot@wanadoo.fr
Web	www.lamalposte.com

Entry 230   Map 4

Normandy

Château de Colombières

A long curving drive, a breathtaking first view, a bridge to a courtyard and there is Monsieur (senior) – charming, witty, dapper. Enter the 18th-century dining room, where breakfasts are served at a table under the gaze of an ancestress, rescuer of Colombières after the Revolution. The suites are three centuries older, one vast and reached via a circular elm-tread stair. The Louis XVI room is as lofty, as sumptuous, its fabrics coordinated, its bathroom with green tiles and medieval tomettes. Garden arbours are equipped with chairs… wander at will, fish in the moat. A privilege to stay here – with Monsieur *tout compris*!

Rooms	3: 1 double, 2 suites.
Price	€150-€200. Suites €150-€240. Extra bed €40.
Meals	Breakfast €10 (child €5). Restaurant 15km.
Closed	Late-October to early-April.

Charles & Claire de Maupeou
d'Ableiges
Château de Colombières,
14710 Colombières, Calvados

Tel	+33 (0)2 31 22 51 65
Email	colombieresaccueil@aliceadsl.fr
Web	www.chateaudecolombieres.com

Entry 231   Map 3

Normandy

Le Château

The château dates proudly from 1580; later, Emile Zola stayed. In the yard, now restored to tremendous shape and character as a garden area for guests, an ancient arched barn houses three beamy bedrooms (admire astounding roof timbers through a trap window). Just beyond the flowering stone steps, the fourth room is in a tiny cottage. These country-elegant rooms are beautiful in Jouy and stripes, restful and private. Madame is a vibrantly warm, well-read, eco-friendly person, who speaks good English, loves having guests and can discourse at fascinating length about the Vikings, the Inuit, the Dukes of Normandy...

Rooms	4: 2 doubles, 1 twin, 1 suite.
Price	€70-€85.
Meals	Dinner with wine or cider, €35. Child €20. Restaurants nearby.
Closed	December to mid-January.

Dominique Bernières
Le Château,
Chemin du Château,
14450 Grandcamp Maisy,
Calvados

Tel +33 (0)2 31 22 66 22
Email marionbandb@wanadoo.fr
Web perso.wanadoo.fr/alain.marion/gbindex.html

Entry 232 Map 3

Normandy

L'Hermerel

Some sort of perfection? A round pigeon tower, a private chapel and lovely hosts complete the picture of this charming, part 15th-century fortified (still working) dairy farm. The lofty beamed rooms and vast fireplaces have been carefully restored and all is unpretentiously stylish with a relaxed atmosphere. Up the old worn stone stair of the interconnecting guest wing are green velvet armchairs, taffeta curtains and vases of wild flowers: the two bedrooms have been decorated beautifully. Come for stunning breakfasts (compotes, farm milk, special jams, several breads), a walled garden to share, and the sea a short walk away.

Minimum two nights at weekends.

Rooms	2: 1 family room, 1 suite.
Price	€70.
Meals	Restaurants in Grandcamp Maisy.
Closed	November-March.

François & Agnès Lemarié
L'Hermerel,
14230 Géfosse Fontenay,
Calvados

Tel +33 (0)2 31 22 64 12
Mobile +33 (0)6 79 44 58 24
Email hermerel@orange.fr
Web www.manoir-hermerel.com

Entry 233 Map 3

Normandy

Ferme-Manoir de la Rivière

Breakfast by the massive fireplace may be oil lamp-lit on winter mornings in this 13th-century fortress of a dairy farm, with its ancient tithe barn and little watchtower. Isabelle is proud of her family home, its flagstones worn smooth with age, its high vaulted stone living-room ceiling, its second-floor rooms, one narrow with a shower in a tower, one with exposed beams and *ciel de lit* drapes. Her energy boundless, she is ever improving her rooms, gives you homemade brioche for breakfast and imaginative Norman cuisine – much supported by delightful Gérard.

Out-of-season cookery weekends. Sawday self-catering also.

Rooms	3: 1 double, 2 triples.
Price	€65-€75.
Meals	Dinner with cider or wine, €27.
Closed	Rarely.

Gérard & Isabelle Leharivel
Ferme-Manoir de la Rivière,
14230 Géfosse Fontenay,
Calvados
Tel   +33 (0)2 31 22 64 45
Mobile   +33 (0)6 81 58 25 21
Email   leharivel@wanadoo.fr
Web   www.lemanoirdelariviere.net

Entry 234   Map 3

Normandy

Manoir de la Fèvrerie

Your blithe, beautiful, energetic hostess is a delight, forever indulging her passion for interior decoration. Her exquisite rooms are a festival of colours, textures, antiques and embroidered linen and the adorable little cottage (with log fire) is ideal for families. It's a heart-warming experience to stay in this wonderful old Normandy farmhouse where the great granite hearth is always lit and breakfast of superb local specialities is served on elegant china; there is a richly carved 'throne' at the head of the long table. A pretty garden behind, in soft countryside a short drive from Barfleur.

Children's room available in main house.

Rooms	4: 3 twins/doubles. 1 family cottage for 4 (2 twins/doubles).
Price	€72-€80. Cottage €130.
Meals	Restaurants 3km.
Closed	Rarely.

Marie-France Caillet
Manoir de la Fèvrerie,
4 route d'Arville,
50760 Ste Geneviève, Manche
Tel   +33 (0)2 33 54 33 53
Mobile   +33 (0)6 80 85 89 01
Email   lafevrerie@orange.fr
Web   www.lafevrerie.fr

Entry 235   Map 3

Normandy

Bruce Castle

Live graciously – even if it's only for a stopover (Cherbourg is 15km away). The Fontanets are a charming and amusing couple and their 1914 neo-classical mansion is full of pretty antiques. From the restrained elegance of the hall a handsome white staircase sweeps up to big, serene bedrooms with garden and woodland views; oriental rugs and crystal chandeliers add another dash of luxury. Breakfast off white porcelain with antique silver cutlery in a charming dining room then retire to the elegant 'library' overlooking the gardens. In the 20-acre grounds are the ruins of an 11th-century castle... to stay here is a massive treat.

Rooms	3 doubles.
Price	€110-€130.
Meals	Restaurant 8km. Simple bistro 3km.
Closed	Rarely.

Anne-Rose & Hugues Fontanet
Bruce Castle,
13 rue du Castel, 50700 Brix,
Manche

Tel	+33 (0)2 33 41 99 62
Mobile	+33 (0)6 72 95 74 23
Email	bruce-castle@orange.fr
Web	www.bruce-castle.com

Entry 236   Map 3

Normandy

Manoir de Bellauney

Even the smallest bathroom oozes atmosphere through its *œil de bœuf*. The youngest piece of this fascinating and venerably ancient house is over 400 years old; its predecessor stood on the site of a monastery, the fireplace in the lovely 'Medieval' bedroom carries the coat of arms of the original owners. To furnish the rooms, your ex-farmer hosts hunted out carved *armoires de mariage*, lace canopies, footstools – and hung tapestry curtains at the windows. They share their energy enthusiastically between this wonderful house, its small dense garden, and their guests. Sheer comfort among warm old stones.

Rooms	3: 1 double, 2 suites for 2-3.
Price	€70-€100. Suites €90-€100.
Meals	Restaurants 4km.
Closed	November-April.

Christiane & Jacques
Allix-Desfauteaux
Manoir de Bellauney,
50700 Tamerville,
Manche

Tel	+33 (0)2 33 40 10 62
Email	bellauney@wanadoo.fr
Web	www.bellauney.com

Entry 237   Map 3

Normandy

Château de Pont Rilly

The Roucherays' passion, talent and attention to detail have wrought a miracle of beauty and harmony. It helps to be a restorer like Jean-Jacques who mixes his own paints; and a decorator like Annick who creates the bedspreads, curtains and cushions. Beautiful breakfast is served in the old kitchen with its monumental fireplace and original spit mechanism; beds in the rooms above sit on rare Marie Antoinette parquet. One overlooks the front moat, paddocks and long drive. There are trout and eel in the stream, donkeys, sheep and goats in the paddocks and Léonne, a friendly peacock, shows up for the welcome.

Rooms	4: 3 doubles, 1 suite.
Price	€150. Suite €200.
Meals	Restaurants 3km.
Closed	Never.

Annick & Jean-Jacques Roucheray
Château de Pont Rilly,
50260 Négreville,
Manche

Tel	+33 (0)2 33 40 47 50
Email	chateau.pont.rilly@gmail.com
Web	www.chateau-pont-rilly.com

Entry 238   Map 3

Normandy

Brown Owl House

Philomena and Pierre – she Irish, he French – are generous, hospitable and fun and you pretty much get the run of their big, solid, 400-year-old farmhouse. The style is contemporary-formal and the atmosphere chatty, laid back and child-friendly. Philomena is a professionally trained cook: book 24 hours ahead and you will be treated to a delectable Anglo-French dinner. The living room, vast and open-plan, is part clear up to the rafters, part overlooked by an attractive mezzanine. The peaceful and immaculate bedrooms have honey-coloured floorboards and views over the immense garden and tree-lined fields.

Rooms	5: 3 doubles, 1 twin sharing 2 bathrooms; 1 family room for 4.
Price	€70-€90.
Meals	Dinner with wine, €30.
Closed	Rarely.

Philomena & Pierre Van der Linden
Brown Owl House,
7 route du Château,
Ferme de la Poissonnerie,
50390 Golleville, Manche

Tel	+33 (0)2 33 01 20 45
Email	contact@brown-owl-house.com
Web	www.brown-owl-house.com

Entry 239   Map 3

Normandy

Le Château

Gravel crunches as you sweep up to the imposing granite château on the Cherbourg peninsula. The beguiling fairytale turrets, Françoise's welcome and Bernard's collection of vintage horse-driven carriages (the whole family love horses) soon work their magic. External stone stairs lead to the red-velvet charm of the 'Chambre Château'; ancient chestnut stairs in the converted outbuilding lead to simple family rooms. In the morning, as you breakfast generously in a light-flooded, pink-panelled family dining room and sip your café au lait, you might like to nod a grateful 'merci' to Bernard's obliging Normandy cows.

Rooms	3: 1 double. Outbuilding: 1 double, 1 family suite for 4.
Price	€110. Family suite €80–€150.
Meals	Restaurant 500m.
Closed	Rarely.

Françoise Lucas de Vallavieille
Le Château,
50700 Flottemanville Bocage,
Manche
Tel   +33 (0)2 33 40 29 02
Mobile   +33 (0)6 99 06 59 82
Email   contact@chateau-flottemanville.com
Web   www.chateau-flottemanville.com

Entry 240   Map 3

Normandy

La Roque de Gouey

A fishing and sailing port and a bridge with 13 arches: a pretty place to stay. The enchanting *longère* is the home of two of our favourite owners: Madame, the same honest open character as ever and Monsieur, retired, who has time to spread his modest farmer's joviality. Your side of the house has its own entrance, dayroom and vast old fireplace where old beams and *tomettes* flourish. The bedrooms up the steepish outside stairs are small, with pretty bedcovers and antiques that are cherished, the ground-floor room is larger, and the breakfast tables sport flowery cloths. Brilliant value.

Rooms	4: 2 doubles, 1 family room for 3, 1 family room for 5.
Price	€55. Family rooms €70–€100.
Meals	Guest kitchen. Restaurants 500m.
Closed	Rarely.

Bernadette Vasselin
La Roque de Gouey,
Rue Gilles Poërier,
50580 Portbail,
Manche
Tel   +33 (0)2 33 04 80 27
Email   vasselin.portbail@orange.fr

Entry 241   Map 3

Normandy

La Vimonderie

Sigrid's big country kitchen and crackling fire are the heart of this fine 18th-century granite house and you know instantly you are sharing her home: the built-in dresser carries pretty china, her pictures and ornaments bring interest to the salon and its Normandy fireplace, and she proudly tells how she rescued the superb elm staircase. A fascinating person, for years a potter in England, she has retired to France and vegetarian happiness; she loves to cook for guests. Bedrooms have colour, unusual antiques and original beams. Five acres of garden mean plenty of space for children and grown-ups alike. Great value.

Minimum two nights.

Rooms	2 doubles.
Price	€50.
Meals	Dinner with wine, from €18. Light supper from €10. Picnics from €5. Guest kitchen.
Closed	January/February.

Sigrid Hamilton
La Vimonderie,
50620 Cavigny, Manche
Tel   +33 (0)2 33 56 01 13
Mobile   +33 (0)6 59 21 48 07
Email   sigrid.hamilton@googlemail.com
Web   www.lavimonderie.com

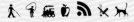

Entry 242   Map 3

Normandy

Manoir de la Porte

A pepperpot turret gives a medieval flourish to the sturdy, creeper-dressed 16th-century manoir. There's a Japanese bridge to the jungly island, a large and luscious garden, two bright, romantic top-floor bedrooms with old-fashioned bathrooms and a tempting sitting area; a fabulously ancient, tiled dining room with huge fireplace, a trio of tables and solid granite walls. Add ethnic rugs and a pair of curly-toed Rajasthani slippers on the stone stairs. Your friendly, chatty, ex-army hosts are great travellers. And Madame is a keen and gifted cook – championing all things local. Apple gâteau for breakfast anyone?

Rooms	2 family rooms for 3.
Price	Family rooms €70-€85.
Meals	Dinner with wine, €21. Kitchen available.
Closed	Rarely.

Annick & Hervé Lagadec
Manoir de la Porte,
50870 Ste Pience, Manche
Tel   +33 (0)2 33 68 13 61
Email   manoir.de.la.porte@wanadoo.fr
Web   www.manoir-de-la-porte.com

Entry 243   Map 3

Normandy

2 Le Bois de Crépi

Madame's welcome is as cheerful and bright as her bedrooms – and she loves to cook. The Gavards' immaculate 1980s house, resting in one pretty acre (lawns, roses, little footbridge over the pond) is the perfect stopover: near the autoroute yet truly tranquil. Borrow bikes and cycle the 'voie verte' to Mont St Michel or spend the day in St Malo. Then come home to friendly table d'hôtes and a great-value menu that reflects the seasons. There's a guest sitting room to retire to, with guide books, games, TV; and bedrooms are under the eaves, warm, simple, characterful, with brand new beds and flowers. Bathrooms gleam.

Rooms	2 family rooms for 2-4.
Price	€50-€57. Extra bed €12. Under 3's free.
Meals	Dinner, 3 courses with wine, €18. Child €10. Restaurants 1km.
Closed	Rarely.

Jean-Paul & Brigitte Gavard
2 Le Bois de Crépi,
Poilley, 50220 Ducey, Manche
Tel   +33 (0)2 33 48 34 68
Mobile +33 (0)6 65 31 99 99
Email   jpgavard@club-internet.fr

Entry 244   Map 3

Normandy

Les Blotteries

Monsieur, formerly a fire officer, is proud of his restored farm (the B&B is his project; Madame works in town). He is an attentive, positive host, full of smiles, jokes and enthusiasm for local food; he creates over 300 pots of jam a year with fruit from the garden! Old granite glints as you pass into the softly-curtained entrance; an original hay rack hangs above. Spacious bedrooms are dotted about the house, stable block or former bakery; the ground-floor family room has large windows overlooking the courtyard. The cream breakfast room is simple and elegant and the fields around are open to all.

Rooms	4: 1 double, 2 triples, 1 family room for 4.
Price	€70-€100. Cot €15.
Meals	Restaurants 1km.
Closed	Rarely.

Laurence & Jean-Malo Tizon
Les Blotteries,
50220 Juilley, Manche
Tel   +33 (0)2 33 60 84 95
Email bb@les-blotteries.com
Web   www.les-blotteries.com

Entry 245   Map 3

Normandy

La Gautraie

Come for a slice of French farmhouse life. Catherine is quietly friendly and provides mouthwatering Norman cuisine – she loves it. Naturally hospitable, she and François cook, serve, clear, and always find time for a glass of calvados with their guests. The old granite stable block, built in 1622, was last modernised in the 1970s. Polished floors, a few heirlooms, a cot in the attic room, a couple of kitchenettes and a dining room with a big table make this suitable for families on a budget. The poetically named but perfectly ordinary Two Estuaries motorway provides quick access one kilometre away.

Rooms	4: 2 doubles, 2 family rooms for 3-4.
Price	€55. Family rooms €70–€80.
Meals	Dinner with wine, €20.
Closed	Christmas.

François & Catherine Tiffaine
La Gautraie,
50240 St James, Manche
Tel +33 (0)2 33 48 31 86
Email ctiffaine@hotmail.fr
Web www.tiffaine.com

Entry 246 Map 3

Normandy

Belle Vallée

Built in 1800, the tall house stands in acres of woods, pastures and landscaped gardens, with outbuildings (the owners' quarters) and cottage. Footpaths meander to a lovely walled orchard, the kitchen garden provides for table d'hôtes, the hens donate the eggs. Inside are corridors alive with books, five delightful bedrooms – vintage beds, polished floors, boudoir chairs, delicious duvets – and an inviting sitting room with a log fire. In the panelled dining room, hospitable Richard and Victoria, both from the catering industry, serve French breakfasts at crisp tables. Domfront on its hill is wonderfully close.

Rooms	5: 3 doubles, 2 quadruples.
Price	€70–€90. Quadruples €90–€120. Extra bed €10.
Meals	Dinner, 4 courses with wine, €23. Restaurants 5-minute drive.
Closed	Rarely.

Victoria & Richard Hobson-Cossey
Belle Vallée,
61700 Domfront, Orne
Tel +33 (0)2 33 37 05 71
Email info@belle-vallee.net
Web www.belle-vallee.net

Entry 247 Map 4

Normandy

Le Mesnil

There are fresh flowers everywhere and your hosts, retired farmers, offer true country hospitality. Peace is the norm, not the exception, in this deeply rural spot, racehorses graze in the pasture and you are unhesitatingly received into a warm and lively extended family. The rooms, in a converted self-contained side wing, have an appropriately rustic air with beams, old wardrobes and tiny kitchenettes. The ground-floor room has a little private garden; up steepish stairs the bedroom is bigger. Breakfast is in the family dining room, with tiled floors and a large fireplace. Children are welcome to visit the family farm next door.

Rooms	2 doubles with kitchenettes.
Price	€54.
Meals	Restaurant 5km.
Closed	Rarely.

Janine & Rémy Laignel
Le Mesnil,
61200 Occagnes,
Orne
Tel +33 (0)2 33 67 11 12

Entry 248 Map 4

Normandy

Le Prieuré St Michel

An atmospheric time warp for the night on the St Michel pilgrim route: traditional décor in the timbered 14th-century monks' storeroom with tapestry wall covering and antiques, or the old dairy, or a converted stable; a huge 15th-century cider press for breakfast in the company of the Ulrichs' interesting choice of art; a chapel for yet more art, a tithe barn in magnificent condition for fabulous receptions, perfectly stupendous gardens, a sort of medieval revival. Your hosts are totally devoted to their fabulous domain and its listed buildings and happy to share it with guests who appreciate its historical value.

Rooms	5: 2 doubles, 1 twin/double, 2 suites.
Price	€110-€125. Suites €140.
Meals	Restaurant 4km.
Closed	Rarely.

Jean-Pierre & Viviane Ulrich
Le Prieuré St Michel,
61120 Crouttes, Orne
Tel +33 (0)2 33 39 15 15
Email leprieuresaintmichel@wanadoo.fr
Web www.prieure-saint-michel.com

Entry 249 Map 4

Normandy

Le Marnis

Barbara's delight in her "corner of paradise" is contagious. In utter peace among the cattle-dotted Norman pastures, here is one brave, outspoken woman, her horse, cats and big waggy Alsatian in a low-lying farmhouse, beautifully rebuilt "from a pile of stones", where old and new mix easily and flowers rampage. The lovely sloping garden is all her own work too – she's getting on but has apparently endless energy. The pastel guest rooms, one upstairs with orchard views, the other down with doors to the garden, are pleasantly floral. The village provides everything, and Sées is nearby.

Babies & children over 10 welcome.

Rooms	1 twin/double.
Price	€65-€70.
Meals	Restaurants in Sées, 15km.
Closed	Rarely.

Barbara Goff
Le Marnis,
Tellières le Plessis,
61390 Courtomer, Orne
Tel   +33 (0)2 33 27 47 55
Email   barbara.goff@wanadoo.fr

🚶 🐱 🐕 🐴 ౫౹

Entry 250   Map 4

Normandy

Les Larry

Just beyond the village of St Quentin de Blavou, this 19th-century farmhouse has long sweeping views across the valley and Norman countryside. Isobel is a bubbly Englishwoman who settled here in 2004; her Shetland and Connemara ponies keep her busy – she teaches, too – but she's still a hands-on hostess. The cosy double has a sloping roof and beams; use the second room, where the bed doubles as a divan, as your sitting room – or sit and chat with Isobel in hers. In fine weather you can breakfast on the terrace and drink in the view. Head out to the countryside for biking and hiking – the peace is divine!

Rooms	2: 1 double, 1 single sharing bathroom (let to same party only).
Price	€50. Singles €40-€45.
Meals	Restaurants 7km.
Closed	Rarely.

Isobel Jagger
Les Larry,
61360 St Quentin de Blavou, Orne
Tel   +33 (0)2 33 73 17 87
Email   isobel.jagger@nordnet.fr
Web   www.chambresdhotesleslarry61360.com

📶 🐱 🐕

Entry 251   Map 4

Le Tertre

Pilgrims have trudged by towards Mont St Michel since the 1500s and the search for inner peace continues: yoga and meditation groups come but never overlap with B&B. Anne talks brilliantly about her exotic travels, is active in the village and pours her creative energy into her house, with the help of an excellent restorer. Both elegantly simple rooms have clear personalities, good beds and sitting spaces, antiques, soft colours and privacy. The Tower Suite, bliss for honeymooners, comes with a six-seater jacuzzi. Stunning views, and super breakfast in the big kitchen, served with love.

Spa in Tower Suite.

Hôtel de Suhard

Bellême – a famously beautiful medieval town of cobbled streets, markets and gourmet restaurants. On its square a tall, shuttered, oh-so-French mansion with a 16th-century pedigree. Interiors are gorgeously unfussy: Louis XV fireplaces, tinkling chandeliers and claw-foot baths. Two bedrooms overlook the walled garden – for breakfasts of fresh fruits and pastries – with views to the countryside; three overlook the road and the quaint town. All are divine. Run by sympathetic Parisian owners with exceptional attention to detail, there are mushroom forays in autumn, order-in dinner on fine china, and three types of coffee for breakfast.

Rooms	2: 1 twin, 1 suite.
Price	€98. Suite €145.
Meals	Restaurants 6km.
Closed	January.

Rooms	5: 2 doubles, 1 twin/double, 2 suites.
Price	£65-£115. Suites £75-£120. Extra bed €25.
Meals	Restaurant 500m. Catered dinner available.
Closed	December-March.

Anne Morgan
Le Tertre,
61360 Montgaudry, Orne
Tel +33 (0)2 33 25 59 98
Email annemorgan@nordnet.fr
Web www.french-country-retreat.com

Josiane Lenoir
Hôtel de Suhard,
34 rue d'Alençon,
61130 Bellême, Orne
Tel +33 (0)2 33 83 53 47
Mobile +33 (0)6 79 64 35 21
Email contact@hotel-de-suhard.fr
Web www.hotel-de-suhard.fr

Normandy

Château de la Mouchère

Art Deco enthusiasts will happily splash out on a stay at this 18th-century château. Bold tiling, muted colours and elegant windows characterise the interior, while magnificent trees and soft parkland promise leafy strolls. Lucky dogs are treated to their own towel and biscuits on arrival – the laundry room with washing and sewing facilities is an added plus – while the sunny south-facing terrace is a birdwatcher's dream. Charming, cultured, generous Roger and Marie-Monique give you homemade jams at breakfast, the best local produce at dinner and keep parkland, gardens and outbuildings pristine.

Rooms	5: 3 doubles, 2 suites for 2-4.
Price	€110–€150. Suites €160–€190.
Meals	Dinner with wine, €30–€40. Restaurant 5km.
Closed	Rarely.

Marie-Monique Huss
Château de la Mouchère,
61130 St Cyr la Rosière, Orne
Tel   +33 (0)2 33 83 02 99
Mobile   +33 (0)6 32 35 92 66
Email   lamouchere@gmail.com
Web   lamouchere.com

Entry 254   Map 4

Normandy

La Cabane du Perche

Up in the branches, on the edge of the huge forest of the Perche, this treehouse might be too comfortable: guests have been known not to come down for days. Fans of quirky furniture – all created to the owners' designs – will love it. There's room for four in a double and two bunks, one just child-size, all hand carved. Shower and basin are made from recycled wine barrels; the compost loo illustrates the green ethos here. Bread, milk, cheese and cider are sourced from local farms and breakfast is served on the terrace. For the active, horse riding is popular – or take a carriage ride in the forest, an unforgettable bit of fun.

Book through Sawday's Canopy & Stars online or by phone.

Rooms	1 treehouse for 4: 1 double, 2 bunks (1 for children only).
Price	£120–£140.
Meals	Restaurants 5km.
Closed	Open all year.

Sawday's Canopy & Stars
La Cabane du Perche,
La Maslotière,
61400 St Mard de Réno, Orne
Tel   +44 (0)1275 395447
Email   enquiries@canopyandstars.co.uk
Web   www.canopyandstars.co.uk/
cabaneduperche

Entry 255   Map 4

Normandy

Château de la Grande Noë

Much to love here: trompe-l'œil marble and Wedgwood mouldings inherited from an Adam-inspired ancestor who escaped the French Revolution; chamber music in the log-fired drawing room; breakfast in a room wrapped in oak panelling inlaid with precious woods; elegant, alcoved bedrooms full of antiques, books, ancestral portraits, soft comforts; a bathroom through a secret door, a loo in a tower. And the delightful Longcamps are a wonderful couple, she vivaciously cultured and musical, he a retired camembert-maker who enjoys his estate. The French-formal garden overlooks paddocks and agricultural plains; walks start a mile away.

It is essential to book well ahead for July and August, and wise for other months.

Do say roughly what time you will arrive (normally after 4pm), as most hosts like to welcome you personally.

Do consider stopping for more than one night where you might otherwise be 'travelling through'.

Rooms	8: 2 doubles, 1 twin, 5 treehouses for 2.
Price	€100-€130. Treehouses €112-€142.
Meals	Restaurants 5km.
Closed	December-March, except by arrangement.

	Jacques & Pascale de Longcamp
	Château de la Grande Noë,
	61290 Moulicent, Orne
Tel	+33 (0)2 33 73 63 30
Mobile	+33 (0)6 87 65 88 47
Email	contact@chateaudelagrandenoe.com
Web	www.chateaudelagrandenoe.com

Entry 256   Map 4

Brittany

Brittany

Épineu

Fear not, the farm mess is forgotten once you reach the cottage and the long rural views beyond. Yvette, generous, sociable, sprightly and very charming, will lead you into her big, wood-floored and -ceilinged country dining room – warmed in winter by the old stone fireplace. It is uncluttered and soberly French. Bedrooms are a good size, the most characterful one is in the main house. The country garden, tended with love and pride, is a delightful space of peace. Breakfasts are legendary and you will be spoiled outrageously; Madame may join you if you are just two. Deep in the countryside, this place is a joy.

Rooms	3: 1 triple. Annexe: 1 double, 1 twin sharing bathroom.
Price	€58. Extra bed €20.
Meals	Restaurant 3km.
Closed	Rarely.

Yvette Guillopé
Épineu,
35890 Bourg des Comptes,
Ille-et-Vilaine
Tel   +33 (0)2 99 52 16 84
Mobile +33 (0)6 25 60 23 22

Entry 257   Map 3

Brittany

Le Presbytère

An old stone parsonage; new generation B&B; a revelation! Pascal and Odile have transformed a plain home into a bold, funky and joyful place to stay. The two suites have mezzanine bedrooms and bathrooms: the Indian Room has authentic antiques, splashes of pink and a superb mosaic; the Design Room a vintage button sofa, Warhol art and a sunken jacuzzi. Both have ultra modern TVs, private decks and garden views. Indulge in homemade waffles, a dip in the plunge pool, a lazy read in the shade of the fruit trees. Or explore the nearby forest – 20 minutes from Rennes. Odile, a free spirit, and Pascal are charming.

Rooms	2 suites.
Price	€75–€105.
Meals	Dinner €20–€25.
Closed	Rarely.

Pascal & Odile Béranger
Le Presbytère, 4 rue du Tertre Gris,
35320 Pancé, Ille-et-Vilaine
Tel   +33 (0)2 99 43 00 75
Mobile +33 (0)6 64 77 61 76
Email beranger.pascal@voila.fr
Web   www.presbytere-chambresdhotesdecharme-
       bretagne.com/

Entry 258   Map 3

Brittany

Château du Quengo

Anne, descendant of an ancient Breton family, and her charming Swiss husband welcome you open-armed to their inimitable house. History, atmosphere and silence rule: private chapel, bio-garden and rare trees outside, carved chestnut staircase, Italian mosaic floor, 1800s wallpaper, about 30 rooms inside. Anne runs willow-weaving classes and plies you with homemade delights; Alfred builds organs and loves animals, gardens and music: the slow life. Bedrooms have antique radiators and are properly old-fashioned, our favourite the family room. No plastic anything, few mod cons – just intelligent, humorous hosts and a beautiful place.

Sawday self-catering also.

Rooms	5: 1 family room for 3; 2 doubles, 2 twins sharing 2 bathrooms.
Price	€50-€80.
Meals	Guest kitchen. Restaurants 1.5km.
Closed	Rarely.

Anne & Alfred du Crest de Lorgerie
Château du Quengo,
35850 Irodouër, Ille-et-Vilaine
Tel   +33 (0)2 99 39 81 47
Email   lequengo@hotmail.com
Web   www.chateauduquengo.com

🚶 🕴 🚃 📶 🗡 🐕 🐈

Entry 259   Map 3

Brittany

La Lande

A delightful find only five minutes from the motorway – a pretty stone and cob longère from the 17th century. Chantal and Franck came here 14 years ago and have been lovingly restoring ever since, creating a happy balance of comfort and charm. Borrow bikes and explore the countryside (mercifully flat) or stroll the gardens and surrounding orchard. Return to a tranquil bedroom with big windows, seagrass matting, a blend of ancient and new furniture and original quirky oils by Franck's father. There's a bistro nearby but, with such well-travelled hosts, why not swap stories over a sumptuous seasonal dinner instead?

Extra bed available.

Rooms	1 double (with separate wc).
Price	€70. Extra bed €18.
Meals	Dinner with wine, €18. Restaurant 3km.
Closed	Rarely.

Chantal & Franck Bauvin
La Lande,
35630 Vignoc, Ille-et-Vilaine
Tel   +33 (0)2 99 69 85 83
Mobile +33 (0)6 31 75 74 57
Email   chantal.bauvin@orange.fr
Web   www.lalandevignoc.com

♿ 🕴 📶 🗡 🐕 🚲

Entry 260   Map 3

Brittany

La Foltière

The setting is magical, the architecture is lovely and the feel is of a hushed and faded stately home. Yet it's not at all precious and children are welcome – note the mazes and bridges, slides and surprises. Tall-windowed bedrooms are big enough to dance in: peachy 'Degas' with its own dressing room, 'Sisley' a symphony in yellow. Breakfast on homemade croissants, parma ham, cheese and a neighbour's homemade jams, then seek out the grounds – magnificent from March to October. Paths meander round the lake and past secret corners bursting with camellias, narcissi, rhododendrons, azaleas, old roses and banks of hydrangea.

Tea room & garden shop open in afternoons.

Rooms	5: 4 doubles, 1 suite.
Price	€158. Suite €178.
Meals	Breakfast €12. Restaurants nearby.
Closed	Christmas.

Alain Jouno
La Foltière,
35133 Le Châtellier,
Ille-et-Vilaine
Tel   +33 (0)2 99 95 48 32
Email   botanique@me.com
Web   www.jardin-garden.com

Entry 261   Map 3

Brittany

La Bossière

Enfolded by cornfields and meadows, at the end of the winding lane, a peaceful old country house with outbuildings, a deep rural escape. English Graham and Jo have found their ideal retreat in La Bossière, surrounded by woodland walks teeming with wildlife. Chutneys and jams come from their own walnuts and fruits, and the veg plot is thriving all year round – dinners are delicious. Find inside a guest sitting/dining room with old beams and granite walls, a wood-burning fire, and a mix of antiques collected worldwide – one a stunning antique four-poster bed. Don't miss Fougères (18km) and the largest fortress in Europe.

Rooms	2: 1 double, 1 four-poster.
Price	€80.
Meals	Dinner with wine, from €28. Restaurants in Louvigné du Désert, 3km.
Closed	Rarely.

Graham & Jo Collins
La Bossière,
35420 Louvigné du Désert,
Ille-et-Vilaine
Tel   +33 (0)2 99 98 13 69
Email   bossiere@btinternet.com
Web   www.la-bossiere.com

Entry 262   Map 3

Brittany

Les Touches

In rolling countryside at the end of the track is an immaculately restored 350-year-old farmhouse. The setting? Three acres of beautifully tended gardens that fall to a babbling brook. In the stone barn are three pretty bedrooms – two cosily under dark beams, the third, for families, with a secluded courtyard aglow with roses and birdsong. Owners Sue and Jerry, new to France, new to B&B, full of plans, love hosting four-course table d'hôtes at their big rustic table. Swings, trampoline and smooth rocks for playing on, an above-ground pool for splashing in, and sofas, books and small log-burner for cosy nights in. Perfect.

Unfenced pool.

Rooms	3: 2 doubles, 1 family room.
Price	€65–€75. Family room €75–€111. Extra bed €18. Cot €10.
Meals	Dinner, 4 courses with wine, €35. Auberge 3km.
Closed	Rarely.

Sue & Jerry Thomas
Les Touches,
35420 St Georges de Reintembault,
Ille-et-Vilaine
Tel   +33 (0)2 99 17 09 91
Email   sue@lestouches.info
Web   www.lestouches.info

Entry 263 Map 3

Brittany

Château de la Ballue

The formal gardens are listed and open to the public, a French reverie of *bosquets* and paths sprinkled with modern sculptures gazing over Mont St Michel. Baroque recitals may ring in the courtyard and Purcell odes float over marble fireplaces, antique paintings, gilded mirrors and orchids. This is no museum, however, but a family home enlivened by children. Sleep deeply in dreamy canopied beds, wake to silver cutlery and a fine continental spread in a blue-panelled breakfast room. Some bedrooms have tented 'cabinets de toilette', birds sing in the *bosquet de musique*. Baroque, family-friendly, enchanting.

Rooms	5: 3 doubles, 1 suite for 2-4, 1 triple.
Price	€195–€215. Suite €240–€295. Triple €280–€335. Extra bed €40.
Meals	Breakfast €18. Restaurants 7km.
Closed	Rarely.

Marie-Françoise Mathiot-Mathon
Château de la Ballue,
35560 Bazouges la Pérouse,
Ille-et-Vilaine
Tel   +33 (0)2 99 97 47 86
Email   chateau@la-ballue.com
Web   www.la-ballue.com

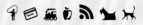

Entry 264 Map 3

Brittany

Le Mesnil des Bois

Lapped by lawn in a deep-forest clearing is a circle of buildings, a 16th-century estate. The charming, amusing Villettes live in the atmospheric manoir, the guests are in the stable block and the renovation is superb. Beautiful bedrooms have lime plaster walls, sleek wooden floors, brocante chandeliers, paintings and vintage bed linen. In the salon, hip sofas wear bright colours and light floods in through high arched windows. Find a spot in the 'village green' courtyard where peonies, perennials and climbing roses grow, and wild deer wander onto the lawn. A little slice of heaven.

Minimum two nights July/Aug & bank holiday weekends.

Rooms	5: 1 double, 1 twin, 3 family rooms for 2-3.
Price	€110-€140. Family room €110-€140.
Meals	Restaurant 1km.
Closed	Mid-November to 1 March.

Martine Villette
Le Mesnil des Bois,
35540 Le Tronchet, Ille-et-Vilaine
Tel   +33 (0)2 99 58 97 12
Mobile   +33 (0)6 82 10 96 11
Email   villette@le-mesnil-des-bois.com
Web   www.le-mesnil-des-bois.com

Entry 265   Map 3

Brittany

Le Presbytère

Inside its walled garden of flower-bordered lawns, orchards and potagers, the vast old priest's house is warm, reassuring and superbly restored. Welcome to a traditional Breton home of ancient beams, twisting staircases, family photos, panelling and ecclesiastical features. Some bathrooms are old-fashioned but each bedroom has character and space – a canopied bed, a striped wall, a garden view; two come with private outside stairs. Madame, a lovely energetic and warmly attentive person, cooks with passion – her dinners are special. A great base for touring St Malo and the bay of Mont St Michel.

Rooms	5: 2 triples, 1 suite for 3; 1 double, 1 twin sharing bathroom.
Price	€60-€70. Triple €85. Suite €100.
Meals	Dinner, 5 courses, €20-€25. Wine €8.50-€30.
Closed	Last two weeks in January.

Madeleine Stracquadanio
Le Presbytère,
35610 Vieux Viel, Ille-et-Vilaine
Tel   +33 (0)2 99 48 65 29
Email   madeleine.stracquadanio@voila.fr
Web   www.vieux-viel.com

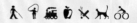

Entry 266   Map 3

Brittany

4 La Hamelinais

The lovely farmhouse, dated 1718, is a genuine, shabby, old-style French B&B: few mod cons but bags of old beams, exposed stones and charm. Marie-Madeleine, who has lived here since childhood, makes it special, preparing a fire in the huge hearth before breakfast, making her own jams, giving her all to garden and orchard. Gentle Jean, retired from the farm, says he "travels through his guests". Up an outside staircase, rooms are old-fashioned, worn and homely (white candlewick on comfy beds), your hosts know and love their region and the sea is close. They are not updating any more but do come before they retire.

Brittany

La Seigneurie

In a seaside town of wide sands and blue sea hides an 18th-century house in a church-side garden: charming Madame's B&B. Across the courtyard, in stable and barn, is the your gorgeous sitting room: a minstrels' gallery, books, magazines, tapestries, an ornate chandelier… and smouldering embers scenting the air. Big bedroom suites are just as enchanting, one on the ground floor, another up private stairs. Fresh flowers and macaroons welcome you, antiques and silver coffee pots delight you, walls are in soft blues and greys, and breakfast arrives in wicker baskets stuffed with local and homemade treats. Seduction by the sea!

Rooms	2: 1 double, 1 triple.
Price	€50-€55. Triple €50-€55.
Meals	Restaurants 4km.
Closed	Rarely.

Rooms	Stables: 1 double, 3 suites for 2-5.
Price	€85. Suites €95-€130.
Meals	Seafood platter with wine, €35-€70. Restaurants 7km.
Closed	Rarely.

Jean & Marie-Madeleine Glémot
4 La Hamelinais,
35120 Cherrueix, Ille-et-Vilaine
Tel +33 (0)2 99 48 95 26
Email lahamelinais@gmail.com
Web www.lahamelinais.com

Françoise Busson
La Seigneurie,
35114 St Benoit des Ondes,
Ille-et-Vilaine
Tel +33 (0)2 99 58 62 96
Mobile +33 (0)6 72 43 06 97
Email contact@la-seigneurie-des-ondes.net
Web www.la-seigneurie-des-ondes.net

Brittany

Malouinière des Trauchandières

This handsome manoir in big peaceful walled gardens has been lovingly restored by Claude, who speaks six languages, and equally well-travelled Agnès; both are charming and gregarious. Theirs is a fascinating house dating from 1510, with French windows opening to a south-facing terrace and a salon lined with rich oak panelling; relax by the blazing fire. Bedrooms, comfortable, traditional and up two sets of stairs, are dominated by dark ships' timbers; the port of St Malo is close, so are golden sand beaches. Breakfast is served beneath the chandelier and there's an annual garden party in the grounds. Marvellous.

Rooms	4: 3 twins/doubles, 1 suite for 3.
Price	€80-€100. Suite €120.
Meals	Hosted dinner with wine, €35. Restaurants in St Meloir, 5-minute drive.
Closed	Rarely.

Agnès François
Malouinière des Trauchandières,
Albiville, St Jouan des Guérets,
35430 St Malo, Ille-et-Vilaine

Tel	+33 (0)2 99 81 38 30
Mobile	+33 (0)6 22 80 47 97
Email	agnesfrancois@hotmail.com
Web	www.les-trauchandieres.com

Entry 269   Map 3

Brittany

Les Mouettes

House and owner are imbued with the calm of a balmy summer's morning, whatever the weather. Isabelle's talent seems to touch the very air that fills her old family house (and smokers are not spurned!). Timeless simplicity reigns; there is nothing superfluous: simple carved pine furniture, an antique wrought-iron cot, dhurries on scrubbed plank floors, palest grey walls to reflect the ocean-borne light, harmonious gingham curtains. Starfish and pebbles keep house and little garden sea-connected, whimsical mobiles add a creative touch. The unspoilt seaside village, popular in season, is worth the trip alone.

Rooms	5: 4 doubles, 1 twin.
Price	€58.
Meals	Restaurants in village.
Closed	Rarely.

Isabelle Rouvrais
Les Mouettes,
17 Grande Rue,
35430 St Suliac,
Ille-et-Vilaine

Tel	+33 (0)2 99 58 30 41
Email	contact@les-mouettes-saint-suliac.com
Web	www.les-mouettes-saint-suliac.com

Entry 270   Map 3

Brittany

Le Clos St Cadreuc

Find peace in this hamlet a pebble's throw from the coast – and driving distance from ten golf courses! There's a welcoming atmosphere in this stone farmhouse, and colour and space in the open-plan dining/sitting room: a friendly place to spend time in. The guest quarters are in the converted stables, very French, very comfortable, with great walk-in showers and hotelly extras; the bright airy mezzanine'd suite 'Viviane' is a triumph. Your warm hosts put Breton dishes on your plate and pour organic wines; between house and stables is a pretty sheltered garden for picnics, potager and DIY barbecues.

Rooms	5: 2 doubles, 1 quadruple, 1 triple, 1 family suite.
Price	€74. Quadruple €74. Triple €80. Family suite €80.
Meals	Dinner with wine, €28.
Closed	Rarely.

Brigitte & Patrick Noël
Le Clos St Cadreuc,
22650 Ploubalay,
Côtes-d'Armor
Tel   +33 (0)2 96 27 32 43
Mobile   +33 (0)6 82 14 94 66
Email   clos-saint-cadreuc@wanadoo.fr
Web   www.clos-saint-cadreuc.com

♁ ♟ ⛟ ☡ ⟆ ✗ ⚲

Entry 271   Map 3

Brittany

Malik

Clad in red cedar, this open-plan Nordic-style house has timber and metal details and sliding glass doors, all in keeping with the woodland feel – and every detail is taken care of. Harmonious covers on excellent beds, oriental wall hangings on restful walls, monogrammed towels, lovely soaps and, across the little footbridge, private seating areas just for you. Breakfast, *un peu brunch*, deliciously Scandinavian, is served in your own little conservatory, with homemade breads and jams. Lovely people and an exquisitely serene house that seems to hug its garden to its heart. A haven on the edge of a small town.

Rooms	2 suites.
Price	€82.
Meals	Restaurants within walking distance.
Closed	January.

Martine & Hubert Viannay
Malik, Chemin de l'Étoupe,
22980 Plélan le Petit,
Côtes-d'Armor
Tel   +33 (0)2 96 27 62 71
Mobile   +33 (0)6 09 92 35 21
Email   malikbretagne@free.fr
Web   www.malik-bretagne.com

♁ ♟ ✗ ⚲

Entry 272   Map 3

Brittany

Le Manoir de la Villeneuve

Embraced by rolling lawns, wooded parkland and sweeping drive, this manor house seems untouched by the 21st century. Light, airy pools of calm – high ceilings, tall windows, polished boards – are furnished with a contemporary elegance while plain walls, beams and tomette floors have been allowed to glow. Beautiful bedrooms have soothing colours, pretty antiques, delicious soaps, beams in some and sloping ceilings; the suite has a vast bathroom and its own salon. Breakfast handsomely at the convivial table, then explore Dinan, St Brieuc, the coast. Return for a dip in the new summer pool. Charming Nathalie oversees all.

Rooms	5: 3 doubles, 1 twin/double, 1 suite for 3.
Price	€75-€140. Suite €75-€140.
Meals	Restaurant 2km.
Closed	Rarely.

Nathalie Peres
Le Manoir de la Villeneuve,
22400 Lamballe,
Côtes-d'Armor

Tel	+33 (0)2 96 50 86 32
Email	manoirdelavilleneuve@wanadoo.fr
Web	www.chambresaumanoir.com

Brittany

Château de Bonabry

An extraordinary old château, built in 1373 by the Viscount's ancestor, with vast, atmospheric bedrooms (not easy to heat!), a lively, loveable couple of aristocratic hosts bent on riding, hunting and entertaining you, fields all around and the sea at the end of the drive. Breakfast till ten on crêpes, croissants and quince jam. Madame is using her energy and taste in renovating some of the rooms; in the suite, original painted panelling, silk curtains and a stag's head on a lustrous wall. Windows tall, portraits ancestral, chapel 18th century, roses glorious – and charming dogs. Unwind and explore the coast.

Sawday self-catering also.

Rooms	2: 1 double with separate bathroom; 1 suite.
Price	€80. Suite €140.
Meals	Bistro in Hillion.
Closed	November-May.

Vicomtesse du Fou de Kerdaniel
Château de Bonabry,
22120 Hillion,
Côtes-d'Armor

Tel	+33 (0)2 96 32 21 06
Email	bonabry@wanadoo.fr
Web	www.bonabry.fr

Brittany

14 rue des Capucins

Big, solid and well-loved, this place wraps you in comfortable, old-world charm. The Pontbriands and their friendly dog are on hand to suggest restaurants, ferry you to the station, yet leave you free to enjoy their home. Downstairs is warm with oak doors and panelling, family antiques, oriental rugs, deep sofas and old leather chairs. The two bedrooms and one bathroom are light and prettily old-fashioned with floral wallpapers and a mêlée of furnishings. St Brieuc is on the doorstep, beaches are 15 minutes away, St Malo and Dinan an hour. And there's a lovely walled garden for summer breakfasts. La vraie France.

Children's rooms & cot available. Close to TGV railway station.

Rooms	2: 1 twin/double; 1 twin/double with separate bathroom.
Price	€65–€80. Child €20.
Meals	Guest kitchenette. Restaurant 5-minute walk.
Closed	November-February.

Serge & Bénédicte de Pontbriand
14 rue des Capucins,
22000 St Brieuc,
Côtes-d'Armor
Tel   +33 (0)2 96 62 08 21
Email   benedictedepontbriand@hotmail.fr
Web   maisondebenedicte.com

Entry 275   Map 3

Brittany

Manoir de Coat Gueno

The 15th-century, country-cocooned manor house is only a short drive from the fishing ports, headlands and long sandy beaches. Wrapped in a rich fluffy towel, gaze out of your lavishly, florally furnished bedroom onto the lawns below. You may hear the crackling of the log fire in the vast stone hearth downstairs, lit by your affable and perfectionist host, the splash and laughter of guests in the pool, or the crack of billiard balls echoing upwards to the tower. The games room and one gorgeous suite are in separate buildings in the grounds. Your attentive host is the perfect French gentleman.

Children over 8 welcome.

Rooms	3: 1 double, 2 suites.
Price	€100–€110. Suites €135–€165.
Meals	Dinner €25. Wine €20.
Closed	September-April.

Christian de Rouffignac
Manoir de Coat Gueno,
Coat Gueno, 22740 Pleudaniel,
Côtes-d'Armor
Tel   +33 (0)2 96 20 10 98
Email   coatguen@aol.com
Web   mapage.noos.fr/coatgueno

Entry 276   Map 2

Brittany

Kerlilou

This may be your dream, too: to leave city jobs, renovate – meticulously, lovingly, yourself, with talent and your well-loved antiques – an ancient farmhouse, then throw it open to like-minded visitors. Pascaline is happy to chat about it, and to cook organic/local dinner at the big kitchen table by the fireplace. She and Patrick are a lovely, anglophile couple, easy, cultured and humorous. Two of the pretty, airy bedrooms are on the ground floor (one through the kitchen); bathrooms have seaweed soap and candles. The setting sun streams out of a dark blue sky onto yellow rapeseed; islands and markets abound. Superb value.

Cots available.

Rooms	5: 1 double, 1 twin/double, 2 triples, 1 family room.
Price	€65–€70. Triples €85. Family room €105.
Meals	Dinner with wine, €25.
Closed	Rarely.

Pascaline & Patrick Cortopassi
Kerlilou,
3 Calvary, 22220 Plouguiel,
Côtes-d'Armor
Tel +33 (0)2 96 92 24 06
Mobile +33 (0)6 17 84 31 08
Email contact@kerlilou.fr
Web www.kerlilou.fr

Entry 277   Map 2

Brittany

À la Corniche

Enter and you will see why we chose this modernised house: the ever-changing light of the great bay shimmers in through vast swathes of glass. Each guest room has its glazed veranda where you can sit and gaze at islands, coastline and sea – stunning. Marie-Clo has enlivened the interior with her patchwork and embroidery, installed a fine new wood-burner in the living space and tea trays in the rooms. It is calm, light, bright; she is attentive, warm and generous, and breakfast is seriously good. A ten-minute stroll brings you to Perros with restaurants and beaches; ideal for couples on a gentle seaside holiday.

Rooms	2 suites.
Price	€90–€95.
Meals	Dinner, €24. Restaurants 400m.
Closed	Rarely.

Marie-Clotilde Biarnès
À la Corniche,
41 rue de la Petite Corniche,
22700 Perros Guirec, Côtes-d'Armor
Tel +33 (0)2 96 23 28 08
Mobile +33 (0)6 81 23 15 49
Email marieclo.biarnes@wanadoo.fr
Web perso.wanadoo.fr/corniche

Entry 278   Map 2

Brittany

Manoir de Kerguéréon

Such gracious hosts with a wonderful sense of humour: you feel you are at a house party; such age and history in the gloriously asymmetrical château: tower, turrets, vast fireplaces, low doors, ancestral portraits, fine furniture; such a lovely garden, Madame's own work. Up the spiral stone staircase are bedrooms with space, taste, arched doors, a lovely window seat to do your tapestry in, good bathrooms; and the great Breton breakfast can be brought up if you wish. Aperitifs among the roses, breakfast before the crackling fire; their son breeds racehorses on the estate and their daughter-in-law runs the B&B. Sheer delight.

Rooms	3: 1 double, 2 twins.
Price	€100. Extra bed €30.
Meals	Restaurants 7km.
Closed	Rarely.

Mr & Mme de Bellefon
Manoir de Kerguéréon,
Ploubezre,
22300 Lannion,
Côtes-d'Armor
Tel   +33 (0)2 96 38 80 59
Mobile   +33 (0)6 03 45 68 55
Email   arnaud.de-bellefon@orange.fr

Entry 279   Map 2

Brittany

Toul Bleïz

There may be badgers and wild boar on the moors but civilisation is a five-minute drive – and you breakfast in a courtyard serenaded by birds. An art teacher in her other life, Julie takes people out painting while Jez concocts delicious vegetarian dishes for your supper. This is a simple Breton cottage with French windows pouring light into a snug and charming ground-floor guest bedroom with a patchwork quilt, lace pillows and little shower room. New for you: a romantic summerhouse in the garden with a wood-burner, armchairs, barbecue and fridge. The village is lovely, the Abbey de Bon Repos is nearby. Great value!

Rooms	1 double.
Price	€60.
Meals	Vegetarian dinner with wine, €22. Picnic available. Summerhouse with kitchenette & BBQ.
Closed	Rarely.

Julie & Jez Rooke
Toul Bleïz,
22570 Laniscat,
Côtes-d'Armor
Tel   +33 (0)2 96 36 98 34
Mobile   +33 (0)6 88 57 75 31
Email   jezrooke@hotmail.com
Web   www.phoneinsick.co.uk

Entry 280   Map 2

Brittany

Manoir de Kerledan

Everyone loves Kerledan, its gargoyles, its sophisticated theatrical décor, its owners' enthusiasm. Peter and Penny have made it stunningly original. Sisal and unstained oak, limed walls, the odd splash of antique mirror or gilded bergère with fake leopard skin create a mood of luxury and calm; slate-floored bathrooms are delicious, candlelit, cut-glass dinners are legendary. Sit by the great dining room fire, stroll in the lovely gardens (baroque courtyard, palisade hornbeam allée, potager), lounge in antique linen in a perfect bedroom and let yourself be pampered by your hosts: arrive as strangers, leave as friends.

Rooms	4: 2 doubles, 1 twin/double, 1 family room.
Price	€90–€135. Family room €105–€145.
Meals	Dinner, 2-3 courses, €23–€28. Wine from €5.
Closed	Mid-November to March.

Peter & Penny Dinwiddie
Manoir de Kerledan,
Route de Kerledan,
29270 Carhaix Plouguer, Finistère
Tel   +33 (0)2 98 99 44 63
Email   kerledan@gmail.com
Web   www.kerledan.com

Entry 281   Map 2

Brittany

Chambres d'Hôtes de Brezehan

Glimpse Lake Drennec from a gap in the hedge before the tree-lined driveway reveals the soft grey stone of the ancient main house – once a weaver's – cloaked in a mass of wisteria, passionflower and roses. This lovely bed and breakfast is run by Catherine and Andreas; charming Catherine's paintings brighten rooms and Andreas' pottery studio sits in perfectly tended gardens. Up a wonderful chestnut staircase, bedrooms are warmly contemporary with earthy tones, some with mezzanine sitting rooms – luxurious. Enjoy organic honey and local jams for breakfast; hike, bike and swim; come home to a delicious log-burning fire.

Rooms	3 doubles.
Price	€58–€73. Extra bed €22.
Meals	Restaurant 5-minute drive.
Closed	Rarely.

Catherine & Andreas Merenyi
Chambres d'Hôtes de Brezehan,
Brézéhant, 29450 Commana,
Finistère
Tel   +33 (0)2 98 78 02 32
Email   contact@bnb-brittany.com
Web   www.bnb-brittany.com

Entry 282   Map 2

Brittany

La Grange de Coatélan

Yolande is a smiling young grandmother of three, Charlick the most sociable workaholic you could find. They are artistic (he paints) and fun. They have beautifully renovated their old Breton weaver's house and converted other ruins into rooms for guests. Their small auberge is mostly doing table d'hôtes now – a single menu of traditional dishes – and the food is brilliant. Bedrooms under the eaves (some steep stairs) have clever layouts, colour schemes and fabrics and an imaginative use of wood. Joyful rustic elegance deep in the countryside, with animals and swings for children's delight.

Minimum two nights in summer.

Rooms	5: 2 doubles, 3 quadruples.
Price	€63–€73. Quadruples €63–€113. Singles €53–€99. Extra bed €7–€25.
Meals	Dinner €23. Wine €17–€57.
Closed	Christmas & New Year.

Charlick & Yolande de Ternay
La Grange de Coatélan,
29640 Plougonven,
Finistère
Tel +33 (0)2 98 72 60 16
Email la-grange-de-coatelan@wanadoo.fr
Web www.lagrangedecoatelan.com

Entry 283　Map 2

Brittany

Manoir de Coat Amour

A dramatic, steep, shrubby drive brings you to a grand old house guarded by stone elephants and a spectacular gem of a chapel: strength and spirit. Set in a paradisiacal park, the Taylors' house overlooks Morlaix yet the traffic hum is minimal, the seclusion total. Chandeliers and antiques, polished floors, Jouy prints and strong colours add to the house-party atmosphere, refined yet comfortable. Jenny and Stafford (she taught textiles) have enjoyed doing their beautiful house in their own style and chat delightedly about it all. Super bedrooms, some connecting, a high colourful guest sitting room, simple luxury.

Minimum two nights July/Aug. Extra beds available.

Rooms	6: 2 doubles, 2 triples, 2 suites for 4-6.
Price	€115–€122. Triple €147–€157. Suites €155–€183. Extra bed €35. Under 2's, €11.
Meals	Dinner with wine, €35–€54. Restaurant 2km.
Closed	Rarely.

Stafford & Jenny Taylor
Manoir de Coat Amour,
Route de Paris,
29600 Morlaix, Finistère
Tel +33 (0)2 98 88 57 02
Mobile +33 (0)6 71 33 68 91
Email stafford.taylor@wanadoo.fr
Web www.gites-morlaix.com

Entry 284　Map 2

Brittany

Domaine de Moulin Mer

Bordeaux shutters against white-washed walls, graceful steps rising to the front door, attendant palm trees... Stéphane has restored this manor house to its full glory. The luxurious rooms are a masterly combination of period elegance and tasteful minimalism, the gardens a riot of shady trees – olives, palms, eucalyptus and mimosas. Across the road you can glimpse the waters of the estuary and a fine old mill. Stéphane, who used to work in Dublin, is an amusing, genial host and a collector of furniture and art. He will cook you (according to availability and his whim) an inventive dinner using fresh local produce.

Rooms	4: 2 doubles, 2 suites.
Price	€80–€100. Suites €120–€140.
Meals	Dinner €35. Wine from €10.
Closed	Rarely.

Stéphane Pécot
Domaine de Moulin Mer,
34 route de Moulin Mer,
29460 Logonna Daoulas, Finistère
Tel   +33 (0)2 98 07 24 45
Email   info@domaine-moulin-mer.com
Web   www.domaine-moulin-mer.com

Entry 285   Map 2

Brittany

La Caloge

On a remote Brittany peninsula... not quite a houseboat, but a boat that's somehow a house. After an illustrious fishing career, La Caloge has come to rest in the country garden of a charming B&B. The roof has been thatched to keep out the weather and inside is a marvel, with polished oak flooring, a fresh blue and white décor and a mast in the middle of the bedroom. You get all the trappings of life on the ocean wave but no risk of seasickness! Rocky cliffs and wild headlands are a minute away, watersports abound in the Baie de Douarnenez, and breakfast is at sweet little tables in the cabin next door.

Book through Sawday's Canopy & Stars online or by phone.

Rooms	1 thatched boat for 2.
Price	£85.
Meals	Shared kitchen in fisherman's cabin. Restaurant 2km.
Closed	Rarely.

Sawday's Canopy & Stars
La Caloge,
Kastell Dinn, Kerlouantec,
29160 Crozon, Finistère
Tel   +44 (0)1275 395447
Email   enquiries@canopyandstars.co.uk
Web   www.canopyandstars.co.uk/caloge

Entry 286   Map 2

Brittany

Manoir de Kerdanet

Irresistible cakes, savouries, fruits and teas are served in a salon with a vast granite fireplace and logs that flicker at the first sign of cold weather. Off a country road, down an alley of trees, and there it is, a beautiful manor house 600 years old, lived in and loved by urbane hosts with a talent for making you feel instantly at home. A spiral stone staircase leads to authentic and timeless bedrooms, comfortable with crisp sheets and woollen blankets, coordinated furnishings and dark Breton antiques. Walkers and sailors will love the coast, there are regattas at Douarnenez, and return happily to easygoing Kerdanet.

Sorry no pets.

Rooms	3: 2 doubles, 1 suite for 4 (1 double, 1 twin).
Price	€100. Suite €130–€190.
Meals	Restaurants 5km.
Closed	Mid-November to mid-March.

Sid & Monique Nedjar
Manoir de Kerdanet,
29100 Poullan sur Mer, Finistère
Tel   +33 (0)2 98 74 59 03
Email   manoir.kerdanet@wanadoo.fr
Web   www.manoirkerdanet.com

Entry 287   Map 2

Brittany

Château du Guilguiffin

Named after the knight who became first Baron in 1010, a fairytale place in its own swathe of wild Brittany. Its opulent rooms and tree-lined approach seduced us utterly. Built with stones from a fortress that once stood here, the château is a jewel of 18th-century architecture – Philippe Davy's family seat. Panelled doors are duck-egg blue, dusky pink or turquoise, rugs are oriental; it's heaven for art connoisseurs. Morning feasts are served on fine Limoges at the 12-seater table; the vast fireplace is lit throughout the year. Settle in here, in the elegant salon or the cosy parlour, or sip drinks on the terrace.

Rooms	5: 4 twins/doubles, 1 suite.
Price	€135–€160. Suite for 2, €150–€160. Suite for 4, €250.
Meals	Breakfast included. Restaurants 15-minute drive.
Closed	Rarely.

Philippe Davy
Château du Guilguiffin,
29710 Landudec, Finistère
Tel   +33 (0)2 98 91 52 11
Email   info@guilguiffin.com
Web   www.guilguiffin.com

Entry 288   Map 2

Brittany

La Ferme de Kerscuntec

In the bucolic heart of the country, yet close to white sand beaches, the 17th-century cider farm has become a delicious B&B. The peaceful bedrooms are modern, fresh and calming, the garden is prolific, your hostess is creative and humorous. Little confections are left out at all times by Anne for guests to enjoy, zinc pots are stuffed with flowers, bathrooms are for lingering in, and sparkling windows frame the fields. Wake to muffins and hedgerow jams, visit the fishing boats in Ste Marine harbour and the grand shops of Quimper, set off for the islands. Crêperies and seafood restaurants abound.

Minimum two nights.

Rooms	3 doubles.
Price	€85-€120.
Meals	Restaurant 2km.
Closed	Rarely.

Anne & Bruno Porhiel
La Ferme de Kerscuntec,
Kerscuntec,
29120 Combrit, Finistère

Tel	+33 (0)2 98 51 90 90
Mobile	+33 (0)6 86 99 78 28
Email	contact@lafermedekerscuntec.fr
Web	www.lafermedekerscuntec.fr

Entry 289 Map 2

Brittany

Lezerhy

A heavenly spot, cradled in a quiet hamlet 200 yards from the river in deepest Brittany. Interesting people: Martine cares for those with disabilities; Philippe pots and teaches aikido; both have time for guests and daughter Melissa occasionally helps out. In an outbuilding, you have your own living room and kitchen and two big, functionally furnished attic rooms decorated in subtle pastels and fitted with good showers. Birds sing, the two cats are among the best ever, there may be a different kind of pastry for breakfast every day, St Nicolas des Eaux has restaurants and kayaks on the river. Cheap, cheerful, bucolic.

Rooms	2 twins/doubles.
Price	€50.
Meals	Guest kitchen. Restaurants 3km.
Closed	November-Easter, except by arrangement.

Martine Maignan & Philippe Boivin
Lezerhy,
56310 Bieuzy les Eaux, Morbihan

Tel	+33 (0)2 97 27 74 59
Email	boivinp@wanadoo.fr
Web	pagesperso-orange.fr/poterie-de-lezerhy

Entry 290 Map 2

Brittany

Talvern

Separated from the road by a grassy courtyard, this honest old farmhouse once belonged to the château. The dividing stone wall encloses a south-facing terrace, a young fruit-treed garden, space for the Gillots' children – and yours – to play, and a potager. Ask gentle Patrick about his vegetables and his face lights up: he was a chef in Paris (do dine in). Christine teaches English and is the talent behind the very fine, quietly original bedroom décor. There are walks in the woods next door, good cycling, resident peacocks, birdlife all around, the sea just 30 minutes away.

Ask about cookery courses October-March.

Rooms	5: 2 doubles, 1 twin/double, 2 suites.
Price	€69-€78. Suites €123.
Meals	Dinner with wine, €24.
Closed	Rarely.

Patrick Gillot
Talvern,
56690 Landévant, Morbihan
Tel +33 (0)2 97 56 99 80
Mobile +33 (0)6 16 18 08 75
Email talvern@chambre-morbihan.com
Web www.chambre-morbihan.com

Entry 291 Map 2

Brittany

La Longère

Arrive as strangers at this stylish retreat 20 minutes from the sea – and leave as friends. Elaine and Paul swapped London for a 18th-century longère surrounded by orchards and fields; then modernised in country-contemporary style. Three attic bedrooms, airy and light, come with roof windows and calming colours, spoiling showers and laundered linen. The sofa'd salon is equally inviting; comfy loungers line the pool. Chat to Elaine as she prepares your dinner, delivered with a flourish to the convivial table. Make the most of the music festivals of Lorient, and all those Brittany gardens that open in summer.

Rooms	3 doubles.
Price	€85-€130.
Meals	Dinner with wine, €25.
	Restaurants 10-minute drive.
Closed	Rarely.

Elaine & Paul Hayden
La Longère,
Kerouallic,
56440 Languidic, Morbihan
Tel +33 (0)2 97 65 13 15
Email info@perfectplacefrance.com
Web www.perfectplacefrance.com

Entry 292 Map 2

Brittany

Ker-Ysta

The old barn has been done in a lovely mix of traditional (old beams and stone walls) and modern: soft grey pleasingly married with more vibrant green, yellow or purple. It's all warm and inviting with views to the big lush garden and a sense of peace. Yolande and her husband came home to Brittany for a simpler life after working hard in buzzy Paris. Quietly bubbly, she is passionate about cooking and interiors so converting an old farmhouse and its outbuildings into a B&B was the ideal plan. Breakfast and dinner (masses of fresh local fish) are at the big table in her kitchen; guests have a cosy sitting room in the barn.

Rooms	4: 3 doubles, 1 family room (2 rooms interconnect). Cot available.
Price	€75–€85. Family room €120–€130. Extra bed €15.
Meals	Dinner with wine, €28.
Closed	Rarely.

	Yolande Le Gall Ker-Ysta, Le Manémeur, 56410 Erdeven, Morbihan
Tel	+33 (0)2 97 55 97 20
Mobile	+33 (0)6 16 71 73 71
Email	contact@ker-ysta.fr
Web	www.ker-ysta.fr

Entry 293   Map 2

Brittany

Kerimel

The standing stones of Carnac are minutes away, beaches, coastal pathways and golf course close by. Kerimel is a handsome group of granite farm buildings in a perfect setting among the fields. Bedrooms are simple beauties: plain walls, some panelling, patchwork bedcovers and pale curtains, old stones and beams. The dining room is cottage perfection: dried flowers hanging from beams over a wooden table, a spring fire in the vast stone fireplace, breakfasts from grand-mère that promise an organic treat each day. A gentle, generous young family with excellent English, and passionately eco-minded.

Rooms	5: 2 twins/doubles, 3 triples.
Price	€80–€90. Triple €80–€90.
Meals	Crêpes supper available €20. Restaurants 3km.
Closed	December–February.

	Nicolas Malherbe Kerimel, 56400 Ploemel, Morbihan
Mobile	+33 (0)6 83 40 68 56
Email	chaumieres.kerimel@wanadoo.fr
Web	www.chambres-kerimel.com

Entry 294   Map 2

Brittany

Kernivilit

Right on the quayside, with the oyster boats under your windows, a very simple but friendly address. French windows open to tiny balconies and bedrooms touch the view; catch the lovely limpid light as you drink coffee on the balcony, listening to the chug-chug of the boats, smelling the sea. Madame worked in England, Germany and the US before coming here to help François farm oysters; he'll take you out in the boats if you ask. Hospitable and generous, alert and chatty, she hangs interesting art in her rooms, lights a fire on cool days and serves a good breakfast (great breads, fine jams) on a terrace shaded by pines.

Brittany

Le Val de Brangon

Wildflower meadows and nut orchards surround this swish farmhouse hotel. If the façade has forfeited a little of its charm, the light from the vast windows compensates in spades, as it settles on eye-catching antiques, modern art and comfy sofas. A big bedroom on the ground floor, all 18th-century French elegance, has its own terrace; swanky bathrooms with spa baths and rain-forest showers are a further treat. Breakfast on homemade cake, fruits and crêpes as you plan the day: a swim in the pool, a trip to Vannes, a hop to the beach. Switched-on Nathalie, your friendly, cheerful hostess, does tasty dinners twice a week.

Children over 12 welcome.

Rooms	3: 1 double, 1 studio & kitchenette, 1 apartment for 3 & kitchenette.
Price	€70. Apartment €80. €70 without breakfast for rooms with kitchenette.
Meals	Restaurant 500m.
Closed	November-February.

Rooms	5 doubles.
Price	£160-£210.
Meals	Dinner with wine, €40 (twice weekly, for 6+). Restaurants 4km.
Closed	14 January-12 February.

Christine & François Gouzer
Kernivilit,
Route de Quéhan, St Philibert,
56470 La Trinité sur Mer, Morbihan

Tel	+33 (0)2 97 55 17 78
Mobile	+33 (0)6 78 35 09 34
Email	info@residence-mer.com
Web	www.residence-mer.com

Nathalie Hubier
Le Val de Brangon,
Lieu-dit Brangon,
56870 Baden, Morbihan

Tel	+33 (0)2 97 57 06 05
Mobile	+33 (0)6 09 79 90 94
Email	vb@levaldebrangon.com
Web	www.levaldebrangon.com

Brittany

Domaine de Coët Bihan

Close to beautiful, medieval Vannes, Jantine and Jacques' house lies in undulating country where horses graze and clematis clambers. Light-filled bedrooms, the most luxurious on the first floor, are crisp and comfy with pukka linen and top-class showers. Feast on crêpes before setting off for walks and climbs and, from the top of wooded summits, views over the Morbihan Gulf. Then a nap in the enclosed garden or an espresso in the tiny salon. If you're enjoying the indoor pool too much to be tempted by a local Michelin-starred restaurant (there are two), Jantine will make you a tasty platter.

Rooms	4 doubles.
Price	€90–€105. Extra bed €15.
Meals	Cold platter, €12–€20. Restaurants 4km. Kitchen & BBQ available.
Closed	Rarely.

Jantine Guégan-Helder
Domaine de Coët Bihan,
Lieu-dit Coët Bihan, Monterblanc,
56250 Vannes, Morbihan
Tel +33 (0)2 97 44 97 22
Mobile +33 (0)6 20 42 42 47
Email domainedecoetbihan@gmail.com
Web www.chambredhotes-vannes.fr

Entry 297 Map 3

Brittany

Château de Castellan

Bucolic fields and forests and not a house in sight. And, at the end of a lane, this modestly grand château-auberge, built in 1732 and once a hideout for counter-revolutionaries. Ring the bell and Madame will come to greet you. Antique church pews, a wide winding stair, pastoral views are the first impressions. The family have one wing, guests are in the middle, on two floors. Rooms are 70s-faded with period-sized beds, one in the attic, the best being the double on the first floor with its painted panelling. Hard-working Madame irons, cleans, cooks (generously and well), smiles… and directs you to the prettiest of ancient villages.

Rooms	3: 1 double, 1 twin, 1 family room for 4. Separate wcs.
Price	€85–€110. Family room €142.
Meals	Dinner in auberge €21. Wine €18–€25.
Closed	November–March.

Patrick & Marie Cossé
Château de Castellan,
56200 St Martin sur Oust,
Morbihan
Tel +33 (0)2 99 91 51 69
Email auberge@club.fr
Web www.castellan.fr.st

Entry 298 Map 3

Western Loire

Western Loire

Château de Coët Caret

Come for a taste of life with the French country aristocracy – it's getting hard to find and the breakfast room is a wonderful place to start the day. Madame greets you on arrival and is on hand when needed. She is a lively, cultured person, involved with the WWF, proud of her château tucked into the woods and its 100 hectares of parkland: serenity guaranteed. Bedrooms are faded but comfortable; *Saumon*, carpeted under the eaves, comes with binoculars for the birds. Your hostess and her son are full of tips and you are in the Brière Regional Park where water and land are inextricably mingled and wildlife abounds.

Rooms	4: 3 doubles, 1 twin.
Price	€100-€115.
Meals	Restaurants 2-10km.
Closed	Rarely.

	Cécile de La Monneraye
	Château de Coët Caret,
	44410 Herbignac, Loire-Atlantique
Tel	+33 (0)2 40 91 41 20
Email	coetcaret@gmail.com
Web	www.coetcaret.com

Entry 299   Map 3

Western Loire

Le Manoir des Quatre Saisons

Jean-Philippe, his mother and sister (who speaks English) are attentive hosts, providing both swimming robes and drinks by the pool. Communal breakfasts are flexible, complete with eggs and cereals as well as local choices. Well-loved, lived-in rooms (some in two-storey cottages in the grounds, some with kitchens) are colourfully coordinated; delightful Jean-Philippe has an eye for detail: stripes, patterns, French flourishes and distant sea views. Beach, river and town are walkable but children will enjoy mucking around in the big dog-friendly garden full of secret corners.

Minimum two nights July/Aug & bank holiday weekends.

Rooms	5: 3 doubles, 1 twin, 1 quadruple.
Price	€75-€95. Quadruple €95-€105. Extra bed €20.
Meals	Restaurants 1.5km.
Closed	Rarely.

	Jean-Philippe Meyran
	Le Manoir des Quatre Saisons,
	744 bd de Lauvergnac,
	44420 La Turballe, Loire-Atlantique
Tel	+33 (0)2 40 11 76 16
Mobile	+33 (0)6 87 33 43 86
Email	jean-philippe.meyran@club-internet.fr
Web	www.manoir-des-quatre-saisons.com

Entry 300   Map 3

Western Loire

Château de Cop-Choux

Where to start: the elegant house built just before the French Revolution (with later towers), the 18-hectare park, the pool, the rolling lawns? Or the 17 marble fireplaces and your friendly hosts? The house is full of light and bedrooms are lofty: fabric floating at tall windows, perhaps an exquisite carved bed. A river runs through the grounds, there are lakes and woods for ramblers, rare ferns for plant buffs, farm animals, even dromedaries in summer. Breakfast comes with a selection of teas in a pretty panelled room and dinner is served at separate tables. All feels calm and serene.

Large cottage sleeps 6 for weekly rental.

Rooms	5: 4 twins/doubles, 1 suite.
Price	€110–€120. Suite €150.
Meals	Breakfast €8. Dinner with wine, €39. Restaurants 12km.
Closed	Rarely.

Patrick Moreau
Château de Cop-Choux,
44850 Mouzeil,
Loire-Atlantique
Tel   +33 (0)2 40 97 28 52
Email   chateau-cop-choux@bbox.fr
Web   www.chateau-cop-choux.com

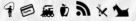

Entry 301   Map 3

Western Loire

Demeure Les Montys

Shhh, don't tell! Not many know of this beautifully symmetrical neoclassical mansion, hidden deep in Loire vineyards. Whoosh back to 1800s high society: stuccoed, panelled rooms, heirlooms, gilded mirrors, Catholic icons, plush blues, golds… and a huge, classical guest suite just for two. The easy-going Libaudières, busy with 12 children, ponies and dog, always find time to whip up breakfast with a smile. So sleep in – or sneak out for sunrise on the photogenic estate: lake, chapel, tennis, birds, trees, vines. Forgive the odd chilly draught or rickety outbuilding: this is as authentic old-style French as you get.

Rooms	1 suite.
Price	€100.
Meals	Restaurants 1km.
Closed	October to mid-April.

Frédérique Libaudière
Demeure Les Montys,
35 impasse des Montys,
44115 Haute Goulaine, Loire-Atlantique
Tel   +33 (0)2 40 03 58 95
Mobile   +33 (0)6 08 45 48 36
Email   lesmontys@yahoo.fr
Web   www.demeure-lesmontys.com

Entry 302   Map 3

Château de la Sébinière

Young, warm, humorous, Anne has exquisite taste, a perfectionist's eye and lovely twin daughters. The house of her dreams, this 18th-century château in its pretty park is a light, sunny and harmonious home. Walls are white or red-ochre, ceilings beamed, bathrooms a blend of old and new. There's an extravagant attention to detail – a pewter jug of old roses by a gilt mirror, a fine wicker chair on an ancient tiled floor. You have your own entrance and the run of the sitting room, log-fired in winter. There may be real hot chocolate at breakfast and, if you wish, a glass of wine on arrival. Nearby Clisson is full of charm.

Rooms	3 doubles.
Price	€105-€125.
Meals	Dinner with wine, €30.
Closed	Rarely.

Anne Cannaferina
Château de la Sébinière,
44330 Le Pallet, Loire-Atlantique
Tel +33 (0)2 40 80 49 25
Mobile +33 (0)6 17 35 45 33
Email info@chateausebiniere.com
Web www.chateausebiniere.com

Entry 303   Map 3

Château de L'Oiselinière

Muscadet was first mentioned in a document dated 1635 found on the premises. Over 600 years this château was owned by four successive families – until the Verdiers acquired it (derelict) and its famous vines. Their passion for the property is infectious, Isabelle has overseen the renovation and her taste is superb. Communal spaces are exquisitely decorated, first-floor guest quarters are stunning and bathroom towels are the château's monogrammed own. A private yard has deckchairs and barbecue; a hot tub is in the offing. Dress up (it's a must) and dine with this fascinating, friendly family; wines are chosen for each course.

Rooms	4 doubles.
Price	€115-€125.
Meals	Dinner with wine, €40.
	Restaurants 1km.
Closed	Rarely.

Georges Verdier
Château de L'Oiselinière,
44190 Gorges,
Loire-Atlantique
Tel +33 (0)2 40 06 91 59
Email contact@chateau-de-l-oiseliniere.com
Web www.chateau-de-l-oiseliniere.com

Entry 304   Map 3

Western Loire

Logis de Richebonne

Monsieur's parents bought this old *logis Vendéen* when he was six. Years later, researching the history of the house, he found his family had owned it in 1670! In the hall, Madame's family tree goes back to the 14th century. Both are warm, welcoming and not at all grand and the old house is full of personal touches: Madame painted the breakfast china and embroidered the beautiful tablecloths. Vast bedrooms have peaceful views and quantities of fresh and dried flowers. The suite is ideal for a family, the huge grounds hold two pretty ponds (unfenced) and a barbecue: you may picnic here. Wonderful all round.

Rooms	3: 2 doubles, 1 suite for 5.
Price	€70.
Meals	Picnic possible.
	Restaurant in village, 1.5km.
Closed	Rarely.

Alain & Françoise de Ternay
Logis de Richebonne,
7 impasse Richebonne,
44650 Legé, Loire-Atlantique
Tel +33 (0)2 40 04 90 41
Email adeternay@wanadoo.fr
Web www.logisderichebonne.com

Entry 305   Map 8

Western Loire

Le Verger

The Broux have revived this fine cluster of granite buildings for their family and the guests they welcome so well. At the end of a private lane, one small ancient house of low heavy beams and big stones makes up your quarters: two divans in the sitting area, bedroom upstairs, hand-painted furniture, loads of personality. Across the yard, in the big square family house where noble stone, timber and terracotta also reign, Annick prepares delicious meals for the long bright table. Outside, flowers and vegetables mix in profusion, a white horse grazes in the field. Lovely people, charming place.

Rooms	1 suite for 2-4.
Price	€49-€79.
Meals	Dinner with wine, €18.
Closed	End-October to Easter.

Annick & Marc Broux
Le Verger,
85530 La Bruffière, Vendée
Tel +33 (0)2 51 43 62 02
Email broux.annick@wanadoo.fr
Web pagesperso-orange.fr/le-verger

Entry 306   Map 8

Château de la Maronnière

Friendly Marie and François have excelled in restoring their luxurious, 18th-century château. Oak parquet is warm underfoot, copper leaf chandeliers light the circular hall and a stuffed fox surprises on the spiral staircase. Many rambling acres of green-fingered Eden await; take a wildlife walk or pluck cherries by the pool. Stylish shared spaces are immaculate with a baby grand in residence: Le Petit Bois has carved antique furniture; La Rotonde is marble grey with unusual panelling. Textiles and trimmings are sumptuous, bath robes fluffy; throw open the shutters and the views pour in. Stroll into Aizenay – or dine here.

Domaine du Revêtison

A 19th-century farmhouse, immaculately converted into a smart B&B. Corinne speaks good English, Steve is British, they give you a family-friendly pool (with poolhouse, bar and games) and nothing is too much trouble. Best of all is Corinne's table d'hôtes at the big convivial table, Vendée style (garlicky bread, bean and lamb stew). Kitchen and dining rooms are linked, bedrooms are country-pretty, towels are white and fluffy and all is splendidly maintained. It's peaceful and remote but the historical theme park Le Puy du Fou is not too far; nor are the glam beaches of Les Sables d'Olonne. Great for sociable families.

Minimum two nights at weekends.

Rooms	4: 1 double, 2 twins/doubles, 1 suite.
Price	€110–€120. Suite €195. Extra child bed €25.
Meals	Dinner with wine, €35. Restaurants 500m.
Closed	Never.

Rooms	4: 1 twin, 3 family rooms for 2-4.
Price	€79. Family rooms €79-€145.
Meals	Dinner €32. Child €15. Restaurants in Chantonnay.
Closed	Rarely.

François-Xavier & Marie-Hélène d'Halluin
Château de la Maronnière,
Route des Sables, 85190 Aizenay, Vendée
Tel   +33 (0)6 25 02 00 55
Email   dhalluinmh@gmail.com
Web   www.chateauvendee.com

Corinne & Steve Wilson
Domaine du Revêtison,
85110 Chantonnay, Vendée
Tel   +33 (0)2 51 09 63 92
Mobile   +33 (0)6 18 93 79 23
Email   revetison@gmail.com
Web   www.domainedurevetison.com

Western Loire

La Joulinière

Wrapped in flowers and lawns in a sleepy Vendée hamlet, this farmhouse looks a treat with its white shutters and bumpy stone. Find leafy terraces, parasols, a pool... inside, a baby grand piano in a country-pretty sitting room where soft, pale fabrics reflect floods of light. There are two cosy suites: Eléonore in the old smithy, with vaulted oak ceilings and stony walls, Guinevere upstairs with a four-poster draped in floaty white. Anthony and Carol, musicians, have an ear for birdsong, eye for décor and heart for B&B. It's like staying with cultured friends in the country, near Chantonnay and the beaches of western France.

Rooms	2 doubles.
Price	€70. Extra bed €10.
Meals	Restaurants 3km.
Closed	End-October to Easter.

Carol & Anthony Langford
La Joulinière,
85390 Bazoges en Parèds, Vendée
Tel   +33 (0)2 51 87 58 93
Mobile   +33 (0)6 78 23 75 04
Email   anthony.langford@yahoo.fr
Web   www.bandbwestfrance.com

Entry 309   Map 8

Western Loire

La Maison de Landerie

Annie used to have her own restaurant in Devon so whether you are outside on her little stone terrace overlooking open fields and forest or inside at her long antique table, it will be a Cordon Bleu breakfast. Multi-talented Annie could open an antique shop as well; her lovingly collected artefacts decorate this sweet little farmhouse like a dream from the past. The vintage linens are sumptuous, the towels are thirsty, the mattresses are from heaven. You can walk to town, pick a trail in the forest or rent a canoe and follow the lazy river Lay. Annie's dinners are renowned, even the Mayor comes to dine.

Rooms	2 doubles.
Price	€60-€65.
Meals	Dinner with wine, €28.
Closed	Christmas.

Annie Jory
La Maison de Landerie,
La Réorthe, 85210 Sainte Hermine,
Vendée
Tel   +33 (0)2 51 27 80 70
Email   richard.jory@wanadoo.fr
Web   www.lalanderie.com

Entry 310   Map 8

La Frelonnière

An elegant country house in a peaceful, pastoral setting – who would not love it? The 18th-century farmhouse, complete with musket holes and open rafters, is informal and delightful. Your English/Scottish hosts are fun, friendly and intimately acquainted with France – they brought their children up here. Now they generously open their living space to guests, their serene pool and their exquisite Monet-style garden. Quietly stylish bedrooms (coir carpets, white walls, fresh flowers, silk flourishes) are divided by a sofa'd library on the landing; dinners, served three times a week, may be romantic or convivial. A gem.

Arrival from 4pm.

Demeure Valeau du Rivage

By Luçon's old port, head through a private courtyard and solid oak door to this calm 15th-century home filled with a sense of fun. Off carved stone stairs is 'Richelieu', a smart duplex double with Italian shower; then 'Suite Pop' with fun feathery lampshades and an outrageously 1970s sitting room. Families will adore the 'Empereur' suite with its balcony room and a further double along a corridor (each with a bathroom). Understated antique furnishings unite homeliness with history. The delightful gardens and inviting pool are child-friendly – as are Isabelle's breakfast pastries! A gem at the gateway to the Coast of Light.

Rooms	2 doubles.
Price	€75.
Meals	Dinner with wine, €30, Fridays and Saturdays; Sunday to Thursday, €15.
Closed	Rarely.

Rooms	3 suites.
Price	€90–€110. Extra bed €20.
Meals	Restaurants 0.5km.
Closed	Rarely.

	Julie & Richard Deslandes
	La Frelonnière,
	85410 La Caillère – St Hilaire du Bois,
	Vendée
Tel	+33 (0)2 51 51 56 49
Mobile	+33 (0)6 70 08 50 26
Email	julie@lafrelonniere.fr
Web	www.bandbvendee.com

	Isabelle & Olivier Cline
	Demeure Valeau du Rivage,
	58 rue du Port,
	85400 Luçon, Vendée
Tel	+33 (0)2 51 30 93 10
Mobile	+33 (0)6 67 18 30 75
Email	valeaudurivage@free.fr
Web	www.chambres-hotes-vendee.com

Western Loire

Le Logis de la Clef de Bois

The town, a *ville d'art et d'histoire*, is one of the loveliest in the Vendée. The house stands in lushness at one end of it. Madame has an easy elegance and her home overflows with taste and glamorous touches, from the fabulous Zuber mural in the dining room to the immaculate fauteuils of the salon. Big paintings, a collection of muslin caps from Poitou, bedrooms that celebrate writers... all point to cultural leanings. 'Rabelais' speaks of the Renaissance and is joyful in trompe l'œil, 'Michel Ragon' is flamboyant in red and white checks. Come down to a royally elegant breakfast and, perhaps, Madame's own cannelés.

Western Loire

Le Rosier Sauvage

The pretty village is known for its exquisite abbey and some of that monastic serenity pervades these rooms. We love the family room under the rafters: massive oak door, cool tiled floor, a touch of toile, a simple mix of furniture. Through the family kitchen, breakfast is at a long polished table in the old stable: linger over cake and compote; the old laundry, its huge stone tub intact, is now a sitting room. Guests can picnic in the many-flowered walled garden, overlooked by the abbey and a glorious cedar tree. Energetic Christine is as charming as her house, which is also home to her husband and twin girls.

Rooms	4: 2 doubles, 2 family suites for 3-5.
Price	€115-€135. Extra bed €26.
Meals	Barbecue & picnic possible. Restaurant 100m.
Closed	Occasionally.

Rooms	4: 1 double, 1 twin, 1 family room for 3, 1 family room for 4.
Price	€48-€51. Family room €48-€54.
Meals	Restaurants within walking distance.
Closed	October-April.

Danielle Portebois
Le Logis de la Clef de Bois,
5 rue du Département,
85200 Fontenay le Comte, Vendée

Tel	+33 (0)2 51 69 03 49
Mobile	+33 (0)6 15 41 04 31
Email	clef_de_bois@hotmail.com
Web	www.clef-de-bois.com

Christine Chastain-Poupin
Le Rosier Sauvage,
1 rue de l'Abbaye,
85240 Nieul sur l'Autise,
Vendée

Tel	+33 (0)2 51 52 49 39
Email	lerosiersauvage@gmail.com
Web	lerosiersauvage.c.la

La Marienne

A perfect blend of serene seclusion and homeliness, this 15th-century priory of warm stonework and beams has been tenderly restored. Charming Françoise dispenses homemade marmalade with advice and smiles, alongside dappled shade and poolside loungers (and open fires in winter). Airy bedrooms, clean-line bathrooms and pure décor induce total relaxation, enhanced by a jacuzzi or hammam (€10). Bedrooms share a tranquil sitting room opening onto beautiful, rustic gardens. You could punt the waterways, cycle country lanes and browse the markets – but La Marienne's hypnotic beauty will tempt you to return.

Rooms	4: 3 doubles, 1 family suite.
Price	€78–€85. Family suite €85–€135.
Meals	Restaurants 10km.
Closed	Rarely.

Françoise Charraud
La Marienne,
14 rue de la Virée-Lesson,
85490 Benet, Vendée

Tel	+33 (0)2 51 51 50 41
Mobile	+33 (0)6 71 77 02 51
Email	charraud.francoise@wanadoo.fr
Web	www.la-marienne.com

Entry 315   Map 8

Demeure l'Impériale

A rare survivor of Cholet's imperial past, when the town flourished on making handkerchiefs, this elegant townhouse was the orangery of a long-gone château. Nothing imperial about Édith, though: she's a natural at making guests feel at home. The bedrooms are bright and beautiful with fine period furniture and modern bathrooms; one sits under the eaves, another overlooks the rose-filled, tree-shaded garden. There are two pretty salons, a glass-roofed dining room in the sunken courtyard, and it's all so spotless you could eat off the parquet. Magnificent breakfasts, excellent dinners; French style and hospitality at its best.

Rooms	3: 2 doubles, 1 suite.
Price	€69–€76. Suite €140.
Meals	Dinner €23. Wine €10–€15.
Closed	Rarely.

Édith & Jean-René Duchesne
Demeure l'Impériale,
28 rue Nationale, 49300 Cholet,
Maine-et-Loire

Tel	+33 (0)2 41 58 84 84
Mobile	+33 (0)6 77 76 75 16
Email	demeure.imperiale@wanadoo.fr
Web	www.demeure-imperiale.com

Entry 316   Map 8

Western Loire

Le Mésangeau

The house is long-faced, and refined; the grounds (superb) come with a fishing pond and 'aperitif gazebo'. The Migons have expertly renovated this unusual house with its barn-enclosed courtyard, two towers and covered terrace. Big, north-facing bedrooms are elegant and comfortable behind their shutters, and keep the housekeepers busy. Expect leather sofas and a suit of armour, colourful beams above antique furniture, two billiard tables, and bikes, ping-pong and drums in the barn. At dinner, French cuisine from Madame, and much entertainment from Monsieur, who collects veteran cars and plays bass guitar.

Rooms	5: 3 doubles, 2 suites.
Price	€90–€110.
Meals	Dinner with wine, €35.
Closed	Rarely.

Brigitte & Gérard Migon
Le Mésangeau,
49530 Drain,
Maine-et-Loire
Tel   +33 (0)2 40 98 21 57
Email   le.mesangeau@orange.fr
Web   www.loire-mesangeau.com

Entry 317   Map 3

Western Loire

Loire-Charmilles

A house and garden full of surprises and a dazzling mix of styles. Chunky beams and old floors are set against slabs of slate, Japanese art and some very modern furniture. Up wooden stairs, through a low doorway (mind your head), bedrooms have huge beds, dimmer switches, antique desks with perspex chairs and ultra-chic bathrooms, one with a repro bath. The enclosed garden teems with roses, mimosa and orchids; breakfast and dinner are on the veranda on warm days or in the huge-windowed orangery; bubbly Nadia cooks on a fireplace grill; she and Jean-Pierre, son Jules and the lovely lab, make this a warm family house.

Rooms	2: 1 double, 1 twin.
Price	€65. 6 nights, €350.
Meals	Dinner with wine, €23.
	Guest kitchenette.
Closed	Rarely.

Nadia Leinberger
Loire-Charmilles, 9 rue de l'École,
49410 Le Mesnil en Vallée,
Maine-et-Loire
Tel   +33 (0)2 41 78 94 74
Mobile   +33 (0)6 77 10 69 66
Email   nadia@loire-charmilles.com
Web   www.loire-charmilles.com

Entry 318   Map 3

Le Manoir de la Noue

On the edge of little Denée, beyond the avenues of a residential estate, discover this: a walled garden resplendent with the colours of the seasons and a 16th-century manor. In 2002 your hosts discovered the world of wine after pursuing other careers; each of their vintages has earned them praise. Now the former barn has become a stylish chambres d'hôtes: bedrooms above, breakfast area below. All is comfortable and characterful: oak beams and bold colour-washed walls, big beds and generous bathrooms. After feasting on Catherine's jams and 'gelées', seek out the lovely village-island of Béhuard.

La Rousselière

A hymn to peace, permanence and gentle living. The superb garden is Monsieur's pride and joy; château-like reception rooms open one into another – glass doors to glass doors, billiards to dining to sitting – like an indoor arcade; family portraits follow you everywhere; Mass is still said once a year in the chapel. But it's never over-grand. Bedrooms are highly individual with their antiques and hand-painted armoires (courtesy of an artistic sister), many bathrooms are new and Madame is the most delightful smiling hostess and a fine cook (veg, meat and eggs all home-grown). Your lovely hosts join you for an aperitif before dinner.

Rooms	4: 2 doubles, 1 twin/double, 1 triple.		Rooms	5: 2 doubles, 2 twins, 1 family room.
Price	€85. Triple €85–€105.		Price	€70–€100. Family room €150.
Meals	Guest kitchen. Restaurant 5km.		Meals	Dinner with wine, €30.
Closed	Rarely.		Closed	Rarely.

Catherine & Olivier de Cenival
Le Manoir de la Noue,
Chemin de la Noue, 49190 Denée,
Maine-et-Loire

Tel   +33 (0)2 41 78 79 80
Mobile   +33 (0)6 84 00 77 89
Email   odecenival@wanadoo.fr
Web   www.domainedeschesnaies.com

François & Jacqueline de Béru
La Rousselière,
49170 La Possonnière,
Maine-et-Loire

Tel   +33 (0)2 41 39 13 21
Mobile   +33 (0)6 60 67 60 69
Email   laurencedeberu@gmail.com
Web   www.anjou-et-loire.com/rousseliere

Entry 319   Map 3

Entry 320   Map 3

Prieuré de l'Épinay

Such happy, interested, interesting people, and meals the greatest fun – local farm chicken and asparagus, raspberries and lettuces from their own organic potager. Facing the big grassed garden, the ancient priory has changed so little that the monks would feel at home here today, though the swimming pool, large and lovely, might be a surprise. Your hosts gladly share their home and its history; lofty ceilings, 15th-century beams, a fascinating *cave*, a rare fireplace. The two-storey rooms in the barn are simple and big, summer breakfasts are served in the chapel. What value!

Ask about wine tours.

Logis de la Roche Corbin

Smack in the middle of old Angers, a secret, special place. Behind a high wall: a cobbled path, a climbing rose, a bunch of lettuces to keep the tortoise happy. Off this delightful courtyard garden is your room, aglow with 18th-century charm; off a French-grey hallway, an exquisite zen-like bathroom. Breakfast is up the magnificent rough-hewn oak stair, in a Japanese-touched room with a rooftop view. Behind this hugely sympathetic restoration of a 16th-century house are a fine, talented couple, Michael, an American painter with a studio over the road, and Pascale from Paris, warm, relaxed and enthusiastic about B&B.

Whole house available July / August.

Rooms	3: 1 suite for 2, 2 suites for 4–5.
Price	€80.
Meals	Dinner with wine, €30. Picnic available.
Closed	October–April.

Rooms	1 double.
Price	€86.
Meals	Occasional dinner with wine, €15-€30.
Closed	Rarely.

	Bernard & Geneviève Gaultier
	Prieuré de l'Épinay,
	49170 Saint Georges sur Loire,
	Maine-et-Loire
Tel	+33 (0)2 41 39 14 44
Email	bernard.gaultier3@wanadoo.fr

	Michael & Pascale Rogosin
	Logis de la Roche Corbin,
	3 rue de la Harpe,
	49100 Angers, Maine-et-Loire
Tel	+33 (0)2 41 86 93 70
Mobile	+33 (0)6 14 78 37 06
Email	logisdelaroche@gmail.com
Web	www.logisdelaroche.com

Château de Montriou

The park will explode your senses — and once the visitors have gone home, what a treat to have it all to yourselves: the lake, the famous sequoia, the waves of crocuses in spring, the tunnel of squashes, ravishing at summer's last flush. The 15th-century château has been lived in and tended by the same family for 300 years and Monsieur and Madame know exactly how to make you feel at home. A spiral stone staircase leads to properly formal bedrooms whose bold colours were design flavour of the period; wooden floors, thick rugs and antiques are only slightly younger. And the venerable library is now a guest sitting room. Unique.

Rooms	5: 3 doubles, 1 double with kitchen, 1 suite for 4 with kitchen.
Price	€85–€130. Suite €165.
Meals	Restaurant 6km.
Closed	Rarely.

Régis & Nicole de Loture
Château de Montriou,
49460 Feneu,
Maine-et-Loire

Tel	+33 (0)2 41 93 30 11
Email	chateau-de-montriou@wanadoo.fr
Web	www.chateau-de-montriou.com

Entry 323　Map 4

Manoir du Bois de Grez

An old peace lingers over the unique fan-shaped yard, the old well, the little chapel: the Manoir oozes history. Your doctor host, an amateur painter, and his gracious, charming wife, much-travelled antique-hunters with imagination and flair, set the tone with a bright red petrol pump and a penny-farthing in the hall. Generous bedrooms (including a superb family room) hung with well-chosen oriental pieces and paintings come in good strong colours that reflect the garden light. You share the big sitting room with your lovely hosts, lots of plants and a suit of armour. The grand gardens are dotted with ornamental trees.

Rooms	4: 2 doubles, 1 twin, 1 family room.
Price	€85–€95. Family room €90–€135.
Meals	Picnic on request. Guest kitchen. Restaurant 1.5km.
Closed	Rarely.

Marie Laure & Jean Gaël Cesbron
Manoir du Bois de Grez,
Route de Sceaux d'Anjou,
49220 Grez Neuville, Maine-et-Loire

Tel	+33 (0)2 41 18 00 09
Mobile	+33 (0)6 22 38 14 56
Email	cesbron.boisgrez@wanadoo.fr
Web	www.boisdegrez.com

Entry 324　Map 4

Western Loire

La Croix d'Étain

Frisky red squirrels decorate the stone balustrade, the wide river flows past the lush garden: it feels like deep country yet this handsome manor has urban elegance in its very stones. Panelling, mouldings, subtly muted floor tiles bring grace, traditional French florals add softness. It looks fairly formal but sprightly Madame adores having guests and pampers them, in their own quarters, with luxury. Monsieur is a hoot, makes jam, loves fishing! Expect plush, lacy, flowery, carpeted bedrooms, three with river views, all with sunny bathrooms. The yacht-side setting is stunning – it could be the Riviera.

Rooms	4: 1 double, 3 twin/doubles.
Price	€85–€100. Singles €60.
Meals	Dinner with wine, €30. Crêperie 50m.
Closed	Rarely.

Jacqueline & Auguste Bahuaud
La Croix d'Étain,
2 rue de l'Écluse,
49220 Grez Neuville,
Maine-et-Loire
Tel   +33 (0)2 41 95 68 49
Email   croix.etain@loire-anjou-accommodation.com
Web   www.loire-anjou-accommodation.com

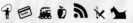

Entry 325   Map 3

Western Loire

Le Moulin de l'Etang

You approach the mill alongside the grand lake: the setting is stunning. Birds trill, the brook babbles and you can breakfast on the patio in summer. Bubbly Maria loves art, food, fashion and gives you two peaceful beamed bedrooms on the lower floor (one bed in the old bread oven!). Sumptuous canopies and cushions are hand-sewn, the feel is boudoir, the bathrooms are freshly modern. Boat and fish on the lake, splash in the above-ground pool, stroll to Noellet (25 minutes). Then it's home for a lovely French/Sicilian supper hosted at the candlelit table; or, on balmy nights, on the barbecue. Wonderful.

Rooms	2: 1 double, 1 family room.
Price	€95. Family room €120.
Meals	Dinner, 5 courses, €25. Wine from €10. Restaurant in Noellet, 3km.
Closed	Rarely.

Maria Mizzi
Le Moulin de l'Etang,
49520 Noellet,
Maine-et-Loire
Tel   +33 (0)2 41 94 47 59
Mobile   +33 (0)6 26 52 28 52
Email   mariamizzi@aol.com
Web   www.lemoulindeletang.com

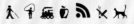

Entry 326   Map 3

Château du Plessis Anjou

Built in the 16th century, Le Plessis has always been in the same family. Inviting rather than imposing, it has been welcoming guests for years. Convivial dinner, at a long table in a grand room garnished with scenes from the Roman Empire, includes produce straight from the potager. Oriental rugs, lofty beamed ceilings, beds turned down at night, water and chocolates by the pillow – many comforts await. It's family-friendly, too: there's a playground and trampoline, rabbits and a goat, a pond brimming with fish and lilies, a hen house – Madame invites children to gather the eggs. Terra Botanica is a 15-minute drive.

Rooms	5: 3 doubles, 2 suites.
Price	€150–€180. Suites €220–€250.
Meals	Hosted dinner €48 (book ahead). Wine €20–€240.
Closed	Rarely.

Valérie & Laurent Renoul
Château du Plessis Anjou,
49220 La Jaille Yvon,
Maine-et-Loire
Tel +33 (0)2 41 95 12 75
Email plessis.anjou@wanadoo.fr
Web www.chateau-du-plessis.com

La Marronnière

This pretty white-shuttered house overlooking the river has been in the family for ever. The vicomte and vicomtesse give you a gracious, smiling welcome and large, serene bedrooms most lovingly revived. Choose a bed tucked into a poppy-papered alcove, or butterflies fluttering pinkly on the walls; all rooms have river views. Madame loves cooking and breakfast is a moveable feast: dining room in winter, terrace in summer. The warmly authentic sitting room provides a winter fire in a stone hearth, Italian ochres, silk drapes, family portraits and – on warm nights – doors open to the Sarthe.

Rooms	4 twins/doubles.
Price	€120.
Meals	Dinner €30. Wine from €20.
Closed	Christmas & Easter.

Jean & Marie-Hélène de La Selle
La Marronnière,
49125 Cheffes,
Maine-et-Loire
Tel +33 (0)2 41 34 08 50
Email j.delaselle@wanadoo.fr
Web www.lamarronniere.fr

Western Loire

La Besnardière

"Divine," says a happy guest. Lovely Joyce brims with knowledge about all things horticultural, cooks beautiful vegetarian food, welcomes art, yoga and meditation workshops in her meditation room and shares her fresh, tranquil, comfortable home with generosity. Beams spring everywhere in the 500-year-old farmhouse, roof and velux windows are new, and the big, warm, book-filled bedrooms are tucked under the rafters, one with steps to a courtyard below. Be charmed by log fires, a soft-pink sofa'd sitting room, a garden full of wildflowers, a donkey, goats, ducks, hens and views.

Rooms	2: 1 double, 1 triple sharing bathroom.
Price	€60.
Meals	Dinner (vegetarian or vegan) with wine, €20.
Closed	Rarely.

Joyce Rimell
La Besnardière,
Route de Baugé,
49150 Fougeré, Maine-et-Loire
Tel   +33 (0)2 41 90 15 20
Email   rimell.joyce@wanadoo.fr
Web   www.holiday-loire.com

Entry 329   Map 4

Western Loire

Les Bouchets

It's spotless now, with all mod cons, gleaming antiques, open fires and vases of fresh flowers. The house was a ruin when the Bignons found it but they managed to save all the old timbers and stones. The result is a seductively warm cheerful house with bedrooms cosy and soft, two upstairs, one with an entrance off a garden where swings invite children to play. Passionate about food, they used to run a restaurant where Michel was chef; note the coppers in the kitchen/entrance hall, and memorabilia in the family sitting room. Géraldine, bright, friendly and organised… and serving beautiful home-grown or local food and the wines of Anjou.

Rooms	3: 1 double, 1 twin/double, 1 family room.
Price	€65-€70. €65-€80. Family room €70-€106.
Meals	Dinner with wine, €27.
Closed	Rarely.

Michel & Géraldine Bignon
Les Bouchets,
49150 Le Vieil Baugé,
Maine-et-Loire
Tel   +33 (0)2 41 82 34 48
Mobile   +33 (0)6 71 60 66 05
Email   bignonm@wanadoo.fr
Web   www.lesbouchets.com

Entry 330   Map 4

Western Loire

Le Logis du Pressoir

Birdsong and sunlight filter through eau de nil shutters into your cosy 18th-century cottage on this former wine pressing estate. A chestnut-panelled haven (pretty curtains, antique furniture, pale linens, a luxurious shower) it's all the work of friendly, knowledgeable Lisa and Mark. Lush parkland conceals four gîtes, whose guests share the heated pool with you. Breakfast amidst wisteria and lavender on your private terrace: summer fruits from the orchard, pâtisserie fresh from the village minutes away. A local restaurant delivers carefree dinners, and Lisa will pack a picnic for forays into historic wine country.

Minimum two nights.

Rooms	1 double.
Price	€75. Singles €65.
Meals	Restaurant 10-minute walk.
Closed	December/January & occasionally.

Lisa & Mark Wright
Le Logis du Pressoir,
Villeneuve, 49250 Brion,
Maine-et-Loire

Tel   +33 (0)2 41 57 27 33
Mobile   +33 (0)6 31 33 74 28
Email   info@logisdupressoir.com
Web   www.logisdupressoir.com

Entry 331   Map 4

Western Loire

La Closerie

Nothing pretentious about this quiet village house – or its owners, genuine country folk who still, after 20 years, love doing B&B. Carmen, retired English teacher, has a great sense of humour; Hervé looks after the vegetables and the hens. Bedrooms, in the old farmhouse or off the shady courtyard, two with their own entrances, are simply decorated with small shower rooms. The suite comes with a sitting room and a sofabed. The sunny conservatory dining room looks over a big bosky garden, full of trees for welcome shade (and swings for children).

Rooms	3: 2 doubles, 1 suite for 2-3.
Price	€62-€65. Suite €65.
Meals	Restaurant 4km.
Closed	Rarely.

Carmen & Hervé Taté
La Closerie,
29 rue d'Anjou,
49160 Saint Philbert du Peuple,
Maine-et-Loire

Tel   +33 (0)2 41 52 62 69
Email   herve.tate@wanadoo.fr
Web   www.bandb-lacloserie.com

Entry 332   Map 4

Western Loire

Domaine de l'Oie Rouge

Recline in bed from the quaint Chambre Camélia and watch the Loire flow by. The 19th-century townhouse sits in a large peaceful garden, and Christiane runs a lovely shop selling all manner of jams, pâtés and excellent produce. One bedroom has an astonishingly ornate 1930s brown-tiled bathroom with its bath bang in the middle, another opens to the garden and trees; all the rooms are lavishly French and art-hung. Monsieur is chef, Madame hosts dinner – great fun when a number of guests are staying. Both your hosts will be happy to help you decide what to see and make the most of your stay.

Rooms	5 doubles.
Price	€80–€98. Extra bed €19.
Meals	Dinner with wine, €27.
Closed	Rarely.

Christiane Batel
Domaine de l'Oie Rouge,
8 rue Nationale,
49350 Les Rosiers sur Loire,
Maine-et-Loire
Tel   +33 (0)2 41 53 65 65
Email   c.batel@wanadoo.fr
Web   domaine-oie-rouge.com

Entry 333   Map 4

Western Loire

Château de Salvert

This highly sculpted neo-gothic folly is home to a couple of unselfconscious aristocrats and lots of cheerful children. The baronial hall is properly dark and spooky, the dining room and salon elegant and plush with gilt chairs and ancestors on the walls. In the vast suite, a sitting area and a library in an alcove. One double has the shower in one turret, the loo in another (off the corridor). All are well decorated with fine French pieces and modern fabrics. The park is huge, wild boar roam, spring boarlets scamper, and Madame plays the piano and holds concerts.

Arrival after 4pm.

Rooms	5: 1 double, 1 suite.
	Cottage: 2 doubles, 1 suite.
Price	€49–€90. Suites €99–€160.
Meals	Dinner €44. Wine €22–€35.
Closed	Rarely.

Monica Le Pelletier de Glatigny
Château de Salvert,
Salvert, 49680 Neuillé,
Maine-et-Loire
Tel   +33 (0)2 41 52 55 89
Mobile +33 (0)6 15 12 03 11
Email   info@salvert.com
Web   www.chateau-de-salvert.fr

Entry 334   Map 4

La Jarillais

Take your cue from two snoozing white terriers – and from charming owners, who laugh easily and love their tranquil old Loire Valley farm. Ringed by roses, wisteria, terrace and pool, 'Coquelicot' exudes French country style: oak beams, red curtains, chimney, spinning wheel. Low-beamed 'Antemis', hugged by vines and daisies, has seagrass rugs on original tiles, a wood-burner, small kitchen. Both have private entrances, modern bathrooms, a cheery shared sitting room. And all is cocooned in meadows, trees, peace. Breakfast on homemade croissants to birdsong and the sight of Saumur's château, a pleasant drive or cycle away.

Château de Beaulieu

Set back from the banks of the river Loire lies a château of character and charm, a perfect reflection of its delightful owners. The house was built in 1727 and the décor, traditional and authentic, captures the romance of that earlier age. Five bedrooms lead off an oak-beamed corridor and range from the dramatic to the cosy and intimate. Find antique armoires, ornate fireplaces, bold colours and dreamy views of the large, tree-brimmed garden – with a lovely pool and a small prospering vineyard. Snuggle down with a book from the library, try your hand at billiards, visit historic Saumur, or visit the châteaux on horseback!

Rooms	2 doubles.
Price	€75-€80. Extra bed €20.
Meals	Restaurant 5km.
Closed	Rarely.

Rooms	5: 4 doubles, 1 suite for 2-4.
Price	€95-€120. Suite €130-€180.
Meals	Restaurants 1km.
Closed	November to Easter.

	Elizabeth & Frank Guibert de Bruet
	La Jarillais,
	Saint Lambert de Levées,
	49400 Saumur, Maine-et-Loire
Tel	+33 (0)2 41 59 03 44
Mobile	+33 (0)6 88 26 81 88
Email	betsy@la-jarillais-saumur.com
Web	www.la-jarillais-saumur.com

	Conor & Mary Coady–Maguire
	Château de Beaulieu,
	98 route de Montsoreau,
	49400 Saumur,
	Maine-et-Loire
Tel	+33 (0)2 41 50 83 52
Email	info@chateaudebeaulieu.fr
Web	www.chateaudebeaulieu.fr

Entry 335   Map 4

Entry 336   Map 4

Western Loire

Manoir de Boisairault

Our inspector had an *Alice Through The Looking Glass* moment as she stepped off the street, through the unremarkable gate and into the wonderful gardens – a series of secret 'rooms' – that surround this elegant, 18th-century, cloistered manor. A labyrinth of caves, typical of the region, lies below and guests sometimes dine there with Jean-Pierre and Béatrice – your cultured, interesting hosts. Pray for the camembert sprinkled with pastis, cooked in the fire's embers – it's divine. Inside are an attractive dining room and three pretty bedrooms; the ground-floor one – all Louis XV – is particularly enchanting.

Rooms	3: 2 doubles, 1 family room for 4.
Price	€110. Family room €95–€155.
Meals	Hosted dinner with wine €35. Children under 10 €15. Restaurants 10 km.
Closed	Rarely.

Jean-Pierre Delmas
Manoir de Boisairault,
8 rue de Pas d'Aubigné,
49260 Le Coudray Macouard,
Maine-et-Loire

Tel	+33 (0)6 08 93 85 61
Email	contact@manoir-de-boisairault.com
Web	www.manoir-de-boisairault.com

Entry 337   Map 4

Western Loire

La Grande Maison d'Arthenay

Micaela was in the hotel trade, Sue worked at a Sussex winery, now they run an idyllic B&B on a former Saumur wine estate. The house dates from 1706, the potager is organic, and the limestone outbuildings create a hollyhock'd garden off which two rustic-chic bedrooms lie. The two in the house are equally lovely, one with an extra bed on the mezzanine: tuffeau walls, deep mattresses, soft beautiful colours. Start the day with a convivial breakfast (fresh figs, eggs from their hens), end it with a wine-tasting dinner at the big table. Sue's wine tours of their own cellars and of the Loire region are unmissable!

Rooms	4: 3 twins/doubles, 1 suite.
Price	€95–€110. Suite €95–€140.
Meals	Dinner with wine, €50.
Closed	November–March.

Micaela Frow & Sue Hunt
La Grande Maison d'Arthenay,
Rue de la Cerisaie, Arthenay,
49700 Les Verchers Sur Layon,
Maine-et-Loire

Tel	+33 (0)2 41 40 35 06
Email	resv@lagrandemaison.net
Web	www.lagrandemaison.net

Entry 338   Map 4

Western Loire

La Maison du Roi René

The famous old auberge has become a charming B&B. Scrunch up the drive serenaded by soft roses to a lovely welcome from Madame. Part medieval, part 18th century, like the village around it, it has corners, crannies and a stunning central stone fireplace. The Valicourts – they speak four languages! – are the happy new owners of these magnificent oak doors and rosy tomette floors; bedrooms are beamed and very pleasing – one opens to the garden, three to the tower. There's a pretty paved terrace for breakfast with viennoiseries and a room of auberge proportions for a light supper of cold meats and local specialities.

Rooms	4: 2 doubles, 1 twin, 1 suite (with sofabed).
Price	€65–€85.
Meals	Supper tray €15. Restaurant 100m.
Closed	Rarely.

Dominique de Valicourt
La Maison du Roi René, 4 Grande Rue,
53290 Saint Denis d'Anjou,
Mayenne

Tel	+33 (0)2 43 70 52 30
Mobile	+33 (0)6 89 37 87 12
Email	roi-rene@orange.fr
Web	www.roi-rene.fr

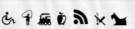

Entry 339   Map 4

Western Loire

Le Logis du Ray

All who stay at the Logis du Ray are wonderfully looked after – and we don't mean only the guests. Warm and caring, Jacques and Martine run a carriage-driving school, own four horses, three carthorses, two Shetland ponies and one Irish cob stallion, and house them in spotless pens and paddocks. Bedrooms are equally immaculate, their lovely old waxed terracotta floors setting off fine antiques and smart colourful fabrics to perfection in refined-traditional French style. The house is handsome in its historic village, your interesting hosts are good fun, the area is both rural and charming. Guests love the breakfasts.

Rooms	2 family rooms for 3.
Price	€75.
Meals	Light supper with wine, €18. Restaurant in village.
Closed	Rarely.

Martine & Jacques Lefebvre
Le Logis du Ray,
53290 Saint Denis d'Anjou,
Mayenne

Tel	+33 (0)2 43 70 64 10
Email	ecoleattelageduray@orange.fr
Web	www.ecoleattelageduray.com

Entry 340   Map 4

Western Loire

Le Rocher

Being the Richecours' only guests means a free run of Madame's delightful conversation (travel, history, houses, gardens, people), her lovingly designed garden (an abundance of old roses), and the delicious house that they have restored with such care and imagination. Your room is in the 17th-century part above the old kitchen, so attractive in its wealth of fitted cupboards and slabs of slate. Character fills the big guest room: original tiles, iron bed, great old timbers. The meadow sweeps down to the river where the family pedalo awaits to take you to the restaurant on the opposite bank. Elegance and great warmth – perfection!

Rooms	1 family room for 2-3.
Price	€90-€150.
Meals	Restaurants within 7km.
Closed	Rarely.

Mme de Richecour
Le Rocher,
Saint Germain de l'Hommel,
53200 Fromentières, Mayenne
Tel +33 (0)2 43 07 06 64
Email eva2richecour@free.fr
Web manoirdurocher.fr

Entry 341   Map 3

Western Loire

Château de Craon

Such a close and welcoming family, whose kindness extends to include you. It's a magnificent place, with innumerable expressions of history, taste and personality, and gracious Loïk and Hélène, young grandparents, treat you like friends. A sitting room with sofas and a view of the park, an Italianate hall with sweeping stone stair, classic French bedrooms in lavender, blue, cream… an original washstand, a canopied bed, a velvet armchair. Everywhere a feast for the eyes; paintings, watercolours, antiques. Outside, 40 acres of river, meadows, lake, ice house, tennis court, pool, and a potager worth leaving home for.

Rooms	6: 3 doubles, 1 twin, 1 single, 1 suite for 2-4.
Price	€100-€160. Single €80. Suite €260.
Meals	Dinner with wine, €30. Restaurants in village, within walking distance.
Closed	November-March.

Loïk & Hélène de Guébriant
Château de Craon,
53400 Craon,
Mayenne
Tel +33 (0)2 43 06 11 02
Email chateaudecraon@wanadoo.fr
Web www.craoncastle.com

Entry 342   Map 3

Western Loire

Château de la Villatte

From the village, a drive rises to the top of the butte where a 19th-century château sits in splendour. Isabelle arrived some years ago and her loving restoration knows no bounds – the fine outbuildings have just been completed – yet still she finds time to enjoy her guests. Dimensions are generous throughout and bedrooms are vast, their parquet floors strewn with rugs. Tall windows overlook the steeply sloping park and the valley below, there are marble fireplaces, paintings in gilt frames, an original claw-foot bath. Breakfast on the balcony or in the grand salon, borrow bikes, or explore the lovely tree'd grounds.

Rooms	2: 1 double, 1 twin/double.
Price	€78-€96. Rooms can interconnect to form suite, €174.
Meals	Cold dinner €20. Wine €14-€39. Summer kitchen.
Closed	Rarely.

Isabelle Charrier
Château de la Villatte,
53970 Montigné le Brillant,
Mayenne
Tel   +33 (0)2 43 68 23 76
Email   info@lavillatte.com
Web   www.lavillatte.com

Entry 343   Map 3

Western Loire

La Rouaudière

Prize-winning cows in the fields, an adorable family in the house, and a wagging farm dog. Thérèse, her farming son and husband (retired) are exceptionally engaging, relaxed people and their conversation is the heart and soul of this place. Dinners are divine, breakfasts in front of the crackling fire are estimable – delicious fresh everything and lashings of coffee. You'll find roses, pergolas, a rare magnolia and birdsong in the garden (Madame is a nature lover and keen plantswoman) and bedrooms that are straightforward, spotless and simple: plain walls, a few antiquey bits and bobs, pretty window boxes. Lovely.

Rooms	3: 1 double, 1 twin, 1 triple.
Price	€55-€60.
Meals	Dinner with wine, €22.
Closed	Rarely.

Maurice & Thérèse Trihan
La Rouaudière,
Mégaudais,
53500 Ernée, Mayenne
Tel   +33 (0)2 43 05 13 57
Email   therese-trihan@wanadoo.fr
Web   www.rouaudiere-megaudais.fr

Entry 344   Map 3

Western Loire

La Garencière

Lovely old stone buildings tumbled with flowers, a few livestock, a pool in a barn with a view: it's a delightful, deep-rural address. These charming young parents – she the fine cook, he the smiling waiter – love their new enterprise and make a spirited team. The two-storey 'boulangerie' – pretty bedsteads, huge old bread oven – is the most characterful of the guest rooms, the vistas are long, the dinners are generous and very, very good. Breakfasts are feasts. Spill outside for pétanque as children explore Wendy house, trampoline, swings and huge space. Great B&B.

Pool available May-Sept.

Rooms	5: 1 double, 3 family rooms for 4, 1 family room for 5.
Price	€70. Family rooms €100–€130. Extra bed €15.
Meals	Dinner with wine or cider, €25. Restaurant 5km.
Closed	Rarely.

Carine & Frédéric Brindjonc
La Garencière,
72610 Champfleur, Sarthe
Tel   +33 (0)2 33 31 75 84
Email   lagarenciere@orange.fr
Web   www.garenciere.fr

Entry 345   Map 4

Western Loire

Éporcé

You may think yourself as lucky to stay in this relaxedly grand place as the owner and his young family to have inherited it, so fine and genuine inside and out. Pure 17th century with a magnificent avenue of trees, moat, lofty beamed ceilings, three salons for guests, it brims with a laid-back lived-in atmosphere – expect antiques, books, pictures, engravings and butterfly collections galore. First-floor rooms are the ones to go for – proper château stuff – and meals are relaxed and easy (unless you go for 'gourmet', family silver and Wedgwood). The gardens are handsome, formal, wonderful.

Chapel & coach house available for weddings.

Rooms	3: 2 doubles, 1 twin/double.
Price	€90–€150.
Meals	Dinner with wine, €40.
Closed	Rarely.

Rémy de Scitivaux
Éporcé,
72550 La Quinte, Sarthe
Tel   +33 (0)2 43 27 70 22
Email   eporce@wanadoo.fr

Entry 346   Map 4

Château de l'Enclos

The Guillous welcome you to their grand château in its elegant setting as long-lost friends. Sociable and fun, they are proud of their parkland with its fine trees, llamas and donkeys, magical Finnish treehouse in a monumental sequoia and new Gypsy caravan, decked, fenced, lantern'd and decorated in cosiest Romany style. Back in the château, a staircase sweeps you up to handsome bedrooms of parquet and rich carpets, writing desks and tall windows; two have balconies. The charming salon opens to a stage-set-perfect garden, and you dine with your hosts in liveliest table d'hôtes style. There's masses to do in little Brûlon.

La Maison du Pont Romain

Cross Monfort's exquisite stone bridge to this pretty house on the banks of the river. Enter the grounds and forget the world in heavenly peace among very old trees. Gentle Madame saved it all from ruin and gives you two comfortable rooms upstairs, privately off the courtyard, both with fine armoires. The suite in the old stables (salon below, bedrooms above) has a charming late 18th-century feel. There are delicious jams at the big table for breakfast and a family salon for guests. Visit Montfort's castle and the lovely, unsung villages and vineyards of the Sarthe. For children? Forest animals at Pescheray and an aquapark in the village.

Rooms	5: 2 doubles, 1 twin, 1 gypsy caravan, 1 treehouse for 2.
Price	€120. Gypsy caravan €140. Treehouse €170.
Meals	Dinner with wine, €45.
Closed	Rarely.

Rooms	3: 2 doubles, 1 suite for 3-4.
Price	€62-€76.
Meals	Dinner with wine, €23.
Closed	Rarely.

Annie-Claude & Jean-Claude Guillou
Château de l'Enclos,
2 av de la Libération,
72350 Brûlon, Sarthe
Tel   +33 (0)2 43 92 17 85
Email jean-claude.guillou5@orange.fr
Web   www.chateau-enclos.com

Chantal Paris
La Maison du Pont Romain,
26 rue de l'Église,
72450 Montfort le Gesnois, Sarthe
Tel   +33 (0)2 43 76 13 46
Email chantal-paris@wanadoo.fr
Web   www.le-pont-romain.fr

Entry 347   Map 4

Entry 348   Map 4

Western Loire

Maison Conti

Relaxed charm fills this regal village house, built by Louis XIV's favourite daughter next to her own château in Montmirail. Trompe-l'œil sets the scene for scrumptious table d'hôtes: homemade soup, local lamb, fruit tarte… in summer, dine peacefully on the terrace then settle by the fire. Double rooms, off a light-bathed corridor, are happy spaces in blue, yellow, green and rose, with period décor and superb bathrooms. Original alcoves and fires sit in limewashed walls and shutters block light – but not church bells, which start at 7am. Rise early to explore the Perche; return to barbecues and badminton on the lawn.

Western Loire

Le Chaton Rouge

Some of the world's fastest cars speed around the Le Mans race track less than ten miles away, but here in St Pierre du Lorouer life is slower. Stay in this elegant townhouse opposite a small church; while the hours away in its courtyard. Or climb the stone steps to a long walled garden where a vegetable patch and raspberry canes provide food for dinner cooked by bright friendly Sarah; tuck in by the fire in winter, and the outdoors dining room in summer. Up a sweep of staircase are the bedrooms, fresh, white and uncluttered, with original tiled floors and oak beams. Super bathrooms have white towels and hand-made soaps.

Guest TV lounge & kitchenette available.

Rooms	4 doubles.
Price	€80–€90. Extra bed €15.
Meals	Dinner, 3 courses with wine, €35. Restaurant nearby.
Closed	Never.

Rooms	4: 2 doubles; 1 double, 1 family suite for 2-4 each with separate bathroom.
Price	€80. Family suite €140.
Meals	Lunch €10. Dinner with wine, €25. Restaurant 20m.
Closed	Rarely.

Richard & Nancy Harrison
Maison Conti,
2 place de l'Église,
72320 Montmirail, Sarthe

Tel	+33 (0)2 43 93 35 26
Email	info@maisonconti.com
Web	www.maisonconti.com

Sarah Carlisle
Le Chaton Rouge, 4 rue du Calvaire,
72150 Saint Pierre du Lorouer,
Sarthe

Tel	+33 (0)2 43 46 21 37
Mobile	+33 (0)6 44 17 23 74
Email	sarah@lechatonrouge.com
Web	www.lechatonrouge.com

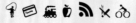

Le Moulin Calme

Weeping willow-fringed millponds dreamy with lilies and irises, a duck house, a charming humpbacked bridge, create a magic waterworld that wraps you in calm. Add quietly spoken Joëlle's excellent cooking (guests return for favourite dishes) using organic produce from the garden and served by ebullient Jean-Luc in the conservatory or by the pond, and you may feel no need to explore the surrounding Loire. There's fishing, a heated pool, swings and a pedalo; young children may need watching. Three exterior staircases lead to rooms in the former millhouse – homely, traditional, with views over water or wooded hills.

Le Prieuré

Bushels of history cling to the beams and vaulted ceilings of the moated priory, snug beneath its old church. Built in the 12th, extended in the 16th, it had monks until the 20th century. Christophe loves telling the history, Marie-France does the decorating, brilliantly in keeping with the elegant old house: oriental rugs on old tiled floors, pale-painted beams over stone fireplaces, fine old paintings on plain walls, good beds under soft-coloured covers. They are attentive hosts, happy to share their vaulted dining room and pretty, peaceful garden, and the road is not an inconvenience.

Rooms	5: 2 doubles, 1 twin, 2 family rooms for 3.
Price	€65. Family rooms €65–€93. Singles €54.
Meals	Dinner €22. Wine €9–€28. Auberge in village.
Closed	Christmas & New Year.

Rooms	3: 2 doubles, 1 twin.
Price	€110–€130. Singles €90–€100.
Meals	Auberge opposite; restaurants nearby.
Closed	November-February, except by arrangement.

	Joëlle Combries
	Le Moulin Calme,
	Gascheau,
	72500 Luceau, Sarthe
Tel	+33 (0)2 43 46 39 75
Email	moulincalme@wanadoo.fr
Web	www.lemoulincalme.com

	Christophe & Marie-France Calla
	Le Prieuré, 1 rue de la Gare,
	72500 Dissay sous Courcillon,
	Sarthe
Tel	+33 (0)2 43 44 09 09
Mobile	+33 (0)6 15 77 84 48
Email	ccalla@club-internet.fr
Web	www.chateauprieure.com

Entry 351   Map 4

Entry 352   Map 4

Western Loire

La Châtaigneraie

Outside is a fairy tale: mellow old stone, white shutters, green ivy, a large leafy garden, a clematis-covered well, a little wood and glimpses of the 12th-century castle round the corner; La Châtaigneraie used to be the servants' quarters. Green-eyed Michèle, modern, intelligent and interested in people, shares the hosting with Michel. The suite is made up of three pastel-hued bedrooms that look onto garden or endless fields. Stay a while and connect – with the soft hills, the woods, the streams, the châteaux. Guests can be as independent as they like and can take one, two or three rooms. Dinner is great value.

Rooms	1 suite of 3 rooms (2 doubles, 1 single).
Price	€65–€120.
Meals	Dinner with wine, €23. Child €12. Restaurant 2km.
Closed	November–March.

Michèle Letanneux & Michel Guyon
La Châtaigneraie,
72500 Dissay sous Courcillon,
Sarthe

Tel	+33 (0)2 43 79 36 71
Mobile	+33 (0)6 16 44 45 97
Email	michelecretagne@yahoo.fr

Entry 353   Map 4

Western Loire

Le Moulin de la Diversière

In a loop of a small river, a honey-coloured mill surrounded by trees, silence and willow-fringed paths leading to two cottages – yours for self-catering or B&B – that Anne and Jean-Marc have lovingly converted in tune with the setting and their green ideals. Outside: a big sloping garden, a play area for your children (and theirs), shady arbours, an above-ground pool. Inside: old tomettes and limewashed walls, cane chairs and fresh flowers, pretty kitchens and showers with pebble floors. Breakfast is brought to your door; table d'hôtes is at your hosts' friendly table, by a roaring fire in winter. Special indeed.

Rooms	3: 1 double, 1 triple. Cottage for 4.
Price	€58. Triple €75. Cottage €65 for 2. Double room connects to triple to form suite: €100–€125 (€395–€655 per week).
Meals	Dinner with wine, €23.
Closed	Rarely.

Anne & Jean-Marc Le Foulgocq
Le Moulin de la Diversière,
72800 Savigné sous le Lude, Sarthe

Tel	+33 (0)2 43 48 09 16
Mobile	+33 (0)6 77 44 79 95
Email	contact@moulin-de-la-diversiere.com
Web	www.moulin-de-la-diversiere.com

Entry 354   Map 4

Loire Valley

Loire Valley

Le Moulin de Lonceux

A placid river sets ancient mill stones grinding and flour flows; ducks dip, swans preen, geese saunter; gardens are beset by roses, herbs, bantams, goats, a hammock. The mill has been ingeniously restored by this hard-working family (she a geologist, he an engineer) into a home and – alongside, separate – a B&B managed with verve. Sleep in stables complete with manger; a flint-walled cider press; a two-room loft suite; a smart Miller's Room with fireplace. Breakfast in the dayroom (sofa, games, candles, log fire) on fresh pastries from home-milled flour (of course). Chartres is close, Paris an easy train ride. A gem.

Loire Valley

Maison JLN

Come to enjoy this gentle, charming family and the serene vibes of their old Chartrain house. Up two steep twisting spirals to the attic, through the family's little prayer room (a shell for each pilgrim who's stayed here), the sweet, peaceful bedroom feels like a chapel itself with its honey floorboards and small windows (no wardrobe). Lots of books; reminders of pilgrimage, just beneath the great cathedral; Madame knowledgeably friendly, Monsieur, who speaks nine languages, quietly amusing, both interested in your travels, both happy to sit and talk when you get back. An unusual and special place, in a timeless town.

Rooms	4: 3 doubles, 1 suite for 2-4.
Price	€105-€170.
Meals	Catered meals & cold tray on arrival, with wine, €15-€25 (on request). Restaurant 3km.
Closed	Rarely.

Rooms	1 twin (with shower & wc on floor below).
Price	€53.
Meals	Restaurants nearby.
Closed	Rarely.

Isabelle Heitz
Le Moulin de Lonceux,
Hameau de Lonceux,
28700 Oinville sous Auneau,
Eure-et-Loir
Mobile   +33 (0)6 70 00 60 45
Email   contact@moulin-de-lonceux.com
Web   www.moulin-de-lonceux.com

Jean-Loup & Nathalie Cuisiniez
Maison JLN,
80 rue Muret,
28000 Chartres, Eure-et-Loir
Tel   +33 (0)2 37 21 98 36
Mobile   +33 (0)6 79 48 46 63
Email   chartres.maison.jln@gmail.com
Web   monsite.orange.fr/maisonjln

Entry 355   Map 5

Entry 356   Map 4

Loire Valley

Moulin de la Ronce

A very fine mill, built in 1555, restored in 2008, beautifully and artfully transformed by Clément and bright smiling Laurence. Expect the best: homemade jams, tea from Paris, eggs from the hens, and, facing a central courtyard, eco-luxurious bedrooms in uncluttered style... an age-old flagged floor, a Philippe Starck bathtub, colourful towels, splashes of art. The waterside setting is timeless, the garden is thronged with weeping willows, there are books to plunder, grapes to pluck, a row boat for the hearty, a day room for summer, a log fire for winter, and, 15 miles away, the glorious cathedral of Chartres.

Rooms	3: 1 double, 1 twin/double, 1 suite.
Price	€150. Suite €200.
Meals	Restaurants 6km.
Closed	Rarely.

Laurence & Clément Krief
Moulin de la Ronce,
28800 Alluyes,
Eure-et-Loir
Email   contact@moulin-de-la-ronce.com
Web   www.moulin-de-la-ronce.com

Entry 357   Map 4

Loire Valley

Chambres d'Hôtes Les Champarts

This was Dagmar's country cottage until she left Paris to settle here. She left her native Germany and adopted France many moons ago. Come for compact, cosy, immaculate B&B set in a charming village. Breakfast is a feast: hot croissants, jams, smoked salmon, farm butter. The cottage garden is cherished and, if you time it right, every old wall will be covered with roses. Up the steep stairs, one bedroom is wood-panelled, the other more typical with sloping rafters; fabrics are flowered and varnished floors symmetrically rugged. Traditional, authentic, friendly, and great fun.

Extra beds available.

Rooms	2: 1 double, 1 suite.
Price	€53. Suite €63.
Meals	Restaurants 3km.
Closed	Rarely.

Dagmar Parmentier
Chambres d'Hôtes Les Champarts,
2 route des Champarts, Blévy,
28170 Maillebois, Eure-et-Loir
Tel   +33 (0)2 37 48 01 21
Email   leschamparts@bab-blevy.com
Web   www.bab-blevy.com

Entry 358   Map 4

Loire Valley

La Soupletière

In woody, watery Sologne, here be happy hard-working cereal farmers. Enter the arms-wide yard, breathe in the harmony of deep old-tiled roofs, the two horses' heads quietly guarding the great barn, the rich country silence, and relax. Your big, white, welcoming ground-floor bedroom has space, 17th-century beams, some nice old furniture, two good reading chairs and a seriously modern, fun bathroom. The generous garden flows into fields and ponds: you can walk straight out. Or explore the towns, châteaux, rivers and cycle paths. Strong, intelligent Marielle has all the best tips on where to go, what to do. Tremendous value.

Extra child bed available.

Rooms	1 double.
Price	€70.
Meals	Restaurants 2km.
Closed	Never.

Marielle Digard
La Soupletière,
45500 St Gondon, Loiret
Tel   +33 (0)6 07 88 12 43
Mobile   +33 (0)6 07 45 95 09
Email   alasoupletiere@orange.fr
Web   www.lasoupletiere.com

Entry 359   Map 5

Loire Valley

Les Vieux Guays

Looking for seclusion? This house sits in 200 acres of woods, its beautiful garden rambling down to the duck-bobbed lake. Alvaro, a tennis professional, and Sandrine returned from Chile to the family home, now alive with two youngsters. They are a poised and friendly couple easily mixing old and modern, bright and dark. Sandrine produces meals for you from an impressive professional kitchen, mostly regional dishes using local organic food. Bedrooms are high quality too: antiques, excellent new bedding, plain walls and floral fabrics. And there's a nice day room, with terrace and fireplace. Very special.

Rooms	5: 2 doubles, 1 twin, 2 family rooms for 4.
Price	€80-€85. Family rooms €120.
Meals	Dinner with wine, €30 (Thurs-Sun only).
Closed	Rarely.

Sandrine & Alvaro Martinez
Les Vieux Guays,
45620 Cerdon du Loiret, Loiret
Tel   +33 (0)2 38 36 03 76
Mobile   +33 (0)6 80 16 53 76
Email   lvg45@orange.fr
Web   www.lesvieuxguays.com

Entry 360   Map 5

Loire Valley

Domaine de la Thiau

A large estate by the Loire, a 19th-century house for the family, a 17th-century one for guests, pheasants and peacocks strutting around the spacious grounds with mature trees. Your hosts – he is a busy vet, she elegantly looks after house, gîtes and you – make it feel welcoming despite the apparent grandeur. Peaceful bedrooms are carefully decorated with carved bedsteads and papered walls – extremely, Frenchly traditional. There's a Victorian-style conservatory for breakfast, furnished with a large oval table and blue velvet chairs. A good address for summer.

Minimum two nights weekends, bank holidays & high season.

Rooms	3: 2 doubles, 1 suite for 3 with kitchen.
Price	€64–€74. Suite €74–€84.
Meals	Catered dinner available for 2+ night stays. Restaurants 4km.
Closed	Rarely.

Bénédicte François
Domaine de la Thiau,
45250 Briare,
Loiret

Tel	+33 (0)2 38 38 20 92
Email	info@lathiau.fr
Web	www.lathiau.fr

Entry 361   Map 5

Loire Valley

Moulin Guillard

Just outside the village of Subligny, not far from Sancerre, is an enchanting blue-shuttered mill where flour was once produced. Now it is a stylish, delightful B&B. Dorothée, a fascinating and cultured woman who once ran a bookshop in Paris, divides her time between an exquisite garden of rare plants and her guests. She offers you a smallish, softly serene double upstairs, and a two-bedroom suite across the way, its private sitting room with piano downstairs. In summer you breakfast between the two, in a barn overlooking the stream and Dorothée's several breeds of free-roaming hen. Dinners are superb.

Rooms	2: 1 double, 1 suite for 4 with sitting room.
Price	€95.
Meals	Dinner €26. Wine from €18.
Closed	Rarely.

Dorothée Malinge
Moulin Guillard,
18260 Subligny,
Cher

Tel	+33 (0)2 48 73 70 49
Mobile	+33 (0)6 61 71 15 30
Email	malinge.annig@orange.fr

Entry 362   Map 5

Loire Valley

La Verrerie

Deep countryside, fine people, fantastic bedrooms. In a pretty outbuilding, the double, with a green iron bedhead, old tiled floor and Provençal quilt, looks onto the garden from the ground floor; the suite's twin has the same tiles underfoot, beams overhead and high wooden beds with an inviting mix of white covers and red quilts. The Count and Countess, who manage forests, farm and hunt, enjoy doing B&B – they are charming and thoroughly hospitable. If you would like to dine in, you will join them for dinner in the main house. Members of the family run a vineyard in Provence, so try their wine.

Rooms	3: 2 doubles, 1 family suite for 2-4.
Price	€75-€110. Family suite €99-€145.
Meals	Dinner with wine, €20-€30. Guest kitchen. Restaurants 10km.
Closed	Rarely.

Étienne & Marie de Saporta
La Verrerie,
18380 Ivoy le Pré,
Cher
Tel +33 (0)2 48 58 90 86
Email m.desaporta@wanadoo.fr
Web www.laverreriedivoy.com

Loire Valley

Demeure des Tanneries

Revel in rich croissants and breads at breakfast – Monsieur was a boulanger/pâtissier, Madame loves to make jams. Dinner is just as good, accompanied by local wines – tasty miniature tartine appetisers, a goat's cheese millefeuille perhaps, a blanquette of turkey, a luscious chocolate tart. Eat in the ruby and gold salon, to a splendid mishmash of antique furniture collected by Monsieur, and polished wood floors, gilt-framed mirrors, crystal chandeliers... somehow it all works. Set off on woodland and vineyard walks, return to a heated pool. A nice friendly spot for an extended stopover as you traverse France.

Children over 8 welcome.

Rooms	2 doubles.
Price	€80-€90. Extra bed €30.
Meals	Dinner with aperitif, €30. Wine €12. Restaurants 5km.
Closed	Rarely.

Paulette Loup
Demeure des Tanneries,
Lit dit Les Billets,
30 route la Chapelotte,
18250 Henrichemont, Cher
Tel +33 (0)2 48 26 19 54
Email info@demeure-tanneries.com
Web www.demeure-tanneries.com

Loire Valley

Moulin de Reigny

The family's wines – citrusy whites and fruity reds – are centre-stage here, and rightly so; three generations of Guilleraults live here. Next comes charming, courteous Geneviève's delicious Sancerrois cuisine, served hand in hand with the appropriate wines at your hosts' table, bathed in evening light from a huge arched window. She takes English lessons to be even more helpful to guests. Then you will walk the short distance through the village to the Caves du Prieuré where the little old mill now houses the peaceful B&B rooms which are utterly simple, old-fashioned and unpretentious. Lovely people, remarkable value.

Rooms	Old Mill: 3 doubles.
Price	€55. Singles €45. Extra bed & baby cot, €25.
Meals	Dinner with wine, €18–€22. Restaurants 8km.
Closed	Rarely.

Geneviève Guillerault
Moulin de Reigny,
2 rue des Fontaines,
Reigny,
18300 Crézancy en Sancerre, Cher
Tel   +33 (0)2 48 79 01 74
Email   jacques.guillerault@wanadoo.fr

Entry 365   Map 5

Loire Valley

Château des Réaux

A neo-gothic castle, gloriously asymmetrical, whose ex-film-world guardians, Michèle and Philippe, love their new life. Outside are semi-wild grounds where six French hens roam and a vegetable garden flourishes; Philippe is a good chef so do eat in. Inside: a stunning fusion of classic and contemporary, a manorial drawing room done in warm minimalist style, a 'smoking room' with comfy sofas, a library/games room to keep you busy. Everything's spacious, including the blissfully serene bedrooms. After feasting on viennoiseries at the convivial table, visit Apremont up the road – you'll fall in love with its delicate wines.

Rooms	4: 2 doubles, 2 suites.
Price	€140–€180. Suites €190–€230.
Meals	Dinner €45. Restaurant 5km.
Closed	Rarely.

Michèle & Philippe Graves
Château des Réaux,
18150 Le Chautay,
Cher
Tel   +33 (0)2 48 74 93 78
Email   lechateaudesreaux@shdnet.fr
Web   www.lechateaudesreaux.fr

Entry 366   Map 10

Loire Valley

Les Bonnets Rouges

Cross the garden courtyard to this venerable 15th-century coaching inn (Stendhal slept here). Beyond the breakfast room, where ancient timbers, wraparound oak panels and stone alcoves dance in mixed-up glory for breakfast amid Turkish rugs, is the staircase up. Bedrooms, wonderfully quaint and nicely tatty, have antique beds (one a four-poster), new mattresses, marble fireplaces and a claw-footed bath. Up steeper, narrower stairs, the pretty attic double has festoons of beams and the loo behind a curtain. Your charming host, Olivier, lives just across the courtyard. Sleep among angels beneath Bourges' unsurpassed cathedral.

Rooms	4: 2 doubles, 2 suites for 3-4.
Price	€72-€80. Suites €80-€110. Extra bed €20.
Meals	Restaurants within walking distance.
Closed	Rarely.

Olivier Llopis
Les Bonnets Rouges,
3 rue de la Thaumassière,
18000 Bourges, Cher
Tel +33 (0)2 48 65 79 92
Email bonnets-rouges@bourges.net
Web bonnets-rouges.bourges.net

Entry 367 Map 10

Loire Valley

La Grande Mouline

In 1989 the Charlons came to raise their family in this rustic haven where the natural garden flows into woods and fields, deer roam and birdlife astounds. Jean Malot is a gentle, attentive host who taught in Tunisia for much of his career and is proud of his conversion of outbuildings for B&B. Nicely unsophisticated bedrooms come with ethnic fabrics and rugs, fresh white walls, tongue and groove panelling – and the odd teddy bear. Breakfast in the main house comes with really good homemade jams and cake. Return after contemplating Bourges to meditate in this sweet corner of God's garden or share the above-ground pool.

Children over 12 welcome.

Rooms	4: 2 triples, 1 quadruple, 1 family room.
Price	Triple €65. Quadruple €80. Family room €80. Extra bed €15.
Meals	Restaurant 3km.
Closed	Rarely.

Jean Malot & Chantal Charlon
La Grande Mouline,
Bourgneuf, 18110 St Éloy de Gy,
Cher
Tel +33 (0)2 48 25 40 44
Email jean-m4@wanadoo.fr
Web pagesperso-orange.fr/lagrandemouline

Entry 368 Map 10

Loire Valley

Domaine de l'Ermitage

In historic Berry Bouy, in the heartland of France, this articulate husband-and-wife team run their beef and cereals farm and Menetou-Salon vineyards (tastings arranged), make their own jam and still have time for their guests. Vivacious and casually elegant, Laurence runs an intelligent, welcoming house. The big, simple yet stylishly attractive bedrooms of her superior 18th-century farmhouse are of pleasing proportions, one up a steep and twisting stair in the brick-and-timber tower, others with views over the graceful park. Guests may use the swimming pool, set discreetly out of sight, between 6 and 7pm.

Rooms	5: 2 doubles, 1 quadruple, 1 triple, 1 twin.
Price	€73–€76. Triple €104. Quadruple €136.
Meals	Restaurants in village.
Closed	Rarely.

Laurence & Géraud de La Farge
Domaine de l'Ermitage,
18500 Berry Bouy, Cher

Tel	+33 (0)2 48 26 87 46
Email	domaine-ermitage@wanadoo.fr
Web	www.hotes-ermitage.com

Entry 369 Map 10

Loire Valley

Domaine de la Trolière

The beautifully proportioned house in its big shady garden has been in the family for over 200 years. The sitting room is a cool blue-grey symphony, the dining room smart yellow-grey with a rare, remarkable maroon and grey marble table: breakfast is in here, dinner, sometimes *en famille*, always delicious, is in the big beamed kitchen. Each stylishly comfortable room has individual character and Madame has a fine eye for detail. She is charming, dynamic, casually elegant and has many cats. Visitors have poured praise: "quite the most beautiful house we've ever stayed in", "the evening meals were superb".

Rooms	4: 3 doubles; 1 double with separate wc.
Price	€51–€71. Extra bed €10.
Meals	Dinner with wine, €25.
Closed	Rarely.

Marie-Claude Dussert
Domaine de la Trolière,
18200 Orval, Cher

Tel	+33 (0)2 48 96 47 45
Mobile	+33 (0)6 72 21 59 76
Email	marie-claude.dussert@orange.fr

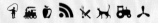

Entry 370 Map 10

Loire Valley

Château de la Villette

More pretty 19th-century hunting lodge than grand château, la Villette sits in 40 idyllic acres of parkland, close to a huge spring-fed lake: borrow the row boat and potter. Capable, hospitable, generous Karin – dynamic gardener, fine cook – loves and cares for each inch of the place. A winding staircase leads to a beauty of a bedroom done in Biedermeier style, with a sloping ceiling and serene views; the second room too is seductive. Feather duvets will cosset you, elegant breakfasts and dinners at the convent table will delight you, and nothing is too much trouble for Karin.

Rooms	2: 1 double; 1 double with separate bathroom.
Price	€80-€90.
Meals	Dinner with wine, €25.
Closed	Rarely.

Karin Verburgh
Château de la Villette,
St Août,
36120 Ardentes, Indre
Tel   +33 (0)2 54 36 28 46
Web   www.romantik-destinations.com

Entry 371   Map 10

Loire Valley

La Croix Verte

Vincent and Élisabeth's serene home lies plumb in the heart of George Sand country. Linger under lime trees in a secret courtyard garden while relishing a plentiful breakfast; enjoy a dinner of home-grown produce; get cosy in the family sitting room before an open fire. A staging post in the 12th century, La Croix Verte stands in the heart of the village but you won't hear a peep as you slumber under a hand-stitched bedcover; the two charming loft bedrooms in natural tones share sofas, books and games. Come for heaps of character, unspoilt countryside, and artist hosts (potter and painter) who are an absolute delight.

Rooms	3: 2 doubles, 1 twin.
Price	€59. Singles €52. Extra bed €20.
Meals	Dinner with wine €23. Restaurant 1.5km.
Closed	Rarely.

Élisabeth & Vincent Portier
La Croix Verte,
Le Bourg,
12 rue des Maîtres Sonneurs,
36400 St Chartier, Indre
Tel   +33 (0)2 54 31 02 71
Email   contact@veportier.com
Web   www.veportier.com

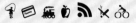

Entry 372   Map 10

Loire Valley

Le Manoir du Menoux

In the heart of a quiet village, through a formal French garden, is a pretty half-timbered house with a Normandy air. Pleasant Marie-Estelle is a straightforward lady with a quiet smile, serving breakfast around a large oak table in the dining room, or outside in summer. Sit listening to the gurgling stream down by the charming summerhouse; in chillier weather, the salons' daybeds make a comfy spot. Up the winding oak staircase are the light and luminous suite 'Diane', southern-coloured 'Manon' gazing over romantic rooftops, and 50s-feel 'Amélie'. Visit snail and chestnut fêtes, and Lake d'Eguzon for nautical things. Lovely.

Rooms	3: 2 doubles, 1 suite for 2-4.
Price	€65–€69. Suite €75–€124.
Meals	Dinner €25. Restaurant within walking distance.
Closed	Last 2 weeks in December.

Marie-Estelle Rives
Le Manoir du Menoux,
15 rue Haute,
36200 Le Menoux, Indre
Tel +33 (0)2 36 27 91 87
Mobile +33 (0)6 60 10 20 57
Email rivesme@wanadoo.fr
Web www.manoirdumenoux.com

Entry 373   Map 9

Loire Valley

Londinium Chambres & Tables d'Hôtes

Friendly hosts offer warm welcomes at this spick 'n' span 18th-century longère. Its huge gardens house fruity orchards and a 300-year-old oak; spy on the birds and Berrichon countryside from the conservatory. The south-facing suite and spacious 'Garden Room' (with chaise longue) are bright and beamed, with parquet floors. Pictures vie with windows whose stunning valley views span 60km; bathrooms are elegant and modern. Take coddled eggs on the terrace or sample Valérie's delicious ice creams. Break the drive south or linger to walk, fish and cycle in the sun. A café, watersports lake and living Roman museum are nearby.

Rooms	3: 2 twins, 1 suite for 4.
Price	€65–€85. Suite €90–€110.
Meals	Dinner €22.50. Restaurants 1.5 km.
Closed	Rarely.

Valérie London
Londinium Chambres
& Tables d'Hôtes,
4 Les Moreaux, Chavin,
36200 Argenton sur Creuse, Indre
Tel +33 (0)2 54 47 71 74
Email londinium.lesmoreaux@gmail.com
Web www.londiniumchambres.com

Entry 374   Map 9

Loire Valley

Domaine du Ris de Feu

No longer part of a defensive frontier of castles, this 15th-century manor and lake is a sanctuary swathed in lush forest. The domain is the pride and joy of Caroline, who runs it to the highest eco and ethical standards, and husband Luc. Artisan builders (still discreetly on site) have restored using natural materials and traditional craft. Your charming fruit loft, on two floors, has oval windows, oak fittings and a wood-burner; upstairs, drift off under organic linen. After breakfast in the old bakery, wander and enjoy, listen to the birdlife, bathe in the lake, hire canoes or bicycles... explore this enchanted kingdom!

Bikes, electric scooters & Citroën 2CVs available to rent.

Rooms	Fruit loft: 1 suite.
Price	€125–€145.
Meals	Dinner from €19. Wine from €12.
Closed	Never.

Luc & Caroline Fontaine
Domaine du Ris de Feu,
36370 Chalais, Indre
Tel +33 (0)2 54 37 87 73
Email contact@lerisdefeu.fr
Web www.lerisdefeu.fr

Entry 375 Map 9

Loire Valley

Château de Forges

Granted to Monsieur's ancestors by Charles VII, this medieval château is rich in atmosphere and architectural beauty. Tour period rooms with deep comforts: an elegant salon with a vast log fire, a vaulted cellar with a hammam and jacuzzi (extra fee), a romantic dining room where you may partake of excellent four-course meals and local tipples. Spacious pastel bedrooms sparkle with period features and joyful views; find big beams, gilt mirrors, a crimson canopy, an antique bath... A green carpet slopes down to the river for swimming or kayaking; beyond the ramparts are the birds and butterflies of La Brenne natural park.

Ask about spa sessions.

Rooms	3 doubles.
Price	€160.
Meals	Dinner with wine, €47 (Mon–Fri only). Restaurant 3km.
Closed	Rarely.

Hugues de Poix
Château de Forges,
36300 Concremiers, Indre
Tel +33 (0)2 54 37 40 03
Email chateaudeforges@orange.fr
Web www.chateaudeforges.fr

Entry 376 Map 9

Loire Valley

Saint Victor La Grand' Maison

The 16th-century château bursts into view from its wooded hilltop, tall turrets and ivy-clad façade towering over the river Anglin. You can saunter down here past the pool and picnic on organic pâté under a 400-year-old oak; just water, trees and birdsong. Inside, read by the fire, tinkle on the baby grand, retire to bed. Deeply comfortable rooms in warm reds, blues and pastels have museum-worthy antiques, plush fabrics, gilt portraits, book-lined walls. Hugely friendly, Madame offers tastings, courses and talks by local savants – and there are gîtes in the grounds. "Simply a delight," says our inspector, "for anybody at all."

Loire Valley

Les Sequoias

Friendly and foodie is this townhouse B&B, on the quiet backstreet of a pretty market town. Here live Marie-Chantal and Colin and a charming black poodle called Pixie. The sequoias that dominate the garden give the house its name, and garden designer Colin is inspired by feng shui (book yourself into a garden design course!). Bedrooms, one yellow, two sky-blue, are spotless and new. Outside is a pool, a log cabin, a super wicker-chaired summer sitting room for guests. As for the food, it's delicious: wild-fruit jelly and viennoiserie at breakfast, generous dishes at dinner, shared with hosts and guests at one big cheerful table.

Rooms	3: 1 double, 2 suites (suites can interconnect).
Price	€115. Suites €150-€200.
Meals	Restaurant 1.5km.
Closed	January-March.

Rooms	4: 2 doubles, 1 twin, 1 suite.
Price	€70. Suite €180.
Meals	Dinner €23. Restaurants within walking distance.
Closed	Rarely.

	Marie Rouet Grandclément
	Saint Victor La Grand' Maison,
	36300 Ingrandes, Indre
Tel	+33 (0)6 03 81 51 37
Email	marie@saintvictorlagrandmaison.fr
Web	www.saintvictorlagrandmaison.fr

	Marie–Chantal & Colin Elliott
	Les Sequoias,
	45 rue de Varennes,
	36210 Chabris, Indre
Tel	+33 (0)2 54 40 15 42
Email	marie-chantal.elliott@orange.fr
Web	www.chabrisloirevalley.com

Entry 377 Map 9

Entry 378 Map 5

Loire Valley

Le Canard au Parapluie Rouge

This pretty 17th-century house has been welcoming guests for most of its history: it was once the Auberge de la Gare; the station has gone but a train occasionally shoots through the sleepy calm. Kathy, from Ohio, and Martin, from Wiltshire, are great fun and will make you feel instantly at home. Each of the sunny little bedrooms has a charm and flavour of its own and the big heavy-beamed living room opens onto an enclosed garden with a well-hidden above-ground pool. Beautiful meals are served in the elegant dining room or out under the trees. Kathy loves cooking and Martin grows the vegetables. It's all absurdly good value.

Rooms	5: 3 doubles, 1 family room for 3; 1 double with separate bathroom.
Price	€55–€85.
Meals	Dinner with wine, €25.
Closed	Rarely.

Martin & Kathy Missen
Le Canard au Parapluie Rouge,
3 rue des Rollets,
36200 Celon, Indre

Tel +33 (0)2 54 25 30 08
Email info@lecanardbandb.com
Web lecanardbandb.com

Entry 379   Map 5

Loire Valley

Le Bouchot

Come not for luxury but for deep country authenticity – and to make friends with a generous, charming, free-thinking family who gave up Paris for this lush corner of France. They have restored, renovated and eco-converted a run-down farm, insulated it with hemp, wattle and daub, then added wood-burning stoves, organic breakfasts… and cats, dogs, horses, hens, donkeys. Bedrooms in outbuildings round the courtyard are wood-clad with sloping ceilings, rudimentary furnishings, mix and match bed linen, the odd rug. Dinner is in the kitchen diner – or the barns when there are campers. A place for new horizons.

Rooms	4: 2 family rooms for 3, 1 family room for 4, 1 family room for 5.
Price	€70.
Meals	Dinner with wine, €25. Restaurant 2km.
Closed	Rarely.

Anne & Jean-Philippe Beau-Douëzy
Le Bouchot, Route de Chaon,
41300 Pierrefitte sur Sauldre,
Loir-et-Cher

Tel +33 (0)2 54 88 01 00
Mobile +33 (0)6 71 57 61 26
Email contact@lebouchot.net
Web www.lebouchot.net

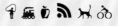

Entry 380   Map 5

Loire Valley

La Gaucherie

A peaceful young family, a gentle welcome, and a beautifully restored, L-shaped farmhouse hidden away in the conifer forests of the Sologne, with plenty of grassed space around it and a pretty orchard. Aurélia, who ran a restaurant and studied art in New York, loves light and simplicity: colours are beige and ecru, furniture wooden and roughly planed. The stable conversion has a rustic sitting room with wood-burning stove and red sofas; floors are terracotta or seagrass, bathrooms are pebbled or mosaic'd. Rejoice in ponies and hens for the children, home-produced eggs and lamb, a lake with boat and a fenced, heated pool.

Rooms	5: 2 doubles, 1 twin/double, 2 suites.
Price	€65–€145.
Meals	Dinner €28.
Closed	Mid-January to mid-February.

Aurélia Curnin
La Gaucherie,
Route de Méry, Dep 76,
41320 Langon, Loir-et-Cher

Tel	+33 (0)2 54 96 42 23
Mobile	+33 (0)6 88 80 45 93
Email	lagaucherie@wanadoo.fr
Web	www.lagaucherie.com

Loire Valley

L'île ô reflets

Just below the troglodyte village of Trôo is a mill in a deliciously green setting. With its river banks, wash houses, barns and wisteria-clad cottages, it has the air of an old-fashioned hamlet. Martial adores it and has continuing plans. He's converted an old turbine which supplies electricity, there's a woodchip burner and the main house has been lovingly restored to perfection. Each fresh, comfortable bedroom is inspired by a La Fontaine fable, and bathrooms are spotless. Outside are terraces and topiary, an orchard and a meadow mown by donkeys. Best of all, the place has its own island, reached by a bridge.

Cots available. Minimum 2 nights.

Rooms	4: 1 double, 1 family room for 3, 2 suites for 3.
Price	€60–€80.
Meals	Restaurants within walking distance.
Closed	Rarely.

Martial Chevallier
L'île ô reflets, Moulin de la Plaine,
2 rue de la Plaine, 41800 Trôo,
Loir-et-Cher

Tel	+33 (0)2 54 72 57 84
Mobile	+33 (0)6 07 99 49 42
Email	martial.chevallier@wanadoo.fr
Web	www.moulindelaplaine.com

Loire Valley

La Villa Médicis

Why the Italian name, the Italianate look? Though the house dates from the 19th century, Queen Marie de Médicis used to take the waters nearby in the 17th. The garden still has a hot spring and the Loire flows regally past behind the huge old trees. Muriel, a flower-lover (artificial blooms as well as fresh) takes wonderful care of guests and knows the area inside out. Comfortable bedrooms, some with brass beds, antique furniture and new parquet, are a tad old-fashioned; bathrooms are being updated. (The surprise 1930s suite is smart.) Downstairs rooms have a typically French elegance.

Loire Valley

16 place St Louis

In the cobbled streets of old Blois, bang in front of the cathedral, with the fascinating château round the corner, stands this elegant townhouse. Inside, an antique staircase twists up three floors of treasures: a retired gramophone, a grandfather clock, bright Malian paintings. The best room at the top has a Turner-worthy view over rooftops to the Loire. Philippe, who loves his old family house, provides big delicious breakfasts in the lovely dining room or, in summer, the flower-run courtyard. Then head for the countryside – or hop in a hot air balloon and spy the châteaux from above. A dreamy place.

Minimum two nights July/Aug.

Rooms	4: 2 twins, 1 triple, 1 suite.
Price	€69. Triple €83. Suite €99.
Meals	Dinner with wine, €32.
Closed	In winter, except by arrangement.

Rooms	3: 1 double, 1 twin, 1 suite.
Price	€80-€90. Suite €130-€140.
Meals	Restaurants in town.
Closed	Rarely.

	Muriel Cabin-Saint-Marcel
	La Villa Médicis,
	Macé, 41000 St Denis sur Loire,
	Loir-et-Cher
Tel	+33 (0)2 54 74 46 38
Email	medicis.bienvenue@wanadoo.fr
Web	lavillamedicis.com

	Philippe Escoffre
	16 place St Louis,
	41000 Blois, Loir-et-Cher
Tel	+33 (0)2 54 74 13 61
Mobile	+33 (0)6 09 65 94 05
Email	16placesaintlouis@orange.fr
Web	www.16placesaintlouis.fr

Entry 383 Map 4

Entry 384 Map 4

Loire Valley

Le Clos Pasquier

Plumb in château country, Blois forest and the Loire on the doorstep, here is what the gracious Nicots left busy jobs for: a beautiful house with chunky beams and stone floors in a sweet, peaceful setting. Delicious furniture and a huge fireplace fit the garden suite; smaller 'Salamandre' and 'Porc-épic' – royal emblems – are minimalist and classy. In the salon are winter fires and tempting jars of sweets; at breakfast you feast on Claire's own brioches, croissants and jams, and smoothies in summer. Explore the Loire on a borrowed bike, delve into historic Blois. Stunning.

Minimum two nights July / Aug.

Rooms	4: 2 twins/doubles, 2 suites.
Price	€115. Suite €135.
Meals	Restaurants in Blois, 6km.
Closed	Rarely.

Laurent & Claire Nicot
Le Clos Pasquier,
10-12 impasse de l'Orée du Bois,
41000 Blois, Loir-et-Cher

Tel	+33 (0)2 54 58 84 08
Mobile	+33 (0)6 07 35 20 14
Email	leclospasquier@orange.fr
Web	www.leclospasquier.fr

Entry 385   Map 4

Loire Valley

Château de Nanteuil

Revered grand-mère's house has faded charm and no châteauesque style or opulence: a few crumbly bits outside, frescoes and trunks in the hall, antlers in the dining room, old floral wallpapers and marble fireplaces in the bedrooms. These are light-filled and unabashedly old-fashioned but there's charm in 'Roi' and 'Rose'; bathrooms are time-warp 70s; river-water murmurs constantly below your window. Most of all, you'll enjoy Frédéric's refreshingly laidback, occasionally mercurial, informality and excellent, cheerful organic dinners – asparagus in season, baked fillet of perch: he really cares about food. Best in summer.

Rooms	5: 2 doubles, 3 family rooms for 2-4.
Price	€75-€95. Family room €80-€120.
Meals	Dinner with wine, €28.
Closed	Rarely.

Frédéric Théry
Château de Nanteuil, 16 rue
Nanteuil, Le Chiteau, 41350 Huisseau
sur Cosson, Loir-et-Cher

Tel	+33 (0)2 54 42 61 98
Mobile	+33 (0)6 88 83 79 84
Email	chateau.nanteuil@free.fr
Web	www.chateau-nanteuil.com

Entry 386   Map 4

Loire Valley

Les Chambres Vertes

Flowers fill the quadrangle formed by the house (16th- and 19th-century) and an old wall; a fountain adds coolness. Your rooms are in the former stables opposite Sophie's house, each with a slate porch; hers has this slate running its full length, giving shelter from sun and rain. Outside the quadrangle is a covered patio for drinks and delicious organic meals, overlooking countryside… all this just a stone's throw from the village. The rooms, on the ground floor, are uncluttered and exquisitely simple, with attractive no-frills bathrooms. The mood is natural, artistic, delightful. Parisienne Sophie lives the dream.

Rooms	3: 2 doubles, 1 twin.
Price	€64–€70.
Meals	Dinner with wine, €26.
Closed	Occasionally.

Sophie Gélinier
Les Chambres Vertes,
Le Clos de la Chartrie,
41120 Cormeray, Loir-et-Cher
Tel   +33 (0)9 73 84 44 55
Email   sophie@chambresvertes.net
Web   www.chambresvertes.net

Entry 387   Map 4

Loire Valley

Le Cormier

Wake in the morning and sigh with pleasure at the beauty of the garden: box hedges and cottage flowers, sweet herbs, poplars and an iris-fringed pond. Then think about breakfasting on garden fruits and homemade banana bread… Californian Michael and Dutch Marie-Louise rescued this long, low farmhouse and barn from ruin; it's hard to imagine more endearing hosts. The suites are exceedingly pretty, with creamy stone walls, overhead beams, dainty fabrics and ethnic rugs; each has its very own salon with kettle, fridge, books, magazines, logs for the fire. One has its own little kitchen. Perfect peace, and not another house in sight.

Minimum two nights.

Rooms	2 suites, 1 with kitchen.
Price	€100–€110.
Meals	Restaurant nearby.
Closed	November-April.

Michael & Marie-Louise Harvey
Le Cormier,
41120 Sambin, Loir-et-Cher
Tel   +33 (0)2 54 33 29 47
Email   michael@lecormier.com
Web   www.lecormier.com

Entry 388   Map 4

Loire Valley

Prieuré de la Chaise

A delight for the senses: stunning ancient buildings outside, Madame's decorations within. The 13th-century chapel, still used on the village feast day, and the 'new' manor house (1500s) are awash with history, 16th-century antiques, tapestries and loveliness – huge sitting and dining rooms, and a winding staircase to the tower room (with a curtained-off loo). One room has a stone fireplace, a fine rug, and limewashed beams. The setting is superb, mature trees shade the beautiful gardens, horses adorn the paddock, you are surrounded by vines; over a simple French breakfast, ask your dynamic hostess to arrange tastings.

Loire Valley

La Roseraie de Vrigny

White shutters, beams, old stones, comfortable bedrooms, organic potager, communal breakfasts and generous hosts – quintessential Sawday's. Ros, musician and philosopher, and John understand what B&B is all about and treat their guests as friends; sup with them on fine French food in the candlelit dining room and you will be charmed. The garden is entrancing too, all rambling roses, contemplative spots, even a little corner that is forever Scotland (like your hosts) and a wooden bridge across a weeping-willow'd stream. Perfectly restful and welcoming after a day contemplating the glories of Chenonceau!

Rooms	5: 2 doubles, 2 suites for 3, 1 suite for 5 (2 showers).
Price	€90. Suite €130-€190.
Meals	Restaurants nearby.
Closed	Rarely.

Rooms	2: 1 double, 1 triple.
Price	€60-€85.
Meals	Dinner €30. Restaurant 1km.
Closed	Rarely.

	Danièle Therizols
	Prieuré de la Chaise,
	8 rue du Prieuré,
	41400 St Georges sur Cher,
	Loir-et-Cher
Tel	+33 (0)2 54 32 59 77
Email	prieuredelachaise@yahoo.fr
Web	www.prieuredelachaise.com

	Rosalind Rawnsley
	La Roseraie de Vrigny,
	3 rue du Ruisseau,
	41400 St Georges sur Cher, Loir-et-Cher
Tel	+33 (0)2 54 32 85 50
Mobile	+33 (0)7 60 45 99 14
Email	rosalind.rawnsley@gmail.com
Web	www.laroseraiedevrigny.com

Loire Valley

Le Moutier

The artist's touch and Jean-Lou's paintings vibrate throughout this house of tradition and originality where you will feel instantly at home. Note one of the bedrooms is accessed via the owner's studio, heaving with paintings and brushes! Of the four, we like best the top-floor one in the house, cosy and bright with white walls, dark green woodwork and a yellow spread over a sturdy brass bed. There's an understated elegance in the sitting and dining rooms, a charming garden, throngs of fruit trees and some loitering hens. Above all, great table d'hôtes: good food and wine generously flow.

Rooms	4: 2 doubles. Studio: 2 doubles.
Price	€70.
Meals	Dinner with wine, €30.
Closed	Rarely.

Martine & Jean-Lou Coursaget
Le Moutier,
13 rue de la République,
41110 Mareuil sur Cher,
Loir-et-Cher

Tel	+33 (0)2 54 75 20 48
Email	lemoutier.coursaget@wanadoo.fr
Web	www.chambresdhotesdumoutier.com

Entry 391   Map 4

Loire Valley

Château-Monastère de la Corroirie

Deep in the Loches forest, a world of feudal enchantment: a ruined monastery, a 12th-century castle, a charming young aristo host. Park by the drawbridge and stroll past the friendly goose, to grassy meadows and a courtyard. 'Monacale' is grey-green with elegant cream linens, 'Seigneurale' has opulent textured reds; both have deep mattresses and simple bathrooms. Enjoy an inventive meal – with vegetables from the organic potager – in the tapestried dining room, then retire to a stylish salon with velvet sofas and flickering fire. With its setting, moat and exceptional antiques, Corroirie exudes history and grandeur.

Rooms	2 doubles.
Price	€85-€125.
Meals	Dinner with wine, €35.
	Restaurants 4km.
Closed	Rarely.

Jeff de Mareüil
Château-Monastère de la Corroirie,
Route de Loches,
37460 Montrésor,
Indre-et-Loire

Mobile	+33 (0)6 80 43 38 75
Email	corroirie@orange.fr
Web	corroirie.com/index.php/fr/chambreshotes

Entry 392   Map 9

Loire Valley

La Palombiere

The handsome 18th-century farmhouse is a short meander through water meadows to the pretty village of St Germain. The tranquil courtyard, full of birdsong, leads to a pretty garden, a surprising and delightful space. Bedrooms are elegant, lofty and spacious, with an uncluttered décor and touches of toile de Jouy; one even has a grand stone fireplace. Your hosts make you feel instantly at home, will recommend favourite strolls and share a book full of maps. Walkers will love it here, history buffs too – don't miss the village's 16th-century château. Come for sociable breakfasts, fireside evenings, excellent tea and copious conversation.

Rooms	3: 1 double, 1 twin/double, 1 suite.
Price	€75–€85.
Meals	Restaurant 3km.
Closed	Rarely.

Jean-Pierre & Marie-Laure
Dellea-Loisance
La Palombiere, 2 impasse de la Garenne,
Bourg de Saint-Germain,
37600 St Jean St Germain, Indre-et-Loire
Tel   +33 (0)6 33 22 66 69
Email lapalombiere37@gmail.com
Web   www.gites-lapalombiere.com

Entry 393   Map 9

Loire Valley

Château de la Celle Guenand

In the heart of an old Touraine village, four hectares of delightful walled park and a fairytale castle that dates from 1442. It's large but not palatial, grand but not ornate, and refreshingly unstuffy. Much is being updated, everything is charming, and Stephen is putting all his energies into his new project. You get top mattresses on king-size beds, bedrooms with beautifully proportioned windows (cool conservative shades for the newest) and delicious quince jams at breakfast. After dinner: brocade sofas in faded reds, books to browse and a piano to play. All this, châteaux by the hatful, and the Brenne National Park.

Rooms	5: 4 doubles, 1 family room for 2-4.
Price	€85–€110. Family room €120–€140.
Meals	Hosted dinner with wine, €26. Restaurant in village.
Closed	October-March.

Stephen Palluel
Château de la Celle Guenand,
14 rue du Château,
37350 La Celle Guenand, Indre-et-Loire
Tel   +33 (0)2 47 94 93 61
Mobile +33 (0)6 76 23 74 77
Email   stephane@chateaucelleguenand.com
Web   www.chateaucelleguenand.com

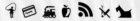

Entry 394   Map 9

Loire Valley

Le Moulin de St Jean

The restored mill in its delicious island setting is all ups and downs, nooks and crannies, big rooms and small, character and variety. Your delightful host John, a Welshman, fled a city job for a quieter life, bringing his love of Loire wines (just ask) and a fondness for entertaining with him. Assorted wallpapers, patterns, frills and furniture – and a welcome bottle of wine – make for a warm, homely feel. Plus new mattresses and good bathrooms, two sitting rooms, numerous DVDs and books, a shady garden, a heated pool – and all the fascinations of the Loire Valley.

Not suitable for young children: unfenced water.

Rooms	4: 2 doubles, 1 twin, 1 suite.
Price	€85–€99. Suite €99-€110.
Meals	Dinner €15-€25. Wine from €10. Restaurant 8km.
Closed	Rarely.

	John Higginson
	Le Moulin de St Jean,
	St Jean St Germain,
	37600 Loches,
	Indre-et-Loire
Tel	+33 (0)2 47 94 70 12
Email	lemoulinstjean@club-internet.fr
Web	www.lemoulinstjean.com

Entry 395   Map 9

Loire Valley

Le Logis du Bief

In a street of fine houses in Loches, a beautifully restored pair of cottages and their superb riverside terrace. This is a very civilised B&B, one for history lovers and foodies. The owner is a collector of fine art; the housekeepers are a friendly French-Moroccan pair (he an excellent chef). Bedrooms house some fine oil paintings, mirrors and antiques, from 'Agnes Sorel' with its own balcony overlooking the river to 'Anne de Bretagne' up the spiral stone stair, a cosy suite with peachy walls. The setting is delicious, the breakfasts are scrumptious, from the homemade jams to the local brioche.

Over 12s welcome.

Rooms	4: 2 doubles, 1 twin, 1 suite for 3.
Price	€90–€115. Suite €110-€140.
Meals	Restaurants 100m.
Closed	Rarely.

	Moha Oulad
	Le Logis du Bief,
	21 rue Quintefol,
	37600 Loches, Indre-et-Loire
Tel	+33 (0)2 47 91 66 02
Mobile	+33 (0)6 83 10 46 64
Email	contact@logisloches.com
Web	www.logisloches.com

Entry 396   Map 9

Loire Valley

La Maison de l'Argentier du Roy

Gaze, as the King's treasurer did, over castles, rooftops and gardens; tranquillity one step from town. This noble stone house in a land of châteaux and vineyards has a regal setting. Choose the 'Belle Epoque' room in the eaves for dreamy escapes, 'Balzac' with its fascinating mosaic tower-shower, or ground-floor 'Jacques Coeur' for grandiose Louis XV styling and an optional connecting salon. Bathrooms are in travertine marble, mattresses are plump, secret passages, tapestries, oak floors and velvet furnishings abound. It's warm, sumptuous and beautifully restored, and run by youthful, charming hosts.

Rooms	3 doubles.
Price	€95–€115.
Meals	Dinner with wine, €39. Restaurants within walking distance.
Closed	Rarely.

Christine & Philippe Rimbault
La Maison de l'Argentier du Roy,
21 rue Saint Ours, 37600 Loches,
Indre-et-Loire

Tel	+33 (0)2 47 91 62 86
Mobile	+33 (0)6 71 63 36 93
Email	postmaster@argentier-du-roy.eu
Web	www.argentier-du-roy.com

Entry 397   Map 9

Loire Valley

Le Clos des Sources

Named after the natural springs that course by, this elegant Tourangeau townhouse sits in a small tranquil village in a green-rivered valley. Bubbly host Laura has a discerning eye; fresh colour schemes, canopy beds, Doisneau prints, local antiques, toile de Jouy bedspreads, wooden floors, exposed brick walls – all come together with imaginative flair. Bedrooms are off a lime tree-shaded courtyard. Terraced above, there's a sunny, walled, grassy garden with fruit trees, a raised swimming pool on a wooden platform and a 'cave' for wine-tasting. Fine fare, lovely river walks, and don't miss the village planetarium.

Rooms	4: 3 doubles, 1 suite.
Price	€80–€100. Suite €100–€125. Extra bed €25.
Meals	Dinner, 4 courses with wine, €35 (Sat nights). Private dinner €25. Picnic €17. Restaurants 12km.
Closed	Rarely.

Laura Crotet
Le Clos des Sources,
2 ruelle des Sources,
37310 Tauxigny,
Indre-et-Loire

Tel	+33 (0)2 47 94 28 34
Email	info@clos-des-sources.fr
Web	www.closdessources.com

Entry 398   Map 4

Loire Valley

Domaine de Beauséjour

Dug into the hillside with the forest behind and a panorama of vines in front, this wine-grower's manor successfully pretends it was built in the 1800s. Venerable oak beams and stone cut by troglodyte masons create a mood of stylish rusticity. Bedrooms are charming, the suite in the main house, the other two in the romantic poolside tower. Find carved bedheads, old prints, vases of fresh and artificial flowers, elegant bathrooms. Your vivacious hostess helps her son run the family wine estate and will arrange a tasting for guests. Picnic in the conservatory or in one of the caves overlooking the valley.

Minimum two nights. Sawday self-catering also.

Rooms	3: 2 doubles. Tower: 1 suite for 3-4.
Price	€70–€90. Suite €120.
Meals	Restaurants 5km.
Closed	Rarely.

Marie-Claude Chauveau
Domaine de Beauséjour,
37220 Panzoult,
Indre-et-Loire
Tel   +33 (0)2 47 58 64 64
Mobile   +33 (0)6 86 97 03 40
Email   dom.beausejour@wanadoo.fr
Web   www.domainedebeausejour.com

Entry 399   Map 9

Loire Valley

La Baumoderie

Anne designed interiors in Paris, Jean-François managed hotels, now they do B&B from their imaginatively restored farmhouse on the top of a hill. Lively, charming people, they serve excellent French dinners in a modern chandelier'd conservatory and give guests two rustic-elegant rooms: one cool and spacious on the ground floor (with just French windows) and a suite at the top of an outside stone staircase; wake to splendid views. You can walk from the house, canoe on the Vienne, taste the wines of Chinon. The garden blends into the landscape, the small village is up the road, and peace reigns supreme.

Rooms	2: 1 double, 1 suite, each with separate shower & wc.
Price	€90–€125.
Meals	Lunch or dinner with wine, €30. Restaurant 4km.
Closed	Rarely.

Anne Tardits
La Baumoderie,
17 rue d'Étilly, 37220 Panzoult,
Indre-et-Loire
Mobile   +33 (0)6 08 78 00 73
Email   anne@labaumoderie.fr
Web   www.labaumoderie.fr

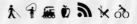

Entry 400   Map 9

Loire Valley

Le Clos de Ligré

This former wine-grower's house sings in a subtle harmony of traditional charm and contemporary chic under Martine's thoroughly modern touch. Sponged walls, creamy beams and eye-catching fabrics breathe new life into rooms with old tiled floors and stone fireplaces – and there are two newer big beamy doubles in the attic. Windows are flung open to let in the light and the stresses of city living are forgotten in cheerful, easy conversations with your hostess, who joins guests for candlelit dinners. Bookcases, billiard table and baby grand, buffet breakfasts at the long table, a pool for the energetic – delightful.

Rooms	5: 4 doubles, 1 family room.
Price	€110.
Meals	Dinner with wine, €35.
Closed	Rarely.

Martine Descamps
Le Clos de Ligré,
Le Rouilly, 37500 Ligré,
Indre-et-Loire
Tel   +33 (0)2 47 93 95 59
Email mdescamps@club-internet.fr
Web   www.le-clos-de-ligre.com

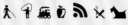

Loire Valley

Le Châtaignier

A pretty old stone farmhouse on the edge of a hamlet, beautifully restored by Odile – and Jean-Joseph who loves his garden. With open lawns, swings, fruit trees and a vast chestnut tree that gives the house its name, it's a joy to spend time in; and there's a summer kitchen. The décor is cool and charming, the bedrooms, each with a private entrance, are inviting. Artistic Odile who speaks good English, presents you with a homemade lavender bag on leaving, a typically delightful touch. Sunny, country-elegant sitting and dining rooms open to the garden, and the fields stretch for miles. Special!

Rooms	2: 1 suite for 2 & sofabed, 1 suite for 4 (2 twin rooms separated by landing).
Price	Suite €70-€106. Suite for 4 €72-€120. Singles €55-€57. Child €18.
Meals	Summer kitchen. Restaurant 3km.
Closed	Rarely.

Odile & Jean-Joseph Crescenzo
Le Châtaignier,
16 rue du Carroi, La Roberderie,
37500 Marcay, Indre-et-Loire
Tel   +33 (0)2 47 93 97 09
Mobile +33 (0)6 71 42 22 15
Email   info@lechataignier.com
Web   lechataignier.free.fr

Loire Valley

Cheviré

Wonderful hosts, wonderful surroundings. You stay in the well-converted stable block of a traditional farmhouse on the edge of a peaceful village – all a-shimmer in the Loire's inimitable light. Welcome to the protected wetlands between the Loire and the Vienne. Pretty, uncluttered bedrooms, each a good size, display a happy mix of old and new; there's space to sit and cook, and new bathrooms gleam. The meadows are full of birds and fritillaries, and the treasures of Chinon await, as do the wines of Bourgueil and Saumur. "Very clean, very friendly, very good breakfasts," say our readers. Superb value, too.

Extra beds available.

Loire Valley

Le Moulin de Touvois

Delightful, good-natured, hospitable Myriam and Jean-Claude have renovated the old miller's house in a blend of styles; now stonework, beams and terracotta mix with good modern furniture. The Moroccan tiled dining table looks great beside the big old stone fireplace; simple, smallish, comfortable bedrooms have tiled or parquet floors and crisp bedding. Best of all is the garden, with its planked bridge, orchard, swings and pool, and shady terrace by the bucolic stream. Three hens contentedly roam, horses dot the paddock, the food is delicious and Jean-Claude arranges visits to wine growers. Wonderful value.

Rooms	Stables: 3: 1 double, 1 triple, 1 quadruple.
Price	€46–€52. Triple €50–€64. Quadruple €52–€80.
Meals	Guest kitchenette. Restaurant 1km.
Closed	Mid-November to mid-March.

Rooms	5: 2 doubles, 2 twins/doubles, 1 quadruple.
Price	€60–€65. Extra bed €15.
Meals	Dinner with wine, €25.
Closed	Mid-November to mid-February.

Marie-Françoise & Michel Chauvelin
Cheviré, 11 rue Basse,
37420 Savigny en Véron,
Indre-et-Loire
Tel +33 (0)2 47 58 42 49
Email chauvelin.michel@wanadoo.fr
Web www.ch-hotes-chevire.fr

Entry 403   Map 4

Myriam & Jean-Claude Marchand
Le Moulin de Touvois,
3 rue du Moulin de Touvois,
37140 Bourgueil, Indre-et-Loire
Tel +33 (0)2 47 97 87 70
Email info@moulindetouvois.com
Web www.moulindetouvois.com

Entry 404   Map 4

Loire Valley

Château d'Hodebert

Silver and flowers on the breakfast table are just what you'd expect in this exquisitely proportioned 17th-century family château, set in its 45 hectares of listed parkland. It is as gracious and sunny as your charming hosts and their four young daughters, Ivana managing house, family and several pets with serene efficiency. You'll find panelling and a log fire in the comfortable sitting room, painted beams in the billiard room, a piano in the dining room, understated elegance and style in the bedrooms, immaculate new bathrooms. It's a rare treat to return from visiting those grand Loire monuments to your own private château.

Rooms	3 doubles.
Price	€120-€150.
Meals	Restaurant 10km.
Closed	Rarely.

Ivana & Hélie de la Bouillerie
Château d'Hodebert,
37370 St Paterne Racan,
Indre-et-Loire

Tel	+33 (0)2 47 29 34 49
Mobile	+33 (0)6 52 72 81 54
Email	contact@chateau-hodebert.com
Web	www.chateau-hodebert.com

Entry 405   Map 4

Loire Valley

20 rue Pilate

In the lovely Loire valley where the intimate and the romantic reign, you have the little house in the garden all to yourselves: a kitchen and a bathroom downstairs, two bedrooms upstairs and a private piece of flower-filled garden for breakfasts. Or you can join your delightful hosts at the long wooden table in the cheerful kitchen where baskets hang from beams. Cultured, dynamic and a superb maker of jams, Ghislaine is involved in visiting artists and writers to this peaceful Touraine town. Be charmed by the genuine welcome, unpretentious comfort, wisteria climbing over the terrace and bird song all around.

Rooms	1 cottage for 4.
Price	Cottage €70-€120.
Meals	Dinner with wine, €30.
Closed	November-March.

Ghislaine & Gérard de Couesnongle
20 rue Pilate,
37370 Neuvy le Roi,
Indre-et-Loire

Tel	+33 (0)2 47 24 41 48
Email	ggh.coues@gmail.com

Entry 406   Map 4

Loire Valley

La Louisière

Simplicity, character and a marvellous welcome make La Louisière special. Madame delights in her role as hostess; Monsieur, who once rode the horse-drawn combine, tends his many roses, and his paintings of the countryside line the walls. A caring and unpretentious couple, both are active in their community. The traditional bedrooms have well-chosen colour schemes and sparkling bathrooms; touches of fun, too. Surrounded by chestnut trees, the farmhouse backs onto the gardens of the château and is wonderfully quiet. Tennis, bikes, tractors, horses to ride and an old-fashioned playground – it's bliss for children.

Rooms	3: 1 twin, 1 triple, 1 suite.
Price	€55-€60.
Meals	Auberge 800m.
Closed	Rarely.

Michel & Andrée Campion
La Louisière,
37360 Beaumont la Ronce,
Indre-et-Loire
Tel   +33 (0)2 47 24 42 24
Mobile   +33 (0)6 78 36 64 69
Email   andree.campion@orange.fr
Web   louisiere.racan.org

Entry 407   Map 4

Loire Valley

Château de Crémille

Deep within a forest lies an elegant little château where swans glide and frogs croak. A staircase curves gracefully to peaceful and traditional bedrooms – all with family stories to tell. Glimpse deer from the room with the roof garden, or choose triple-aspect Chambre de la Tour. Aldric is your host, cook, and delightful dinner companion. Gaze at parkland views; enjoy a welcoming aperitif in the tower's salon with wood fire; feast in a chandelier'd dining room. Catch the eerie bark of stags – and enjoy forest forays when hunting season's over. Dramatic setting, a family feel – and a splendid wire-haired terrier!

Rooms	3: 2 doubles, 1 family room.
Price	€120-€130. Family room €295.
Meals	Dinner with wine, €20-€38. Restaurant 10km.
Closed	November-April.

Aldric De La Brosse
Château de Crémille,
37130 Mazières de Touraine,
Indre-et-Loire
Tel   +33 (0)2 47 24 00 32
Email   cremille@orange.fr
Web   www.chateaudecremille.fr

Entry 408   Map 4

Loire Valley

La Cornillière

Just 15 minutes from the centre of Tours yet deep in the countryside where deer, and the occasional wild boar, invite themselves into the garden from the surrounding woods. The Espinassous live in the 18th-century vigneron's house and have turned an outhouse into a delightfully rustic guest suite – antique furniture, terracotta floor – with all creature comforts. Croissants and fresh bread will be delivered to you each morning and the large gardens are yours to explore, including the formal walled garden, Monsieur's pride and joy. These are friendly, cultured people; happy to advise on visits.

Sawday self-catering also.

Rooms	Suite for 2–4.
Price	€95–€150.
Meals	Picnic in garden on request. Restaurants nearby.
Closed	Rarely.

	Catherine Espinassou
	La Cornillière,
	Mettray, 37390 Tours,
	Indre-et-Loire
Tel	+33 (0)2 47 51 12 69
Mobile	+33 (0)6 70 94 70 05
Email	kakimail@orange.fr
Web	www.gites-lacornilliere-touraine.com

Entry 409   Map 4

Loire Valley

Le Chat Courant

A handsome 18th-century family house on the river Cher just opposite Villandry and with its own lovely garden (whose birdsong drowns out any occasional train noise). Bedrooms are pretty and stylish: the double in the converted cottage opens to the swimming pool, the suite in the main house has fine antique furniture. Éric – who is also a keen photographer – has created garden enchantment here with old species of apple trees, a walled vegetable garden, a wisteria-clad pergola, a formal boxed flower garden, and a semi-wild garden beyond, all surrounded by woodland and pasture where the families' horses peacefully graze.

Rooms	2: 1 family suite for 2–5. Summer house: 1 double.
Price	€70–€75. Family suite €100.
Meals	Restaurant 5 minutes by car.
Closed	Rarely.

	Éric Gaudouin
	Le Chat Courant,
	37510 Villandry,
	Indre-et-Loire
Tel	+33 (0)2 47 50 06 94
Mobile	+33 (0)6 37 83 21 78
Email	info@le-chat-courant.com
Web	www.le-chat-courant.com

Entry 410   Map 4

Loire Valley

Château de l'Hérissaudière

You could get used to country-house living here, French-style. Madame, charming, cultured, welcomes you as family. Wrapped in 18 acres of parkland, the manor is all light, elegance, bold paintings and fresh flowers. Relax in the sunny salon or the splendid library. Bedrooms are spacious, gracious and subtly themed, Empire perhaps, or rich Louis XV. Bathrooms have the original tiling and marble floors. Tuck into a gourmet breakfast while Madame recommends local restaurants for dinner. Ping-pong and pool are in the grounds, with wild cyclamen and giant sequoias, and the old chapel has become a summer kitchen.

Rooms	5: 2 doubles, 3 suites.
Price	€120–€135. Suite €130–€180.
Meals	Summer kitchen. Restaurant 3km.
Closed	Rarely.

Claudine Detilleux
Château de l'Hérissaudière,
37230 Pernay,
Indre-et-Loire
Tel +33 (0)2 47 55 95 28
Mobile +33 (0)6 03 22 34 45
Email lherissaudiere@aol.com
Web www.herissaudiere.com

Loire Valley

Château du Vau

At the end of a long bumpy drive is a house of great character run with good humour: delightful philosopher Bruno has turned his family château into a stylish refuge for travellers. Two large, light bedrooms have been redecorated with seagrass and family memorabilia round splendid brass bedsteads; others remain, very comfortably, in their traditional, distinguished garb. And then there are the beautifully crafted treehouses: oriental in the oak tree, African in the cedar, breakfast hampers delivered at the end of a rope… Dinners showcase estate produce. There's a fine pool, and a golf course bang opposite.

Rooms	7: 3 doubles, 1 family room, 1 triple, 2 treehouses for 2.
Price	€130. Family room €140. Triple €140. Treehouses €140.
Meals	Dinner with wine, €42. Summer buffets in garden €26.
Closed	Rarely.

Bruno Clément
Château du Vau,
37510 Ballan Miré,
Indre-et-Loire
Tel +33 (0)2 47 67 84 04
Email info@chateau-du-vau.com
Web www.chateau-du-vau.com

Loire Valley

Les Mazeraies

Beautifully sculpted from the same ancient cedar trees that stalked the splendid grounds 100 years ago, this thoroughly contemporary mansion on the old château foundations in the Garden of France is a real delight. Humour, intelligence and love of fine things inhabit this welcoming family and their guest wing is unostentatiously luxurious in rich fabrics, oriental and modern furniture, good pictures and lovely, scented, cedar-lined bathrooms. Ground-floor rooms have a private terrace each, upstairs ones have direct access to the roof garden. Marie-Laurence is utterly charming.

Rooms	4: 1 double, 2 twins/doubles, 1 suite for 3-4.
Price	€100.
Meals	Restaurants nearby.
Closed	Rarely.

Marie-Laurence Jallet
Les Mazeraies,
34 route des Mazeraies,
37510 Savonnières, Indre-et-Loire

Tel	+33 (0)2 47 67 85 35
Email	les.jallet@wanadoo.fr
Web	www.lesmazeraies.com

Entry 413   Map 4

Loire Valley

Les Hautes Gâtinières

High on a cliff above the Loire, house and garden gaze over village, valley and vines. Les Hautes Gâtinières may be modern imitating old, but we chose it for Jacqueline's five-star hospitality. All is immaculate and meticulous within: glossy wooden floors, smart wallpapers, French repro furniture. There's a big living area with a tiled floor warmed by rugs, and views over the large sloping garden, perfect for children (and Api, the fluffy white dog) to romp in. Giant breakfasts, a lovely welcome and a delightful restaurant just down the hill – great value for the Loire. Châteaux, gardens, vineyards beckon.

Rooms	3: 2 doubles, 1 suite for 4.
Price	€59. Suite €99.
Meals	Restaurants in village, 500m.
Closed	Rarely.

Jacqueline Gay
Les Hautes Gâtinières,
7 chemin de Bois Soleil,
37210 Rochecorbon, Indre-et-Loire

Tel	+33 (0)2 47 52 88 08
Email	gatinieres@wanadoo.fr
Web	www.gatinieres.eu.ki

Entry 414   Map 4

Loire Valley

La Falotière

A cave suite! Hewn long ago into the rock beside a bell-topped presbytery, deliciously cool and light, it's a spacious retreat. Step from private courtyard to sitting room with big fireplace and old bread oven, smart wicker chairs, red lamps, tiled floors. Burrow through to a cushioned, red-carpeted bedroom sculpted into whitewashed rock; soak in a theatrical free-standing bath. Locals and walkers: your delightful hosts serve home-laid eggs at breakfast, enjoy sharing their lovely shady garden and this intriguing town, wedged in a gully ten minutes from Tours amid the Loire's vineyards and châteaux. Private, unique, fantastic.

Rooms	1 suite.
Price	€130. Child bed €15.
Meals	Restaurant 150m.
Closed	Rarely.

Dominique & Jean-Pierre Danderieux
La Falotière,
51 rue du Docteur Lebled,
37210 Rochecorbon, Indre-et-Loire

Mobile	+33 (0)6 50 65 41 49
Email	contact@falotiere.com
Web	www.falotiere.com

Entry 415 Map 4

Loire Valley

Château de Nazelles

Even the pool is special: a 'Roman' bath hewn out of the hillside with a fountain and two columns, set on one of several garden levels that rise to the crowning glory of vines where grapes are grown by natural methods. The young owners brim with enthusiasm for their elegant, history-laden château, built in 1518 to gaze across the Loire at Amboise. Every detail has been treated with taste and discretion. Rooms, two in the main house, two smaller in the adorable old pavilion, are light and fresh with lovely wooden floors, the suite carved from the rock itself – and there's a big living room with books, internet and games.

Rooms	6: 4 doubles, 2 suites for 4.
Price	€115-€150. Suite €260-€300.
Meals	Summer kitchen. Restaurants 3km.
Closed	Rarely.

Véronique & Olivier Fructus
Château de Nazelles,
16 rue Tue la Soif,
37530 Nazelles,
Indre-et-Loire

Tel	+33 (0)2 47 30 53 79
Email	info@chateau-nazelles.com
Web	www.chateau-nazelles.com

Entry 416 Map 4

Loire Valley

Manoir de la Maison Blanche

Your 17th-century manor sits in blissful seclusion yet you can walk into the centre of old Amboise. Annick is the perfect host, loves people, loves life, and gives you three fabulous, generous, lofty bedrooms in a converted outbuilding. One is tiled and beamed with a small patio overlooking the garden, another, under the eaves, reached via an outdoor spiral stair, is charming. The garden is surprisingly huge, bursting with roses and irises that may make their way to your room. Look out for the 16th-century pigeon loft – a historical rarity. Delicious breakfasts, super rooms, and châteaux all around. One of the best.

Rooms	3: 2 triples, 1 family room.
Price	€90.
Meals	Guest kitchenette. Restaurants within walking distance.
Closed	Rarely.

Annick Delécheneau
Manoir de la Maison Blanche,
18 rue de l'Épinetterie,
37400 Amboise, Indre-et-Loire

Tel	+33 (0)2 47 23 16 14
Mobile	+33 (0)6 88 89 33 66
Email	annick.delecheneau@wanadoo.fr
Web	www.lamaisonblanche-fr.com

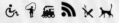

Entry 417   Map 4

Loire Valley

Belleroche

Faint sounds sometimes drift upwards from the embankment far below but Belleroche remains serene. Only a 15-minute walk from the centre of Amboise, this fine house stands poised and aloof in a three-hectare terraced garden high above the Loire, with great views to the other side from the highest point. You can wander on paths linking different levels of roses, peonies and fruit trees. The exquisite bedrooms and the guest sitting room, once the old library, also overlook the river. So, too, does a little 18th-century pavilion under the lime trees where Florence may serve breakfast on sunny mornings. A heavenly place.

Rooms	2: 1 suite, 1 double each with separate bath.
Price	€120. Suite €100–€150.
Meals	Restaurants nearby.
Closed	Mid-October to mid-April.

Florence Janvier
Belleroche,
1 rue du Clos de Belleroche,
37400 Amboise, Indre-et-Loire

Tel	+33 (0)2 47 30 47 03
Mobile	+33 (0)6 73 89 60 16
Email	belleroche.amboise@orange.fr
Web	www.belleroche.net

Entry 418   Map 4

Loire Valley

Château de Pintray

Instant charm at the end of the long leafy avenue. This intimate château glows with personality and peculiarity yet this is no museum-piece: delightful Anne looks after the B&B while Jean Christophe produces some of the region's best sweet and dry white wines; enjoy the tastings. Stuffed full of character, bedrooms have super comfy beds on carpeted floors and bathrooms big old roll top tubs and walk-in showers. Tuck in to a splendid breakfast at the convivial table – alongside the Guignol puppet theatre! – before setting off for the great châteaux: Chenonceau, Amboise, Villandry and Azay le Rideau, all within an hour's drive.

Rooms	3: 2 doubles, 1 family room.
Price	€110. Family room €110-€160.
Meals	Restaurant 2km.
Closed	Rarely.

Anne Ricou & Jean Christophe Rault
Château de Pintray,
RD 283, Lussault sur Loire,
37400 Amboise, Indre-et-Loire
Tel +33 (0)2 47 23 22 84
Email marius.rault@wanadoo.fr
Web www.chateau-de-pintray.com

Entry 419 Map 4

Loire Valley

Le Vieux Manoir

Imagine visiting the château at Amboise, then staying in a manoir from whose cellars runs a secret tunnel to the château's grounds. Gloria ran a B&B in Boston before resettling in France to fulfil a dream of restoring a 17th-century jewel. Rooms are filled with fascinating brocante and family antiques, bedrooms bow to the ladies, one with its hand basin sitting in an antique dresser, and bevelled mirrors and hand-made tiles sparkle in the bathrooms. You breakfast convivially in a conservatory that opens to a French-formal town garden, and the two cottages in the grounds are impeccable – perfect for families with children over five.

Rooms	8: 5 doubles, 1 triple, 2 cottages for 2-4.
Price	€145-€185. Cottages €220-€295.
Meals	Restaurants in town.
Closed	November-February. Call for out of season reservations.

Gloria & Robert Belknap
Le Vieux Manoir,
13 rue Rabelais,
37400 Amboise,
Indre-et-Loire
Tel +33 (0)2 47 30 41 27
Email info@le-vieux-manoir.com
Web www.le-vieux-manoir.com

Entry 420 Map 4

Loire Valley

Le Pavillon de Vallet

The 18th-century tuffa stone is pale and fragile, the lawns run down to the Cher, wisteria covers the gazebo; monks once lived here, the serenity endures. New to B&B, delightful Éric injects his designer flair and love of antiques, his cultural curiosity and his sense of fun into his welcoming house and sparkling conversation. An interesting diplomat, Michel is often away. Guests have a lofty, chequer-tiled living room full of light and well-being, "or make yourself tea in the kitchen". The bread-oven bedroom is sweet with painted beams and private courtyard; in another, large twin beds await beneath a canopy of joists. Superb.

Minimum two nights.

Rooms	3: 2 doubles, 1 twin/double.
Price	€110–€130. Extra person €20.
Meals	Occasional dinner on demand. Restaurant 1km.
Closed	Rarely.

Éric Lesigne
Le Pavillon de Vallet,
4 rue de l'Aqueduc,
37270 Athée sur Cher, Indre-et-Loire

Tel	+33 (0)2 47 27 38 18
Mobile	+33 (0)6 25 25 47 12
Email	pavillon.vallet@orange.fr
Web	www.pavillondevallet.com

Entry 421 Map 4

Loire Valley

Manoir de Chaix

Up a quiet lane, embraced by woodland and fields, an exceedingly fine manor house with dovecot, orchard, barn, pool and flourishing potager. Warm friendly Christian, ex sommelier, welcomes you in; on Saturdays his wife (a Parisian chef!) treats you to table d'hôtes. Spacious beamed bedrooms – four reached via a stone turret stair – are full of traditional comfort, and the dining room is inviting, with blazing logs, light-flooded windows and a great big convivial table. This is the Loire and there are châteaux by the hatful: Chenonceau, Loches, Amboise, Azay le Rideau, Villandry. A great find, and good value.

Rooms	8: 4 doubles, 2 twins, 1 triple, 1 family suite for 2-4.
Price	€75–€90. Triple €97–€102. Family suite €111.
Meals	Dinner with wine, €27. Restaurants 5km.
Closed	Rarely.

Francis Fillon & Christian Poil
Manoir de Chaix,
Lieu dit Chaix,
37320 Truyes,
Indre-et-Loire

Tel	+33 (0)2 47 43 42 73
Email	manoirdechaix@sfr.fr
Web	www.manoir-de-chaix.com

Entry 422 Map 4

Loire Valley

Moulin de la Follaine

A smart metal gate opens to courtyard and garden beyond: Follaine is a deeply serene place. Ornamental geese adorn the lake, the tended garden has places to linger, colourful bedrooms have antique furniture, fabulous mattresses and lake views; one opens to the garden. Upstairs is a lovely light sitting room – and a guest fridge for picnics in the garden. Amazingly, the old milling machinery in the breakfast area still works – ask and Monsieur will turn it on for you; there are relics from the old hunting days, too. Your hosts, once in the hotel trade, know the area intimately and are utterly charming.

Sawday self-catering also.

Rooms	3: 1 double, 2 suites.
Price	€75–€80. Suite €80–€120.
Meals	Bar-restaurant 800m; choice in Loches.
Closed	November–March.

Danie Lignelet
Moulin de la Follaine,
2 chemin du Moulin,
37310 Azay sur Indre,
Indre-et-Loire
Tel   +33 (0)2 47 92 57 91
Email   moulindelafollaine@wanadoo.fr
Web   www.moulindelafollaine.com

Entry 423   Map 4

Loire Valley

Le Belvédère

Madame, ex-air hostess and English teacher, treats you to superb breakfasts, and is a mine of information on the region. From plain street to stately courtyard magnolia to extraordinary marble-walled spiral staircase with dome atop – this is a *monument historique*, a miniature Bagatelle Palace with a circular salon, in the centre of sleepy Bléré. The light, airy, elegant rooms, small and perfectly proportioned, are soft pink and grey; lean out and pluck a grape from the vine-clad pergola, prettily illuminated at night. Monsieur was a pilot and still flies vintage aircraft; ask about flights over the Loire châteaux.

Minimum two nights preferred. Children over 12 welcome.

Rooms	3: 2 doubles, 1 suite for 4.
Price	€100–€120. Suite €150. €10 supplement for one night.
Meals	Restaurants in Bléré.
Closed	Occasionally.

Dominique Guillemot
Le Belvédère,
24 rue des Déportés,
37150 Bléré,
Indre-et-Loire
Tel   +33 (0)2 47 30 30 25
Email   lebelvedere37@gmail.com
Web   lebelvedere-bednbreakfast.com

Entry 424   Map 4

Loire Valley

Les Moulins de Vontes

"Magical," say readers. Three old mills side by side on a glorious sweep of the Indre, boats for messing about in, wooden bridges to cross from one secluded bank to another, a fine view of the river from the terrace. No dinners so gather a picnic en route and your entertaining hosts will happily provide cutlery, rugs and anything else you need. The airy, elegant, uncluttered rooms are in historic style and have stunning river views (the rushing water becomes a gentle murmur at night). Bathrooms sparkle. Billiards in the sitting room, home honey for breakfast, swimming and fishing in the river, eco-aware owners. Heaven.

Minimum two nights.

Loire Valley

La Lubinerie

Built by Elizabeth's grandfather, its typical brick-and-tile face still looking good, this neat townhouse is a spirited mixture of nostalgic and modern. Strong colours and delicate muslin, elegant mirrors and her own patchwork, and a fascinating collection of paintings, prints, old cartoons and… teapots. Elizabeth lived for years in England, collected all these things and calls her delicious rooms 'Earl Grey', 'Orange Pekoe', 'Darjeeling'. Your hosts love sharing their stories and knowledge with guests. Two lovely dogs, a friendly little town, a sweet cottagey garden – and, we are told, the best croissants ever.

Rooms	3: 1 twin, 2 doubles, each with separate wc.
Price	€140.
Meals	Restaurants 2.5km.
Closed	October-March.

Rooms	3: 2 doubles, 1 suite for 4.
Price	€75-€85. Suite €85-€144.
Meals	Restaurants 3km.
Closed	Rarely.

Odile & Jean-Jacques Degail
Les Moulins de Vontes,
37320 Esvres sur Indre,
Indre-et-Loire

Tel	+33 (0)2 47 26 45 72
Mobile	+33 (0)7 78 11 87 66
Email	info@moulinsdevontes.com
Web	www.moulinsdevontes.com

Entry 425   Map 4

Elizabeth Aubert-Girard
La Lubinerie, 3 rue des Écoles,
37320 Esvres sur Indre,
Indre-et-Loire

Tel	+33 (0)2 47 26 40 87
Mobile	+33 (0)6 82 89 00 95
Email	lalubinerie@orange.fr
Web	www.lalubinerie.com

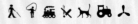

Entry 426   Map 4

Poitou – Charentes

Poitou - Charentes

Château de la Roche Martel

At the apex of three provinces, a sensational launch pad for Anjou, Touraine and Poitou. There's character and history in spades (Henry III is buried here), mullioned windows, a rare covered wooden gallery, a horse in the paddock, century old trees. And now, delightful new owners, she a Polish picture restorer, he an expert on Plantagenet history. Bedrooms glow with gorgeous fabrics and tadelakt walls, the larger double with a four-poster and fine stone fireplace, the smaller in a pretty round tower. All feels generous, the bathrooms are splendid (one with a rare antique wc) and salons face north and south – take your pick!

Minimum two nights November-February.

Rooms	3: 1 double, 1 family room, 1 single.
Price	€120. Family room €140-€165. Single €90. Extra bed €25.
Meals	Restaurant 6km.
Closed	Rarely.

Alicja & Dominique de Cornulier Lucinière
Château de la Roche Martel,
86120 Roiffé, Vienne
Tel   +33 (0)5 49 22 36 31
Mobile   +33 (0)6 83 43 46 34
Email   larochemartel@orange.fr
Web   www.larochemartel.com

Poitou - Charentes

L'Aumônerie

This old hospital priory beside the original moat (now a boulevard bringing new neighbours) has eight drama-packed centuries to tell. The L'Haridons have put back several original features and the old stone spiral stair leads up to one of the suites: big sitting room, huge stone fireplace, low oak door to pretty, beamed bedroom with extra bed. The family suite (up outside stairs) has a big sitting room and bedrooms decorated in jazzy shades of red. The small ground-floor double is utterly charming but Madame's pride and joy is her immaculate box-hedged vegetable garden. You breakfast in her lawn-view conservatory.

Rooms	3: 1 double, 1 suite for 2-3, 1 family suite for 2-6.
Price	€55. Suites €60-€90. Children under 3 free of charge.
Meals	Restaurants within walking distance.
Closed	Rarely.

Christiane L'Haridon
L'Aumônerie,
3 bd Maréchal Leclerc,
86200 Loudun, Vienne
Tel   +33 (0)5 49 22 63 86
Mobile   +33 (0)6 83 58 26 18
Email   chris.lharidon@wanadoo.fr
Web   www.l-aumonerie.biz

Poitou - Charentes

Domaine de Bourgville

Time slows down here. In the converted stable block of a 17th-century 'gentilhommière' the style is gentle, provincial France, in tune with the rolling countryside of forests, hamlets and hills. The first-floor bedrooms wrap you in a soft embrace of old French bedsteads and shiny seagrass, flowers, rush-seated chairs and views to garden or terrace; all is intimacy and calm. Breakfast in the airy sitting room with its comfortable, well-chosen furnishings; John is a superb cook so stay for dinner. Explore medieval Chinon, walk the trails, then return to the rambling garden. Supremely restful, truly hospitable.

Rooms	4: 3 doubles, 1 twin.
Price	€50-€65.
Meals	Dinner with wine, €28. Restaurant/bar in village.
Closed	Rarely.

	John & Glyn Ward
	Domaine de Bourgville,
	Allée de Bourgville,
	86420 Mont sur Guesnes, Vienne
Tel	+33 (0)5 49 98 74 79
Mobile	+33 (0)6 61 71 92 97
Email	b-b.bourgville@wanadoo.fr
Web	www.vie-vienne.com

Entry 429   Map 9

Poitou - Charentes

Château de la Motte

Nothing austere about this imposing, lovingly restored 15th-century castle. A wide spiral stone staircase leads to grandly high yet simply decorated rooms where family furniture, vast stone fireplaces and rich canopies, finely stitched by talented Marie-Andrée, preserve the medieval flavour; bathrooms are state of the art. The lofty, light-filled sitting room is engagingly cluttered, the elegant dining room witnesses excellent, organic, home cooking and enlightened conversation with your dynamically green, cultured and charming hosts. Everyone is welcome here, families included.

Sawday self-catering also.

Rooms	5: 1 double, 1 twin, 1 triple, 2 suites for 2.
Price	€95. Suite €105-€125. Triple €105-€150. Extra bed €25.
Meals	Dinner with wine, €30. Child under 12, €20.
Closed	Mid-November to mid-March.

	Jean-Marie & Marie-Andrée Bardin
	Château de la Motte,
	2 La Motte, 86230 Usseau, Vienne
Tel	+33 (0)5 49 85 88 25
Mobile	+33 (0)6 19 03 35 35
Email	chateau.delamotte@wanadoo.fr
Web	www.chateau-de-la-motte.net

Entry 430   Map 9

Poitou - Charentes

Manoir de la Boulinière

Laughter echoes in this 15th-century country manor where descendants of Scottish royalty once lived. Share with Alain, Marie-Pierre and son Henri the great gothic windows, the stone-flagged floors, the huge fireplaces, a living room replete with period pieces and their art collection. Alain is generous with the Loire valley's secrets, Marie-Pierre offers cookery mornings; table d'hôtes dinners burst with fresh herbs. The walled garden, too, is delightful, with giant cedar, plums, cherries, vines, a pretty gazebo. Two-room suites, up spiral stairs, revel in canopied beds, gorgeous bathrooms and a heady sense of history.

Poitou - Charentes

La Grenouillère

In an unexpectedly lovely cluster of old buildings on a residential road, a wonderful B&B. Impossible not to be charmed by these warm, easy, good-hearted people who offer you extremely good food, flowing wine, meals on a shady terrace in summer and, always, flowers on the table. The bedroom in the converted woodshed has beams, a colourful tiled floor and a view over the garden – rambling and delightful with a long pond and weeping willows. More rooms await in the house across the courtyard where Madame's charming mother lives (and makes delicious jam). There's even a Mongolian yurt – and a beautiful river boat to sleep in.

Rooms	2 family suites for 4-6.
Price	€130. Extra bed (12+ years) €60. Under 2s free. Travel cot available.
Meals	Dinner €35. Child under 12, €20. 'Birthday' dinner, €50 with champagne.
Closed	Rarely.

Rooms	7: 3 doubles, 2 triples, 1 yurt for 4 (with kitchen), 1 riverboat for 2.
Price	€50-€57. Yurt €95-€140. Riverboat €85-€100.
Meals	Dinner, 4 courses with wine, €29.
Closed	Rarely.

Marie-Pierre & Alain Guillon-Hardyau
Manoir de la Boulinière,
7 Manoir de la Boulinière,
86230 Usseau, Vienne
Tel   +33 (0)5 49 85 07 49
Mobile   +33 (0)6 87 03 58 84
Email   manoir.bouliniere@hotmail.fr
Web   www.manoirdelabouliniere.fr

Annie & Noël Braguier
La Grenouillère,
17 rue de la Grenouillère,
86220 Dangé St Romain, Vienne
Tel   +33 (0)5 49 86 48 68
Email   lagrenouillere86@orange.fr
Web   lagrenouillere86.com

Entry 431   Map 9

Entry 432   Map 9

Poitou - Charentes

Château de La Plante

You'll be charmed by this graceful stone château, looking proudly over the countryside to the wooded Vienne valley. 'La Plante' refers to the vines that were harvested for wine by Madame's ancestors. Period elegance drifts through rooms where the family grew up, leaving canopied beds, parquet floors and the odd empty picture frame in bedrooms lovingly named after great-grandmothers. Serenity reigns supreme; breakfast is in the old music room, a fittingly classic cream-blue affair. Join your hosts for an aperitif on the balustraded terrace or under the spreading lime tree. If houses could sing, this one surely would.

Rooms	4: 1 twin/double, 2 doubles; 1 family suite for 4 with separate wc.
Price	€80–€110. Family suite €130.
Meals	Restaurants 10-minute drive.
Closed	Rarely.

Patrick & Françoise Dandurand
Château de La Plante,
86540 Thuré, Vienne
Tel   +33 (0)5 49 93 86 28
Email   patrick.dandurand@orange.fr
Web   www.chateaudelaplante.fr

Entry 433   Map 9

Poitou - Charentes

Manoir de Vilaines

An oasis in the middle of rolling fields and wooded copses is an elegantly proportioned manor farmhouse, home to a hard-working family with a great sense of hospitality. Sleep in a super-comfortable bed, wake to a delicious breakfast at the big oval table overlooking the garden's cherry tree (home-produced apple juice, local honey…). In the two end wings are the biggest family suites, and the décor is traditional in keeping with the period of the house – long drapes, calm colours, folded bathrobes on immaculate beds. Outside is the paddock where the old carthorse lives, beyond is the market town of Mirebeau. Great value.

Rooms	4: 1 double, 1 suite for 3, 1 suite for 4, 1 suite for 5.
Price	€59. Suite: €72 for 3, €85 for 4, €98 for 5. Singles €42.
Meals	Restaurant 4km.
Closed	Rarely.

Géraldine Simonnet
Manoir de Vilaines,
Vilaines, 86110 Varennes, Vienne
Tel   +33 (0)5 49 60 73 93
Email   manoirdevilaines@orange.fr
Web   manoir-de-vilaines.com

Entry 434   Map 9

Poitou - Charentes

Château de Labarom

A great couple in their genuine family château of fading grandeur; mainly 17th century, it has a properly aged face. From the dramatic hall up the superbly bannistered staircase, you reach the salon gallery that runs majestically through the house. Here you may sit, read, dream of benevolent ghosts. Bedrooms burst with personality and wonderful old beds. Madame's hand-painted tiles adorn a shower, her laughter accompanies your breakfast (organic garden fruits and four sorts of jam); Monsieur tends his trees, aided by Polka the dog – he's a fount of local wisdom. A warm, wonderful, authentic place.

Rooms	3: 2 doubles, 1 twin.
Price	€74–€84. Child €20, in connecting room.
Meals	Auberge nearby; choice 3km; Michelin star 8km.
Closed	Rarely.

Éric & Henriette Le Gallais
Château de Labarom,
Route de Thurageau,
86380 Cheneché, Vienne
Tel   +33 (0)5 49 51 24 22
Mobile   +33 (0)6 83 57 68 14
Email   labarom@labarom.com
Web   www.labarom.com

Entry 435   Map 9

Poitou - Charentes

La Roseraie

Country B&B with one foot in the town: Neuville is a mere stroll. Warm and generous, Heather and Michael live in an elegant townhouse in four enclosed acres with orchard, vegetable garden and two rows of vines. The sitting area is cosy, the pool is fabulous, the bedrooms are immaculate, restful and calm: seagrass floors, white tub chairs, a carved bedhead, a balcony here, a patio off the garden there. Put the world to rights over Heather's delicious dinner served at the big table, or under the pergola in summer: gîte and B&B guests combine. Doves coo, Jack Russells frolic, Poitiers is the shortest drive.

Sawday self-catering also.

Rooms	5: 3 doubles, 2 family suites for 4–5.
Price	€68–€88. Family suites €120–€165.
Meals	Dinner with wine, €28.
Closed	Rarely.

Michael & Heather Lavender
La Roseraie,
78 rue Armand Caillard,
86170 Neuville de Poitou, Vienne
Tel   +33 (0)5 49 54 16 72
Email   heather@laroseraiefrance.fr
Web   www.laroseraiefrance.fr

Entry 436   Map 9

Poitou - Charentes

La Pocterie

A "passionate gardener" is how Martine describes herself, with a soft spot for old-fashioned roses: they ramble through the wisteria on the walls and gather in beautifully tended beds. The 'L' of the house shelters a very decent pool (alarmed) while furniture is arranged in a welcoming spot for picnics. Martine works but will see you for breakfast (in the delightful dining room or under the pretty arbour) or in the evening: she's the one with the big smile. A fresh, polished and peaceful retreat with Futuroscope minutes away. Bikes and tennis nearby, and a huge range of day trips to choose from: excellent for families.

Rooms	2: 1 double, 1 triple.
Price	€70. Triple €80.
Meals	Restaurants 3km.
Closed	Rarely.

Michel & Martine Poussard
La Pocterie,
86210 Vouneuil sur Vienne, Vienne

Tel	+33 (0)5 49 85 11 96
Mobile	+33 (0)6 76 95 49 46
Email	martinelapocterie@orange.fr
Web	lapocterie.chambres.free.fr

Entry 437 Map 9

Poitou - Charentes

Les Pierres Blanches

A simple unpretentious house built with century-old beams, in gardens bright with perennials, mature trees and swimming pool. Madame, friendly and charming, makes her own cakes and jams at a large table in the open-plan dining room with a cheery fire in winter. You have your own sitting room with cool beige walls, beams, a red sofa and armchairs, and pottery by family members, while the large ground-floor bedroom is light and airy, prettily painted in fresh apple green and with a romantic, canopied bed; this leads to a private decked terrace with a blue table and chairs. You are near to the medieval delights of Chauvigny.

Rooms	1 double.
Price	€65.
Meals	Restaurant 2km.
Closed	Rarely.

Nicole Gallais-Pradal
Les Pierres Blanches,
86210 Bonneuil Matours, Vienne

Tel	+33 (0)5 49 85 24 75
Email	les.pierres.blanches@orange.fr
Web	www.les-pierres-blanches.fr

Entry 438 Map 9

Logis du Château du Bois Doucet

Naturally, graciously, aristocratically French, owners and house are full of stories and eccentricity. Beautiful treasures abound: a jumble of ten French chairs, bits of ancient furniture, pictures, heirlooms, lamps in a stone-flagged salon, a properly elegant dining room, old dolls and family hunting buttons. There are statues inside and out and bedrooms with personality; the two-storey suite in the main house is fit for a cardinal. Monsieur's interests are history and his family, Madame's are art and life, and the garden is listed, a symphony in green. Feel part of family life in this delightful people- and dog-orientated house.

La Brasserie

Nod 'Bonjour' to the bereted gents by the gate, amble up the garden and enter the pages of the novel *Chocolat*: La Brasserie's vast staircase and mosaic floors have the feel of an authentic French shop. This is actually an old brewhouse – now a B&B with eco leanings: expect solar panels and power from the whirring village mill. Friendly Carol and John are rooted to this community and happily offer local tips over organic breakfasts – about châteaux, beautiful walks and sunflower fields. Guest stairs lead to four spotless, floral-themed bedrooms; original, outsize room-keys unlock a gloriously Gallic retreat.

Extra bed available.

Rooms	3: 1 family room with wc on ground floor. Wing: 1 double, 1 family room for 4-6.
Price	€80-€90. Family room €150.
Meals	Dinner with wine, €30.
Closed	Rarely.

Rooms	4: 1 double, 2 family rooms, 1 suite.
Price	€60-€65. €75-€80 for 3. Singles €45.
Meals	Restaurants 3km.
Closed	November-March.

	Vicomte & Vicomtesse de Villoutreys de Brignac
	Logis du Château du Bois Doucet,
	86800 Lavoux, Vienne
Tel	+33 (0)5 49 44 20 26
Mobile	+33 (0)6 75 42 79 78
Email	mariediane1012@yahoo.fr

	Carol & John Gardiner
	La Brasserie,
	86500 Saulgé, Vienne
Tel	+33 (0)9 62 03 23 39
Mobile	+33 (0)6 79 40 46 35
Email	enquiries@labrasserie-vienne.com
Web	www.labrasserie-vienne.com

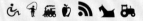

Entry 439   Map 9

Entry 440   Map 9

Poitou - Charentes

La Théophilière

You reach the village house from the back, up a long tree-lined drive. Jean-Louis, genial and twinkly, keeps vegetables and chickens; Geneviève is a perfectionist. Their traditional Poitevin farmhouse, rendered a sunny ochre, has a modern conservatory along its width and rooms opening off either side. Simply dressed bedrooms are in immaculate old-school style; the canopy over the double bed was made for a great-grandmother's wedding. Breakfast features a dozen homemade jams, supper is a treat: Poitevin farci, pork cooked in honey, fruit tart from garden produce – following a delicious pine aperitif.

Rooms	3: 1 double, 1 family room; 1 twin with separate wc.
Price	€57–€62. Family room €84–€99. Singles €53–€58.
Meals	Dinner with wine, €20. Restaurant nearby.
Closed	Rarely.

Geneviève & Jean-Louis Fazilleau
La Théophilière,
86400 Champniers, Vienne
Tel   +33 (0)5 49 87 19 04
Email   jeanlouis.fazilleau@free.fr
Web   www.chambres-hotes-poitou-charentes.fazilleau.fr

Poitou - Charentes

Château de Tennessus

It's all real: moat, drawbridge, dreams. Two steep stone spirals to "the biggest bedroom in France": granite windowsills, giant hearth, canopied bed, shower snug; on the lower floors of the keep, the medieval family room: vast timbers, good mattresses, arrow slits for windows. Furniture is sober, candles are lit, fires always laid, and you breakfast – beautifully – at a massive table on 14th-century flagstones. The whole place is gloriously authentic, the charming gardens glow from loving care (medieval potager, modern pool), the views reach far, and Pippa is a bundle of energy and generosity.

Children over 6 welcome.

Rooms	3: 2 doubles (one with kitchenette), 1 family room.
Price	€120–€145.
Meals	Gourmet picnic basket with wine, €29.50. Restaurants 500m.
Closed	Christmas.

Nicholas & Philippa Freeland
Château de Tennessus,
79350 Amailloux, Deux Sèvres
Tel   +33 (0)5 49 95 50 60
Email   tennessus@orange.fr
Web   www.tennessus.com

Poitou - Charentes

La Petite Bêchée

In the middle of a remote green valley, this beautifully restored building girdled by mature trees happens to be part of an alpaca farm; you are free to wander across the river and through swathes of grassland in search of a picnic spot. Josephine's welcome reflects the loved and lived-in qualities that you'll find everywhere: snuggled under beams in the sitting room, or up the oak staircase to the cosy country bedroom. Before heading off to find medieval France, enjoy breakfast on the garden terrace hung with wisteria or in the dining room… but it's all so peaceful you may decide to stay put after all.

Extra single bed available downstairs.

Rooms	1 suite.
Price	€85.
Meals	Plat du jour €12-€15. Restaurants 4km.
Closed	Rarely.

Josephine Colclough
La Petite Bêchée,
Le Moulin de La Bêchée, Le Plessis,
Deux Sèvres,
79400 Auge, Deux Sèvres
Tel   +33 (0)5 49 75 53 19
Email beechy.colclough@orange.fr
Web   www.rural-gites-france.com

Entry 443   Map 9

Poitou - Charentes

Le Logis de Bellevue

You're within strolling distance of one of the prettiest towns in the Marais Poitevin. The blue-shuttered lodge has been transformed by this happy, hospitable British couple into a colourful home with the guest suite on the first floor: white walled, wooden floored, clean-limbed and spotless. The garden is immaculate too, with lawns and colourful borders, croquet, table tennis and (shared with gîtes) super pool. Garden fruits make an appearance at breakfast in homemade juices and jams; clever Marylyn even makes brioche. Dinner might include goat's cheese from the area and lamb from the farmer next door. A treat.

Rooms	1 family suite for 2-4.
Price	€90-€170.
Meals	Dinner with wine, €35. Child €17. Restaurants 400m.
Closed	Christmas.

Marylyn & Anthony Kusmirek
Le Logis de Bellevue,
55 route de Benet,
79510 Coulon,
Deux Sèvres
Tel   +33 (0)5 49 76 75 45
Email kusmirek@orange.fr
Web   www.lelogisdebellevue.com

Entry 444   Map 8

Poitou - Charentes

Maison des Algues

In a residential area, behind private gates on the outskirts of Rivedoux Plage, is a single-storey hotel, whitewashed, shuttered and impeccably maintained. Nothing is too much trouble for Christian and Jocelyne, who will pick you up from the airport and insist on giving you the best: white towels for the bathroom, coloured towels for the pool, pâtisseries for tea. Bedrooms open to a wicker-chaired terrace and are roomy, restful and flooded with light. Spin off on a bike (there are ten, all free) and acquaint yourself with the island – the whitewashed houses of La Flotte, the fabulous white sands, the chic shops of St Martin.

Poitou - Charentes

Le Beach House

Ever dream about your own cabin on an island with glorious sunsets and views to the horizon? This one has a private dune to boot – and a first-row balcony seat from which to contemplate the waves or the sparkling Milky Way. Breakfasts are superb, aperitifs come from the honesty bar, and everything is shipshape in the little blue and white cabin ten steps from the house: quietly stylish wicker furniture and luxurious linen. Antoinette is huge fun, Philippe knows his oysters, there's a pool here, a colourful port nearby, and plashy waves to lull you to sleep at night.

Minimum stays apply: please see website.

Rooms	5: 3 doubles, 2 suites (interconnecting).
Price	€125-€215.
Meals	Guest kitchen. Restaurants within walking distance.
Closed	Rarely.

Rooms	2: 1 double. Cabin: 1 double.
Price	€125-€155.
Meals	Occasional dinner with wine, €30. Restaurant 1km.
Closed	November-March.

Christian & Jocelyne Gatta-Boucard
Maison des Algues, 147 rue des Algues,
17940 Rivedoux (Île de Ré),
Charente-Maritime

Tel	+33 (0)5 46 68 01 23
Mobile	+33 (0)6 88 48 35 80
Email	information@maison-des-algues.com
Web	www.maison-des-algues.com

Antoinette & Philippe Girard
Le Beach House, Plage de la
Faucheprère, La Cotinière, 17310
St Pierre d'Oléron, Charente-Maritime

Tel	+33 (0)5 46 47 19 70
Mobile	+33 (0)6 86 82 38 39
Email	contact@lebeachhouse.com
Web	www.lebeachhouse.com

Poitou - Charentes

La Grande Barbotière

Between the fruit trees a hammock sways, breakfast is served next to a sparkling pool and sculpted chickens peck. Tucked behind gates in the heart of a bustling village is a *maison de maître* of elegance and charm. Your hosts (she half Belgian, he from Yorkshire) have a wicked sense of humour and have created a luxurious and eclectic décor – gazelle antlers, pebbled showers, delicious French linen – for suites with private terraces. Table tennis, croquet, toys for children, bikes to borrow, jasmine, lavender and, everywhere, that spirit-lifting light that you find on this cherished stretch of coastline.

Minimum two nights. Children under 4 welcome.

Rooms	2 suites.
Price	€95–€200.
Meals	Restaurants 4km.
Closed	Rarely.

Christopher & Jacqui McLean May
La Grande Barbotière,
10 rue du Marais Doux,
17220 St Vivien, Charente-Maritime

Tel	+33 (0)5 46 43 76 14
Mobile	+33 (0)6 43 12 11 04
Email	info@mcleanmay.com
Web	www.lagrandebarbotiere.com

Entry 447   Map 8

Poitou - Charentes

A l'Ombre du Figuier

A rural idyll, wrapped in birdsong. The old farmhouse, lovingly restored and decorated, is simple and pristine; its carpeted rooms under eaves that are polished to perfection overlook a pretty garden where you may picnic. Your hosts are an interesting couple of anglophiles. Thoughtful, stylish Madame serves generous breakfasts of homemade jams, organic breads, cheeses and cereals under the fig tree in summer. Monsieur teaches engineering in beautiful La Rochelle; follow his suggestions and discover its lesser-known treasures. Luscious lawns are bordered by well-stocked beds, and there's a garage for your car. Great value.

Rooms	2: 1 family suite for 2-6.
	Annexe: 1 family room for 2-4.
Price	€62–€132.
Meals	Guest kitchen. Restaurant within
	walking distance. Auberge 3km.
Closed	Rarely.

Marie-Christine & Jean-François Prou
A l'Ombre du Figuier,
43 rue du Marais, 17230 Longèves,
Charente-Maritime

Tel	+33 (0)5 46 37 11 15
Mobile	+33 (0)6 79 35 55 12
Email	mcprou@wanadoo.fr
Web	www.alombredufiguier.com

Entry 448   Map 8

Poitou - Charentes

La Villa Cécile

Stroll from the church to Cécile and Gérard's peaceful garden and its sweet-scented roses. They are charming people and theirs is a happy, house. The newly built traditional Charentais exterior belies the chic contemporary look inside where wood, glass and leather sit in harmony with good modern art. Your sitting/dining room has big windows onto terraces; light-filled bedrooms are immaculate and luxurious, one with its own terrace and huge bath, another with a circular bed. Breakfast on the terrace is a treat – homemade everything from pancakes to yogurt, deliciously different each day; Zack the friendly dog may join you.

Free private parking bookable in advance. Minimum two nights during summer holidays.

Rooms	3: 2 doubles, 1 twin/double.
Price	€90–€130. Sauna €15 p.p. Hot tub €10 p.p.
Meals	Restaurants within walking distance.
Closed	Never.

Cécile Thureau & Gérard Blumberg
La Villa Cécile,
1 rue de Puyravault, 17700 Vouhé,
Charente-Maritime

Tel	+33 (0)5 46 00 61 50
Mobile	+33 (0)6 75 85 00 34
Email	lavillacecile@orange.fr
Web	www.lavillacecile.fr

Entry 449   Map 8

Poitou - Charentes

Le Clos de la Garenne

Charming owners and animals everywhere, from boxer dog to donkey to hens! Brigitte and Patrick gave up telecommunications for their dream of the country and the result is this heart-warming, small-village B&B. Avid collectors, they have decorated their roomy 16th-century house with eclectic flair, and old and new rub shoulders merrily; discover doll's house furniture and French cartoon characters, old armoires and antique treasures. Harmony breathes from walls and woodwork, your hosts are endlessly thoughtful, food is exotic organic (and delicious), and families are truly welcome.

Minimum three nights July/Aug.

Rooms	4: 2 doubles, 1 suite for 6. Family cottage (in same street) for 5.
Price	€71–€81. Suite €71–€172. Cottage €71–€131.
Meals	Dinner with wine, €27. Teenager €22. Child €12.
Closed	January/February.

Brigitte & Patrick François
Le Clos de la Garenne,
9 rue de la Garenne,
17700 Puyravault,
Charente-Maritime

Tel	+33 (0)5 46 35 47 71
Email	info@closdelagarenne.com
Web	www.closdelagarenne.com

Entry 450   Map 8

Poitou - Charentes

Les Grands Vents

In a lovely village in the heart of cognac country, beside a sleepy road, the old farmhouse has simple limewashed walls and French country décor. New to B&B and very enthusiastic, Virginie, who has an interiors boutique in town, and Philippe, a cabinet-maker, will be changing things gradually. You have your own entrance and living room but your happy hosts want you to feel completely at home. Bedrooms, with views onto a big garden, are large, fresh and catch the morning or evening sun. There's a lush pool, turquoise water surrounded by velvet greenery, and a covered terrace for simple summer breakfasts. Good value.

Rooms	2: 1 family room, 1 suite.
Price	€62. Extra bed €20.
Meals	Restaurants in St Mard, 3km, and Surgères, 8km.
Closed	Rarely.

Virginie Truong Grandon
Les Grands Vents,
17380 Chervettes,
Charente-Maritime
Tel   +33 (0)5 46 35 92 21
Mobile +33 (0)6 07 96 68 73
Email   adaunis@orange.fr
Web   www.les-grands-vents.com

Entry 451   Map 8

Poitou - Charentes

Les Hortensias

Behind its modest, wisteria-covered mask, this 17th-century former wine-grower's house hides a charming interior – and a magnificent garden that flows through orchard to topiary, a delight in every season. Soft duck-egg colours and rich trimmings make this a warm and safe haven, light airy bedrooms are immaculate (one with its original stone sink, another with a pretty French pink décor), the bathrooms are luxurious, the walls burst with art and the welcome is gracious, warm and friendly. Superb value, scrumptious dinners and blackcurrants from the potager – Madame's sorbets are the best.

Rooms	3: 2 doubles, 1 triple.
Price	€62. Triple €69-€83. Extra bed €17.
Meals	Dinner with wine, €24. Summer kitchen. Restaurant in village.
Closed	Christmas & 1 January.

Marie-Thérèse Jacques
Les Hortensias,
16 rue des Sablières,
17380 Archingeay,
Charente-Maritime
Tel   +33 (0)5 46 97 85 70
Email jpmt.jacques@wanadoo.fr
Web   www.chambres-hotes-hortensias.com

Entry 452   Map 8

Poitou - Charentes

Palmier Sur Cour

Enter the handsome townhouse off the street. Calm descends, scented roses waft the air, period details abound. Fireplaces, cornices, deep skirtings, a light-flooded grey-stone staircase with iron balustrading leading ever upwards… Delightful Hélène, creator of all this serenity, has decorated each lovely lofty bedroom in classic French style. Wake to happy feasts of homemade cakes, fresh cut fruits and great coffee at one big table, or out on the terrace. Beaches and seafoods beckon, and the port of Rochefort (which lies within the charmed triangle of La Rochelle, Saintes, Royan) is an interesting town in itself.

Minimum two nights.

Rooms	3: 1 double, 2 family rooms for 3-4.
Price	€79-€84. Family room €105-€149.
Meals	Guest kitchenette. Restaurants within walking distance.
Closed	Never.

Hélène Coulon
Palmier Sur Cour,
55 rue de la République,
17300 Rochefort, Charente-Maritime

Tel	+33 (0)5 46 99 55 54
Mobile	+33 (0)6 65 78 40 76
Email	contact@palmiersurcour.com
Web	www.palmiersurcour.com

Entry 453   Map 8

Poitou - Charentes

Le Logis du Port Paradis

Seafood is fresh from the Atlantic, the palm-ringed pool shimmers and five light-filled rooms exude your hosts' love of the sea. Clustered round a family home a short drive from Royan's sandy beaches, the nicely independent rooms and family suites have terraces, gleaming showers, ingenious headboards (sail canvas, slate, terracotta), a seaside feel. If you're lucky, Monsieur will cook – tuna carpaccio, fresh sole, gratin aux fraises – joining guests at one long table overlooking the pool; Madame may share stories of oyster farming. Plump down afterwards on cherry sofas or step out to the flower garden for fresh air and stars.

Rooms	5: 3 doubles, 2 suites.
Price	€68-€73. Suite €90-€130.
Meals	Dinner with wine, €32. Restaurants 3km.
Closed	Rarely.

Nadine Bauve
Le Logis du Port Paradis, 12 route du Port Paradis, 17600 Nieulle sur Seudre, Charente-Maritime

Tel	+33 (0)5 46 85 37 38
Mobile	+33 (0)6 09 71 64 84
Email	logis.portparadis@wanadoo.fr
Web	www.portparadis.com

Entry 454   Map 8

Poitou - Charentes

Ma Maison de Mer

Sink into a cream sofa with a chilled après-plage beer and soak up the nautical chic. Built in the 1920s in a quiet tree-lined street (150m from a lovely beach, 400m from 'centre ville') Ma Maison has been renovated by bubbly Emma, who lives here with her young family. Find seashell collages and elegant wicker chairs, an intimate bar, and bedrooms super-fresh and inviting, some with mosquito nets, others with ceiling fans. The four-course set menu (summer only) changes daily so you can look forward to some wonderful seafood, and if you need an excuse to stay, take a boat across the Gironde from Royan to sample the Medoc wines.

Rooms	5: 4 doubles, 1 twin.
Price	€75–€155.
Meals	Dinner with wine, €35, on request (June-September only).
Closed	Rarely.

Emma Hutchinson
Ma Maison de Mer,
21 av du Platin,
17420 Saint Palais sur Mer,
Charente-Maritime

Tel   +33 (0)5 46 23 64 86
Email   reservations@mamaisondemer.com
Web   www.mamaisondemer.com

Entry 455   Map 8

Poitou - Charentes

La Flotte

Soak up the peace of this handsome estate and nature reserve, where a pretty stone studio is freshly baked in Charentaise sunshine. Cuddle up by the fireplace in a simple, white beamed living room, listening to coo-cooing wood pigeons, rustling trees — or in a cosy bedroom with poppy cushions. Rugs are fluffy, curtains stripy, the open kitchen well equipped and a little terrace perfect for breakfast and barbecues. Beyond lie sprawling grounds, vines, sunflowers, a pool... Wander to pretty Mortagne harbour; beaches, wineries and golf are close. Lovely Amanda looks after you, from three-course dinners to fishing in the lake.

Minimum one week June-September.

Rooms	Studio: 1 twin/double with kitchenette.
Price	€90–€135. €630–€945 per week.
Meals	Dinner, 3 courses with wine, €25. Restaurant 2km.
Closed	Rarely.

Tim & Amanda Walsh
La Flotte,
17120 Boutenac Touvent,
Charente-Maritime

Tel   +33 (0)5 46 90 63 34
Mobile   +33 (0)6 77 29 17 20
Email   info@laflottefrance.com
Web   www.laflottefrance.com

Entry 456   Map 8

Poitou - Charentes

Poitou - Charentes

Château de la Tillade

It's clear that Michel and Solange like people; they immediately put you at ease in their comfortable home. The château sits at the top of an avenue of lime trees; the vineyards here have produced grapes for cognac and pineau for two centuries. Solange holds painting courses; her artistic flair is reflected in her love of fabrics. Bedrooms are marvellously individual, each like a page out of Michel's memory book, steeped in family history. Meals around the family table are a delight with conversation in English or French; lavish, but without stuffiness. A rare opportunity to get to know a pair of charming French aristocrats.

La Rotonde

Stupendously confident, with priceless river views, this city mansion seems to ride the whole rich story of lovely old Saintes. Soft blue river light hovers into high bourgeois rooms to stroke the warm panelling, marble fireplaces, perfect parquet (the studios are less fine). Double glazing, yes, but ask for a room at the back, away from river and busy road. The Rougers love renovating and Marie-Laure, calm and talented, has her own sensitive way with classic French furnishings: feminine yet not frilly, rich yet gentle. Superb (antique) linen and bathrooms, too, breakfasts with views and always that elegance.

Rooms	4: 1 twin, 3 family rooms for 3-4 (one room with wc just outside room).		Rooms	4: 2 doubles, 1 twin, 2 studios (with kitchenettes) for 2.
Price	€90-€120. Extra bed €23.		Price	€100.
Meals	Dinner with wine, €38. Restaurant 12km.		Meals	Restaurants in town centre.
Closed	Rarely.		Closed	Rarely.

	Vicomte & Vicomtesse Michel de Salvert Château de la Tillade, Gémozac, 17260 St Simon de Pellouaille, Charente-Maritime			**Marie-Laure Rouger** La Rotonde, 2 rue Monconseil, 17100 Saintes, Charente-Maritime
Tel	+33 (0)5 46 90 00 20		Mobile	+33 (0)6 87 51 70 92
Email	contact@la-tillade.com		Email	laure@laboutiquedelarotonde.com
Web	www.la-tillade.com		Web	www.laboutiquedelarotonde.com

Entry 457   Map 8

Entry 458   Map 8

Poitou - Charentes

Le Manoir Souhait

Built by a cognac merchant in 1888 (outbuildings contain the presses), the mellow manoir has pretty porcelain in elegant cabinets, sprigs of lavender on fat pillows, white-painted beams, a majestic antique bed, a sparkling chandelier: Liz's attention to detail is irresistible. That includes lavish dinners on which guests heap praise, and breakfasts of fresh fruits, charcuterie, viennoiseries and griddled muffins. Further treats await outside in the form of badminton, table tennis, swings and a terraced heated pool. A luxurious B&B run by friendly super-organised English hosts, Liz and Will.

Sawday self-catering also.

Rooms	3: 1 double, 2 suites for 2-4.
Price	€98. Suite €120-€178.
	Extra bed €12. Cot €7.
Meals	Dinner, 4 courses, €33.
Closed	Rarely.

Will & Liz Weeks
Le Manoir Souhait,
7 rue du Château d'Eau,
17490 Gourvillette, Charente-Maritime

Tel	+33 (0)5 46 26 18 41
Mobile	+33 (0)6 08 48 27 34
Email	weeks@manoirsouhait.com
Web	www.manoirsouhait.com

Entry 459   Map 9

Poitou - Charentes

Le Bourg

Stone cottages, nodding hollyhocks, ducks in the lane: Mareuil epitomises rural France, and the house sits in its heart. Arrive to a sweeping drive, an immaculate pool, a grand façade and Ron and Vanessa, who have travelled the world. After a final posting in Paris they have landed in sunny Charente, and are happy. Bedrooms are bright, airy and comfortable, with cosy bathrooms; dinners, in the ample dining room, are gastronomic, cosmopolitan, entertaining and preceded by pineau de Charente. You are surrounded by sunflowers and vines and Cognac is close. Friendly, interesting, great fun.

Rooms	3 twins/doubles.
Price	€85-€95.
Meals	Dinner with wine, €30.
Closed	Rarely.

Vanessa Bennett-Dixon
Le Bourg,
16170 Mareuil,
Charente

Tel	+33 (0)5 45 66 29 75
Email	lebourg-charente@wanadoo.fr
Web	www.lebourg-charente.com

Entry 460   Map 9

Poitou - Charentes

Le Chiron

The big old well-lived-in house is all chandeliers, ceiling roses and heavy dark furniture. The 'Toile de Jouy' triple has a rustic elegance, 'La Rose' is... pink. Bathrooms are more functional than luxurious but with so much natural beauty to hand who wants to stay in anyway? Madame's regional cooking is a treat, served in a conservatory big enough for many. Genuinely welcoming, your farmer hosts stay and chat (in French, mostly!) when they can. They'll also show you the fascinating old cognac still. Big, off the beaten track and great for families (they run a campsite next door).

Rooms	6: 2 doubles, 1 twin, 2 triples, 1 family suite for 4.
Price	€50. Family room €80.
Meals	Dinner with wine, €20.
Closed	Rarely.

Micheline & Jacky Chainier
Le Chiron,
16130 Salles d'Angles,
Charente
Tel +33 (0)5 45 83 72 79
Email mchainier@voila.fr

Entry 461   Map 9

Poitou - Charentes

Logis des Jardins du Chaigne

Lush gardens cascade into Cognac vineyards (giant lilies, snowy roses, topiary, a lavender-lined stream, lake, tennis, a pool with bar)... a superb setting for summer concerts, a garden-loving public and this handsome brandy château. As gracious as their historic home, Béatrice and Philippe welcome you with exquisite objets, a gardening library, and convivial table d'hôtes with fresh herbs. Sweep upstairs to a galleried landing and luxurious bedrooms with soft linen and monogrammed towels. Wake to sunrise over vineyards and myriad pleasures: fêtes, markets, beaches, cognac and peace.

Children over 12 welcome.

Rooms	5: 2 doubles, 2 suites, 1 apartment for 2.
Price	€130–€150. Suite €120–€150. Apartment €100–€120.
Meals	Dinner €35. Restaurant 2km.
Closed	Rarely.

Philippe & Béatrice Marzano
Logis des Jardins du Chaigne,
Le Chaigne,
16120 Touzac, Charente
Tel +33 (0)5 45 62 33 92
Email philippe.marzano@wanadoo.fr
Web www.logisdesjardinsduchaigne.com

Entry 462   Map 9

Poitou - Charentes

Le Chatelard

This is a gem of a place to stay, both grand and intimate. Béatrice inherited the exquisitely French neo-gothic château and she lovingly protects it from the worst of modernisation (though the hurricane took its toll and trees have had to be replanted). Sleep between antique linen sheets, sit in handsome old chairs and be charmed by a bedroom in a tower. The sitting room has that unusual quirk, a window over the fireplace, the dining room a panelled ceiling studded with plates. Béatrice, a teacher, and Christopher, a lecturer in philosophy, are interesting, cultured hosts who enjoy eating with their guests.

Rooms	4: 1 double; 1 double, 1 twin, 1 family suite for 6 each with separate wc.
Price	€60–€70. Family suite €80–€120. Extra bed €10. Singles €50.
Meals	Dinner with wine, €25. Restaurant 1km.
Closed	Rarely.

	Béatrice de Castelbajac & Christopher Macann
	Le Chatelard,
	16480 Passirac, Charente
Tel	+33 (0)5 45 98 71 03
Email	c.macann@wanadoo.fr
Web	www.chateaudepassirac.jimdo.com

Poitou - Charentes

Château de Lavaud

Superlatives cannot do justice to French/Californian Florence and Robert's ten-year renovation of this delicious château. Five hectares of woods and gardens roll down to a waterfall and river while historic Montbron sits on the hill above. Behind, a gorgeous pool. Spacious rooms – globally themed, full of personality – are divine. Natural pigments hug lime and straw walls, old shutters make bathroom doors, vintage sinks carry snappy taps perfectly. Take breakfast royally – or dine – in a panelled dining room with long views. Repose in the sunny living room, the snug cinema room, the poolside salon. Magical!

Rooms	4: 2 doubles, 2 twins/doubles.
Price	€110–€150. Extra bed €25.
Meals	Lunch €15–€20. Dinner with wine, €35. Restaurant 1km.
Closed	Rarely.

	Florence Manderscheid
	Château de Lavaud,
	16220 Montbron, Charente
Tel	+33 (0)5 45 23 93 54
Mobile	+33 (0)6 99 25 12 47
Email	f.manderscheid@gmail.com
Web	www.chateau-de-lavaud.com

Poitou - Charentes

La Fontaine des Arts

Along the narrow street in the charming, bustling town, through the heavy oak gates, under the ancient arch, is a cottage by the Charente with a little boat for trips up the river. Beautifully coiffed Marie-France combines the glamour of the city with the warmth of a country hostess: guests love her. Breakfast in the conservatory alongside Gérard's easel and piano, or in the courtyard by the pretty fountain pool. Décor is quintessential French: shiny gold taps, striped and flowered walls, a white dressing table. There's a shared guest kitchenette – and a surprising open-gallery bathroom in the double. One night just isn't enough.

Rooms	3: 1 double, 1 twin, 1 triple.
Price	€66-€73.
Meals	Guest kitchenette. Restaurant within walking distance.
Closed	Rarely.

Marie-France Pagano
La Fontaine des Arts,
13 rue du Temple,
16230 Mansle, Charente

Tel   +33 (0)5 45 69 13 56
Mobile +33 (0)6 12 52 39 86
Email   mfpagano@wanadoo.fr
Web   www.la-fontaine-des-arts.com

Entry 465   Map 9

Poitou - Charentes

La Cochère

Cool off by the lush pool, listen to the clacking and cheering of summer Sundays' boules. Katie, husband Nat and Bob the St Bernard are the proud protectors of this dreamlike place where the long breakfast table groans with fresh compotes and croissants and the tranquil garden (their delight) sparkles with lanterns at dusk. In the old coach house, antique iron beds wear floral quilts and crisp linen, and pretty stone peeps through timeworn render. Who wouldn't fall for this heart-warming blend of sophisticated and rustic in a sleepy farming village, once a horse-trading centre? Don't miss the fascinating Jardins Européens project.

Rooms	4: 2 doubles, 1 twin. Studio for 3 (May-Sept only).
Price	€65. Singles €55.
Meals	Occasional dinner €25. Owners' restaurant in Verteuil, 6km.
Closed	Christmas.

Katie Anderson
La Cochère,
Le Bourg,
16700 Salles de Villefagnan,
Charente

Tel   +33 (0)5 45 30 34 60
Email   la.cochere@wanadoo.fr
Web   www.lacochere.com

Entry 466   Map 9

Poitou - Charentes

Le Pit

What a remote, interesting and gentle place – heaven for walkers, and for children. Pets doze by the fire, llamas munch on the hillside. Simple, floral bedrooms are in a converted outbuilding (with parking right by), the larger one overlooking the lake. Dinner is unusual (venison pâté perhaps), delicious (produce from the precious vegetable garden) and preceded by a glass of local pineau. Alex left London for French farming with a difference, capable Hélène looks after you, and there are many little corners of rustic charm and colour from which to enjoy the fascinating surroundings. Fun and hugely welcoming.

Rooms	2: 1 double, 1 quadruple.
Price	€55. Quadruple €55-€100.
Meals	Dinner with wine, €27.
Closed	Rarely.

Alex & Hélène Everitt
Le Pit,
Lessac, 16500 Confolens, Charente
Tel   +33 (0)5 45 84 27 65
Mobile   +33 (0)6 30 34 14 11
Email   everitt16@aol.com
Web   www.lepit.fr

Entry 467   Map 9

Aquitaine

Aquitaine

Château Bavolier

The classic pale-stone building lies low among unfussy lawns and trees. Inside, the space, light and simplicity of décor are striking. Your charming talented hostess uses a restrained palette to give a floaty, dreamy quality: beige and white paint, pale-straw sisal, impressive decorations (she has beautifully restored some hand-painted panelling). The first bedroom is beautiful in white, gilt and black Louis XVI. The second is enormous, breathtaking, with myriad windows, play of dark and light across the huge brass bed and monochrome oils of Paris. And in each a magnificent chandelier. Amazing.

Rooms	2 doubles.
Price	€110–€160.
Meals	Restaurant nearby.
Closed	October–March.

Ann Roberts
Château Bavolier,
33920 St Christoly de Blaye,
Gironde

Tel	+33 (0)5 57 42 59 74
Email	info@chateau-bavolier.com
Web	www.chateau-bavolier.com

Entry 468   Map 8

Aquitaine

Château de la Grave

Come for three sweeping bedrooms, two balconies with vineyard views, a stone entrance hall — and a wrought-iron terrace for a glass of the Bassereaus' own dry white semillon (their red is superb, too). They are a hard-working, caring and confident couple in an 18th-century château with too much good taste to make it sumptuous, thank heavens. It is relaxed and easy with six friendly cats, and horses in the fields. Breakfast is on the terrace, wine-tasting courses in the magnificent *salle de dégustation*. The small pool is for evening dippers rather than sun-worshippers. Good value.

Rooms	3: 1 double, 1 triple, 1 family room for 4.
Price	€85–€110. Triple €110–€130. Family room €150.
Meals	Restaurants in Bourg, 2km.
Closed	December–March; 2 weeks in August.

Philippe & Valérie Bassereau
Château de la Grave,
33710 Bourg sur Gironde,
Gironde

Tel	+33 (0)5 57 68 41 49
Email	reservation@chateaudelagrave.com
Web	www.chateaudelagrave.com

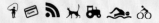

Entry 469   Map 8

Aquitaine

Le Castel de Camillac

Perched above vineyards and the lazy Dordogne, a perfect mini-château. Madame has restored its 18th-century spirit with passion, giving rooms delicious drama: panelled walls, vast tapestries, Turkish rugs, elegant antiques. Bedrooms, gleaming with polished wood and lush fabrics, feel like intimate family rooms while head-ducking beams and odd-shaped but sparkling bathrooms add to the charm. Breakfast in the voluptuous dining room or on the terrace, swim in the discreet circular pool, play tennis on the floodlit court, enjoy a round of billiards by the wood-burner. A rich experience, 30 minutes from Bordeaux.

Rooms	3 doubles.
Price	€90–€105. Extra bed €15–€20.
Meals	Guest kitchenette available. Restaurant 2km.
Closed	Occasionally.

Élisabeth Frape
Le Castel de Camillac,
1 Camillac,
33710 Bourg, Gironde
Mobile +33 (0)6 74 31 15 85
Email elisabeth.frape@lecasteldecamillac.com
Web lecasteldecamillac.com

Entry 470   Map 8

Aquitaine

Domaine du Freyche

A bend in the winding Dordogne creates the serene Île de Carney where this house stands. Views stretch from the domaine across vast flood plains where deer forage, silhouetted against the setting sun. Bedrooms are quirky – two baths sit side by side in 'Mountain' – while the Airstream caravan, boldly decorated in sugar pink and bubblegum green, makes a stunning third room. Makers of organic bed linen and fans of classic cars – you can hire theirs out – the friendly Riperts have many strings to their bow. Take your own horse (it's been an equestrian centre for years) or sample the wines in St Émilion. Superb.

Rooms	3: 1 double, 1 twin/double, 1 Airstream caravan for 2.
Price	€100.
Meals	Restaurants nearby.
Closed	Rarely.

Carole Ripert
Domaine du Freyche, Lieu dit le Freyche,
33240 Lugon & l'Île du Carnay, Gironde
Tel +33 (0)6 15 22 52 25
Mobile +33 (0)6 18 03 80 37
Email contact@domainedufreyche.com
Web www.domainedufreyche.com

Entry 471   Map 9

Aquitaine

Château de la Vieille Chapelle

A long, leafy lane brings you to a secluded and sumptuous estate, its backdrop sweeping vineyards and raw 12th-century stone. It's an idyllic retreat, a perfect balance of shabby and chic. Each river-view bedroom is smartly decorated with state-of-the-art wet rooms and beds you can simply sink into. In the château's galleried dining room, the discreet Madame Mallier serves light meals or full dinners, and suggests exclusive tours of the renowned cellars. Explore the vineyards, fish, recline, and let yourself be hypnotised by the fast-running (but unfenced) river and the beauty of glorious Bordeaux.

Gluten-free meals available. Smoking allowed (except in bedrooms).

Rooms	3: 1 double.
	Outbuildings: 2 doubles.
Price	€75. Singles €70. Cot €10.
	Extra bed €20.
Meals	Dinner €14–€35. Wine €6.40–€35.
Closed	Rarely.

Fabienne & Frédéric Mallier
Château de la Vieille Chapelle,
4 Chapelle, 33240 Lugon & l'Île
du Carnay, Gironde
Tel   +33 (0)5 57 84 48 65
Mobile   +33 (0)6 17 98 19 56
Email   best-of-bordeaux-wine@chateau-de-la-vieille-chapelle.com
Web   www.chateau-de-la-vieille-chapelle.com

Entry 472   Map 9

Aquitaine

Château Lavergne Dulong

This 19th-century mansion has become a sumptuous stopover in Sylvie's hands. Go through the neo-gothic façade and step into a surprising baroque-furnished hall complete with sculptures and a staircase that sweeps you up to lavish, lovely, expansive rooms where gilt mirrors, neatly placed club chairs and superb linens heighten your sense of indulgence. Sylvie gives tasting tours of her cellar and vineyard, and it's a ten-minute drive to the tram that ferries you into Bordeaux. Or meander by the summerhouse and spread out lazily on a poolside recliner, until sleep or appetite beckons you away – dinners are a treat.

Rooms	2: 1 twin, 1 suite.
Price	€135–€165. Suite €155–€195.
	Extra bed €25..
Meals	Brunch €20. Dinner €45 (Fri/Sat only, minimum 4). Wine €5.50–€16.
	Summer kitchen.
Closed	December–February.

Sylvie Dulong
Château Lavergne Dulong,
23 route du Courneau,
Montussan, 33450 Bordeaux,
Gironde
Tel   +33 (0)5 56 72 19 52
Email   contact@chateau-lavergne-dulong.com
Web   www.chateau-lavergne-dulong.com

Entry 473   Map 8

Aquitaine

83 rue de Patay

Martine may have just one room but she's used to making guests feel welcome: she owns a restaurant in the middle of the old town. Le Loup has been serving local specialities since 1932: you will probably want to pay a visit. This old stone townhouse is a welcome retreat after days visiting the city (ten minutes by tram) or those renowned vineyards. Martine has given it a light modern touch which works well. Your cosy little bedroom is approached up a curved stone staircase and you have the floor to yourselves. It overlooks a small courtyard garden and has a desk and other pieces stencilled by a friend.

Rooms	1 twin/double.
Price	€70.
Meals	Martine's restaurant 'Le Loup' near Cathedral.
Closed	Rarely.

Martine Peiffer
83 rue de Patay,
33000 Bordeaux,
Gironde
Tel   +33 (0)5 56 99 41 74
Mobile +33 (0)6 19 81 22 81
Email   mpeifferma95@numericable.fr

Entry 474   Map 8

Aquitaine

La Villa Chaleemar

In an up-and-coming neighbourhood of the wine capital of France, near the renowned Jardin Public and the revived dockside, is a super-contemporary B&B. Impeccable Leena lives with her daughters on one side of the courtyard – glass glides open to loungers and bamboo – while guests' quarters are on the other, reached via a sweeping concrete stair. Find a limewashed dining table for organic breakfasts, leather seating before the fire and bleached bedrooms flooded with light, two with space for a slatted table and chairs. There's an entry code so your independence is guaranteed – and grand old Bordeaux lies at your feet.

Rooms	3 doubles.
Price	€79–€95.
Meals	Restaurant 200m.
Closed	Rarely.

Leena Negre
La Villa Chaleemar,
67 rue Mandron,
33000 Bordeaux, Gironde
Tel   +33 (0)5 57 87 33 07
Mobile +33 (0)6 87 67 23 57
Email   contact@villa-chaleemar.com
Web   www.villa-chaleemar.com

Entry 475   Map 8

Aquitaine

Ecolodge des Chartrons

A many-splendoured delight: city-centre and eco-friendly, with lovely materials and the warmth of simplicity. Your relaxed and friendly hosts have put their earth-saving principles to work, stripping the wonderful wide floorboards, insulating with cork and wool, fitting solar water heating and sun pipes to hyper-modern shower rooms, organic linen and blankets to beds and providing all-organic breakfasts. At the bottom of this quiet road flows the Garonne where cafés, shops and galleries teem in converted warehouses (English wine merchants traded here 300 years ago) and a mirror fountain baffles the mind.

Two parking places only.

Rooms	5: 2 doubles, 2 twins/doubles, 1 triple.
Price	€117–€138. Triple €159–€175.
Meals	Restaurant 100m.
Closed	Rarely.

Véronique Daudin
Ecolodge des Chartrons,
23 rue Raze,
33000 Bordeaux, Gironde

Tel	+33 (0)5 56 81 49 13
Mobile	+33 (0)6 99 29 33 00
Email	veronique@ecolodgedeschartrons.com
Web	www.ecolodgedeschartrons.com

Entry 476   Map 8

Aquitaine

Adare House

An elegant 19th-century Bordelais townhouse, a breath away from the immaculate Jardin Public. Step in and wend your way up a stone staircase to stylish, cosy rooms with polished floorboards, rattan armchairs and bone china for fine biscuits and exotic teas. Breakfast in a graceful guest dayroom or on a pint-sized terrace plump with petunias: fruit salad, tasty compotes, scrumptious courgette and walnut cake. Explore Bordeaux on bike or stroll to the Place du Parlement where restaurants spill, minstrels stroll, and people stop and stare. A pocket Eden run by lovely people. (It would be wise to ring ahead to arrange parking.)

Rooms	2: 1 twin/double, 1 family room for 2-4.
Price	€90. Family room €115.
Meals	Restaurants nearby.
Closed	Rarely.

Mary Pratt
Adare House,
8 rue Émile Zola,
33000 Bordeaux, Gironde

Tel	+33 (0)5 57 34 43 05
Mobile	+33 (0)6 15 49 64 04
Email	mikenmarypratt@free.fr
Web	www.bordeaux-bnb.com

Entry 477   Map 8

Aquitaine

L'Esprit des Chartrons

A delicious vintage townhouse in chic Chartrons, metres from the Garonne quays where Bordeaux's bourgeoisie once traded: 21st-century design blends with wine-soaked history. Playful bedrooms are named after famous local writers: glamorous 'Montaigne' with bubble tub; red-brick, industrial-style 'Montesquieu'; light-filled 'Mauriac'. There are private terraces for tête-à-têtes, swish Italian bathrooms for pampering, a leafy sun terrace and a stylish stove-warmed salon for breakfast (crisp pastries, real hot chocolate). On a quiet lane, with covered parking, yet a stroll from restaurant-lined streets and World Heritage sites.

Rooms	3: 2 doubles, 1 twin/double.
Price	€110–€150.
Meals	Restaurants nearby.
Closed	Never.

Brigitte Gourlat
L'Esprit des Chartrons,
17 bis rue Borie,
33300 Bordeaux, Gironde

Tel	+33 (0)5 56 51 65 87
Mobile	+33 (0)6 82 20 20 67
Email	brigitte.gourlat@numericable.fr
Web	www.lespritdeschartrons.fr

Entry 478   Map 8

Aquitaine

Au Cœur de Bordeaux

New to B&B after a charity career, Sébastien and Aude charm all who discover their gem of a chambres d'hôtes, a picturesque stroll from Bordeaux's UNESCO-listed old town. Be dazzled by chandeliers sprinkling light on chintzy wallpapers, glitzy pink-yellow mock Regency chairs, plush velour and oriental rugs, eclectic antiques in cosy rooms with mini bars. If you need to spread out, choose the family suite or exquisite 'Issan'. Wake to generous breakfasts with country ham and special cheese. Four or more may choose table d'hôtes with produce fresh from Capucins market – a fine alternative to restaurants outside the door.

Rooms	5: 3 doubles, 1 suite for 2-4, 1 family suite.
Price	€95–€130. Suites €125–€155.
Meals	Occasional dinner with wine, €30 (min. group of 4). Restaurants nearby.
Closed	Rarely.

Sébastien Cazenave
Au Cœur de Bordeaux,
28 rue Boulan,
33000 Bordeaux, Gironde

Tel	+33 (0)6 89 65 84 21
Email	contact@aucoeurdebordeaux.fr
Web	www.aucoeurdebordeaux.fr

Entry 479   Map 8

Aquitaine

L'Arène Bordeaux

Within strolling distance of the most beautiful spots in Bordeaux is this elegant townhouse in a residential street. Handsome colours and discreet décor blend with herringbone parquet, cosy shared spaces are classically furnished, the Roman arena views are stunning. Lofty and evocatively named bedrooms ('Margaux', 'St Émilion') have sumptuous beds, accent chairs or three-piece suites, espresso machines, iPod docks and chic bathrooms in grey slate. Your friendly hosts offer wine in the garden on arrival, homemade jams at breakfast and all their best tips. Markets, antiques, boutiques, bistros and bars lie at your feet.

Minimum two nights at weekends.

Rooms	5 twins/doubles (2 rooms interconnect).
Price	€95–€200.
Meals	Restaurants 3-minute walk.
Closed	Rarely.

Jean Marie Terroine
L'Arène Bordeaux,
29 rue Émile Fourcand,
33000 Bordeaux, Gironde
Tel   +33 (0)5 56 52 05 85
Mobile +33 (0)6 16 06 48 31
Email   larenebordeaux@gmail.com
Web   www.larenebordeaux.com

Entry 480   Map 8

Aquitaine

Château Lestange

Come for the grape harvest! We are full of admiration for Anne-Marie, who keeps this proud old place and its vineyards afloat. Built in 1645, it was 'modernised' after the Revolution, but the faded Louis XV paintwork and imperfect tiles simply add to its charm. Beautiful wooden floors, panelled walls and old furniture create a well-lived-in feel, and the very private family suites, furnished with mirrors and portraits Anne-Marie is still unearthing from the attic, are capacious. Bathrooms are incongruously modern. Breakfast in a vast room beneath a grand mirror; stroll to dinner in the restaurant down the road.

Minimum two nights.

Rooms	2 family rooms.
Price	€130–€220.
Meals	Restaurant in village.
Closed	Rarely.

Anne-Marie Charmet
Château Lestange,
33360 Quinsac, Gironde
Mobile +33 (0)6 73 00 86 19
Email   charmet@chateau-lestange.com
Web   www.chateau-lestange.com

Entry 481   Map 8

Aquitaine

La Palombière

Head south, like the migratory *palombes* (doves) that give this luxurious perch its name. In the woods of Château Lestange, your dreamy treehouse comes with fresh flowers, sumptuous linen and touches of antiquity (doorknobs straight from the château). There's a wood-burner for cool nights, a romantic bed and a trapdoor to the mezzanine for children and sleeping bags – what a thrill. (They also get giant beanbags, French TV and the best view.) In summer, wake to breakfast on your terrace delivered by invisible hands; in winter, breakfast is in the château. Nearby is a river restaurant that serves the very best local produce.

Book through Sawday's Canopy & Stars online or by phone.

Rooms	Treehouse for 5: 1 double, mezzanine with 3 beanbags for children.
Price	£135-£210.
Meals	Restaurant 2km.
Closed	Open all year.

Sawday's Canopy & Stars
La Palombière,
Château Lestange,
33360 Quinsac, Gironde

Tel	+44 (0)1275 395447
Email	enquiries@canopyandstars.co.uk
Web	www.canopyandstars.co.uk/palombiere

Entry 482   Map 8

Aquitaine

Château de Courtebotte

Off a country lane a romantic 17th-century château stands in wooded grounds with glorious views to the glassy waters of the river Dordogne. Myriad charming features include open hearths and high ceilings, spotless bathrooms and lavish bedrooms; one room comes with a covered balcony, another has a four-poster and an antique commode… Breakfast on the terrace in fine weather; delicious dinners can be booked ahead. The inviting pool (unfenced) is shared with guests from the neighbouring gîte. Your hosts, friendly and delightful, know the best producers for vineyard tours – don't miss them. Stroll to shops and restaurants.

Rooms	5: 3 doubles, 1 suite, 1 twin/double.
Price	€115-€260. Suite €200-€250.
Meals	Breakfast €12. Dinner with wine, €35. Restaurant 1km.
Closed	20 December-31 March.

Isabelle Jehanno
Château de Courtebotte,
1 Courtebotte,
33420 St Jean de Blaignac, Gironde

Tel	+33 (0)5 57 84 61 61
Email	contact@chateaudecourtebotte.com
Web	www.chateaudecourtebotte.com

Entry 483   Map 9

Aquitaine

Château Claud–Bellevue

On the edge of a sleepy village, a 17th-century priory with a lych gate to the church. Mellow stone walls are lapped by groomed lawns and gravel paths; a central fountain plays; beyond are 17 hectares of vines. Your hosts, new to chambres d'hôtes and full of plans, give you an effusive welcome and delicious rooms: gilt-edged prints on rustic walls and goosedown as soft as a cloud. The treats continue at table for Madame, from Venezuela, is cordon-bleu trained; expect cheeses, fruits, charcuterie and homemade breads, granola and conserves. Discover the wines of St Émilion and visit the beautiful gardens of Sardy.

Minimum two nights.

Rooms	3: 2 doubles, 1 twin/double.
Price	€95–€125.
Meals	Light dinner with wine, €22. Afternoon tea included. Restaurants 3km.
Closed	Rarely.

Ana Bockmeulen
Château Claud-Bellevue,
31 le Bourg,
33350 Belves de Castillon
St Emilion, Gironde

Tel	+33 (0)5 57 49 48 23
Email	ana@chateauclaudbellevue.com
Web	www.chateauclaudbellevue.com

Entry 484   Map 9

Aquitaine

Clos de la Barbanne

One for wine buffs. This 1860s farmhouse — restored in slick, minimalist style — sits in a boutique vineyard, a cork's pop from oenophile haven. Monsieur Gerber shows guests round his cellars and talks grapes in the airy communal lounge. Madame serves breakfast when you fancy and dinners in private parlours on request — and there are Michelin stars in St Émilion. Just four doubles keep things quiet, all crisp and modern; exposed stone walls and books on wine add a sense of place. The garden, with an indoor pool, is a work in progress, but the view — rolling country, braided with vines — is the fine, finished article.

Rooms	4 doubles.
Price	€130–€180.
Meals	Dinner €40–€60. Wine €10–€30. Restaurants 5km.
Closed	Rarely.

Annie Gerber
Clos de la Barbanne,
2 les Grandes Pièces,
33570 Montagne, Gironde

Tel	+33 (0)5 57 24 08 79
Mobile	+33 (0)6 27 05 27 13
Email	a.gerber@clos-de-la-barbanne.net
Web	www.clos-de-la-barbanne.net

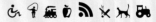

Entry 485   Map 9

Aquitaine

Domaine de Barrouil

As befits its calling, this old wine-grower's house stands in a sea of vines whose liquid fruits you will taste. Inside the colourful and immaculate house, greens, reds and creams set off gilt-framed mirrors, fine bathrooms, and bedcovers made by Madame. Your hosts believe in big thick towels too. Madame's superb French dinners, served in the beautifully tiled dining room, may bring echoes of more exotic lands. She is charming and chatty, a former English teacher; he, a former journalist, knows masses about wine; they'll bend over backwards to help. Ask about watercolour painting classes.

Rooms	3: 2 doubles, 1 family suite for 2-4.
Price	€55-€90.
Meals	Dinner with wine, €30.
Closed	Rarely.

Annie & Michel Ehrsam
Domaine de Barrouil,
Bossugan,
33350 Castillon La Bataille,
Gironde
Tel   +33 (0)5 57 40 59 12
Email   info@barrouil.com
Web   www.barrouil.com

Entry 486   Map 9

Aquitaine

Château de Carbonneau

Big château bedrooms bedecked in soft linens with splashes of splendid detail, a fine old bed in the 'Peony' room, huge bathrooms done with rich tiles – here is a self-assured family house where quality is fresh, history stalks and there's plenty of space for three young Ferrières and a dozen guests. Visit Wilfred's winery and taste the talent handed down by his forebears. Jacquie, a relaxed dynamic New Zealander, provides tasty alternatives to the ubiquitous duck cuisine and a relaxed approach to dining; a dab hand at interiors, she has also cultivated a luminescent, airy guest sitting room near the orangery.

Rooms	5: 2 doubles, 3 twins/doubles.
Price	€90-€135.
Meals	Dinner €27. Wine €8-€20.
Closed	December-February.

Jacquie Franc de Ferrière
Château de Carbonneau,
33890 Pessac sur Dordogne,
Gironde
Tel   +33 (0)5 57 47 46 46
Mobile   +33 (0)6 83 30 14 35
Email   carbonneau@orange.fr
Web   www.chateau-carbonneau.com

Entry 487   Map 9

Aquitaine

Chambre d'Hôtes de La Batellerie

Luxuriate in period splendour in a 1750s riverfront mansion: tapestries, open fires, panelled walls, oriental rugs, fine antiques, chandeliers and a white gravel fountain'd courtyard. Add 21st-century luxuries: king-size beds in big beamed bedrooms, power showers, claw foot baths, and – joy of joys – a leafy indoor pool. Monsieur's 27 years as a New York chef show at breakfast, a feast of mini croissants and charcuterie; Madame, from Thailand, has thankfully put dinners on the menu. Across the river from this former wine warehouse then town hall lies a bustling market town of slate roofs and church spires. Great value for the decadence.

Minimum two nights. Extra bed available.

Rooms	4: 3 doubles, 1 family suite for 2-4.
Price	€90-€125. Family room €110-€125.
Meals	Dinner from €15. Restaurants within walking distance.
Closed	Rarely.

Éric Lagrange
Chambre d'Hôtes de La Batellerie,
2 rue Onésime, Reclus, 33220 Port
Ste Foy & Ponchapt, Gironde

Tel	+33 (0)9 60 43 36 07
Mobile	+33 (0)6 16 64 35 65
Email	info@labatellerie.com
Web	www.labatellerie.com

Entry 488   Map 9

Aquitaine

La Gravouse

A genuine bienvenue feel floods this 18th-century farmhouse. Perhaps it's the afternoon tea on one of the glorious terraces, the sprawling parkland and 360-degree views of oaks and roses, the pool, peace and cherry trees whose fruits appear in breakfast conserves. Book the suite for gracious beams, scrubbed stone, a log-burner by a well-stocked bookcase; choose the 'Loft' for its lovely open-plan bathroom-cum-bedroom. Market towns dot the Dordogne's banks, vineyards and châteaux entice, and your warm hosts welcome you to the easygoing sophistication of southwest France… Fiona is a keen gardener, and teaches yoga. Idyllic.

Rooms	2: 1 double, 1 suite.
Price	€100. Suite €130.
Meals	Light dinner with a glass of wine, €17. Afternoon tea, €10. Restaurants 4km.
Closed	December/January.

Fiona Valpy
La Gravouse,
33220 St André & Appelles,
Gironde

Tel	+33 (0)5 57 41 28 18
Email	lagravouse@gmail.com
Web	www.lagravouse.com

Entry 489   Map 9

Aquitaine

La Girarde

In a gentle countryside of wooded valleys, near the pretty market town of Ste Foy la Grande, this smartly renovated farmhouse has its origins in the wine industry; no surprise: St Émilion lives and breathes wine. You will be impeccably looked after by English hosts whose caring attention is reflected in immaculate double-glazed windows, geo-thermally heated floors and delicious seasonal meals. Choose between two bedrooms on the ground floor and two under the roof; all have big comfy beds and super bathrooms. Outside: a park-like garden edged with grand weeping conifers, and a lovely sheltered saltwater pool.

Rooms	4: 2 doubles, 2 twins/doubles.
Price	€105–€120.
Meals	Dinner €27. Wine €15–€45. Children's meals available, €7.
Closed	Rarely.

	Trish Tyler
	La Girarde,
	33220 St Quentin de Caplong,
	Gironde
Tel	+33 (0)5 57 41 02 68
Mobile	+33 (0)6 76 07 97 43
Email	bienvenue@lagirarde.com
Web	www.lagirarde.com

Entry 490 Map 9

Aquitaine

L'Autre Vie

At a swanky chalet cocooned in vines and fruit trees, soak up peace and privacy from the vast deck or sparkling pool. Swish, minimalist-white bedrooms are named after chic cities where your young Australian hosts have lived. 'New York's glass wall streams panoramic vineyard views; 'Sydney' has French windows to the morning sun. Sleek bathrooms have huge showers and Elemis lotions, gardens melt into the famed vineyards of St Émilion and Pomerol, whose wines you can sip while snacking on charcuterie or sizzling meat on the barbecue. Justin and Vanessa provide it all so you can simply, as their motto goes, "relax and enjoy."

Rooms	3 doubles.
Price	€90–€140.
Meals	Lunch/dinner hampers from €15. Wine from €4. Restaurants 7km.
Closed	Rarely.

	Vanessa Parr
	L'Autre Vie,
	Champ de la Grave,
	33190 Camiran, Gironde
Tel	+33 (0)6 46 44 79 41
Email	contact@autre-vie.com
Web	www.autre-vie.com

Entry 491 Map 9

Aquitaine

La Cigogne

Croaking frogs, prune-drying paraphernalia and a wacky springwater pool – this is rural, unstuffy, great fun. In its leafy garden, La Cigogne (the name of the nearby stream) is a typical farmhouse, inherited by Véronique and modernised by this charmingly natural couple to give simple and wonderfully individual guest rooms, each with its own vine- and rose-shaded terrace. There's a cosy sitting room for winter evenings; the huge barn, its old mangers still intact, makes a comfortable retreat – with billiards – for damp summer days. Yves, a talented golfer, is happy to give you a free lesson and cycle paths pass the door.

Rooms	2 doubles.
Price	€65–€80.
Meals	Dinner with wine, €25.
Closed	November-March.

Yves & Véronique Denis
La Cigogne,
5 le Grand Janot,
33580 Ste Gemme, Gironde

Tel	+33 (0)5 56 71 19 70
Mobile	+33 (0)6 75 93 66 32
Email	lacigogne.33@orange.fr
Web	www.chambres-lacigogne.fr

Entry 492   Map 9

Aquitaine

Chambres d'Hôtes Janoutic

Charming Jean-Pierre finds the finest organic produce for his table. From croissants to charcuterie, 'poulets fermier' to orchard jams (apricot, blackcurrant, redcurrant, fig), it sounds delicious. This is a well-restored old farmhouse in the hamlet of Janoutic, two miles from the motorway, a great little stopover between Bordeaux and Toulouse. We like the two bright, carpeted bedrooms upstairs best, their rustic rafters hung with tobacco leaves in memory of old farming days; all have big walk-in showers. There's more: leather sofas and a great log fire; a wild garden with an aviary and a pool for newts and birds.

Rooms	3: 2 doubles, 1 family room for 3.
Price	€70. Family room €70–€96.
	Extra bed €26. Singles €60.
Meals	Dinner €28. Child under 12, €19.
Closed	Rarely.

Jean-Pierre Doebele
Chambres d'Hôtes Janoutic,
2 Le Tach,
33124 Aillas, Gironde

Mobile	+33 (0)6 81 97 02 92
Email	jpdoebel@club-internet.fr
Web	www.chambresdhotesjanoutic.com

Entry 493   Map 9

Aquitaine

Peyraguey Maison Rouge

Born and raised amid the Sauternes' vine-clothed hills and châteaux, the Belangers know Bordeaux wines intimately. Monsieur may offer a tasting on your second night in this authentic old wine-grower's house; for deeper insights, book an œnology course (min. 4). Tour châteaux, kayak down the Ciron, follow Bordeaux's wine trail past the 12 top Grands Crus Classés and St Émilion. Return to a dip in the pool, a game of ping-pong, grilled duck in the village auberge and a book by the fire in the elegant sitting room where wine scenes dot warm stone walls and champagne-coloured curtains glimmer. A genuine French vineyard stay.

Rooms	3: 2 doubles, 1 twin.
Price	€75–€105. Extra bed €25.
Meals	Restaurants 2km.
Closed	Never.

Annick & Jean-Claude Belanger
Peyraguey Maison Rouge,
33210 Bommes Sauternes,
Gironde

Tel	+33 (0)5 57 31 07 55
Email	belanger@club-internet.fr
Web	www.peyraguey-sauternes.com

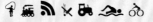

Entry 494   Map 9

Aquitaine

Le Domaine de l'Escuderia

Monsieur milks 100 Friesian cows, Madame breeds horses happily. Their maison de maître was a wreck in storm-torn woodland before they rolled up their sleeves. Now it has country-pretty rooms with iron four-posters and massage showers, a modern guest kitchen, sofas on the veranda, a bubbling hot tub… one extravagance in an eco-friendly restoration. Breakfast on farm milk and homemade flan, borrow bikes for a spin down to Lac Biscarosse, tempt the ponies with a carrot, jog around sprawling grounds and unkempt woods – or kite-surf off Atlantic beaches, half an hour away. Country fun for all the family.

Extra beds available.

Rooms	4: 3 doubles, 1 family room for 2-5.
Price	€64–€70. Family room €79–€89.
Meals	Guest kitchen. Restaurant 3km.
Closed	Never.

Emmanuelle Gallouet
Le Domaine de l'Escuderia,
Route de Blaise,
40160 Parentis en Born, Landes

Mobile	+33 (0)6 61 42 58 83
Email	contact@lescuderia.com
Web	www.lescuderia.com

Entry 495   Map 8

Aquitaine

Maison d'Agès

Madame deploys boundless energy to ply you with exquisite food from the potager, myriad teas, lovely antique-filled, sweet-coloured bedrooms (with her own framed embroidery): she adores entertaining, Monsieur is a delight. This noble manor with colonial verandas stands among fabulous old hardwoods and acres of pines. Nature rejoices, horses grace the paddock, hens range free, beautiful species of wild heather and gorse grow wild. A huge open fire, a panelled sitting room and an embracing of Slow Food (grown organically, harvested locally, eaten in season and tasting delicious) tell it perfectly.

Cash only. Minimum two nights July/Aug.

Rooms	1 double.
Price	€95. Extra bed €20.
Meals	Dinner with wine, €25.
Closed	Rarely.

	Élisabeth Haye
	Maison d'Agès,
	40110 Ousse Suzan, Landes
Mobile	+33 (0)6 86 87 56 08
Email	maisondages@gmail.com
Web	www.hotes-landes.fr

Entry 496   Map 13

Aquitaine

Domaine de Sengresse

In the undiscovered Landes, two hours from Spain, a remote and ravishing 17th-century domaine. A solid stone house, a cathedral-like barn, an elegant pool, red squirrels in many luscious acres and a 'petite maison' whose bread oven served the area's farms: such are the riches in store. A Godin stove and six-oven Aga feed today's guests in gourmet style (from a wonderful array of homemade produce), the rooms are bathed in light and everything sparkles, from the luxurious bedrooms with their calming colours to the library brimful of books. More country hotel than B&B, run by the loveliest people.

Sawday self-catering also.

Rooms	5: 3 doubles, 2 twins.
Price	€110–€135. Singles €95–€135.
Meals	Dinner with wine, from €30.
Closed	Rarely.

	Michèle & Rob McLusky
	& Sasha Ibbotson
	Domaine de Sengresse,
	Route de Gouts,
	40250 Souprosse, Landes
Tel	+33 (0)5 58 97 78 34
Email	sengresse@hotmail.fr
Web	www.sengresse.com

Entry 497   Map 13

Aquitaine

Château de Bezincam

An atmosphere of dream-like tranquillity wafts over this grand and appealing old French country house with its elegant doors and polished oak floors. Just outside the park gates is the beautiful river Adour, abundant in bird and wildlife — every ten years or so it comes and kisses the terrace steps. The gilt-mirrored bedroom overlooks the water and a great spread of meadows where animals graze. There is a vast choice for 'flexitime' breakfast on the terrace or in the rustic-chic dining room. Madame was a publisher in Paris for many years.

Rooms	1 double.
Price	€75.
Meals	Restaurants 2km.
Closed	Rarely.

Claude Dourlet
Château de Bezincam,
600 quai de Bezincam,
Saubusse les Bains,
40180 Dax, Landes

Tel   +33 (0)5 58 57 70 27
Email   dourlet.bezincam@orange.fr
Web   www.bezincam.fr

Entry 498   Map 13

Aquitaine

Maison Capcazal de Pachioü

Fall asleep by a crackling fire, wake to the clucking of the hens. You'll love this isolated house, with its original panelling (1610) and its contents accumulated by the family for 12 generations: portraits from the 17th century onwards, spectacular bedrooms with canopied antique beds, strong colours, luscious armoires, embroidered linen. One luminous bathroom has a marble-topped washstand, the living room is handsome with twin grandfather clocks and huge stone fireplace, and François has stepped into his mother's shoes seamlessly, nurturing goats, donkeys, pets and guests; brilliant dinners, too.

Rooms	4 doubles.
Price	€50-€90.
Meals	Dinner with wine, €22.
Closed	Rarely.

François Alberca-Dufourcet
Maison Capcazal de Pachioü,
606 route de Pachioü,
40350 Mimbaste,
Landes

Tel   +33 (0)5 58 55 30 54
Email   francois.alberca@wanadoo.fr
Web   www.capcazaldepachiou.com

Entry 499   Map 13

Aquitaine

Domaine de Peyron

The family estate — a pretty cluster of beautifully maintained buildings — has been feted in design magazines; you can tell that Maylis adored creating her interiors. Three themed bedrooms lie peacefully in the barn, alongside a glowing salon. One is wood-panelled, like a swish ski lodge; one, with ceiling fan and draped four-poster, has its heart in Africa; all are luxurious. Frolic in the pool with wonderful views, retire to the terrace and watch the sun set. Maylis is a bundle of energy, loves children, loves people and is a great cook: dinners are intimate or convivial, breakfasts are feasts.

Babysitting available.

Rooms	3 doubles.
Price	€85–€90.
Meals	Lunch €26. Dinner €38. Wine €16–€45. Picnic baskets on request. Guest kitchenette.
Closed	Rarely.

	Maylis & Louis Cottard
	Domaine de Peyron,
	240 chemin de Bordes,
	40700 St Cricq Chalosse, Landes
Tel	+33 (0)5 58 79 85 64
Mobile	+33 (0)6 32 31 90 47
Email	lcottard@wanadoo.fr
Web	www.domainedepeyron.com

Entry 500 Map 13

Aquitaine

Domaine de la Carrère

Wow! Country-house grandeur: with its oak panelling, parquet floors and ancient beams this house feels solid, strong and in keeping with its illustrious past and royal connections. Built during the reign of Louis XIV, it was the village Mairie or town hall before the current owners moved in. Bedrooms are classically elegant with high ceilings, carved bedheads, flamboyant drapes; bathrooms are high luxe. Quiet corners display plump sofas while the garden is lush with terraces, lawns and a dreamy pool. Historic Pau is 20 minutes away and glorious Biarritz 40; return to Fritz's fabulous dinner amid candles and cut glass.

Rooms	5: 4 doubles, 1 twin.
Price	€95–€125.
Meals	Dinner with wine, €35.
Closed	Rarely.

	Fritz Kisby & Mike Ridout
	Domaine de la Carrère,
	54 rue la Carrère, 64370 Arthez de Béarn,
	Pyrénées-Atlantiques
Tel	+33 (0)5 24 37 61 24
Mobile	+33 (0)6 32 96 34 62
Email	info@domaine-de-la-carrere.fr
Web	www.domaine-de-la-carrere.fr

Entry 501 Map 13

Aquitaine

La Closerie du Guilhat

Through the iron gates, up the tree-lined drive to an astonishing kingdom of plants of all shapes and sizes: a hidden garden of exotica. Weave your way through rhododendrons and magnolias, bananas and bamboos to secret benches for quiet reading and the Pyrenees as a backdrop – sheer delight for all ages. To the sturdy Béarn house with solid old furniture and traditional décor Marie-Christine has added her own decorative touches; bedrooms are spotless. Table tennis is shared with gîte guests, dinners are delicious. The other-worldliness is restorative yet the lively spa town of Salies is a bike-ride away.

Rooms	3: 1 double, 1 twin, 1 suite for 3 adults or 2 adults & 2 children.
Price	€58–€64. Suite €75–€85.
Meals	Dinner €22. Wine from €16
Closed	Rarely.

Marie–Christine Potiron
La Closerie du Guilhat,
64270 Salies de Béarn,
Pyrénées-Atlantiques
Tel   +33 (0)5 59 38 08 80
Email   guilhat@club-internet.fr
Web   www.closerieduguilhat.com

Entry 502   Map 13

Aquitaine

Maison Marchand

A lovely face among all the lovely faces of this listed village, the 16th-century Basque farmhouse, resuscitated by its delightful French/Irish owners, is run with well-organised informality. Dinners round the great table are lively; local dishes are excellent. Light, well-decorated bedrooms, each with their own terrace, have beams, exposed wafer bricks, thoughtful extras. Summer breakfast is on the covered terrace in the beautiful walled garden with peaceful reading spots and three friendly cats. Your hosts delight in sharing their culture of pelote basque, rugby, real tennis, horses… and their passion for all things Basque.

Rooms	3: 2 doubles, 1 family room (1 double & 2 extra beds).
Price	€70–€90. Family room €70–€110. Extra bed €20.
Meals	Dinner with wine, €25.
Closed	Mid-November to mid-March.

Valerie & Gilbert Foix
Maison Marchand, Rue Notre Dame,
64240 La Bastide Clairence,
Pyrénées-Atlantiques
Tel   +33 (0)5 59 29 18 27
Mobile +33 (0)6 82 78 50 95
Email   maison.marchand@wanadoo.fr
Web   pagesperso-orange.fr/maison.marchand

Entry 503   Map 13

Aquitaine

Les Volets Bleus

High in these ancient hills stands a beautiful new farmhouse built with old Basque materials. Chic, clever Marie has made a perfect creation. The décor has been meticulously studied, a magical effect achieved. Through the double-arch door, a flagged entrance hall, then a terrace with charming rattan chairs. Up stone staircases are bedrooms in restful colours with wood or tiled floors, gilt mirrors, embroidered sheets, ancestral paintings; exquisite bathrooms have iron towel rails and aromatic oils. Marie is an accomplished gardener so retreat to her garden for a read or a swim – or lounge in the salon on deep sofas. Heaven.

Rooms	4: 2 doubles, 1 twin, 1 suite.
Price	€110–€170. Suite €140–€186.
Meals	Restaurants 1.5km.
Closed	December-February.

Marie de Lapasse
Les Volets Bleus,
Chemin Etchegaraya,
64200 Arcangues,
Pyrénées-Atlantiques
Mobile +33 (0)6 07 69 03 85
Email maisonlesvoletsbleus@wanadoo.fr
Web www.lesvoletsbleus.fr

Entry 504 Map 13

Aquitaine

Bidachuna

The electronic gate clicks behind you and 29 hectares of forested peacefulness are yours – with wildlife. Open wide your beautiful curtains next morning and you may see deer feeding; lift your eyes to feast on long vistas to the Pyrenean foothills; trot downstairs to the earthly feast that is Basque breakfast; fall asleep to the hoot of the owl. Shyly attentive, Isabelle manages all this impeccably and keeps a refined house where everything gleams; floors are chestnut, bathrooms are marble, family antiques are perfect. Pop off to lovely St Jean de Luz for lunch or dinner, return to this manicured haven and blissful cossetting.

Rooms	3: 2 doubles, 1 twin.
Price	€120. Singles €110.
Meals	Restaurant 6km.
Closed	Mid-November to mid-March.

Isabelle Ormazabal
Bidachuna,
Route D3, Lieu dit Otsanz,
64310 St Pée sur Nivelle,
Pyrénées-Atlantiques
Tel +33 (0)5 59 54 56 22
Email isabelle@bidachuna.com
Web www.bidachuna.com

Entry 505 Map 13

Aquitaine

Villa Le Goëland

It is lush, lavish, inviting. Dominating the ocean, yards from the beaches of glamorous Biarritz, the only privately owned villa of its kind to have resisted commercial redevelopment has opened its arms to guests. Turrets were added in 1903; Paul's family took possession in 1934; now he and his wife, young, charming, professional, are its inspired guardians and restorers. Be ravished by oak floors, magnificent stairs, tall windows and balconies that go on for ever. Two bedrooms have terraces, beds are king-size, bathrooms are vintage or modern, breakfasts flourish sunshine and pastries. And the surfing is amazing.

Rooms	4: 3 doubles, 1 suite for 3.
Price	€150–€270.
Meals	Breakfast €10 (free on presentation of a Sawday guide). Restaurant 20m.
Closed	November–February.

	Paul & Élisabeth Daraignez
	Villa Le Goëland, 12 plateau de l'Atalaye, 64200 Biarritz, Pyrénées-Atlantiques
Tel	+33 (0)5 59 24 25 76
Mobile	+33 (0)6 87 66 22 19
Email	info@villagoeland.com
Web	www.villagoeland.com

Entry 506   Map 13

Aquitaine

La Bergerie d'Anne-Marie

Basque houses have a charm all of their own. This one is steeped in green hills and its views are panoramic, with thrilling sightings of the sea. Bruno, once a magazine photographer in Paris, knows and loves his neck of the woods and looks after guests with aplomb; his table d'hôtes is a delight. Bedrooms have the same fabulous views, the 'Squirrel Room', with mirrors and Louis XVI pieces, the most pleasing to the eye. The suite is ideal for a family, with interlinking rooms and a gorgeous old bath down four stairs. Cruise the coastal road, hop into Spain, return to an aperitif on the intimate terrace.

Minimum two nights.

Rooms	2: 1 double en suite; 1 suite for 3 with shared bathroom.
Price	€110–€140. Suite €185. Pets €20.
Meals	Dinner with wine, €30. Restaurant 1km.
Closed	November.

	Bruno Krassinine
	La Bergerie d'Anne-Marie, Chemin de Goyetchea 1285, La Croix des Bouquets, 64122 Urrugne, Pyrénées-Atlantiques
Tel	+33 (0)5 59 20 79 44
Email	bkrassinine@free.fr
Web	www.labergeriedannemarie.venez.fr

Entry 507   Map 13

Aquitaine

Domaine de Silencenia

The ideal place for discovering the Basque country. The house cornerstone, the magnificent magnolia, the towering pines were all planted on one day in 1881. A heated pool and a lake (with fountain, boat, trout and koi carp) are set in spacious parkland, and a billiard room, sauna and small gym (for a small charge) are on tap. This sensitive restoration includes a honeymoon room, a pretty pine four-poster, a desk made from wine cases and respect for the original chestnut panelling. Philippe, aided by his young wife Ruth, is proud of his 'table gourmande'. He knows about wine, too: his cellar is brilliant. Be charmed.

Rooms	5: 3 doubles, 2 triples.
Price	€90.
Meals	Dinner with wine, €30.
Closed	Rarely.

Philippe Mallor
Domaine de Silencenia,
64250 Louhossoa,
Pyrénées-Atlantiques
Tel   +33 (0)5 59 93 35 60
Mobile   +33 (0)6 72 63 81 66
Email   domaine.de.silencenia@orange.fr
Web   www.domaine-silencenia.com

Entry 508   Map 13

Aquitaine

Domaine Lespoune

Renovated with panache in unsung Pays Basque, this 18th-century manor calms and charms. Easy-going and interesting, Nicole and Yves poured their hearts into its restoration: panelling, tiled and wooden floors, original doors, and added modern touches: colourwashed walls, contemporary art, walk-in showers. The ground-floor bedroom has a striking black-and-white tiled floor and a private terrace; the rooms upstairs are palely soft (one with veranda). Breakfast under the spreading magnolia, spend the day fishing, return to Nicole's beautiful food – and a Navarrenx cigar in the garden.

Use of sauna & spa included with 2-night stay.

Rooms	5: 3 doubles, 1 twin, 1 suite for 2–4 (1 double, 1 twin).
Price	€75–€95. Suite €95–€105. €10 supplement for one night July/August.
Meals	Dinner with wine, €25–€38.
Closed	Mid-November to mid-March.

Yves & Nicole Everaert
Domaine Lespoune,
20 route de Camblong,
64190 Castetnau Camblong,
Pyrénées-Atlantiques
Tel   +33 (0)5 59 66 24 14
Email   contact@lespoune.fr
Web   www.lespoune.fr

Entry 509   Map 13

Aquitaine

Maison L'Aubèle

The Desbonnets transformed their grand 18th-century village house after finding it and this sleepy village in the Pyrenean foothills: both house and owners are quiet, elegant, sophisticated and full of interest. He collects precious old books, she binds them, and the furniture is a feast for the eyes. As you breakfast off fine china ask what you need to know about the region, and do delve into their tempting library. The light, airy bedrooms have more interesting furniture on lovely wooden floors. 'La Rose' is very chic, 'La Verte' is a dream, large and luminous with views of the mountains and a 'waltz-in' bathroom.

Rooms	2 doubles.
Price	€70.
Meals	Restaurants 4km.
Closed	Rarely.

Marie-France Desbonnet
Maison L'Aubèle, 4 rue de la Hauti,
64190 Lay Lamidou,
Pyrénées-Atlantiques
Tel   +33 (0)5 59 66 00 44
Mobile   +33 (0)6 86 22 02 76
Email   desbonnet.bmf@infonie.fr
Web   www.laubele.fr

Entry 510   Map 13

Aquitaine

La Bastide Estratte

In six remote hectares of woodland with Pyrenean peaks beyond, a solid slate-roofed farmhouse. Enter the wide stone arch into a beautiful balcony-fringed, flagstoned courtyard: sip a cappuccino among ornamental acers, japonicas, box hedges as Virginia creeper winds her way over the walls. Inside, a patina of light greys, olives and ecru provides a studied canvas for polished floors, white sofas, porcelain in bookcases, fine fittings and herbal prints. Lovely, lively Chantale will help with Jurançon wine routes, excellent restaurants and fantastic walks. If it's all too cool, hop in the jacuzzi.

Minimum two nights.

Rooms	3 doubles.
Price	€85. Singles €75. Extra bed €30.
Meals	Restaurants 10km.
Closed	Rarely.

Chantale Albert
La Bastide Estratte, Chemin de Bas Afittes,
64360 Lucq de Béarn,
Pyrénées-Atlantiques
Tel   +33 (0)5 59 34 32 45
Mobile   +33 (0)6 22 64 16 55
Email   chantale.albert@nordnet.fr
Web   www.labastide-estratte.com

Entry 511   Map 13

Aquitaine

Château de Lamothe

An idyll of indulgence whose grandiose interior makes you feel like royalty but whose playful touches make you feel at home. Breakfast in a dining room of gilt mouldings and candelabras, then slink off to the billiard room, the home cinema, the plush aubergine salon. A lavish Designers Guild décor complements flat-screens and walk-in showers, while Pyrenean backdrops frame expansive gardens – the pool is fabulously discreet. Your charming Dutch hosts prepare evening meals of local specialities or dishes from their global travels; they'll tell you the places to go, the wine to drink. A beguiling place that you'll long to return to.

Aquitaine

Maison Rancèsamy

Painters love this haven and respond to Isabelle's own gentle talent; she is the loveliest hostess. From terrace and pool you can see for ever into the Pyrenees – sunlit snowy in winter, all the greens in summer. Beside the 1700s farmhouse, the barn conversion shelters artistic, uncluttered, stone-walled bedrooms and incredible views. The superb dining room – Isabelle's trompe-l'œil floor, huge carved table – reflects the origins (Polish, French, South African) of this happy, relaxed couple. On balmy summer evenings, the food (book ahead) is deliciously garden-aromatic: Simon is a powerful, eco-aware gardener. Wonderful.

Minimum two nights July / Aug.

Rooms	5: 4 doubles, 1 family room for 4–6.		Rooms	5: 2 doubles, 1 twin, 2 family rooms.
Price	€225–€275. Family room €275–€335.		Price	€75–€90. Family room €108–€125.
Meals	Dinner €47.50. Wine €20–€125. Restaurant 5km.		Meals	Dinner with wine, €32.
Closed	Rarely.		Closed	Rarely.

	Laurent Nederlof			Simon & Isabelle Browne
	Château de Lamothe,			Maison Rancèsamy,
	64400 Moumour,			Quartier Rey, 64290 Lasseube,
	Pyrénées-Atlantiques			Pyrénées-Atlantiques
Mobile	+33 (0)6 88 28 38 61		Tel	+33 (0)5 59 04 26 37
Email	laurentnederlof@gmail.com		Email	missbrowne@wanadoo.fr
Web	www.chateau-de-lamothe.eu		Web	www.missbrowne.com

Entry 512   Map 13

Entry 513   Map 13

Aquitaine

Clos Mirabel

Fifteen minutes from city lights, yet surrounded by vineyards. French-Canadian André is a retired diplomat, Ann worked in travel, Emily goes to the village school. They fell in love with Clos Mirabel five years ago, now they delightedly welcome guests. The 18th-century manor is flanked by a winery and gatehouse; the interiors are light, airy and restful, their gracious proportions enhanced by Ann's elegant eye. A spiral staircase links the Gustavian apartment's three levels, there's a pool terrace with breathtaking Pyrenean views and breakfast honey comes from André's bees. Outstanding.

Aquitaine

Ancienne Laiterie

Insects buzz, birds twitter and owls hoot from the barn: the setting is lushly rural. Clare delights in her garden too, all rambling roses and peonies, a stream at the end of the field, a fenced pool beyond the potager. Inside the old Béarn farmhouse a stylish shabby chic rules (more chic than shabby!) with French country furniture and elegant pastels. The bedroom is sweetly simple, the oval bathtub is a delight. Clare keeps hens, gives you homemade bread at breakfast and honey from the beekeeper; she also makes fabulous ice cream. Don't miss market day in Oloron Ste Marie – a town of history, charm and gushing rivers.

Minimum two nights.

Rooms	3: 2 doubles, 1 apartment for 4 (with kitchen).
Price	€95–€159. Apartment €139–€140. Extra bed €35.
Meals	Restaurants 3km.
Closed	Rarely.

Rooms	Gîte: 1 double, 1 twin/double (for 2 adults or 3 children).
Price	€130. Singles €90.
Meals	Dinner with wine, €20–€45. Afternoon tea €12. Restaurants, 3km.
Closed	Rarely.

Ann Kenny & André Péloquin
Clos Mirabel, 276 av des Frères Barthélémy, Jurançon, 64110 Pau, Pyrénées-Atlantiques
Tel +33 (0)5 59 06 32 83
Mobile +33 (0)6 79 59 04 91
Email info@closmirabel.com
Web www.closmirabel.com

Clare Stephens
Ancienne Laiterie, Chemin Cabarrouy, Quartier Laring, 64360 Monein, Pyrénées-Atlantiques
Tel +33 (0)5 59 80 07 49
Mobile +33 (0)6 10 34 34 91
Email anciennelaiterie@gmail.com
Web www.laiteriefrance.com

Entry 514   Map 13

Entry 515   Map 13

Aquitaine

Castel de Fonpré

Breakfast under the plane trees, venture to Lourdes or out to lunch, then glide in the pool or gaze at distant mountains. There's a rolling-hill approach to this fine maison de maître, set among oaks and chestnuts, still with its bell to ring home the workers. Pamela and David, and two gentle dogs, welcome you to high moulded ceilings and traditional comforts, calming colours and pristine bathrooms. This is for nature lovers, from the wonderful artwork to the wooden floors to the sun-drenched rooms; top rooms have an escapist, treehouse feel. You'll remember Fonpré's serenity and rustling trees long after you leave.

Rooms	3: 1 double; 1 twin/double, 1 twin sharing bathroom.
Price	€60–€80.
Meals	Restaurants 7km.
Closed	Rarely.

Pamela Kinslow
Castel de Fonpré,
64350 Arricau Bordes,
Pyrénées-Atlantiques

Tel	+33 (0)5 59 68 25 50
Email	info@frenchcountryholiday.net
Web	www.frenchcountryholiday.net

Entry 516   Map 14

Aquitaine

Manoir Beaujoly

The medieval manor surveys fertile land rich in tales of knights and kings: a stunning hilltop setting. Horses graze, quails potter and guests gather by the pool in a ruined granary to barbecue trout from the river or duck from the market. The cool, thick-walled building wears its no-frills minimalism well: rough stone, hefty beams, a roll top bath, canvas wardrobes, ancient bullet holes... and 'open' bathrooms behind screens. There's a great fire in the monastic sitting room where delightful Dutch-German hosts serve breakfasts of cheese and charcuterie. Rampage, like those medieval Templars, across glorious 'French Tuscany'.

Minimum three nights.

Rooms	5 twins/doubles.
Price	€100–€120.
Meals	Restaurants 4km.
Closed	December–March.

Karin Ulrike Waltermann
Manoir Beaujoly,
47340 Hautefage la Tour,
Lot-et-Garonne

Tel	+33 (0)5 53 01 52 51
Mobile	+31 (0)6 50 20 39 77
Email	waltermann@kriskras.nl
Web	www.beaujoly.com

Entry 517   Map 14

Aquitaine

Domaine de Rambeau

Handsome and enticing, this 18th-century manor house is perched on a hillside with views of silken wheat fields and distant valleys. But feast your eyes on the star of the show: an all-bells-and-whistles pool. Inside: an air of decadent splendour – even a knight in armour – where all is tasteful, relaxed and spacious in sitting, dining and bedrooms – just watch out for some low beams (and ask for an extra single if you need one). There's lovely artisan bread and homemade jams for breakfast, scrumptious dinners from generous owners and acres of parkland to mosey around – home to a huge and friendly black pig.

Extra beds available. New Wellness Centre.

Rooms	3 doubles.
Price	€120. Extra bed €20.
Meals	Breakfast €10. Dinner, 3 courses with wine, €25. Restaurant 4km.
Closed	Rarely.

Kim Reeves
Domaine de Rambeau,
47260 Castelmoron sur Lot,
Lot-et-Garonne
Tel +33 (0)5 53 79 38 43
Mobile +33 (0)6 13 95 39 52
Email reeves.kim@hotmail.fr
Web www.domainederambeau.com

Entry 518   Map 14

Aquitaine

Manoir de Levignac

Walk through the hall into the handsome country kitchen and thence into the peaceful grounds: with nature reserve, views and resident donkey. Or stay and dine, beautifully, in a room with a big fireplace, pottery pieces and carved cupboard doors. In the sitting room, terracotta tiles, kilim rugs and grand piano give a comfortably artistic air. Adriana is Swiss-Italian, Jocelyn is South African; they are thoughtful and kind and do everything well. You'll have a lush bedroom with rural views, a sitting room and an immaculate bathroom. Outside, a small pine wood, a daisy-sprinkled lawn and a pool surrounded by palms.

Rooms	2 suites for 4.
Price	€70–€80.
Meals	Dinner with wine, €25.
Closed	Rarely.

Jocelyn & Adriana Cloete
Manoir de Levignac,
St Pierre sur Dropt,
47120 Duras,
Lot-et-Garonne
Tel +33 (0)5 53 83 68 11
Email cloete@wanadoo.fr
Web manoir.de.levignac.free.fr

Entry 519   Map 9

Aquitaine

Château Lavanau

The Uharts aren't just playing at being farmers, as the wine crates beside their pink-washed farmhouse prove. After spending 15 years in Paris, they now produce 100,000 bottles of Côtes de Duras a year; Paul – half French – is happy to guide you round the vineyard. There's an art studio, too: Juliana trained at St Martin's and runs courses. The bedrooms are simple and very charming, with old country furniture and splashes of colour. A half wall separates each room from its narrow stylish bathroom. There's also a small kitchen where you can prepare snacks. And a garden just leaving its infancy.

Rooms	5: 3 doubles, 2 twins.
Price	€70–€80.
Meals	Restaurant 1km.
Closed	Rarely.

Juliana & Paul Uhart
Château Lavanau,
Les Faux, 47120 Loubès Bernac,
Lot-et-Garonne
Tel +33 (0)5 53 94 86 45
Mobile +33 (0)6 74 97 57 04
Email juliana.uhart@googlemail.com
Web www.chateaulavanau.com

Entry 520   Map 9

Aquitaine

Manoir de Roquegautier

In a beautiful park with rolling views, this gracious house is wondrously French. Drapes, swags and interlinings all by Brigitte, and memorable rooms in the tower with their own entrance and spiral stone stair. There are claw-footed baths and huge old basins and taps, and each top-floor suite has one round tower room. Bliss for families: swings, games room and discreet pool, gazebos around the garden and mature trees to shade your picnic lunches. Delicious food fresh from the family farm are shared with your hosts, but note: the French language may dominate at dinner.

Rooms	4: 2 doubles, 2 family suites: 1 for 3, 1 for 4.
Price	€84–€92. Family room €120–€133.
Meals	Dinner €26. Child €12. Wine €6/0.5L
Closed	November-Easter.

Brigitte & Christian Vrech
Manoir de Roquegautier,
Beaugas,
47290 Cancon,
Lot-et-Garonne
Tel +33 (0)5 53 01 60 75
Email roquegautier@free.fr
Web www.roquegautier.fr

Entry 521   Map 9

Aquitaine

Domaine du Moulin de Labique

Soay sheep on the drive, ducks on the pond, goats in the greenhouse and food *à la grand-mère*. Shutters are painted with *bleu de pastel* from the Gers and the 13th-century interiors have lost none of their charm. In house and outbuildings there are chunky beams, seagrass on ancient tiles, vintage iron bedsteads, antique mirrors, and wallpapers flower-sprigged in raspberry, jade and green. Outside are old French roses and young alleys of trees, a bamboo-fringed stream, a restaurant in the stables, an exquisite pool. Wonderful hosts, the Bruxellois owners loved this place for years; now they are its best ambassadors.

Rooms	6: 3 doubles, 2 twins, 1 suite for 4.
Price	€110–€135. Suite €190.
Meals	Dinner €31. Wine €16–€30.
Closed	Rarely.

Patrick & Christine Hendricx
Domaine du Moulin de Labique,
Saint Vivien,
47210 Villeréal,
Lot-et-Garonne

Tel +33 (0)5 53 01 63 90
Email moulin-de-labique@wanadoo.fr
Web www.moulin-de-labique.net

Entry 522 Map 9

Aquitaine

Le Prieuré du Château de Biron

Beneath the imposing fortress, the church gazes over the little village, hiding this very old priory. Cross the tiny cobbled courtyard to an ornate knocker on a nail-studded door. You're greeted in a stone floored hall and ushered up an elegant stair. Fireplaces take pride of place in huge first-floor rooms, along with exposed stone walls, the glow of antiques, fine linens and shades of powder blue and pale gold: Élisabeth has exquisite taste. Timbers fly across the palely gracious rooms under the roof; heavenly views reach across the fields. Harmonious, rich, thoroughly welcoming and not to be missed.

Rooms	5 + 1: 3 suites, 2 family rooms, 1 apartment for 3.
Price	€125–€165. Apartment €165–€185.
Meals	Dinner €30. Restaurant 50m.
Closed	Mid-November to February.

Élisabeth Vedier
Le Prieuré du Château de Biron,
Le Bourg,
24540 Biron, Dordogne

Tel +33 (0)5 53 61 93 03
Mobile +33 (0)6 84 31 38 38
Email leprieurebiron@gmail.com
Web www.leprieurebiron.com

Entry 523 Map 9

Aquitaine

Château Gauthié

Outside a perfect bastide village, a château B&B run with warmth and energy. Stéphane cooks brilliantly and loves wine; Florence is enormous fun, a breath of fresh air. Restful, light-filled, traditional bedrooms have white bathrooms. An infinity pool overlooks the lake below, above it perches the treehouse, its balcony gazing over meadows and cows, its mother tree thrusting two branches through the floor. Solar-lit paths lead you down through the trees at night, a breakfast basket is winched up in the morning. Now there's a second treehouse – with two storeys! Play badminton, fish in the lake, spin off on a bike, bask in the hot tub.

Minimum two nights. Self-catering treehouse: 1 week minimum in summer.

Rooms	6: 4 doubles, 1 twin, 1 treehouse for 2. Self-catering treehouse for 2-5 (1 double, 3 singles).
Price	€90–€115. Treehouse €120–€165. Self-catering treehouse €1,000–€1,500 per week.
Meals	Dinner, 4 courses with wine €40. Wine list €15–€50.
Closed	Mid-November to March.

	Florence & Stéphane Desmette
	Château Gauthié,
	24560 Issigeac Monmarvès,
	Dordogne
Tel	+33 (0)5 53 27 30 33
Email	chateau.gauthie@laposte.net
Web	www.chateaugauthie.com

Entry 524 Map 9

Aquitaine

Châteaux dans les Arbres

Three mystical, magical castles in the trees – you couldn't be further from camping! Rémi, the owner, is a master craftsman, his 'châteaux' have been a year in the making and, with the Dordogne unfurling around you and the rustle of the wind in the trees, you're in for the most amazing stay. Bathrooms are chic, breakfasts are winched up in baskets, there's a great chef to hand should you want one, and a stunning infinity pool below. Children have bunks, everyone has a vast terrace – with hot tub – and 'Hautefort' has its own adorable kitchen. Surely the finest treehouses in France.

Book through Sawday's Canopy & Stars online or by phone.

Rooms	3 treehouses: 1 for 2, 1 for 4. Treehouse for 6: 2 doubles, 2 bunks.
Price	£186–£230.
Meals	Restaurant 2km.
Closed	Rarely.

	Sawday's Canopy & Stars
	Châteaux dans les Arbres,
	Domaine de Puybéton,
	24440 Nojals & Clotte, Dordogne
Tel	+44 (0)1275 395447
Email	enquiries@canopyandstars.co.uk
Web	www.canopyandstars.co.uk/danslesarbres

Entry 525 Map 9

Aquitaine

Le Clos d'Argenson

Laurence and Pascal's marvellous renovation of this handsome fin-de-siècle townhouse, in strolling distance of Bergerac's Place de la Republique, has kept many original features: marble fireplaces and polished wooden floors, a library with an antique pool table, a ceiling-rose chandelier in the grand salon. Choose a garden-facing suite for quiet and leafy views of courtyard and divine pool; in the morning, descend a fantastic curving staircase to the dining room or balcony for a breakfast of local treats. At least once, sit down to dinner with this delightful French family and enjoy the best of regional cuisine.

Aquitaine

Le Colombier de Cyrano & Roxane

Surprises abound in this quaint, creaky, 16th-century townhouse. Flamboyantly colourful rooms with rooftop views get their own front doors and bathrooms: expect slouchy comfort with a peppering of decadence. Snaffle the room with the covered balcony terrace – and hammock – and you won't miss a garden. Fill up on brioche and homemade jams in a relaxed living area before exploring Bergerac; back for a snifter and a story with your entertaining hostess before ambling out for a *repas soigné*. Full of higgledy-piggledy theatrical charm – and worth a bit of street noise for the wonderful, central position.

Rooms	4 suites: 3 for 2, 1 for 4.
Price	€120-€130. Singles €100-€105.
Meals	Occasional dinner €27. Restaurants within walking distance.
Closed	November-April.

Rooms	2 doubles.
Price	€73-€83. Extra bed €25-€45.
Meals	Restaurants within walking distance.
Closed	Rarely.

Pascal & Laurence Amelot
Le Clos d'Argenson,
99 rue Neuve d'Argenson,
24100 Bergerac, Dordogne
Mobile +33 (0)6 12 90 59 58
Email leclosdargenson@gmail.com
Web www.leclosdargenson.com

Betty Reed
Le Colombier de Cyrano & Roxane,
17 place de la Myrpe,
24100 Bergerac, Dordogne
Tel +33 (0)5 53 57 96 70
Mobile +33 (0)6 81 65 97 87
Email bluemoon2@club-internet.fr
Web www.lecolombierdecyrano.fr

Entry 526 Map 9

Entry 527 Map 9

Aquitaine

Le Relais de la Myrpe

A joy to stay on the oldest square in Bergerac, where heavily beamed houses stand cheek by jowl and locals toss boules under the plane trees as the tourists snap away. Up the wonky staircase is your small, private, studio-style living space, full of quaint comfort and Xavière's colourful brocante. She speaks excellent English, lives close by and runs a bric-a-brac shop on the ground floor. You get an unexpectedly capacious bedroom at the top overlooking the leafy square; beams abound, scatter rugs adorn the polished boards and there's a big curtained-off shower. Foie gras, truffles and wine are yours to discover.

Rooms	2: 1 double, 1 single (with daybed) sharing bathroom & 2 wcs.
Price	€55–€75. €300–€400 per week.
Meals	Restaurant 50m.
Closed	Never.

Xavière Simand-Lecouve
Le Relais de la Myrpe,
18 place de la Myrpe,
24100 Bergerac, Dordogne
Mobile +33 (0)6 29 18 03 84
Email xavierelamyrpe@hotmail.fr
Web www.relaisdelamyrpe.com

Entry 528 Map 9

Aquitaine

Le Logis Plantagenet

A medieval house, part of an earlier château, stands in a tree-lined square in old Bergerac, a minute's walk from the lovely limpid river – a peaceful, town-centre address. Your well-travelled and welcoming hosts, who live opposite, give you light-filled bedrooms painted in soft colours with pretty rugs on polished floors, excellent beds, full-length baths and fabulous linen. Breakfast is served in the courtyard garden in summer and in the large kitchen in winter. After a day visiting châteaux and gardens and tasting fine wines, return to two delightful country-house sitting rooms.

Rooms	4: 1 double, 1 studio, 2 twins.
Price	€95.
Meals	Dinner with wine, €28. Restaurants nearby.
Closed	Rarely.

Bruce & Rosetta Cantlie
Le Logis Plantagenet,
5 rue du Grand Moulin,
24100 Bergerac, Dordogne
Tel +33 (0)5 53 57 15 99
Email bruce.cantlie@wanadoo.fr
Web www.lelogisplantagenet.com

Entry 529 Map 9

Aquitaine

Château des Baudry

Steeped in 500 years of history, the four solid wings of this distinguished château enclose a grand central courtyard where water shimmers with tiny fish. In a dining room wrapped in blue wallpaper and ribbon you'll discover that Hélène's cooking *à la grand-mère* is more than delicious, it's a reason to be here. Breakfast is among terracotta and citrus trees; bedrooms are large, traditional, framed by lofty beams, aglow with antiques and soft quilting. Views of Italiante gardens give way to more untouched countryside; pillars by the pool guide the eye to Dordogne vistas. And they are a wonderful, eco-committed couple.

Rooms	5: 1 double, 4 twins/doubles.
Price	€128–€150.
Meals	Breakfast €13. Dinner €35. Wine €12–€35.
Closed	Rarely.

Hélène Boulet & François Passebon
Château des Baudry,
24240 Monestier, Dordogne
Tel   +33 (0)5 53 23 46 42
Email   chateaudesbaudry@orange.fr
Web   www.chateaudesbaudry.com

Entry 530   Map 9

Aquitaine

La Ferme de la Rivière

The large farmhouse auberge sits alone and surrounded by its fields in a hamlet of a dozen houses. The Archer family honour tradition; he is a poultry breeder, she is an industrious (decidedly non-vegetarian) cook and the recipes for handcrafting pâtés and foie gras are their heirlooms. Readers talk of fabulous meals and delicious aperitifs…The honey stones of the building are impeccably pointed and cleaned, bedrooms have functionality rather than character, shower rooms are large and pristine and there's an open-fired sitting room just for guests. Good for families (a climbing frame in the garden). Utterly French.

Rooms	2: 1 double, 1 triple.
Price	€58.
Meals	Dinner with wine, €21.50.
Closed	November–February.

Marie-Thérèse & Jean-Michel Archer
La Ferme de la Rivière,
24520 St Agne, Dordogne
Tel   +33 (0)5 53 23 22 26
Email   archer.marietherese@wanadoo.fr
Web   www.lafermedelariviere.com

Entry 531   Map 9

Aquitaine

La Rebière d'Or

The Dordogne laps sleepily alongside this renovated bijou château with its own slipway, majestic grounds and swish pool. Roam freely through living areas lavished with antiques and boudoir trinkets. Woodland and river cameo views unfold from large, comfortable Edward-style bedrooms where artistic charm abounds – even in the bathrooms. Breakfast on fresh fruit brochettes in the dining or piano room – or outside where peacocks parade. You're a stone's throw from the busy market town of Mouleydier and a leg stretch away from good eateries. In a suburb, a surprising haven of tranquillity – with grandeur and style in spades.

Minimum two nights. Children over 12 welcome.

Rooms	2 doubles.
Price	€120–€125. Extra bed €25.
Meals	Restaurant 50m.
Closed	Rarely.

Catherine Fournel
La Rebière d'Or,
13 rue de la Rocade,
24520 Mouleydier, Dordogne
Tel   +33 (0)5 53 58 23 05
Mobile   +33 (0)6 13 77 33 83
Email   contact@rebiere-dor.com
Web   catherinefournel.free.fr

Entry 532   Map 9

Aquitaine

Terre et Toi

Hand-built, sewn, cut, plumbed and oiled, the guest cottage displays Sara's passion for eco-building and natural style. Two airy bedrooms have whitewashed walls of straw and earth, lime and hemp, polished wet rooms with composting loos – and views over a lake and poplar grove from the bed and terrace. Heart-shaped windows, flower motifs, flowing white drapes: all in harmony with nature. Sara's talents include delicious organic vegetarian meals; and your own kitchen. Walk, canoe, taste wines, hop on a train to Bordeaux – and take time to admire the many birds in the wildlife-happy gardens.

Rooms	Cottage: 2 twins/doubles & kitchen.
Price	£70–£85 for 2.
Meals	Vegetarian dinner, 3 courses, €20; main course €10. Guest kitchenette. Restaurant 8km.
Closed	Rarely.

Sara Daniels
Terre et Toi,
24700 St Géraud de Corps,
Dordogne
Tel   +33 (0)5 53 80 14 13
Email   saradaniels@hotmail.fr
Web   www.terre-et-toi.com

Entry 533   Map 9

Aquitaine

Le Moulin de Leymonie du Maupas

The Kieffers did the utterly successful restoration of their remote Dordogne mill themselves, their gardening past speaks softly in the herb-scented patio and the little brook trembles off past grazing horses to the valley. Inside, levels juggle with space, steep stairs rise to small rooms of huge character with stone and wood walls, rich rugs and selected antiques; loos are tiny. Your sitting room is seductive with its logs on the fire and timbers overhead. Add a relaxed, bubbly welcome, organic dinners served with crisp linen and candles, homemade bread and jams for breakfast, and you have great value.

Children's room available.

Rooms	2: 1 double, 1 twin.
Price	€85. €70 per night for 2-night stay.
Meals	Dinner €15–€20. Wine €9.
Closed	Rarely.

Jacques & Ginette Kieffer
Le Moulin de Leymonie du Maupas,
24400 Issac,
Dordogne
Tel   +33 (0)5 53 81 24 02
Email   jacques.kieffer2@wanadoo.fr
Web   perso.wanadoo.fr/lemoulindeleymonie

Entry 534   Map 9

Aquitaine

Pauliac

The exuberant hillside garden, full of blossom and bamboo, has gorgeous views of sunflowers and an overflowing stone plunge pool. John and Jane's talents are a restful atmosphere, great dinners, and interiors that are a brilliant marriage of cottage simplicity and sparks from African throws and contemporary paintings. Beautiful bedrooms have a separate entrance. Delightful, energetic Jane offers superb, imaginative food in the sun-splashed veranda with its all-season views, or the bright, rustic dining room with roaring log fire – and early suppers for children. Lovely people in a tranquil view-drenched spot.

Cookery & painting courses.

Rooms	4: 2 doubles, 1 twin, 1 suite for 4.
Price	€80–€85. Suite €80–€110.
Meals	Dinner €25. Wine €10.
Closed	Rarely.

Jane & John Edwards
Pauliac,
Celles, 24600 Ribérac, Dordogne
Tel   +33 (0)5 47 23 40 17
Mobile   +33 (0)6 88 13 06 27
Email   info@pauliac.fr
Web   www.pauliac.fr

Entry 535   Map 9

Aquitaine

Briançon

The 14th-century walnut mill is a house full of riches and light, and the English garden, blessed with a burbling brook, is resplendent with rare plants. Inside, sofas wear colourful throws, boho-stylish bedrooms burst with personality and shower rooms have retro touches. Dinners, served at the big old country table, sound enticing: wines from Michael's cellar, produce from Katie's potager, herbs and garlic scattered with studied abandon, and plenty for vegetarians. Katie and Michael, from London, have created a sophisticated yet laid-back home and it's a treat to stay.

Aquitaine

La Bastide de Chapdeuil

Keep your eyes peeled or you'll miss the tiny sign as you wind along the village lanes: La Bastide is not be missed. The 18th-century house, restored with comfort in mind, is modern, friendly and has dashes of luxury; kids and grown-ups will love the home cinema, gardens, long pool, and the al fresco dining. Bedrooms are blissful, bathrooms sumptuous, and Franck is all gentle courtesy. He and eco-minded Michaëlla offer organic whenever possible, so you breakfast on village bread, homemade jams and yogurt, and dine on Perigordin goodies such as confit and asparagus. Markets, medieval towns, abbeys – take your pick!

Rooms	5: 3 doubles; 2 twins sharing bathroom.
Price	€100–€150. Twin €85–€100.
Meals	Dinner €35. Restaurant 2km.
Closed	December-March.

Rooms	5: 4 doubles, 1 family room for 4.
Price	€70–€90.
Meals	Dinner with wine, €26. Restaurants 2km.
Closed	Rarely.

Katie Armitage
Briançon,
24320 Verteillac,
Dordogne
Tel   +33 (0)5 53 91 38 40
Email   katie@elliottarmitage.com
Web   www.elliottarmitage.com

Franck & Michaëlla Pinel
La Bastide de Chapdeuil,
La Pouze, 24320 Chapdeuil,
Dordogne
Tel   +33 (0)5 53 91 25 44
Email   labastidedechapdeuil@laposte.net
Web   www.labastidedechapdeuil.com

Entry 536   Map 9

Entry 537   Map 9

Aquitaine

La Cachette

Small but perfectly formed, this rural bolthole, complete with a farm wagon in the yard, is just far enough off the tourist trail for total peace. Up steep stairs, two cosy oak-beamed bedrooms with ensuite shower rooms share the eaves of the 18th-century granite farmhouse. Ron and Jennifer live in the modern extension with their cat and couldn't be more charming or more helpful. You can breakfast on the terrace overlooking the sloping lawns of the garden, or opt for the comfort of the guests' sitting/dining room – a welcoming space with a wood-burning stove and a vast collection of DVDs for cosy nights in.

Minimum two nights.

Rooms	2 doubles.
Price	€55. Singles €45.
Meals	Dinner with wine €20. Restaurant 5km.
Closed	December-February.

Jennifer Sweetman
La Cachette,
Sarlandelle, 24270 Sarlande,
Dordogne
Tel +33 (0)5 53 62 94 24
Email sweetrasjas@yahoo.co.uk
Web lacachettedordogne.co.uk

Entry 538 Map 9

Aquitaine

Les Hirondelles

Carine, half-Greek, energetic, charming and fun, makes you feel welcome in the sunny kitchen of her restored farmhouse on the top of a hill. She enjoys cooking French and international dishes and makes amazing walnut jam. Simple, dim-lit, inexpensive bedrooms are in a converted barn set back from the house, each with a terrace delineated by concrete planters. The pool is far enough away not to disturb your siesta. Spend two or three nights and get to know this beautiful village and the whole area; Carine knows the best places to go.

Minimum two nights July/Aug.

Rooms	4: 2 doubles, 2 twins.
Price	€50-€55.
Meals	Dinner, 3 courses with wine, €19.
Closed	November-April.

Carine Someritis
Les Hirondelles,
Le Maine, 24510 Ste Alvère,
Dordogne
Tel +33 (0)5 53 22 75 40
Email leshirondelles.carine@orange.fr
Web www.les-hirondelles-dordogne.jimdo.com

Entry 539 Map 9

Aquitaine

Le Moulin Neuf

Watch the ducks waddle by on their way to the lake. Robert's greeting is the first line of an ode to hospitality written in warm stone and breathtaking gardens, set to the tune of the mill stream. Immaculate rooms in the guest barn are comfortingly filled with good beds and fresh flowers, bathrooms are sheer luxury, and views sweep over the lawns. Wake up to a royal breakfast of delicious breads, croissants, pâtisseries, homemade jams, succulent fruits and tiny cheeses served on white tablecloths on the vine-shaded terrace. All is lovingly tended, the river flows under the house, all in perfect peace.

Ask about pets. Over 10's welcome. Minimum three nights in winter.

Rooms	5: 2 doubles, 1 twin/double, 1 suite, 1 family room for 3.
Price	€85–€89.
Meals	Restaurant in Paunat, 1km.
Closed	Rarely.

Robert Chappell
Le Moulin Neuf,
Paunat,
24510 Ste Alvère, Dordogne

Tel	+33 (0)5 53 63 30 18
Email	moulin-neuf@usa.net
Web	www.the-moulin-neuf.com

Entry 540   Map 9

Aquitaine

Le Domaine de La Millasserie

Near lovely lively Trémolat, and the Dordogne with its watery charms, is this elegant, immaculate B&B. American Byrne and Alain from Bordeaux have swapped literature and antiques for hospitality – and they do it well. Alongside their honey-hued 18th-century manor overlooking the woods, the B&B wing in traditional style houses four generous rooms. French windows open to private terraces, huge beds are dressed in toile de Jouy, gorgeous antiques glow: armoires, paintings and mirrors. Lazy breakfasts, on the terrace or by the pool, offer fresh fruits, croissants, viennoiseries, strong French coffee and good English tea.

Minimum two nights. Children over 16 welcome.

Rooms	4 doubles.
Price	€95.
Meals	Restaurants 5km.
Closed	Rarely.

Byrne Fone & Alain Pioton
Le Domaine de La Millasserie,
24150 Mauzac & Grand Castang,
Dordogne

Tel	+33 (0)5 53 57 78 01
Email	byrnefone@wanadoo.fr
Web	www.bandbfrancedordogne.com

Entry 541   Map 9

Aquitaine

Manoir de la Brunie

An elegant village manor in a glorious setting: the views are stupendous. The owners live in Paris but the genial manager will introduce you to a fine living room full of warm bright colours overlooking a sweeping lawn (play the piano, browse the books) and excellent bedrooms. The tower suite and small double have a modern feel, the other rooms, huge and high-ceilinged, are more classical; all have subtle colours, new wood floors, space for armchairs and sofas, and good lighting. Breakfasts are fresh, bathrooms delightful... there's a heated pool shared with gîte guests, a river beach nearby, riding next door.

Chauffeured 2-day gourmet packages available.

Rooms	5: 3 doubles, 1 twin/double, 1 suite.
Price	€65–€99. Extra bed €17.
Meals	Breakfast €8–€12. Dinner with wine, €27.
Closed	December/January.

Joyce Villemur
Manoir de la Brunie,
La Brunie,
24220 Le Coux & Bigaroque,
Dordogne
Tel   +33 (0)5 53 31 95 62
Email   manoirdelabrunie@wanadoo.fr
Web   www.manoirdelabrunie.com

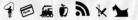

Entry 542   Map 9

Aquitaine

La Guérinière

Once a charterhouse, this good-looking Perigord house, peacefully atop a hill facing Domme in private parkland, is a tribute to the rich sober taste of the area. Inside reflects outside: the same dark timbers against pale stone and the owners have redecorated the bedrooms most charmingly, gradually replacing the modern furniture with country antiques; the feel is warmly authentic. Moreover, they used to run a restaurant: we hear great reports of the food. There's a big table for house guests and you may find more gourmets in the beamed dining room (outsiders are occasionally allowed in). A gem.

Sawday self-catering also.

Rooms	5: 1 double, 2 twins, 1 triple, 1 quadruple.
Price	€90–€105. Triple €130–€140. Quadruple €155–€170.
Meals	Dinner €28. Wine from €20.
Closed	November–March.

Brigitte & Christophe Demassougne
La Guérinière,
Baccas, 24250 Cénac & St Julien,
Dordogne
Tel   +33 (0)5 53 29 91 97
Email   contact@la-gueriniere-dordogne.com
Web   www.la-gueriniere-dordogne.com

Entry 543   Map 9

Aquitaine

Château de Puymartin

Neither dream nor museum, Puymartin is a chance to act the aristocrat for a spell, and survey the day visitors from your own wing. The fireplace in the tapestried baronial dining room would take a small tree, painted beams draw the eye, the carved stone staircase asks to be stroked, the furniture is authentic 17th-century Perigordian, history oozes from every corner. Bedrooms are vastly in keeping – twin four-posters, a faded ceiling painting, a loo in a turret, thick draperies. The elderly, ever-elegant Comtesse is friendly and very French; her son helps in the château and speaks good English; both are delightful.

Rooms	2: 1 twin, 1 family room.
Price	€150. Family room €120. Extra bed €30.
Meals	Restaurant 5km.
Closed	November-March.

Comtesse de Montbron
Château de Puymartin,
24200 Sarlat la Canéda,
Dordogne
Tel   +33 (0)5 53 59 29 97
Email   chateaupuymartin@gmail.com
Web   www.chateau-de-puymartin.com

Entry 544   Map 9

Aquitaine

Les Chambres de la Voie Verte

Steps curl up and around the old stone walls and lead to four rooms, each delightful, each with its own outside entrance. Find soft purples, greens, greys, rose reds, comfortable new beds and state-of-the-art bathrooms with walk-in showers. From the top floor, views stretch over the town's Perigordian rooftops, to Montfort château beyond. Enjoy breakfast off white Limoges china at the long table in the house next door (and on the terrace on warm days). The friendly owners also run the bar and florist's on either side; extrovert Madame revels in her projects. The old railway track for cycling to Sarlat and Souillac is near.

Rooms	4: 2 doubles, 2 twins.
Price	€70-€80. Extra bed €20.
Meals	Restaurants in town.
Closed	Rarely.

Annie Boyer
Les Chambres de la Voie Verte,
24200 Carsac Aillac,
Dordogne
Mobile   +33 (0)6 70 09 38 95
Email   annie.boyer43@orange.fr
Web   www.chambres-de-la-voie-verte.com

Entry 545   Map 9

Aquitaine

Les Charmes de Carlucet

An 18th-century house with a poignant history: Jewish families were sheltered here during the Second World War. Now the welcoming Edgars – he French, she English – live here with their children. In a vast walled garden on the edge of the village, the house has been completely renovated. Living and dining rooms are cool compositions of natural stone, white walls, pale fabrics; pitch-ceilinged, L-shaped bedrooms under the eaves have gleaming floors, spotless bath or shower rooms, fans for summer. Should you tire of the heated pool or new sauna, you can stroll to the clipped hedges of Eyrignac.

Sawday self-catering also. Extra beds available.

Rooms	2 doubles.
Price	€99–€119. Extra bed €20.
Meals	Restaurant 500m.
Closed	Rarely.

Éric & Helen Edgar
Les Charmes de Carlucet,
24590 St Crépin & Carlucet,
Dordogne

Tel	+33 (0)5 53 31 22 60
Email	lescharmes@carlucet.com
Web	www.carlucet.com

Entry 546   Map 9

Do let owners know when booking if you intend to bring your pet – particularly if it's not a dog!

Let's you know that an owner has their own pet on the premises, it may not be a cat!

France has more National and Regional parks than you might guess. Try www.parcs-naturels-regionaux.tm.fr

Limousin

Limousin

Maison Marie-Thérèse

The face could only be French, framed by wisteria in its sweet *jardin de curé*. Pat and Mike, who welcome you with pleasure, tales of life and reviving laughter to their almost colonial nest (willow pattern, old prints, deep English comfort), could only be English. The great conservatory floods you with light from leafy garden and wooded hills beyond. The top floor is yours: pretty, raftered bedrooms with superb beds, character and no clutter. Don't miss dinner: they ran a restaurant in Yorkshire. Breakfast is what you want when you want. Proper family B&B in a lovely part of France where Lac Vassivière beckons.

Rooms	2: 1 double, 1 twin sharing bath/shower room.
Price	€65–€75.
Meals	Dinner with wine, €20.
Closed	Rarely.

Pat & Mike Reynette-James
Maison Marie-Thérèse,
16 rue des Garennes,
87470 Peyrat le Château,
Haute-Vienne
Tel   +33 (0)5 55 69 32 47
Email   Info@maisonmarietherese.com
Web   maisonmarietherese.com

Entry 547   Map 10

Limousin

Magnac

In an ancient manor of enormous personality, your live-wire hostess, once a Parisian designer, now paints porcelain, organises cultural events and struggles to renovate the family house and its wild park with deep respect for its originality. Utterly endearing in its battered aristocracy, it is one room deep: light pours in from both sides onto heavy floorboards, 18th-century panelling and a delightful tower cocktail room. The traditional-style bedroom in the main house is vast, the snugger suite in the half-timbered orangery is ideal if you'd rather be independent.

Children over 12 welcome.

Rooms	2: 1 twin/double, 1 suite.
Price	€95. Suite €95–€140.
Meals	Dinner with wine, €40.
Closed	November to mid-May.

Catherine & Bertrand de la Bastide
Magnac,
87380 Magnac Bourg,
Haute-Vienne
Mobile   +33 (0)6 03 08 79 19
Email   cathdelabastide@gmail.com

Entry 548   Map 9

Limousin

Moulin de Marsaguet

The nicest people, they have done just enough to this proud old building to make it look as it did 200 years ago when cannon balls were forged here. The farm is relaxed and natural, the bedrooms quaint, they have ducks and animals (including Lusitanian horses), three teenagers and a super potager. And they make pâtés and 'confits' by the great mill pond, hanging the hams over the magnificent hearth in their big stone sitting room with its old-fashioned sofa. Relish the drive up past the tree-framed lake (boating possible) and stone outbuildings and the prospect of breakfast made with home-grown ingredients.

Ask about pets.

Rooms	3 twins/doubles.
Price	€60.
Meals	Dinner with wine €22. Restaurant 3km.
Closed	November to mid-April.

Valérie & Renaud Gizardin
Moulin de Marsaguet,
87500 Coussac Bonneval,
Haute-Vienne
Tel +33 (0)5 55 75 28 29
Mobile +33 (0)6 26 16 34 47
Email renaudvalerie.gizardin@orange.fr
Web www.moulindemarsaguet.com

Entry 549 Map 9

Limousin

Les Drouilles Bleues

High on a granite hill, with views to swell your heart, the low stone house and its greenly rocky garden creak with age and history. As does the whole region. Paul and Maïthé, a most intelligent and attentive couple, take their hosting to heart, greeting with homemade treats, revelling in — and joining — the people who gather at their convivial and tasty dinner table. In converted outbuildings, handsome bedrooms large and smaller, are simple, a touch old-fashioned and done with care and soft colours. All have working fireplaces, sleeping quarters on mezzanines, good shower rooms. Deeply, discreetly, welcoming.

Rooms	3: 2 doubles, 1 suite for 4.
Price	€68. Suite €90–€145. Under 5's free.
Meals	Dinner with wine, €25. Child under 12, €15.
Closed	Rarely.

Maïthé & Paul de Bettignies
Les Drouilles Bleues,
La Drouille,
87800 St Hilaire les Places,
Haute-Vienne
Tel +33 (0)5 55 58 21 26
Email lesdrouillesbleues@gmail.com
Web drouillesbleues.free.fr

Entry 550 Map 9

Limousin

Château Ribagnac

Patrick and Colette are intelligent, thoughtful and enthusiastic, and their splendid château, built in 1647, is a treat. With a growing family in London, this was their dream – superbly achieved. In fine big rooms, the conversion is authentic and elegantly comfortable: rugs on oak floors, old and newish furniture, superb new bathrooms (one loo in its turret). Ask for a lighter room with views over park and lake. Fruit and veg grow in their organic garden, the local meat is succulent, there is a deep commitment. Conversation flows with the wine.

Rooms	5 suites for 2-5.
Price	€90-€160.
Meals	Dinner with wine, €45.
Closed	Rarely.

Patrick & Colette Bergot
Château Ribagnac,
87400 St Martin Terressus,
Haute-Vienne
Tel +33 (0)5 55 39 77 91
Email reservations@chateauribagnac.com
Web www.chateauribagnac.com

🕆 ✉ 👶 📶 ✗ 🐕 🚲

Entry 551   Map 9

Limousin

Château du Fraisse

After 800 years of family and estate symbiosis, Le Fraisse is a living history book, mainly a rustic-grand Renaissance gem by the great Serlio – pale limestone, discreetly elegant portico, Henry II staircase and an astonishing fireplace in the vast drawing room. Your cultured hosts, two generations now, will greet you with warmth, happily tell you about house and history and show you to your room: fine furniture, paintings and prints, traditional furnishings; one bathroom has a fragment of a 16th-century fresco. If you return late at night you must climb the steep old spiral stair to your room as the main door is locked.

Rooms	4: 1 double, 1 twin, 1 suite for 3, 1 suite for 4.
Price	€90. Suite €95-€215.
Meals	Restaurants 6km.
Closed	Mid-December to mid-January.

Marquis & Marquise des Monstiers Mérinville
Château du Fraisse,
Le Fraisse, 87330 Nouic,
Haute-Vienne
Tel +33 (0)5 55 68 32 68
Email infos@chateau-du-fraisse.com
Web www.chateau-du-fraisse.com

🕆 📶 🐕 🐕

Entry 552   Map 9

Limousin

La Flambée

You will find simple French value and a sweet, hard-working young couple on this organic smallholding. They genuinely like sharing their country fare, created from home-grown vegetables and home-reared lamb, duck, pigeon and rabbit (delicious pâtés). Myriam cares for their children, potager and guests and is redoing the rooms with fun and colour; Pierre, a builder by trade, looks after the animals and myriad house improvements. The 18th-century roadside farmhouse has characterful old wood – a great oak staircase, beams, timber framing – family clutter, fireplaces, peaceful bedrooms and a garden full of toys.

Children over 12 welcome. Extra bed available.

Rooms	4: 1 double, 1 family room for 3, 2 family rooms for 4.
Price	€45. Family room for 3, €55. Family room for 4, €65.
Meals	Dinner with wine, €18.
Closed	Rarely.

	Pierre & Myriam Morice
	La Flambée,
	Thoveyrat,
	87300 Blond,
	Haute-Vienne
Tel	+33 (0)5 55 68 86 86
Email	chambrehote@freesurf.fr
Web	www.laflambee.info

Entry 553   Map 9

Limousin

La Pissarelle

In a green and lovely corner of France, discover the wee hamlet where Annie's family have always farmed. Here she and Wolfgang, who worked with NATO and speaks impeccable English, have returned to renovate a highly personal, treasure-filled farmhouse with a cosily simple Petite Maison for guests just across the patio. Having lived all over the world, they adore having visitors at their table in the former cattle byre or in the new veranda – and hope you might park your horses in their field. Before the vast ex-château fireplace, you will be regaled with tales of local life and exotic lands afar. A fascinating couple.

Extra single. Baby bed & high chair available.

Rooms	Cottage for 4: 1 double, 1 twin.
Price	Cottage €50–€100.
Meals	Dinner with wine, €25. Lunch, 2 courses, €12.50. Picnic €6. Restaurant 3km.
Closed	Rarely.

	Wolfgang & Annie Oelsner
	La Pissarelle, La Clupte,
	23430 Châtelus le Marcheix,
	Creuse
Tel	+33 (0)5 55 64 30 58
Mobile	+33 (0)6 73 00 26 68
Email	lapissarelle@gmail.com
Web	www.lapissarelle.com

Entry 554   Map 9

Limousin

Château de Memanat

Roger and Pauline are passionate about their château. It is fabulously comfortable yet keeps strict faith with its past. Bedrooms are light and beautifully furnished, one with its own sitting room; bathrooms are superb. The food's great, too: Pauline adores cooking and uses local and organic suppliers. Opt for the simple menu and she and Roger will dine with you; go for gourmet and they'll join you for dessert. The grounds are vast: 1km of trout river, a walled garden with play area and solar-heated pool, and parkland planted with specimen trees by guests of the first owner, the scientist Dr Louis Queyrat. Absolutely marvellous.

Limousin

La Petite Maison

Come for romance and good, honest food: home-reared quails, rabbits, organic veg, fresh-laid eggs, honey from the hives. Chris catches wild boar and fish, Joanne cooks – deliciously – from handwritten recipes and serves in the 1670s dining room or on the sun terrace overlooking a wooded valley. Chandeliers dangle from big old beams and a wood-burner glows... bedrooms are swagged and draped, with free-standing double baths and fluffy gowns – give free rein to your imagination! This fertile land abounds in lakes (fishing, canoeing) and trails (foot, bike and horse). Aubusson of tapestry fame is ten minutes away.

Ask about Valentine weekends.

Rooms	2 suites.
Price	€95–€110.
Meals	Dinner €34. Wine €15.
Closed	Christmas & New Year.

Rooms	3 doubles.
Price	€75.
Meals	Dinner with wine €25. Restaurants 11km.
Closed	Rarely.

Roger & Pauline Ketteringham
Château de Memanat,
Memanat,
23250 Chavanat, Creuse
Tel +33 (0)5 55 67 74 45
Email enquiries@memanat.com
Web www.memanat.com

Christopher & Joanne Spencer
La Petite Maison,
Chassing Cheval,
23200 St Avit de Tardes, Creuse
Tel +33 (0)5 55 66 49 07
Email mrandmrsspencers@googlemail.com
Web lapetitemaisonlimousin.com

Entry 555   Map 10

Entry 556   Map 10

Limousin

Maison Numéro Neuf

Lisa and Duncan from England have embraced life in southern La Souterraine. She is the least ruffled, most contented of chefs; he serves wines with finesse; both love house, children, guests, and their secret garden with hens. Now, at last, the renovation of the former residence of the Marquis de Valady is complete. So much to enjoy: the fine proportions, the sweeping balustrade, the antique mirrors, the crystal-drop chandeliers, the pale walls, the glowing parquet… and superb breakfasts and dinners. If Lisa pops a hot water bottle into your bed it will be encased in white linen: the hospitality here is exceptional.

Rooms	3: 2 doubles; 1 twin, sharing shower.
Price	€80–€115. Twin €65–€75.
Meals	Dinner €22–€45. Wine €18.
Closed	Rarely.

Duncan & Lisa Rowney
Maison Numéro Neuf,
Rue Serpente,
23300 La Souterraine, Creuse
Tel   +33 (0)5 55 63 43 35
Email   reservations@maisonnumeroneuf.com
Web   maisonnumeroneuf.com

Entry 557   Map 9

Limousin

Maison Grandchamp

In an historic town, you are welcomed by a charming, cultured couple to a 400-year-old house of fascinating origins. Thrill to Marielle's tales – her ancestors built and extended the house, their portraits hang in the panelled drawing room: find time for François' knowledge of geography and the environment. Up the elegant spiral stairs, bedrooms are in proper but unpompous château style, big, soft and quiet. Breakfast is in the beamy 16th-century dining room, by the cosy kitchen fire or in the terraced garden overlooking jumbled rooftops, or in the luminous veranda. Then explore glorious Corrèze.

Overflow room for 2 available.

Rooms	3: 2 twins/doubles; 1 twin/double with separate bathroom.
Price	€80–€90. Extra bed €25.
Meals	Dinner with aperitif & wine €29–€32. Restaurants within walking distance.
Closed	January–March.

Marielle & François Teyssier
Maison Grandchamp,
9 place des Pénitents,
19260 Treignac, Corrèze
Tel   +33 (0)5 55 98 10 69
Mobile   +33 (0)6 59 05 09 46
Email   teyssier.marielle@wanadoo.fr
Web   www.hotesgrandchamp.com

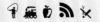

Entry 558   Map 10

Limousin

La Farge

The stone hamlets take you back to another age along the rugged valleys. The delightful Chibals have adopted the country and nationality, the stones and the peace, updating them with their English sense of fine finish: an ancient cart carefully restored before being flooded with flowers, new windows fitted with the latest fly screens, first-class beds and showers. Fresh pastel bedrooms have honey-boarded floors and a teddy each; modern pine mixes with antique oak; the kitchen's solid farmhouse table, wood-burner and super food are at the heart of this house. Heaven.

Minimum two nights. Sawday self-catering also.

Rooms	3: 2 doubles; 1 twin with separate bathroom.
Price	€65.
Meals	Dinner with wine, €32.50.
Closed	Rarely.

Jean-Luc & Hélène Chibal
La Farge,
19400 Monceaux sur Dordogne,
Corrèze

Tel	+33 (0)5 55 28 54 52
Email	info@chezarchi.com
Web	www.chezarchi.com

Limousin

Jeanne Maison d'Hôtes

Where tree-clad hills surge up from valleys and sprinklings of fortified towns cling gloriously to hilltops you find this turreted, redstone village. Hidden from tourist bustle behind high walls is a green shady garden, roses in abundance, a 15th-century tower and three floors of living space. Big bedrooms have sisal and sofas, heavy old armoires, the odd redstone wall and one, a stone terrace; white bathrooms sparkle. She did PR in Paris, he was a restaurateur, both are fine, interesting hosts and speak good English. You eat well; mushrooms are gathered in season and Brigitte is proud of her breakfast gâteaux.

Rooms	5: 3 doubles, 2 twins/doubles.
Price	€98.
Meals	Dinner with wine, €35.
Closed	Rarely.

Brigitte & Pascal Monteil
Jeanne Maison d'Hôtes,
BP 28 Le Bourg,
19500 Collonges la Rouge, Corrèze

Tel	+33 (0)5 55 25 42 31
Email	info@jeannemaisondhotes.com
Web	www.jeannemaisondhotes.com

Auvergne

Auvergne

Château Neureux

With bucolic views to hills, pastures, lake and stream, a perfect little 18th-century getaway. It is now home to a Dutch film director and an American ballerina, a hospitable, delightful pair. Past deep-red walls and a beaded Deco chandelier find big elegant bedrooms that mix French classicism with Dutch sobriety, ornate wallpapers with louvered French shutters. As you tuck into breakfast's pâtisseries, gaze through tall windows to the vast estate where peacocks and donkeys roam, wild deer and foxes saunter, and a pool (shared with the gîte guests) tempts behind orchard walls. Rent bikes, stride into the hills, fish on the lake...

Rooms	5: 2 doubles, 2 twins/doubles, 1 suite for 2-4.
Price	€110-€130.
Meals	Restaurant 1km.
Closed	Rarely.

Roeland Kerbosch & Valerie Valentine
Château Neureux,
03320 Lurcy Lévis, Allier
Tel   +33 (0)9 64 41 55 30
Email   info@chateauneureux.com
Web   www.chateauneureux.com

🚶 ⚲ 🗐 🚂 📶 ✕ 🐱

Entry 561   Map 10

Auvergne

Jaffière

Down the leafy little lane, the gates will be thrown open and two low-slung dogs will shout "Welcome!" Well integrated in the village, your Anglo-Scots hosts are the friendliest possible, the old farmhouse and barn stand in a big youthful garden (Richard is loving his new job...) that disappears into rolling golden cow pastures and copses. The house is deliciously personal, the pretty raftered rooms full of cosy comfort, the big shared bathroom light and warm. Frances not only fills the place with Scottish laughter, she also makes a mean breakfast treat while Richard basks quietly. You won't regret booking dinner, either. Great value.

Extra double room available. Children over 8 welcome.

Rooms	2: 1 double, 1 twin sharing bathroom (let to same party only).
Price	€60. Singles €45. Extra bed €25.
Meals	Dinner with wine, €20.
Closed	Rarely.

Frances & Richard Sladden
Jaffière,
03160 St Aubin le Monial, Allier
Tel   +33 (0)9 75 40 17 13
Email   jaffiere@gmail.com
Web   www.jaffiere.com

🚂 🍶 ✕ 🐱

Entry 562   Map 10

Auvergne

Domaine d'Aigrepont

Madame greets you warmly outside the original 1640s manor that her ancestors built overlooking the Allier valley. Round a grassy courtyard, the manor, chapel and handsome guest wing float in a sea of terraced gardens surging with lavender, jasmine, roses, vines and a pool. Named after family heroes, bedrooms breathe authenticity with high beams, beautiful antiques, oriental rugs, fireplaces, snow-white linen and new bathrooms, one with a bulls-eye to the courtyard. Breakfast on homemade brioche, dive into the valley for walks, gardens, vineyards and thermal baths, then off to Moulins for dinner.

Auvergne

St Louis

Right on the border of Burgundy, this farmhouse is surrounded by acres of flat and loamy pastureland. The open feel continues indoors: you can spread out in the vast hallway and its gallery, and the big flagstoned sitting rooms while the kids spill into the huge lawned garden. Breakfast convivially on fresh bread and homemade jams in the fine dining room, explore the nooks of the pretty villages nearby and return to restful country-cottage bedrooms with quilted beds and sparkling showers. Alix's elegant 80-year-old mother has discovered her inner artist here: you too may find the inspiration you seek.

Rooms	4: 2 doubles, 1 twin, 1 twin/double.
Price	€130. Singles €120.
Meals	Catered meals available. Restaurant 5km.
Closed	October-April.

Rooms	2: 1 twin/double, 1 twin.
Price	€70-€90.
Meals	Dinner €25. Restaurants 10km.
Closed	End September to Easter, except by arrangement.

	Édith de Contenson
	Domaine d'Aigrepont,
	Aigrepont, 03000 Bressolles, Allier
Tel	+33 (0)6 80 05 51 02
Email	postmaster@chambres-d-hotes-en-bourbonnais.com
Web	www.aigrepont.com

	Lendon & Alix Meaby
	St Louis,
	Lieu-dit Varennes,
	03230 Beaulon, Allier
Tel	+33 (0)4 70 44 08 12
Mobile	+33 (0)6 84 19 90 71
Email	alixdemonspey@lcltd.co.uk
Web	www.b-and-bstlouis.weebly.com

Entry 563   Map 10

Entry 564   Map 10

Auvergne

Château de Clusors

Atop a hill, this small château has gazed on untouched countryside since the 14th century. Steeped in history (Henri is full of stories; Madame de Montespan once stayed here), the place is still a working farm: friendly and down-to-earth, Madame manages a herd of Charolais cows. Up the spiral stone stair are big bedrooms with fine furniture and excellent modern bathrooms; breakfast is set before family portraits and a bookcase stocked with leather-bound tomes. Outside: a large garden with orchard and pool; rest in the shade of a lime tree and admire the magnificent view. Wonderfully, authentically French.

Kitchen available if rooms let to same party.

Rooms	2 triples.
Price	Triple €100. Extra bed €20.
Meals	Charcuterie & vegetable platter, €10. Restaurants 1km.
Closed	Rarely.

Christine & Henri Thieulin
Château de Clusors,
03210 St Menoux, Allier

Tel	+33 (0)4 70 43 94 69
Mobile	+33 (0)6 70 79 27 75
Email	henri.thieulin@orange.fr
Web	www.chateaudeclusors.com

Entry 565 Map 10

Auvergne

Cognet

Billowing hilly pastures wrap the hamlet in sensuality. Built in 1886 as a rich man's summer place, here is a generous, sophisticated house informed by Madame's broad cultural interests, her father's paintings and her fine Provençal furniture that looks perfect beside the beautiful original panelling and wide fireplace. Up steep shiny stairs, the guest space is a sweep of pine floor and ceiling; light floods over sitting area, big pine bed, old chest; a proud tree shades the splendid shower room. Deep rest, super breakfast and conversation, Romanesque jewels to visit, beauty sessions in Vichy – a must.

Rooms	1 twin/double.
Price	€70.
Meals	Light supper with wine first night, €15. Wine €10. Restaurants 5km.
Closed	November–February.

Bénita Mourges
Cognet,
03300 La Chapelle, Allier

Tel	+33 (0)4 70 41 88 28
Mobile	+33 (0)6 98 47 54 48
Email	maison.cognet@free.fr
Web	maison.cognet.free.fr

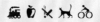

Entry 566 Map 10

Auvergne

Château du Ludaix

Pure château with a touch of humour, Ludaix is glamorous, dramatic and utterly welcoming. David and Stephanie have boundless energy, love people (they run a training company) and lavish care on house and guests. David is exploring the archives ("Ludaix is a living history book"), rebuilding the ancient waterworks and shady walks in the wood. Stephanie's talent cossets the rich warm rooms with English and French antiques ancient and modern, myriad hats, clocks and costumes, the odd tented ceiling. Gorgeous rooms, imaginative bathrooms, delicious food, great conversation – and lots more...

Extra rooms for groups & seminars. Whole house available.

Rooms	4: 2 suites for 2, 1 for 3, 1 for 4.
Price	Suite €120. €150 for 3. €180 for 4.
Meals	Dinner, 4 courses with wine, €40.
Closed	January/February.

David Morton & Stephanie Holland
Château du Ludaix, Rue du Ludaix,
03420 Marcillat en Combraille,
Allier

Tel	+33 (0)4 70 51 62 32
Mobile	+44 (0)7739 431918
Email	stephanie@rapport-online.com
Web	www.chateauduludaix.com

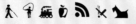

Entry 567   Map 10

Auvergne

La Rambaude

A generous and handsomely decorated family house: the volcanoes gave their lava for dining room and staircase floor slabs; the hall is resplendent with hand-blocked wallpaper by Zuber. Ancestors gave their names to bedrooms, where their faded photographs and intricate samplers fill the walls; others left some fine old ornaments and pieces of furniture and built the stupendous brick barns that shelter the garden. Élisabeth is dynamic, intelligent and full of wry humour, once a trace of shyness has worn off, and serves her deliciously wholesome breakfast in the garden, studded with wild violets in spring.

Rooms	2 doubles.
Price	€74–€78.
Meals	Restaurants 2km.
Closed	November-March, except by arrangement.

Élisabeth Beaujeard
La Rambaude,
8 route de la Limagne, Chaptes,
63460 Beauregard Vendon,
Puy-de-Dôme

Tel	+33 (0)4 73 63 35 62
Email	elisabeth.beaujeard@orange.fr
Web	www.la-rambaude.com

Entry 568   Map 10

Auvergne

Château de Vaulx

Is it real or a fairy tale? Creak along the parquet, swan around the salon, sleep in one tower, wash in another. It's been in the family for 800 years, well-lived-in rooms have peace and romantic furnishings — worthy of the troubadours who sang here. Breakfast on home-hived honey, brioche, yogurt, eggs, cheese, get to know your delightful young hosts who are nurturing it, as their parents did, with joy — and updating a bit. Visit the donkey, walk from quiet lawn into sweeping view, tuck into Philippe's tasty cuisine. Feeling homesick? Have a drink in Guy's cellar 'pub' with its collection of beer mats. A dream of a place.

Arrival from 5pm.

Rooms	3: 2 doubles, 1 family room.
Price	€80. Family room €100. Extra bed €20.
Meals	Dinner with wine, €25–€30.
Closed	November–April.

Guy & Régine Dumas de Vaulx, Philippe & Martine Vast
Château de Vaulx,
63120 Ste Agathe, Puy-de-Dôme
Tel   +33 (0)4 73 51 50 55
Mobile +33 (0)6 42 01 11 94
Email   ph.vast@orange.fr
Web   www.chateaudevaulx.fr

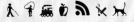

Entry 569 Map 10

Auvergne

Domaine de Gaudon - Le Château

Out in wildest Auvergne, tranquillity and the unexpected: a fortified farm next door, new Medici urns outside, 19th-century splendour inside — glossy oak panelling, fine stucco, original glowing blue paint. Alain and Monique, endearingly natural and communicative, have created a setting of astonishing brass, gilt and quilted glamour for their French antiques. Add splendid bathrooms, dazzling breakfasts, specimen trees, serenading frogs, bats, birds and insects (some in frames), herons fishing in the ponds — in the park. Children and adults love it, one and all.

Wellness Centre opens in 2013.

Rooms	5: 3 doubles, 1 twin, 1 suite.
Price	€110. Suite €130. Extra bed €25.
Meals	Supper trays available. Restaurant 4km.
Closed	Rarely.

Alain & Monique Bozzo
Domaine de Gaudon - Le Château,
63520 Ceilloux,
Puy-de-Dôme
Tel   +33 (0)4 73 70 76 25
Email   domainedegaudon@wanadoo.fr
Web   www.domainedegaudon.fr

Entry 570 Map 10

Auvergne

Château Royal de Saint-Saturnin

A volcanic region is the perfect cradle for this magnificently turreted and castellated fortress, high on the forested fringes of one of France's most beautiful villages. A stone spiral, worn with age and history, leads to five swish bedrooms in the oldest wing. The Louis XIII suite, its bathroom tucked into a tower, spans the castle's width; views are to tumbling rooftops and gardens and parkland behind. The vaulted dining room, decked with gleaming coppers, is the background for relaxed breakfast spreads, and your hosts are friendly and well-travelled. Once owned by Catherine de Médici, now open to the public.

Auvergne

Les Frênes

Perched above Saint Nectaire, the old farmhouse has stupendous views from its hillside garden of the Romanesque jewel below and woods and mountains soaring beyond. Monique, chatty and knowledgeable, enthuses her guests with descriptions of the Auvergne in perfect English. She doesn't pretend to offer luxury, just the cosy comfort of a real home. You stay in an attached one-bedroom cottage with a shower and kitchen area downstairs. Breakfast is in Monique and Daniel's vaulted dining room, full of exposed beams and stone; eat copiously and enjoy the humour, zest and kindness of a couple who were born to hospitality. Astonishing value.

Rooms	5: 2 doubles, 3 suites.
Price	€200–€240. Suite €240–€270. Special rates for 2+ people in suites, and for stays of 2 nights or more.
Meals	Breakfast €15 (€10 for child under 10). Restaurant 1.5km.
Closed	Mid-November to end March.

Rooms	1 cottage for 2.
Price	€55.
Meals	Restaurants in St Nectaire, 2km.
Closed	Rarely.

Emmanuel & Christine Pénicaud
Château Royal de Saint-Saturnin,
Place de l'Ormeau,
63450 St Saturnin, Puy-de-Dôme
Tel   +33 (0)4 73 39 39 64
Email chateaudesaintsaturnin@yahoo.fr
Web   www.chateaudesaintsaturnin.com

Monique Deforge
Les Frênes,
Sailles, 63710 St Nectaire,
Puy-de-Dôme
Tel   +33 (0)4 73 88 40 08
Email daniel.deforge@orange.fr
Web   pagesperso-orange.fr/deforge/lesfrenes

Entry 571   Map 10

Entry 572   Map 10

Auvergne

La Closerie de Manou

The rambling old house sits solid among the ancient volcanoes of Auvergne where great rivers rise and water is pure (it's in the taps here). There's a fine garden for games, a family-sized dining table before the great fireplace and a mixed bag of friendly armchairs guarded by a beautiful Alsatian stove in the salon. The décor is properly, comfortably rustic, bedrooms are lightly floral, no bows or furbelows, just pretty warmth and good shower rooms. Maryvonne, intelligent and chatty, knows and loves the Auvergne in depth and serves a scrumptious breakfast. A great find for walkers.

Minimum two nights July/Aug.

Rooms	5: 2 doubles, 1 twin/double, 1 family room, 1 suite.
Price	€85–€90. Family room & suite €85–€120. Extra bed €30. Whole house available.
Meals	Restaurant in village, 0.3km.
Closed	Mid-October to March.

Françoise & Maryvonne Larcher
La Closerie de Manou,
Le Genestoux, 63240 Le Mont Dore,
Puy-de-Dôme
Tel +33 (0)4 73 65 26 81
Mobile +33 (0)6 08 54 50 16
Email laclomeriedemanou@orange.fr
Web www.laclomeriedemanou.com

Entry 573   Map 10

Auvergne

Château de Pasredon

Whichever splendid room is yours – we loved the four-poster 'Jouy' with its waltz-in bathroom – you will feel grand: here a superbly inlaid armoire, there an exquisite little dressing room, everywhere shimmering mirrors, fabulous views of uninterrupted parkland, ancient trees, older volcanoes, acres of space for those who like to read in a secluded spot to the magical sound of birdsong. The vast, panelled, period-furnished drawing and dining rooms are quite dramatic. A perfectly cultured, relaxed hostess, Madame makes you feel instantly at ease and helps you plan your day over a delicious breakfast. Really very special.

Rooms	3: 2 doubles, 1 twin.
Price	€85–€110.
Meals	Restaurants 2km.
Closed	Mid-October to mid-April.

Henriette Marchand
Château de Pasredon,
63500 St Rémy de Chargnat,
Puy-de-Dôme
Tel +33 (0)4 73 71 00 67
Email chateau.de.pasredon@orange.fr

Entry 574   Map 10

Auvergne

Le Relais de la Diligence

They are listed as an equestrian stopover – horses spend the night in the field behind – and walkers and cyclists are extremely welcome too. Laurette, gentle and humorous, is proud of her rooms, which are authentically, charmingly French, and Peter is a talented craftsman: note the decorative wood-burner in the sitting room. Their shared interest in restoration comes together in this old village inn with its carefully restored beams, warm colours and sweet painted furniture. Breakfast is lovely with homemade jams; good simple suppers are enjoyed at the refectory table. You'll feel very much at home.

Members of the French federation of horse-trekking stopovers (FRETE).

Rooms	3: 1 double, 1 family room for 3, 1 family room for 4.
Price	€55. Family room for 3, €60. Family room for 4, €85.
Meals	Dinner with wine, 3 courses, €18; 4 courses, €21.
Closed	Rarely.

Peter & Laurette Eggleton
Le Relais de la Diligence,
Le Bourg,
63630 St Bonnet le Chastel,
Puy-de-Dôme

Tel	+33 (0)4 73 72 57 96
Email	leseggleton@aliceadsl.fr
Web	www.relais-diligence.com

Auvergne

La Jacquerolle

Built on the ramparts of the ancient town, just below the medieval Abbey whose August music festival draws thousands, the big, atmospheric old house has been lined with wood and lovingly filled with flowers in every form – carpets, curtains, wallpaper, quilts. It is a soft French boudoir where mother and daughter, quietly attentive, welcome their guests to sleep in cosy bedrooms, some with wonderful views out to the hills, all with firm beds and good little bathrooms. (Ask for the largest.) French country cuisine is served on bone china with bohemian crystal before a huge stone fireplace.

Rooms	3: 1 double, 1 family room, 1 twin.
Price	€70-€80.
Meals	Dinner with wine, €25.
Closed	Rarely.

Carole Chailly
La Jacquerolle,
Rue Marchédial,
43160 La Chaise Dieu,
Haute-Loire

Tel	+33 (0)4 43 07 60 54
Email	lajacquerolle@hotmail.com
Web	lajacquerolle.com

Auvergne

Château de Chazelles

Off the beaten track amid the mountains of the Auvergne, a renovated château, an understated gem. Outside are romantic, child-friendly walled gardens awash with lime trees, pines and weeping birch; inside are large, light, impeccable bedrooms with sublime views. Ornate four-posters, Jouy-print wallpaper, framed 30s fashion ads and fine painted furniture exude stylish comfort, deep roll top baths are delicious after a day's hiking, the lovely sitting room has books, maps and guides to supplement your delightful, well-travelled hosts' tips for trekking, riding and exploring – and Frank's travel pics are stunning.

Rooms	3: 1 double, 1 suite for 2-4, 1 suite for 4-6.
Price	€75.
Meals	Dinner with wine, €25. Picnic lunch available. Restaurant 4km.
Closed	November-March.

Cathy Wainwright
Château de Chazelles,
43130 St André de Chalencon,
Haute-Loire
Tel   +33 (0)4 71 58 49 17
Email   info@chateau-chazelles.com
Web   www.chateau-chazelles.com

Entry 577   Map 11

Auvergne

Château de Durianne

At the entrance to the gorges of the Loire is the House of Durianne where garrisons of soldiers once kept watch; the Chambons have poured heart and soul into rescuing the family château. Nothing had been touched for a century; in the attics was 120-year-old wallpaper which they lovingly re-used. Now the place, its portraits and antiques, feels like home. The huge bedroom overlooks a farm where they keep sheep, the cultivated garden leads to the orchard, the village is just down the lane. Breakfast is generous (homemade tarte, juice from their apples) and you may be joined by delightful Françoise for coffee and a chat.

Rooms	1 family suite for 2-4.
Price	Family suite €70-€80. Whole castle €800 per week (June-August).
Meals	Dinner with wine, €20. Restaurant 3km.
Closed	Rarely.

Françoise du Garay
Château de Durianne,
43700 Le Monteil, Haute-Loire
Tel   +33 (0)4 71 02 90 36
Mobile +33 (0)6 80 70 59 32
Email   info@chateaudedurianne.com
Web   www.chateaudedurianne.com

Entry 578   Map 11

Auvergne

Charmance

Who said time warp? Only 30 years old, this voluminous villa is a festival of fabric flowers and powerful repro furniture, ornaments, plaster statues, hanging baskets – and the milk of human kindness. Madame is the warmest, most attentive great-grandmother you could wish for. She loves her fascinating area with passion and knowledge, starting with the splendid Romanesque church of St Paulien in rich volcanic stone. Upstairs: big rafters, carved beds, good mattresses, a magnificent dark-tiled bathroom and your own reading/TV space; downstairs: two salons, a fine terrace and garden. The road is imperceptible at night.

Extra bed available.

Rooms	1 suite for 2-3.
Price	€80-€140. Extra bed €50.
Meals	Restaurant 4km.
Closed	Never.

Léa Gibert
Charmance,
42 av de la Rochelambert,
43350 St Paulien,
Haute-Loire
Tel   +33 (0)4 71 00 44 25

Entry 579   Map 10

Auvergne

Chez l'Autre

The church bells stop at 10pm and peace descends on this medieval village high in the Auvergne, and on the Jollivets' fascinating, rambling house whose features range from 8th-century to 21st. Explore steps, passages and leafy inner patios; tread flagstones under hefty beams; browse books by the fire; pop champagne from your minibar. Two traditional bedrooms, one in the house under the rafters, have terraces with village views. Your artistic and educated hosts restore antiques, are flexible on meals (charcuterie platter to gourmet table d'hôtes), and share tips on the valley's attractions: art, archaeology, the great outdoors.

Rooms	2: 1 family room for 2-3.
	Annexe: 1 family room for 2-3.
Price	Family room €120. Extra bed €15.
Meals	Hosted dinner with wine, from €25.
	Restaurants 10km.
Closed	Rarely.

Bernard Jollivet
Chez l'Autre,
43380 Chilhac, Haute-Loire
Tel   +33 (0)4 71 77 49 98
Email jollivetb@free.fr
Web   www.chez-lautre.com

Entry 580   Map 10

Auvergne

Ferme des Prades

A real creaky old farmhouse – warm, atmospheric, unpretentious. A sweet, down-to-earth couple, Françoise and Philippe welcome company: their sons are away studying, and this is 'la France profonde'! The farm covers 150 hectares; walk for hours through pure air and inspiring landscapes – you need not see another soul. The house, destroyed in the French Revolution, was rebuilt by Napoleon's confessor. Within its solid walls are stripped floors and panelling, big rooms, comfortably worn sofas, fine armoires, muslin curtains – and Françoise's bedside tables fashioned from milk churns. Convivial dinners are great value. A treat.

Rooms	5: 3 doubles, 2 family rooms for 4-6.
Price	€64-€90.
Meals	Dinner with wine, €25.
Closed	Rarely.

Françoise & Philippe Vauché
Ferme des Prades,
Les Prades, Landeyrat,
15160 Allanche, Cantal
Tel   +33 (0)4 71 20 48 17
Mobile   +33 (0)6 88 30 79 67
Email   les-prades@wanadoo.fr
Web   www.fermedesprades.com

Entry 581   Map 10

Auvergne

La Chalinhôte

Hike, snow-shoe, fish, ride from a handsome house in a delightful village. Inside all is fresh, spotless and contemporary. This is an exemplary B&B run by friendly young hosts as green as can be, who offer you wholesome local breakfasts and adult dinners (early supper for children) at a big pine table beneath a carved country ceiling. No-nonsense, no-rugs bedrooms, three on the top floor, have soothing colours; mattresses are top-class, showers are Italian and the big family suite is filled with light. Take coffee to the pretty front garden where the birds chirrup in the Auvergne air and the church clock chimes on the hour.

Rooms	4: 1 double, 1 twin/double, 1 family room for 3, 1 family suite for 4.
Price	€60. Family room €70-€115. Under 4's free.
Meals	Dinner with wine, €20. Child under 12, €10. No charge for under 4's.
Closed	Christmas.

Olivier & Angélique Bueb
La Chalinhôte,
Le Bourg,
15170 Chalinargues, Cantal
Tel   +33 (0)4 71 20 93 25
Email   contact@lachalinhote.fr
Web   www.lachalinhote.fr

Entry 582   Map 10

Auvergne

Château de Lescure

On the southern slope of Europe's largest extinct volcano, where nine valleys radiate, stands an atmospheric 18th-century château guarded by a medieval tower where two rustic vaulted bedrooms soar. The twin has the right furbelowed drapery and, in the big inglenook kitchen, Sophie, a committed environmentalist, serves home-smoked ham, veg from her organic garden, fruit from her orchard. Michel's passions are heritage conservation and blazing trails across the hills straight from the door. They are bilingual hosts who may invite you to join in bread-making, cooking, visiting their medieval garden...

Minimum two nights in summer.

Rooms	3: 1 twin; 1 double with separate shower; 1 double with shower downstairs.
Price	€90. Extra bed €30.
Meals	Dinner with wine, €20–€30. Child €10.
Closed	December/January.

Michel Couillaud & Phoebe Sophie
Verhulst
Château de Lescure,
15230 St Martin Sous Vigouroux,
Cantal
Tel   +33 (0)4 71 73 40 91
Email   michel.couillaud@gmail.com
Web   sites.google.com/site/chateaudelescure

Entry 583   Map 10

Auvergne

La Roussière

Not another house in sight. Just the Cantal hills and a chattering stream. Brigitte and Christian live here with their son and have done much of the restoration themselves. Christian is a genius at woodwork: his golden staircase and panelling sit happily with mellow stone, old armoires, ancient ceiling hooks... There's an Alpine air to the place. Beds are excellent, meals 'en famille' are a delight: great food, good wine, mineral water from the spring. Be calmed by a serene, rustic elegance. There's an organic vegetable garden, green rolling hectares, a haven for wildlife; perfection.

Minimum two nights July/Aug.

Rooms	3: 1 double, 1 suite for 2–3, 1 suite for 3–4.
Price	€75–€95. Suite €90–€160.
Meals	Dinner with wine, €26.
Closed	Rarely.

Christian Grégoir & Brigitte
Renard
La Roussière,
15800
St Clément, Cantal
Tel   +33 (0)4 71 49 67 34
Email   info@laroussiere.fr
Web   www.laroussiere.fr

Entry 584   Map 10

Auvergne

Maison de Massigoux

So near the town, you stand beside the donkeys in clean country air and gaze down onto unreal street lights. The 1720s gentleman's residence is full of contrasts: the original time-polished timbers of the rustic-elegant staircase, ancient rafters over neat little bedrooms in the converted loft with pretty, muted colours and good modern showers (the family suite is less contemporary), Christiane's traditional dishes between hayrack and carved sideboard. The talk of old country life is fascinating and the dogs are lovely. This is the heart of wide, wild Auvergne: walk from the door, explore unsung villages, châteaux and nature parks.

Minimum two nights in family suite.

Rooms	5: 4 doubles; 1 family suite with separate shower.
Price	€70–€80. Family suite €70–€130. Extra bed €30. Child €20.
Meals	Dinner with wine, €18 (not in August). Restaurant 2km.
Closed	Rarely.

Christiane & Michel Mouret
Maison de Massigoux,
Chemin de Massigoux,
15000 Aurillac, Cantal
Tel +33 (0)4 71 48 70 25
Mobile +33 (0)6 81 31 66 24
Email massigoux@orange.fr
Web www.massigoux.com

Entry 585   Map 10

Auvergne

Les Ombrages

A fine old merchant's house in a remote little Auvergne town is the new home of your well-travelled Franco-Finnish hosts. After years of urban high flying, they are loving their quiet life among the trees and birds of the big rambling garden, the guests who come to share it all with them, and their two lively, low-slung dogs. Original timber floors warm the generous, simply comfortable rooms, brass and four-poster beds are fabulously big (Krister is Viking-tall), delicious breakfast is by the old kitchen wood burner or in the long light dining room. Walk, bike, discover myriad treasures, then return for Christine's happy French cooking.

Rooms	4: 2 doubles, 1 twin, 1 quadruple.
Price	€52–€62. Quadruple €72–€92. Extra bed €15.
Meals	Dinner with wine, €24.
Closed	Rarely.

Krister & Christine Rosendahl
Les Ombrages,
Rue d'Empeyssine,
15700 Pleaux, Cantal
Tel +33 (0)4 71 40 47 66
Mobile +33 (0)6 04 16 75 60
Email info@les-ombrages-cantal.com
Web www.les-ombrages-cantal.com

Entry 586   Map 10

Auvergne

Maison d'Hôtes de Charme La Fournio

The approach is mysterious and magical, the views to the Auvergne are spectacular, and your host likes nothing better than to share with you his enchanting home. Cherrywood glows with beeswax, copper pots shine, 18th-century floor boards creak and gorgeous old roses grow around the door. Albert is also a passionate cook, of local sausages and Cantal cheeses, homemade jams and tasty fruit purées. Listen to birds — and cow bells — from the garden, discover lovely Argentat on the Dordogne, settle in with cards by the wood-burner, retire to delicious beds dressed in hand-embroidered linen. Exquisite!

Children welcome. Cot available.

Rooms	3: 1 double, 1 family suite for 3. Cottage: 1 family suite for 3 (wc on lower floor).
Price	€95. Family room €70-€90. Cottage €90-€110.
Meals	Dinner with wine, €23. Restaurant 2km.
Closed	Rarely.

Albert Marc Charles
Maison d'Hôtes de Charme La Fournio,
Escladines, 15700 Chaussenac,
Cantal

Tel	+33 (0)4 71 69 02 68
Mobile	+33 (0)6 81 34 91 70
Email	albert.charles@wanadoo.fr
Web	www.lafournio.fr

Entry 587   Map 10

Listen to *Les Chansons D'Auvergne* before you travel. John Williams did a beautiful recording with Nana Mouskouri — long ago.

Advice on eating: 'eat food, not too much, mostly plants'. (Ref Michael Pollan). Tricky, though, in France!

A tip for parents of young children: some B&B owners will gladly let you pitch a tent for the children.

Midi – Pyrénées

Manoir de Malagorse

The refined manoir in its idyllic setting smiles again, thanks to Anna and Abel. Now bedrooms are statements of simple luxury – muted colours, quilted bedcovers – and the great kitchen is a wonder to behold: a massive fireplace, a vaulted ceiling, cookery courses in summer. Dine at the big table, or intimately if you prefer. Anna's table decorations are a match for Abel's exquisite food: napkins tied with twine, candles tall and dramatic. Book in for wine tastings and professional massages, and bring the family – children are very welcome and it's wonderful all year round. In winter they run an Alpine restaurant.

Moulin de Goth

The 13th-century mill – imaginatively, magically restored by its Australian owners – guards a garden of rare peace and beauty. Lily pads and lawns, willows, water and a sculpted horse – it is ineffably lovely. Humorous and exuberant Coral can cook you a lovely meal; Bill's life experiences make for interesting conversation. Big, dramatically raftered rooms have decorative iron beds, soft fabrics, antique chests. The stone-walled dining room, its arrow slits intact, is stunningly barrel-vaulted – but meals are mostly in the enchanting garden. Readers adore this place.

Children over 8 welcome.

Rooms	6: 3 doubles, 1 family room, 2 suites.
Price	€130–€185. Family room €160–€260. Suite €220–€390. Child bed €25. Under-ones stay free.
Meals	Light lunch from €20. Dinner €42. Wine from €20.
Closed	Rarely.

Rooms	2: 1 double, 1 triple.
Price	€80–€85. Triple €80–€105.
Meals	Dinner with wine, €27–€31.
Closed	Rarely.

Anna & Abel Congratel
Manoir de Malagorse,
46600 Cuzance, Lot

Tel	+33 (0)5 65 27 14 83
Mobile	+33 (0)6 76 74 86 08
Email	acongratel@manoir-de-malagorse.fr
Web	www.manoir-de-malagorse.fr

Coral Heath-Kauffman
Moulin de Goth,
46600 Creysse, Lot

Tel	+33 (0)5 65 32 26 04
Mobile	+33 (0)6 98 63 41 80
Email	coral.heath@orange.fr
Web	www.moulindugoth.com

Entry 588　Map 9

Entry 589　Map 9

Midi - Pyrénées

Maison de Bibby

On holiday from New Zealand, Anna fell in love with this 12th-century house and a new life opened up; she sold her art gallery (much of it landed here, most strikingly) and set about renovating. She brings an easygoing generosity to B&B – guests can join in cooking solid simple soups or casseroles, she may invite some locals to dine with you, she knits hot water bottle sleeves. The drop-dead gorgeous house is quirky, too, with deeply comfortable rooms. Up winding narrow stairs, Louis XVI chairs stand on rush-matted boards and heavy curtains hang at ancient windows. You will surely fall in love with it – and with its wonderful owner.

Minimum three nights.

Rooms	2 doubles.
Price	€120.
Meals	Dinner with wine, €20. Restaurants within walking distance.
Closed	Rarely.

Anna Bibby
Maison de Bibby,
Rue de l'Eglise,
46600 Martel, Lot
Tel   +33 (0)5 65 37 76 26
Email   annabibby@hotmail.fr
Web   www.maisondebibby.com

Entry 590   Map 9

Midi - Pyrénées

Château de Termes

The views! Sublime when the mists hang in the valleys and the sun glints on the summits. Your hospitable hosts, he a small-plane instructor who offers flying for guests, she quietly busy with her ten gîtes, have created a marvellous escape for families. More domestic than grand, their 1720s château promises three good rooms (two with bath and loo in the bedroom), a garden, a pool, play areas, short tennis, a big terrace, a small bar. Floors are stripped wood or chunky terracotta, furniture 'distressed', the suite opens to the garden, the whimsical doubles are in the tower. Kids love it.

Rooms	3: 2 doubles, 1 family suite.
Price	€64-€85. Family suite €68-€85.
Meals	Breakfast €7.50. Dinner with wine, €20-€25 (available July/Aug). Restaurant 4km.
Closed	November-March.

Pierre & Sophie Nadin
Château de Termes,
St Denis,
46600 Martel, Lot
Tel   +33 (0)5 65 32 42 03
Email   infos@chateau-de-termes.com
Web   www.chateau-de-termes.com

Entry 591   Map 9

Moulin de Fresquet

On the edge of Gramat, down a private drive, a gorgeous old mill and a big welcome from a hospitable couple. Cushioned loungers furnish sloping lawns down to the stream, the water flows beneath your feet and you will relax the second you arrive. Warm inviting bedrooms, four reached down a spiral stair, and most opening to the garden, are distinguished by taffeta curtains and fine tapestries; the private suite lies in a charming outbuilding. Gardens are a treat – a charming collection of rare ducks wander through the grounds. The region is much loved, but please note, the surroundings, whilst beautiful are not suitable for small children.

Free secure private parking available.

Le Moulin de Latreille

The mill is 13th century and Cistercian, the owners are talented and attentive, the setting is magical. Kingfishers and wild orchids, herons, hammocks and happy dogs… and it is just as wonderful inside. Furniture has been renovated and painted, books peep from alcoves, bathrooms are delightful, and you get a little private sitting room with a wood-burner. Down its own bumpy track from the village, with timeless views of cliffs, woods and weir, let the chorus of birdsong and the rush of the millrace wash over you; they even generate their own electricity. Heaven in Quercy.

Minimum two nights. Unfenced water.

Rooms	5: 1 double, 2 twins/doubles, 2 suites.
Price	€69-€118. Suites €99-€138.
Meals	Restaurants 800m
Closed	November-March.

Rooms	2 doubles.
Price	€85.
Meals	Dinner with wine, €25. Light lunches & picnics available. Restaurant in village.
Closed	December-February.

	Gérard & Claude Ramelot
	Moulin de Fresquet,
	46500 Gramat, Lot
Tel	+33 (0)5 65 38 70 60
Email	info@moulindefresquet.com
Web	www.moulindefresquet.com

	Giles & Fi Stonor
	Le Moulin de Latreille,
	Calès, 46350 Payrac, Lot
Tel	+33 (0)5 65 41 91 83
Email	gilesetfi@gmail.com
Web	moulindelatreille.com

Midi - Pyrénées

Château de Milhac

To the top of the village, through the great gates... and there it stands, a high, dry-moated château, small, enchanting, built in 1440, sacked at the time of the Revolution. Some towers are still in ruins, the rest has been exquisitely revived. Up an outside stair is a beautiful suite with cream stone walls and a baldaquin bed, up a further (winding) stair is a slipper bath – and shower; a 16th-century tapestry furnishes a limewashed wall. These gentle Norwegian hosts live and breathe art and antiques. On one terrace is a pool (for lengths not lilos); on another, a table waiting for breakfast. The views are a glory, the comforts divine.

Minimum two nights.

Rooms	1 suite.
Price	€130.
Meals	Restaurants within walking distance.
Closed	Rarely.

Pascal Nyborg
Château de Milhac,
46300 Milhac, Lot
Tel   +33 (0)5 65 37 17 75
Email   pascal@nyborg.no
Web   www.chateau-de-milhac.fr

Entry 594   Map 9

Midi - Pyrénées

La Théronière

This mellow stone 19th-century farmhouse, secure in its delightful grounds, is within walking distance of the pretty market town of Prayssac: you have the best of all worlds. Bedrooms, subtly hued and flower-themed, are lovely, 'Gardenia' on the ground floor, 'Lavande' with a Juliet balcony. After a day's canoeing on the Lot, lapping up the honey'd streets of Sarlat, the region's markets and the cave paintings of Lascaux, it's delicious to return to cool gardens and a pool. Friendly and civilised, Karen and Tony are well-versed in looking after guests and enjoy sharing their home.

Rooms	5: 4 doubles, 1 single.
Price	€75.
Meals	Dinner with wine, €28. Restaurants in Prayssac, 1km.
Closed	Rarely.

Karen & Tony Durant-Pritchard
La Théronière,
Route de Théron,
46220 Prayssac, Lot
Tel   +33 (0)5 65 20 15 47
Email   info@theroniere.com
Web   www.theroniere.com

Entry 595   Map 9

Midi - Pyrénées

Saby

Barbara and Angus welcome you with open arms to an imposing country house in big gardens with heaps of terraces and a lovely pool. Inside are white walls, exposed stones, original beams, splashes of colour, lots of character and objets from the owners' travels including agrarian items and a pair of gothic doors! There's one guest bedroom in the house – big, comfortable and on the ground floor – and two in the barn sharing a living space and a kitchen. Bathrooms are excellent and contemporary. Breakfasts include homemade jams and local honey; and there's a restaurant in the village you can walk to.

Children over 12 welcome.

Rooms	2: 1 suite. Barn: 2 doubles (let to same party only) & kitchen.
Price	€65-€85. Barn: €85-€140.
Meals	Occasional dinner with wine, €27. Restaurants 2km.
Closed	Rarely.

Angus & Barbara McPherson
Saby,
46700 Mauroux, Lot
Tel +33 (0)5 65 23 47 11
Email barbara@cerneygardens.com

Entry 596   Map 9

Midi - Pyrénées

Mondounet

The golden Lot stone glows and the wonderful view from the breakfast terrace sweeps over two valleys. On a peaceful through road with just the postman going by, the 17th-century farmhouse has been restored to its original character, including outbuildings for gîte guests. Make friends round the fenced-in salt-purified pool, or over dinner, served before the generous fire. Zoé will charm you, see you have a good time, serve breakfast when you like. Peter plays the guitar and sings – his musical evenings are great fun. Off the lovely living room is the bedroom, simple, spacious, delightful – as is the whole place.

Rooms	1 double.
Price	€65.
Meals	Dinner with wine, €22.
Closed	Rarely.

Peter & Zoé Scott
Mondounet,
46800 Fargues, Lot
Tel +33 (0)5 65 36 96 32
Email scotsprops@aol.com
Web www.mondounetholidaysandhomes.com

Entry 597   Map 14

Midi - Pyrénées

Téranga

This happy, secluded house is charged with childhood memories. Agnès, vivacious ex-English teacher, and Francis, wine-lover and retired architect, have filled the rooms with Senegalese touches and take immense pleasure in welcoming guests. Bedrooms have wooden floors and ethnic hangings, the gardens hide a delicious pool and the long vine-strewn veranda is the perfect spot for breakfast gâteaux and jams. Discover restaurants in old Pradines, history in lovely Cahors (a short drive), and the river Lot for watery adventures.

Minimum two nights.

Rooms	2 doubles.
Price	€74.
Meals	Restaurants 10-minute walk.
Closed	November-March.

Agnès & Francis Sevrin-Cance
Téranga,
303 av Adeline Cubaynes,
46090 Pradines, Lot

Tel	+33 (0)5 65 35 20 51
Email	chambres.teranga@orange.fr
Web	www.chambresteranga.com

Entry 598 Map 9

Midi - Pyrénées

Domaine de Labarthe

These vital, welcoming, interesting people, who are in the wine trade and grow walnuts, have turned one wing of the handsome old family house into elegant B&B rooms, two in subtle designer colours, one in traditional cosy French style. The two-storey pigeonnier would be perfect for a small family. Laurence's dinners alone are worth the visit, then there's the fine pool on the olive-studded terrace, the rose garden and Italianate formality rolling past walnut groves to the Lot countryside, gastronomy and wine, old villages and unmissable Cahors. Such wealth.

Minimum two nights in summer.

Rooms	4: 1 double, 2 twins/doubles, 1 duplex suite for 2-3 with kitchenette.
Price	€115-€120. Suite €130.
Meals	Occasional dinner, 3 courses, €25.
Closed	Rarely.

Laurence & Guillaume Bardin
Domaine de Labarthe,
46090 Espère, Lot

Tel	+33 (0)5 65 30 92 34
Email	contact@domaine-de-labarthe.com
Web	www.domainedelabarthe.com

Entry 599 Map 9

Midi - Pyrénées

Mas de Garrigue

Match natural Irish hospitality with the personality of a many-layered French house and you have a marriage made in heaven. Sarah creates fine pâtés from the pigs Steve raises on the veg patch in winter and serves them with onion jam made with onions grown there in summer: they care deeply about their food and its sourcing. The big, unusual house has an elegance all its own: vast rooms, supremely beamed and raftered, are furnished with quiet taste, Irish antiques and the occasional contemporary flourish; beds are the best you've ever slept in, each bathroom a poem. They are a lovely, witty couple, generous to a fault.

Minimum two nights July/Aug. Minimum groups of 6 in winter.

Rooms	4: 3 doubles, 1 twin.
Price	€95–€110.
Meals	Dinner with wine, €35.
Closed	November–March.

Sarah Lloyd & Steven Allen
Mas de Garrigue,
La Garrigue,
46160 Calvignac, Lot
Tel   +33 (0)5 65 53 93 31
Email   info@masdegarrigue.com
Web   www.masdegarrigue.com

Entry 600   Map 10

Midi - Pyrénées

Les Jardins de la Contie

Ken and Sabine have rescued a ruined hamlet and created a place of rustic charm. It is delightfully quirky, very comfortable, all knobbly-stone walls, flagged floors, beams, arches and inglenooks. Traditional bedrooms in separate buildings, each with a private outdoor spot, have country antiques, cosy beds, good linen. In the huge breakfast room you feast on hams, cheeses and fruit from their trees: the lush gardens are full of them, fragrant shrubs too, so pick a lounger and settle in. Lovely people, big saltwater pool, great walks from the house, views to die for – yet the shortest drive from civilisation.

Rooms	2: 1 double, 1 suite for 2 with kitchenette.
Price	€60–€95.
Meals	Restaurants 3km.
Closed	November–March.

Sabine & Ken Lazarus
Les Jardins de la Contie,
La Contie,
46100 Lunan, Lot
Mobile   +33 (0)6 11 64 78 57
Email   sablaz@nordnet.fr
Web   www.lacontie.com

Entry 601   Map 10

Midi - Pyrénées

Les Chimères

In a wonderful hilltop village is a big old house with a painted wrought-iron gate and matching shutters – inside and out oozes character and history. Find magazines, books, paintings, antiques, playing cards, flowers, pottery on dressers, cats on chairs and a huge fireplace in the kitchen where lovely Lisanne creates great meals and breakfasts to remember (breads, brioche, fruits, yogurts, cheese, ham and divine jams). Big bedrooms, reached via 12th-century stone stairs, are equally charming. Bathrooms are luxurious, bathrobes are colourful, there are fans, books and irons – and gorgeous views from garden and house.

Rooms	2: 1 double, 1 twin.
Price	€60-€68. Singles €48. Extra bed €10.
Meals	Dinner with wine, €27. Child under 12, €12. Restaurants within walking distance.
Closed	Rarely.

Lisanne Ashton
Les Chimères,
23 av Louis Bessières,
82240 Puylaroque,
Tarn-et-Garonne

Tel   +33 (0)5 63 31 25 71
Email   aux-chimeres@orange.fr
Web   www.aux-chimeres.com

Entry 602   Map 14

Midi - Pyrénées

Green Chambre d'Hôte

Under pollution-free skies, amid acres of meadow and woodland, a green paradise unfolds. Taking on a hunter's shack, this couple renovated their patch simply and with love and attention. Sid and Laura are a delight, as is their colourful organic garden. Landscape gardeners and experts on wildlife, they are also virtually self-sufficient; home-grown veggie cuisine for supper, solar powered everything and natural pest control. Overlooking lavender garden and vine-covered terrace is a cosy bedroom. Watch birds by day, listen to frogs sing at night, immerse yourself in unspoilt beauty.

Extra single bed available.

Rooms	1 double.
Price	€55-€80. Child bed €15.
Meals	Dinner (vegetarian) with wine, €20. Picnic lunch available. Restaurants 10-minute drive.
Closed	Rarely.

Laura & Sid Havard
Green Chambre d'Hôte, Lausoprens,
82140 St Antonin Noble Val,
Tarn-et-Garonne

Tel   +33 (0)5 63 30 53 77
Mobile   +33 (0)6 31 99 94 31
Email   green.havard@gmail.com
Web   www.greenchambredhote.com

Entry 603   Map 14

Midi - Pyrénées

La Résidence

Your charming hosts love being part of village life – and what a village: medieval to the core and with a famous Sunday market. It is a joy to stay in a townhouse in the heart of it all, with an airy hall and a great spiral staircase, rosy floor tiles and old stone walls, and views to a delicious, sculpture-rich garden. Three of the big tranquil bedrooms overlook the garden, another has a divine terrace with rooftop views; sunlight dapples the soft colours and uncluttered spaces, modern paintings and old country pieces. Seriously into food, Sabine and Evert do excellent dinners – by arrangement only.

Studio available.

Rooms	5: 3 doubles, 2 twins.
Price	€85–€103.
Meals	Restaurants nearby.
Closed	Rarely.

Evert & Sabine Weijers
La Résidence,
37 rue Droite,
82140 St Antonin Noble Val,
Tarn-et-Garonne
Tel   +33 (0)5 63 67 37 56
Email   info@laresidence-france.com
Web   www.laresidence-france.com

Entry 604   Map 15

Midi - Pyrénées

Les Granges Tourondel

Past vineyards and woodland, zoom in on the warm stones of Tourondel: perfect rustic simplicity with modern trimmings. The two ground-floor rooms open to the garden, the upper rooms have timbered ceilings; all have spotless bathrooms. No feminine frills but uncluttered surfaces, tiled and wooden floors, and far-reaching views. Host Thierry is generous in spirit and deed, and the skills he developed as a Head Chef mean you'll enjoy hearty meals – and organic produce grown on his land. He has an exuberant passion for music so dinners can end in a musical flourish… and dozing off by the open fire. Great value.

Rooms	4: 2 triples, 2 family rooms.
Price	Triple €60–€65.
	Family room €70–€85.
Meals	Dinner with wine, €22.
	Restaurants 5km.
Closed	Rarely.

Thierry Caulliez
Les Granges Tourondel,
Bourdayrou, 82800 Bruniquel,
Tarn-et-Garonne
Tel   +33 (0)5 63 24 17 31
Mobile   +33 (0)6 87 08 80 04
Email   thierry@tourondel.com
Web   www.tourondel.com

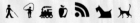

Entry 605   Map 14

Midi - Pyrénées

Le Mas des Anges

An exciting venture for a super couple who are squeaky-green too, running their organic vineyard. You find a very pretty house surrounded by lovely shrubs, a pool, and a separate entrance to each bedroom with terrace. Ground-floor rooms have fabulous colours, big good beds, bathrooms with thick towels. The sitting area is airy and modern with stacks of books, magazines and interesting sculpture and art. Sophie gives you a huge breakfast with homemade bread and jams, fresh fruit, cheeses and yogurt. Mountauban is only 7km away and you are near enough to amazing Albi for a day trip.

Rooms	3: 2 doubles, 1 family room for 3-4.
Price	€75. Family room €95-€105.
Meals	Restaurants in Montauban, 7km.
Closed	Rarely.

Juan & Sophie Kervyn
Le Mas des Anges,
1623 route de Verlhac Tescou,
82000 Montauban, Tarn-et-Garonne

Tel	+33 (0)5 63 24 27 05
Mobile	+33 (0)6 76 30 86 36
Email	info@lemasdesanges.com
Web	www.lemasdesanges.com

Entry 606   Map 14

Midi - Pyrénées

Bonjour Haut

Surveying a world of fields, woods and sky, guarded by a vast oak tree, the venerable farmhouse breathes generosity and style. No wonder the globe-trotting Bodys are infectiously happy to settle here and preserve its authenticity. The pretty country kitchen is where delightful Harriet cooks and serves meals when it's chilly on the terrace; John builds quietly outside. The big open hearth in the sitting room tells us this was once the kitchen, the mix of rustic and antique is perfect. Yours is the wonderful attic: heavily beamed, soft white all over, lit by myriad windows, graced with antique beds – and a full, open bathroom.

Cot available.

Rooms	2: 1 family room for 2-4; 1 double with shared bathroom.
Price	€65. Family room €75-€155. Child €10.
Meals	Dinner with wine, €20. Restaurant 8km.
Closed	Rarely.

Harriet & John Body
Bonjour Haut,
82220 Labarthe,
Tarn-et-Garonne

Tel	+33 (0)5 63 26 08 58
Mobile	+33 (0)6 25 05 69 69
Email	hbody@mac.com
Web	www.bonjour-haut.com

Entry 607   Map 14

Midi - Pyrénées

Tondes

Warm country people, the Sellars left a Sussex farm for a smallholding in deepest France to breed sheep, goats and poultry the natural way: no pesticides, no heavy machines, animals roaming free. Their hard work has earned them great respect locally and their recipe for a simple rewarding life includes receiving guests happily under the beams, by the wood-burning stove, in pretty-coloured, country-furnished rooms with super walk-in showers. While Julie creates homemade marvels from her farmhouse kitchen, you relax on the terrace with a glass of homemade orange liqueur and admire the garden – as wonderful as all the rest.

Rooms	2: 1 double, 1 family room.
Price	€60. Extra bed €15.
Meals	Dinner with wine, €25.
Closed	Rarely.

Julie & Mark Sellars
Tondes,
82400 Castelsagrat,
Tarn-et-Garonne
Tel +33 (0)5 63 94 52 13
Email willowweave@orange.fr

Entry 608   Map 14

Midi - Pyrénées

Au Château

A beguiling mix of grandeur and informality. The house is filled with light and life, thanks to this young Anglo-French family. Softly contemporary bedrooms, two in a separate building, are airy spaces that mix the best of modern with the loveliest of traditional: pale beams and white plaster walls, bold colours, luxurious silks, elegant antiques. There's a country-style breakfast room and a kitchenette so you can make your own suppers – then eat al fresco on the terrace. Visit historic towns, explore the Canal du Midi, let the kids roam free in the garden, stroll the charming village.

Rooms	5: 1 double, 1 triple, 1 family room, 2 suites for 2-3.
Price	€64–€83.
Meals	Cold dinner with wine, €12. Guest kitchenette. Restaurants 5-minute walk.
Closed	Rarely.

Kathrin Barker
Au Château,
1 bd des Fossés de Raoul,
82210 St Nicolas de la Grave,
Tarn-et-Garonne
Tel +33 (0)5 63 95 96 82
Email kathrin.barker@sfr.fr
Web www.au-chateau-stn.com

Entry 609   Map 14

Le Petit Feuillant

Magret de canard, beans from the garden, wines from the Côtes de Gascogne, melons from over the hill: table d'hôtes (and lots of French guests) is pure pleasure for David and Vikki. In a hilltop, out-of-the-way village, this well-restored house and barn, with its several terraces and outstanding views, has become a B&B of huge comfort and charm. Find old stone walls and tiled floors, whitewashed beams and weather-worn shutters, soft colours and uncluttered spaces, and homemade croissants for breakfast. Foodies come for the cookery courses, astronomers for the night skies. Great value.

Minimum two nights July/Aug.

Rooms	5: 3 doubles, 1 triple, 1 family room (2 doubles, 1 single).
Price	€60-€90. Triple €80-€100. Family room €70-€130.
Meals	Dinner with wine, €25. Auberge within walking distance.
Closed	Rarely.

	David & Vikki Chance
	Le Petit Feuillant,
	Le Bourg,
	82120 Gramont,
	Tarn-et-Garonne
Tel	+33 (0)5 81 78 17 00
Email	david.chance@neuf.fr
Web	www.gasconyhotels.co.uk

Entry 610   Map 14

L'Arbre d'Or

How nice to find a chambre d'hôtes that offers dinner every day (do book though), and a big garden, and a pool, in the centre of bastide Beaumont. Young, friendly and fun, Chantal and Serge are enchanted with their new B&B life. Chantal's artful sense of colour and texture brings new soul to the old place, super hangings drape the beds and renovated bathrooms seduce. The lovely heart of this old town is at the door of the handsome, well-proportioned 17th-century gent's res where tall windows let in floods of light and elegant old stairs creak as they should. Superb value, and surely the finest ginkgo biloba tree in France.

Extra bed available.

Rooms	4: 2 doubles, 2 triples.
Price	€63-€71. Triples €73-€99. Extra bed €21-€23.
Meals	Dinner €22. Wine from €5. Restaurants 1km.
Closed	Rarely.

	Chantal & Serge Néger
	L'Arbre d'Or, 16 rue Despeyrous,
	82500 Beaumont de Lomagne,
	Tarn-et-Garonne
Tel	+33 (0)5 63 65 32 34
Mobile	+33 (0)7 70 08 18 86
Email	contact@maison-hote-82.com
Web	www.maison-hote-82.com

Entry 611   Map 14

Midi - Pyrénées

La Lumiane

Such a surprise to step off a side street into a delightful garden with loungers, pool and sweet-smelling shrubs. Chatty Alain and chef Gisèle have restored this gracious house with style: rooms in the main house, up the stunning spiral staircase, breathe tradition and space, old fireplaces, big windows and antiques; those in the garden annexe have a sweetly contemporary feel. All have an uncluttered mix of florals and stripes and simple, spotless bathrooms. Eat well on local, seasonal produce in the formal dining room or on the terrace by candlelight, wake to the sound of the church bells. Much authenticity and charm.

Rooms	5 doubles.
Price	€64–€69.
Meals	Dinner with wine, €26.
Closed	Rarely.

Alain & Gisèle Eman
La Lumiane,
Grande Rue, 32310 St Puy, Gers
Tel +33 (0)5 62 28 95 95
Mobile +33 (0)6 78 18 32 24
Email info@lalumiane.com
Web www.lalumiane.com

Entry 612   Map 14

Midi - Pyrénées

Belliette

On a hill near the winding Douze river sits a 300-year-old farmhouse. It is gorgeous inside and out. Arum lilies run along the half-timbered façade, an ancient bread oven and rose-brick chimney stand at its core, beautifying each simple bedroom. The Cormiers' affection for Gascon culture and armagnac shines through. Join them for an evening meal, be serenaded by your engaging host and his guitar. Outside, deer roam and there's a delightful chicken coop full of feathery inhabitants. Catch a wisp of the Pyrenees on a clear day, enjoy vales-lovely walks, historic Eauze, summer markets and summertime jazz in Marciac.

Rooms	3: 1 double, 1 triple, 1 suite.
Price	€70. Triple €70–€90.
	Suite €80–€100. Under 3's free.
	Folding cot & baby equipment available.
Meals	Dinner with wine, €22. €10 for under 15s.
Closed	Rarely.

Marie Cormier
Belliette,
Cutxan,
32150 Cazaubon, Gers
Tel +33 (0)5 62 08 18 68
Email marie.cormier32@gmail.com
Web www.belliette.fr

Entry 613   Map 14

Maison d'Hélène

In an ancient much-loved village with a stream running through is an ivy-clad house of serenity and charm. Here lives Debbie, a landscape gardener and interior designer from London, owner of a lovely cat. Find comfort and refinement at every turn: glowing old floors, impeccable country furniture, a leopard skin thrown in for good measure. First-floor bedrooms come with spacious sweet-smelling bathrooms (one at the bottom of the beautiful stairs) and the enticing little garden has a pool. Breakfast out here on homemade jams (fig/walnut/plum), then dine in the village. Beyond are markets to explore, armagnacs to try. Wonderful.

Children over 10 welcome.

Rooms	2 doubles, each with separate bathroom.
Price	€55.
Meals	Restaurants in village.
Closed	Rarely.

Deborah Hart
Maison d'Hélène,
Route de Cazaubon,
32240 Estang, Gers
Tel   +33 (0)5 62 69 59 53
Email deborahhart2@me.com

Entry 614   Map 14

Lieu dit Fitan

Complete quiet, beautiful gardens, charmed pool – and Dido, who loves people, an inspiration to us all. In 1999 this was a derelict barn in the undulating Gers countryside; the restoration is a wonder. At the door, a superb space opens before the eyes, English antiques gleam, the fine modern kitchen sparkles (use it for a small fee). In two luscious bedrooms, one up, one down, raw stones punctuate soft yellow walls, patchwork cheers, books tempt. Dido paints (studio available), has travelled thousands of miles, loves colours and cooking fresh, light food, and is highly cultured. A corner of paradise, it even smells heavenly.

Rooms	2: 1 double, 1 twin.
Price	€70-€80.
Meals	Dinner with wine, €35. Use of kitchen €8.
Closed	Rarely.

Dido Streatfeild-Moore
Lieu dit Fitan,
32230 Louslitges, Gers
Tel   +33 (0)5 62 70 81 88
Email deedoenfrance@wanadoo.fr
Web   www.chezdeedo.com

Entry 615   Map 14

Midi - Pyrénées

Laouarde

In rolling Armagnac country: a former wine estate, an 1823 house with watchtower views. Simon and Catherine swapped London for warm limestone and blue shutters, beautiful sash windows and oak parquet, and 25 acres of meadows, orchards and peace. Wonderful breakfasts (compotes from the garden, delectable croissants) are taken by the open fire or on the pool terrace, and Simon's dinners are mouthwatering. Up the beeswax-polished stair are delicious bedrooms full of personality, from country-pretty to elegant Bourbon. Read, listen to music, take an aperitif in the walled courtyard, explore this amazing region.

Rooms	4: 2 suites, 1 twin, 1 single.
Price	€85–€110. Suite €95–€120. Single €55–€65.
Meals	Dinner €35 (Sunday-Wednesday). Restaurants 1km.
Closed	November-April, except by arrangement.

Simon & Catherine Butterworth
Laouarde,
32190 Vic Fezensac, Gers
Tel +33 (0)5 62 63 13 44
Email info@laouarde.co.uk
Web www.laouarde.com

Entry 616 Map 14

Midi - Pyrénées

Espasot

Well-tended sunflower fields roll beside tree-lined winding lanes: Gers, between Bordeaux and Toulouse, is remote and peaceful. This modest old turkey farm stands amid spreading oaks – and magnolias, limes, palms. Up ancient stairs are pristine rooms with walk-in showers, saved from minimalism by oak floors and soft beiges, blues or browns. Madame danced for the Amsterdam Ballet and offers large late breakfasts and the lowdown on walks, rides, music festivals and markets. It's five minutes to a 'prix fixe' menu in the village square. Coming soon: cookery courses by a Dutch Michelin chef in a new outdoor kitchen and lounge.

Rooms	4: 3 doubles, 1 suite.
Price	€80–€100. Singles €60–€80.
Meals	Dinner, 3 course with wine, €25. Restaurant in town.
Closed	Rarely.

Josiane Geys
Espasot,
32190 Belmont-Gers, Gers
Tel +33 (0)5 62 06 40 87
Email josiane.geys@orange.fr
Web www.espasot.nl

Entry 617 Map 14

Domaine de Peyloubère

The waterfall, the wild orchids, the swimming pool, the hosted dinners – there's no other place like it. Years ago Theresa and her late husband fell for this big romantic house, its wildlife-rich domaine and its centuries-old cedars; the enthusiasm remains undiminished, the sensitive restoration shows in every room. But the sober buildings don't prepare you for the explosion inside... late 19th-century painter Mario Cavaglieri spread his love of form and colour over ceilings and doors. Now 'his' suite has vast space, fine antiques, a dream of a bathroom, dazzling murals. Heaven for children – or an anniversary treat.

Sawday self-catering also.

Le Loubet

Surrounded by undulating wheat fields a mile from a small town is an 1850s farmhouse with symmetrical turrets, and gardens in which children can run around. Your hosts – he Irish, she with good English, and three children – welcome you in to a big airy upper-floor living space just for you: practical table, sofas with throws, DVDs, TV. Bedrooms with balconies and views are simple and spotlessly clean, one with a kitchenette and washing machine; it's ideal for families. Set off after breakfast to visit the maze garden close by – or the aquatic game centre on the lake, certain to delight teens.

Rooms	2 suites.
Price	€80–€110.
Meals	Dinner with wine, €30.
Closed	Rarely.

Rooms	2: 1 double; 1 twin/double with kitchenette & separate shower.
Price	€65. Under 2's free.
Meals	Restaurant in L'Isle Jourdain, 2km.
Closed	Rarely.

	Theresa Martin
	Domaine de Peyloubère,
	32550 Pavie - Auch, Gers
Tel	+33 (0)5 62 05 74 97
Email	martin@peyloubere.com
Web	www.peyloubere.com

	Géraldine Scannell
	Le Loubet,
	32600 L'Isle Jourdain, Gers
Tel	+33 (0)5 62 07 48 32
Mobile	+33 (0)6 89 97 19 31
Email	info@leloubet.com
Web	www.leloubet.com

Midi - Pyrénées

Le Relais de Saux

Bernard Hères inherited ancient Saux from his parents and, with the help of his late wife, opened it to guests. He knows the area thoroughly and will guide you to fine walks in the Pyrenees. High on a hill facing Lourdes and dazzling peaks, arrive in the garden, bright with lawns, terraces and quiet corners… or relax in deep armchairs in a beamed salon with a lush garden view. Bedrooms with carpeted bathrooms come in traditional mood – draped bed heads, darkly papered walls – while the two big second-floor rooms sit cosily beneath lower ceilings. (A word of warning: be careful as you leave the dual carriageway on arrival.)

Rooms	5: 3 doubles, 2 twins/doubles.
Price	€85-€96.
Meals	Restaurant 2km.
Closed	Occasionally.

Bernard Hères
Le Relais de Saux,
Route de Tarbes,
Le Hameau de Saux, 65100 Lourdes,
Hautes-Pyrénées
Tel   +33 (0)5 62 94 29 61
Email   contacts@lourdes-relais.com
Web   www.lourdes-relais.com

Entry 620   Map 14

Midi - Pyrénées

Eth Berye Petit

Beauty, harmony, tranquillity… all who stay, long to return. The grand old village *maison de maître*, in Henri's family for centuries, opens to soft green rolling meadows and the majestic Pyrenees – the finest view in all France! Ione, graceful, smiling mother of two, ushers you up the venerable stair to wonderful warm bedrooms in pastel hues – one with a balcony – and luscious beds wrapped in antique linen. The living room, where a fire roars and a fine dinner is served on winter weekends, is a delight to come home to after a day's skiing or hiking. For summer? A dreamy garden. Exceptional.

Rooms	3: 1 double, 1 twin, 1 suite.
Price	€59. Suite €64-€82.
Meals	Dinner with wine, €23. Auberge 100m.
Closed	24 December- 2 January.

Henri & Ione Vielle
Eth Berye Petit,
15 route de Vielle,
65400 Beaucens,
Hautes-Pyrénées
Tel   +33 (0)5 62 97 90 02
Email   contact@beryepetit.com
Web   www.beryepetit.com

Entry 621   Map 14

Midi - Pyrénées

La Ferme du Buret

In an enchanting Heidi-esque valley in the Haute (but gently rolling) Pyrénées is a long low stone cattle stable tucked into the hills, with a barn attached. Each superb structure houses two guest bedrooms. From lofty beams to floor, interiors are lined with thick wide planks of cedar, chestnut, acacia and oak; rustic-chic fabrics and sleek bathroom fittings add to the spare, but never spartan, charm. Cathy is a champion skier and can ski-guide you, Pierre is an inspired chef of regional dinners served indoors or out at an enormous table with magnificent views. Sports and thermal spas abound, the scenery makes the heart sing.

Rooms	4: 2 twins/doubles, 2 family rooms.
Price	€90-€110. Extra bed €20.
Meals	Dinner with wine, €25.
Closed	Mid-November to January (open Christmas to New Year).

Pierre & Cathy Faye
La Ferme du Buret,
65130 Asque,
Hautes-Pyrénées
Tel   +33 (0)5 62 39 19 26
Mobile   +33 (0)6 86 77 33 71
Email   info@lafermeduburet.com
Web   www.lafermeduburet.com

Entry 622   Map 14

Midi - Pyrénées

Domaine de Jean-Pierre

Madame is gracefully down to earth and her house and garden an oasis of calm where you may share her delight in playing the piano or golf (3km) and possibly make a lifelong friend. Built in Napoleon's time, her house has an elegant hall, big airy bedrooms and great bathrooms, while fine furniture and linen sheets reflect her pride in her ancestral home – a combination of uncluttered space and character. The huge triple has space to waltz in and the smallest bathroom; the colours chosen are peaceful and harmonious; and breakfast comes with an array of honeys and civilised conversation. Great value.

Rooms	3: 2 doubles, 1 triple.
Price	€60. Triple €80.
Meals	Restaurants 3km.
Closed	Rarely.

Marie-Sabine Colombier
Domaine de Jean-Pierre,
20 route de Villeneuve,
65300 Pinas, Hautes-Pyrénées
Tel   +33 (0)5 62 98 15 08
Mobile   +33 (0)6 84 57 15 69
Email   marie@domainedejeanpierre.com
Web   www.domainedejeanpierre.com

Entry 623   Map 14

Midi - Pyrénées

La Souleillane

Fabienne and Jean-Luc have done an amazing restoration, and guest rooms at 'Sunnyside' are appropriately big and bright: the cheery yellow family room in the house, the restful doubles in the barn. Having young boys of their own, they make children very welcome and give them the run of the walled garden. Your hosts work so you may be left alone in the morning; come evening, Fabienne enjoys cooking and chatting round the table while Jean-Luc, Pyrenean born and bred, is an interesting source of mountaineering escapades. No sitting room but a large covered terrace for summer. And there's cross-country skiing nearby. Lovely.

Extra family room for 4 available.

Rooms	3: 1 double. Barn: 2 doubles.
Price	€60. Extra bed €10.
Meals	Dinner with wine, €19.
Closed	Rarely.

Fabienne & Jean-Luc Garcia
La Souleillane,
4 rue de l'Ancienne Poste,
65150 St Laurent de Neste,
Hautes-Pyrénées

Tel	+33 (0)5 62 39 76 01
Email	info@souleillane.com
Web	www.souleillane.com

Entry 624 Map 14

Midi - Pyrénées

Ancienne Poste Avajan

Up the long winding mountain road to a renovated lodge with a deck for lounging and a garden in the offing – it's hard to imagine the post was ever sorted here! Sojourns are packaged for sport-orientated winters and summers, a chef provides energy-charged Alpine breakfasts and dinners, and James offers free two-day ski and snow tours. An outward bound professional par excellence, he loves what he does and makes this place buzz. There's a big dining-cum-sitting room with leather sofas, wood-burner and bar, a snug for quiet moments and six bedrooms in countrified modern style. All feels comfortable, inviting, great fun.

Minimum four nights.

Rooms	6: 2 doubles, 2 triples, 1 twin, 1 bunk room.
Price	Half-board: €256. Bunk room €197. Catered summer & winter activity packages. Full-board €890–€899 p.p. per week; half-board from €699 p.p. per week.
Meals	All prices half-board for 2 per night.
Closed	Rarely.

James Dealtry
Ancienne Poste Avajan,
65240 Avajan,
Hautes-Pyrénées

Tel	+33 (0)5 62 40 53 17
Mobile	+33 (0)6 09 49 73 80
Email	james@ancienneposteavajan.com
Web	www.ancienneposteavajan.com

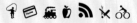

Entry 625 Map 14

Midi - Pyrénées

La Genade

Up in her beloved mountains with the wild streams splashing and an unbroken view of 13th-century Lordat, Meredith loves sharing her heaven. A passionate climber, skier and cyclist, she rebuilt a ruined auberge: old stones and new wood, craggy beams, precious furniture and a cheery fire make it rustic, warm and elegant. Under truly American care, rooms have fine linens, oriental rugs and books. The welcome is genuine, breakfast is fresh and generous, dinners are animated and delicious. Walkers and cyclists should stay a week, and there's a repair room specially for bikes. Remarkable value.

Children over 6 welcome. Minimum two nights (minimum one for cyclists).

Rooms	3: 2 doubles, 1 twin.
Price	€55-€65. Twin €70. Extra bed €10.
Meals	Dinner with wine, €20-€24.
Closed	Rarely.

Meredith Dickinson
La Genade,
La route des Corniches,
09250 Axiat, Ariège
Tel   +33 (0)5 61 05 51 54
Mobile   +33 (0)9 62 29 51 52
Email   meredith.dickinson@orange.fr
Web   www.chambre-dhote-pyrenees-lagenade.com

Entry 626   Map 14

Midi - Pyrénées

Las Coumeilles

A Pyrenean paradise, an idyllic and remote spot for nature lovers and birdwatchers – great walks start from the door. Look out over extensive grounds, pretty lanes and glorious countryside, relax with a pre-dinner drink by the wood-burner, tuck into breakfast on a private sun terrace. Uncover rare orchids nearby, dip into the heated pool, play tennis, feast in an open-air summer kitchen. Jump at dinner if proffered – Tom is curry king, Trish is the unparalleled queen of desserts. The spotless bedrooms will charm you, towels abound; nab the 'Moon Room' for superlative views. You'll love the Ariège – and its capital, Foix.

Rooms	3: 1 double, 1 twin, 1 family room (3 doubles) for 2-6.
Price	€65-€75. Family room €115-€130. Extra bed €10.
Meals	Dinner, 3-4 courses with wine, €20-€25. Light supper €13. Restaurants 2km.
Closed	December/January.

Tom & Trish Littmann
Las Coumeilles,
Le Village, 09300 Leychert, Ariège
Tel   +33 (0)5 61 02 61 94
Mobile   +33 (0)6 72 37 16 57
Email   tomlittmann@hotmail.com
Web   www.ariegebedandbreakfast.com

Entry 627   Map 14

Midi - Pyrénées

Impasse du Temple

Breakfast among the remains of a Protestant chapel, sleep in a townhouse, one of a terrace built in 1758; John and Lee-Anne are its second owners. Delightful, humorous Australians, they are restoring their elegant mansion and loving it. Graciously high ceilings, a sweeping spiral staircase, lovely great windows in an oasis of ancient, stream-kissed oaks... arrive as strangers, leave as friends. The food is fantastic and the pastel-shaded bedrooms are generous, with just enough antiques; one even has the vast original claw-footed bath. The attention to detail is exceptional and guests sing their praises.

Sawday self-catering also.

Rooms	5: 2 doubles, 2 triples, 1 suite.
Price	€80–€90. Suite €116–€130. Extra bed €25.
Meals	Dinner €25. Wine €9–€20. Restaurant nearby.
Closed	Rarely.

John & Lee-Anne Furness
Impasse du Temple,
09600 Léran, Ariège
Tel +33 (0)5 61 01 50 02
Mobile +33 (0)6 88 19 49 22
Email john.furness@wanadoo.fr
Web www.chezfurness.com

Entry 628 Map 15

Midi - Pyrénées

La Ferme de Boyer

Your hosts, fun, humorous and with interesting pasts, have filled the big rambling farmhouse with polished mahogany and family memorabilia and the garden with shrubs and lawns. He was once a helicopter engineer and loves classic cars, she is a Cordon Bleu cook; both designed furniture for first-class hotels and worked for hotels in Paris. Now they run a sparkling B&B. Bedrooms are sunny and charming, more English than French with pastoral views, the family room is large and self-contained, Harriet's dinners are convivial and delicious, and sweet Mirepoix is just down the road.

Separate family suite for 4 & kitchenette available.

Rooms	2: 1 double, 1 twin.
Price	€65–€80.
Meals	Dinner with wine, €30.
Closed	Rarely.

Robert & Harriet Stow
La Ferme de Boyer,
09500 Coutens - Mirepoix, Ariège
Tel +33 (0)5 61 68 93 41
Mobile +33 (0)6 22 04 05 84
Email ferme.boyer@wanadoo.fr
Web www.fermeboyer.iowners.net

Entry 629 Map 15

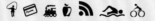

Midi - Pyrénées

Gratia

Luscious texture combinations of original floor tiles discovered, virgin, in the attic and stupendous carpentry: loving hands crafted Gratia in the 1790s; flair and hard work brought it back from ruin in the 1990s. Jean-Paul's motto 'less is more' informs the wonderful uncluttered bedrooms with their pretty beds and linens; Florence, chic and charming, will do physiotherapy in the great attic studio – mats, music, massage; the ethos is 'polished and cool', the attitude is determinedly green, breakfast is perfect. Chill out on the manicured lawn by the saltwater pool, converse delightfully, depart thoroughly renewed.

Rooms	3 doubles.
Price	€90-€120.
Meals	Restaurants 3km.
Closed	Mid-September to April.

Florence Potey & Jean-Paul
Wallaert
Gratia,
09210 Lézat sur Lèze, Ariège
Tel   +33 (0)5 61 68 64 47
Email   ferme.gratia@wanadoo.fr
Web   www.ariege.com/gratia

Entry 630   Map 14

Midi - Pyrénées

Chaumarty

Head up, up to a hilltop farmhouse with panoramic views to the Pyrenees and a lovely family who've spent 12 years fixing up their eco-friendly home. It's all hemp, lime, wood and terracotta, solar energy, a natural swimming 'bassin', horses, a donkey, a sand pit and a swing for your kids to share with theirs... such fun. Inside are two big, beamed guest rooms with country antiques, good beds and walk-in ochre showers. Sink into an easy chair by the wood-burner and browse books that reveal a passion for all things bio... as do family dinners with Italian-Swiss Stefano and Violaine from Bordeaux. Great value, too.

Rooms	2: 1 double, 1 family room.
Price	€60-€75. Family room €80-€95.
Meals	Dinner with wine, €18. Restaurant 5km.
Closed	Rarely.

Violaine & Stefano Comolli
Chaumarty,
31550 Gaillac-Toulza,
Haute-Garonne
Tel   +33 (0)5 61 08 68 64
Email   chaumarty@free.fr
Web   www.chaumarty.com

Entry 631   Map 14

Midi - Pyrénées

Les Pesques

Surrounded by rolling farmland, at the end of a quiet lane, a gorgeous old manor house in a luxuriant garden – a happy place and home. Brigitte has decorated in peaceful good taste and all is charmingly cluttered, each country antique the right one. Unsophisticated bedrooms have white walls, vintage iron beds, fresh white linen and old terracotta floors; one has a wisteria-draped balcony; the newest smiles in soft nuances of colonial blue. A dreamy, comfortable, joyful house run by Brigitte, who concocts lovely fresh meals from vegetables from the potager and eggs from the hens. Great value.

Rooms	3: 1 double, 1 twin, 1 family room.
Price	€60.
Meals	Dinner with wine, €20.
Closed	Rarely.

Brigitte & Bruno Lebris
Les Pesques,
31220 Palaminy,
Haute-Garonne
Tel   +33 (0)5 61 97 59 28
Email   reserve@les-pesques.com
Web   www.les-pesques.com

Entry 632   Map 14

Midi - Pyrénées

Au Delà du Temps

The owners, ex-wine-growers from the Charente, love their new life in the lush Pyrenees, on the outskirts of this turn-of-the-century spa town. Outside: a small harmonious Japanese style garden with a swimming pool. Inside: three alpine suites clad in pale pine, cosy, warm with excellent bathrooms – perfect for families. A lovely breakfast of croissants, brioche, apple tart, served with candles and Scandinavian touches, sets you up for some hearty hiking and skiing: Luchon's lift whisks you to the top of the mountain. Or go shopping in Spain, or wallow in the town's spa; your friendly hosts know their patch well.

Rooms	3: 1 suite for 2 with kitchen, 1 suite for 2-4, 1 suite for 2-4 with kitchen.
Price	€84-€122.
Meals	Restaurants 15-minute walk.
Closed	Mid November-mid December.

Frédérique & François Roy
Au Delà du Temps,
28 av de Gascogne,
31110 St Mamet, Haute-Garonne
Tel   +33 (0)5 61 89 13 53
Mobile   +33 (0)6 18 64 14 29
Email   suedcognac@wanadoo.fr
Web   www.gite-luchon.com

Entry 633   Map 14

Midi - Pyrénées

La Maison du Lac

This grand Gascogne house, with its yellow ochre façade, was saved from ruin by the Charons. They faithfully restored it and are generous enough to share! French and English antiques from Patrick's Gloucester grandmother meet textiles from North Africa, where Nicole's roots are. Guests have the salon – once the kitchen – with its wide stone hearth and billiard table. Oak floored rooms are elegant; twin beds can be added to the open-plan suite for a family. You can breakfast on the terrace, in the summer dining room or by the pool. Nicole is a talented cook and does noon-time grillades from her summer kitchen, and dinner on the south-facing terrace.

Minimum two nights.

Château de Séguenville

Séguenville, a 13th-century château rebuilt in 1653, has been in Marie's family for years – we love its slightly frayed charm. And its decoration – simple, elegant and full of personality, just like its owner! Galleried bedrooms have marble fireplaces and creaky floors, a painted ceiling was recently unearthed. Outside are a swimming pool and a terrace with ancient-parkland views; visit the chateau's windmill, still grinding flour. Marie, who has children of her own, particularly enjoys having families to stay. Ask about her gourmet dinners, or spin off on a bike into stunning countryside.

Rooms	4: 2 doubles, 1 twin, 1 suite.
Price	€80. Suite €90. Singles €70-80. Extra bed €10.
Meals	Dinner with wine, €25. Restaurant 2km.
Closed	December to Easter.

Rooms	5: 3 doubles, 1 family room, 1 suite.
Price	€120. Suite €135. Family room €200.
Meals	Dinner, 3 courses, €30. Wine from €7.
Closed	15 December-15 January.

	Patrick & Nicole Charon
	La Maison du Lac,
	Lieu dit Michalet,
	31350 Boulogne sur Gesse,
	Haute-Garonne
Tel	+33 (0)5 61 88 92 16
Email	nicole.charon@hotmail.fr
Web	www.lamaisondulacgascogne.com

	Marie Lareng
	Château de Séguenville,
	Région de Toulouse,
	31480 Cabanac Séguenville,
	Haute-Garonne
Tel	+33 (0)5 62 13 42 67
Email	info@chateau-de-seguenville.com
Web	www.chateau-de-seguenville.com

Entry 634   Map 14

Entry 635   Map 14

Midi - Pyrénées

La Villa les Pins

In a vast parkland of deciduous trees is a house of marble floors and crystal chandeliers, built by Marie's father in grand old French style. The salon has a huge stone fireplace lit on cool days, the bedrooms are plush with fitted carpets, canopied beds and floral walls, and Marie, ex-hotelier, warm, friendly and quietly spoken, is a natural hostess. Wake to delicious jams and viennoiserie served at dressed tables; catch the bus from Vacquiers and spend the day in Toulouse; return to soak in a deep scented tub before popping out for dinner in the village. Space and comfort abound.

Rooms	5: 2 doubles, 2 suites, 1 twin.
Price	€85-€95.
	Suite €105-€155.
Meals	Restaurant 2km.
Closed	Rarely.

	Marie Daigre
	La Villa les Pins,
	1660 route de Bouloc,
	31340 Vacquiers, Haute-Garonne
Tel	+33 (0)5 61 84 96 04
Email	villalespins@9business.fr
Web	www.lavillalespins.com

Midi - Pyrénées

La Ferme d'en Pécoul

Talented Élisabeth makes jams, jellies and liqueurs, pâté, confit and foie gras, keeps hens and is wonderfully kind. Almost-retired Noël gently tends the potager as well as the fields; wrap yourself in the natural warmth of their Lauragais farmhouse. The first floor is lined with new wood, there's an airy guest sitting room and two comfy bedrooms with tiny showers. Summer meals are outside, enjoyed with your hosts. One dog, two cats, fields as far as the eye can see – and exquisite medieval Caraman (once rich from the dye cocagne) just down the road. Great value.

Minimum two nights weekends & summer holidays. Single child's room on request.

Rooms	2 doubles.
Price	€48.
Meals	Dinner with wine, €18.
Closed	Rarely.

	Élisabeth & Noël Messal
	La Ferme d'en Pécoul,
	31460 Cambiac, Haute-Garonne
Tel	+33 (0)5 61 83 16 13
Mobile	+33 (0)6 78 13 18 07
Email	enpecoul@wanadoo.fr
Web	pagesperso-orange.fr/enpecoul

Midi - Pyrénées

Les Loges de St Sernin

Vast welcoming comfort lies in store behind those superb wooden doors in the heart of Toulouse – and no expense spared. Madame, living on the third floor, is a poppet: petite, delightful, up to speed with this vibrant town. Big peaceful guest bedrooms spread themselves across the floor below, each with warm colours, a huge bed, an antique mirror, luxurious linen. Breakfast is served on a balcony in good weather, as early or as late as you like it. Period detail abounds: inside shutters, marble fireplaces, sweeping parquet, tall windows beautifully dressed – Madame aims to please. Marvellous!

Minimum two nights at weekends March-October.

Rooms	4: 2 doubles, 2 twins.
Price	€125-€140. Extra bed €25-€35.
Meals	Restaurants within walking distance.
Closed	Rarely.

Sylviane Tatin
Les Loges de St Sernin,
12 rue St Bernard,
31000 Toulouse, Haute-Garonne
Tel   +33 (0)5 61 24 44 44
Mobile +33 (0)6 60 35 80 43
Email   logesaintsernin@live.fr
Web   www.leslogesdesaintsernin.com

Entry 638   Map 14

Midi - Pyrénées

Chambres d'Hôtes Les Brunes

Swish through large wooden gates into a central courtyard and garden filled with birdsong to find lovely Monique and her 18th-century family home, complete with tower. Bedrooms are up the spiral stone tower staircase which oozes atmosphere; all are a good size ('Le Clos' is enormous) and filled with beautiful things. Antiques, beams, rugs, gilt mirrors and soft colours give an uncluttered, elegant feel; bathrooms are luxurious, views from all are lovely. You breakfast on homemade cake, farm butter and fruit salad in the handsome farmhouse kitchen.

Minimum two nights during school holidays preferred.

Rooms	4: 2 doubles, 2 twins.
Price	€92-€148.
Meals	Guest kitchenette. Restaurant 5km.
Closed	Rarely.

Monique Philipponnat-David
Chambres d'Hôtes Les Brunes,
Hameau les Brunes,
12340 Bozouls, Aveyron
Tel   +33 (0)5 65 48 50 11
Mobile +33 (0)6 80 07 95 96
Email   lesbrunes@wanadoo.fr
Web   www.lesbrunes.com

Entry 639   Map 10

Midi - Pyrénées

Monteillet-Sanvensa

A lovely old stone mini-hamlet next door to a working farm in the calm green Aveyron where there is just so much space. Two simply decorated but charming rooms, each with their own terrace, look out over a typical medieval château. One guest room is white and yellow with a walk-in shower, the other washed-pink and white, with a super bathroom and a small kitchenette; both are cool and airy. The garden is full of flowers, the rolling views stupendous, and Monique is fun, easy-going and eager to please. Relax in one of the many shady areas in summer with a drink or a book and enjoy the birdsong.

Rooms can interconnect.

Rooms	2 doubles, one with kitchenette.
Price	€50.
Meals	Occasional dinner with wine, €22. Light suppers available, from €15.
Closed	2 weeks in September.

Monique Bateson
Monteillet-Sanvensa,
12200 Villefranche de Rouergue,
Aveyron
Tel +33 (0)5 65 29 81 01
Mobile +33 (0)6 89 28 60 76
Email monique.bateson@orange.fr

Entry 640   Map 15

Midi - Pyrénées

Les Tapies

Alive with the energy of its sporty hosts, this old family house is set in a lovely park with trees and a stream. Inside: parquet floors and high ceilings, glorious shocking-pink hall walls, an oak staircase and light spacious suites; and two beamed doubles that capture the spirit of the house as it always was. The easy-going owners love having guests, Marianne whips up a different pastry or cake for breakfast each day (eat by the pool under the giant beech trees), and Louis will tell you all about his beloved region: there's tree-climbing, sailing and walking to be done. A proper home full of kindness and fun.

Rooms	4: 2 doubles, 2 family rooms.
Price	€75-€85. Family room €110-€140.
Meals	Restaurant 1km.
Closed	Rarely.

Louis & Marianne Mouries-Martin
Les Tapies,
12630 Agen d'Aveyron, Aveyron
Tel +33 (0)5 65 42 73 57
Mobile +33 (0)6 11 66 16 80
Email mourieslouis@wanadoo.fr
Web perso.wanadoo.fr/lestapies

Entry 641   Map 15

Midi - Pyrénées

Quiers - Ferme Auberge

Escape to vast pastures and sensational views. This is an outdoorsy place and is brilliant for families: canoe, climb, hang-glide, spot birds, hunt orchids. The farm feels rustic, charming and somewhat shambolic – but in the nicest way. Bedrooms, a short walk down a steepish track, sit snugly in the old 'bergerie'; expect shiny terracotta floors, old beams, freshly painted walls, simple pine beds. In the main house are tapestries and country antiques smelling of years of polish. Here, Véronique and her chef brother produce wonderful big meals of home-grown organic produce.

Rooms	5: 2 doubles, 2 twins, 1 family room.
Price	€65.
Meals	Dinner €20-€24. Wine €10-€22. Restaurants in Millau.
Closed	November-April.

Véronique Lombard
Quiers - Ferme Auberge,
12520 Compeyre,
Aveyron
Tel   +33 (0)5 65 59 85 10
Email   quiers@wanadoo.fr
Web   www.quiers.net

Entry 642   Map 15

Midi - Pyrénées

Montels

The rolling Languedoc hills are wild and ancient, and the views from the little garden are lovely… you can even watch paragliders launching from the cliff. It matters little that Madame speaks no English: she is so kind and welcoming. In this modern house she gives you two bedrooms, bright, sweet and spotless, and a very delightful third, just up the track in her daughter's house, complete with its own terrace and views. The family used to tend sheep and you can still enjoy Madame's 'lafloune', a sheep's-milk cake, at breakfast. Great value for money – and there's a lovely new conservatory for guests.

Rooms	3: 1 triple, 1 family room for 4. House up track: 1 double.
Price	€50. Family room €80.
Meals	Restaurants in Millau, 3km.
Closed	Rarely.

Henriette Cassan
Montels,
12100 Millau,
Aveyron
Tel   +33 (0)5 65 60 51 70

Entry 643   Map 15

Midi - Pyrénées

Le Gouty

A lovely old farmhouse on two levels, a terrace at the back for meals (lots of produce from sweet neighbours) and the dreamiest sunsets and views – Phillipe and Lynda, embarking on a new life in France, love the house, the community and the region. Guest bedrooms, each in a renovated farm building, have chestnut floors and reclaimed beams, the showers are super-large, and one bedroom has its own terrace – raise a glass to the view! You are in heart of the sparsely populated Aveyron – 'la France profonde.' Homemade yogurt and fig jam at breakfast, apple juice from the village and wonderful walks from the door.

Rooms	2 doubles.
Price	€55.
Meals	Dinner €22.50. Restaurant 10km.
Closed	Rarely.

Phillipe & Lynda Denny
Le Gouty,
12380 Pousthomy, Aveyron
Tel   +33 (0)5 65 49 40 31
Mobile   +33 (0)6 42 48 47 58
Email   le.gouty@nordnet.fr
Web   legouty.webplus.net

Entry 644   Map 15

Midi - Pyrénées

Aurifat

Good furniture, books and paintings are thoroughly at home in this multi-stepped, history-rich house (the watchtower is 13th-century) where all is serene and inviting. Each freshly decorated room has its own private entrance, the twin has a cosy sitting area, the double a terrace for sun-drenched views. Walking distance to everything, the house is on the southern slope of Cordes (borrow a torch for a night time stroll), the pool is delicious and there's a barbecue alongside the guest kitchen. Terrace breakfasts (spot the deer) are enchanting; nothing is too much trouble for these lovely hosts.

Minimum two nights.

Rooms	2: 1 double, 1 twin/double.
Price	€80.
Meals	Kitchen & BBQ available. Restaurants within walking distance.
Closed	October-April.

Ian & Penelope Wanklyn
Aurifat,
81170 Cordes sur Ciel,
Tarn
Tel   +33 (0)5 63 56 07 03
Email   aurifat@gmail.com
Web   www.aurifat.com

Entry 645   Map 15

Midi - Pyrénées

Clos de Lacalm

Warmly generous, born to do B&B, Sally and Kirk have carefully restored a lovely old place, a classic vigneron's house in a sweep of open countryside six minutes from hilltop Cordes sur Ciel. The guest suite is divine, thanks to crisp linen, curtains and calm colours, good books, pretty antiques and deep comfy chairs. Sally serves summer breakfasts of fruits, croissants, homemade cakes and jams on a beautiful terrace alongside sweet lavender and clipped box. Drop in on Gaillac's superb market (Fridays), spin off on a bike (they have two for guests), cool off by the pool: it's yours to adore.

Rooms	1 suite for 3.
Price	€95-€145.
Meals	Restaurant in Cestayrols, 3.5km.
Closed	Rarely.

Kirk & Sally Ritchie
Clos de Lacalm,
Lacalm Haute,
81150 Cestayrols, Tarn
Tel   +33 (0)5 63 56 28 05
Email   info@closdelacalm.com
Web   www.closdelacalm.com

Entry 646   Map 15

Midi - Pyrénées

Château Cestayrols

For 400 years, this château was in the same family of wine makers. Now it is the characterful home of Murray and Jan, your fascinating well-travelled hosts. The inviting guest bedrooms are full of light, with painted beam ceilings, elegantly floral fabrics and the finest bed linen. Tucked off the secluded garden is a small terrace area where breakfast is served in summer, and a pretty walled pool; you are welcome to relax here as long as you wish, or sink into deep sofas inside. You're in the heart of Gaillac wine country, and stunning Albi – UNESCO heritage site – is nearby.

Rooms	2: 1 double, 1 suite for 2-4.
Price	€95. Suite €95-€140.
Meals	Restaurant 50m.
Closed	November-April.

Murray & Jan Turnbull
Château Cestayrols,
81150 Cestayrols, Tarn
Tel   +33 (0)5 63 56 95 33
Email   t-bull@wanadoo.fr
Web   www.chateau-cestayrols.com

Entry 647   Map 15

Midi - Pyrénées

Château de Mayragues

A paradise of history, culture, tranquillity and vines. Inside those stern walls you clamber up old stone stairs to the open sentry's gallery, enter your chamber and gasp at the loveliness of the room and the depth of the view. Beyond the fine old timbers and stonework, glowing floor, furniture and fabrics, your eyes flow out over luscious gardens, woods and vines. Alan is a softly-spoken Scot, Laurence a charming Parisienne; both are passionate about their prize-winning restoration, their musical evenings and, of course, their wonderful organic wines. Such a treat.

Minimum two nights. Sawday self-catering also.

Midi - Pyrénées

Artichaud

Gaillic vines and Bastide villages surround this back-from-the-road, eco-renovated farmhouse, which, under Liliane and Jos's expert eye, is an almost totally organic concern. Jos looks after the garden while Liliane's domain is the potager; a passionate cook, she grows produce for their table d'hôtes, including gourmet choices. Rooms are cosy with antique furniture; all look out to the garden. Breakfast on the terrace with your hosts: homemade yogurt, preserves, croissants, and bread from their neighbours. Then laze by the pool – or curl up by the wood-burner in the reading room. Fantastic walking here – ask Jos for his tips.

Rooms	2 + 1: 1 double, 1 twin. Cottage for 4.
Price	€100–€110. Cottage €550–€650 per week.
Meals	Restaurants within 4km.
Closed	December-March.

Rooms	3: 1 double, 1 twin, 1 suite.
Price	€75–€80. Suite €90–€95. Singles €68–€73.
Meals	Hosted dinner €29 (not Thurs/Fri). Restaurants 5km.
Closed	Rarely.

Laurence & Alan Geddes
Château de Mayragues,
81140 Castelnau de Montmiral,
Tarn
Tel +33 (0)5 63 33 94 08
Email geddes@chateau-de-mayragues.com
Web www.chateau-de-mayragues.com

Liliane & Jos Delanote
Artichaud, Castel et Merlarié,
81140 Castelnau de Montmiral,
Tarn
Tel +33 (0)5 63 57 20 42
Email liliane@artichaud.fr
Web www.artichaud.fr

Entry 648   Map 15

Entry 649   Map 15

Midi - Pyrénées

Mas de Sudre

George and Pippa are ideal B&B folk – relaxed, good-natured, enthusiastic about their corner of France, generous-spirited and adding lots of extras to make you comfortable. Set in rolling vineyards and farmland, Sudre is a warm friendly house with beautiful furniture, shelves full of books, big inviting bedrooms and a very lovely garden full of sunny/shady fragrant corners in which you can sleep off delicious breakfast. The more energetic may leap to the pool, boules, bikes or several sorts of tennis and you are genuinely encouraged to treat the house as your own. French guests adore this very British B&B.

Rooms	3: 2 doubles, 1 twin.
Price	€80.
Meals	Restaurants nearby.
Closed	Rarely.

Pippa & George Richmond-Brown
Mas de Sudre,
81600 Gaillac, Tarn
Tel   +33 (0)5 63 41 01 32
Email masdesudre@wanadoo.fr
Web   www.masdesudre.com

Entry 650   Map 15

Midi - Pyrénées

Combettes

Come for an absolutely fabulous French bourgeois experience: a wide 16th century stone staircase deeply worn, high ceilings, southern colours, loads of stairs, interesting *objets* at every turn. Add the owners' passion for Napoleon III furniture, oil paintings and ornate mirrors and the mood, more formal than family, is unmistakably French. Bedrooms, some with rooftop views, are traditional and very comfortable; breakfast is served overlooking the old part of Gaillac. A treat to be in the heart of town, with utterly French people. Madame is a darling and it's excellent value for money.

Rooms	5: 3 doubles, 1 twin, 1 suite.
Price	€60. Suite €75. Singles €45.
Meals	Restaurants 30m.
Closed	Rarely.

Lucile & Marie-Pierre Pinon
Combettes,
8 place St Michel,
81600 Gaillac, Tarn
Tel   +33 (0)5 63 57 61 48
Email contact@combettesgalliac.com
Web   www.combettesgalliac.com

Entry 651   Map 15

Midi - Pyrénées

Domaine du Buc

Bright, smiling Brigitte is proud of her lovely 17th-century domaine, in the family for 100 years. An imposing stone staircase leads to wonderful big bedrooms with original parquet and grand mirrors, period beds, subtle paint finishes and 19th-century papers, and quirky treasures discovered in the attic: sepia photographs, antique bonnets, vintage suitcases. Showers are top-range Italian and the old arched billiards room makes a perfect salon. It's unusually, richly authentic, the breakfasts are locally sourced and delicious and you are eight miles from Albi, World Heritage Site. A huge treat.

Extra rooms available. Minimum two nights July / August.

Rooms	3 twins/doubles.
Price	€100–€120.
Meals	Restaurant 1.5km. Guest kitchen.
Closed	December to mid-March.

Brigitte Lesage
Domaine du Buc,
Route de Lagrave,
81150 Marssac sur Tarn, Tarn
Tel   +33 (0)5 63 55 40 06
Mobile   +33 (0)6 70 14 96 47
Email   contact@domainedubuc.com
Web   www.domainedubuc.com

Entry 652   Map 15

Midi - Pyrénées

Les Buis de St Martin

The dogs are as friendly as their owner, the birds chortle in their aviary, the Tarn runs at the bottom of the garden: it's a dream place. Jacqueline has lived here for 30 years and is delighted to please you and practise her English. You'll love the understated luxury of soft mushroom hues in bedrooms and bathrooms, the quilting on the excellent beds, the good paintings, the floaty muslin at the windows that look over the garden. Meals are served at one friendly table in the luminous white dining room – gleaming antiques on old tiles – or on the lovely teak-furnished patio.

Minimum two nights in summer. Sawday self-catering also.

Rooms	2 twins/doubles.
Price	€110–€120.
Meals	Dinner with wine, €30.
Closed	Rarely.

Jacqueline Romanet
Les Buis de St Martin,
Rue St Martin,
81150 Marssac sur Tarn, Tarn
Tel   +33 (0)5 63 55 41 23
Mobile   +33 (0)6 27 86 29 48
Email   jean.romanet@wanadoo.fr
Web   www.lesbuisdesaintmartin.com

Entry 653   Map 15

Midi - Pyrénées

Lamartco

Way off the beaten track but so delightful. Sylvie and Pierre have recreated the past in their brilliantly authentic restoration of a crumbled old farmhouse and Sylvie's kitchen is a poem: a cooking area in the farmer's old fireside bed, shelves groaning with goodies from Pierre's flowing garden. Pierre has a great sense of humour and loves to speak English: suppers (with local wines) are wonderful. They have put their hearts into this place – antique plates, dolls, bric-a-brac, sweetly rustic bedrooms with armoires, Provençal prints, rush-seated chairs; and a terrace for the garden room. Glorious Albi is 30km.

Rooms	2: 1 triple. Garden: 1 double.
Price	€50–€60. €100 for 2, including dinner and breakfast.
Meals	Dinner with wine, €20.
Closed	Rarely.

Sylvie & Pierre Dumetz-Manesse
Lamartco,
St Marcel, Padiès,
81340 Valence d'Albigeois, Tarn
Tel   +33 (0)5 63 76 38 47
Email   lamartco@wanadoo.fr
Web   www.lamartco.com

Midi - Pyrénées

Barbiel

You will settle quickly here. Tim and Tracy are relaxed and welcoming, all smiles and ease, the house is calming and there's a terrace for lazy breakfasts in the garden with stunning views over rolling hills. Independent ground-floor bedrooms are in the barn: aqua-washed walls, white cotton sheets, a cool mix of modern and antique furniture, zippy bathrooms with thick towels, even a tiny kitchenette for picnics or snacks. For gorgeous dinners at one big table you go to the main house where Tracy's sense of style is splashed all over a stunning art-filled sitting room. Albi is a must-see.

Rooms	2: 1 double, 1 twin/double.
Price	€55–€60.
Meals	Dinner with wine, €22. Light supper from €12. Guest kitchenette.
Closed	Rarely.

Tim & Tracy Bayly
Barbiel,
81340 Assac, Tarn
Tel   +33 (0)5 63 56 97 12
Mobile   +33 (0)6 41 69 26 06
Email   ttbayly@gmail.com
Web   www.tranquiltarn.co.uk

La Barthe

Your Anglo-French hosts in their converted farmhouse welcome guests as friends. The pastel-painted, stencilled rooms are smallish but beds are good, the hospitality is wonderful and it's a deliciously secluded place; take a dip in the raised pool or set off into the country on foot or by bike. The Wises grow their own vegetables and summer dinners are hosted on the terrace overlooking the lovely Tarn valley, in a largely undiscovered part of France where birds, bees and sheep serenade you. Watch the farmers milking for roquefort and don't miss Albi, with its huge and magnificent cathedral – it's no distance at all.

Rooms	2: 1 double, 1 family room.
Price	€50.
Meals	Dinner with wine, €22.
Closed	Rarely.

Michèle & Michael Wise
La Barthe,
81430 Villefranche d'Albigeois,
Tarn
Tel   +33 (0)5 63 55 96 21
Email labarthe@chezwise.com
Web   www.chezwise.com

Entry 656   Map 15

Borio Nove

Bubbly and well-travelled, Lu and Freddie are the perfect B&B hosts and their characterful house on the hillside has a pretty courtyard garden and stunning views. Inside you find a remarkably English style with a roaring fire, deep comfortable sofas, lamps in quiet corners, lovely paintings, fresh flowers and oodles of books. Bedrooms are dressed in soft creams with wooden floors, pleasant bathrooms, comfortable beds and antiques from all over the world; it's like staying with family friends. Meals are jolly affairs at flexible times round the big table – and Freddie knows his wines.

Minimum two nights.

Rooms	2: 1 double, 1 twin/double.
Price	€78-€90.
Meals	Dinner with wine, €18-€30.
Closed	December-February.

Freddie & Lu Wanklyn
Borio Nove,
Bouscayrens, 81120 Lombers,
Tarn
Tel   +33 (0)5 63 55 36 94
Email luwanklyn@aliceadsl.fr
Web   www.borionore.com

Entry 657   Map 15

Midi - Pyrénées

Château de Ronel

Pass the pink garlic fields, through the iron gate and into immense grounds with ancient trees, old roses and a natural pool. The building dates from the 18th-century and has a large pale blue fire-warmed dining room with a communal wooden table and old church benches. Lovely Lydie gives you homemade bread from the cob oven for breakfasts and delicious suppers, Christophe has done all the renovations himself and a sitting room is in the making. Big dreamy first-floor bedrooms (one the old chapel) have stone walls, pastel colours and lovely antiques; bathrooms are atmospheric. Very good value.

Rooms	2 doubles.
Price	€100–€110.
Meals	Dinner with wine, €28. Child €16. Picnic €8–€12. Restaurant 5km.
Closed	Rarely.

Christophe & Lydie Gay
Château de Ronel,
81120 Roumegoux, Tarn
Tel   +33 (0)5 63 55 75 40
Mobile +33 (0)6 14 78 21 06
Email postmaster@chateauderonel.fr
Web   www.chateauderonel.fr

Entry 658   Map 15

Midi - Pyrénées

Chambre d'hôtes de Cadalen

Twin pigeonniers signal journey's end, a honey-coloured house below the ramparts of medieval Lautrec. Alain and Hugo have created an elegant refuge of quiet grandeur, tiled floors, books, beams and abundant antiques, shared with a charming quartet of cats and dogs. Toile de Jouy and draped beds give spacious bedrooms a traditional elegance, unfussy bathrooms are spotless. Book ahead for a sumptuous dinner of home-grown veg and local produce, including the town's famous pink garlic. Breakfast and dinner are taken with your hosts in the dining room or on the terrace, above lush lawns patrolled by peacocks.

Rooms	3: 1 double, 1 suite for 1, 1 suite for 2.
Price	€95. Suite €85–€95.
Meals	Dinner with wine, €28. Restaurant 5-minute drive.
Closed	Never.

Hugo Weinberg & Alain Rouquier
Chambre d'hôtes de Cadalen,
81440 Lautrec,
Tarn
Tel   +33 (0)5 63 75 30 02
Email h.weinberg@wanadoo.fr
Web   www.cadalen81.com

Entry 659   Map 15

Midi - Pyrénées

La Terrasse de Lautrec

Le Nôtre-designed gardens backing a graceful house, with terraces overhanging the village ramparts: the beauty and the peace are restorative. Seek out the secluded shady corners and roses, the box maze, the pond brimming with waterlilies, the pool that looks over the hills. As you swan through the frescoed dining room and the drawing room with its 1810 wallpaper you feel you've stepped back into another age. Dominique, warm and intelligent, treats you to the cooking of the region. Retire to a stunning drawing room, or a large, luminous bedroom filled with ochre and gilt.

Minimum two nights July/Aug.

Rooms	4: 2 doubles, 1 twin, 1 suite.
Price	€80–€110. Suite €120–€130.
Meals	Dinner with wine, €30. Reservation required, 4 guests minimum, weekdays only.
Closed	November-March.

Dominique Ducoudray
La Terrasse de Lautrec,
9 rue de L'Église,
81440 Lautrec,
Tarn

Tel   +33 (0)5 63 75 84 22
Email   d.ducoudray@wanadoo.fr
Web   www.laterrassedelautrec.com

Entry 660   Map 15

Midi - Pyrénées

Domaine d'en Naudet

Superb in every way, and such a sense of space! The domaine, surrounded by a patchwork-quilt countryside, was donated by Henri IV to a hunting crony in 1545 – and was in a parlous state when Éliane and Jean fell for it. They have achieved miracles. A converted barn/stable block reveals four vast and beautiful bedrooms (two with private wicker-chaired terraces), sensuous bathrooms and a stunning open-plan breakfast/sitting room. In the grounds, masses for children and energetic adults, while the slothful may bask by the pool. Markets, history and beauty surround you, and Éliane is a lovely hostess.

Minimum two nights July/Aug.

Rooms	4: 2 doubles, 2 twins.
Price	€95.
Meals	Guest kitchen. Restaurant 3km.
Closed	Rarely.

Éliane & Jean Barcellini
Domaine d'en Naudet,
81220 Teyssode,
Tarn

Tel   +33 (0)5 63 70 50 59
Mobile +33 (0)6 07 17 66 08
Email   contact@domainenaudet.com
Web   www.domainenaudet.com

Entry 661   Map 15

La Métairie au Bosc

Hospitable Brigitte was in banking; Albert knows his wines, and is chef; both love to travel: note the many oriental touches. Richly delicious dinners are hosted at a slab of polished marble next to the open-plan kitchen, in this long, magnificent, Pyrenean farmhouse with its old barn intact. Sliding doors open to a vast stone veranda, a summer delight: views roll across garden, pool, fields and hills. Bedrooms revel in parquet, paintings and French marqueterie; bathrooms have baths and double basins. Bikes and golf clubs to borrow, fireside billiards for cosy nights in. The comfort and care are superb.

Rooms	4: 3 doubles, 1 suite.
Price	€100. Suite €130.
Meals	Dinner with wine, €40. Restaurants in Revel, 7km.
Closed	Rarely.

Brigitte Heyche
La Métairie au Bosc,
Le Bosc,
81700 Garrevaques, Tarn
Tel   +33 (0)5 63 75 23 61
Mobile   +33 (0)6 87 41 91 58
Email   contact@metairie-le-bosc.com
Web   www.metairie-le-bosc.com

Entry 662   Map 15

La Villa de Mazamet & Le Petit Spa

A 'coup de foudre' caused Mark and Peter to buy this grand 1930s house in walled gardens, a few minutes' walk from the market town of Mazamet. Renovation revealed large light interiors of wood-panelled walls, parquet floors and sweeping windows. Furnished with modern elegance, the ground floor invites relaxation in comfy sofas or quiet corners. Bedrooms, with sumptuous beds and fine linen, are calmly luxurious; bathrooms are Art Deco gems. Your hosts are interesting, relaxed and well-travelled, meals in the restaurant are gastronomic. Ideal for Carcassonne, Albi and all those medieval villages.

Minimum two nights. Children over 14 welcome.

Rooms	5: 3 doubles, 2 twins/doubles.
Price	€95-€150.
Meals	Dinner €32.50. Wine from €14.
Closed	Rarely.

Peter Friend & Mark Barber
La Villa de Mazamet & Le Petit Spa,
4 rue Pasteur, 81200 Mazamet,
Tarn
Tel   +33 (0)5 63 97 90 33
Mobile   +33 (0)6 25 50 56 91
Email   info@villademazamet.com
Web   www.villademazamet.com

Entry 663   Map 15

Languedoc – Roussillon

Languedoc - Roussillon

La Maison de Marius

Fascinating Quézac is a pilgrimage 'street-village' with many cobbles and a lovely old bridge over the Tarn. The house sits prettily at its heart, all warm and lived-in – old stones, beams and a light fresh feel. The rooms have artistic flourishes; the bathrooms are super. Dany is a poppet, adores embellishing her home (country fabrics, hand-painted furniture) and spoiling her guests with gâteau de noix from her walnuts and delicacies from her impressive vegetable patch. Sit on the lovely terrace, surrounded by spring flowers, or rose garden where only birds, water and wind are to be heard. A wonderful area – stay a while.

Rooms	5: 4 doubles, 1 family room for 4.
Price	€90-€120. Family room €68-€90.
Meals	Dinner with wine, €25.
Closed	November-March.

Danièle Méjean
La Maison de Marius,
8 rue du Pontet,
48320 Quézac, Lozère

Tel	+33 (0)4 66 44 25 05
Mobile	+33 (0)6 83 37 62 33
Email	dany.mejean@wanadoo.fr
Web	www.maisondemarius.fr

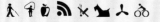

Entry 664   Map 15

Languedoc - Roussillon

Transgardon en Cévennes

A light-filled valley and utter solitude. Eco-minded Pascal and Frédérique fell in love with this remote hamlet, then restored the main house and a guest cottage (two more are under way). He uses their own veg and local meat to create divine meals; she makes bread and brioches for breakfast, with honey from their bees. Swim in the stream under the old bridge (catch a trout in the rockpool?). On cool evenings, hunker down by the stove in the main house. Bliss awaits you in your stone cottage down the path over the bridge: crisp linen, an Italian shower, an extra mezzanine bed. Hike, cycle, explore... or do nothing.

Rooms	Cottage: 1 double. Extra bed on mezzanine.
Price	Cottage €110-€135. Singles €90. Under 5's free.
Meals	Dinner with wine, €25. Restaurants 9km.
Closed	Rarely.

Frédérique & Pascal Mathis
Transgardon en Cévennes,
Transgardon,
48240 St Privat de Vallongue,
Lozère

Tel	+33 (0)4 34 25 90 23
Email	transgardon@transgardon.fr
Web	www.transgardon.fr

Entry 665   Map 15

Languedoc - Roussillon

Château Massal

The château façade flanks the road, the many-terraced garden rambles behind, with views across river and red-roofed town. Up a stone spiral are big beautiful bedrooms with a château feel; walnut parquet and mosaic floors along with strong-coloured walls set off family furniture to perfection; one has a bathroom in the tower; one houses an ancient grand piano: it's enchanting. Madame, one of an old French silk family who have been here for several generations, is as elegant and charming as her house; a fine cook, too. She will show you where to find really good walks, exciting canoeing, and wildlife.

Child's bed available.

Rooms	4 doubles.
Price	€68-€98.
Meals	Dinner with wine, €28 (for groups of 4+).
Closed	Mid-November to March.

Françoise & Marie-Emmanuelle du Luc
Château Massal,
Bez & Esparon,
30120 Le Vigan, Gard
Tel +33 (0)4 67 81 07 60
Email francoiseduluc@gmail.com
Web www.cevennes-massal.com

Entry 666 Map 15

Languedoc - Roussillon

Villa Virinn

Melons and cherries in season, homemade marmalade and fig jam all year. Douglas is the chef, Geoff the greeter and gardener, both are warm hosts loving the French life. Their big new house, private and peaceful, is a short stroll from the small hilltop town: walk in for dinner and return to a candlelit garden. Inside, all is fresh, comfortable, unflashy; beds have painted headboards and matching tables, walls are blue, soft green, pale honey; those off the garden have terraces. Colourful flowers and loungers round the pool, an honesty bar, a vineyard view: the excursions are great but the temptation is to stay.

Extra twin room available.

Rooms	2: 1 double, 1 twin/double.
Price	€90.
Meals	Hosted dinner €25. Wine €10.
Closed	October-April.

Geoff Pople & Douglas Tulloch
Villa Virinn,
Chemin de Bercaude,
30360 Vézénobres, Gard
Tel +33 (0)4 66 83 27 30
Email geoffanddoug@villavirinn.com
Web www.villavirinn.com

Entry 667 Map 16

Languedoc - Roussillon

Mas Vacquières

Thomas and Miriam have restored these lovely 18th-century buildings with pretty Dutch simplicity, white walls a perfect foil for southern-toned fabrics in bedrooms reached by steep stone stairs. Mulberry trees where silkworms once fed still flower; the little vaulted room is intimate and alcoved, the big soft salon a delight. Tables on the enchantingly flowered terrace under leafy trees and a lawn sloping down to the stream make perfect spots for silent gazing; and table d'hôtes is a delight. Share the pool, sheltered in its roofless barn, with gîte guests and your charming hosts; it's all so relaxed you can stay all day.

Languedoc - Roussillon

Les Marronniers

In love with their life and their 19th-century *maison de maître*, John and Michel welcome guests with exuberant gaiety. John is a joiner with a fine eye for interior design; Michel, quieter, takes care of beautiful breakfasts. From the classic tiles of the entrance hall to the art on the walls to the atmospheric lighting at night, every detail counts. Generous breakfast is elegantly served under the chestnut trees, after which you can wander off to join in lazy Provençal village life, or visit Avignon, Uzès, Lussan – your wonderful hosts know all the best places.

Rooms	3: 2 doubles, 1 twin/double.		Rooms	4: 2 doubles, 2 twins.
Price	€85–€110.		Price	€105–€130.
Meals	Dinner €35.		Meals	Restaurant 5km.
Closed	Rarely.		Closed	Rarely.

	Thomas & Miriam van Dijke			**John Karavias & Michel Comas**
	Mas Vacquières,			Les Marronniers,
	Hameau de Vacquières,			Place de la Mairie,
	30580 St Just & Vacquières, Gard			30580 La Bruguière, Gard
Tel	+33 (0)4 66 83 70 75		Tel	+33 (0)4 66 72 84 77
Email	info@masvac.com		Email	info@lesmarronniers.biz
Web	www.masvac.com		Web	www.lesmarronniers.biz

Entry 668   Map 16   Entry 669   Map 16

Languedoc - Roussillon

La Magnanerie

This happy, artistic, relaxed couple welcome guests to their light-filled former silk farm, splashed with Moroccan colour and ethnic *objets*. It has pretty ochre-coloured plates, a long wooden table on an uneven stone floor, an ancient sink, beams twisting, glimpses of age-old village rooftops, a ravishing courtyard, big, pretty, uncluttered bedrooms, a roof terrace looking over Provence. Michèle paints, manages tranquilly and adores cooking; Michel, passionately active in sustainable development, knows his wines and the local community; their talk is cultural and enriching.

Rooms	3: 2 doubles, 1 family room.
Price	€60. Family room €70-€100. Children under 10 stay free.
Meals	Dinner with wine, €24.
Closed	Rarely.

Michèle Dassonneville & Michel
Genvrin
La Magnanerie,
Place de l'Horloge,
30580 Fons sur Lussan, Gard

Tel   +33 (0)4 66 72 81 72
Email   mimi.genvrin@orange.fr
Web   www.atelier-de-fons.com

Entry 670   Map 16

Languedoc - Roussillon

Pont d'Ardèche

An ancestor built this fine fortified farmhouse 220 years ago: proudly worn, it still stands by the Ardèche with its own small beach. Inside, in sudden contrast, are a cavernous entrance hall, a stone staircase lined with portraits, and pale plain bedrooms above, saved from austerity by Ghislaine's painted furniture and friezes. There's no sitting room but a homely kitchen for good breakfast breads and jams. The squirrel-run park invites lingerers, and there's a delicious oval pool shared with gîte guests. Pierre can accompany you on canoe trips: this is a lovely sociable family who enjoy all their guests.

Rooms	3: 1 double, 1 family room (1 double & bunkbeds), 1 triple.
Price	€70. Family room €70-€90. Triple €80-€95. Child under 10, €10. Extra bed €15.
Meals	Guest kitchen. Dinner with wine, €25.
Closed	Rarely.

Ghislaine & Pierre de Verduzan
Pont d'Ardèche,
30130 Pont St Esprit, Gard

Tel   +33 (0)4 66 39 29 80
Email   pontdardeche@aol.com
Web   www.pont-dardeche.com

Entry 671   Map 16

Languedoc - Roussillon

Le pas de l'âne

Sheltering under umbrella pines, an ordinary house with an extraordinary welcome. Fun for food-lovers and families; even the parrot greets you with a merry 'bonjour'. Anne, a Belgian ex-antique dealer in London, is chef; gregarious Italian Dominique is host; both are intelligent and humorous. Dinners are fabulous affairs, full of joy and fresh delights: garden strawberries, home-laid eggs, homemade spiced oils. We like the upstairs bedrooms best; the double has its own terrace. Four cats, two dogs, a pool, a big garden – heaven for kids in summer. And all those gorges and southern markets to discover.

Rooms	3: 1 double, 1 twin, 1 twin/double.
Price	€60–€80.
Meals	Dinner with wine, €23.
Closed	Rarely.

Anne Le Brun
Le pas de l'âne,
209 chemin du Pas de l'Âne,
Combe, 30200 Sabran, Gard
Tel   +33 (0)4 66 33 14 09
Mobile   +33 (0)6 30 68 62 03
Email   pasdelane@wanadoo.fr
Web   www.pasdelane.com

Entry 672   Map 16

Languedoc - Roussillon

Clos de la Fontaine

The earthy colours of the south glow at every turn of this beautifully restored old house beneath the ancient fort: red-gold stone, restful white limewashed walls, terracotta tiles; the blue light filters in through garden greenery to highlight the fruit of a passion: your hosts' abundant and changing collection of modern art (works for sale) and designer furniture. She has a highly creative approach to décor; he is an excellent cook; both love opening their home to visitors, sharing the pleasure and the art. All the rooms are exquisite, with yet more original art, a lovely fireplace, old doors… Just 15 minutes from Uzès.

Minimum two nights. Not suitable for under 12s because of pool & artworks.

Rooms	4: 2 doubles, 2 twins/doubles (each with separate wc).
Price	€110. Singles €90. Extra bed €30.
Meals	Dinner, 4 courses, €25 (Sat, Mon & Weds only). Wine €2-€3/ glass. Restaurant within walking distance.
Closed	October-March.

Michel & Annick Rey
Clos de la Fontaine,
3 rue du Lavoir,
30330 St Laurent la Vernède, Gard
Tel   +33 (0)4 66 72 97 85
Mobile   +33 (0)6 13 97 82 64
Email   michel.rey66@orange.fr
Web   www.closdelafontaine-provence.com

Entry 673   Map 16

Languedoc - Roussillon

L'Espérou

Imagine a fine old house with mullioned windows in a golden hamlet five minutes from Uzès. Delight in paintings, portraits, carpets, mirrors, and a fine collection of hats up the wide stone stairs to a grandly beautiful two-bedroom suite. The rooms overlook lush lawns, white roses and southern pines: an oasis with an elegant pool and loungers awaiting aperitifs. Your hosts, passionate about baroque music, opera and treasured old things, offer you lovely lazy breakfasts on immaculate china and an indulging bathroom with Christian Dior towels. For Provençal magic, explore the shops, galleries and market of Uzès.

Rooms	2 doubles sharing bathroom (rooms can interconnect to form suite).
Price	€160-€230.
Meals	Restaurants nearby.
Closed	Rarely.

Jacques Cauvin
L'Espérou, Hameau St Médiers,
30700 Montaren & St Médiers,
Gard

Tel	+33 (0)4 66 63 14 73
Mobile	+33 (0)6 64 14 48 89
Email	contact@lesperou.com
Web	www.lesperou.com

Entry 674   Map 16

Languedoc - Roussillon

Domaine de Marsault

At the end of an avenue of fine plane trees is this most elegant family mansion, joyfully revived by Jean-Pierre Salle. Step into a stone-flagged hallway and a vast salon, awash with light from high windows overlooking the garden beyond. Two bedrooms sharing a big bathroom with a wonderful old bath are equally plush, while the big boldly coloured suites have dressing rooms, marble fireplaces and gleaming armoires. A generous, delicious breakfast is served at round tables under parasols or at the big polished dining table. The cherry on the cake? Lovely honey-stoned Uzès awaits at the end of a well-used vineyard track.

Minimum two nights.

Rooms	5: 2 doubles, 2 suites, 1 double sharing bathroom (let to same party only).
Price	€190. Suite €230. Extra double €130.
Meals	Restaurants 2km.
Closed	Mid-October to mid-March, except Truffle Fair in January.

Jean-Pierre Salle
Domaine de Marsault,
30700 Uzès, Gard

Tel	+33 (0)4 66 22 53 92
Email	info@domainedemarsault.com
Web	www.domainedemarsault.com

Entry 675   Map 16

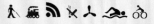

Languedoc - Roussillon

Mas d'Oléandre

Lovely, long stone buildings enfold the convivial two-tier courtyard, great trees shade the pool, the Cévennes hills march off beyond. It is enchanting. Your welcoming young Dutch hosts have created a beautiful unpretentious place to stay; the garden, the lawn round the pool, the glowing old furniture inside, the silvery weathered teak out. Bedrooms, each with its own piece of terrace, light and white with splashes of colour, feel separate from one another round the courtyard and Esther keeps it all utterly pristine. Gather your own picnic at glorious Uzès market and bring it back here. Breakfast and dinner are delicious.

Rooms	4: 2 suites; 2 doubles, each with separate shower.
Price	€77-€137.
Meals	Dinner with wine, €32.50.
Closed	Mid-November to early March.

Léonard Robberts & Esther Küchler
Mas d'Oléandre,
Hameau St Médiers,
30700 Montaren & St Médiers,
Gard

Tel	+33 (0)4 66 22 63 43
Email	info@masoleandre.com
Web	www.masoleandre.com

Entry 676 Map 16

Languedoc - Roussillon

Les Bambous

Circles of delight, ten minutes from Avignon. Joël & Michèle love welcoming guests to their glowing little house in an unpretentious Provençal town, and the charming peaceful courtyard shaded by bamboo and bourgainvillea. He paints portraits and pastels, she cooks – linger over delicious food at the big mosaic table. In the courtyard studio is a delightful mix of soft limed walls and ethnic treasures from winter travels: a Peruvian wall hanging, an African sculpture. You have an inviting king-size bed, a pebble-floored shower, a bright kitchenette, a gently curving staircase to a bed-sitting area above. Such value!

Rooms	2: 1 studio with kitchenette, 1 family room for 2-4.
Price	Studio €65. Family room €70-€105.
Meals	Dinner with wine, €25.
Closed	January.

Joël & Michèle Rousseau
Les Bambous,
21 rue de la Mairie,
30131 Pujaut, Gard

Tel	+33 (0)4 90 26 46 47
Mobile	+33 (0)6 82 93 06 68
Email	rousseau.michele@wanadoo.fr
Web	www.lesbambous.net

Entry 677 Map 16

Languedoc - Roussillon

Les Écuries des Chartreux

Villeneuve is a mini Avignon without the crowds. In a stable block next to a 13th-century monastery you find these charmingly furnished, beautifully kempt guest quarters, smelling of beeswax. All is coolness, elegance and light: stone walls, terracotta floors, rustic beams, Provençal antiques. Two suites have mezzanines, all have perfect kitchenettes so you can self-cater if you prefer. No pool but a delectable courtyard garden. Pascale gives you breakfast in the main house and all the attention you require – including an aperitif before you head out for the evening. This is heaven.

Rooms	3 suites: 1 for 2, 1 for 3, 1 for 4, each with kitchenette.
Price	€93-€166.
Meals	Restaurants 50m.
Closed	Rarely.

Pascale Letellier
Les Écuries des Chartreux,
66 rue de la République,
30400 Villeneuve lès Avignon, Gard
Tel   +33 (0)4 90 25 79 93
Email   pascale.letellier@orange.fr
Web   www.ecuries-des-chartreux.com

Languedoc - Roussillon

La Claire Demeure

Surrounded by great plane trees that have never been pruned, a charming southern home. The stone vaulted salon bears witness to the days of the Knights Templar; the sofas are comfy, the fireplace glows in winter, the piano (not grand) is ready to play. Kind Claire, friendly and refined, gives you elegant bedrooms with flagged floors and high windows, fine linen, fresh flowers, a sprinkling of antiques – and simple generous family suppers enhanced by her husband's wines. He knows all about Gigondas and Châteauneuf-du-Pape so don't miss the vineyards. This is a wonderful area where markets, cafés and galleries abound.

Rooms	2 doubles.
Price	€69-€88.
Meals	Dinner with wine, €15 (reservation required). Restaurants 10km.
Closed	Mid-November to mid-March.

Claire Granier
La Claire Demeure,
1424 route de Jonquières,
30490 Montfrin, Gard
Tel   +33 (0)4 66 37 72 48
Mobile +33 (0)6 74 50 86 84
Email   claire.tytgat@wanadoo.fr
Web   www.laclairedemeure.com

Languedoc - Roussillon

Alfonso's Wagon

Once home to Alfonso the daredevil leopard-tamer (so Nella, the owner, would have you believe), this colourful *roulotte* is a hundred years old. It's a whirl of fairy lights, vintage finds, mirrors and gorgeous cushions, circus-y postcards, prints and books, and a musical library of Gypsy jazz. A cupboard in the bedroom reveals a bright pink loo and basin closet, the gas shower is a dash outside to a hut. And your outdoor kitchen table overlooks the horses' training ring of this busy stud farm; you will be really well cared for. The medieval village of Sauve is nearby – don't miss it.

Book through Sawday's Canopy & Stars online or by phone.

Languedoc - Roussillon

Burckel de Tell

It's an old house in a little market town – but step off the narrow street and you enter another world. First the courtyard, a source of light and greenery and the open breakfast barn hung with Régis' paintings. Up a stone spiral lined with tapestries lie two tempting rooms and a lovely smell of wax-polished stone floors. Expect fine old doors, windows that seem to frame pictures and a newly-revived Bechstein: you can tell that an artist and an art historian live here, it has huge visual appeal and music is vital to them. There's a terrace on the roof, too. Don't miss Calvisson's Sunday market.

Minimum two nights July/Aug.

Rooms	1 Gypsy wagon for 2.
Price	£80-£105.
Meals	Breakfast £10. Restaurants 4km.
Closed	November-March.

Rooms	3: 1 double, 2 suites.
Price	€65. Suite €70-€75.
Meals	Dinner with wine, €20. Restaurant in Calvisson.
Closed	Rarely.

	Sawday's Canopy & Stars
	Alfonso's Wagon,
	Chemin de Vernedes,
	Toupiargues,
	30260 Sardan, Gard
Tel	+44 (0)1275 395447
Email	enquiries@canopyandstars.co.uk
Web	www.canopyandstars.co.uk/alfonso

	Régis & Corinne Burckel de Tell
	Burckel de Tell,
	48 Grand'Rue,
	30420 Calvisson, Gard
Tel	+33 (0)4 66 01 23 91
Email	burckeldetell@hotmail.fr
Web	www.bed-and-art.com

Entry 680   Map 16

Entry 681   Map 16

Languedoc - Roussillon

Envie de Sud

Right in the heart of this sunny southern town is a wine-grower's house of warmth and charm. Graceful Florence, hostess and mother, has poured energy and soul into its restoration, respecting the history and adding spice and colour. There are three bedrooms upstairs and one opening to the garden, all with special colours and polished plaster walls, perfect bedding and bathrooms of character. Outside is bliss: a gravelled walled garden, a stone basin pool, a spiral stairway to a sundeck by the rooftops. Enjoy compotes and crêpes for breakfast, and vibrant suppers at the table with your hosts and guests.

Extra beds available. Ask about parking.

Rooms	4: 1 twin/double, 2 family rooms, 1 double.
Price	€75–€90.
Meals	Hosted dinner €18. Wine €6. Summer kitchen. Restaurants close by.
Closed	Rarely.

	Florence Loiseleur
	Envie de Sud,
	22 rue Broussan,
	30600 Vauvert, Gard
Tel	+33 (0)4 66 51 59 84
Email	enviedesud@gmail.com
Web	www.enviedesud.com/

Entry 682   Map 16

Languedoc - Roussillon

Mas de Barbut

Danielle's family home is stunning, imaginative, decorated with élan. Great travellers, the Gandons have gathered fascinating things in a strikingly harmonious way; bedrooms are Mexican, Mandarin or Provençal, outstanding bathrooms have fabulous tiles. Different food, a different table decoration every day: they love cosseting guests. The summer sitting room has a pebble floor, the stone bassin is overlooked by slatted oak loungers, there's a sweet spot for drinks by the river and the frond-shaded courtyard is bliss. Near the sea yet away from it all – and restaurants in lovely St Laurent. A treat from start to finish.

Rooms	5: 2 doubles, 2 triples. Studio: 1 double.
Price	€110–€120. Triple €110–€120. Studio €130.
Meals	Occasional dinner with wine, €35.
Closed	Rarely.

	Danielle & Jean-Claude Gandon
	Mas de Barbut,
	30220 St Laurent d'Aigouze, Gard
Tel	+33 (0)4 66 88 12 09
Mobile	+33 (0)6 64 14 28 52
Email	contact@masdebarbut.com
Web	www.masdebarbut.com

Entry 683   Map 16

Languedoc - Roussillon

Château Roumanières

Potted olive trees proudly stand to attention outside this 13th-century bastide with its lovely old stonework and bamboo-shaded courtyard. It's this young family's refined home: salon with charming fireplace and sofas, winter garden with luscious plants and tiled floor, and roof terrace. Intimate, big-bedded rooms with village views have new-as-a-pin bathrooms and separate loos. Make friends round a rotund breakfast table in a vaulted dining room: local honey, homemade cake, charcuterie. Enjoy the quiet square, or tootle off to Montpellier or Nîmes. Return to Saturday's gourmet dinner – ambrosial.

Rooms	5: 2 doubles, 1 family room, 2 suites.
Price	€85–€120. Family room €85–€120. Suite €115–€140.
Meals	Dinner €20–€42. Restaurants nearby.
Closed	Rarely.

Amélie Giorgetti-Gravegeal
Château Roumanières,
Place de la Mairie,
34160 Garrigues, Hérault

Tel	+33 (0)4 67 86 49 70
Email	gravegeal.amelie@wanadoo.fr
Web	www.chateauroumanieres.com

Entry 684   Map 16

Languedoc - Roussillon

Au Soleil

Catherine is as elegant and welcoming as her house. Once involved in theatre PR, she now devotes her energies to guests and house; it's a treat to stay in her village-centre *maison de maître*. Behind the front door, caressed by sweet jasmine, find sunlight, space and simplicity, fine pieces of brocante and a sitting room with deep orange sofas. Bedrooms are peaceful and calm, with kilim rugs on glowing terracotta, and windows overlook the rooftops of a lush inner courtyard where cat and dog doze. Simple Mediterranean food is served with pleasure; and on Sundays in summer the bulls race through town.

Rooms	3 doubles.
Price	€65–€75.
Meals	Dinner with wine, €22. Restaurant 100m.
Closed	Rarely.

Catherine Maurel
Au Soleil,
9 rue Pierre Brossolette,
34590 Marsillargues, Hérault

Tel	+33 (0)4 67 83 90 00
Email	catherine.maurel@ausoleil.info
Web	www.ausoleil.info

Entry 685   Map 16

Languedoc - Roussillon

Le Mas de l'Olivier

Silvi's bubbling enthusiasm for receiving and cooking – breakfast, lunch and dinner, all delicious – will inspire you to join in. Her arranging and decorating skills make the fine old wine-grower's house a generous and original place to stay. Find big rooms, quiet colours and stunning old floor tiles in the first-floor 'apartment' (where three rooms share a bathroom). Lou Poustalou, the fireplaced and terraced 'grangette' by the pool, is a delight for an independent family, with a handy kitchenette. In summer, the jumbly, bowery garden is ideal for cool evening drinks before convivial dinner outside.

Rooms	5: 1 double; 3 doubles sharing bathroom (2 rooms interconnect). Grangette: 1 family room for 3 (with kitchenette).
Price	€80–€100. Family room €100–€120.
Meals	Lunch €20. Dinner €20–€25. Wine €25–€40.
Closed	Rarely.

Silvi Leichtnam
Le Mas de l'Olivier,
Rue du Laurier-tin,
34400 Vérargues,
Hérault
Mobile   +33 (0)6 43 11 33 62
Email   slibersa@orange.fr
Web   www.lemasdelolivier.fr

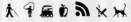

Entry 686   Map 16

Languedoc - Roussillon

Castle Cottage

On the edge of an unspoilt forest, in a garden flooded with hibiscus where 40 tortoises roam (no touching please)… it's hard to believe you're a tram ride from Montpellier. The house is recent, the vegetation lush, the tempting pool (mind the alarm) set among atmospheric stone 'ruins'. In the house are small but comfortable beds in pretty rooms (shuttered in summer) full of family pieces and colour, a good shower room and doors to the terrace. Outside is the 'pavilion', is a sweet little uncluttered house for two. Your hostess loves this place passionately, her garden is an oasis even in winter and the beach is nearby.

Minimum two nights at weekends. Cottage: minimum three nights.

Rooms	3: 2 doubles, sharing shower & separate wc. Cottage for 2.
Price	€92–€108. Cottage €81–€135 (€566–€946 per week). Under 5's free. Extra bed €32.
Meals	Breakfast €10. Restaurants in Montpellier, 3km.
Closed	Rarely.

Dominique Cailleau
Castle Cottage,
289 chemin de la Rocheuse,
34170 Castelnau le Lez, Hérault
Tel   +33 (0)4 67 72 63 08
Mobile   +33 (0)6 75 50 41 50
Email   castlecottage@free.fr
Web   castlecottage-chambresdhotes.com

Entry 687   Map 15

Languedoc - Roussillon

Domaine de Pélican

In summer, vignerons drop by for Monday tastings – followed by a special dinner: book to join in. This eco-leaning wine estate has a mulberry-lined drive and a real family atmosphere: he is quiet and gentle, she energetic and charming. In the old barn, bedrooms have soft-coloured walls, some beds on mezzanines (no windows but glazed doors), pretty shower rooms. Old honey-coloured beams protect the dining room – a dream that gives onto the terrace and rows of vines beyond. Cool off in the saltwater pool, or wild-swim in the river Hérault. Ideal for those interested in good wine, peacefulness and proper French country cuisine.

Rooms	4: 1 double, 1 suite for 4; 1 double, 1 twin, each with fold-out bed.
Price	€62–€72.
Meals	Dinner €24. Restaurant in village.
Closed	Rarely.

Isabelle & Baudouin Thillaye du Boullay
Domaine de Pélican,
34150 Gignac,
Hérault
Tel   +33 (0)4 67 57 68 92
Email   domaine-de-pelican@wanadoo.fr
Web   www.domainedepelican.fr

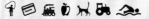

Entry 688   Map 15

Languedoc - Roussillon

Des Lits sur la Place

Right on the square of the old town, with views over rooftops and hills beyond, is a lovely old house in a rich ochre red, decorated simply and with devotion to detail. The charming young owners, former photographers from Paris, run a restaurant to the side: the menu is short, the dishes delicious. Hike in the unspoilt hills, visit vibrant Montpellier, explore the wild wooded hills, then return to big peaceful bedrooms on the second floor, painted and polished in soft earthy colours, with fine old cross beams and chic Italian showers. Breakfast at the long table will delight you: homemade yogurts, jams, pain d'épice.

Rooms	5: 3 twins/doubles, 2 family rooms for 2-4.
Price	€62–€72. Family room €93–€122.
Meals	Lunchtime bistro menu, €19. Dinner from €26. Wine from €20. Restaurants 10-minute drive.
Closed	Rarely.

Marion & Thierry Deloulay
Des Lits sur la Place,
12 place de la Croix,
34600 Hérépian, Hérault
Tel   +33 (0)4 67 23 16 84
Mobile   +33 (0)6 41 61 43 44
Email   contact@deslitssurlaplace.fr
Web   www.deslitssurlaplace.fr

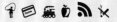

Entry 689   Map 15

Languedoc - Roussillon

Maison de Bacchus

Find your way to a tranquil side street of this enchanting old, twisty, stone-built Languedoc village, knock on the door, climb the stairs from the deep dark hall, and gape at the space and light of the living quarters. Jean and David, who've lived in Pomérols for 11 years, built a fine big house within ancient timbers and old stone walls and love sharing it, as well as their local knowledge. Charming, uncluttered bedrooms come with lots of storage space and pretty modern shower rooms; the generous living room and its terrace invite farniente – but your friendly hosts will inspire you to get out and explore: there's so much to see.

One-night stays welcome.

Rooms	3: 1 suite for 2-4; 2 doubles sharing shower.
Price	€70-€80. Suite €85-€125.
Meals	Restaurants within walking distance.
Closed	Rarely.

David & Jean Black
Maison de Bacchus,
12 rue des Pompes,
34810 Pomérols, Hérault

Tel	+33 (0)4 67 01 44 15
Mobile	+33 (0)7 57 50 24 45
Email	jeanpomerols@gmail.com
Web	www.pomerols-chambres-d-hotes.com/

Entry 690   Map 15

Languedoc - Roussillon

The Village House

A tall narrow house, unpretentious and spotless, run by unpushy hosts who live and work here so are always around for you. The oldest part is attached to the 14th-century ramparts of the sleepy market town which stands in a sea of Languedoc vineyards. Serene rooms are set round the charming first-floor guest terrace: the smaller one cool and light with white floor tiles, the master room splendid with its big bathroom and balcony over the square. An excellent place to stay, inexpensive, stylish, discreet, it has a winter living room, too. Historic Pézenas has markets and boutiques galore, and the mountain bikes are free.

Minimum two nights.

Rooms	2 doubles.
Price	€60-€65.
Meals	Restaurants 2km.
Closed	Rarely.

John Cook & Jean-Maurice Siu
The Village House,
3 rue du Théron,
34320 Gabian,
Hérault

Tel	+33 (0)4 67 24 77 27
Email	contact@thevillagehouse.info
Web	www.thevillagehouse.info

Entry 691   Map 15

Languedoc - Roussillon

Château de Murviel

The château is perched on the pinnacle of the village, surveying mellow rooftops, sweeping vineyards and hills. Soft, plastered walls, honey-coloured floorboards, pale stone floors and bleached-linen bed curtains create a feeling of warmth, modernity and light – unexpected in such an old place. If your host is away, a lovely housekeeper takes good care of you and serves breakfast in a cobbled, fountain'd courtyard dotted with lemon trees and oleander; there's a super guest kitchen, too. Whether you are interested in wine or the Cathars, this is an extremely charming place to lay your head.

Two nights preferred in high season. Whole house available.

Rooms	4: 1 double, 2 triples, 1 suite.
Price	€80–€110.
Meals	Kitchen available. Restaurant 0.5km.
Closed	January.

Yves Cousquer
Château de Murviel,
1 place Georges Clémenceau,
34490 Murviel lès Béziers, Hérault
Tel +33 (0)4 67 32 35 45
Mobile +33 (0)6 07 42 47 08
Email chateaudemurviel@free.fr
Web www.murviel.com

Entry 692 Map 15

Languedoc - Roussillon

Les Mimosas

The O'Rourkes love France, wine, food, their fine house in this enchanting old village and the dazzling countryside around. Enter a high cool hall with old stone stairs leading to fresh, delicately decorated bedrooms with showers and good art on the walls. Rooms at the back face south with views to the hills. You can walk, ride, climb rocks; swim, canoe in the river; visit the local market and the unusual succulent garden. Then return for drinks on the terrace with your friendly hosts, he an architect, both keen on history, art and travel. They'll readily advise on restaurants near and far. "A little slice of heaven."

Rooms	4 doubles.
Price	€75.
Meals	Restaurants in Roquebrun.
Closed	November–January.

Martin & Jacqui O'Rourke
Les Mimosas,
Avenue des Orangers,
34460 Roquebrun, Hérault
Tel +33 (0)4 67 89 61 36
Mobile +33 (0)6 42 33 96 63
Email welcome.lesmimosas@wanadoo.fr
Web www.lesmimosas.net

Entry 693 Map 15

Languedoc - Roussillon

La Souche

Vineyards melt into wildflower'd hills, cliffs and copses: a kaleidoscope of views and colours where you sleep 'comme une souche' – like a log. Especially after Marianne's fresh fish suppers with Languedoc wine, served beautifully on the garden terrace or by the fire. She and Hennie have preserved the frescoes, decorative tiles, marble stairs and fires of their 1890s *maison de maître*, adding fresh, white bedrooms upstairs with Hennie's handcrafted mosaics and views over vines and hamlet. Walk, ride, canoe down the Canal du Midi, perfect your boules toss, and catch up on books by the mulberry-shaded pool.

Minimum two nights.

Rooms	4: 2 doubles, 2 twins/doubles.
Price	€85–€100.
Meals	Dinner, €22–€25. Wine €12. Restaurant 4km.
Closed	Rarely.

Marianne Mulckhuyse & Hennie Vellekoop
La Souche,
Hameau de Castelbouze,
34360 St Chinian, Hérault
Tel   +33 (0)4 67 38 10 77
Email   info@lasouche.com
Web   www.lasouche.com

Languedoc - Roussillon

La Métairie Basse

In these wild, pastoral surroundings with great walking and climbing trails, you bathe in simplicity, stream-babble and light. Your hosts, hard-working walnut and chestnut growers, have converted to 'bio' and sell delicious purées and jams. The guest barn is beautifully tended: country antiques, old lace curtains, new bedding and blue tones relax the eye; there's a fireplace and a full kitchen too. Monsieur has a big friendly handshake, Madame is gentle and welcoming, and breakfast on the shady terrace includes cheese or walnuts or honey. The wonderful Cathar city of Minerve is a 40-minute drive. Amazing value.

Rooms	2: 1 double (with sofabed), 1 family room for 3.
Price	€58. Family room €68.
Meals	Guest kitchen. Restaurants 3km.
Closed	October-March, except by arrangement.

Éliane & Jean-Louis Lunes
La Métairie Basse,
Hameau de Prouilhe,
34220 Courniou, Hérault
Tel   +33 (0)4 67 97 21 59
Mobile   +33 (0)6 11 38 07 68
Email   info@metairie-basse.com
Web   www.metairie-basse.com

Languedoc - Roussillon

Mas du Soleilla

Famous wines and wild drifting views across vineyards and pines out to the sea – of course the Romans loved it here. Reclining on the terrace with a glass of delicious estate wine, you could be one of them. A typical day begins with fresh grape juice and breakfast at a splendid great marble table and ends, after a sumptuous meal in the nearby auberge, with you following the lanterns back to bed in big, cool, limewashed rooms. A dynamic Swiss couple, Christa and Peter know everything about the area, from cathedrals to markets, but the first stop is always the cellar: the wines have been famous here for 2000 years.

Minimum two nights.

Rooms	5: 2 doubles, 3 twins/doubles.
Price	€105–€145.
Meals	Restaurant 500m.
Closed	Never.

Christa Derungs & Peter Wildbolz
Mas du Soleilla,
Route de Narbonne Plage,
11100 Narbonne, Aude
Tel   +33 (0)4 68 45 24 80
Email   chambres@mas-du-soleilla.com
Web   www.mas-du-soleilla.com

Entry 696   Map 15

Languedoc - Roussillon

Château Haute-Fontaine

Vineyards crossed with wild walks circle this unpretentious, sea-breezy château, home to sociable British hosts beyond a pine-flanked drive. Explore the garrigue-rich estate, tour the fascinating cellar. There is elegance, symmetry and an embracing inner courtyard for breakfast; jasmine clambers, herbs tumble and tables cluster – mingle with guests from the three gîtes. Slumber in the former grape-pickers' dwelling in 'Syrah', 'Marsanne', 'Vermentino' or 'Merlot'. Beds are wicker or wrought iron, shower rooms large and shared. There are terracotta tiles, ochre walls and a kitchen for twilight feasts... and coasts and culture await.

Rooms	4: 2 doubles, 1 single, 1 triple, all sharing 2 bathrooms and wcs.
Price	€72–€82. Triple €93. Single €56.
Meals	Guest kitchen. Dinner with wine, €15–€20. Restaurant 1km.
Closed	September to Easter.

Paul & Penelope Dudson
Château Haute-Fontaine,
Domaine de Java, Prat de Cest,
11100 Bages, Aude
Tel   +33 (0)4 68 41 03 73
Email   haute-fontaine@wanadoo.fr
Web   www.chateauhautefontaine.com

Entry 697   Map 15

Languedoc - Roussillon

Domaine du Griffon

Step confidently from the village street into this light, uncluttered house. Michel, Christophe, his mother Denise (a fine pastry cook) and their beloved pets are loving their new life here. The salon is soft and inviting, the big, gently-coloured bedrooms are full of light and space, the pergola shades your evening glass of wine. Dine in quiet pink elegance with your charming cultured hosts: one big table, succulent regional dishes made with market produce, served with good local wines (Michel grew up in a vineyard; he and Christophe had a couple of restaurants...). The sun shines 300 days a year; Cistercian Fondfroide is a must.

Rooms	5: 3 doubles, 2 twins/doubles.
Price	€78-€90. Extra bed €20. Pets €5.
Meals	Dinner with wine, €30. Restaurant 6km.
Closed	Rarely.

Michel Dyens & Christophe Malguy
Domaine du Griffon,
8 route de Ferrals,
11200 Boutenac, Aude
Tel +33 (0)4 68 27 07 29
Email domaine-du-griffon@wanadoo.fr
Web www.domaine-du-griffon.com

Entry 698   Map

Languedoc - Roussillon

Le Vieux Relais

Valerie and Mike poured hearts and souls into refurbishing their 18th-century coach house. Old door hinges gleam, tiled floors sweep across the big, welcoming, fresh-faced bedrooms, each with its own sitting area and ceiling fan to keep you cool. There's a cosy guest sitting room and a flower'd courtyard garden with – joy of joys – a pool; homemade cake for tea, fabulous dinners with local wines, barbecues on a shady terrace. Your friendly English hosts have stacks of time for you and know all about local events and restaurants. Books for readers, maps for walkers: they always go the extra mile.

Minimum two nights June-Sept.

Rooms	5: 1 double, 1 twin, 1 family room for 2-5, 2 suites.
Price	€70-€80. Family room €70-€135. Suite €75-€85.
Meals	Dinner with wine, from €25. Picnics available.
Closed	Rarely.

Valerie & Michael Slowther
Le Vieux Relais,
1 rue de l'Étang,
11700 Pépieux, Aude
Tel +33 (0)4 68 91 69 29
Email mike@levieuxrelais.net
Web www.levieuxrelais.net

Entry 699   Map 15

Languedoc - Roussillon

Languedoc - Roussillon

Métairie Montplaisir

Amélie throws open her ancient smallholding to all. You can hang around the modern kitchen where delicious and inventive meals are produced (by Maman) and wines chosen for your supper (locals come too). Or snooze in front of the fire in the large living room with mirrors and French windows to the garden. Quirky bedrooms (one has a bio-ethanol fireplace) have bright colours, sitting spaces, modern and antique furniture, funky paintings on the walls; the stunning loft apartment has its own terrace. You can have a massage here, then doze in the garden or float in the pool – but you might want to visit Carcassonne and Cathar castles!

Extra child beds available.

Domaine St Pierre de Trapel

Coming in from the magnificent gardens, catch the scent of herbs as you walk through the house. The delightful owners, lively, educated, well-travelled, moved here from east France for a more relaxing way of life and climate. Using exquisite taste, they have combined original 18th-century elegances with new necessities in big bedrooms and bathrooms of pure luxury, each with its own soothing colour scheme. Tranquil in all seasons, with relaxing outdoor spots for all, a superb 150-year-old cedar, olive trees, a swimming pool surrounded by roses and a lovely covered terrace. A place of beauty, elegance and space.

Rooms	5: 2 doubles, 2 suites, 1 loft for 2-5 with kitchen.
Price	€150-€170. Suite €180-€220. Loft €230-€250. Extra bed €30.
Meals	Dinner, 3 courses, €30. Wine €18-€40. Ask about picnic hampers and light lunch. Restaurant in village.
Closed	Christmas.

Rooms	5: 3 doubles, 1 twin, 1 suite.
Price	€95-€140. Suite €90-€170.
Meals	Restaurants 5km.
Closed	November-March, except by arrangement.

	Amélie Roujou de Boubée
	Métairie Montplaisir,
	2 av René Cassin,
	11600 Conques sur Orbiel, Aude
Tel	+33 (0)4 68 25 87 16
Mobile	+33 (0)6 33 74 62 17
Email	contact@metairiemontplaisir.com
Web	www.metairiemontplaisir.com

	Christophe & Catherine Pariset
	Domaine St Pierre de Trapel,
	Route de Villedubert,
	11620 Villemoustaussou, Aude
Tel	+33 (0)4 68 77 00 68
Email	cpariset@trapel.com
Web	www.trapel.com

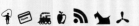

Entry 700   Map 15

Entry 701   Map 15

Languedoc - Roussillon

Villelongue Côté Jardins

Painters, poets, nature-lovers love this place, where history and romance combine. Dark 16th-century passages and uneven stone floors open into heavily beamed rooms sympathetically revived. Bedrooms are big and simply refined in their white cotton and old armoires, the newest on the ground floor. Views are to the ancient trees of the park or the great courtyard and ruined Cistercian abbey. Sisters Renée and Claude, warm, knowledgeable, generous, were born here and provide convivial breakfasts and dinners. Wild gardens and duck ponds, lazy cats, and lovely walking paths into the landscape.

Languedoc - Roussillon

La Forge de Montolieu

Napoleonic cannonballs were once fashioned in this striking country forge, set in a secluded valley where flowers and bird-filled forests give way to waterfalls and trout-rich pools. Later, textiles emerged from its creamy walls… Now home to a charming Franco-American family, it's a wonderful renovation project with four country-pretty bedrooms, new Italian showers and a kitchenette in the guest wing. Charles' photos hint at their passion for the place, and you'll learn more over a lazy brunch, a family supper or five-course dinner – organic with seasonal veg. Walk the dogs through a pocket of woods to book-happy Montolieu.

Rooms	3: 1 double, 1 twin, 1 family room for 3.
Price	€65.
Meals	Dinner with wine, €25. No dinner July/August.
Closed	Christmas.

Rooms	4: 2 doubles, 1 triple, 1 twin.
Price	€75-€90. Triple €80-€110. Cot €15.
Meals	Cooked breakfast €5. Dinner €18-€30. Wine €4-€25. Guest kitchenette. Restaurant 2km.
Closed	Rarely.

	Claude Antoine & Renée Marcoul
	Villelongue Côté Jardins,
	11170 St Martin le Vieil,
	Aude
Tel	+33 (0)4 68 76 09 03
Email	villelongue-cote-jardins@orange.fr
Web	www.villelongue-cote-jardin.com

	Charles Cowen
	La Forge de Montolieu,
	Hameau de Franc,
	11170 Montolieu, Aude
Tel	+33 (0)4 68 76 60 53
Email	info@forgedemontolieu.com
Web	www.forgedemontolieu.com

Entry 702   Map 15

Entry 703   Map 15

Languedoc - Roussillon

Château La Villatade

An enormous 19th-century wine vat (where, in times past, hundreds of tonnes of grapes were turned into wine) is the novel tasting room for the aromatic wines still made at this traditional farmhouse. Sophie and Denis invite you to share their home and their passion for wine-making; their welcome is irresistible. The 'Forge' and the 'Walker' suites are charming, modern, immaculate, with limewashed walls and terracotta floors, and the grounds are idyllic: horses in the paddock, a potager, teeming trout and a natural pool, bliss for a swim on a hot day. Mountains, caves and gorges wait to be explored, Carcassonne is wonderfully close.

Rooms	2 suites.
Price	€90-€100.
Meals	Dinner with wine, €20.
Closed	January.

Sophie & Denis Morin
Château La Villatade,
La Villatade,
11600 Sallèles Cabardès, Aude
Tel +33 (0)4 68 77 57 51
Email villatade@wanadoo.fr
Web www.villatade.com

Entry 704   Map 15

Languedoc - Roussillon

Chez Providence

Once part of the medieval village ramparts, now a thoroughly comfortable B&B in a deeply rural, mountain village near Carcassonne. Your Anglo/Dutch hosts are discreetly friendly. Bathrooms are modern, bedrooms traditional and pretty with invitingly dressed beds, good sitting spaces, polished floors and exposed stone walls. The attic room is a favourite with couples; the suite, usefully, has two separate rooms which can take six. You'll breakfast (perhaps on the balcony with wooded village views) and dine well: regionally and organically, in the smart dining room. Relax in the peaceful furnished garden across the quiet road.

Rooms	3: 1 double, 1 family room for 2-4, 1 family suite (2 twins/doubles; 2 extra sofabeds).
Price	€60. Suite €60-€90. Family suite €70-€100. Singles €50-€65. Extra bed €20. No charge for under 3's in cot.
Meals	Dinner, 3 courses with wine, €25 (under 12's half price).
Closed	Never.

Christina Press & Nico Janssen
Chez Providence,
9 rue de la Piala,
11390 Cuxac Cabardès, Aude
Tel +33 (0)4 68 25 32 24
Email info@chezprovidence.com
Web www.chezprovidence.com

Entry 705   Map 15

Languedoc - Roussillon

La Rougeanne

Monique has endless energy and adores people, Paul-André is quiet and charming, together they promise you a wonderful stay. They bought the old wine-grower's estate on the edge of town in a most parlous state – but look at it now! The sitting room is stylish, restful, flooded with light and washed with pearl grey, the bedrooms are quietly luxurious; Monique has a way with interiors. Have breakfast by the lavender in summer, then discover hilltop bastides and the castles of the Cathars... monumental Carcassonne is up the road. Return to a garden within gardens and distant views, an orangery and a pool. Bliss.

Rooms	5: 3 doubles, 1 twin, 1 family room.
Price	€81–€120. Family room €81–€180. Extra bed €30.
Meals	Restaurants within walking distance
Closed	Rarely.

Monique & Paul-André Glorieux
La Rougeanne,
8 allée du Parc,
11170 Moussoulens, Aude
Tel +33 (0)4 68 24 46 30
Mobile +33 (0)6 61 94 69 99
Email info@larougeanne.com
Web www.larougeanne.com

Entry 706   Map 15

Languedoc - Roussillon

Violette & Félicie

In the garden of a château are two Gypsy wagons with colourful pasts – and presents. Grand 140-year-old Félicie sits by a big fig tree, a fantasy in purple, red and gold. A few metres away, pink, yellow and blue Violette is just 100. Original fittings blend with the new: fabulous wallpaper, a tiny fridge, electric heat. Both *roulottes* have a double bed and a secret closet with loo and basin; you have a key to your real bathroom next to the pool in the former cloister. Enjoy organic table d'hôtes with creative hosts, and Molière on the lawn in summer. Near medieval Mirepoix and Carcassonne.

Book through Sawday's Canopy & Stars online or by phone.

Rooms	2 Gypsy wagons for 2.
Price	£62–£79.
Meals	Dinner with wine, €25. Restaurants 10km.
Closed	Open all year.

Sawday's Canopy & Stars
Violette & Félicie,
Château de Fajac la Selve,
11420 Pech Luna, Aude
Tel +44 (0)1275 395447
Email enquiries@canopyandstars.co.uk
Web www.canopyandstars.co.uk/chateaudefajac

Entry 707   Map 15

Languedoc - Roussillon

Le Domaine de Puget

Janie and John are warm, genuine, wonderful hosts. The house, the space, the stars, the views that reach to the Pyrenees – let their gentle delight in it all rub off on you. The old mellow stone buildings are centred on an open courtyard, two guest rooms are in the main house, the suite has its own garden, and all are done in modern rustic style, with very pretty views. Outside are shady gardens and walking paths, orchard, lake and lovely pool; inside are deep comfy sofas. John is chef, treating you to regional, seasonal (often organic) food and a different wine to try each night; you can also visit the producers.

Minimum two nights July / Aug.

Rooms	5: 2 doubles, 1 twin, 1 family room for 2-4, 1 suite for 2-4.
Price	€75-€85. Suite €120-€150. Family room €120-€150.
Meals	Dinner €35. Wine from €10. Restaurants 15-minute drive.
Closed	Rarely.

Janie & John Haward
Le Domaine de Puget,
11270 Gaja la Selve,
Aude
Tel   +33 (0)4 68 60 26 30
Email   john@lepuget.com
Web   www.lepuget.com

Entry 708   Map 15

Languedoc - Roussillon

Domaine les Magasins

Quite a setting – on the Canal du Midi. Boats bob and Carcassonne calls. Sweep through huge gates to Luc and Marianne's beautiful home, once a hub of activity where grain was loaded on to brave little barges. Now, all is calm, and bedrooms are spacious and stylishly minimalist – nab the family room or the suite with a terrace. Have breakfast by a wonderful pool (cosy if the two gîtes are full); come evening, share colonial-style sitting and dining rooms with your gentle hosts. You can mosey along the canal for supper – or Luc will drop you 5km away and the restaurant owner will deliver you back!

Children over 12 welcome.

Rooms	4: 2 twins/doubles, 1 family room for 4-5, 1 suite.
Price	€90-€95. Family room €90-€170. Suite €100-€110. Extra bed €20-€25.
Meals	Restaurants nearby.
Closed	Rarely.

Luc & Marianne Pringalle
Domaine les Magasins,
Port de Bram,
11150 Bram, Aude
Tel   +33 (0)4 68 79 49 18
Mobile   +33 (0)6 74 53 49 07
Email   zensud11@gmail.com
Web   www.domainelesmagasins.fr

Entry 709   Map 15

Languedoc - Roussillon

Château de la Prade

Lost among the cool shadows of tall sunlit trees beside the languid waters of the Canal du Midi is a place of understated elegance and refinement. Sitting in 12 acres, the 19th-century house is more 'domaine' than 'château' – formal hedges, fine trees, ornamental railings – though the vineyards have long gone. Swiss Roland runs the B&B, George looks after the gardens: they are kind and discreetly attentive hosts. Dinner is served on beautifully dressed tables, breakfasts are a treat, bedrooms have tall windows, polished floors, an immaculate, uncluttered charm. Half a mile from the road to Carcassonne but so peaceful.

Rooms	4 twins/doubles.
Price	€95-€115.
Meals	Dinner €26. Wine €17-€36.
Closed	Mid-November to mid-March.

Roland Kurt
Château de la Prade,
11150 Bram,
Aude

Tel	+33 (0)4 68 78 03 99
Email	chateaulaprade@wanadoo.fr
Web	www.chateaulaprade.eu

Entry 710   Map 15

Languedoc - Roussillon

Domaine Michaud

Stylish Jolanda from Holland looks after you beautifully in these ancient buildings in a pastoral setting with views of the Pyrenees and mature trees. The big living room has a fireplace, tapestries on the walls, antique furniture and a terrace for breakfast. Dinner (for locals too) is always a surprise and usually a home-grown one; and you can socialise or be private. Bright, lovely bedrooms, some with stone walls, most with views, one in romantic whites. The pool is just below so it may be splashy during the day. There's a self-catering studio-apartment too, in the main house with its own terrace.

Minimum two nights preferred.

Rooms	5 + 1: 4 twins/doubles. Apartment for 2.
Price	€89-€115. Apartment €685-€955 per week. Cot €15. €10 supplement for one night.
Meals	Breakfast €10 for apartment guests. Dinner, 3 courses, €30. Restaurant 4km.
Closed	Rarely.

Jolanda Danen
Domaine Michaud,
Route de la Malepère, Roullens,
11290 Carcassonne, Aude

Mobile	+33 (0)6 44 29 42 30
Email	info@domainemichaud.eu
Web	www.domainemichaud.eu

Entry 711   Map 15

Languedoc - Roussillon

Les Marguerites

Dine deliciously and convivially at one big table – by the log fire or under the stars. On the edge of the historic little spa town of Alet les Bains is this grand old mansion and sparkling B&B – throw open elegant shutters for sunshine and views. Here live Antoinette (daughter of a renowned restaurateur) and Keith (fount of local knowledge), in love with the Languedocian life, bringing up a young family. Outside find a fabulous play area, little tables for breakfast and century-old trees. The bedrooms are big, airy, uncluttered and charming; the suite has a long sunny balcony, the village has an outdoor pool. Heaven!

Minimum two nights. All children welcome.

Rooms	4: 3 doubles, 1 family suite for 4.
Price	€65–€105. Suite €105–€140.
Meals	Dinner €25. Wine €12–€25. Restaurant within walking distance.
Closed	Rarely.

Keith & Antoinette Fairhurst
Les Marguerites,
57 av Nicolas Pavillon,
11580 Alet les Bains, Aude
Tel +33 (0)4 68 20 53 56
Email Antoinette@les-marguerites.fr
Web www.les-marguerites.fr

Entry 712   Map 15

Languedoc - Roussillon

La Rassada

In a corner of Corbières where wild orchids flourish and eagles soar stands Philippa's eco-friendly barn. Once used for drying rosemary and thyme, it's now a modern home, open to the rafters with massive windows and heady views. Simple, comfy, contemporary ground-floor rooms with big glass doors open to the garden, while the kitchen opens to the terrace – for breakfasts of brioche, jams, muesli, all organic and homemade. Your charming host is a heavenly cook so dinners too are a treat. Perfect for nature-loving families and walkers – and the coast is close. Ask for a picnic and you can be as free as a bird all day.

Minimum stay four nights for two (two nights for four people).

Rooms	2: 1 double, 1 twin, sharing bathroom (let to same party only).
Price	€80–€90.
Meals	Dinner with wine, €20. Restaurants 15-min drive.
Closed	December/January.

Philippa Benson
La Rassada,
Route d'Opoul,
11510 Feuilla, Aude
Tel +33 (0)4 68 42 82 56
Email philippa@feuillanature.com
Web www.feuillanature.com

Entry 713   Map 15

Languedoc - Roussillon

L'Orangerie

The most charming town with a bustling market, and lovely restaurants… you stay in the heart of it all. Through huge green gates enter a pretty courtyard with flowering pots, the orange tree (as announced) and here is a true 18th-century *maison de maitre* with original terrazzo floors. Calm and relaxed, Sylvie and Claude offer a charming sitting room with a reading corner and comfy seating, and bright inviting bedrooms, one with a terrace. Breakfast in the dining room or in the courtyard brings seasonal fresh fruits, cake and homemade jams. Dinner can be served here too – in best traditional French style.

Languedoc - Roussillon

Les Buis

Carlos's rather grand house is in the colourful village centre; you enter from the narrow street to mosaic floor and marble stair. The attractive bedrooms have a classic feel too with antiques, armchairs and decorative fireplaces, some with big views of the lovely garden below with its open pool. When it's warm, the stone balustraded terrace is where you breakfast, on an impressive sweet and savoury spread. You can withdraw to the red salon or to the less formal library; or take off for the Canigou massif with its hiking trails and curious Orgues formations. It's a 20-minute drive to Perpignan, 30 to a good beach.

Rooms	4: 3 doubles, 1 family room.
Price	€65-€100.
Meals	Dinner with wine, €27.
Closed	Rarely.

Rooms	4: 2 doubles,1 twin, 1 triple (2 rooms), all with separate baths and wcs.
Price	€85-€125. Triple €135-€155. Extra bed €30.
Meals	Restaurant 250m.
Closed	Rarely.

	Sylvie & Claude Poussin
	L'Orangerie, 3T rue Ludovic Ville, 66600 Rivesaltes, Pyrénées-Orientales
Tel	+33 (0)4 68 73 74 41
Mobile	+33 (0)6 09 82 75 87
Email	maisonhoteslorangerie@wanadoo.fr
Web	maisonhoteslorangerie.com

	Carlos Monteiro
	Les Buis, 37 rue Carnot, 66130 Ille sur Têt, Pyrénées-Orientales
Tel	+33 (0)4 68 57 67 43
Mobile	+33 (0)6 09 01 34 31
Email	contact@lesbuis.com
Web	www.lesbuis.com

Entry 714   Map 15

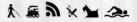

Entry 715   Map 15

Languedoc - Roussillon

Castell Rose

A beautiful, pink marble gentleman's house in its own parkland on the edge of a very pretty town between the sea and the mountains; the views are superb. Evelyne and Alex are both charming and give you large graceful bedrooms with calm colour schemes, good linen, tip-top bathrooms and elegant antiques. After a good breakfast, wander through the flourishing garden with its ancient olive trees to find a spot beside the lily pond, or just float in the pool. It's a five-minute stroll to village life, or take the yellow train up the mountain from Villefranche for more amazing views.

Rooms	5: 3 doubles, 1 twin, 1 family room.
Price	€85–€99. Family room €119–€139.
Meals	Restaurant 500m.
Closed	Rarely.

Evelyne & Alex Waldvogel
Castell Rose,
Chemin de la Litera,
66500 Prades,
Pyrénées-Orientales
Tel +33 (0)4 68 96 07 57
Email castellroseprades@gmail.com
Web www.castellrose-prades.com

Entry 716 Map 15

Languedoc - Roussillon

Maison Prades

Informal, vibrant and fun is this peaceful townhouse with big sunshiney rooms. Already well-integrated into the community, the charming new owners – Robson Brazilian, Benoît Belgian – are super well-travelled and following their dream: to run a laid-back but stylish B&B. They've opened up the garden, pruned back the trees, introduced teak tables for breakfast and loungers for leisure. Original features have been restored, wooden floors uncovered, bedrooms refurbished and the whole house handsomely revived. Robson is a keen cook and table d'hôtes dinners have an international flavour – as well as being fun!

Off-road parking for 4 cars. Minimum two nights July/Aug.

Rooms	5: 2 doubles, 1 twin/double, 1 triple, 1 family room for 2-4.
Price	€65–€80. Triple €55–€85. Family room €55–€110. Singles €55–€75. Extra bed €15.
Meals	Dinner, with wine €25, Mon & Weds. Restaurants 5-minute walk.
Closed	Rarely.

Robson Santana
Maison Prades,
51 av du Général de Gaulle,
66500 Prades, Pyrénées-Orientales
Tel +33 (0)4 68 05 74 27
Mobile +33 (0)6 19 01 27 86
Email info@maisonprades.com
Web www.maisonprades.com

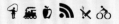

Entry 717 Map 15

Languedoc - Roussillon

Languedoc - Roussillon

Sanglier Lodge

An easy place to be: quiet, classically cosy but not staid. Peter and Mike's 18th-century village house showcases their art finds and taste and simply invites retreat. They are gracious, helpful hosts. Sip wine by the big wood-burner in the softly-lit sitting room, dip in the perched pool, doze on the shaded terrace. Bedrooms seduce gently; linen is luxurious; bathrooms modern. Breakfast and dine (gastronomically, out of season) at separate, well-dressed tables. You're quickly in the wilds for great walking and an hour each from Perpignan, Mediterranean beaches and the Dali Theatre-Museum in Figueres.

Minimum two nights.

Mas Pallarès

In a beautiful wooded valley five minutes from Céret is this ancient farmhouse with stepped gardens and a child-perfect stream. Birds sing, wisteria blooms, views sweep across the wooded valley and Lizzie has worked hard to ensure everyone has their own corner of calm; the B&B rooms have lovely big balconies. The mood is easy and the rooms are friendly: old floor tiles, inviting colours, country antiques, spotless showers. Lizzie's breakfasts are feasts and the fenced pool and summer kitchen are shared with apartment guests who self-cater. Céret's market is fantastic; legendary Collioure is a hop away.

Minimum two nights.

Rooms	4: 3 twins/doubles, 1 suite.
Price	€59-€69. Suite €80-€95. Extra bed €15.
Meals	Restaurant within walking distance (open during day only). Other restaurants 7km.
Closed	Rarely.

Rooms	2: 1 double, 1 suite with kitchenette.
Price	€80-€115. Suite €95-€140.
Meals	Summer kitchen. Restaurant 1km.
Closed	Rarely.

	Peter Laird
	Sanglier Lodge,
	6 route Royale,
	66230 Le Tech,
	Pyrénées-Orientales
Tel	+33 (0)4 68 81 04 23
Email	sanglierlodge@aol.com
Web	www.sanglierlodge.com

	Lizzie Price
	Mas Pallarès,
	66400 Céret,
	Pyrénées-Orientales
Tel	+33 (0)4 68 87 42 17
Email	lizzie@ceret-farmhouse-apartments.com
Web	www.ceret-farmhouse-apartments.com

Entry 718   Map 15

Entry 719   Map 15

Languedoc - Roussillon

Château d'Ortaffa

Medieval Ortaffa sits in a pocket of sunshine between the Pyrenees and the lively port of Collioure, and this big old wine-maker's château perches on its fortified walls. Breakfast on the terrace comes with a stunning tableau of mountains and sea with village rooftops tumbling below. Slip into a beautifully restored house whose elegant, pastel-shaded library and guest rooms display your hosts' love of antiques and fine art: your room may have Picasso prints, quirky graffiti, bookshelves, an antique child's bed, remnants of the former chapel... Roll down to the port for seafood, slide south along the coast to Spain.

Minimum two nights.

Rooms	4: 2 doubles, 1 suite, 1 family suite for 4-5.
Price	€95-€120. Suite €100. Family suite €120. Extra bed €30.
Meals	Restaurant in village.
Closed	Rarely.

Michelle & Alain Batard
Château d'Ortaffa,
8 rue du Château,
66560 Ortaffa, Pyrénées-Orientales
Tel   +33 (0)4 68 37 95 01
Email   chateau.ortaffa@gmail.com
Web   www.chateau-ortaffa.com

Entry 720   Map 15

Rhône Valley – Alps

Rhône Valley - Alps

Le Couradou

Diana, bright and gifted, and Jos, a charming geologist, came from cool populous Belgium to empty rustic Ardèche and set about transforming this fine big silk-farm house into a warm home. Outside, vineyards and the distant Cévennes, inside, wonderful vaulted 15th-century ceilings, split-level living spaces and four big bedrooms creatively and luxuriously put together with the local gifts of stone walls, country antiques, southern fabrics and wrought iron – there's even a sunken bath in one room. Gorgeous views from private terraces, a beautiful garden and a super pool complete the experience.

Minimum five nights in high season.

Rooms	4: 2 doubles, 2 triples.
Price	€90-€130. Extra bed €35.
Meals	Dinner with wine, €39.
Closed	October-April.

Diana Little & Jos Vandervondelen
Le Couradou,
Le Chambon,
07150 Labastide de Virac, Ardèche
Tel +33 (0)4 75 38 64 75
Email infos@lecouradou.com
Web www.lecouradou.com

Rhône Valley - Alps

L'Évidence

Amid the terraced hills and chestnut forests of the Ardèche is a rambling multi-levelled farmhouse squirrelled away on the village edge, with mountains beyond. A pleasure to step inside and find three fresh bedrooms: 'Zanzibar', reached through a slick jacuzzi'd bathroom, is big and Africa-infused; 'Oslo', right at the top, is all cool blues; cosy 'Jaïpur' (once a goat cellar) is womb-like and intimate, ideal for romancers. Breakfast in bed, or take bread and brioche to the kitchen. Suppers of seasonal bounty can be booked too, saving a drive to a restaurant – and there's a little pool. Smiley Christine, new to B&B, is a delight.

Rooms	3 doubles.
Price	€80-€120. Extra bed €65.
Meals	Lunch or picnic €15. Dinner with wine, €28. Restaurant 10km.
Closed	Rarely.

Christine Moser
L'Évidence,
Peyreplane, 07380 Prades, Ardèche
Tel +33 (0)4 75 94 15 89
Mobile +33 (0)6 22 62 62 82
Email christine.moser@l-evidence.com
Web www.l-evidence.com

Rhône Valley - Alps

Les Roudils

Breakfast like kings among the butterflies in an idyllic place. High up in the nature-rich regional park of Monts d'Ardèche the views are inspiring, the peace supreme. At the end of the long windy road, the house, built of stone and wood from the chestnut forests, has been lovingly restored to offer authentic bedrooms full of light and soft simplicity. Informal and fun, Marie makes heavenly preserves (apricot, rosemary), Gil makes aperitifs and honeys (chestnut, heather, raspberry). Come for sunshine and music, a great Cévenol fireplace and exceptionally warm hospitable people and their three cats. Paradise!

Rooms	3: 2 doubles, 1 suite.
Price	€70-€75. Suite €70-€115.
Meals	Kitchen available. Restaurant 8km.
Closed	November-March.

Marie & Gil Florence
Les Roudils,
07380 Jaujac, Ardèche
Tel +33 (0)4 75 93 21 11
Email le-rucher-des-roudils@wanadoo.fr
Web www.lesroudils.com

Entry 723   Map 11

Rhône Valley - Alps

Château de Fontblachère

Framed by a forested valley and mountainous horizons, this 17th-century château marries Provençal peace with deep comfort and style. Bernard greets you in a courtyard whose manicured hedges and white roses dissolve into parkland: a panoramic pool, Japanese fish pond, tennis court, jacuzzi… Under vaulted ceilings are more treats: a log fire, piano, candles, art, and Turkish cushions in the orangery where you may dine on iced melon soup and quail. Sprightly Bernard cooks, serves, pours and chats all the while. Immaculate rooms have space for families and the valley cries out for walking, riding and fishing in the river.

Rooms	5: 3 family rooms, 1 for 3, 1 for 4, 1 for 5.
Price	Family room €100-€150.
Meals	Dinner with wine, €35. Restaurants 3km.
Closed	October-April.

Bernard Liaudois
Château de Fontblachère,
07210 St Lager Bressac, Ardèche
Tel +33 (0)4 75 65 15 02
Email chateau@fontblachere.com
Web www.chateau-fontblachere.com

Entry 724   Map 11

Rhône Valley - Alps

Maison Hérold

Enjoy every bend through wild Ardèche to this elegant old bourgeois house, built on the remains of an ancient stronghold; feel the strength of the land; hear the untamed water piling past. You will be greeted by sweetly endearing people (teacher and nurse) who have renovated their family home with a fine eye, then be shown up the graceful curling staircase to a room with 19th-century antiques, modern bathroom and soul-cleansing views. A spring rises in the garden, delicious breakfast is in the pretty dining room. Writer Hérold received many literati and Ravel composed his 'Valse' here. Atmospheric and definitely special.

Rooms	2: 1 double, 1 suite.
Price	€65. Suite €80.
Meals	Restaurant 200m.
Closed	Rarely.

Joselyne & Patrick Moreau
Maison Hérold,
Lapras, 07270 St Basile, Ardèche
Tel   +33 (0)4 75 06 46 09
Email   contact@maisonherold.com
Web   www.maisonherold.com

Entry 725   Map 11

Rhône Valley - Alps

Le Veyroux de Longefaye

Wonderful to wind through the cherry and apricot orchards of the Ardèche hills – especially in spring – to the peaceful old farmhouse at the end of the track, and a friendly welcome from interesting Swiss hosts. Well-travelled, they have personalised their home with eclectic paintings, prints, books and kilims. You sleep in secluded stylish quarters downstairs, then wake to a feast of pancakes, fruits, local brown bread and jams under the sweet linden tree – or in the huge lofty kitchen amid sleek red units and rustic wood and stone. Take a massage, slip into the pool, visit the beekeeper next door, lap up the views.

Rooms	2: 1 double, 1 twin/double.
Price	€75-€85.
Meals	Restaurant 10-minute drive.
Closed	October-April.

Bernard & Dominique Betrancourt
Le Veyroux de Longefaye,
07570 Désaignes, Ardèche
Tel   +33 (0)4 75 06 61 74
Email   leveyroux@orange.fr
Web   www.leveyrouxdelongefaye.com

Entry 726   Map 11

Domaine du Fontenay

Simon's lifelong ambition was to become a wine-maker in France, now his wines are highly regarded; enjoy the tastings in the cellar. Huge care is been taken by these owners to make you comfortable and well-informed. In a separate building are four super bedrooms with excellent mattresses, big showers, rugs on old terracotta tiles and astonishing views from this hilltop site; and each bedroom has an excellent folder with all the local info. In summer, breakfast is served at check-clothed tables on the big terrace. This is a great area for good-value gourmet restaurants so enjoy them – and ask about 'La Route Magique.'

Rooms	4: 1 triple, 3 suites.
Price	Triple €73–€86. Suite €73–€96. Cot available free of charge.
Meals	Kitchen available. Restaurant nearby.
Closed	Rarely.

Simon & Isabelle Hawkins
Domaine du Fontenay,
Fontenay, 42155 Villemontais, Loire
Tel   +33 (0)4 77 63 12 22
Mobile   +33 (0)6 81 03 30 33
Email   info@domainedufontenay.com
Web   www.domainedufontenay.com

Entry 727   Map 11

Domaine du Château de Marchangy

Down an avenue of oaks and through grand gates to a perfectly proportioned house. Light pours into intimate, immaculate guest rooms on the first and loft floors of the ivy-clad guest wing; be charmed by big rugs on pale wood floors, harmonious colours, delightful armoires, stylish *objets*, gorgeous fabrics, garden flowers and, in the irresistible guest salon, a huge log fire in winter. Rise at your leisure for château breakfasts and fruits from the orchard, served by the pool in summer, in whinnying distance of the horses. Your smiling hostess looks after you wonderfully.

Minimum two nights July/Aug.

Rooms	3 suites.
Price	€105–€125.
Meals	Picnic on request. Restaurants 10-minute drive.
Closed	Rarely.

Marie-Colette Grandeau
Domaine du Château de Marchangy,
42190 St Pierre la Noaille, Loire
Tel   +33 (0)4 77 69 96 76
Email   contact@marchangy.com
Web   www.marchangy.com

Entry 728   Map 11

Maison d'hôtes de La Verrière

Hugging the edge of a beautiful valley in Beaujolais, the high views from nearly every room of this serenely secluded family home are magnificent. Whether waking in your quirky country bedroom, meeting guests at the breakfast table (sampling yogurt cake and nine homemade jams) or swimming in the natural salt pool among wild mountain flowers, the valley is always there – particularly beautiful in autumn. Grégoire's guided walks start from the house. Both he and Christine love having guests to stay, and their French cuisine is so good (never the same dish twice) there's no reason to dine anywhere else.

La Folie

You'll sleep in a rustic stone tower with windows onto beauty. La Folie, inspired by Pascal and Pascaline's Indian travels, is decked with flamboyant trinkets and curiosities; they've been carving and restoring *roulottes* (traditional showmen's wagons) for years. You have your own bathroom and a hand-carved balcony onto a dizzying landscape with gorgeous rambles. You share the salon downstairs (rich dark furniture, eclectic books), and the big kitchen with guests staying in the wagons outside. Enjoy the pretty garden, friendly pets and breathtaking views of the Beaujolais hills.

Book through Sawday's Canopy & Stars online or by phone.

Rooms	5: 3 twins/doubles, 1 triple, 1 quadruple.
Price	€75. Triple €90. Quadruple €110. Singles €60. Pets €5. Under 2's €6 (includes use of cot, highchair etc).
Meals	Dinner €28, with wine. Restaurant 15km.
Closed	Rarely.

Rooms	1 double in tower.
Price	£60-£95.
Meals	Use of kitchen. Restaurant 6km.
Closed	November-March.

	Christine Gesse & Grégoire Lamy
	Maison d'hôtes de La Verrière,
	69430 Les Ardillats, Rhône
Tel	+33 (0)4 74 04 71 46
Email	christine.gesse@orange.fr
Web	a.la.verriere.pagesperso-orange.fr

	Sawday's Canopy & Stars
	La Folie,
	La Serve, 69860 Ouroux, Rhône
Tel	+44 (0)1275 395447
Email	enquiries@canopyandstars.co.uk
Web	www.canopyandstars.co.uk/folie

Entry 729   Map 11

Entry 730   Map 11

La Croix de Saburin

To-die-for views soar over endless streaks of vines to Mounts Brouilly and, even, Blanc: a dream of a setting. Built in regional style against the hillside is this very French, contemporary-smart house. Sociable and perfectionist, Monique and Jean-Michel began B&B when they retired; bedrooms are pretty with chalky mango-wood tables and sparkling bathrooms. Guests are spoilt with the salon: tea-making kit and plenty of books. Rare birds, orchids and butterflies dwell in the valley below; cycling, wine tasting and Lyon are close by. Dine with the family on salade Lyonnaise and chicken in champagne. Intimate and stunning.

Rooms	2: 1 double, 1 family room.
Price	€68. Family room €68–€85. Extra bed €17.
Meals	Dinner with wine, €25.
Closed	Rarely.

Jean-Michel & Monique Legat
La Croix de Saburin, Saburin,
69430 Quincié en Beaujolais,
Rhône

Tel	+33 (0)4 74 69 02 82
Mobile	+33 (0)6 08 50 19 03
Email	jean-michel.legat@orange.fr
Web	lacroixdesaburin.free.fr

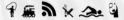

Entry 731   Map 11

Les Pasquiers

Come to meet Laurence, her daughter and two sweet cats in this beautiful home in a wine-country village setting. Oriental rugs and fine antiques rub shoulders with contemporary art, gorgeous books lie around for everyone to peruse, there's a grand piano in the drawing room, heaps of CDs, and a stunning spacious dayroom in the attic. Bedrooms are sunny, beds wear beautiful linen, bathrooms are fashionably screened, and the garden is divine – languid terraces, organic potager, summerhouse, pool. Delightful Laurence loves to cook and both breakfasts and dinners are scrumptious. One of the best!

Rooms	5: 2 doubles, 2 twins, 1 quadruple.
Price	€88. Quadruple €88. Extra bed €20. Meals for over 7's, €12. Children under 7, free.
Meals	Dinner with wine, €35.
Closed	Rarely.

Laurence Adelé-Gandilhon
Les Pasquiers,
69220 Lancié, Rhône

Tel	+33 (0)4 74 69 86 33
Mobile	+33 (0)6 83 42 86 60
Email	welcome@lespasquiers.com
Web	www.lespasquiers.com

Entry 732   Map 11

Domaine La Javernière

Through the huge wrought-iron gates into a courtyard lined with delectable roses and a house filled with history and soul. In the heart of Beaujolais country, this huge bourgeois residence is owned by wine distributor Thibault who treats guests as friends and runs it with an easy charm. Great Grandpapa's portrait hangs in the hall, there are books, photographs, art and sculpture everywhere, a piano if you wish, and space to roam: nowhere is out of bounds. Bedrooms are gracious, sunny and sprinkled with antiques, bathrooms range from swish Italian to cute and tiny under the eaves. Gastronomy and vineyards abound.

Rooms	4: 2 doubles, 1 twin, 1 suite for 4-5.
Price	€90-€140.
Meals	Restaurant 600m.
Closed	November-March.

Thibault Roux
Domaine La Javernière,
69910 Javernière, Rhône
Mobile   +33 (0)6 66 05 90 52
Email   contact@la-javerniere.fr
Web   la-javerniere.fr

Entry 733   Map 11

Château de Chambost

It takes little to imagine the owners aristocratic ancestors residing in this rural, 16th-century hillside château. Traditional going on lavish, it's still fit for Lyonnais elite, its five bedrooms decked out in toile de Jouy and period furniture; one's still adorned with original 1850s parrot-flocked wallpaper. In the basement lies another gem: a striking umbrella-vaulted dining room where vivacious hostess Véronique serves homemade aperitifs and beef reared on the château's estate. The cows have bagged most of the garden, but you can retire to the elegant sitting room to plan countryside forays beyond.

Rooms	5: 2 doubles, 2 twins, 1 family room.
Price	€90-€100. Family room €115.
Meals	Dinner with wine, €25. Restaurant 15km.
Closed	Last 2 weeks in July.

Vivien & Véronique de Lescure
Château de Chambost,
69770 Chambost Longessaigne,
Rhône
Tel   +33 (0)4 74 26 37 49
Mobile   +33 (0)6 30 52 04 84
Email   infos@chateaudechambost.com
Web   www.chateaudechambost.com

Entry 734   Map 11

Rhône Valley - Alps

Les Hautes Bruyères

Once settled on this wooded hilltop in restfully subdued, country-smart comfort, you can't imagine that super-urban Lyon is only 10 minutes away. Karine's converted farm buildings are sophisticated yet simple – and so is she, with a genuine interest in other people and a flair for interiors. With 2,000 years of European history in its bones and a solid reputation for good food, Lyon has myriad treasures to see and taste. After a day of discovery or work, in city or countryside, relax in the green and birdsung garden or the elegant Italianate pool area. Tomorrow there will be delicious breakfast in the 'auberge' dayroom.

Rooms	5: 2 doubles, 1 twin/double, 2 suites.
Price	€145–€250. Suite €175–€280. Extra bed €35.
Meals	Restaurants in Lyon, 6km. Guest kitchenette. Bocuse cookery school in village: weekday bookings.
Closed	Rarely.

Karine Laurent
Les Hautes Bruyères,
5 chemin des Hautes Bruyères,
69130 Écully, Rhône

Tel	+33 (0)4 78 35 52 38
Mobile	+33 (0)6 08 48 69 50
Email	contact@lhb-hote.fr
Web	www.lhb-hote.fr

Entry 735 Map 11

Rhône Valley - Alps

Domaine des Charmilles

The Villons' villa has the good luck to have a pretty view across the river and feels marvellously rural. In the leafy grounds the cottage has two suites, one for a couple, one for a family, each impeccably furnished and contemporary: a mod-con kitchen, a chic palette, telly, games, lots of space. Breakfast, in the big house whenever you fancy, is homemade and truly delicious. Super dinners too (Lyonnais on request), local wines selected by Monsieur, and barbecues in summer. Dogs, donkey and miniature goats entertain little ones, as do swings beneath century-old trees. Lovely Lyon is a 20-minute drive.

Ask about weekly rental.

Rooms	2: 1 double, 1 suite.
Price	€100–€160. Suite €100–€180. Extra person €20.
Meals	Dinner €25. Wine €15. Restaurant 1km.
Closed	Never.

Caroline Villon
Domaine des Charmilles,
Le Clavel, 1061 route de Lyon,
69390 Vernaison, Rhône

Tel	+33 (0)6 11 71 91 40
Email	info@domaine-charmilles.com
Web	www.domaine-charmilles.com

Entry 736 Map 11

Rhône Valley - Alps

Château de Tanay

Surrounded by flat lands, a magnificent château in acres of parkland with pool. Inside is equally splendid. A sleek modern décor illuminates fine stonework and medieval beams, there's a games room for children, a grand piano for musicians and a convivial dining table; in summer, take breakfast by the moat beneath the willow. Spend the day in charming old Lyon or treat the family to the Parc des Oiseaux... return for a château tour with your hosts, trot off for dinner at the local pizzeria. Big tasteful bedrooms lie in the courtyard stables but the family suite is in the château itself – with an amazing massage bath.

Extra bed available.

Rooms	5: 1 family suite.
	Stables: 4 twins/doubles.
Price	€95-€130. Suite €160.
Meals	Dinner with wine, €20.
	Pizzeria in village, 1km.
Closed	Rarely.

Benoît Haym
Château de Tanay,
Chemin de Tanay,
01600 St Didier de Formans, Ain
Tel   +33 (0)9 53 36 87 42
Mobile +33 (0)6 63 94 70 27
Email   info@chateau-tanay.com
Web   www.chateau-tanay.com

Entry 737   Map 11

Rhône Valley - Alps

Ancienne École du Chapuy

In the rural quiet of forests, lakes and unsung villages sits this old school house, peaceful by the road. Classily converted by Marie-Christine and Alain, it has a warm, happy atmosphere. Up a winding staircase, pastel bedrooms with fine bedding and handsome bedsteads look out to lush pastures. Bathrooms glitter in sea greens and have huge bathtubs. Pleasing contrasts of bright fabrics, striking modern pieces and antiques in the sitting room; breakfasts are superb. Make the most of (flat) cycling, then tuck into those good old French clichés, frogs' legs and snails – local specialities! Intimate, charming.

Rooms	2: 1 double, 1 family room for 4.
Price	€65-€130.
Meals	Restaurant 2km.
Closed	November-March.

Alain Privel & Marie-Christine Palaysi
Ancienne École du Chapuy,
Les Bruyères, Châtillon sur Chalaronne,
01400 Romans, Ain
Tel   +33 (0)4 74 55 63 30
Mobile +33 (0)6 83 86 82 68
Email   ecoleduchapuy@hotmail.fr
Web   www.ecoleduchapuy.com

Entry 738   Map 11

Château de Marmont

An amazing avenue of plane trees delivers you to an authentic château experience – yet the people are the best part of it. Madame is a joy, laughing, enthusing, creating delicious cakes and jams for breakfast, her house as colourful as she is. Monsieur is quietly helpful. Up the grand stairs to a fine room with Persian carpets, trompe-l'œil walls, antiques, books and fresh flowers. Madame pours tea from silver into porcelain and artfully moves the butter as the sun rises; at night she'll light your bedside lamp, leaving a book open at a chosen page for you to read after a game of (French) Scrabble. Step back in time…

Le Clos du Châtelet

Sweeping gardens overlook the valley, the garden is full of sequoias, and an outbuilding is home to a collection of antique bird cages. Bedrooms are peaceful havens of elegantly muted colours: 'Joubert' in pink-ochre, its twin wrought-iron four-posters dressed in toile de Jouy; 'Lamartine' in palest aqua. All have polished wooden floors and gently sober bathrooms. There's much comfort here: an open fire in the sitting room, period furniture, prints, antlers on the wall and a delicious air of calm. Dinner is by candlelight in an atmospheric dining room with a wonderful old terracotta floor. Peace, charm and spectacular views.

No credit cards.

Rooms	2: 1 double, 1 family suite for 3-5.
Price	€95.
Meals	Restaurant 3km.
Closed	Rarely.

Rooms	4: 3 doubles; 1 double with separate bath
Price	€98-€118.
Meals	Dinner €35. Wine €20-€35.
Closed	Rarely.

	Geneviève & Henri Guido-Alhéritière
	Château de Marmont,
	2043 route de Condeissiat,
	01960 St André sur Vieux Jonc, Ain
Tel	+33 (0)4 74 52 79 74
Web	www.chateau-marmont.info

	Madame Durand-Pont
	Le Clos du Châtelet,
	01190 Sermoyer, Ain
Tel	+33 (0)3 85 51 84 37
Email	leclosduchatelet@free.fr
Web	www.leclosduchatelet.com

Entry 739   Map 11

Entry 740   Map 11

Rhône Valley - Alps

La Ferme du Champ Pelaz

Deeply rural is this gentle land where distant peaks tantalise and three generations of Smiths live in the big, creeper-smothered 19th-century farmhouse. Guests have their quarters in the middle with Michael and Linda at one end, daughter Katey and her children at the other. The owners know all about the area (Michael specialises in golf breaks) and can guide you towards the best alpine walks. Bedrooms are cosy and pretty, pastel-painted, wooden floored, a good size and ideal for all. There's a pool for summer heat and a big log fire and deep sofas in the living room for cool nights.

Minimum two nights in summer.

Rooms	4: 2 triples; 2 doubles (sharing wc on landing).
Price	€70-€90.
Meals	Restaurant 5-minute drive.
Closed	Rarely.

Michael & Linda Smith
La Ferme du Champ Pelaz,
57 chemin de la Biolle, Pesey,
74150 Thusy, Haute-Savoie
Tel   +33 (0)4 50 69 25 15
Mobile +33 (0)6 31 85 55 54
Email champ-pelaz@wanadoo.fr
Web   www.champ-pelaz.com

Entry 741   Map 11

Rhône Valley - Alps

Chalet Châtelet

The cow-belled Vallée d'Abondance envelops this pretty pine chalet, the result of years of your hosts' creative energy. Oak floors, soft shapes and high ceilings hug reclaimed furniture and works by other members of this arty family. Warmth comes from a Finnish stove and solar panels – an eco-lover's dream and you still find bliss in the hot tub (along with spectacular views). Expect cultured chat in the intimate dining room and Suzie's range-cooked local and organic food. Bedrooms have stunning views too, and dreamy bathrooms; gaze to mountains you climbed, snow-shoed or skied that day. Heavenly.

Weekly winter prices vary throughout the season. Short breaks available.

Rooms	4: 2 doubles, 2 triples.
Price	€90-€150. Winter half-board: €520-860 p.p. per week.
Meals	Dinner with wine, €30.
Closed	Rarely.

Pascal & Suzie Immediato
Chalet Châtelet,
74360 Bonnevaux,
Haute-Savoie
Tel   +33 (0)4 50 73 69 48
Email info@chalet-chatelet.com
Web   www.chalet-chatelet.com

Entry 742   Map 12

Rhône Valley - Alps

La Ferme du Château

Still more farming village than resort, Abondance links seamlessly with the Portes du Soleil so the skiing is superb. Christine from England fell in love with the place 13 years ago and now runs an elegant farmhouse-chalet with a top-floor living space in the vast old hayloft. She offers cooked breakfasts for skiers, tasty food all year round, a central fireplace for cosiness and a mezzanine for kids to play. Close to restaurants and shops, the house has its back to the traffic, its face to the mountain, and a few bedrooms open to terrace and fenced garden. Hike, bike – or brave the zip wire that spans the entire valley!

Extra beds available.

Rooms	6 twins/doubles.
Price	€60-€80.
Meals	Dinner, 3 courses with wine, €25.
Closed	November.

Christine Allenet
La Ferme du Château,
Chef Lieu,
74360 La Chapelle d'Abondance,
Haute-Savoie

Tel	+33 (0)6 81 40 80 26
Email	info@savoiefaire.co.uk
Web	www.savoiefaire.co.uk

Entry 743   Map 12

Rhône Valley - Alps

La Ferme du Lac Vert

Cow hides and fur, restored timbers and a sculpted stair, delectable canapés and cocktails that explode in the mouth – live dangerously at the funkiest chalet in the Portes du Soleil. Quirky cow horn sculptures add personality, bathrooms ooze luxury and Lucy and Rob are full of joie de vivre. In winter the shuttle whisks you to the slopes, in summer there are cow bells and cycle trails. Return to three fabulous living spaces (one with a bar on runners, one with a fireplace for warming vin chaud), a hot tub on the terrace, and bedrooms that are simply divine; one has an opium bed shipped from Indonesia.

Minimum four nights.

Rooms	8: 3 doubles, 2 twins, 3 family rooms.
Price	€86-€156 for 2. Winter half-board: €710-€1,250 p.p. per week.
Meals	Restaurant 500m.
Closed	Rarely.

Lucy Mundell
La Ferme du Lac Vert,
169 Vieille Route,
Montriond, 74110 Morzine,
Haute-Savoie

Tel	+33 (0)4 50 79 49 33
Email	ski@skizeen.com
Web	www.skizeen.com

Entry 744   Map 12

Rhône Valley - Alps

Chalet APASSION

Perched on the mountainside above the lovely old resort of Samoëns, a luxury ski chalet so new that fresh pine scents the air. Majestic views stretch from the terraces and balcony, and a cedar hot tub is the perfect place to soak away the day's strain: skiing and snowboarding in winter, biking and hiking in summer. Glossy bedspreads and scatter cushions finish pristine rooms, while in the open-plan sitting/dining room, plush leather sofas sit in the glow of a real fire. Breakfast is just as relaxed – simply let attentive owners Vicky and Rob know when you'd like it. Delightful dinners are on request.

Minimum two nights in summer, three nights in winter.

Rooms	5 twins/doubles.
Price	€120–€144. Winter half-board: €690–€1,240 p.p. per week (includes resort shuttle).
Meals	Dinner with wine, €33 (3 courses & canapés, €48). Winter half-board. Restaurants 1km.
Closed	Rarely.

Rob & Vicky Tarr
Chalet APASSION,
77 chemin du Battieu, Vercland,
74340 Samoëns, Haute-Savoie

Tel	+33 (0)4 50 18 68 33
Mobile	+33 (0)6 06 70 81 57
Email	robandvicky@apassion.com
Web	www.apassion.co.uk

Entry 745   Map 12

Rhône Valley - Alps

Ferme du Ciel

High above the valley and pretty Samoëns, the huge old chalet-style farmhouse as been expertly renovated to reveal soaring beams, a great woody open-plan living space, a shiny modern kitchen and big lofty bedrooms; also, a log fire in winter, a lovely balcony-terrace in summer. The whole place oozes comfort and style in patterned rugs, heated floors, crisp white linen. Your hard-working hosts and two lovely labs are very present for B&B guests or decently discreet if you self-cater. There are a hot tub, a sauna and a garden swimming pool. Beyond are lakes and mountains, fresh air and cowbells – and beauty galore.

Minimum three nights in winter.

Rooms	6: 1 double, 4 twins/doubles (each with extra double sofa bed), 1 family room for 5.
Price	€130–€160. Family room €180. Winter half-board: €940–€1,550 p.p. per week.
Meals	Catered (half-board) all year.
Closed	Rarely.

Andrew & Su Lyell
Ferme du Ciel,
773 route Mathonex, Mathonex,
74340 Samoëns, Haute-Savoie

Tel	+33 (0)4 50 58 44 57
Mobile	+33 (0)6 21 19 74 83
Email	info@fermeduciel.com
Web	www.fermeduciel.com

Entry 746   Map 12

Chalet Odysseus

The village has character; Chalet Odysseus
has much besides. There's comfort in soft
sofas, check curtains, bright rugs and open
fire, and swishness in sauna and small gym;
a chef cooks for you once a week in winter,
and your relaxed English hosts who look
after you well (Kate, too, is a fine cook)
breed border collies on site. They have the
ground floor of this brand-new chalet; you
live above. Cheerfully pretty bedrooms come
with the requisite pine garb, two have
balconies that catch the sun, the tiniest comes
with bunk beds for kids. Great for an active
family break, whatever the season.

Minimum two nights.

La Ferme du Soleil

The hamlet of four old wooden houses (two
chalets, two farm buildings) is high up,
impossibly pretty, detached from the bustling
world, with views to lift spirits and a deep
silence in which to contemplate such beauty.
In winter, you are a stroll from the top of a
chair lift and a quick slide from the bottom of
several, so you can stop skiing when you're
ready for a blazing log fire and a delicious
bite. In summer you can wander the
mountains to enjoy the flowers and the bell-
ringing cows. The word 'idyll' really does
apply. Big, cosy, beautiful, open and convivial
– another dream realised.

Minimum seven nights.

Rooms	5: 3 doubles, 1 twin, 1 bunk room.	
Price	€90. Winter half-board: €140-€200 for 2 per night.	
Meals	Dinner with wine, €40.	
Closed	Rarely.	

Rooms	5: 2 doubles, 2 twins, 1 family studio for 3.
Price	€100-€124. Family room €100-€124. Winter half-board prices for 2. Half-board €700-€865 p.p. per week. Summer: self-catered (8) €1,440-€2,160; studio €720 for 2 (child €120). Prices per week.
Meals	Winter: half-board. Summer: self-catered.
Closed	May to early June; Nov to early Dec.

Kate & Barry Joyce
Chalet Odysseus, 210 route de Lachat,
74300 Les Carroz d'Araches,
Haute-Savoie

Tel	+33 (0)4 50 90 66 00
Mobile	+33 (0)6 85 77 06 54
Email	chaletodysseus@wanadoo.fr
Web	www.chaletodysseuslachat.com

Veroni Gilbert
La Ferme du Soleil, Les Gettiers,
74450 Le Grand Bornand,
Haute-Savoie

Tel	+33 (0)9 52 76 34 01
Mobile	+44 (0)7789 947024
Email	lafermedusoleil@hotmail.com
Web	www.lafermedusoleil.com

Entry 747   Map 12

Entry 748   Map 12

Rhône Valley - Alps

Chalet Le Panoramic

They pick you up from Geneva, then whisk you to the chalet just above the village, right on the piste, with a charming bar-auberge across the way. It doesn't get much better than this and Lisa and Simon head a happy team. There's heaps of space for kids and adults, bedrooms are cosy (two with balconies, most with views), bathrooms shine, sofas are snooze-worthy and ski posters add style. In a huge room with a piste-side panorama (skiers to one side, village to the other) the wine flows, the piano plays, the logs crackle and the cakes, canapés and dinners are divine. Toast your good fortune in the hot tub under the stars.

Winter bookings only. Minimum seven nights.

Rooms	9: 3 twins/doubles, 3 triples, 3 family rooms.
Price	€202-€320. Triple €202-€320. Family room €202-€320. Half-board prices for 2: €710-€1,110 p.p. per week. (With airport transfer €860-€1,260 p.p.)
Meals	Catered only. Tea, aperitifs & drinks included.
Closed	May to mid-December.

	Lisa Clark
	Chalet Le Panoramic,
	74230 La Clusaz,
	Haute-Savoie
Tel	+44 (0)1534 863630
Email	lisa@snowlife.co.uk
Web	www.snowlife-laclusaz.com

Entry 749   Map 12

Rhône Valley - Alps

Proveyroz

Josette has boundless energy, is a great walker, adores her mountain retreat in this lovely valley and cooks very well indeed. Her chalet rooms, all wood-clad of course, are bright and welcoming in blue, white and orange; they have unusually high ceilings, good storage and plenty of space. In the open-plan living area, huge windows open to a small sun-soaked terrace and a little garden while the mixture of old and modern furniture plus bits and pieces of all sorts gives the whole place a comfortable, family feel; the vast fireplace is a winter delight. Skiing is the big thing round here, Annecy is close and Geneva an hour away.

Rooms	2: 1 double; 1 triple with separate wc.
Price	€55. Triple €65.
Meals	Dinner with wine, €20.
Closed	Rarely.

	Josette Barbaud
	Proveyroz,
	74230 Manigod, Haute-Savoie
Tel	+33 (0)4 50 44 95 25
Mobile	+33 (0)6 70 55 63 60
Email	josette.barbaud@sfr.fr
Web	josette.barbaud.free.fr

Entry 750   Map 12

Rhône Valley - Alps

Chalet Chovettaz

Join this outgoing family in their big high-mountain chalet, new-built for warmth and comfort. Chatty, gregarious, motherly Fiona serves real English tea with luscious brownies and then takes care of hearty meals all year round. Fancy fabrics and animal prints stand out among traditional English furniture and family ornaments; two wood-burners warm the generous living area. Kids can hide in the snug while you warm your toes in the hot tub. A wraparound balcony lets you drink in sunlight and alpine views: Mont Blanc is a mile as the crow flies. There's skiing a short hop away and hiking paths outside the door.

Minimum two nights in winter. Weekly prices available.

Rooms	4: 2 twins/doubles; 1 double with separate shower; 1 children's quadruple (on mezzanine).
Price	€110–€130. Quadruple €110–€190. Winter half-board: €150–€190 p.p. (includes transport to lifts).
Meals	Dinner with wine, €45. Packed lunch €13.
Closed	Rarely.

Fiona & Christopher Hopkinson
Chalet Chovettaz, 30 chemin de La Chovettaz d'en Haut, 74170 Les Contamines Montjoie, Haute-Savoie

Tel	+33 (0)4 50 47 73 05
Mobile	+33 (0)6 27 39 02 70
Email	enquiries@skicontamines.com
Web	www.skicontamines.com

Entry 751 Map 12

Rhône Valley - Alps

La Touvière

Mountains march past Mont Blanc and over into Italy, cows graze in the foreground, the place is perfect for exploring this walkers' paradise. Myriam, bubbly and easy, adores having guests with everyone joining in the lively, light-hearted family atmosphere. In the typical old and unsmart Savoyard farmhouse, the cosy living room is the hub of life. Marcel is part-time home improver, part-time farmer (just a few cows now). One room has a properly snowy valley view, the other overlooks the owners' second chalet, let as a gîte; both are a decent size, homely but not basic, while shower rooms are spotless. Remarkable value.

Rooms	2 doubles.
Price	€60.
Meals	Restaurant 3km.
Closed	Rarely.

Marcel & Myriam Marin-Cudraz
La Touvière,
73590 Flumet, Savoie

Tel	+33 (0)4 79 31 70 11
Email	marcel.marin-cudraz@wanadoo.fr
Web	www.touviere.fr

Entry 752 Map 12

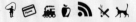

Rhône Valley - Alps

Chalet Savoie Faire

At the top of a thrillingly steep road are mountains, clear skies and world-class cross-country skiing – but who'd guess that behind the grey façade of this old Savoyard farmhouse is a luxurious B&B? Friendly owners Hugh and Nikki – she runs wonderful cookery courses – have put everything into the renovation and each room has charming touches. The arched diner (once the cowshed) is chandelier-hung and atmospheric; the sitting room has a toasty fire and a rug to snuggle toes in; the bedrooms are a delight (the big family suite is on the first floor) with chunky-chic furniture from old timbers. Bathrooms are a wow.

Rhône Valley - Alps

La Portette

Up the winding mountain road to the church square and the top of the village, and a beautiful old farmhouse owned by Liza and Andy. The enticing family suite is reached from the street, more comfy bedrooms lie above. At the top… great cosy sofas beneath a pitched wooden roof, a long table for fabulous meals, big carved balconies for breathtaking views. In winter, two friendly ski hosts take over, life moves up a gear, every bedroom is filled and you are whisked to the télécabine in three minutes. The snowy slopes of Les Arcs and La Plagne are yours to discover; in summer, you can bike, hike and lake-swim.

Discounts for under 16's & over 65's.

Rooms	3: 1 double, 1 double (links with bunk room); 1 twin with separate bathroom.
Price	€68–€110. Bunk room €70–€90. Half-board option: summer €2,500; winter €2,800; prices per week for 2.
Meals	Dinner, 3 courses with wine, €28. Restaurant 1km.
Closed	Rarely.

Rooms	6: 2 doubles, 1 family room (1 double, 1 bunk room); 1 double, 2 twins sharing bathroom.
Price	€60. Winter half-board: €420–€600 p.p. per week (includes transport to lifts).
Meals	Dinner with wine, €25. Picnic lunch €7. Restaurant 2km.
Closed	Rarely.

	Nikki Shields-Quinn
	Chalet Savoie Faire,
	Fontaines-Naves,
	73260 La Léchère, Savoie
Tel	+33 (0)4 79 24 54 28
Email	nicoleshields13@hotmail.com
Web	www.chaletsavoiefaire.com

	Liza Omar
	La Portette,
	Montorlin, 73210 Bellentre, Savoie
Tel	+33 (0)4 79 07 34 31
Mobile	+33 (0)6 10 78 11 33
Email	liza@mountainsinc.com
Web	www.mountainsinc.com

Entry 753   Map 12

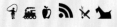

Entry 754   Map 12

Rhône Valley - Alps

Maison Coutin

A year-round Alpine dream. In summer it's all flowers, birds and rushing streams. In winter you can ski cross-country, snow-walk or take the ski lift, 500m away, to the vast ski field of Les Arcs. La Plagne is close, too. Delicious, mostly organic, food is cooked in the wood-fired oven. Your friendly, sporty hosts have known the valley all their lives, have three children and will be helpful with yours. View-filled bedrooms are traditionally dark-beamed and attractively, imaginatively furnished. There's a smallish comfortable dayroom with a fridge. Great value and a deeply eco-friendly ethos.

Dietary requirements catered for on request. Ask about child rates & half-board summer rates.

Rooms	3 family suites: 1 for 3, 1 for 4, 1 for 6.
Price	€58-€64 for 2. €18-€22 extra adult. Winter half-board: €581-€654 for 2 per night.
Meals	Dinner with wine, €21. Child €8-€16. Restaurant 200m.
Closed	Rarely.

	Claude Coutin & Franck Chenal
	Maison Coutin,
	Chemin de la Fruitière,
	73210 Peisey Nancroix, Savoie
Tel	+33 (0)4 79 07 93 05
Mobile	+33 (0)6 14 11 54 65
Email	maison-coutin@orange.fr
Web	www.maison-coutin.fr

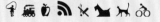

Entry 755   Map 12

Rhône Valley - Alps

Maison Caramel

There are many chalets in the Alps, but this one is special. The building, a former stable and workshop, was once owned by carpenter brothers; now you might find a luxurious modern bed next to rustic bunks beautifully made from recycled timbers. Gaze down the valley, up the peaks or over the jutting village rooftops. Inside, for quirkery and vistas, go for a room at the top: cabin beds in the eaves, snug mezzanines, a roll top bath with forest and glacier views. The skiing in Paradiski is fabulous, but there's so much else too: canoeing, hiking, marmot-spotting... a veritable adventurer's paradise.

Winter: 4 extra rooms & family rooms on upper floor. Half-board optional all year.

Rooms	5: 2 doubles, 2 twins, 1 family room.
Price	€80-€110. Family room €100-€140. Winter half-board: €550-€750 p.p. per week.
Meals	Dinner with wine, €35. Picnic lunch €10. Restaurants within walking distance.
Closed	Rarely.

	Alvaro Gil
	Maison Caramel,
	Chemin des Glières,
	73210 Landry,
	Savoie
Mobile	+33 (0)6 26 80 77 67
Email	info@maisoncaramel.com
Web	www.maisoncaramel.com

Entry 756   Map 12

Rhône Valley - Alps

La Ferme d'Angèle

Savoyard charm oozes from this 1830s chalet. Think flagstones and furs, antlers and candles, wooden headboards and hearts, balconies and billowing window boxes. Romantic 'La Gentiane' is in the mazot, 'Edelweiss' is perfect for families. Relax in the starlit hot tub amid swaying larch; thaw in the sauna. With breakfast crêpes à l'ancienne, tartiflette, fire-smoked ham and strawberry soup for dinner, Valérie loves to spoil. Intimate tables dot an atmospheric stone-walled living room, ski instructor Olivier will point you towards the best pistes. In summer, keen cyclists may want to tackle the Petit St Bernard pass.

Minimum two nights in school holidays.

Rhône Valley - Alps

Chalet Colinn

Mylène and Elizabeth love the outdoors, hence their five-year fight to reincarnate a fallen ruin as a luxury mountain retreat. Join them for gourmet dinner under soaring, raftered ceilings in the grand living space which hovers above Tignes dam. Or soak in the terrace hot tub under the stars; there's a sauna too. Urban rusticity, mountain chic: the place reeks Italian style yet is, unbelievably, hidden in this tiny hamlet. For daytime adventure: the slopes at Val d'Isère, or Tignes, or the Vanoise park. Just ask Elizabeth, off-piste skier extraordinaire.

Snow tyres/chains recommended in winter.

Rooms	5: 1 double, 1 family room for 3, 3 family rooms for 4.
Price	€160. Family rooms €225-€300. Winter: half-board prices for 2. Singles €90. Child €60.
Meals	Dinner €25. Wine €20.
Closed	Rarely.

Rooms	5: 3 twins/doubles, 2 triples.
Price	€190-€400. Winter half-board for 2 per night. €700-€1,200 p.p. per week (includes ski pass).
Meals	Dinner €35. Wine from €13.
Closed	Rarely.

Valérie & Olivier Graziano
La Ferme d'Angèle,
73700 Séez, Savoie

Tel	+33 (0)4 79 41 05 71
Mobile	+33 (0)6 07 67 43 20
Email	contact@ferme-angele.com
Web	www.ferme-angele.com

Elizabeth Chabert & Mylène Charrière
Chalet Colinn,
Le Franchet de Tignes, BP 125,
73150 Val d'Isère, Savoie

Tel	+33 (0)4 79 06 26 99
Email	contact@chaletcolinn.com
Web	www.chaletcolinn.com

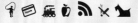

Entry 757   Map 12

Entry 758   Map 12

Rhône Valley - Alps

Rhône Valley - Alps

Chalet Solneige

A six-minute tootle down the hill from little Vaujany is Solneige: charming on the outside, stylish within. Here live hosts Pieter and Therese – Dutch, Swiss, great at languages, warm and fun. The hub is the vaulted living room: squishy taupe sofas and candles, convivial table, log fire, even a trunk of dressing up clothes... all ages love it here. For summer there's a fruit tree'd garden; for winter, the glorious Alpe d'Huez (Vaujany's gondola whisks you up in a trice); delicious food is served year round. Bedrooms are fresh-contemporary with bathrobes for the hot tub and dreamy views: raise your glass to the stars.

Dogs welcome in 2 bedrooms only.

Montchâteau

Views swoop across the green rolling landscape of the National Park as far as the eye can see; sit on the glazed veranda and drink it all in. High in the hills, utterly peaceful, this 19th-century hunting lodge is 15 minutes from lakes, 30 minutes from slopes, and 40 minutes from Grenoble: a special situation. Your gently attentive hosts give you large tranquil bedrooms in uncluttered French style – Rococo-repro here, Louis XV there – and super-spoiling bathrooms. Downstairs are plush leather chesterfields on a sweeping floor, a marble fireplace, English TV, and thrice-weekly meals at the big table.

Minimum two nights July/Aug.

Rooms	6: 1 double, 1 twin, 1 twin/double, 2 family rooms for 3, 1 family suite for 2-4.
Price	€78. Family room €110-€140. Family suite €120-€140. Winter half-board: €525-€795 p.p. per week. Dogs €5 (must book).
Meals	Dinner €25 (most nights). Winter: catered (half-board). Wine €18-€25. Restaurants in village, 2km.
Closed	November.

Rooms	4: 3 doubles, 1 family room.
Price	€59-€79. Family room €79.
Meals	Dinner with wine, €25 (Fri, Sat & Mon only; cold supper available rest of week). Restaurant 4km.
Closed	Rarely.

	Therese Gasser
	Chalet Solneige,
	Lieu-dit de Pourchery,
	38114 Vaujany, Isère
Tel	+33 (0)4 76 79 88 18
Email	solneige@wanadoo.fr
Web	www.solneige.com

	Hazel Watson
	Montchâteau,
	Reyssabot,
	38620 Merlas, Isère
Tel	+33 (0)4 76 66 16 82
Email	hazel@montchateau.com
Web	www.montchateau.com

Entry 759   Map 12

Entry 760   Map 11

Rhône Valley - Alps

Le Traversoud

Rooms are named after painters; lovely 'Cézanne' lies under the eaves on the top floor. Nathalie, warm, bright and amusing, and attentive Pascal welcome you to their farmhouse, guide you up the outside stairs to colourful, comfortable bedrooms and spotless shower rooms (a sauna, too) and treat you to some of the best home cooking in France, served at a long table; even the brioche is homemade. The garden overflows with grass and trees, crickets chirrup, the Bernese Mountain dog bounds, the donkeys graze and the exuberant courtyard is a safe space for your children to join Pascal and Nathalie's. Wonderful, informal B&B.

Longeville

There is a gentle elegance about this house and the people who live in it, including three sleek cats and two friendly dogs. Of Scots and Irish origin, the Barrs have spent their adult years in France running a wooden toy business. Their love for this 1750s farmhouse shows in their artistic touch with decorating, their mix of old and modern furniture, their gorgeous big bedrooms done in soft pale colours that leave space for the views that rush in from the hills. A high place of comfort and civilised contact where dinner in the airy white living room is a chance to get to know your kind, laid-back hosts more fully.

Rooms	3: 1 twin, 2 family rooms.
Price	€58. Family rooms €74–€90. Under 10's, €10.
Meals	Dinner with wine, €25.
Closed	Rarely.

Rooms	2 twins/doubles.
Price	€50–€80.
Meals	Dinner with wine, €25.
Closed	Rarely.

Nathalie & Pascal Deroi
Le Traversoud,
484 chemin Sous l'École,
38110 Faverges de la Tour, Isère
Tel   +33 (0)4 74 83 90 40
Mobile   +33 (0)6 07 11 99 42
Email   deroi.traversoud@orange.fr
Web   www.le-traversoud.com

Mary & Greig Barr
Longeville,
5 Longeville,
38300 Succieu, Isère
Tel   +33 (0)4 74 27 94 07
Mobile   +33 (0)6 87 47 59 46
Email   mary.barr@wanadoo.fr

Entry 761   Map 11

Entry 762   Map 11

Rhône Valley - Alps

Domaine de Gorneton

The most caring of B&B owners: he, warmly humorous and humble about his excellent cooking; she, generous and outgoing. Built high on a hill as a fort in 1646, beside the spring that runs through the magnificent garden (a genuine Roman ruin, too), their superb old house is wrapped round a green-clad courtyard. Inside, levels change, vast timbers span the dining room, country antiques sprawl by the fire in the salon. In an outside single-storey building are traditional, rather sombre guest rooms with pristine bathrooms – and a bedhead from Hollywood in the best room. Family friendliness in deep country 15 minutes from Lyon.

Rooms	4: 3 doubles, 1 suite.
Price	€120–€180.
Meals	Dinner with wine, €40.
Closed	Rarely.

Mr & Mme Fleitou
Domaine de Gorneton,
712 chemin de Violans,
38670 Chasse sur Rhône, Isère

Tel	+33 (0)4 72 24 19 15
Mobile	+33 (0)6 99 81 72 08
Email	gorneton@wanadoo.fr
Web	www.gorneton.com

Entry 763   Map 11

Rhône Valley - Alps

Château de Pâquier

Old, mighty, atmospheric – yet so homely. Enormous rooms, high heavy-beamed ceilings, large windows with sensational valley views; terraced gardens and animals; impressive bedrooms (handsome wardrobes, underfloor heating) up an ancient spiral staircase that sets the imagination reeling. Twice a week Hélène prepares dinner for guests in her modernised 17th-century tower kitchen (wood-fired range, stone sink, cobbled floor) where she makes her bread, honey, jams and walnut aperitif. Jacques and their daughter run an auberge next door – so do eat there too. And drink wine from the Rossis' own vineyard near Montpellier.

Rooms	5: 4 twins/doubles, 1 family room.
Price	€80. Family room €86–€140.
Meals	Dinner €20–€29. Wine €5/litre. Family auberge next door.
Closed	Rarely.

Jacques & Hélène Rossi
Château de Pâquier,
Chemin du Château,
38650 St Martin de la Cluze, Isère

Tel	+33 (0)4 76 72 77 33
Email	chateau.de.paquier@free.fr
Web	chateau.de.paquier.free.fr

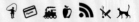

Entry 764   Map 11

Rhône Valley - Alps

Clos de la Sauvagine

A modern-traditional hillside house with owners who go above and beyond for their guests; literally, a breath of fresh air. Once you've trekked and climbed all you can, come home to cosy pine-clad bedrooms with plump duvets and soft lighting – in the main house or in the chalet. The intricate, sloping garden glows with flowers, trees, vegetables, birds, little winding pathways and views to die for; sip wine on the terrace, flip open a book. Henri and Janine, both incredibly kind and generous, share their homely open-plan living area with you. An immaculate, pampering, very beautiful place – and Henri designed the house.

Over 10's welcome.

Rooms	2: 1 double (with separate wc). Cottage for 4 (1 double, 1 mezzanine twin).
Price	€120. Cottage €110–€180. Singles €90.
Meals	Dinner €25. Restaurant 10km.
Closed	November–April.

	Janine & Henri Bonneville
	Clos de la Sauvagine,
	La Chapelle,
	38650 Château Bernard, Isère
Tel	+33 (0)4 76 34 00 84
Mobile	+33 (0)6 08 60 18 61
Email	henribonneville@orange.fr
Web	www.closdelasauvagine.com

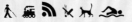

Entry 765   Map 11

Rhône Valley - Alps

Les Marais

Opt for the simple country life at this friendly farm, which has been in the family for over 100 years and has returned to organic methods. A couple of horses, a few hens and, when there's a full house, beautiful meals of regional recipes served family-style, with homemade chestnut cake and 'vin de noix' aperitif. Monsieur collects old farming artefacts and Madame, although busy, always finds time for a chat. The bedrooms are in a separate wing with varnished ceilings, antique beds, some florals; baths are old-fashioned pink, new showers delight Americans. At the foot of the Vercors range, French charm, utter peace.

Rooms	4: 1 double, 1 twin, 1 triple, 1 family room for 4.
Price	€55–€60. Triple €70. Family room €98.
Meals	Dinner with wine, €18 (Not Sundays).
Closed	Rarely.

	Christiane & Jean-Pierre Imbert
	Les Marais,
	26300 St Didier de Charpey, Drôme
Tel	+33 (0)4 75 47 03 50
Mobile	+33 (0)6 27 32 23 65
Email	imbert.jean-pierre@wanadoo.fr
Web	pagesperso-orange.fr/les-marais

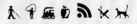

Entry 766   Map 11

Rhône Valley - Alps

Les Péris

Here is the grandmother we all dream of, a woman who cossets her guests, puts flowers and sweets in the bedrooms and sends you off with walnuts from the farm. In the family for ten generations, the old stone house facing the mountains is a happy and delightful home. Join family, friends and guests round the long kitchen table for walnut cakes at breakfast and daughter Élisabeth's delicious *menu curieux* that uses forgotten vegetables. Roomy, old-fashioned bedrooms with armoires breathe a comfortable, informal air. Great for kids: a garden for wild flowers and a duck pond for splashing in.

Rhône Valley - Alps

Chambres d'Hôtes Morin Salomé

A feast of colour and art, surrounded by breathtaking views, the Morin house is a visual treat, and is owned by a charming couple. He has created the windows and ironwork of the pergolas, she has tiled, fresco'd and frieze'd bathrooms, bedrooms and kitchen, with skill and imagination. Bedrooms are all river-side, brilliantly done, and fun. Dine on the terrace at one long table amongst a fabulous collection of pots and clambering plants, with the magnificent cliff beyond and rushing river sounds. A second terrace with ponds and goldfish almost drips over the river – the perfect solace. Tons to do nearby. Stunning.

Rooms	3: 1 double, 1 suite for 3, 1 family room for 4.	Rooms	4: 2 doubles, 1 family room, 1 triple.
Price	€50. Family suite €50–€70. Family room €50–€90.	Price	€70.
Meals	Dinner with wine, €20.	Meals	Dinner with wine, €27.50. Restaurant 5-minute walk.
Closed	Never.	Closed	Rarely.

	Madeleine Cabanes & Élisabeth Berger		Frédéric & Salomé Morin
	Les Péris,		Chambres d'Hôtes Morin Salomé,
	D154 - Route de Combovin,		26 rue du Temple,
	26120 Châteaudouble, Drôme		26340 Saillans, Drôme
Tel	+33 (0)4 75 59 80 51	Tel	+33 (0)4 75 21 43 95
		Mobile	+33 (0)6 14 18 75 89
		Email	morin-salome@orange.fr
		Web	www.chambres-hotes-morin-salome.fr

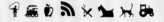

Entry 767   Map 11

Entry 768   Map 11

Rhône Valley - Alps

La Moutière

Surrounded by gorgeous gardens, the bastide sits large and square amid old outbuildings concealing perfectly converted gîtes. Bare stone façades and limestone trims under a Provençal roof set the tone for simple, fresh, uncluttered interiors: new limestone floors, white furniture, neutral tones and flashes of unexpected colour. Bedding is sumptuous, bathrooms fashionably funky, views from the beautiful pale blue pool glide pleasingly over rows of poplars and fields of lavender. Your wonderfully exuberant Belgian hostess gives convivial weekly dinner parties under the chestnut trees during high season. Divine.

Rooms	3 twins/doubles.
Price	€105-€125.
Meals	Dinner €38. Guest kitchen. Restaurant 3km.
Closed	Rarely.

Françoise Lefebvre
La Moutière,
Quartier Moutière,
26230 Colonzelle, Drôme
Tel   +33 (0)4 75 46 26 88
Mobile +33 (0)6 76 94 90 25
Email lamoutiere@gmail.com
Web   www.lamoutiere.com

Entry 769   Map 16

Rhône Valley - Alps

La Fontaine Bleue

With its warm terracotta façade, blue shutters, beams and whitewashed walls, this old southern townhouse makes a pleasant change from most B&Bs. The lovely English owners have lived in this land of lavender, olive trees and wine for over 20 years and have restored the house beautifully in Provençal style. Original stairs lead to both bedrooms and a large salon with a working fireplace; the terrace overlooks the walled town garden, an enchanting mass of flowers and shaded pergola – a perfect spot for your evening wine. You're perfectly placed for mountain river swimming and gorges to explore.

Not suitable for young children.

Rooms	2 doubles.
Price	€70-€78.
Meals	Dinner with wine, €32. Restaurants within walking distance.
Closed	Rarely.

Susan King
La Fontaine Bleue,
19 bd Clemenceau,
26170 Buis les Baronnies, Drôme
Tel   +33 (0)4 75 28 21 79
Email susan.king@hotmail.fr
Web   www.la-fontaine-bleue.fr

Entry 770   Map 16

Rhône Valley - Alps

La Lauren

Below, glorious views stretch south over the Sault plateau, west to Mont Ventoux. Here, surrounded by lavender fields, all is whisper-quiet. Warm friendly Christine has renovated her 17th-century sheep farm with extreme care and furnished it with walnut antiques and rich deep brocade – character oozes from every pore. She has a large garden, a handsome whippet, and serves six homemade jams at breakfast under the trees or in the baronial hall. Just for guests: teal velvet armchairs, a Renaissance fireplace and down-steps bedrooms with deep colours, splendid beds, south-facing views. Special for writers, artists, romantics.

Minimum two nights July/Aug.

Rooms	2: 1 double, 1 family room (1 double, 1 twin).
Price	£95. Family room £160.
Meals	Guest kitchenette. Restaurant 9km.
Closed	November-April.

Christine Gourbin
La Lauren,
Route de Séderon,
26570 Ferrassieres, Drôme
Tel   +33 (0)6 25 79 33 56
Email   kris.lauren@yahoo.fr
Web   www.la-lauren.com

Entry 771   Map 16

If you are walking in the mountains you should know about France's wonderful Réfuges – where you can sleep.

Our *Go Slow France* is a Treat. Get a copy before travelling, and prepare to meet remarkable people.

Walkers should take a look at www.ffrandonnee.fr for excellent information. The IGN maps are superb, too.

Provence – Alps – Riviera

Provence - Alps - Riviera

Mas St Joseph

Come for the view of row upon row of peaks fading into the distance, the walking, the welcome and the Slow Food. Hélène and Olivier bought the old *mas* and its sloping terrain, restored it with love, then moved in and began taking guests. Olivier is the walker and knows all the trails; the countryside is spectacular. One bedroom has the old bread oven in the corner; another was the stable, the old manger proves it; all are rustic and charming. Delicious, delightful table d'hôtes is held on the terrace in warm weather or in the lovely old barn. Further treats: massage treatments, a hot tub and a pool. And, oh, those views!

Rooms	5: 1 double, 1 triple, 2 suites for 4, 1 gypsy caravan.
Price	€65. Triple €84. Suite €103. Gypsy caravan €65.
Meals	Dinner with wine, €22.
Closed	Mid-November to March.

Hélène & Olivier Lenoir
Mas St Joseph,
04200 Châteauneuf Val St Donat,
Alpes-de-Haute-Provence
Tel   +33 (0)4 92 62 47 54
Mobile   +33 (0)6 60 04 70 66
Email   contact@lemassaintjoseph.com
Web   www.lemassaintjoseph.com

Entry 772   Map 16

Provence - Alps - Riviera

Le Jas du Bœuf

Here is Haute Provence bliss surrounded for miles by forests, vineyards and lavender and with stunning views of the Lubéron. Les and Wendy have restored the big 17th-century farmhouse to perfection and love having guests. Choose between traditional bedrooms in the house and two breathtakingly modern, wood and glass poolside lodges that pull the outside in. Star attractions are Wendy's art and design courses, yet a multitude of sports, delightful villages, gardens and markets call you. Then chill out by the infinity pool or in the exotic sunken siesta house. Exquisitely minimalist, wonderfully remote and welcoming.

Rooms	5: 3 doubles, 2 lodges for 2.
Price	€80-€115. Lodge €95-€130.
Meals	Dinner with wine, €35. Summer kitchen. Restaurants 3km-8km.
Closed	Never.

Wendy & Les Watkins
Le Jas du Bœuf,
Lieu-dit Parrot,
04230 Cruis,
Alpes-de-Haute-Provence
Tel   +33 (0)4 92 75 84 78
Email   jasduboeuf@googlemail.com
Web   www.colourdimensions.com

Entry 773   Map 16

Provence - Alps - Riviera

Le Clos de Rohan

Cloaked in a valley sweet with lavender lies an 18th-century farmhouse with ingeniously restored barns — find lavender stalks in the plaster! Lovely generous rooms have classy bathrooms, iron beds, crisp linen, a patio and terrace each, and views over valley and hills fat with bees. The chic two-storey suite comes with an open fire and a kitchenette, the double is more rustic, and there's a shared living room with a cosy wood-burner. In a courtyard garden heady with blooms breakfast on homemade honey, cherries, plums, and daydream by the small pool. Provence at its bucolic best.

Provence - Alps - Riviera

La Belle Cour

The moment you enter the gorgeous big courtyard you feel at home. Angela and Rodney's welcome is second to none: cheerful and open, warm and humorous. On medieval foundations, this 18th-century staging post for pilgrims is all exposed stone and beams, its décor traditional/rustic; you'll love the embracing living rooms, the open fire, the cosy library with surround-sound music. Bedrooms overlook the courtyard and have private staircases; wallow in luscious fabrics and colours and intriguing treasures like the exquisite Japanese silk paintings. Truly special, right in a friendly village with restaurants and a swimming pool.

Rooms	2: 1 double, 1 suite.
Price	€85-€100. Extra bed €15-€30.
Meals	Dinner with wine, €25. Guest kitchen.
Closed	Rarely.

Rooms	2 doubles.
Price	€90-€105.
Meals	Restaurants within walking distance.
Closed	November-March.

Françoise Cavallo
Le Clos de Rohan,
04150 Simiane la Rotonde,
Alpes-de-Haute-Provence

Tel	+33 (0)4 92 74 49 42
Mobile	+33 (0)6 20 06 59 76
Email	francoise.cavallo@terranet.fr
Web	www.le-clos-de-rohan.eu

Rodney & Angela Heath
La Belle Cour,
Place Daniel Vigouroux,
04280 Céreste,
Alpes-de-Haute-Provence

Tel	+33 (0)4 92 72 48 76
Email	angela.heath@orange.fr
Web	www.labellecour.com

Entry 774   Map 16

Entry 775   Map 16

La Maison du Guil

The 16th-century stone and timber priory, the oldest house in this remote narrow hamlet, has the same glorious views as ever, out over the rooftops to the surrounding peaks. Inside is all stone and timber, too, beautifully architect-renovated and furnished with a cleancut imaginative eye. The big living room has a stunning arched stone ceiling, the perfect foil for high-modern scarlet chairs and table cloths. Delighted with their Alpine venture, the charming new young owners will offer you a big traditional bedroom or a funkier cave-like room with stone nooks for lights and a sunken shower. Splendid.

Minimum three nights July/Aug.

L'École Buissonnière

A stone jewel set in southern lushness and miles of green vines and purple hills. Country furniture – a particularly seductive choice of Provençal chairs – is polished with wax and time; big whitewashed bedrooms are freshly sober; birds sing to the tune of the aviary outside. One balconied bedroom, in the mezzanined old barn, has a saddle and a herdsman's hat from a spell in the Camargue; ask about John's travels. He rightly calls himself a Provençal Englishman, Monique is warmly welcoming too, theirs is a happy house, where German is also spoken. Wonderful Vaison la Romaine is four miles away.

Rooms	4: 2 doubles, 2 family rooms.
Price	€120-€130. Child €45.
Meals	Dinner €35 inc. aperitif & coffee. Wine from €5. Restaurant 3km.
Closed	Rarely.

Rooms	3: 2 doubles, 1 family room.
Price	€63-€73. Family room €63-€99.
Meals	Guest kitchen. Restaurant in village, 1km.
Closed	Early November to March.

Tom Van De Velde
La Maison du Guil,
La Font, 05600 Eygliers,
Hautes-Alpes
Tel   +33 (0)4 92 50 16 20
Email   info@lamaisonduguil.com
Web   www.lamaisonduguil.com

Monique Alex & John Parsons
L'École Buissonnière,
D75, 84110 Buisson,
Vaucluse
Tel   +33 (0)4 90 28 95 19
Email   ecole.buissonniere@wanadoo.fr
Web   www.buissonniere-provence.com

Entry 776   Map 12

Entry 777   Map 16

L'Évêché

Narrow, cobbled streets lead to this fascinating and beautifully furnished house that was once part of the 17th-century Bishop's Palace. The Verdiers are charming, relaxed, cultured hosts – he an architect/builder, she a teacher. The white walls of the guest sitting room-library are lined with modern art and framed posters, and the cosy, quilted bedrooms, all whitewashed beams and terracotta floors, have a serene Provençal feel. Views fly over beautiful terracotta rooftops from the balconied suite, and handsome breakfasts are served on the terrace, complete with exceptional views to the Roman bridge.

Rooms	5: 3 twins/doubles, 2 suites for 2-3.
Price	€84-€92. Suite €115-€160.
Meals	Restaurants nearby.
Closed	2 weeks in both November & December.

Aude & Jean-Loup Verdier
L'Évêché,
14 rue de l'Evêché, Cité Médiévale,
84110 Vaison la Romaine, Vaucluse

Tel	+33 (0)4 90 36 13 46
Mobile	+33 (0)6 03 03 21 42
Email	eveche@aol.com
Web	www.eveche.com

Entry 778   Map 16

La Maison aux Volets Rouges

Step off the street into the 'red-shuttered' house to be wrapped in its warm embrace. Rooms are big with tiled floors, beams and antiques; family photographs line the stairs; there's an open fire for cool days, a courtyard for warm ones. High-beamed bedrooms have good storage and individual touches – a brass bed, an arched window, a teddy bear on the baby's bed. Garden and pool are a three-minute walk, restaurants a short stroll. Borrow a bike, play tennis at the local club (no charge), drop in on the glories of Avignon and Aix. Delightful, energetic Brigitte has impeccable English and breakfasts are delicious.

Rooms	2: 1 double; 1 double with separate shower.
Price	€70.
Meals	Restaurants within walking distance.
Closed	Rarely.

Brigitte Woodward
La Maison aux Volets Rouges,
2 place de l'Église,
Les Farjons, 84100 Uchaux,
Vaucluse

Tel	+33 (0)4 90 40 62 18
Email	b.woodward@hotmail.fr
Web	www.lamaisonauxvoletsrouges.com

Entry 779   Map 16

Provence - Alps - Riviera

Provence - Alps - Riviera

Dar Mona

Meander through pine forests and vineyards where all is peaceful under breezy blue Provençal skies. Here lies a stunning modern house settled into a slope: lavender-laden bees buzz around terraced gardens with panoramic views, and an exquisite pool and decked area sit within ochre walls. Honeymooners will love the B&B room with its huge views and leisurely breakfasts on the terrace; families can spread out in the cottage. There's also a poolside studio, and a Gypsy caravan; the whole place exudes ethnic chic. Bag them all and sleep 14 – Mona and Marcel the dog will move out should you fancy the house too! Heaven.

Justin de Provence

One night is not enough to take in all that Isabelle and Philippe have laid on for you in their imposing Provençal farm and grounds, a 15-minute walk from Orange: tiled, styled, quilted, shuttered and wrought bedrooms; bathrooms with attitude (screened, free-standing baths); and former outbuildings sheltering hammam, jacuzzi, indoor swimming pool (there's a large outdoor pool too), fitness room, tiny Pagnol-esque café and a small shop (brocante, lavender soaps). Isabelle's sculptures pop up all over, her breakfasts are copious and mostly outdoors, there's a guest kitchen, and (of course!) a boulodrome.

Rooms	4: 1 double. Studio for 2. Gypsy caravan for 3. Cottage for 5-7.
Price	€120. Gypsy caravan €120. Cottage €120-€250.
Meals	Dinner with wine, €28. Restaurants 2km.
Closed	Rarely.

Rooms	5: 4 doubles, 1 twin.
Price	€120-€205.
Meals	Restaurants nearby.
Closed	Rarely.

Mona Lengellé
Dar Mona,
80 route de Valbonnette,
84220 Piolenc, Vaucluse
Mobile +33 (0)6 27 63 69 64
Email moniquelengelle@yahoo.fr
Web www.darmona.com

Isabelle & Philippe Berbudeau
Justin de Provence,
Chemin du Mercadier,
84100 Orange, Vaucluse
Tel +33 (0)4 90 69 57 94
Email contact@justin-de-provence.com
Web www.justin-de-provence.com

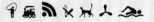

Entry 780 Map 16

Entry 781 Map 16

Provence - Alps - Riviera

L'A Propos

Step through the looking glass into a world of refined French elegance; the smell of fresh coffee drifting through the salon, the click of a heel on polished parquet. White is softened by 19th-century features, earthy fabrics and the odd wacky touch: walls clothed in blown-up black-and-white postcards. There are three private parks for cypress shaded wanderings, a heated pool, a balneotherapy, a boules pitch, a buddha for peace and harmony. Large rooms are classic–contemporary, with ample bathrooms attached. Beyond are ancient ruins, vibrant markets, canoeing on the Ardèche, wine tasting in Châteauneuf-du-Pape.

Provence - Alps - Riviera

La Maison des Remparts

Built into the honey-coloured walls of this fortified village, a stylish refuge decorated with a restraint that lets the ancient walls and beams tell their own story. The house is arranged around a secluded courtyard with an azure pool at its centre, overlooked by a big bright living room. Bedrooms are a symphony of pale colours and crisp white linen, elegance and space; unashamedly gorgeous, they have bathrooms to match. Enjoy a madly indulgent breakfast around the oak table in the stone-flagged kitchen, specially set up for guests. The owners don't live here, but bubbly Ludivine makes you feel beautifully at home.

Rooms	5: 1 double, 4 suites for 1-4.
Price	€110–€160. Suite €175–€250.
Meals	Lunch €16. Dinner à la carte, €35. Wine €18–€80. Restaurants 150m.
Closed	Rarely.

Rooms	5: 1 double, 2 family rooms for 2-4, 2 suites.
Price	€160. Family room €140–€280. Suite €160–€280. Extra bed €40.
Meals	Guest kitchen. Restaurants walking distance.
Closed	Rarely.

Estelle Godefroy-Mourier
L'A Propos,
15 av Frédéric Mistral,
84100 Orange, Vaucluse

Tel	+33 (0)4 90 34 54 91
Mobile	+33 (0)6 10 33 06 32
Email	info@lapropos.com
Web	www.lapropos.com

Ludivine Rivallin
La Maison des Remparts,
74 cours Louis Pasteur,
84190 Beaumes de Venise, Vaucluse

Tel	+33 (0)4 90 62 75 49
Email	contact@lamaisondesremparts.com
Web	www.lamaisondesremparts.com

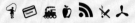

Entry 782   Map 16

Entry 783   Map 16

Provence - Alps - Riviera

Le Clos St Saourde

What a place! Outdoors turns inwards here, spectacularly: many walls, ceilings, even some furniture, are sculpted from solid rock. The décor is minimalist and luxurious with a flurry of natural materials and lots of quirky touches: the wrought-iron lamps and lanterns, the clever lighting, the solar pools. Indulge yourself in a private spa (if you have booked the treehouse) or in a breathtaking grotto bathroom. This lovely couple will tell you all about visits, vineyard tours, activities (fancy rock-climbing, a massage?) and restaurants in their exquisite area. They serve delicious gourmet platters with the right wines.

Rooms	5: 2 doubles, 2 suites for 2-3 (with sofabeds),1 treehouse for 2.
Price	€180–€260. Suite €220–€290. Treehouse €370–€470. Extra bed €40.
Meals	Gourmet platter with wines, €50. Summer kitchen. Restaurant 2km.
Closed	Rarely.

Jérôme & Géraldine Thuillier
Le Clos St Saourde,
Route de St Véran,
84190 Beaumes de Venise, Vaucluse
Tel   +33 (0)4 90 37 35 20
Mobile   +33 (0)6 99 41 44 19
Email   contact@leclossaintsaourde.com
Web   www.leclossaintsaourde.com

Entry 784   Map 16

Provence - Alps - Riviera

Le Mas de la Pierre du Coq

What's especially nice about this 17th-century farmhouse is that it hasn't been over-prettified. Instead, it has the friendly, informal elegance of a house that's lived in and loved; grey-painted beams, soft stone walls, seductive bathrooms. The Lorenzes loved it the moment they saw it; it reminded gentle Stéphan of the house he grew up in. Bustling Martine starts your day with a terrific breakfast, Stéphan shows you the walks from the door. The gardens, sweet with roses, oleanders and lavender, are shaded by ancient trees and the pool and views are glorious. Stay for as long as you can; book excellent dinners in advance.

Rooms	4: 1 double, 1 suite, 2 twins.
Price	€125–€150. Suite €200.
Meals	Dinner with wine, €40.
Closed	August.

Stéphan & Martine Lorenz
Le Mas de la Pierre du Coq,
434 chemin de Sauzette,
84810 Aubignan, Vaucluse
Tel   +33 (0)4 90 67 31 64
Mobile   +33 (0)6 76 81 95 09
Email   lorenz.stephane@wanadoo.fr
Web   www.masdelapierreducoq.com

Entry 785   Map 16

Provence - Alps - Riviera

Mas Pichony

Summer evenings are spent beneath the ancient spreading plane tree while sunset burnishes the vines beyond the slender cypresses and the old stones of the 17th-century *más* breathe gold. Laetitia and Laurent have given the farmhouse style and charm, beautifying it with country antiques, books and vibrant colours. The rooms are done with good taste, too. Two children, five horses and a trio of cats complete the delightful picture. Laetitia serves good Provençal food at the big, convivial table; turn your back to the parked cars and the roofed area by the pool is a delicious place to sit and soak up daytime views.

Rooms	5: 3 doubles, 2 twins/doubles.
Price	€108–€120. Singles €94–108. Extra bed €40.
Meals	Dinner with wine, €32.
Closed	November–March.

Laetitia & Laurent Desbordes
Mas Pichony, 1454 route de St Didier,
84210 Pernes les Fontaines,
Vaucluse
Tel   +33 (0)4 90 61 56 11
Mobile   +33 (0)6 99 16 98 58
Email   mas-pichony@wanadoo.fr
Web   www.maspichony.com

Entry 786   Map 16

Provence - Alps - Riviera

La Nesquière

The gardens alone are worth the detour: trees and greenery galore, riots of roses, all flourishing in a huge many-terraced park by a river. The 18th-century farmhouse harbours a fine collection of antiques – one of Isabelle's passions – tastefully set off by lush indoor greenery and lovely old carpets on ancient tile floors. Softly old-elegant rooms have hand-embroidered fabrics and genuine old linens, including Provençal quilts – truly exquisite – with splashes of red, orange and beige against white backgrounds. A warm, gracious welcome from Isabelle and her family.

Rooms	5: 3 twins/doubles, 2 family rooms for 4.
Price	€115–€140. Family room €105–€125.
Meals	Dinner with wine, €40 (Sat & Tues).
Closed	Mid-December to mid-January.

Isabelle de Maintenant
La Nesquière, 5419 route d'Althen,
84210 Pernes les Fontaines,
Vaucluse
Tel   +33 (0)4 90 62 00 16
Mobile   +33 (0)6 79 72 43 47
Email   lanesquiere@wanadoo.fr
Web   www.lanesquiere.com

Entry 787   Map 16

La Bastide Rose

Once an ancient mill on the river Sourge, this pink-hued house has a relaxed but regal air. The grounds are huge, with their own island, swimming pool and an orangery where a seasonal breakfast is served. Inside, character abounds. There's a sitting room that was once an ancient kitchen and distinctive bedrooms, one with its own terrace, another with antiques and a sitting room. All have modern bathrooms. The library is stocked with books, and occasional exhibitions are held (almost more hotel than B&B!). Lovely Poppy can point you to the best walks and finest markets, or leave you to linger in this fabulous place.

Minimum two nights 15 June-30 Aug.

Rooms	5: 3 twins/doubles (two can interconnect), 2 suites.
Price	€150-€220. Suite €210-€290. Extra bed €35. Pets €10.
Meals	Breakfast €18. Lunch €25-€30. Dinner €32-€50. Wine €20-€140. Restaurant 7km.
Closed	Mid-January to mid-March.

Poppy Salinger
La Bastide Rose,
99 chemin des Croupières,
84250 Le Thor, Vaucluse

Tel	+33 (0)4 90 02 14 33
Mobile	+33 (0)6 78 43 57 33
Email	contact@bastiderose.com
Web	www.bastiderose.com

Entry 788 Map 16

Le Mas de Miejour

Fred and Emma are wonderful hosts, sommeliers with a passion for wine who have escaped their city pasts. The guest bedrooms of their delightful old *mas* are all different, all serene: one on the ground floor with a painted brass bed and a white appliquéd bedcover, another with Senegalese fabrics; the family suite spreads itself over two floors. The land here is flat with a high water table so the gardens, sheltered by trees and waving maize, are ever fresh and green. It's a beautiful, artistic place to relax, your littl'uns can play with theirs, the pool is delicious and the food a delight.

Sawday self-catering also.

Rooms	3: 2 doubles, 1 family room for 4 (1 double, 1 twin).
Price	€85-€115. Family room €130-€185.
Meals	Restaurants 3km.
Closed	November-March, except by arrangement.

Frédéric Westercamp &
Emmanuelle Diemont
Le Mas de Miejour, 117 chemin du Trentin,
84250 Le Thor, Vaucluse

Tel	+33 (0)4 90 02 13 79
Mobile	+33 (0)6 68 25 25 06
Email	masdemiejour@hotmail.com
Web	www.masdemiejour.com

Entry 789 Map 16

Provence - Alps - Riviera

A l'Ombre du Palais

Gaze from the veranda, aperitif in hand, on the Palais des Papes and Notre Dame des Dômes; Sabine's house is in Avignon's old heart. Inside… a riot of russets, reds and saffrons, bright modern paintings and Louis XVI pieces, stylish orchids and tumbling cushions – a décor as generous as Sabine herself. Bedrooms, flamboyant and generous, vary greatly in size and are peaceful and private; we adored 'Kandinsky' and 'De Staël'. Sabine loves guests and house in equal measure, and gives you breakfast where and when you want it – including that veranda. Dinners are exquisite and delicious.

Minimum two nights.

Rooms	5: 2 doubles, 1 twin, 1 twin/double, 1 family room for 3.
Price	€115–€185. Family room €145–€165. Extra bed €40.
Meals	Dinner €40. Wine €10–€12. Restaurants within walking distance.
Closed	January/February.

	Sabine Ferrand
	A l'Ombre du Palais,
	Place du Palais des Papes,
	84000 Avignon, Vaucluse
Tel	+33 (0)6 23 46 50 95
Email	sabine.ferrand@wanadoo.fr
Web	www.alombredupalais.com

Entry 790   Map 16

Provence - Alps - Riviera

Sous L'Olivier

Old stonework rules the scene, big arched openings have become dining-room windows, a stone hearth burns immense logs in winter, and all is set round a pretty courtyard. Charming young bon viveur Julien, apron-clad, started his career chez Paul Bocuse, a starred reference: breakfasts are sumptuous affairs and convivial dinners are worth a serious detour. Gentle Carole is behind the very fresh, Frenchly decorated bedrooms. Flat agricultural land spreads peacefully out around you; the big, child-friendly, saltwater pool is arched with canvas shading and surrounded by giant pots and plants. Lovely people, fabulous food.

Rooms	5: 3 doubles, 2 suites.
Price	€90–€220. Suite €90–€220. Extra beds available €30.
Meals	Dinner with wine, €30.
Closed	Rarely.

	Carole, Julien, Hugo & Clovis Gouin
	Sous L'Olivier,
	Quartier le Petit Jonquier,
	84800 Lagnes, Vaucluse
Tel	+33 (0)4 90 20 33 90
Email	souslolivier@orange.fr
Web	www.chambresdhotesprovence.com

Entry 791   Map 16

La Villa Augustine

From the expertly mixed cocktails to the pool with a view, the spoiling is magnifique! Guy and Christophe are passionate about cooking, entertaining and 20th-century art and design; their villa was built in 1912, their enthusiasm is infectious. Dine on the terrace amid Baccarat crystal and pressed linen, sink into a sumptuous sofa (there are many), sweep up the staircase to bed. Each room is furnished in a given style: 'Années 1940s' with walls, lamps and chandelier all in green, 'Art Deco Neo Classique' with two terraces. No description could do justice to the communal spaces, and the terraced garden is magical.

Minimum two nights at weekend. Children over 15 welcome.

Terrasses du Luberon

Be inspired by the views, which sweep from pool and dining terrace over vineyards, orchards and fields to breezy Mont Ventoux: plan walks or cycle rides through Provençal villages. The house sprawls in the steep Bonnieux hills, a stroll from the village, tree-wrapped in rural peace – play pétanque before dinner. New owners, back from Réunion, are busy with a veg garden, cartoon collections (Tintin guards the breakfast buffet) and looking after guests; tips range from hikes to markets to Michelin-star restaurants. Rooms have private patios, space for extra beds and a shared kitchen and laundry.

Minimum three nights in high season.

	La Villa Augustine		Terrasses du Luberon
Rooms	5 doubles.	Rooms	5: 2 doubles, 3 twins/doubles.
Price	€120-€200.	Price	€110-€145.
Meals	Dinner €39. Wine €22-€102. Restaurants nearby.	Meals	Restaurants within walking disctance. Guest kitchen.
Closed	January/Febuary.	Closed	November-February.

Guy Sanchez
La Villa Augustine,
25 quai du Midi,
84400 Apt, Vaucluse
Tel   +33 (0)4 90 06 16 95
Email contact@lavillaaugustine.com
Web   www.lavillaaugustine.com

Marie Laure & Jean Marc Caspar
Terrasses du Luberon,
Quartier Les Bruillères,
84480 Bonnieux, Vaucluse
Tel   +33 (0)4 90 75 87 40
Email information@lesterrassesduluberon.fr
Web   www.lesterrassesduluberon.fr

Entry 792   Map 16

Entry 793   Map 16

Provence - Alps - Riviera

Le Jardin de Tim

After people-watching in the pretty, chic and celeb-popular Provençal village, buzz open the gates and return to an oasis of classy, landscaped peace. It is a superbly renovated old house done in harmonics of beige and coffee with colourful highlights and fabulous bathrooms. Exotic rooms are large, luscious and lovely. Enormous, split-level, high-contemporary 'Darjeeling' is worth the extra pennies with its private terrace and glass stairs up to a super-luxury bathroom. Philippe, a warm, gentle designer and dog-lover, speaks perfect English; his delightful French assistant Cathy will greet you if he's away: you will be well looked after.

Minimum two nights July/Aug.

Provence - Alps - Riviera

Mas des Tourterelles

Let the peace and the greenery wash over you, here on the residential outskirts of town; the beautiful, bustling centre of St Rémy is mere minutes away. The Aherns have thrown themselves into life in the Alpilles, Richard restoring the farmhouse with its honey-coloured stone, beams and tiles, Carrie adding the deceptively simple touches — pale walls, linen curtains, sisal carpets, splashes of colour. Bedrooms are restful spaces, utterly delightful. Cool off by the pool or under the vine-covered bower, look forward to dinner in town, a short stroll.

Minimum two nights. Sawday self-catering also.

Rooms	5: 2 doubles, 2 family rooms, 1 suite.
Price	€120–€200. Family room €200–€250. Suite €280–€350.
Meals	Dinner €35. Restaurants within walking distance.
Closed	January/February.

Rooms	4: 3 doubles, 1 twin.
Price	€110–€125.
Meals	Restaurants within walking distance.
Closed	Rarely.

	Philippe Arpels
	Le Jardin de Tim,
	Impasse de la Vieille Fontaine,
	13810 Eygalières,
	Bouches-du-Rhône
Tel	+33 (0)9 63 23 90 83
Email	contact@lejardindetim.com
Web	www.lejardindetim.com

	Richard & Carrie Ahern
	Mas des Tourterelles,
	21 chemin de la Combette,
	13210 St Rémy de Provence,
	Bouches-du-Rhône
Tel	+33 (0)4 32 60 19 93
Email	richard.ahern@sfr.fr
Web	www.masdestourterelles.com

Provence - Alps - Riviera

Mas de la Croix d'Arles

St Rémy is Provence on a plate: the ancient streets, artists, restaurants, the colourful weekly market, lush valleys and clear light which inspired Van Gogh. A short walk down the canal, a properly Provençal farmhouse distils this peace in a bubble of olives, vines and fruit trees. Tucked away in a pale stone bungalow are two light-filled B&B rooms, whose slate tiles, painted beams and fiery red splashes give a chic twist to Provençal style. You share a plunge pool with gîte guests, and breakfast on the terrace with lovely Jordane, who'll spill the area's best-kept secrets from hilltop Les Baux to the ochre-tinged Lubéron.

Provence - Alps - Riviera

Mas du Vigueirat

High plane trees flank the drive to the dusky pink, grey-shuttered farmhouse and inside all is light, simplicity and elegance. Bedrooms are uncluttered spaces of bleached colours, limed walls and terracotta floors, and views are over the beautiful garden or meadows. The high-beamed dining room/salon is a calm white space with a corner for sofas and books and if the weather's warm you'll take breakfast under the plane tree; after a dip in the pool or a jaunt on the bike, enjoy one of Catherine's delicious lunches. St Rémy (galleries, Van Gogh museum) is just up the road; Arles and Avignon are close.

Minimum two nights.

Rooms	2: 1 double, 1 twin.
Price	€75-€90.
Meals	Restaurant 1km.
Closed	Rarely.

Rooms	4: 3 doubles, 1 suite (July/August only).
Price	€135-€155. Suite €185.
Meals	Picnic available. Poolside meal in summer, €15-€20. Restaurants 3km.
Closed	Christmas.

	Jordane Marsot
	Mas de la Croix d'Arles, Chemin des Servières, 13210 St Rémy de Provence, Bouches-du-Rhône
Tel	+33 (0)4 90 90 04 82
Mobile	+33 (0)6 28 98 30 56
Email	masdelacroixdarles@sfr.fr
Web	www.masdelacroixdarles.com

	Catherine Jeanniard
	Mas du Vigueirat, 1977 chemin du Grand Bourbourel, Route de Maillane, 13210 St Rémy de Provence, Bouches-du-Rhône
Tel	+33 (0)4 90 92 56 07
Email	contact@mas-du-vigueirat.com
Web	www.mas-du-vigueirat.com

Entry 796 Map 16

Entry 797 Map 16

Provence - Alps - Riviera

Mas de Ravert

At last: a genuine old family-run farmhouse in Provence, close to everything but away from the crowds. Muriel discreetly welcomes you into the sitting/dining room... with its raftered ceiling, grand piano and billiard table decked in Bordeaux red felt, it's quite a conversion from the old goat barn. All is contemporary, nothing is too cluttered, not even the pièce de résistance, the 'Littérature' suite, wonderfully private and cool. Look out for the dancing prints of Provençal artist Léo Lelée on the stairway, as you descend for breakfast on the terrace or a dip in the pool, protected from the Mistral by tall cypress trees. Charming.

Provence - Alps - Riviera

Le Mas d'Arvieux

Carolyn and Alex, lovers of the outdoor life and well-travelled, have now put their elegant stamp on this generous manor house in Provence. Big bedrooms, one in the tower wing, one with a carved mezzanine, have beams and stone walls, fine old armoires, luxurious bathrooms, long views. There's a ground-floor room that's fine for wheelchair users and Arvieux's orchards drip with olives and luscious jam-worthy fruit. Peaceful out of season, it's a great set-up for families in high summer and the whole house can be booked. Cookery and art classes can be arranged, and you're close to Avignon's treasures.

Rooms	4: 2 doubles, 1 twin, 1 suite for 4.
Price	€80–€100. Suite €150. Extra bed €20.
Meals	Restaurant 2km.
Closed	Rarely.

Rooms	6: 2 doubles, 1 suite, 2 triples, 1 studio.
Price	€105. Suite €135. Triple €130. Studio €130.
Meals	Occasional dinner with wine, €35. Restaurant 3km.
Closed	Rarely.

	Muriel Bérard
	Mas de Ravert, Chemin de la Thèze, Route de St Rémy, 13103 St Etienne du Grès, Bouches-du-Rhône
Tel	+33 (0)4 90 49 18 11
Mobile	+33 (0)6 50 75 29 04
Email	masderavert@wanadoo.fr
Web	www.masderavert.fr

	Alex & Carolyn Miller
	Le Mas d'Arvieux, Route d'Avignon, 13150 Tarascon, Bouches-du-Rhône
Tel	+33 (0)4 90 90 78 77
Email	mas@arvieux-provence.com
Web	www.arvieux-provence.com

Entry 798   Map 16

Entry 799   Map 16

Provence - Alps - Riviera

24 rue du Château

On a medieval street near one of the finest castles in France, two *maisons de maître* are joined by an ochre-hued courtyard and a continuity of taste. It's an impeccable renovation that has kept all the soft patina of stone walls and tiles. No garden, but a courtyard for candlelit evenings and immaculate breakfasts. Calming, gracious bedrooms have fine old furniture and beams, perfect bathrooms, crisp linen. While you can be totally independent, your relaxed and courteous hostess knows the most wonderful places to visit – don't miss the Cathédrale D'Images at Les Baux. Deeply atmospheric.

Minimum two nights.

Provence - Alps - Riviera

Galerie Huit

In the ancient heart of Arles, a fascinating 17th-century mansion. Warm vibrant Julia is curator of aesthetics, cultured conversation and a gallery that combines art with hospitality. Flagstones, fireplaces and original panelling abound, homemade jams at breakfast accompany a stylish tea selection and occasional dinners are paired with wine from friends' vineyards. And staircases wind past Chinese scrolls to your suite: exquisite tommette tiles, dreamy *ciel de lit*, restored frescoes, marble touches and a small mosaic shower room with a gilded mirror. Explore Arles, a town ripe for discovery, enjoy the Camargue wilds!

Minimum two nights.

Rooms	4: 2 doubles, 2 twins.
Price	€80-€100.
Meals	Restaurants in town.
Closed	November-March.

Rooms	1 suite.
Price	€95-€150. Extra bed €30.
Meals	Occasional dinner with wine, €35. Restaurants nearby.
Closed	Rarely.

	Martine Laraison
	24 rue du Château,
	13150 Tarascon, Bouches-du-Rhône
Tel	+33 (0)4 90 91 09 99
Email	ylaraison@gmail.com
Web	www.chambres-hotes.com

	Julia de Bierre
	Galerie Huit,
	8 rue de la Calade, 13200 Arles,
	Bouches-du-Rhône
Mobile	+33 (0)6 82 04 39 60
Email	contact@galeriehuit.com
Web	www.galeriehuit.com

Entry 800   Map 16

Entry 801   Map 16

Provence - Alps - Riviera

Mas de la Rabassière

Amazing views to the coast, fanfares of lilies at the door, Haydn inside and 'mine host' smiling in his 'Cordon Bleu' chef's apron. Vintage wines and a sculpted dancer grace the terrace table. Cookery classes with house olive oil and easy airport pick-up are all part of the elegant hospitality, aided by Thévi, Michael's serene assistant from Singapore. Big bedrooms and a drawing room with a roaring fire are comfortable in English country-house style: generous beds, erudite bookshelves, a tuned piano, Provençal antiques... and tennis, croquet, a pool. A little fading around some edges but stacks of character.

No credit cards.

Rooms	2 doubles.
Price	€145.
Meals	Dinner with wine, €50.
Closed	Rarely.

Michael Frost
Mas de la Rabassière,
2137 chemin de la Rabassière,
13250 Saint Chamas,
Bouches-du-Rhône

Tel +33 (0)4 90 50 70 40
Email michaelfrost@wanadoo.fr
Web www.rabassiere.com

Entry 802 Map 16

Provence - Alps - Riviera

Les Arnauds

Come for a lovely old laid-back stone house, with pretty views of fields and hills. Here lives Sheila, with cats, dog, donkey, and a duck who shares the pool! You can share the family's living space or retreat to the guest sitting room, but summer evenings will be spent outside, drinking in the scents and peace. Breakfasts with delicious peach, cherry and apricot jams set you up for the festivals and flower markets of Aix (6km). Return to comfortable beds on carpeted floors and ceiling fans to keep you cool. Time it right (July/October) and you can join in with the lavender and olive harvests: great fun.

Rooms	3: 2 doubles, 1 suite.
Price	€80-€120. Suite €115-€125.
Meals	Restaurant 3km.
Closed	Rarely.

Sheila Spencer
Les Arnauds, 1902 chemin
du Pont Rout, 13090 Aix
en Provence, Bouches-du-Rhône

Tel +33 (0)4 42 20 17 96
Mobile +33 (0)6 78 90 38 85
Email shspencer@gmail.com
Web www.lesarnauds.com

Entry 803 Map 16

Le Clos des Frères Gris

In through the gates of Hubert's exquisitely tended, well-tree'd gardens: you'd never guess the centre of Aix was seven minutes away. Polyglot Caroline is a people person whose hospitality goes beyond her warm welcome. A passion for antiques and a talent with fabrics and colours are evident (her quilt shop is in the chapel); bedrooms marry comfort and cool elegance, fine linens and thick towels; breakfast is memorable. Admire the rose and herb gardens on the way to boules or pool, then set off to discover the music and markets of Aix. A jewel of a bastide, a home from home, worth every sou.

Minimum two nights.

Domaine de Valbrillant

The old bastide overlooks Mont St Victoire and combines country calm with autoroute convenience. Make a wish at the well (in sumptuous gardens where small dogs play) then ascend stone steps to swish furnishings, flagged floors and burnt-orange walls. Wake to delicious breakfasts as a pastry-laden Lazy Susan spins and Robert reels off café tips. Up curved stairs are evocative rooms, all vast: bookcases recess into nooks, lamplight hits beams, curtains open to panoramas. With three gîtes in the spacious grounds, Anne says she's great with people but terrible at business! We love her approach and assure you – this is superb value.

Rooms	4 doubles.
Price	€110–€200.
Meals	Restaurant 1km.
Closed	November-March.

Rooms	3: 2 suites for 2-3, 1 family room for 4.
Price	Suites €75–€95. Family room €85–€165.
Meals	Restaurant 2km.
Closed	Never.

Caroline & Hubert Lecomte
Le Clos des Frères Gris,
2240 av Fortune Ferrini,
13080 Luynes - Aix en Provence,
Bouches-du-Rhône

Tel	+33 (0)4 42 24 13 37
Email	freres.gris@free.fr
Web	freres.gris.free.fr

Anne & Robert Poujol
Domaine de Valbrillant,
13590 Meyreuil,
Bouches-du-Rhône

Tel	+33 (0)4 42 58 46 76
Mobile	+33 (0)6 87 28 39 46
Email	robert.poujol@9online.fr
Web	www.domainedevalbrillant.com

Provence - Alps - Riviera

Provence - Alps - Riviera

La Bartavelle

French Myriam and English Alastair, kind helpful hosts, live with exceptional views across the valley and sunrises framed by oak woods in their traditionally styled modern farmhouse, a testament to deft planning. Ground-floor bedrooms spread themselves round a lovely central pool and a walled terrace loaded with pot plants while an airy sitting room provides music, mod cons and reading space. Alastair knows the history of the region off by heart and every path and trail; trek up through the woods to the ridge-perched village of Mimet, with charming restaurants and views to Marseille and the sea.

Mas Ste Anne

On its hilltop on the edge of pretty Peynier, the old *mas* stands in glory before Cézanne's Montagne Sainte Victoire: pull the cowbell, pass the wooden doors and the red-shuttered farmhouse rises from beds of roses. Beautifully restored, it once belonged to the painter Vincent Roux and memories of his life live on, thanks to your gracious and very helpful hostess. The 'Roux' room is the nicest, all beams, terracotta tiles, fantastic ochre/green bathroom down the hall and delicious garden view. The house has a wonderful old-fashioned patina and the gardens are perfectly kept.

Older children welcome. Minimum two nights.

Rooms	5: 2 doubles, 2 twins, 1 suite for 2-3.		Rooms	2: 1 double; 1 double with separate bathroom.
Price	€75–€85. Suite €75–€105.		Price	€100–€120.
Meals	Guest kitchen. Restaurant 3km.		Meals	Summer kitchen. Restaurants in village.
Closed	Rarely.		Closed	First 3 weeks in August.

Myriam & Alastair Boyd
La Bartavelle,
348 chemin des Amandiers,
13105 Mimet,
Bouches-du-Rhône
Tel   +33 (0)4 42 58 85 90
Email   info@labartavelle.com
Web   www.labartavelle.com

Jacqueline Lambert
Mas Ste Anne,
3 rue d'Auriol,
13790 Peynier,
Bouches-du-Rhône
Tel   +33 (0)4 42 53 05 32
Email   stanpeynier@yahoo.fr
Web   www.massainteanne.com

Entry 806   Map 16

Entry 807   Map 16

Provence - Alps - Riviera

Château d'Eoures

Just outside bustling Marseilles is a haven of civilisation and tranquillity. This 18th-century bastide, in Jean-Lou's family for generations, is surrounded by dappled grounds – enjoy peacocks, rabbits, hens, a swimming pool among the trees and irresistible wicker-furnished terraces. Music room, library, salon – the house is yours and your hosts love nothing better than to spoil you. Expect lavish breakfasts, delicious dinners and romantic rooms… a marble fireplace, a gilt mirror, a *ciel de lit* bed with beautiful linen. Don't miss Aubagne, for fêtes, festivals, fountains – and Marcel Pagnol's atmospheric house.

Provence - Alps - Riviera

La Demeure Insoupçonnée

New hosts Julie and Jean-Claude love life at their fresh, leafy oasis in juicy-sounding Cassis. Everything is beautiful: the Cap Canaille views, the pool (with dolphin detail) and a rare tranquillity in this idyllic, much-visited area. Bougainvillea and sea scents are moments away as is the buzzing village centre. Spacious bedrooms are bright, unusual stones pock walls. One has a four-poster and mini kitchen for snacks; the rock-hewn bathrooms make luxurious caves. Deep sleeps precede continental or charcuterie breakfasts… restful mornings merge into one. Bliss out in the pool, hammock or drive the stunning Route des Crêtes.

Rooms	2: 1 double; 1 family suite for 2-5 with separate bathroom.
Price	€150. Family suite €100–€250.
Meals	Dinner with wine, €29. Summer kitchen. Restaurant 5km.
Closed	Rarely.

Rooms	3: 2 doubles, 1 suite.
Price	€130–€190. Suite €160–€200. Extra bed €30.
Meals	Restaurant 1km.
Closed	Rarely.

	Mr & Mme Chouvet
	Château d'Eoures,
	53 rue Arnould, 13011 Marseille,
	Bouches-du-Rhône
Tel	+33 (0)4 91 44 24 53
Email	contact@chateau-eoures.com
Web	www.chateau-eoures.com

	Julie Kopp
	La Demeure Insoupçonnée,
	21 montée de la Chapelle,
	13260 Cassis, Bouches-du-Rhône
Tel	+33 (0)4 42 82 35 78
Mobile	+33 (0)6 31 10 73 12
Email	lademeureinsoupconnee@gmail.com
Web	www.la-demeure-insoupconnee-cassis.com

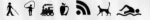

Entry 808   Map 16

Entry 809   Map 16

Provence - Alps - Riviera

Provence - Alps - Riviera

La Bastide du Moulin

Follow narrow streets to the top of the village, pass tall gates and there is the bastide in tranquil gardens. Find six spacious rooms in the main house, and one even larger near the sparkling pool, perfect for couples or families. All come in romantic pastel shades, with terracotta tiled floors and bright chic bathrooms, and most with their own terrace. A beautiful place for lazy days... a large covered space with tables for breakfast and dinner, a shady arbour for quiet reading, views of rolling hills. There are medieval buildings close by, beaches five minutes away and wines from the Bandol vineyards.

Le Clos de la Chèvre Sud

Carole's flair for design shows not only in the comfy, traditional décor but also in the wonderfully quirky touches such as the wok recycled as a bathroom basin. Colour-washed rooms are cosy and inviting, in beiges, ochres, reds, greys and blues. For summer, there's a broad sheltered terrace for breakfasting, dining, lazing and enjoying the views – the sea on one side, the forested hill on the other, a riot of flowering shrubs and trees in between. Patrice is a doctor and osteopath while Carole, a nurse, runs the spa and massage centre; both are charming and fun. Perfect – and there's a stunning pool.

Maximum three nights B&B. Kitchen available with suite during summer (min. five nights).

Rooms	7: 3 doubles, 4 suites.	Rooms	3: 2 doubles, 1 suite.
Price	€130-€180. Suite €145-€300. Extra bed €30.	Price	€120.
		Meals	Dinner €35. Wine list from €22. Dinner obligatory Fri & Sat (or min. one evening during stay).
Meals	Lunch €25. Dinner €40. Wine €25-€150. Restaurant nearby.		
Closed	Rarely.	Closed	Rarely.

Marie-Noëlle & Jérôme Pipon
La Bastide du Moulin,
20 chemin des Aires Ste Madeleine,
83740 La Cadière d'Azur, Var

Tel   +33 (0)4 94 05 43 97
Email   marie-noelle.pipon@orange.fr
Web   www.bastide-du-moulin.com

Patrice & Carole Zoro
Le Clos de la Chèvre Sud,
255 chemin du Pas de la Chèvre Sud,
83740 La Cadière, Var

Tel   +33 (0)4 94 32 31 54
Mobile   +33 (0)6 27 63 69 64
Email   clochesud@wanadoo.fr
Web   www.closdelachevre.com

Entry 810   Map 16

Entry 811   Map 16

Bastide Ste Trinide

You'll love the simple lines and bright, airy décor of this renovated 18th-century farmhouse that once belonged to Pascale's grandparents. Prepare to be seduced by reds, whites and chocolate touches, fine linens, exposed beams, a choice of terraces for cooling breezes. One delight is the captivating chapel across the courtyard, another is the vibrant art: walls throughout are splashed with the canvasses of a family friend. You'll also love the blissful quiet up here in the hills, though the beaches are minutes away. Walks, riding, golf, exotic gardens, zoo; let your charming young hosts help you explore.

La Cordeline

Owned by lawyers down the centuries, the fadingly elegant *hôtel particulier* stands in the quiet heart of the old town. Isabelle, a physiotherapist and keen cook, fell in love with it all, moved here in 2005 and now has a young family. One side looks over the street, the other over the walled garden (a fountained haven in the town centre) and you enter to warm old honeycomb tiles under a vaulted ceiling. The big bedrooms are being gradually updated, old-style charm giving way to a more modern take. In winter you can snuggle down by a log fire and read in peace.

Weekend packages include massage & beauty sessions.

Rooms	2: 1 double, 1 twin/double.
Price	€70–€90.
Meals	Restaurants nearby.
Closed	Rarely.

Rooms	4: 3 doubles, 1 triple, all with separate wc.
Price	€70–€105. Extra bed €20.
Meals	Dinner with wine, €29.
Closed	Rarely.

	Pascale Couture & Grégoire Debord
	Bastide Ste Trinide,
	1671 chemin Chapelle Ste Trinide,
	83110 Sanary sur Mer, Var
Tel	+33 (0)4 94 34 57 75
Email	contact@bastidesaintetrinide.com
Web	www.bastidesaintetrinide.com

	Isabelle Konen-Pierantoni
	La Cordeline,
	14 rue des Cordeliers,
	83170 Brignoles, Var
Tel	+33 (0)4 94 59 18 66
Email	lacordeline@wanadoo.fr
Web	www.lacordeline.com

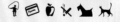

Entry 812   Map 16

Entry 813   Map 16

Une Campagne en Provence

In spring, water gushes through myriad irrigation channels dug by the Knights Templar! Martina and Claude, proud possessors of the European Ecolabel, have planted 3,750 trees on their vast estate. The bastide keeps its fortress-like proportions and, like its owners, has bags of charm. Simple furnishings are lit by huge windows, floors are terracotta, and breakfasts and dinners put the accent on Provençal produce and their own wine. A pool with a view, a sauna, a Turkish bath, a well-stocked library, a mini cinema in the cellar... an isolated paradise for all ages, overseen by a charming young family, two geese and one dear dog.

Pool open May-October.

La Bastide des Templiers

This modern home is pure Provence: yellow walls, blue shutters, a backdrop of tree-covered hills. Inside it's full of light, and the bedrooms come in a rag-rolled palette of colours with Balinese furniture gathered from exotic travels. Breakfast is at the Templar-style table with fresh pastries and local jams. Outdoors is even finer, listening to the cicadas with a chilled pastis... there's a terrace and a pond, a shaded pool, a Mediterranean garden and a jacuzzi – Joel, a massage therapist, will work your worries away. Walk in the knights' footsteps in Bras, explore the caves at Sainte Beaume, head for the coast.

Minimum two nights (low season), three nights (high season). Children over 15 welcome.

Rooms	5: 3 doubles, 1 suite. 1 studio with kitchenette.
Price	€93-€125. Suite €120-€142. Studio €127-€160. €15 supplement for one night.
Meals	Dinner with wine, €34. Restaurant 3km.
Closed	January to mid-March.

Rooms	5 doubles.
Price	€75-€110. Singles €65-€85. Extra bed €15.
Meals	Restaurants 1km.
Closed	December/January.

Martina & Claude Fussler
Une Campagne en Provence,
Domaine le Peyrourier,
83149 Bras, Var

Tel	+33 (0)4 98 05 10 20
Email	info@provence4u.com
Web	www.provence4u.com

Harald Goerg
La Bastide des Templiers,
980 chemin du Rail sur le Chemin,
83149 Bras, Var

Tel	+33 (0)4 94 77 61 97
Mobile	+33 (0)6 17 35 85 08
Email	service@bastide-des-templiers.com
Web	www.bastide-des-templiers.com

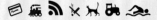

Entry 814   Map 16

Entry 815   Map 16

Provence - Alps - Riviera

Domaine de la Blaque

The first and only property in the Var to be offically classified 'éco'! You are surrounded by nature at its best, and your lovely hosts have that artistic flair which puts the right things together naturally: palest pink-limed walls and white linen; old-stone courtyard walls with massed jasmine and honeysuckle; yoga groups and painters with wide open skies. Indeed, Jean-Luc is passionate about astronomy, Caroline is a photographer, they produce olives, truffles and timber, organise courses and love sharing their remote estate with like-minded travellers. Each pretty, independent room has its own little terrace.

Domaine de St Ferréol

Old, genuine and atmospheric are the words for this wine estate. Breakfast is the highlight of Armelle's hospitality and she's full of ideas for excursions, Monsieur happily sharing his knowledge of the area. They are a warm, lively and cultured couple, their working vineyard has a timeless feel, their wine tastings are most civilised events. Glorious views to Pontevès castle from the first-class, authentically Provençal bedrooms; they and the breakfast room (with mini-kitchen) are in a separate wing but, weather permitting, breakfast is on the terrace. Peace and privacy in a beautiful old house, superb walking, an outdoor pool.

Rooms	2: 1 double, 1 twin, each with kitchenette.
Price	€85–€98.
Meals	Restaurants 2.5km.
Closed	Rarely.

Rooms	3: 2 twins/doubles, 1 suite.
Price	€72–€85. Suite €102–€132.
Meals	Guest kitchen available. Restaurant 1.5km.
Closed	Mid-November to February.

	Caroline & Jean-Luc Plouvier Domaine de la Blaque, 83670 Varages, Var
Tel	+33 (0)4 94 77 86 91
Mobile	+33 (0)6 25 32 22 81
Email	la.blaque@gmail.com
Web	www.lablaque.com

	Guillaume & Armelle de Jerphanion Domaine de St Ferréol, 83670 Pontevès, Var
Tel	+33 (0)4 94 77 10 42
Email	saint-ferreol@wanadoo.fr
Web	www.domaine-de-saint-ferreol.fr

Entry 816   Map 16

Entry 817   Map 16

Provence - Alps - Riviera

Château Nestuby

Bravo, Nathalie! – in calm, friendly control of this gorgeous, well-restored 18th-century bastide. One whole wing is for guests: the light, airy, vineyard-view bedrooms, pastel-painted and Provençal-furnished with a happy mix of antique and modern (including WiFi), the big bourgeois sitting room (little used: it's too lovely outside), the spa on the roof terrace and the great spring-fed tank for swims. Jean-François runs the vineyard, the tastings and the wine talk at dinner with sweet-natured ease. Utterly relaxing and very close to perfection.

Minimum three nights July / Aug.

Rooms	5: 1 double, 1 twin, 1 triple, 1 family room, 1 suite.
Price	€85. Extra bed €18.
Meals	Dinner with wine, €27.
Closed	Mid-December to February.

Nathalie & Jean-François Roubaud
Château Nestuby,
4540 route de Montford,
83570 Cotignac, Var
Tel   +33 (0)4 94 04 60 02
Mobile +33 (0)6 86 16 27 93
Email   nestuby@wanadoo.fr
Web   www.nestuby-provence.com

Entry 818   Map 16

Provence - Alps - Riviera

La Maison de Rocbaron

Who would not love this beautifully restored stone bergerie in a riot of greenery and flowers, with terraces dotted about gardens and pool? Jeanne and Guy's welcome is warm and easy; he keeps guests happy over an aperitif as she delivers a dinner not to be missed. The glorious black fig of Solliès is one of her specialities; both Jeanne and Guy are passionate about Slow Food. Various staircases lead to elegant rooms, symphonies of pinks, whites and florals. An early dip, a feast of a breakfast, and you're ready for the day's adventures. A happy place in harmony with the world – in a peaceful Provençal village.

Rooms	5: 3 doubles, 2 suites for 2-4.
Price	€80-€118. Suite €98-€128.
Meals	Dinner with wine, €40. Guest fridge & microwave. Restaurants in village.
Closed	December-February.

Jeanne Fischbach & Guy Laguilhemie
La Maison de Rocbaron,
3 rue St Sauveur,
83136 Rocbaron, Var
Tel   +33 (0)4 94 04 24 03
Email   contact@maisonderocbaron.com
Web   www.maisonderocbaron.com

Entry 819   Map 16

La Grande Lauzade

This ancient monastery, bought at auction by Corine's great-grandfather, was a working wine estate. Now Corine and Thierry, extrovert musician, live here with their young family and pets, becoming ever more 'green' amid their wildish, well-tree'd grounds. Blues and whites predominate in big lofty rooms (some up twisty stairs) furnished with some exquisite and often fascinating pieces, such as the chicken-hatching box on legs, carved in fine wood. Distinct traffic hum from the terrace but so much to do on the spot: darts, table tennis, billiards, boules and pool… and convivial breakfasts each morning.

Rooms	3: 1 double, 1 suite, 1 triple.
Price	€95–€160.
Meals	Restaurants 1km.
Closed	Rarely.

Corine & Thierry Varipatis
La Grande Lauzade,
83340 Le Luc en Provence, Var
Tel   +33 (0)4 94 60 74 35
Email   contact@lagrandelauzade.com
Web   www.lagrandelauzade.com

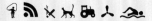

Entry 820   Map 16

Villa de Lorgues

Expect the unexpected in this stately 18th-century townhouse. From the basement spa to the traditional living rooms – level with the delicious garden and terrace – to the bedrooms at the top, all is pure enchantment. A red lantern here, zany birdcages there, four-posters, fireplaces and candles just where you least expect them. Bedrooms combine superb comfort with an elegant minimalist décor. Come evening, fairy lights wink along the wrought-iron balustrades from top to bottom. Claudie juggles a busy freelance career with talent, taste, a warm welcome and a fabulous sense of humour.

Minimum two nights July/Aug.

Rooms	2 doubles.
Price	€130–€180.
Meals	Restaurants within walking distance.
Closed	January-March.

Claudie Cais
Villa de Lorgues,
7 rue de la Bourgade,
83510 Lorgues, Var
Tel   +33 (0)6 61 47 67 02
Email   villadelorgues@gmail.com
Web   www.villadelorgues.com

Entry 821   Map 16

Provence - Alps - Riviera

La Sarrazine

Sumptuous gardens on multiple levels, a wonderful variety of trees and flowers, and terraces for quiet moments: paradise at its best, with views thrown in. One spacious double is all creams, with white sheets beautifully embroidered; there are blues, reds and yellows elsewhere, and an uncluttered cosiness. Guests share a large, relaxed sitting/dining room with a fireplace and a terrace. Lively Hilary has won a seat on the village municipal council: looking after both guests and community comes easily to her. Tennis and boules here, and Lorgues' restaurants and weekly market a short walk. Delightful.

Minimum three nights.

Rooms	3: 1 double, 2 twins/doubles.
Price	€95-€135.
Meals	Dinner €20-€30. Wine €15.
Closed	Rarely.

Hilary Smith
La Sarrazine,
375 chemin du Pendedi,
83510 Lorgues, Var
Tel +33 (0)4 94 73 20 27
Mobile +33 (0)6 77 15 63 24
Email reservations@lasarrazine.com
Web www.lasarrazine.com

Entry 822   Map 16

Provence - Alps - Riviera

La Bastide du Pin

It's a glamorous drive up from Nice to this gorgeous hideaway, set among gardens of lavender with views as far as the eye can see. Bedrooms are spacious and elegant with an understated feel, there's a beautiful shaded patio with only a fountain to disturb you, and billiards and books for evenings in. But best of all is Pierre, your interesting and attentive host, who gives you gorgeous breakfasts in a big dining room and holds court at dinner once a week in summer. A great spot from which to stroll into Lorgues, with its abbey, buzzing market, shops and bars; it's particularly alluring in spring.

Rooms	6: 4 doubles, 1 twin/double, 1 family room for 2-3.
Price	€90-€160. Family room €110-€165.
Meals	Occasional summer dinner with wine, €30-€40. Restaurants in Lorgues, 2km.
Closed	Rarely.

Pierre Gissinger
La Bastide du Pin,
1017 route de Salernes,
83510 Lorgues, Var
Tel +33 (0)4 94 73 90 38
Email contact@bastidedupin.com
Web www.bastidedupin.com

Entry 823   Map 16

45 boulevard des Pêcheurs

From your private terrace atop this intriguing house, gaze past the umbrella pines and out to the sky-blue bay – it's a real tonic. The many-windowed parquet-floored bedroom, restfully done in soft colours, feels like a lookout tower. Good bathroom, too. Breakfast is served in the family dining room or on the main terrace; the luxuriant garden and superb pool area lie beyond while the wide, welcoming, uncluttered salon has nice old French furniture and ship's binoculars for those views. Your hosts – charming, active and attentive Claudine and Serge, who used to work in boats – are helpful and unintrusive. The centre is a 15-minute walk.

Minimum two nights.

Un Air de Rien

Overlooking the plane-tree'd village square, this reverently renovated town hall is Provençal-perfect; bunting flutters, pétanque clunks, time slows. Bedrooms are rustic chic – brickwork, wrought-iron chandeliers, beams; bathrooms impress with marble basins, super smellies and sleek fixtures. Bright paintings add pools of colour. Both from Belgium, Lionel brings wine knowledge and humour – enjoy a glass of Provençal wine or famous Belgian beer on the lovely terrace; Caroline quietly cares for guests and two small children. Their hospitality is reflected in beautiful breakfasts and the fine wine and tapas bistro.

Minimum two nights.

Rooms	1 double.
Price	€80-€90.
Meals	Restaurants nearby.
Closed	Rarely.

Rooms	2 doubles.
Price	€105-€120. Extra bed €30.
Meals	Wine, beer & tapas bar on site. Restaurants within walking distance.
Closed	December-March.

	Claudine & Serge Draganja
	45 boulevard des Pêcheurs,
	Super-Lavandou,
	83980 Le Lavandou, Var
Tel	+33 (0)4 94 71 46 02
Mobile	+33 (0)6 16 17 03 83
Email	draganja@orange.fr
Web	www.chambrehotes-draganja.com

	Lionel & Caroline Thomsin
	Un Air de Rien,
	3 place de la Libération,
	83610 Collobrières, Var
Tel	+33 (0)4 94 28 17 73
Email	lionel@unairderien.com
Web	www.unairderien.com

Entry 824   Map 16

Entry 825   Map 16

Le Pré aux Marguerites

Built in the 1950s in Provençal style, the house was the family's holiday home when Frédéric was a child. Your captivating host was an interior designer in New York; now he runs this cliffside B&B. Breakfasts are convivial and copious, on the terrace or by the pool. You could spend all day here, up among the mimosas and palms, under the pines overlooking the sea…. there's even a path down to a private beach. The largest suite faces the sea, the other comes with a sloped beamed ceiling; both have polished antiques. Don't miss hilltop villages Ramatuelle and Gassin – popular in summer but ever enchanting.

Rooms	2 suites with kichenette.
Price	€150-€300.
Meals	Dinner €45. Wine from €15.
Closed	January-March.

Frédéric Jochem
Le Pré aux Marguerites,
1 av du Corail,
83240 Cavalaire, Var
Tel   +33 (0)4 94 89 11 20
Email   fjochem@aol.com
Web   www.bonporto.com

Entry 826   Map 16

Le Clos du Pierredon

On the edge of charming Grimaud, in a road dotted with gated mansions, is an imposing but pretty former farmhouse, terracotta with green shutters. It stands in spacious grounds with a swimming pool lower down; take a dip, relax under the palms. Lovely Heather, gentle and stylish, serves summer breakfasts on the terrace outside; for dinner, village restaurants are a hilltop stroll. Or, out of season, nip into St Tropez (in high summer, cycling would be the faster option!). Smallish bedrooms come with their own entrances, one has a little terrace, another a balcony, and bathrooms are pristine, two with splendid new showers.

Rooms	3 doubles.
Price	€150.
Meals	Restaurant nearby.
Closed	Rarely.

Heather & Kevin Jennings
Le Clos du Pierredon,
249 chemin St Joseph,
83310 Grimaud, Var
Mobile   +44 (0)7889 452 296
Email   jennings@cardiac-concerns.com
Web   www.grimaudvacation.com

Entry 827   Map 16

Clos Saint Clement

This old stone house, oozing Provençal charm, was once a magnanerie where silkworms were raised. Now it's dedicated to your delight! The only hardship is choosing which bedroom to take: all are stylish and pale-hued, with high ceilings and ancient beams, and light streaming through shutters to illuminate beautiful old furniture. All have tiled bathrooms with extra towels for the pool – shimmering in the large garden amongst the fruit trees, figs and olives. Owners Suzanne and Pierre join you for convivial continental breakfasts at a long marble table on the terrace, or in the cool of the terracotta-flagged salon. Wonderful.

Minimum three nights July/Aug. Children over 8 welcome.

L'Hirondelle Blanche

The beach is over the road, St Tropez a boat-trip away: charming out of season. Quite a character, Monsieur Georges enjoys painting, music, wine and old houses; he renovated this typical palmy 1900s Riviera villa himself. His paintings hang in the quirky sitting room, wines may appear for an evening tasting. Each room has a personal touch: a hat pinned to the wall, a fishing net on a wall; some have little balconies; bathrooms are basic with healthily rough eco-friendly, line-dried towels; breakfast is good. Despite the road, you don't need a car: fly in, train in, take a taxi or come by bike.

Cleaning every two days. TGV station 10-minute walk.

Rooms	4: 3 doubles, 1 triple.
Price	€115-€130. Triple €115-€165. Singles €104-€119.
Meals	Dinner, 4 courses with wine, €35. Restaurant 1.2km.
Closed	Mid-October to mid-March. (Can be open for groups of 8+.)

Rooms	4: 3 doubles, 1 triple.
Price	€99-€189.
Meals	Breakfast €5-€15. Restaurants within walking distance.
Closed	Mid-October to April.

Pierre & Suzanne Anselot
Clos Saint Clement,
83680 La Garde Freinet, Var
Tel   +33 (0)6 51 82 00 52
Email   contact@clossaintclement.com
Web   www.clossaintclement.com

Georges & Florence Methout
L'Hirondelle Blanche,
533 bd du Général de Gaulle,
83700 St Raphaël, Var
Tel   +33 (0)4 98 11 84 03
Email   kussler-methout@wanadoo.fr
Web   www.hirondelle-blanche.fr

Entry 828   Map 16

Entry 829   Map 16

Provence - Alps - Riviera

Lou Rigaou

On the edge of a perched Provençal village on a wooded hillside, time flows at another pace: the peacefulness is striking. Your colourful bedroom comes with its own entrance and terrace, so it really is a room of your own; views reach over a flower-strewn garden to woods beyond. There's even a little swimming pool for a cooling plunge as cicadas chirp in the trees. Sylvie, who lives in the main house, loves her guests, is a mine of local information and spirits breakfast onto your terrace without your even noticing. A ten-minute stroll brings you to the heart of the village; a one-hour drive has you in St Tropez.

Extra bed available.

Rooms	1 double.
Price	£65-£75. Extra bed €20.
Meals	Restaurants 800m.
Closed	Rarely.

Sylvie Bruniau
Lou Rigaou,
Les Clots, 83830 Claviers, Var
Tel   +33 (0)4 94 47 81 42
Mobile   +33 (0)6 63 44 55 98
Email   sylviebruniau@wanadoo.fr
Web   users.skynet.be/locations/Sylvie

Entry 830   Map 16

Provence - Alps - Riviera

La Guillandonne

A very long drive, anticipation, then the house, the river, the cool forest. These lovely, civilised people, a former teacher of English and an architect, have treated their old house with delicacy and taste. Standing so Italianately red-ochre in its superb *parc* of great old trees and stream, it could have stepped out of a 19th-century novel. The interior speaks for your hosts' caring, imaginative approach (polished cement floors, rustic Salernes tiles). Bedrooms are full of personality, elegant and colourful; the living room is exquisite with vintage Italian hanging lamps and Le Corbusier chairs.

Sawday self-catering also.

Rooms	3: 2 doubles, 1 twin.
Price	€90.
Meals	Restaurants 1.5km.
Closed	Rarely.

Marie-Joëlle Salaün
La Guillandonne,
731a route des Tourettes,
83440 Tourrettes, Var
Tel   +33 (0)4 94 76 04 71
Mobile   +33 (0)6 24 20 73 09
Email   guillandonne@wanadoo.fr

Entry 831   Map 16

Les Canebières

The mountain drive is amazing, the setting is stupendous. Olive groves, cultivated terraces, sloping lawns, and a gorge below. There's an (unfenced) pool, acres to explore and three ancient dwellings woven delightfully into one. Guests live in the house; Molly, artist, sailor and free spirit, lives in the shepherd's hut alongside. American by birth, she loves children, animals, people, produces her own olive oil and has cooked on yachts for years – you are in good hands. Interiors are country traditional, one bedroom is Balinese, the suite is nautical, there are books, games, DVDs, toys, a piano, a lute – and a harp made by Molly!

Villa Suzanne

Provençal-smart is the style: the handsome townhouse was built in 1870 with its imposing black and red door and marble window lintels. Helen's colourful, classy and eclectic furnishings are in keeping. Artistic, much-travelled and bubbling with enthusiasm, she easily shares her time between physiotherapy (in-house), art and her B&B. Red, yellow and apricot bedrooms are deeply appealing, so is the view over the old town and cathedral beyond the small garden. The road (you won't notice it at night) leads to the hilltop and seaside wonders of Provence while the scent factories and al fresco eateries of Grasse are a stroll away.

Rooms	3: 2 doubles, 1 suite.
Price	€85–€105. Suite €105–€125.
Meals	Dinner with wine, €35. Restaurants 3km.
Closed	Rarely.

Rooms	2: 1 double, 1 family room for 2-4.
Price	€95. Family room €100–€140.
Meals	Restaurant within walking distance.
Closed	Rarely.

	Molly Holt
	Les Canebières,
	Route de St Cézaire,
	83440 Mons, Var
Tel	+33 (0)4 93 60 22 69
Mobile	+33 (0)6 45 54 64 94
Email	landfall.molly@gmail.com

	Helen Mcleod
	Villa Suzanne,
	41 bd Victor Hugo,
	06130 Grasse,
	Alpes-Maritimes
Tel	+33 (0)6 85 46 56 71
Email	helenmcleod@wanadoo.fr

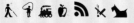

Entry 832   Map 16

Entry 833   Map 16

Le Relais du Peyloubet

A hint of Tuscany seeps through this ancient farmhouse, its shutters and terracotta tiles, standing on a hillside wrapped in olive groves. Once growing flowers for Grasse perfumers, its delicious terraces and orchards are now tended by Roby while Xavier, a pâtissier, whisks up the fabulous breakfasts. Dinners are do-it-yourself in the summer kitchen overlooking the peaceful hills. Beamed and parquet-floored bedrooms, all with private terraces, are furnished in country Provençal style. There are shady seats in the woods, glorious views, boules, pool, and the coast 20 minutes. Blissfully calm, easy and welcoming.

Lou Candelou

Terracotta roofs peep over lush foliage in this residential area to hills and the heavenly Mediterranean. A huge mimosa guards the small friendly house of local stone and blue shutters; arrive by narrow private road to a lovely welcome from Boun and her daughter. Fresh, charming rooms with ethnic cottons, painted furniture and spotless bathrooms lead to a potted terrace. Enjoy a feast of pastries, fresh fruit, exotic conserves on the big balcony with views; make your own picnic or barbecue in the kitchen by the guest sitting room; pull yourself away and hop on a train to the coast.

Whole apartment available in winter. Min. two nights (weekends & high season). Extra bed available.

Rooms	5: 1 double, 2 suites, 2 twins/doubles.	Rooms	3 doubles.
Price	€75-€115. Suite €85-€125.	Price	€60-€80. €15 supplement for one night. Extra bed €20.
Meals	Summer kitchen. Restaurant 3km.	Meals	Guest kitchen available - reservation required.
Closed	Mid-November to mid-March.	Closed	Rarely.

	Xavier & Roby Stoeckel		**Mme Bougie**
	Le Relais du Peyloubet,		Lou Candelou, 57 av St Laurent,
	65 chemin de la Plâtrière,		06520 Magagnosc,
	06130 Grasse, Alpes-Maritimes		Alpes-Maritimes
Mobile	+33 (0)6 16 90 67 39	Tel	+33 (0)4 93 36 90 16
Email	relais-peyloubet@wanadoo.fr	Mobile	+33 (0)6 03 86 45 58
Web	www.relais-peyloubet.com.fr	Email	loucandelou@neuf.fr
		Web	www.loucandelou.com

Entry 834   Map 16

Entry 835   Map 16

Bastide Valmasque

The coral-coloured house is hard to miss. Friendly Philippe and Claudia met in India, and the influence of the subcontinent is everywhere. Indian canopies and daybeds are guarded by sacred stone cows amongst fruit trees, palms and lawns. Living and dining rooms have a hint of Bollywood — jewel coloured upholstery and mirrored furniture sizzle against pale walls. Bedrooms are spacious, bright and modern, each with charming decorative touches and a colour scheme that extends into the compact bathrooms. Breakfast indoors or on one of the terraces, then set off for Cap d'Antibes beaches: the road is close by.

l'Air du Temps

Tucked away down a cul-de-sac, built by the hands of the Scassaus themselves and a short walk from the beaches, is this pretty Provençal house. One room has a sparkly chandelier and smoky-pink walls, another a sauna and private terrace. Outside: plenty of terrace to dine on, a kitchenette to whip up your dinner in and a chuckling green parrot, Ramón, who loves guests. The charming owners have lived here for years and are in love with their region; understandably so. Catch a ferry to St Tropez, visit the medieval villages, wander the lavender-perfumed mountains or come for the jazz in July. Delightful.

Minimum two nights. Extra bed available.

Rooms	5: 3 doubles, 2 suites.
Price	€75–€115. Suite €110–€140. Extra bed €25.
Meals	Restaurant nearby.
Closed	Rarely.

Rooms	4 doubles.
Price	€100–€150.
Meals	Restaurants within walking distance. Summer kitchen.
Closed	November-March.

Philippe Bonan
Bastide Valmasque,
1110 route d'Antibes,
06410 Biot, Alpes-Maritimes

Tel	+33 (0)4 93 65 21 42
Email	bastidevalmasque@gmail.com
Web	www.bastidevalmasque.com

Rose-Marie Scassau
l'Air du Temps,
La Chenaie, 283 av des Eucalyptus,
06160 Juan les Pins,
Alpes-Maritimes

Tel	+33 (0)4 93 61 27 43
Email	airdutemps06160@yahoo.fr
Web	villaairdutemps.com

Entry 836   Map 16

Entry 837   Map 16

Provence - Alps - Riviera

Villa Estelle

In a town filled with medieval memories, on one of the prettiest streets in France (probably), is gorgeous Villa Estelle. Once the old inn of the town, where painters flocked (and still do), it's opened up for evening drinks so locals can enjoy this part of their heritage. The previous owner, an interior designer, has left behind Moroccan-coloured rooms filled with pretty furniture, huge bathrooms and a cosy sitting room. Outside, a huge sunny courtyard with views spilling over rooftops out to sea. Ramble around the idyllic streets of the "Montmartre of the Riviera"; bubbly Fiona looks after you immaculately. Superb.

Rooms	5: 2 doubles, 3 family rooms.
Price	€120-€130. Family room €130-€180. Minimum 2 nights in high season (April- September).
Meals	Restaurants within walking distance.
Closed	Never.

Fiona Kennedy
Villa Estelle,
5 montée de la Bourgade,
06800 Cagnes sur Mer,
Alpes-Maritimes

Tel	+33 (0)4 92 02 89 83
Email	info@villa-estelle.com
Web	www.villa-estelle.com

Entry 838   Map 16

Provence - Alps - Riviera

La Locandiera

Built for holidays and for early 20th-century entertaining, this Côte d'Azur villa is a literal stone's throw from the fishing port and beach, and charming Madame Rizzardo has forsaken Venice to restore it. Her open-plan living room has an aura of witty conversation, dry cinzano and stylish cigarette holding (now a thing of the past, of course). Three of the cool, fresh, traditionally furnished bedrooms look straight out to sea over a walled garden whose jasmine-sweet corners are furnished for shaded retreat. Heaps of restaurants and smart places are reachable on foot.

Rooms	5: 2 doubles, 1 twin, 2 suites.
Price	€120-€150. Suite €150-€180.
Meals	Restaurant 100m.
Closed	Last 2 weeks in November.

Daniela Rizzardo
La Locandiera, 9 av Capitaine
de Frégate Vial, 06800 Cagnes
sur Mer, Alpes-Maritimes

Tel	+33 (0)4 97 22 25 86
Mobile	+33 (0)6 27 88 17 40
Email	daniela@lalocandieracagnes.com
Web	www.lalocandieracagnes.com

Entry 839   Map 16

Provence - Alps - Riviera

Terrasses du Soleil

All the charm of a restored medieval hilltop village above the bustle and beach of Cagnes. The Bouvets' home was a 60s night club fashionable with celebrities, and traces remain: fine terrace breakfasts (home baking a speciality) happen next to the dance floor. Rooms are distributed up and down stairs and come in different styles: retro, Provençal, classic, each with a trim loggia or balcony and distant sea, mountain and rooftop views. Forget the car: Madame, a local expert, will help you negotiate excellent public transport links to Antibes, Monaco, Cannes and beyond.

Minimum two nights July / Aug.

Rooms	4: 2 doubles, 2 suites.
Price	€110-€130. Suites €115-€135.
Meals	Restaurants 5-minute walk.
Closed	November to mid-December.

Catherine Bouvet
Terrasses du Soleil, Place Notre Dame de la Protection, Le Haut de Cagnes, 06800 Cagnes sur Mer, Alpes-Maritimes

Tel	+33 (0)4 93 73 26 56
Email	catherine.bouvet@terrassesdusoleil.com
Web	www.terrassesdusoleil.com

Entry 840   Map 16

Provence - Alps - Riviera

Le Mas St Antoine

On the residential outskirts of St Paul de Vence is a characterful B&B run by the effervescent Maric. An artist, she has joyfully decorated each of her guest rooms, our favourites being the two in the house: a gorgeous, and spacious, Asian / Venetian suite, and 'Panoramic' that lives up to its name (and has a bath tub in its bedroom). All come with a private terrace and a summer kitchen so you can breakfast or lunch in peace, then bask around the splendid pool. The legendary hilltop village, all tourist boutiques, bars and cobble-stoned beauty, is an easy stroll. Nice and beaches are a bus ride away.

Minimum four nights.

Rooms	4: 2 doubles, 2 suites.
Price	€100-€120. Suites €110-€130. Extra bed €50.
Meals	Private summer kitchens. Restaurants in village.
Closed	October-April.

Maric Trojani
Le Mas St Antoine, 1133 chemin St Etienne, 06570 St Paul de Vence, Alpes-Maritimes

Tel	+33 (0)4 93 32 50 84
Mobile	+33 (0)6 03 61 12 15
Email	contact@lemassaintantoine.com
Web	www.lemassaintantoine.com

Entry 841   Map 16

La Forge d'Hauterives

This place purrs with the sunny indulgence of the Côte d'Azur, whose beaches lie over the hills. Standing strong and proud in the heart of a medieval perfume-makers' village, the Provençal bastide was restored from near-ruin by Madame: find harmonious pale colours, natural materials, family antiques, flowers, a pool. A designer, hostess and talented cook, she serves summer breakfasts amid vines and lavender, and caters for groups with family recipes of honeyed lamb or veal casserole – delicious. There are trout in the river, craft shops by the castle, a restaurant in the priory. Nice and St Paul de Vence are near.

Minimum two nights.

Rooms	5: 4 doubles, 1 family room.
Price	€100-€180. Family room €230-€260. Extra bed €35.
Meals	Dinner with wine, €40. Restaurants 150m.
Closed	Rarely.

Anne d'Hauterives
La Forge d'Hauterives, 44 rue
Yves Klein, 06480 Saint Paul
de Vence, Alpes-Maritimes
Tel   +33 (0)4 93 89 73 34
Mobile   +33 (0)6 82 82 84 45
Email   anne.dhauterives@newatoo.net
Web   www.laforgedhauterives.com

Entry 842   Map 16

Le Clos de St Paul

A young Provençal house on a lushly planted and screened piece of land where boundary hedging is high. In a guest wing, each pretty bedroom has its own patio, and there's a wonderful summer kitchen for guests to share. Smiling Madame has furnished with great simple taste – anthracite greys, mellow yellows, painted chairs, the odd antique. She genuinely cares that you have the best, offers a welcome glass of rosé on her stunning shaded terrace and serves a very fresh breakfast in the garden. The lovely large mosaic'd pool is refreshingly discreet. Great value.

Minimum two nights. All rooms have a terrace.

Rooms	3: 1 double, 1 twin/double, 1 twin/double with kitchenette.
Price	€75-€110. Pets €5.
Meals	Summer kitchen. Restaurant 1km.
Closed	Rarely.

Béatrice Ronin Pillet
Le Clos de St Paul,
71 chemin de la Rouguière,
06480 La Colle sur Loup,
Alpes-Maritimes
Tel   +33 (0)4 93 32 56 81
Email   leclossaintpaul@hotmail.com
Web   www.leclossaintpaul.com

Entry 843   Map 16

Histoires de Bastide

It must have been rustic enough in its hunting lodge days but the lovely old stone building is now the most luxurious country-antique guest house you could wish for. Big unfussy rooms in soft restful colours and textures, the best beds, superb bathrooms with tiling to die for, a richly Provençal garden and pool: everything seems part of the fabric of the place. Sandrine cares deeply that it all be perfect and takes great care of you, with the help of darling three-year-old Romaric. The historic Riviera playgrounds are at your feet, the pretty hilltop villages at your back, Sandrine's spa and hammam ready when you return.

The Frogs' House

Quiet, green, frog-sung air, sight-lines over rooftops to mountains, valley and sea, a brand-new renovation done by a passionately committed young couple in an unspoilt village. Corinne, from La Réunion, and Benoît, a local boy, met in Australia. They will point (or take) you to fabulous hikes for all, from timid to trained; promote local produce and biodiversity; serve superb Provençal and Creole food; organise natural-wine tastings. And they know the local craftspeople. The atmosphere is all fresh simplicity with spotless white paint, new pine furniture — and friendship. A real place.

3-day full-board stays available.

Rooms	5: 3 doubles, 2 twins/doubles.
Price	€150–€240. Extra bed €30.
Meals	Breakfast €10–€15. Restaurants 2km.
Closed	Rarely.

Rooms	7: 3 doubles, 3 twins/doubles, 1 suite.
Price	€76–€98. Suite €125–€153.
Meals	Restaurants in village.
Closed	Mid-November to mid-December; mid-January to mid-March.

Sandrine Otto
Histoires de Bastide, Chemin du
Moulin à Farine, 06140 Tourrettes
sur Loup, Alpes-Maritimes

Tel	+33 (0)4 93 59 08 46
Mobile	+33 (0)6 67 79 08 73
Email	info@histoiresdebastide.com
Web	www.histoiresdebastide.com

Benoît & Corinne Couvreur
The Frogs' House,
35 rue du Saumalier,
06640 St Jeannet,
Alpes-Maritimes

Tel	+33 (0)4 93 58 98 05
Email	info@thefrogshouse.fr
Web	www.thefrogshouse.fr

Entry 844 Map 16

Entry 845 Map 16

Villa Kilauea

A grand Mediterranean villa that looks so settled in Nice's lush western hills you'd never know it was a 21st-century creation. There are balustrade-edged terraces, panoramic views and a blissful pool. Bedrooms above the pool house have a zen-like calm: wrought-iron four-posters draped in muslin, teak floors, white walls; orchids and silks hint at the exotic. The 'Lavender Room' in the main house opens to the garden and is as feminine as the rest. Nathalie, the perfect host, kind, gentle and generous to a tee, delights in juggling family life with her B&B. Nice is a ten-minute drive down the hill.

Villa L'Aimée

In one of the most authentic parts of Nice, a short tram ride from the city's rich culture (buses also stop virtually at the gate), Villa L'Aimée was built in 1929 and is typical of its period. Toni's decoration has restored its wonderful shapes and details to their original opulence. Warm, cultured and much-travelled – one of her lives was in the art world – she has created delightful bedrooms in subtle colours with damasks and silks, fine linen, tulle canopies and beautiful furnishings, exuding an air of old luxury. The original parquet is breathtaking, the breakfasts are superb.

Children over 10 welcome.

	Villa Kilauea		Villa L'Aimée
Rooms	3 doubles.	Rooms	3: 2 twins/doubles, 1 twin.
Price	€130–€160.	Price	€110–€135.
Meals	Restaurants in Nice, 10-minute walk.	Meals	Restaurants within walking distance.
Closed	Rarely.	Closed	December-March.

	Nathalie Graffagnino		**Toni Redding**
	Villa Kilauea,		Villa L'Aimée,
	6 chemin du Candeu,		5 av Piatti, 06100 Nice,
	06200 Nice, Alpes-Maritimes		Alpes-Maritimes
Tel	+33 (0)4 93 37 84 90	Tel	+33 (0)4 93 52 34 13
Mobile	+33 (0)6 25 37 21 44	Mobile	+33 (0)6 71 82 67 72
Email	contact@villakilauea.com	Email	bookings@villa-aimee.co.uk
Web	www.villakilauea.com	Web	www.villa-aimee.co.uk

Entry 846 Map 16

Entry 847 Map 16

Provence - Alps - Riviera

La Parare

Cradled in summer by cicada chant and the gentle wind, cocooned in winter in a romantic log-fired bedroom, you will be bewitched by the subtle mix of clean-cut modernity and fine oriental detail that your much-travelled polyglot hosts have achieved in this craggy old house. Breakfast in bed anyone? Bathtub for two? Elegant gourmet dinner? All of these and more: Karin from Sweden and French/Dutch Sydney love pampering people. The rough hills outside highlight the delicacy inside, the natural walled pool, the stunning bathrooms, the civilised conversation at dinner. Worth every centime.

Provence - Alps - Riviera

Les Cyprès

Glorious views stretch over countryside and town from Frances's apricot-coloured villa. Its beautiful big garden bears olives, flowers and fruit in profusion – fig, cherry, strawberry… discover secret areas for dining or hiding away with a book. Bedrooms are traditional and minimalist with pretty bedspreads and smart bathrooms, and breakfast is scrumptious: bread, brioche, homemade jams galore. Explore the fascinating old town, tootle over to Nice, and get back in time for Frances's truly delicious four-course dinners. Whet your whistle with an aperitif in the cosy-rustic sitting room… prepare to be spoiled!

Minimum two nights July/Aug.

Rooms	4 doubles.
Price	€130–€160.
Meals	Dinner €30–€45 (once or twice a week).
Closed	Rarely.

Rooms	3 doubles.
Price	€85–€90. Extra bed €25.
Meals	Dinner, 4 courses with wine, €25. Restaurant 1km.
Closed	Christmas.

	Karin & Sydney van Volen
	La Parare,
	67 calade du Pastre,
	06390 Châteauneuf Villevieille,
	Alpes-Maritimes
Tel	+33 (0)4 93 79 22 62
Email	karin@laparare.com
Web	www.laparare.com

Entry 848 Map 16

	Frances Thompson
	Les Cyprès,
	289 route de Châteauneuf,
	06390 Contes,
	Alpes-Maritimes
Tel	+33 (0)6 46 27 54 95
Email	contact@lescypres.fr
Web	www.lescypres.fr

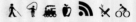

Entry 849 Map 16

Corsica

Chambres d'Hôtes à Vallecalle

Welcome to the master house in Vallecalle, on the village edge, an eagle's nest with long exquisite valley views. Here live Paul Henri and Myriam, warm, witty, welcoming, living the dream, raising a family, happy to advise you on their beloved adopted land – the food, the culture – or leave you in peace to explore their home, beautiful in its simplicity. Bedrooms, two with 18th-century floorboards, are spacious and gracious. The terraced gardens have oranges, olives, a hammock, corners for shade and sun, and, below, a river to bathe in. Myriam's dishes, always delicious, can be delicate, intriguing or hearty. Stay in!

Rooms	3: 1 double, 1 family room for 4, 1 suite for 5 (single in living room).
Price	€63. Family room €68-€100. Suite €68-€136.
Meals	Dinner with wine, €23. Restaurant 7km.
Closed	Never.

Myriam & Paul Henri Gaucher
Chambres d'Hôtes à Vallecalle,
Village de Vallecalle,
20232 Vallecalle, Haute-Corse
Tel +33 (0)4 95 37 60 60
Email phgaucher@sfr.fr
Web www.chambresencorse.com

Entry 850 Map 16

ON WHEELS

ALFONSO'S WAGON
Montpellier - **Entry 680**

VIOLETTE
Near Carcasonne - **Entry 707**

LA CABANE DU PERCHE
Normandy - **Entry 255**

OUT IN THE WILDERNESS

UP IN THE TREES

LA PALOMBIÈRE
Near Bordeaux - **Entry 482**

FELICIE
Near Carcasonne - **Entry 707**

Alastair Sawday has been publishing books for over twenty years, finding Special Places to Stay in Britain and abroad. All our properties are inspected by us and are chosen for their charm and individuality and, now, with twenty-one titles to choose from there are plenty of places to explore. You can buy any of our books at a reader discount of 25%* on the RRP.

List of titles	RRP	Discount price
British Bed & Breakfast	£15.99	£11.99
British Bed & Breakfast for Garden Lovers	£19.99	£14.99
British Hotels and Inns	£15.99	£11.99
Pubs & Inns of England & Wales	£15.99	£11.99
Venues	£11.99	£8.99
Cotswolds	£9.99	£7.49
Devon & Cornwall	£9.99	£7.49
Wales	£9.99	£7.49
Ireland	£12.99	£9.74
Dog-friendly Breaks in Britain	£14.99	£11.24
French Bed & Breakfast	£15.99	£11.99
French Self-Catering	£14.99	£9.74
French Châteaux & Hotels	£15.99	£11.99
Paris	£9.99	£7.49
Italy	£15.99	£11.99
Portugal	£12.99	£9.74
Spain	£15.99	£11.99
Morocco	£9.99	£7.49
India	£11.99	£8.99
Go Slow England & Wales	£19.99	£14.99
Go Slow France	£19.99	£14.99

*postage and packaging is added to each order

How to order:
You can order online at: www.sawdays.co.uk/bookshop/
or call: +44(0)1275 395431

Wheelchair-accessible places

Wheelchair-accessible
At lest one bedroom and bathroom accessible for wheelchair users. Phone for details.

Alastair

Sawday's

'More than a bed
for the night…'

Britain
France
Ireland
Italy
Portugal
Spain

www.sawdays.co.uk

Self-Catering | B&B | Hotel | Pub | Canopy & Stars

If you have any comments on entries in this guide, please let us have them. If you have a favourite house, hotel, inn or other new discovery, please let us know about it. You can return this form, email info@sawdays.co.uk, or visit www.sawdays.co.uk and click on 'contact'.

Existing entry

Property name: ______________________

Entry number: Date of visit: ___ / ___ / ___

New recommendation

Property name: ______________________

Address: ______________________

____

Tel: ______________________

Your comments

What did you like (or dislike) about this place? Were the people friendly? What was the location like? What sort of food did they serve?

____

____

____

____

____

____

____

____

Your details

Name: ______________________

Address: ______________________

Postcode: ______________ Tel: ______________

Please send completed form to ASP, The Old Farmyard, Yanley Lane, Long Ashton, Bristol BS41 9LR

Languedoc - Roussillon

Mas d'Oléandre

Lovely, long stone buildings enfold the convivial two-tier courtyard, great trees shade the pool, the Cévennes hills march off beyond. It is enchanting. Your welcoming young Dutch hosts have created a beautiful unpretentious place to stay; the garden, the lawn round the pool, the glowing old furniture inside, the silvery weathered teak out. Bedrooms, each with its own piece of terrace, light and white with splashes of colour, feel separate from one another round the courtyard and Esther keeps it all utterly pristine. Gather your own picnic at glorious Uzès market and bring it back here. Breakfast and dinner are delicious.

Rooms	4: 2 suites; 2 doubles, each with separate shower.
Price	€77–€137.
Meals	Dinner with wine, €32.50.
Closed	Mid-November to early March.

Léonard Robberts & Esther Küchler
Mas d'Oléandre,
Hameau St Médiers,
30700 Montaren & St Médiers,
Gard

Tel   +33 (0)4 66 22 63 43
Email   info@masoleandre.com
Web   www.masoleandre.com

Entry 676   Map 16

Languedoc - Roussillon

Les Bambous

Circles of delight, ten minutes from Avignon. Joël & Michèle love welcoming guests to their glowing little house in an unpretentious Provençal town, and the charming peaceful courtyard shaded by bamboo and bourgainvillea. He paints portraits and pastels, she cooks – linger over delicious food at the big mosaic table. In the courtyard studio is a delightful mix of soft limed walls and ethnic treasures from winter travels: a Peruvian wall hanging, an African sculpture. You have an inviting king-size bed, a pebble-floored shower, a bright kitchenette, a gently curving staircase to a bed-sitting area above. Such value!

Rooms	2: 1 studio with kitchenette, 1 family room for 2-4.
Price	Studio €65. Family room €70–€105.
Meals	Dinner with wine, €25.
Closed	January.

Joël & Michèle Rousseau
Les Bambous,
21 rue de la Mairie,
30131 Pujaut, Gard

Tel   +33 (0)4 90 26 46 47
Mobile   +33 (0)6 82 93 06 68
Email   rousseau.michele@wanadoo.fr
Web   www.lesbambous.net

Entry 677   Map 16

1. Region
2. Write-up Written by us, after inspection.
3. Rooms Assume rooms are en suite. If not, we say 'with separate bath' or 'sharing bath'.
4. Price The price shown is the one-night price for two sharing a room with breakfast. A price range incorporates room/seasonal differences. We also give single occupancy rates – the amount payable by one person staying in a room for two.
5. Meals Prices are per person. **All meals must be booked in advance.** Most often you may bring your own wine.
6. Closed When given in months, this means for the whole of the named months and the time in between.
7. Symbols Treat each one as a guide rather than a statement of fact. Check important facts when booking.
8. Entry and map numbers

List of symbols

- At least one bedroom & bathroom accessible for wheelchair users. Phone for details.
- At least one bedroom and bathroom accessible without steps.
- Children of all ages are welcome. Cots, highchairs, etc, are not necessarily available.
- Credit cards accepted, most commonly Visa and MasterCard.
- Within 10 miles of a bus/coach/train station and owner can arrange collection.
- Good vegetarian dinner options (arrange in advance at B&Bs).
- Wireless internet access available for guests.
- The premises are licensed.
- No smoking anywhere in the property.
- Owners' pets live on the property.
- Guests' pets can sleep in the bedroom (not on the bed).
- Working farm or vineyard.
- Some, if not all, bedrooms are air-conditioned
- Swimming pool on the premises; use may be by arrangement.
- Bikes on the premises to hire or borrow.
- Tennis court on the premises; use may be by arrangement.

Exchange rate, January 2013
£10=$16.30=€12.31

For many years Alastair Sawday Publishing has been 'greening' the business in different ways. Our aim is to reduce our environmental footprint as far as possible and with almost everything we do we have environmental implications in mind. In recognition of our efforts we won a Business Commitment to the Environment Award in 2005, a Queen's Award for Enterprise in the Sustainable Development category in 2006, and the Independent Publishers Guild Environmental Award in 2008.

The buildings

In 2005 we created our own eco offices by converting some old barns to create a low-emission building. Heating and lighting the building, which houses over 40 employees, now produces only 0.28 tonnes of carbon dioxide per year. Not bad when you compare this with the six tonnes emitted by the average UK household.

Photo: Tom Germain

We achieved this through a variety of innovative and energy-saving building techniques, some of which are described below.

Insulation By laying insulating board 90mm thick under the roof tiles and floor, and lining the building with plastic sheeting, it is almost totally air-tight.

Heating We installed a wood pellet boiler from Austria in order to be largely fossil-fuel free.

Water We installed a 6,000-litre tank to collect rainwater from the roofs for reuse. Two solar thermal panels on the roof provide hot water.

Electricity Our electricity has long come from the Good Energy Company and is 100% renewable.

Materials Virtually all materials are non-toxic or natural, and our carpets are made from (80%) Herdwick sheep wool from National Trust farms.

Doors and windows Outside doors and new windows are wooden, double-glazed and beautifully constructed in Norway. Old windows have been double-glazed.

However, becoming 'green' is a journey and, although we began long before most companies, we realise we still have a long way to go.